A History of
Psychological
Theories

ROSS STAGNER

EMERITUS PROFESSOR OF PSYCHOLOGY
WAYNE STATE UNIVERSITY

A History of Psychological Theories

MACMILLAN PUBLISHING COMPANY

NEW YORK

Collier Macmillan Publishers

LONDON

Macmillan Publishing Company
866 Third Avenue, New York, New York 10022

Collier Macmillan Canada, Inc.

LIBRARY OF CONGRESS CATALOGING IN PUBLICATION DATA

    Stagner, Ross (date)
     A history of psychological theories.

    Includes index.
    1. Psychology—Philosophy. I. Title. [DNLM:
    1. Psychological Theories—history. BG 81 S779h]
    BF38.S67 1988   150'.1   87-20378

Printing: 1 2 3 4 5 6 7 8   Year: 8 9 0 1 2 3 4 5 6 7

ISBN 0-02-415390-7

For Margaret

Preface

Psychologists have an honored tradition of "explaining" the behavior of a person by examining the historical background of the individual. The case history is an essential part of clinical work. The history of a company is often the key to understanding conflicts in the workplace. Psychologists exploring international conflicts also find historical explanations to be important even when they need supplements from other data sources.

The same logic leads me to believe that a richer understanding of contemporary theories about psychology can be attained by looking at the history of theories and theorizing. A theory is, after all, a cognitive structure, a product based on empirical data which have been transformed and conceptualized. Processes of differentiation, abstraction, assimilation, accommodation, reasoning, and strategy formation play parts in every instance of theory construction. It seems to me obvious that psychological science should help us to understand psychological theorizing.

While theories are cognitive, psychologists are human beings and as such have emotions and aspirations. Some of the processes involved in personality development, such as Oedipal conflicts, identification, and perceptual defense, have influenced the development of specific persons and their ideologies. This is a sensitive area, and I have tried to rely on the psychologist's autobiography or contemporary accounts of behavior rather than indulging my imagination.

The book is organized to illuminate the dialectical conflict between advocates of introspection, or the study of human experience, and behavior observation, the study of human action. The most encouraging feature of writing this account has been the recognition that integrative theories are emerging in which experience and behavior play appropriate parts.

I have been led to this project by teaching a course called History of Systems of Psychology to graduate students at Wayne State University.

By degrees, over the years, this course developed from expounding the ideas of structuralists, behaviorists and others, into an examination of the dynamics of dissenters from traditional theory, and an explication of the aspects of cognitive psychology which throw light on the formulation of a new theoretical position.

Another feature which grew over time was the introduction of material from applied psychology. My students were unhappy with a treatment of theories which seemed remote from clinical, industrial, community or legal problems. I have therefore made a systematic effort to identify applications of each theory, not at length, but probably enough to convince a skeptical student that theories can be practical. In my experience this has led to lowered resistance to studying history and theories; in the long run, I have faith that it will result in improvements in the practice of psychology as a profession.

Every book about history presents a mixture of fact and opinion. But every fact is dependent upon an observer; hence, the production of a history is an exercise in the selection of topics, ideas, persons, and evidence. This book represents "history as I see it." This is true also of all other books on the topic. No one can list all of the psychologists who may have contributed in a small or large way to the development of the science; nor would space permit the examination of every "theory" that has been published. Looking at this confused and ambiguous picture, the historian selects items which can be systematized into a coherent picture. Selective perception, then, is a major determinant of any such history. Perceptual defense is another process, operating this time to exclude logic or data which would undermine the preferred position of the historian.

Chronology is of course important; we assume that history moves only in one direction in time, so that earlier developments may modify later views, but not *vice versa*. Yet there are many theoretical systems evolving simultaneously. I have tried to solve this problem of organization by selecting one system, e.g., behaviorism, but then developing ideas chronologically within that category. I then introduce a competing theory (Gestalt) and show chronologically how it evolved.

My book is primarily about human behavior and experience. I do not deny that research on animal behavior has contributed to progress in psychology, but it has seemed to me that the study of human beings takes precedence. This does not mean that I am anti-Darwinian; I assume that there is some kind of continuity in the development of species. But I also suspect that *Homo sapiens* may have species-specific attributes which could not have been predicted from any amount of research on animals. At any rate, humans are complex enough without trying to solve questions of inter-species continuity.

One more restriction on subject-matter should be mentioned. This is a book about systems of psychology, and specific theories are fitted into systems. This means that there are many "micro-theories" which do not lend themselves to categorizing and so have been omitted. There are currently theories about information-processing, attribution theory, cognitive dissonance theory, adaptation-level theory, personal distance theory, and so on and on. In some cases I have packaged one of these into a system, perhaps doing violence to the micro-theory. In other cases I have simply opted to omit the material. I repeat, every history is selective, and I have preferred to seek meaningful patterns rather than encyclopedic coverage.

Particular interest may attach to my extensions of some of these patterns. I have segregated certain ideas and labeled them "neo-structuralism," "neo-behaviorism" and "neo-analysis." The criteria for these categories are set forth in the appropriate chapters; my labels do not agree with some earlier usages, but I see my logic for inclusion as persuasive.

Another innovation is the inclusion of theories about individual differences, mainly "intelligence" and "personality." In my view the macro-theories labeled behaviorism, Gestalt, etc., have direct ties to the individual-differences area, but these have been ignored. I hope that some of the logical extrapolations I pose will be found to improve understanding of those fields. Similarly, I have extended the discussion of psychoanalysis, behaviorism, and humanistic psychology to link the general theory with applications in psychotherapy and behavior modification. This addition was intended primarily to meet a need expressed by clinical students to anchor their applied training to general theory.

The teaching of theory is not achieved by having students read a book. For this reason I have prepared an Instructor's Manual to accompany this volume, in which I describe some unusual exercises calculated to activate some of those cognitive processes which I have cited as steps in the theorizing process.

This book has taken shape over a period of many years, and my obligations to many colleagues over that time are too numerous for specific acknowledgments. I do wish to thank some of them for help on this specific manuscript; Dr. E. D. Lawson, Ms. Andrea Disbro and Derek Tackitt of State University College, Fredonia, New York, who prepared Figure 17.1 for me; Dr. M. Marlyne Kilbey and the Wayne State University Department of Psychology for logistical support; Dr. L. T. Benjamin, Jr., for access to some of his excellent files. To dozens of colleagues who contributed reprints and manuscripts I can only express my deep appreciation. For the errors and omissions in the book I must accept sole responsibility.

I would like to thank the following people for reviewing the book in manuscript: Jane A. Halpert, DePaul University; C. Alan Boneau, George Mason University; James L. Pate, Georgia State University; Nicholas L. Rohrman, Colby College; Randall M. Potter, Clarion University of Pennsylvania; and Michael Wertheimer, University of Colorado at Boulder.

Ross Stagner

Contents

CHAPTER 5

Germany: The Emergence of Scientific Psychology

CHAPTER 6

American Psychology Before Titchener: William James

CHAPTER 7

Titchener and Structuralism   *113*

CHAPTER 8

Functionalism   *138*

CHAPTER 9

Early Behaviorism

CHAPTER 1

Theories, Theorizing, and Theorists

We humans enjoy constructing theories. Long ago people developed theories about the lights that shine in the night sky. We devised theories about the difference between a living person and a dead person, and about why a baby resembles (or does not resemble) one or both parents. Folklore records theories about thunder and lightning, about steam and ice, about war and peace.

Theorizing about how knowledge is acquired and how habits are formed has gone on for thousands of years, along with speculations about anger, fear, and love. It is, however, only a little more than a century since the logic and technology of "science" have been focused on human behavior and experience. This is the referent for the adage that psychology has a long past but only a short history. The long past is made up of informal observations, reflections, and reasoning, during a period when instruments and methods for arriving at more precise data had not been developed. Thus, psychology as a science is generally said to have originated in 1879, when the German philosopher-psychologist Wilhelm Maximilian Wundt (1832–1920) opened the first laboratory formally dedicated to the investigation of psychological phenomena. The short "history" of psychology is devoted to developments since that time.

Laboratory routines and techniques, as well as the invention of specialized devices, have been important in the progress of other natural sciences. Astronomy made tremendous strides after Galileo constructed a telescope. Progress in physics was speeded by the manufacture of reliable pumps, thermometers and the like. Our learning about chemistry was accelerated by the availability of temperature and pressure controls. This technological element has also influenced the growth of psychology. Since 1879 psychological laboratories have become progressively more sophisticated with regard to the application of stimuli and the recording of responses.

Given this dramatic change in the *quality* of the evidence collected in the last century, one may ask why we do not simply ignore the theorizing that went on in earlier centuries. A persuasive answer is that psychology is a developmental science, concerned with origins and sequences of growth in mental and behavioral functions. In applying the logic of developmental research to psychology itself, we must look back into the distant past. Just as we seek to understand specific persons in terms of their childhood experiences, so it seems logical that we try to understand the science of psychology through an investigation of the paths along which the study of psychology has traveled.

Development as Differentiation

Developmental psychologists hold that one essential aspect of organismic development is the process of differentiation. The fertilized ovum develops into sets of specialized tissues serving distinct functions. A child's general linguistic capacity may specialize into a talent for poetry, or for history. A noisy, self-assertive youngster often becomes an exhibitionistic adult. As a general rule, development proceeds from the general to the specific.

Similar trends are observable in the history of science. At the time of the flowering of Periclean Athens, philosophy embraced all of what we call human knowledge. A philosopher was one who loved wisdom, and wisdom was equated to knowledge. Aristotle has often been described as the last human being to possess all of the currently available knowledge.

But philosophy had begun to differentiate even in Aristotle's time. The astronomers were beginning to specialize in detailed instrumentation, in the measurement of time, and in theories of cosmology. At some point—any date chosen would be arbitrary—the role of the astronomer came to be distinguished from that of the philosopher. By the time of Copernicus (see Figure 1.1), it was clear that philosophy could no longer claim astronomy as part of its realm of expertise.

The same happened with physics. As instrumentation, experimentation, the accumulation of empirical observations, and speculation multiplied, the physicists split from philosophy and established themselves in a separate discipline. Similar processes led to the recognition of chemistry and biology as independent areas of human knowledge, no longer dominated by philosophical thinking. Psychology was the last of these sciences to become independent. Although most historians agree that 1879 marks the beginning of a scientific psychology, it is important to note that at Harvard University, psychology was treated as a subdiscipline of philosophy until 1932. At Oxford University in England, there was no post labeled "professor of psychology" until even later.

The specialization process has not ended. Today we must distinguish not only between clinical and counseling psychologists, but between ex-

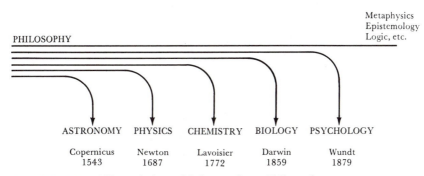

FIGURE 1.1   Differentiation of Sciences from Philosophy

As observers abstract a given attribute (e.g., the stars) from the mass of information in the environment, they begin to develop specialized methods of study, to collect data, and to devise theories. At some point it becomes apparent that the new science can no longer be considered to be merely a specialized aspect of philosophy. The dates shown above are arbitrary but identify some outstanding development which is convenient for purposes of dating.

perimental and physiological, or between social and community psychologists. And just as this process of differentiation has reduced communication and mutual understanding among the other natural sciences, it is having unfortunate consequences for cooperation among the various psychological specialties.

Differentiation is not the only developmental principle. Integration begins to reunite the specialized parts. In the embryo, nerve cells and muscle cells go their separate ways for some time and then link up to form functional tissues. The same tendency toward establishing connections across boundary lines is observable in science. Chemistry differentiated from physics about two hundred years ago, but in the twentieth century, physical chemistry has evolved as a specialty that bridges the artificial gap between the two fields. In the history of psychology, we shall observe differentiation of the field followed by integration, as persons working in separate areas find that they need knowledge from the specialties of others. The growth of any science is likely to show this dialectical process as one area expands and then a countermovement fosters closer cooperation with related specialties.

Why Construct Theories?

An eminent American psychologist, B. F. Skinner, once published an article entitled "Are Theories of Learning Necessary?" (1950). As the title implied, his conclusion was that theorizing is indeed unnecessary,

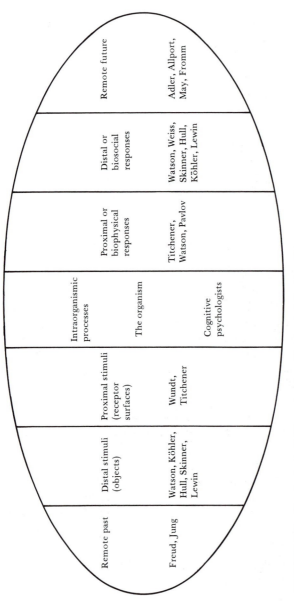

FIGURE 1.2 Psychological Theories in a Temporal Perspective

Theories may focus on different spatial and temporal perspectives. Psychoanalysts (Freud, Jung) emphasize the distant past of a person; others concentrate on the immediate present. Some theories have concentrated on nerve-muscle responses while others study changes in person-environment relations. A few stress the remote future as one determinant of thought and behavior. (*Suggested by a diagram in Brunswik, 1939.*)

and that researchers should merely gather facts. Critics have examined Skinner's other publications and concluded that he had been theorizing throughout his professional career (see Chap. 11). In his studies of reinforcement schedules, he did not take into account the phases of the moon or variations in the chemical composition of the pellets of food used. A researcher must have a theory about *which changes* in the environment offer a reasonable prospect of affecting behavior. The theorist may, of course, be unconscious of this guiding theory.

Theories pervade applied psychology, too. Employers have theories about the desires of workers, and politicians have theories about voters. Parents theorize about plausible explanations for the strange behavior of their children, and the offspring are known to speculate about what makes their parents tick.

Theory as Causality

As in the examples just cited, most theories bear on the question of cause and effect. If pain is regularly followed by crying, we theorize that the pain caused the response. However, we must avoid the logical error of assuming that sequence proves causation. If a particular dance is followed by rain, it is not necessarily true that the dance caused the rain. At least, we need many more observations to confirm this induction. And even repetition is not conclusive. One of the most dependable sequences in human history is that sunrise is always followed by sunset, but this does not prove that one caused the other. Logicians have a phrase, *post hoc, ergo propter hoc* ("after this, therefore on account of this") to label this kind of fallacious reasoning. Sequence does not prove causation.

An alternative use of theory as causality is found in views that emphasize the immediate situation. People may change their behavior on learning that they are in a group of very religious people, or as a consequence of watching those around them. Groups have a strong influence on the opinions and behavior of the members. After a football game, the crowd may riot and do damage that most individuals would avoid if not in a crowd.

Still a third approach to the theory–causality relationship is to focus on the future. I may have a theory that one of my students has a dream of being a famous scientist someday, and I explain his work behavior as a function of that aspiration. Theories, then, may emphasize the past, the present, or the future, in trying to explain human behavior.

This variation in temporal perspective was diagrammed by Egon Brunswik as shown in Figure 1.2. Brunswik (1939) tied the different theory–time relations to familiar schools of psychological theory. Freud and the psychoanalysts focused on the extreme past, the very early childhood of the person being studied. (Jung even extended this focus to include the racial past.) Behaviorists focus on the near past and the immediate present. Gestalt theory relies almost entirely on the present situation, the field within which a person is behaving, as the "cause" of the response. (The term *distal* refers to distant objects, i.e., outside the person. The term *proximal* identifies a stimulus on a receptor surface, i.e., different from the object "out there.") Structuralists such as E. B. Titchener concentrated their efforts almost entirely on the proximal stimuli. Psychologists developing theories that explain behavior in terms of remote future ambitions are mostly in the humanistic psychology category, although Alfred Adler, a psychoanalyst, also offered a theory using this humanistic approach.

Is one of these temporal perspectives more accurate than another? At present, we can say only that each is useful in an appropriate context. Clinical psychologists have a tendency to prefer past-oriented theories, and counseling specialists like the future orientation. Industrial psychologists typically rely on present-focused theories but concede that both past and future variables may affect present behavior.

Theory and Reality

The term *theory* is also applied to a way of uncovering a concealed reality. Appearances, as the saying goes, are deceiving. A critic may say of a public figure, "She is really running for governor but is not ready to announce it." School psychologists "explain" a boisterous pupil's behavior by saying, "He is really asking for attention."

The notion that a theory somehow cuts through appearances to an underlying reality is not confined to psychology. Consider the chemist who says, "Water is *really* a compound of hydrogen and oxygen," or the physicist who says, "Matter is really just electrons, protons, mesons, quarks, and so on, spinning madly, in mostly empty space." Each is saying something, not about causation, but about a concealed "reality."

Jesting Pilate might have asked, "What is reality?" If so, he would have been wise not to wait for an answer. Consider this book. It may be described as *"really* paper with marking on it in black ink." But a chemist might see it as *"really* a bunch of hydrocarbon molecules." And the physicists would probably say "it is *really* a bunch of electrons and other subatomic particles spinning in empty space."

What is the book "really"? The best answer we can give is that it is all of these. Reality depends on which point of view we adopt, which frame of reference is applied. Einstein's theory of relativity asserts that physical measurements are always relative to the point from which they are made. One of his epigrams was "Theory determines what observations are to be made."

Incidentally, it is important to note that many psychologists who try to share the prestige of physics in their appeal to observers to accept psychology as a science fail to keep pace with the progress of physics. For example, Rollo May (1967) wrote of a conversation with Werner Heisenberg (he of the "indeterminacy" theorem). The physicist "emphasized his belief that our classical, inherited view of nature as an object 'out there' is an illusion, that the subject is always part of the formula, that the man viewing nature must be figured in, the experimenter into his experiments or the artist into the scene he paints. . . . 'Of course, you psychologists in your discipline have always known this,' he added." May carefully avoided confirming this assessment, noting mentally that "the inseparable relation between subject and object he was describing was exactly what much contemporary psychology had been trying strenuously to avoid" (p. 10). The skepticism of Aristotle, of Descartes, and of Freud regarding our naive assurance that we know reality has been lost on many American psychologists.

There is, of course, an important difference between the subject matter of physics or chemistry and the subjects studied by psychology: no molecule of water has ever been known to object to electrolysis; human subjects, by contrast, often rebel at the treatments they are subjected to by psychological experimentation.

Theorizing as a Psychological Process

Psychologists have examined the activities of other scientists in constructing theories. A physicist, for example, begins with a specific observation or observations. One aspect of the evidence is singled out for examination; thus, the wavelength of light may be abstracted as the focus of attention. Comparisons are made between the behavior of lights of different wavelengths, as in interference patterns. The physicist may then develop a theory on the unobserved features of light that "explain" the interference phenomena.

Psychologists can also observe their colleagues engaged in theorizing. The basic events are the same as in physics. Perceiving, or loving, or learning may provide specific data. Some feature or attribute is selected for study. Some hypothesis is developed (e.g., that boys have a marked tendency to love females resembling their mothers). This hypothesis may then be fitted into a larger theory dealing with child development.

Observation

Every theory begins with data. Generally, one seeks to make observations of a variety of events involving the object or person under scrutiny. Conditions of observation are varied systematically: we can study perceiving in the laboratory, or on the athletic field, or in political activities. Experiments normally imply a careful control of conditions; field research tries to extract important material from the mass of irrelevant items.

Abstraction

The theorist seeks to identify *one* specific attribute under study. This might be the physical quality of a stimulus, or the occurrence of a reinforcement, or the operation of a social influence. The same data may lend themselves to different theories as different attributes are abstracted for special study.

Differentiation

Once a detail has been abstracted from the total situation, the observer can establish differences. One could compare children living with one parent and children living with two parents. Or one could compare the speed of recognizing words and nonsense syllables, or liking a person whose attitudes resemble one's own versus liking a person with opposing attitudes. The comparison of different stimuli may suggest an explanation of the differences in behavior.

Assimilation

The theorist typically tries to extend a novel theory as widely as possible. To Freud, all pleasures were ultimately sexual. To Pavlov, all learning was essentially conditioning. Piaget (1926) held that a young child forms a schema of a sensorimotor kind, such as "A ball will roll on the floor." Then this schema is transferred to other objects: "A wheel will roll on the floor. A block will not roll on the floor." The child then develops a theory: "If it has a circular visual shape, it will probably roll." At the level of complex theory, a psychologist may say, "If one person finds himself or herself in a group, all of whose members hold a certain view, this person will change to agree with that view." Assimilation simply means that as soon as one finds a good generalization, there is a tendency to add other items so that the generalization extends as far as possible.

Accommodation

A generalization soon reaches a limit. As a person's experience widens, new experiences will refuse to assimilate with the earliest theory. A child may discover that soap bubbles are round but won't roll. A modification of the hypothesis becomes necessary. A social psychologist may learn that individuals of certain varieties reject a group consensus. Piaget's concept of accommodation is that a schema may have to be modified to fit the evidence. Thus the "round . . . roll" theory is changed to exclude filmy round objects. Accommodation, then, is a modification of a theory to account for evidence. When B. F. Skinner (1938) proposed that we distinguish reflexes from operants, he was pointing to evidence that required modification of the original hypothesis of Ivan Pavlov.

Concept Formation

Once a detail has been abstracted, it provides a basis for a concept. Early astronomers noted that some stars were "fixed," always in the same relative positions. Others were "wanderers" and were called *planets*. *Two* concepts replaced the *single* concept of a star. Many single concepts of popular psychology have been replaced by multiple concepts in scientific psychology. "Eating" is a normal phenomenon, but "bulimia" is a specific variation on eating with its own unique features.

When psychologists first began using laboratory methods, concepts like *sensation* and *image* were taken from popular writings and fitted into specific procedures. Later, terms like *reinforcement, insight,* and *transfer of training* were evolved. The history of psychology is, to a considerable extent, a history of major concepts.

Differences in concepts are related to differences in point of view. Watson's concept of a reflex as any response elicited by a stimulus in the absence of prior learning fitted with his definition of psychology as the study of observable behavior. Freud's approach was quite different. Figure 1.3 illustrates how Freud arrived inductively (i.e., by observation) at

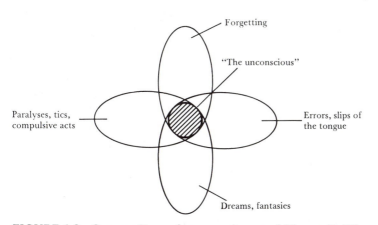

FIGURE 1.3　Concept Formation as an Aspect of Theory Building

From specific observations, such as dreams, errors, and forgetting of selected memories, Freud abstracted the common attribute, lack of conscious awareness of the circumstances determining the behavior. This common attribute he labeled "unconscious process" or "The Unconscious."

his concept of *unconscious process*. He recorded instances of the forgetting of familiar names, errors and slips of the tongue, dreams, and hysterical symptoms, all of which had in common the attribute that the person was unaware of a reason for the behavior. The concept of *unconscious behavior* could then be extended to logical lapses and other new examples of this unconscious determinism.

As I have just suggested, one of the first tendencies of a psychologist who has just devised an attractive new concept is to generalize it to a wider range of examples. This is an example of Piaget's assimilation. One observes behavior and tries to fit it into existing categories (i.e., concepts). In some cases, behavior will be noted that cannot be fitted into the concept. At this point, *accommodation* becomes necessary; the psychologist splits the existing concept and defines the two so that they can be kept separate. Let us use Skinner again as an example: He devised two new concepts, Type S and Type R responses. Type S included the knee jerk, sneeze, salivation, and so on, and the common attribute was control by an external stimulus. Type R responses included movements of the arms, legs, lips, and so on, which occurred independently of any external stimulus.

Each theory is couched in terms of its own set of concepts. It is important for the student to learn what these concepts are and how they compare across theories, but not to mix them indiscriminately. Each concept is embedded in a theory and carries with it a variety of assumptions. To mix Freud's concept of cathexis with Skinner's concept of variable reinforcement is to compound confusion.

Other concepts cut across theories. These are logical rather than substantive; for example, the concept of *determinism* is one accepted by all psychologists (although some define it more loosely than do others).

Determinism

Perhaps the first great conceptual innovation in the study of natural events was the idea of *determinism*. This was the principle that events in nature are outcomes of natural causes, not of spiritual intervention. We must understand that in early Greek history, antideterministic beliefs were widespread. The behavior of a mountain stream was influenced by a resident sprite, as was true also of trees and thunderstorms. Larger phenomena, such as ocean storms or volcanoes, were explained as eccentricities of the gods. Science is impossible within such a formulation, as the laws painstakingly developed by observation can be violated at any time at divine whim.

By the time of Plato and Aristotle, most of this primitive animism had disappeared, at least among the intellectuals. Whereas Socrates was treated severely for questioning the gods, his successors simply ignored the issue and got away with it. Generally, from this time (roughly 300 B.C.) onward, determinism was accepted as being applicable to the physical world.

The psychological world was not as judiciously treated. Homer had described the gods as intervening to deceive humans with illusions, to drive them mad with lust or terror, or to induce behavior unpredictable from the individual's past pattern. By the time of Aristotle, it was safer to treat humans as having innate impulses toward wealth and power, not necessarily impulses of divine inspiration, and also to deal with pride, vanity, and cruelty as properties of humans, not imposed from outside. Today psychologists in general would agree that human actions should be understood in a purely human frame of reference, rather than being blamed on Satan or on God. This means not that psychologists have developed generally acceptable theories about motives and emotions, but only that these theories now fall within the deterministic frame of reference and are treated as phenomena open to rational explanation if sufficient data are available.

A Psychological Experiment

Determinism is assumed by all scientific psychologists. However, there are many ways of describing or conceptualizing the "cause" of a certain bit of behavior. To illustrate this point, I like to use a widely discussed experiment in which a pigeon is taught to walk a figure 8. The experimenter achieves this goal by watching the pigeon carefully and providing a reward (usually, food) when the response is in the desired direction. The process is called *shaping,* and a patient experimenter can shape this complex behavior.

There are, however, several different determinants here. Physical structure is one: an animal that could not walk would not be a good target for this experiment. A second determinant is the presence of food: pigeons will respond, and will remember the response, when food is a consequence. The third determinant is the experimenter: decisions about which movements can be fitted into the desired pattern (and hence, rewarded) depend on experimental judgment.

Multiple Causation

The pigeon's behavior is determined by a variety of factors, some inside the organism, some in the environment. Early behaviorists espoused a simplistic notion of determinism in which a single stimulus led to a single response. I shall demonstrate later that this phenomenon occurs very rarely, if at all. Most of the phenomena studied by psychologists are instances of multiple causes and multiple responses.

Figure 1.4 shows an alternative way of thinking about stimulus and response. In any situation, many stimuli affect the organism. Some of these are blocked, ignored, or excluded in some way. The organism may

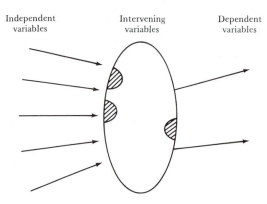

FIGURE 1.4   One Model of the Relationship of Independent, Intervening and Dependent Variables.

Information and stimulation affect the organism (the lens) within which
there are filters excluding some kinds of inputs. There may also be inhibitions which block some potential responses, the dependent variables.
This conceptualizes behavior as an interactive function of environment
and organism.   *(Suggested by a diagram in Brunswik, 1952).*

also emit a variety of responses, but some of these may be inhibited. In
the pigeon experiment, the experimenter tries to control the stimuli (e.g.,
light, sound, odors, and temperature). There is also an effort indirectly
to control the responses; if the bird starts preening or trying to fly, the
withdrawal of food will inhibit these undesired responses.

Human analogies are easy to find. College students in a classroom
receive not only external stimuli from the instructor, their classmates,
and outside noises, but internal stimuli such as hunger, a stomachache,
or other bodily changes. The student also emits many responses, which
may include taking notes, daydreaming of future pleasures, writing a
letter to a friend, or reading a comic book. One of the themes to be
developed in this book is the increase in the complication of theories to
take account of these multiple inputs and outputs.

It will be noted that Figure 1.4 is divided into three parts, labeled
"Independent variables," "Intervening variables," and "Dependent variables." *Independent* of this scheme means not under the student's control;
the sunlight outside, the instructor's vocal patterns, and the noises made
by nearby classmates are examples. *Dependent* variables are so called because they depend on the organism. *Intervening* variables are processes
assumed to go on inside the person; not surprisingly, as these cannot be
directly observed, they are the focus of marked disagreements among
theorists.

This analysis indicates why psychologists prefer to avoid terms like
cause and *effect*. Each action has many causes, and there may be a variety

of effects. To take a simple example, if a parent punishes a child for misbehavior, one effect may be to inhibit the act; another may be to elicit hostility, anger, and rebellion.

Parsimony

Given this complication in the cause–effect or stimulus–response relationship, the theorist may be tempted to hypothesize the operation of a variety of forces inside the organism, each of which would explain some of the observations. Early American psychologists fell into this logical trap. They suggested that each of the major human activities could be explained by an instinct, an inherited need to behave in this way. Thus, humans had an instinct for hunting, construction, acquisition, territoriality, and dozens of other activities. Critics found it objectionable that so many hypothetical entities should be concocted. They opposed these complicated assumptions with Ockham's razor, otherwise known as the law of parsimony. William of Ockham (1300–1349) proposed the logical rule that one should not multiply causes "unnecessarily"; in other words, we should keep things simple, but not oversimplified. The rule is thus difficult to follow, as a case can always be made that this extra "cause" is necessary.

Theory as Metaphor

The foregoing pages have sketched some features of theories as logic. But scientists devise theories to communicate with others; generally, the theorist hopes to convince others that this is a valid approach. It is important, then, to consider theory as communication.

Communication is facilitated if one can find a good figure of speech—a metaphor—for the theory. The metaphor has to be taken from familiar phenomena. For example, the Greeks proposed a theory that the sun was a flaming chariot driven across the sky by Helios. Chariots were common objects, fires were well known; the metaphor was well adapted to communicate.

Virtually all theories are based on some kind of metaphor, implicit or explicit. Modern physics gives us a metaphor of the atom as a kind of miniature solar system, with a nucleus (the sun) and orbiting particles (the planets) such as electrons, pions, mesons, and quarks. No theorist would suggest that the metaphor is exact; rather, it supplies a kind of model on which one can hang various kinds of experimental evidence to make it "clearer."

The metaphor must be taken from fairly common experience; otherwise, it does not communicate. A theory of problem solving in terms of the Martian process of grokking would not be useful because no one (except some science-fiction fans) can imagine what *grokking* refers to. Metaphors used by psychological theorists vary widely. William James referred to habit as the "enormous flywheel" of society; most of his readers knew that a flywheel was a stabilizer that reduced fluctuations in machine operation. Behaviorists often use the telephone switchboard metaphor: one plugs in a stimulus, and a distant phone rings (the response). At various times, Freud used a membrane metaphor (for separating conscious from unconscious processes), a hydraulic metaphor (for the pressures of instincts against societal inhibitions), and a geographic metaphor for id, ego, and superego.

Egocentric Theorizing

The metaphor chosen by a theorist will derive from personal experiences and will reveal something about the theorist's thought patterns. It was a Greek philosopher, Xenophanes, who offered the insightful comment that "The gods of the Ethiopians are swarthy and flat-nosed, the gods of the Thracians fair-haired and blue-eyed." In other words, the kind of explanatory figures one constructs will reflect one's everyday experience. Aristotle noted, "Men say that the Gods have a king, because . . . they imagine, not only the form of the Gods, but their ways of life to be like their own" (*Politica*, 1958, p. 280).

Scientists are also egocentric. Their theorizing reflects their personal experiences. Many essays about Sigmund Freud trace elements of his theories to details of his own biography. Friends of John B. Watson described him as having very poor mental imagery; thus it was not surprising that he found much of the theorizing of his predecessors about conscious phenomena to be foolish, as he could not find these in his own experiences.

The metaphor involved in a theory is not always important. However, it is desirable that we remember that a metaphor is exactly that, a figure of speech, not a mechanical model of the event to be explained. Thus no behaviorist meant that a plug-in connection like a switchboard was involved in learning; rather, this was a convenient way of thinking about connecting a stimulus with a response. A second caution is that one should avoid mixing metaphors. A telephone switchboard that is also given some of the properties Freud ascribed to his hydraulic pressure system will leave the reader confused. Metaphors can be used but must not be mixed.

The Process of Theorizing

Theorizing, I have suggested, is a typical cognitive process. It is continuous, but it can be analyzed. We can conveniently divide it into concept formation, hypothesis production, the devising of empirical tests, and the construction of theoretical systems.

Concepts hardly need further elaboration. The only point worth repeating is that each theorist is apt to derive distinctive concepts, and if these are not kept separate, confusion will result.

Hypothesis formation is the process of predicting how a particular concept will vary with different conditions. A classic example is the principle that an association of two events will be stronger the more frequently these two are experienced together.

A collection of hypotheses sharing common concepts, common assumptions about relationships, and compatible predictions about outcomes constitutes a theory. Sometimes this is called a *theoretical system.* Usages are unclear; generally accepted definitions are difficult to find. For simplicity, I shall use the term *theory* to refer to an assumed relationship among variables, although this relationship may be specific or general.

Theories go through stages of development. In the following chapters, I shall indicate how behavioristic, Gestalt, and psychoanalytic theories have been changing as new empirical findings and new logic affect the validity of the original theory.

The Hypotheticodeductive Method

One of the most elaborate examples in psychology of formal theorizing is the "hypotheticodeductive" method used by C. L. Hull in his theory of human behavior. His method, based on strictly logical principles, consisted in arriving inductively at a general postulate that had promise of being widely relevant to some aspect of behavior. From this general postulate, deductions of plausible consequences could be made. For example, from the postulate regarding primary reinforcement (Hull, 1951, p. 20), it is possible to deduce a corollary regarding secondary reinforcement (p. 28).

Opinions differ among psychologists about the value of the hypotheticodeductive (or inductive-deductive) method. Certainly no one has followed Hull's example by deriving elaborate formal statements of stimulus, drive, habit, reinforcement, and so on. It is possible that Hull's influence in psychology would have lasted longer if he had not been so precise in formulating his theory and the predictions that came from it. Testable statements permit one to validate a theory, but they also make it possible to disprove the theory. The sweeping generalizations made by many theorists are often so vague that no real test is possible.

Prediction

It is generally held that the soundest validation of a theory depends on the prediction of an event. The argument is that if the phenomenon has been accurately conceptualized, and if the antecedent conditions have been specified, the event predicted will occur. Thus psychologists spend many hours of effort testing predictions about the speed of learning, predictions about veridical and distorted perceptions, and predictions about interferences with memory. On a more applied level, they may test predictions about advertising appeals, the motivation of factory workers, and the relationship of early trauma to later personality disorder.

There is one major weakness of predictive tests: the convinced theorist often "sees" evidence favoring her or his theory when others do not. This is why theories have to be tested by critics rather than by proponents.

Postdiction

A somewhat larger group of "tests" of theories depends on *postdiction;* that is, one looks at the background of a juvenile delinquent (for example) and infers that the cause of his or her antisocial behavior was an abusive parent. This is a very inadequate test because there are dozens of other variables in the biography, many of which were potential determinants. A particularly poor example of postdiction is exemplified by the statement "This response occurred frequently; therefore it must have been reinforced." The theorist *assumes* that the theory is correct, so if behavior occurred, the reinforcer can be assumed. This is not to say that one should not examine a problem carefully to see if such a factor can be identified; it is only to point out that one does not prove a theory by asserting it to be true.

Control

Some theorists argue that the best validation of a theory lies in control, that is, in being able to manipulate the environment so that the behavior occurs on demand or is blocked on demand. This is a more compelling form of prediction, in that the experimenter can demonstrate control empirically by inserting the independent variable at the chosen time and place. This distinguishes scientific from popular psychology. It was the great contribution of Wilhelm Wundt that he took the study of sensing and perceiving out of the armchair and into the laboratory. Application of precisely measured stimuli, under conditions such that the observer could not know which stimulus would come next, provided evidence that the independent variable consistently produced a relevant dependent variable, such as a sensation of color or sound.

Not all sciences involve control; geology, for example, has few variables subject to human manipulation. Astronomy is another example. In such cases, we fall back on *understanding* as the test of the truth of a theory. Prediction is available in some cases, although it does not work well (or hasn't yet) for earthquakes or volcanoes. Ethical considerations prevent us from doing many psychological experiments to test theories. No one deliberately deprives babies of food, comfort, and caressing simply to test a theory of personality development. These ethics account for some of the imprecise formulations in the area of personality and social psychology; predictions can be made, but deliberate experimental control is forbidden by social conventions and ethics.

Theory as Prescription

A substantial amount of theorizing about psychology takes the form of *prescriptions,* such as "Psychology should be the study of the relations of behavior to physiology," or "The purpose of psychological research should be to find the basic elements in mental processes." Freud would argue that the study of psychology deals with the effect of unconscious processes on behavior.

This "prescriptive" approach to psychology was pioneered by R. I. Watson (1971). It is a suitable format for characterizing the various approaches to psychology, as such prescriptive statements are offered by all major theorists. Watson offered a set of 18 prescriptions, which in his opinion encompassed all of the variants on theories of psychology. In Table 1.1, Watson's prescriptions are listed in the form of bipolar pairs

TABLE 1.1   Prescriptions for Psychology as Proposed by Watson

These terms should be thought of as being preceded by the phrase, "Psychology should be defined as the study of . . ."		
Conscious mentalism	versus	Unconscious mentalism
Objective contents		Subjective observations
Determinism		Indeterminism
Functionalism		Structuralism
Empiricism		Rationalism
Inductive reasoning		Deductive reasoning
Mechanism		Vitalism
Objective methodology		Introspective methodology
Molecularism		Holism (molarism)
Monism		Dualism
Naturalism		Supernaturalism
Nomothetic laws		Idiographic laws
Peripheral processes		Central processes
Purism		Utilitarianism
Quantitativism[a]		Qualitativism
Rationalism		Irrationalism
Staticism (cross-sectional study)		Developmentalism
Staticism (enduring features)		Dynamicism (features causing change)

[a]Many of these terms were invented by Watson for the sake of brevity. A more complete definition of each is given in Watson (1971).

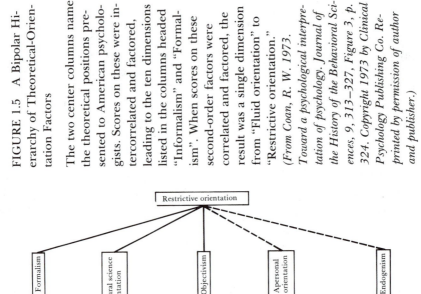

FIGURE 1.5 A Bipolar Hierarchy of Theoretical-Orientation Factors

The two center columns name the theoretical positions presented to American psychologists. Scores on these were intercorrelated and factored, leading to the ten dimensions listed in the columns headed "Informalism" and "Formalism". When scores on these second-order factors were correlated and factored, the result was a single dimension from "Fluid orientation" to "Restrictive orientation."

(From Coan, R. W. 1973.
Toward a psychological interpretation of psychology. Journal of the History of the Behavioral Sciences, 9, 313–327, Figure 3, p. 324. Copyright 1973 by Clinical Psychology Publishing Co. Reprinted by permission of author and publisher.)

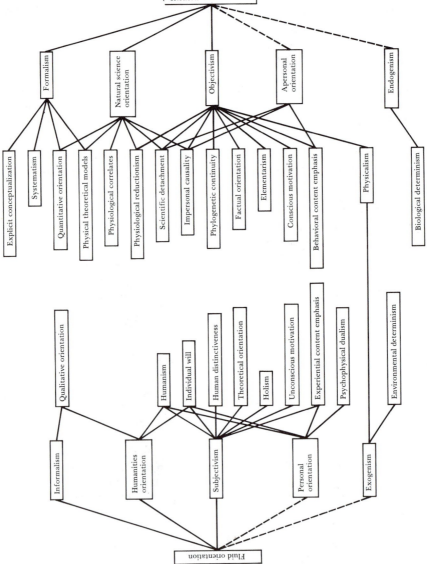

of concepts, such as "objective contents" versus "subjective observations." Behavioristic psychologists prefer the first, but many other varieties of psychological experts endorse the second. The analysis of psychological theorizing, then, may be systematized around these prescriptions.

Coan's Research

Watson assumed that his prescriptions would cluster, that is, that persons who accepted one of these prescriptions would tend to accept others. R. W. Coan (1968) investigated this hypothesis. He listed fifty-four well-known theorists and asked a sample of members of the American Psychological Association (APA) to describe each theorist on each of some thirty-four dimensions derived from Watson's earlier publications. A factor analysis of the responses elicited six clusters of psychological theories: (1) subjectivistic versus objectivistic; (2) holistic versus elementaristic; (3) personal versus transpersonal; (4) quantitative versus qualitative; (5) dynamic versus static; and (6) endogenist versus exogenist. The meaning of these terms will become clearer as we examine Coan's later studies.

Coan also (1968) prepared a list of 120 statements of "what psychologists should do," again based on Watson's list. These statements were sent to several hundred psychologists randomly chosen from the APA membership. Replies were received from 298—a large enough group so that we can feel considerable confidence that the results reflect significant groupings within American psychology. The responses to each item were intercorrelated with those to every other item; a factor analysis produced 17 dimensions along which prescriptions varied. These are shown in the two inner columns of Figure 1.5. Thus, humanism is opposed to scientific detachment, unconscious motivation is opposed to conscious motivation, environmental determinism is opposed to biological determinism, and so on.

Coan then computed factor scores for each respondent on each of the 17 factors, and intercorrelated these, followed by factor analysis. The result was an identification of five second-order factors, that is, highly generalized dimensions along which the prescriptions could be arranged. These are shown in the outer columns of Figure 1.5. It appears that an emphasis on natural science is opposed to an emphasis on "humanism" or a "humanities" orientation; subjectivism is contrasted to objectivism, and so on. In a very broad perspective, then, Coan concluded that psychologists tend to favor either a "restrictive" approach that would confine psychological research and speculation within rather strictly defined concepts and methods of investigation, or a "fluid" orientation, embracing more phenomena as acceptable for study, using more field observation and individual case studies, using impressionistic observation instead of laboratory investigation, and so on.

Kimble's Research

A somewhat similar study was conducted by G. A. Kimble (1984). Although the format used was different from Coan's, the variables (theoretical leanings) were closely parallel to Coan's. Kimble was intrigued by C. P. Snow's famous description of the "two cultures," humanities and science, and the divergence between them.

To obtain samples of psychologists likely to differ on Snow's "two cultures" dichotomy, Kimble took advantage of a feature of APA membership. The Association has 42 divisions corresponding to specialty areas such as clinical, industrial, experimental, and other areas. Some psychologists join several divisions, but most elect membership in only one, thus suggesting a concentration of interest and involvement in that phase of psychology. Kimble sent questionnaires to psychologists belonging only to one division, hoping to get homogeneous groups. The results for two divisions, experimental psychology and psychotherapy, are shown in Figure 1.6.

A glance at the figure shows marked differences in the kind of prescription one endorses for psychology, and these differences parallel dif-

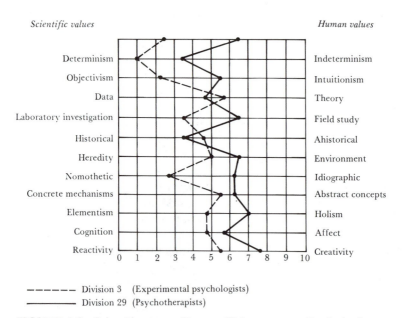

```
------ Division 3   (Experimental psychologists)
———— Division 29  (Psychotherapists)
```

FIGURE 1.6   Scientific versus Human Values among Psychologists

This shows responses of experimental psychologists and of psychotherapists to propositions paralleling those of Figure 1.5. Note the consistent leaning of experimentalists to the "tough-minded" side and of therapists to the "tender-minded" orientation. *(Data courtesy of Dr. G. A. Kimble.)*

ferences in membership. The psychotherapists consistently leaned toward the "human values" while the experimentalists favored the "scientific" values shown. The data tend to confirm Snow's hypothesis; psychologists, like other professional groups, are dividing into distinctive categories according to the values they perceive to be most important. And these values, in turn, are dictating preferences with regard to theoretical formulations, research, and applications.

Psychology of the Psychologist

A student of personality, looking at the results of the Coan and Kimble studies would suspect that there are noncognitive factors that influence individual choices of prescriptions. William James (1907) proposed that psychologists can be sorted into "tender-minded" and "tough-minded." The former are subjective, interested in helping, averse to quantification, and impressionistic; the latter favor objectivity and laboratory research, want to measure and quantify, and insist on instrumental recording whenever possible.

Coan (1973) attempted to test the James hypothesis. He obtained responses from about a hundred psychologists (from his sample of 298 APA members) to R. B. Cattell's 16-PF Inventory. One of Cattell's scores is labeled "Tender-minded vs. Tough-minded," and Coan did get differences in the predicted direction; that is, the tender-minded chose statements fitting on the left side of Figure 1.5; the tough-minded preferred positions falling on the right. However, the differences were not very large.

From still another fraction of his group of respondents, Coan obtained answers to some life-history questions. A few of the more intriguing findings were that for males, a father described as "controlling" favored developing an objectivist orientation; if, in addition, the father was "demanding," the theoretical leaning included an emphasis on behavior and physicalism. For females, the father seemed to be a particularly important determinant of a quantitative orientation. Of some interest is Coan's finding that the psychologists' reported relations to their mothers did not predict any theoretical tendency. One might conclude that professional issues are still "male" concerns, even for women entering psychology as a profession.

Reflecting on his investigations, Coan (1973) concluded that "It is really very difficult to escape the notion that our positions are governed to a high degree by individual temperament" (p. 325). This should not be surprising. Psychologists are human, and therefore, they have emotions, aspirations, sensitivities, and inhibitions. In later chapters, I present evidence that these personal variables have indeed influenced the development of psychological theory.

CHAPTER 2

Classical Backgrounds

Modern American psychological theory carries remnants of three major classical philosophies. These are respectively, the Greek concern with cognition, the Hebrew emphasis on emotion, and the Hindu focus on consciousness.

The sheer volume of material available on these three trends is so large that only capsule summaries can be included here. Some attention will be given to the connections between these philosophies and elements of modern psychology. However, later chapters will include more specific references where they are appropriate.

Many of the prescriptive dimensions summarized in Table 1.1 can be traced to ancient origins. And many practices of modern applied psychology share these same origins. Obviously, the student can study the current state of psychology without a knowledge of the ancestral roots, but a deeper understanding is likely to result if these recent developments are linked to their beginnings.

Classical Greece

The word *psychology* is of Greek origin. It derives from the word *psyche,* meaning "breath," which can also be translated as "soul." *Psyche* was contrasted with *soma* ("body"). *Logos,* meaning *word,* came to be the identification of a field of study.

Why did the Greeks feel it necessary to assume the existence of a soul? It is generally agreed that primitive cultures distinguish soul from body on the basis of at least four kinds of evidence: (1) dreams; (2) loss of consciousness; (3) delirium; and (4) death. Specifically, the Greeks noted that in a dream one may travel thousands of miles and have strange experiences, although companions state that the body has not moved from the spot; one may have hallucinations in which the dead rise up; in a fever, one is chased by terrifying monsters; after a blow on the head, one loses consciousness and so is unaware of surrounding activity. Finally, the body weighs exactly the same a few minutes after death as before death, yet something obviously is missing. The soul is a theoretical entity created to explain all of these phenomena.

It should be noted that the theory of an immortal soul did not arise in classical Greece before Plato. Some scholars suspect that this idea migrated from India to Greece in the aftermath of Alexander's invasion of India about 330 B.C. The Hindu doctrine of reincarnation obviously involves a soul that survives after the death of the body, reincarnates in one form or another until it finally reaches Nirvana, peaceful reunion with the cosmic soul. Plato seems to have accepted some version of this philosophy, along with the theory of innate ideas, to which we can trace the doctrine of human instincts.

Appearance Versus Reality

A major problem for the Greeks was the difference between appearance and reality. The senses, they held, could not be trusted (although some philosophers disagreed). Democritus, for example, believed that a tiny replica of the real object, called an *eidolon*, entered into the human body by way of a sense organ and was stored somewhere inside. This meant that humans really perceived objective truth. However, the *eidola* in storage rubbed against each other and were transformed, the result being errors of memory.

Modern readers find the *eidolon* theory naive. Obviously, a tiny chair does not find its way into my eye when I look at a chair. But consider: physics tells us that photons, submicroscopic particles, bounce off the object and stimulate the retina. In other words, there is a kind of parallel to the *eidolon* even in today's thinking.

Democritus is also famous for his anticipation of modern atomic theory. He denied the reality of conscious experiences and espoused an objectivistic monism. One of the most widely quoted of his assertions is related to this problem: "By convention sweet is sweet, by convention bitter is bitter, by convention hot is hot, by convention cold is cold, by convention color is color. But in reality there are atoms and the void. That is, the objects of sense are supposed to be real, and it is customary to regard them as such, but in truth they are not. Only the atoms and the void are real".

This statement, of course, sounds surprisingly like the answers given by modern physics. This book is not "real"; it is only a bunch of protons, electrons, mesons, and quarks and mostly empty space (the void). Sensory qualities such as sweet and colored do not exist for physics; only vibrations and molecules are real to the atomic physicist.

Democritus went further with his argument, even speculating about the shape and size of the "atoms" giving rise to certain sensations. The

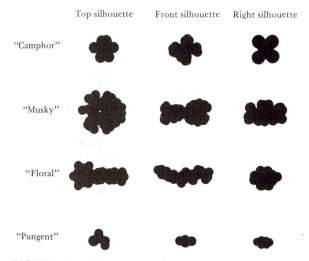

FIGURE 2.1   Shapes of Molecules Determine Sensory Qualities

Was Democritus a prophet? He speculated that the shapes of "atoms" determined the qualities of tastes and odors. Research by Amoore (1964)
showed that molecular shape determined odor quality. *(From Amoore,
1964, Fig. 5, p. 467; by permission of author and New York Academy of Sciences.)*

atoms producing a sour or acid taste, he wrote, were "angular, winding,
small and thin." When we recognize that he never saw an atom, his courage is impressive. But again, his approximation to modern science is
astounding. In Figure 2.1 are reproduced some observations on the shapes
of the chemical molecules giving rise to sensations of odor. Although
these have no resemblance to Democritus' description, they still confirm
the intuition of the wise old Greek that the physical shape of the stimulus and our conscious sensation are somehow intimately related.

Determinism—the belief that both physical and mental events are determined by prior circumstances and are not capricious phenomena generated by divine intervention into human affairs—appeared early in Greek
speculation. The materialism of Democritus, who interpreted the "soul"
as being made up of atoms essentially like those of the body, but finer,
smoother, and more spherical, is a case in point. He held that there is
no such phenomenon as "free will," and that all human behavior could
be traced strictly to prior events.

The philosopher Zeno (c. 300 B.C.) is credited with a famous defense
of determinism. The story is that Zeno had a slave who had been stealing
from him. When he got out his whip to punish the miscreant, the slave
protested, "But master, it was determined that I should steal. So I am

not responsible and should not be punished." To which Zeno replied firmly, "And it is determined that I shall punish thee."

Democritus has held that the kind of sensation a person experienced was a function of the kinds of atoms making impressions on the sense organs. He explicitly noted that color, taste, smell, and so on were not real; he thus banished conscious data from the world of science. We can compare his definition of sensing, which omitted consciousness, with that offered by W. T. Powers (1973): "When I refer to perception, I mean in general the entire set of events, following stimulation, that occurs in the *input* part of the brain, all the way from sensory receptors to the highest centers in the cerebral cortex" (p. 35). Note that the term *color*, for example, cannot enter this definition. Optical stimuli vary in wavelength, not in color. Retinal cells manifest electrochemical activity, not color. And this is true for the fibers in the optic nerve, the subcortical nuclei, and the cerebral cortex. Consciousness and perceptual qualities are sunk without a trace.

Heraclitus

As Democritus forecast the behaviorist, Heraclitus was an early advocate of the idea that everything is conflict and change: "A man cannot step twice in the same river" means that the river is constantly changing, that all the molecules are flowing away, and that no situation ever exactly repeats itself. Heraclitus might have added that the man is not the same: his cells are changing, and his accumulated experiences make him a different person. Critics of the concept of a constant personality can agree with this construction of reality.

Pythagoras

Another modern theme in classic garb is mathematical precision and quantification. Pythagoras believed that "quantity, specifically number, was the key to all reality" (Murphy, 1968, p. 5). This certainly is true of the modern physicist's metaphysics: mathematical relations are the underlying basics of the real world. From the Pythagorean love of numerical relations, Murphy commented, came our modern obsession with numbers: "A *p* value . . . of .05 is significant, but a .06 is not significant. . . . There had to be thirty subjects to make possible the use of a Pearson correlation coefficient" (p. 19). Murphy went on to cite other misuses of numbers in modern psychology, such as the assumption of continuity when the evidence of discontinuity is obvious (Murphy ridicules the statistician who says there are 2.3 children in the average American family).

Interestingly, this Pythagorean obsession with numbers tied in with the debate over sensory illusions; Greek architects learned how to vary

the width and height of columns to provide an illusion of perfect verti-
cality. The appearance of symmetry was achieved by an asymmetrical
physical reality.

Alcmaeon

The earliest physiologist, a theorist whose ideas are debated even today,
was Alcmaeon of Crotona (c. 450 B.C.) He engaged in the dissection of
animals and asserted that the nerves carried information from the sense
organs to the brain. He also designated the brain as the place where
memories were stored and reorganized, so that the person could infer
relationships that were not directly perceived.

Alcmaeon was influenced by Pythagoras, at least with respect to the
latter's concern about numerical relationships. As the strings of a lyre
must be in certain relations to each other if they are to produce pleasant
sounds, so the components of the human body were governed by mathematical laws. Health was a state of equilibrium, and if this equilibrium
were disturbed by accident or disease, it was the task of the body to try
to restore this balance. Thus, fever represented an excess of heat, and
the treatment was to cool the patient; other conditions indicated excessive dryness and could be treated with water, and so on. Everything depended on diagnosing the correct disturbance of equilibrium and finding the procedure that would restore equilibrium.

Alcmaeon's ideas about therapy persisted over many centuries. His
general principle of equilibrium gave rise to the modern principle of
homeostasis and to various opponent-process theories of vision and of
affectivity.

The chronological sequence of some of these early Greek thinkers is
given in Table 2.1. Some of these philosophers, although interesting in
themselves, have not affected the development of theories of psychology
and hence are not mentioned in the text.

Socrates and Plato

Considering his fame, one is astonished to learn how little we know about
Socrates (469–399 B.C.) and his ideas. He described himself as a gadfly,
needling the complacent Athenians with his pointed questions and dev-
astating analogies. But he left behind him a debate that continues today:
Was he merely a mouthpiece for Plato, or was Plato merely a steno-
grapher recording Socrates' pearls? The *Dialogues* are ostensibly records
of Socrates educating the youth of Athens by asking leading questions;
but each of the *Dialogues* comes to us over the signature of his student,
Plato.

The difficulty of sorting ideas, crediting some to Socrates and some to
Plato, began with Plato himself. Plato wrote, "There is not and never will

TABLE 2.1   Some Important Figures in Greek Philosophy

The following list includes the major philosophers whose speculations have influenced the development of Western thought, specifically in relation to human behavior and human experience. The phrases given can function as "tag lines" or memory cues to help you relate this individual to the major psychological theses developed in the text.

PHILOSOPHER	KEY PHRASES
Heraclitus (500 B.C.)	All is change; the basic principle of life is conflict.
Parmenides (500 B.C.)	Thought is enduring; perception is transitory
Pythagoras (582–507 B.C.)	Only mathematics is real; magic numbers.
Anaxagoras (499–428 B.C.)	All animate organisms are capable of reason.
Alcmaeon (500 B.C.)	Quest for equilibrium; tension reduction, homeostasis.
Empedocles (495–435 B.C.)	Temperament depends on bodily fluids; objects give off emanations to the senses.
Protagoras (481–411 B.C.)	We know only what we experience; sensations are due to movements of sense organs.
Democritus (460–370 B.C.)	The only reality is the atom; all else is illusion.
Socrates (470–399 B.C.)	Self-knowledge, self-development, self-consistency; satisfaction is found only in the "good," which involves ethics.
Plato (427–347 B.C.)	Only form is real; experiences are illusory. Humans are both rational and divine. Soul is good; body is bad.
Aristotle (384–322 B.C.)	Observation is the key to understanding; all knowledge comes through the senses. Soul is identified with function. Hierarchy of motives: nutritive, sensitive, rational.
Zeno (340–265 B.C.)	Virtue is knowledge; all events are rigidly determined.
Epicurus (342–270 B.C.)	Mechanistic theory of behavior; atomism; believe only your senses; the true pleasures are those of reason; eliminate fear of death, fear of the gods.

be a work of Plato; the works which now go by that name belong to Socrates, embellished and rejuvenated" *(Second Epistle)*.

Perhaps it is not important to decide on authorship. The ideas are the treasure, and we have these well presented. We can leave arguments over credits and priorities to the living.

The central task of philosophy, according to Socrates, is to understand how we know our world. This is the question of epistemology: a logical analysis of knowing, a way of distinguishing appearance from reality.

In an oft-cited dialogue, Socrates led a slave through a series of questions to the proof of the Pythagorean theorem (the problem of the square of the hypotenuse). Socrates used this method to demonstrate his thesis that the slave knew the theorem but did not know that he knew; in brief, the slave had innately the solution to the problem but had to become conscious of it. Knowledge, then, is a kind of reminiscence, teasing into awareness ideas that were there all along.

In this conception of knowledge, the processes of studying, learning, and repetition are of minor importance; reason and reflection are paramount. Thus, Socrates laid the foundation for *rational* psychology as opposed to the *empirical* psychology of laboratories and field observations.

It is tempting to make an analogy with the process of psychotherapy. The patient says, "Tell me why I am miserable." The therapist replies, "Only you know the answer, but perhaps I can help you dig it out." Socrates taught us the importance of asking the right questions.

Socrates warned his students not to trust their senses for evidence of truth. The senses report on appearances but cannot get at the underlying reality. To use a modern example, your senses will never reveal to you that this book is composed of electrons and protons. Merely listening to political speeches will never lead you to a wise judgment about policy decisions. Reason is the crucial process. You may be well or ill, standing or sitting, clothed or naked; the *real* you is something other than these appearances.

However, this does not mean that reality is only an idea; that, Socrates claimed, is a "bottomless pit of nonsense." Thus, we face the obligation to use our senses. We learn by observing. Memory makes records of experience like inscriptions on a wax tablet. Contiguity and frequency are important in the recording of events and the establishing of associations. Observation *plus* reason may lead to awareness of reality.

The Zeitgeist I have suggested that theories are affected by the socioeconomic environment, or the "spirit" of the times. Plato's views may well have been shaped by the historical context of his life. D. N. Robinson (1981) pointed out that Plato's views set forth in *The Republic* reflect the situation after Athens was defeated by Sparta. Just as Prussia (Germany) dominated western Europe in the last half of the nineteenth century, so Sparta dominated Greece during the fourth century B.C. Thus, the Spartans—"strong, self-denying, regimented, orderly, traditional"— became the models used by Plato in his hypothetical perfect state. This is the Plato who proposed that citizens be classified as gold, or silver, or brass and iron, made so by heredity and the gods, some to rule, some to serve. Plato also proposed arranged marriages and controlled breeding to improve the genetic quality of the citizenry.

Socrates had proposed that reason should rule over the passions. According to Robinson (1981), the historical situation accounted for this attitude: "Noting the sad fate of a people moved by passion, they [Socratics] devoted themselves to impersonal reason and argued well enough for what came to be known as *Rationalism* to make it the 'official' philosophy until the seventeenth century" (p. 55).

Plato pictured Socrates as the skeptic, incessantly asking questions designed to make the listener examine established beliefs. (It was this tendency to question religious and political institutions that led to Socrates' sentence of death.)

Knowledge Along with this skepticism about existing beliefs, the Socratics expressed doubts about humans' knowledge of their environment. The famous fable of the cave illustrates this doubting attitude, which questions the connection between perception and reality. Imagine, Plato suggested,

> human beings living in an underground den . . . here they have been from their childhood, and have their legs and necks chained so that they cannot move, and can only see before them, being prevented by the chains from turning round their heads. Above and behind them a fire is blazing [and between the prisoners and the fire there are] men passing . . . carrying all sorts of vessels, and statutes, and figures of animals. [The prisoners] see only the shadows of these things, or of one another, which the fire throws on the opposite wall. (*Republic*, p. 273)

Thus, said Plato, we know reality only by distorted shadows; we cannot know reality directly.

Here again, the Greeks anticipated modern thought. Vision does not give us direct contact with external objects; vibrations reach the eye, activate retinal cells, and produce electrical fields in the cortex; vision reflects reality indirectly, not at all as a direct picture. The same holds for taste, smell, hearing, and touch. We try to get direct evidence of what is real, but because all knowledge has to come through the senses, we cannot know reality directly.

Can we know reality at all? Plato held with Pythagoras that there were certain truths that had a deeper reality than sensory evidence. This reality was of forms, not of objects. Consider the idea of a triangle. One can draw right triangles, acute triangles, isosceles triangles, and so on. No one of these is the perfect triangle, but the idea of a perfect triangle can still exist (see Figure 2.2). The idea, or form, is thus independent of sensation; Plato believed that these were innate, coming with the soul from some cosmic reality not directly available to the human senses. This detail of Plato's philosophy is believed by many scholars to have come from the East, from India or Persia, with which the Greeks had many contacts.

An amusing sidelight on Plato's fable of the cave is that the philosopher suspected that many individuals do not wish to face reality. In the fable, he tells of a prisoner who escapes and sees what the outside world

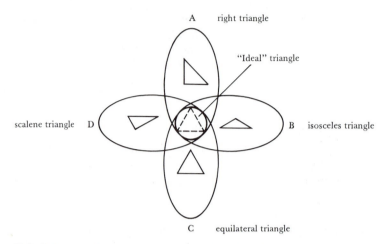

FIGURE 2.2   Plato's Conception of the Ideal Triangle

One can experience many kinds of triangles, but it is impossible to draw an abstract triangle representing the mathematical definition. The ideal triangle is a rational abstraction from many observed, concrete triangles. (Compare Figure 1.3, p. 9.)

is "really" like. On his return, he tries to explain the reality to his fellows, but they think he has lost his senses by exposure to the external environment.

Plato's belief in the "reality" of form as opposed to appearance can be illustrated in another way. What, he asked, is the relationship between a pile of logs and a ship? The answer is in the form, or the plan, of a ship, which existed before the logs were hewn into shape and fitted together to make the ship. Forms are the basic reality; the objects that reflect these forms are ephemeral and changing. This hypothesis runs through all of science. A psychologist who says that the child's fear of dogs is "really a conditioned reflex" is trying to identify a hypothetical reality behind the overtly observable behavior of the child.

In Plato's thinking, an innate idea is activated by some external stimulus; that is, if one has experiences with a triangle, these will elicit the idea of a pure triangle as opposed to a single specific triangle (see Figure 2.2). If an experience does not fit an innate pattern, we are puzzled and usually forget the incident.

Aristotle

Aristotle appears to have been an early example of the "Oedipus complex" influence on theorizing. He rebelled against Plato's belief in innate ideas, or the hereditary determination of thought. He was the first explicitly empirical theorizer; that is, he insisted that *all* knowledge comes through the senses. He did not share the skepticism of Plato, as exemplified in the fable of the cave. Nevertheless, Aristotle was well aware that the senses were unreliable. He pointed out that the information emanating from the object made an impression on a sense organ, and that what was really known was what was recorded, not what was out there in the external world. He believed in inductive reasoning from observations to generalizations, as an alternative to innate ideas; but he was also a logician, the founder of the syllogism, and a firm believer in the primacy of reason when it seemed to break with observation.

It is difficult to guess whether the Plato–Aristotle split was due to ideas or to emotions. As Plato had no difficulty in praising his mentor, Socrates, it seems likely that he and Aristotle clashed. Contemporaries described Aristotle as having a "sharp and bitter" tongue, so it may well be that personal friction was the major influence in this early controversy.

Regarding the soul, already the central concept in theories about human psychology, Aristotle's view resembled Plato's in some ways, differed sharply in others. Plato had assumed that the soul came from a cosmic soul and returned there after death. Aristotle considered soul to be a function of the body. Plato had treated the soul as having three parts, the nutritive (e.g., desires for food), the locomotor (spirit and courage), and reason. Aristotle likewise wrote of three varieties of soul, but characterized them as vegetative, animal, and human. The vegetative soul was involved in nutrition and reproduction; the animal, in sensitivity and locomotion; the human, in reason. Aristotle anticipated the hierarchy theories of motivation, writing that the lower-level needs must be satisfied before we can pay attention to and strive for ideals and intellectual goals. The most important distinction of all is that Plato treated the soul as *form*—that is, the patterning of thought and behavior—whereas Aristotle identified the soul with *function*. The eye, for example, is an organ, but seeing is its function; thus, we can say, seeing is soul as far as the eye is concerned. For Plato, the soul of a ship would be its pattern, its design; for Aristotle, it would be the function of sailing.

Implicit in the foregoing distinctions is the underlying philosophy. Plato was an idealist and a nativist; his reality was basically a matter of the innate ideas activated as the person encounters stimuli and responds to them. Aristotle was an empiricist, for whom ideas were arrived at inductively, from experience; in his view, the mind at birth was a *tabula nuda,* a blank wax slate on which experience will write as the child grows. Plato's view is best represented in modern times by C. G. Jung's postulate of a racial unconscious; Aristotle started a tradition now best represented by behaviorism and some phenomenological theorists.

Both great Greeks set forth theories of motivation. Plato emphasized pleasure and pain, but he also noted pride, security, and conformity as important drives. He was cynical about politicians, saying that they exploited the masses for their selfish benefit. It may be that he anticipated the gestalt principle of closure: "Desire is a consciousness of incompleteness." However, for Plato, the attainment of physical goals led only to a temporary satisfaction; the dependable pleasures were those of the soul.

Aristotle was even more explicit regarding human motives. In his *Rhetoric,* he counseled orators how to sway their audiences and politicians how to influence the citizenry. Of this remarkable book, G. Murphy (1968) wrote, "It makes very modern reading to scan the way in which the passions of mankind, particularly those that the orator would sway—fear, pride, rage, shame, self-justification, and so on—are spelled out" (p. 56).

The foregoing discussion does not begin to identify all of the points on which the classic Greeks anticipated the major issues of twentieth-century psychology. What one should remember is that the Greek texts became the staple of study for scholars down through the centuries and hence shaped the psychological views of René Descartes, John Locke, David Hume, John Stuart Mill, and even Wilhelm Wundt.

The Judaic Tradition

Although American psychology has emphasized cognition and thus heavily reflects the Greek concern with how we know the world around us, current thought also introduces dynamics and psychopathology. This latter aspect derives more from Hebrew than from Greek ideas.

The Hebraic tradition postulates a soul and, like the Greek, relates it to life or breath. The Hebrew scriptures use two terms, *nefesh* to refer to any living creature, and *ru'ah* to identify human life. *Ru'ah* was associated with the impulse toward a higher spiritual life, toward idealistic thought and action, mobilizing power and energy for certain goals. However, the Hebrew tradition included the specific principle that a human being had a soul that was a divine gift; for this concept, the word was *neshamah.*

As in Greece, the early Hebrew literature is ambiguous on the immortality of the soul. The *Encyclopedia Judaica* suggests that, in Hebrew tradition, humans are not descended from the gods, as in Greek doctrines, nor are they the product of blind natural forces (the Darwinian approach). Rather, they are descended from angels. Interestingly, in ancient Palestine, the metaphysical view of humans was monistic: there was not, in these early writings, a dualism of body and soul; rather, there was a unified entity that could be viewed from two different viewpoints, as physical and as psychical.

Humans differ from the lower animals, according to this theory, with respect to reason, creativity, and awareness of God. Also, of course, they have free will. This idea conflicts with the idea of the long line of determinists stretching back to Democritus and forward to behaviorism, that belief in free will inhibits the development of a scientific psychology, as the relation of antecedent conditions to consequent acts may be disrupted at any time by a free (undetermined) choice.

Classical Judaism did not include immortality as an attribute of the soul. Rather the emphasis was on immortality through one's children and later generations. However, there is an interesting parallel to the Greek tradition in that Sheol (like Hades) is a kind of shadowy ghostlike realm in which disembodied souls have a foggy, fuzzy existence.

A sharp break with the Greek view, however, relates to innate ideas. Where Plato had postulated innate ideas such as mathematics, ethics, and logic, the Hebrews postulated an innate knowledge of good and evil, pointing up the major difference in the Judaic and Greek traditions: an overwhelming concern about cognition, for understanding of the world, among the Greeks, versus a concern about emotions and ethics among the Hebrews.

Belief in the divine revelation of truth is antithetical to a concern about observation and reflection as the sources of true knowledge. If truth is divinely revealed, there is no need for science. For if, by chance, observation contradicts the revelation, then the scientist will be attacked as antireligious.

Consequently, most of the psychological material in the Old Testament relates to emotions such as shame and guilt. It is no surprise that Sigmund Freud, whose psychoanalytic theory focused on these emotions, was steeped in the Judaic literature and showed a concern about dynamics, as opposed to reason, as the keystone of human psychology. Analytic theory has constantly emphasized the irrational in human behavior and has ignored the inductive and deductive search for an understanding of reality.

The Hebrew conception of God, however, was actually somewhat more rational than that of the Greeks. Whereas, in the Iliad, the gods are forever tricking one side or the other with illusions and hallucinations, such incidents occur rarely in the Hebrew Scriptures.

The differences in the psychological assumptions of the classical Greek and Hebrew literature have not been thoroughly explored. There is some evidence, however, that the active interchange of scholars between the United States and Israel will fill this gap. A monograph by Kaplan, Schwartz, and Kaplan (1984) examines some of these issues, notably, ideas about parent–child relations, marital relations, and the autonomy of the individual personality. Given the influence of religion in the early history of the United States, such discussions may lead to a better understanding of how the field of psychology has evolved in this country.

Patristic Psychology

It is difficult to disentangle the ideas and influences of early Christian writers from those of classical Judaism. Initially, of course, the Christian version differed only slightly from the Hebrew doctrines. But with time, substantial changes were introduced.

The major writings of this period (roughly, A.D. 100–1500) were by the Christian fathers (hence, *patristic*). St. Paul was the first influential thinker in this group; later important thinkers were Origen, St. Augustine, and St. Thomas Aquinas.

Human nature was viewed differently in the new religion. Every person was a child of God, hence the concept of universal fellowship was launched on its uncertain course. This concept did not change behavior; just as Greeks and Hebrews killed off their enemies, so the Christians slew theirs. Salvation was the primary goal of life; although good works could marginally improve one's chances of heaven, it was the acceptance of Christ and faith in the new gospel that opened the door. The soul was firmly pronounced to be immortal; both Greeks and Hebrews had vacillated on this issue.

The *Zeitgeist* effects in the spread of Christianity are well known. The Roman masses lived in poverty, as did most of the Mediterranean world. Exploitation by the aristocracy and pillage by the barbarians made it seem futile to pursue materialistic goals. The martyrdom of prominent Christians may actually have attracted converts because of admiration for their bravery and integrity.

Motivation

Sigmund Freud obtained much of his theory of motivation from the Hebrew tradition, but it differed little from the early Christian version. The power of the sex drive was acknowledged, but sex was uniformly denounced by the Christian leaders as seducing people (generally, males) away from the paths of righteousness. Origen, one of the outstanding writers of the early Church, castrated himself so that he would not be obsessed with sexual impulses. St. Augustine, after a somewhat licentious early life, renounced sexual pleasures and devoted his energies to forwarding the doctrines of the new religion.

Learning

The contrast of patristic with Aristotelian psychology is most apparent with respect to epistemology. Mostly, it could be described as Neoplatonic, that is, as emphasizing innate ideas, reflection, and meditation, rather than observation of nature. By self-examination one could acquire knowledge and also could arrive at conclusions regarding the relations of human beings to God.

One of the ironies of this period was that, whereas the *ideas* of Plato were absorbed into Church doctrine and into the philosophic writings of the time, it was Aristotle who was revered as the master philosopher. Historians have no generally accepted explanation for this development. The preference for neo-Platonism, with an authoritarian approach to government and an emphasis on innate ideas, makes sense in a religious organization based on belief in divine revelation. One hypothesis is that Plato's association with the skeptical Socrates caused the Church fathers to avoid invoking his name. Aristotle, although famous, was less closely identified with skepticism. Further, most of Aristotle's works had been lost in the collapse of the Roman Empire, hence, the contradiction of his views and those of Plato was virtually unknown.

Another interesting sidelight on the history of the period is the role of the Arab conquest in salvaging Greek classics. Many Greek writings were destroyed in the great fire in the library at Alexandria around A.D. 200. However, Arabic translations of these Greek masterpieces had been sent to other locations; thus, our knowledge of classical Greece is due to the respect for scholarship of the early Arabs. During the Saracen occupation of Spain, for example, Christian scholars came to Cordova to study, thus initiating the series of events leading to the Renaissance.

St. Augustine (354–430) distinguished between knowledge and wisdom (which had been more-or-less synonymous for the classical Greeks). For Augustine, knowledge was earthbound, an awareness of temporal things, whereas wisdom was based on a knowledge of eternal things. The earthbound processes of perceiving and remembering might help an individual to cope with the problems of survival, but wisdom was the attribute by which humans found their way to God.

The uses of introspection were first and most sensitively explored by St. Augustine. An example is his discussion of forgetting, which can be summarized in this way: I may say that I have forgotten a friend's name; I try recalling names from memory, and eventually, I recognize one as the one I am seeking. Now, how can I recognize it if I have forgotten it? And if I have forgotten it, how has it reappeared in my consciousness? These are questions of thresholds, as in modern information-processing research, and also of inhibition, as explored in Freudian psychology.

Introspection, of course, leads to other problems. According to Augustine, people are born with a knowledge of right and wrong, of good and evil. The perception of an act as right or wrong does not depend on the familiar five senses, but on another, "inner" sense. In a curious sentence, Robinson (1981) characterized this inner sense: "It, unlike the five senses, perceives itself perceiving as it perceives each of the separate senses perceiving" (p. 122). This problem agitated William James, who tried to introspect on himself introspecting, without success; and it intrigued Gordon Allport, who distinguished this aspect of self from the individual's self-image or self-concept.

Dualism

The early Christian theory of reality was dualistic: body was matter; soul was not. Generally speaking, the body was evil and the soul good. It was taken for granted that the soul could direct the body most of the time; under stress, the body might overrule the soul, as in the case of a strong sex drive. No attention was given to the paradox that the material could not affect the nonmaterial, or vice versa. Descartes and his successors worked at this dilemma, without much success.

Thomistic Psychology

St. Thomas Aquinas (1225–1274) was the last of the great Christian theoreticians, at least in relation to psychology. Although generally endorsing the ideas of St. Paul, Origen, and St. Augustine, he conceded more to empirical observation than his predecessors. Only the more important of his ideas can be sketched here:

1. Aquinas accepted the traditional distinction between knowledge and wisdom, but he analyzed the problem in a novel fashion. Experience, he proposed, is of particulars only; it cannot give knowledge of the universal. Like Plato, he stressed the importance of abstract ideas. He did not, however, endorse the notion that these were innate. They could be arrived at by the power of reason, which takes particular experiences and abstracts universal forms (truths) from them. Even animals can learn particular acts, but only humans have the power of reason and hence can arrive at divine truths.

2. Although lower animals are prisoners of instinct, humans have more freedom. The body has a nervous system that can transmit to the soul information about the external world, thus permitting complex learned activities that are superior to the innate patterns of the lower species.

3. Because they are endowed with reason, human beings can abstract form from appearance. Form is not given in the sensory impressions of any phenomenon but must be abstracted from the information provided by particulars. Aquinas anticipated Gottfried Wilhelm Leibniz by using the term *agens intellectus* ("active intellect") to identify the agency that processes sensory data. Appearances are deceptive; only the intellect can decide on an underlying reality. Curiously, Aquinas contradicted himself at times; one passage reads, "We perceive directly reality itself," a conclusion at odds with his earlier position.

Many critics have pointed out that Aquinas was anti-intellectual. Robinson (1981) concluded his discussion by saying that it was logically necessary for Aquinas to wind up opposing experimentation and the empirical observation of natural events. Just as free will makes a strict determinism impossible, so experimentation constituted a threat to deduced reality. Although the Renaissance saw an erosion of this attitude among Church leaders, it has not entirely vanished today.

The Hindu Contribution

Historians of psychology have tended to concentrate on the Greeks, partly because Western civilization seems to be a continuation of their culture, including their emphasis on cognition. This tradition held until after World War II as regards American psychology. In the 1950s and 1960s there was a sudden upsurge of interest in the Hindu ideology of consciousness, meditation and mastery of the environment by withdrawing from it. "Consciousness-raising" became popular. Drugs became a part of the movement to explore "altered states of consciousness." It is possible that an impetus came from American soldiers who had been stationed in India, Burma and Thailand during the war and brought back these eastern customs with them.

Classical Indian theories, like Hebraic thought, are closely bound to religious doctrines. However, we can sort out the psychological strains from the aspects that need not concern us because they have not affected contemporary psychology.

A. C. Paranjpe (1984) noted that there were two major currents in Indian philosophy in its early history: Yoga and Vedanta. Because they are similar with respect to human nature and human behavior, we can ignore this distinction.

Both Indian philosophies emphasize the fallibility of the senses, the untrustworthy character of our knowledge of the external world, and the fallacy of trying to fathom its secrets. The road to truth, they hold, lies in withdrawal from the environment and meditation on the hidden truths of reality. There is an obvious similarity, here, to both the classical Greek and the Judaic traditions, but in different aspects. The Greeks wanted to study nature at close hand to penetrate illusion, whereas the Hindu tradition favors contemplative meditation as the path to understanding. Similarly, the Judeo-Christian legacy praised the meditative life, but the focus of meditation was on the nature of God, not on nature itself.

The clash between objectivism and subjectivism, noted briefly in the preceding chapter, has its place in Hindu psychology. The emphasis here is on the irrelevance of matter. Reality is consciousness. J. Woodroffe (1959), a Sanskrit scholar, offered the parallel to modern physics, which dematerializes matter: "While western philosophers have held that the Reality behind these phenomena is unknowable," he wrote, "the Vedanta affirms that it is knowable and is consciousness itself" (p. 325). This view anticipates the subjective idealism that asserts that the only real world is the world as it is perceived.

Paranjpe (1984), whose treatment of Yoga and Vedanta is comprehensive, took the position that this abolition of matter is ambiguous. In the framework of Vedantic thinking, cognitive constructions may be real; they "are illusory *only* when seen from the level of the absolute knowledge (parā vidyā) which is attained in the state of Nirvikalpa Samādhi" (p. 293). Thus, Vedanta accepts the idea of levels of reality, as well as the possibility of living in a shared reality with other persons, whereas the subjective idealists of Western philosophy had a problem with the concept of a reality that could be shared with others. (George Berkeley solved this problem by asserting that, as God perceives all reality all the time, there is a single reality that would be the same as that known to another person.)

Perhaps because of this uncertainty about the existence of a real physical world, the Yogis and the Vedantists have never explored the possibility of applying an experimental approach to consciousness. Meditation, in the sense of trying to understand the world, is a standard practice, and many hours are spent in training the neophyte in deep meditation and trance states. It is this emphasis on altered states of consciousness that seems to have underlain the widespread Western interest in Hindu philosophies since World War II.

The claim that yogic training enables one to have control over many bodily functions normally not susceptible of conscious control is another linkage of East and West. Recent studies of biofeedback have claimed to replicate feats described by Yogis in slowing down breathing, heart rate, metabolism, and so on. Although the data are less than firmly convincing, the shared interest of Indian and Western scholars is relevant.

A more detailed account of Vedanta—as well as a brief summary of a school called Lokayata, which was the only early Indian venture into empiricism, and which never gained much credence in the face of the subjectivistic bias that characterizes the other Indian schools—can be found in G. S. Brett's *History of Psychology* (1912). Brett also speculated about the relevance of Hebrew influences on Western psychology; regrettably, both the Hindu and the Hebrew sections were deleted in the more widely distributed abridged edition of this important book.

Did the Oriental philosophies have a true impact on the development of scientific psychology, specifically in America? The evidence is clearly affirmative. In the first place, we note that Gustav Fechner was greatly attracted to a variant of the Hindu doctrines. In a book called *Zend-Avesta*, he developed the idea of body and soul as a single entity viewed from different perspectives; the title comes from the religious literature of the Parsis, Zoroastrianism.

William James, often called the father of American psychology, was interested in Yoga and read some of the literature available in the West in the middle of the nineteenth century. However, he denied having tried "Yoga discipline," although he admitted some experimenting with it. "You are mistaken about my having tried Yoga discipline," he. wrote to a friend in 1906; "I have read several books . . . and in the slightest possible way tried breathing exercises" (1960, p. 275). It seems likely that he encouraged other psychologists to become familiar with the Hindu tradition, although any actual use of these ideas had to wait until the last half of the twentieth century.

Paranjpe (1984) pointed out that Yoga also anticipated Gestalt theory in its handling of the part–whole problem. "Although an object as a whole (such as a water jar) is identical with the parts of which it is composed, it has some properties (e.g., its capacity to contain water) which are different from those of its parts" (p. 288–289).

On the whole, with its concept of levels of analysis and of reality, Yoga seems to have anticipated some of modern systems theory. Saral (1983) commented that "there exist many ways of perceiving and categorizing reality" (p. 52). And he added that, in the Hindu philosophy, "the truth is not the monopoly of any single creed or cult" (p. 52–53). One wishes that Western religions had developed such a tolerance for clashing doctrines.

Culture and Psychology

The culture of classical India, like that of India today, is quite different from the Western pattern. The extended family is both large and psychologically powerful. This fact has operated against the Western philosophy of individualism and egocentrism. As Murphy and Murphy (1968) wrote:

> With the development of the family and caste system in India, there is the development of a psychology of caste, and of clan, in which individuality is hardly ever mentioned. . . . Both in the philosophy and in the great epic poems of India, the law of the extended family and the nation takes precedence over personal obligations. (pp. 224–225)

Murphy and Murphy thus deduced that the practice of isolated meditation may be a means of escaping from a complex network of social obligations (which would suggest that an innate aspect of human nature is a demand for some individual freedom). They interpreted a meditator's isolation as

> a process by which his own severe, pure, and eternal individuality will be set free in order to be absorbed ultimately into the nameless, but perfect, bliss which is available for those whose social existence has been purified and stripped bare, down to the ultimate pure reality of a selfhood which is no longer an individual self but only a divine spark. (p. 225)

In summary, we can say that the Indian tradition is one in the "tender-minded" tradition, with a focus on self-observation, changes in states of consciousness, withdrawal from an unpleasant outer world, and depreciation of the physiological drives. This tradition contrasts sharply with the Western orientation toward hard science, rigid determinism, and physiological reductionism, a "tough-minded" view of psychology. The Hebrew approach is closer to that of India, but with an escape from trouble by unity with God instead of a loss of individuality in a cosmic principle.

As I have commented earlier, classical psychologies dealt almost exclusively with consciousness. It is the orientation toward reality and the role of consciousness that distinguishes the three traditions sketched so briefly and inadequately here. Western psychology is extraverted and, in general, assumes that reality is objective, and is independent of the observer. Indian psychology holds that reality depends heavily on the observer, although it is possible to experience a reality shared with others. Hebrew tradition includes an awareness of the fallibility of both sensing and reasoning and emphasizes, more than the Greek or Indian philosophies, the relation of the individual with God. As we shall see, the fusing of these divergent ways of thinking has not come easily, and attempts to mingle them have sometimes led to unpleasant consequences.

Cross-cultural Comparisons

Paranjpe (1984) analyzed the cultural backgrounds of psychological theories, primarily contrasting the Greek and Hindu approaches. However, the conceptual framework he offered can be applied to any such comparison. He devised a six-point scale, or list of crucial issues, as follows:

1. The assumption of the lawfulness of nature.
2. Assumptions or ontological propositions borrowed from philosophy.
3. Attitudes about the relation of man to nature.
4. Assumptions about human nature.
5. Assumptions about the human condition.
6. Values concerning the desirable human condition. (p. 57)

With respect to Point 1, Paranjpe commented that all three of the traditions (the Hindu, Hebrew, and classical Greek) assume the lawfulness of events, or scientific determinism. The Hebrew and Hindu cultures are more tolerant of the idea of supernatural intervention, but basically, they are both deterministic.

With regard to Point 2, Paranjpe found both monistic and dualistic positions represented in both Greek and Hindu thinking. The Hebrew stance is preponderantly dualistic, underlining the separation of body and spirit or mind. Among the Hindu writings, Sankhya is dualistic and Advaita monistic. Regarding Point 3, Paranjpe commented that the Greek and Western tradition favors a mastery of nature by human beings; science and technology are instruments for domesticating nature and bending it to serve human needs. The Hebraic pattern gives rather more attention to the submission of humans to natural catastrophes (e.g., drought and sickness) as punishments visited on them by God for their sins. The Indian culture, he suggested, favors merging humans with nature, that is, adapting to natural conditions and understanding nature through meditation, not struggling to control or overpower nature.

Point 4 emphasizes the nature of human nature. Both East and West assume that pleasure and pain are central, but the Western tradition focuses on the external stimuli that induce such feelings, whereas the Indian tradition highlights the human being as enjoyer and as sufferer. But the Indian philosophers reject egocentric individualism, treating each person as an offshoot of cosmic unity seeking peace in reunion with that unity. The West, of course, asserts the primacy of the individual and the legitimacy of egoistic aims. These assertions are linked to a moral obligation to help others (often ignored in practice), whereas the Hindu emphasis is on an abandonment of selfish goals while withdrawing from society and also from any altruistic concerns.

Linked to this issue is the question of human rationality or irrationality. Western theorizing elevates rationality for the most part (as in most of the American theories, such as structuralism, behaviorism, and Gestalt.) An exception is psychoanalytic theory, which stresses the irrational determination of behavior. The Bhagavad-Gita, like Freud, warns us that emotions and desires may distort perception and memory, leading to loss of rationality, and to death. The Hebraic ethos resembles this approach.

Point 5 concerns the human condition. The Hindu tradition assumes that all is suffering. The eternal cycle of birth and death is the only true reality, and the foremost aim of humans is to escape from it. Hebrew scholars would generally endorse this view. However, Paranjpe contrasted the Hindu and Hebraic attitudes toward suffering. In the Hindu version, suffering is a path to knowledge; in the Garden of Eden myth, suffering is the consequence of seeking knowledge. Sin, shame, and guilt are Hebraic and Western themes, that are not found in Hinduism.

What is the desirable human condition (Point 6)? Plato proposed an important distinction between pleasures such as the restoration of bodily equilibrium (by eating, drinking, and so on) and "higher" pleasures of an intellectual or esthetic character. Freud proposed that the ultimate pleasure is sexual gratification, which can be sublimated into Plato's higher category. Hinduism does not reject physical or sexual pleasures; however, it holds that the highest pleasure is an intense mystical experience, an "oceanic feeling." The Hebrew tradition also places the highest pleasure on a mystical level, as in the feeling of unity with God.

Paranjpe summed up his analysis of the Greek and Hebraic traditions in this way: "The Greek thinkers emphasized the general over the particular; the problems of man *qua man* seemed more important to them than the problems of particular persons in their particular predicaments. Here the abstract notion of essence is placed over existence; the rational ability of man is separated from his intuitions and feelings" (p. 19). A plaint that we shall find again in the literature on humanistic psychology is that our culture pits reason against emotion, thus dividing the personality and crippling it. "By contrast," Paranjpe wrote, "the Hebraic spirit places emphasis on the concrete man in his wholeness. Passionate involvement of man with his mortal existence is important. . . . The ideal man of Hebraism is the man of faith, not the man of reason cherished by Plato and Aristotle" (p. 19).

It is not particularly useful to try to harmonize these traditions, but it is valuable to keep them in mind as we examine the varieties of psychological theorizing that have stemmed from these origins. Obviously, "scientific" psychology embodies the Greek ethos and a "tough-minded" orientation; "humanistic" psychology incorporates more of the Hindu and Hebrew traditions and exemplifies the "tender-minded" approach to human thought and action.

CHAPTER 3

France: The Rise of Mechanism

So far the "long past" of psychology has been speculative rather than experimental. The Scholastic psychology, which reached its peak in the work of St. Thomas Aquinas, was a body of generalizations based on introspection by the writer with an occasional reference to observed behavior. The idea of controlled experimentation in the physical sciences had been around for some time, but no one had proposed experimental study of human thinking or behaving.

The rediscovery of Aristotle's writings in the Moorish library at Cordova dates to the fourteenth or fifteenth centuries, a hundred years after Aquinas. Aristotle's strictures regarding the importance of observation and record-keeping undoubtedly stimulated many of the scholars of this period to begin research on physical objects, mass, motion, heat, and so on. Similarly, chemistry began to take shape as the "natural philosophers" studied oxides and other chemical combinations which could be transformed by heating or cooling. The idea of a deterministic world, one in which a specified antecedent led invariably to an identifiable consequent, was rescued from oblivion and initiated what we call the Renaissance.

This scientific beginning did not affect the domain of human thought and behavior until the time of René Descartes (1596–1650). Descartes accepted the thesis that the universe was mechanistic or deterministic, and he extended this belief to human behavior. It thus seems reasonable to identify France as the locus for the emergence of mechanistic psychology.

How did a mechanistic psychology originate? Its roots, of course, are in Aristotle's emphasis on the body and its functions, with his definition of the soul as function. Seeing, he wrote, is the function of the eye, and so we can call seeing "the soul of the eye." This ingenious argument for ending the exasperating dualism of body and soul went underground during the Middle Ages but reappeared at the time of the Renaissance.

Another factor that may have set the stage for mechanism was boredom with discussions of consciousness. Scholars were probably looking for some new problems on which to sharpen their wits. Consciousness having been explored interminably, behavior was chosen for study.

We should recognize the contribution of Leonardo da Vinci in making this possible. Leonardo (1452–1519) opened up the possibility of developing a model of human behavior as a complicated machine. His studies of anatomy and his analogy of the skeleton to a system of levers offered guidance to those who wanted to forget about consciousness in favor of research on human and animal behavior. Leonardo also anticipated other features of what I have called "tough-minded" psychology; for example, he sought mathematical expressions for almost every process he explored. Likewise, he was an earnest advocate of experiment, within the limited facilities available in his time.

A little after Leonardo, Nicolaus Copernicus (1473–1543) promulgated his mechanistic theory of astronomy. He rejected the thesis that the earth was the center of the universe; instead, he showed that our knowledge of planetary motion required placing the sun at the center, with the earth revolving around it along with the other planets. As scholars got used to the idea of a mechanistic universe, the idea of mechanistic laws for human behavior became at least tolerable.

Galileo Galilei (1564–1642), in addition to his work on astronomy and on falling bodies, revived the atomic theory propounded by Democritus almost two thousand years earlier. He conceived of the world as "a multitude of minute particles having certain shapes and moving with certain velocities." He reversed Aristotle's dictum that rest was the "natural state" of objects and that they moved only while energy was being applied to them. Galileo proposed the hypothesis that an object in motion would continue to move until stopped by friction or some other obstacle.

Other exciting things were happening in science. Francis Bacon (1561–1626) was preaching empiricism and experimentation. William Harvey (1578–1657) studied the circulation of the blood and argued that the heart acted like a pump. Table 3.1 expands this brief listing of the distinguished scholars revitalizing science after nearly two millennia of oblivion. But the hidden agenda was more than a mechanical view of behavior: If the body moved like a machine, why not the mind as well?

René Descartes

The first Renaissance figure to make important contributions to psychological theory was René Descartes (1596–1650). Like Aristotle, Descartes had one of those wide-ranging minds that absorbed most of what was

TABLE 3.1   Major Scientists of the Renaissance Period[a]

Person	Contribution
Leonardo da Vinci (1452–1519)	Anatomy; capillary action; engineering.
Nicolaus Copernicus (1473–1543)	Heliocentric theory of astronomy.
Tycho Brahe (1546–1601)	Determination of planetary orbits.
Francis Bacon (1561–1626)	Empiricism; experiments and systematic observations of nature.
Galileo Galilei (1564–1642)	Telescope; mechanistic approach to psychology; falling bodies; mathematical treatment of data.
Johannes Kepler (1571–1630)	Planetary orbits; optics.
William Harvey (1578–1657)	Circulation of the blood.
René Descartes (1596–1650)	Analytic geometry; behavior as reflex action.
Antonie van Leeuwenhoek (1632–1723)	Microscope.
Isaac Newton (1642–1727)	Laws of motion; theory of gravitation; calculus; optics, color mixture, and wave theory of light.
Luigi Galvani (1737–1798)	Electrical nature of nerve impulse.

[a]The time period covered is longer than that usually alloted to the Renaissance, but these are the scientists who made scientific psychology possible.

known or speculated about in his lifetime. He made important contributions to mathematics and was deeply interested in medicine and physiology. Although present-day psychologists recall Descartes mainly to deplore his detrimental effects on the development of the field of psychology, they concede in doing so that he was an important figure in the history of the discipline.

A Focus on Behavior

Many historians would argue that the most important contribution of Descartes to the modern field of psychology was his espousal of the study of behavior. We know that his influential predecessors had concentrated almost exclusively on soul, mind, or consciousness; to propose studying human behavior was almost a revolution in itself.

Along with Descartes's interest in human action went a preference for mechanism. He was influenced by Galileo, whose work in astronomy and physics underscored the utility of a mechanistic approach to the physical universe. But there may also have been a more personal influence on Descartes's leanings toward mechanistic explanations of behavior. He had been a sickly child and was somewhat pampered by the monks who had supervised his early education. He was allowed to sleep much later than the other boys, and to read much more than they. In adolescence, he suffered from some lengthy illness, and while recuperating he spent a good deal of time strolling in the Royal Gardens at St. Germain-en-Laye, near Paris. Here, engineers and sculptors had collaborated to erect robotic statues, figures representing animals, humans, and gods that could move and make sounds. Water under pressure flowed through hidden pipes, and when the visitor stepped on a pedal, the statue responded mechanically. Thus, Neptune might wave a trident, Triton blow a horn, or a warrior turn his head and lift his weapon. By his own account, Descartes found these mechanical devices intriguing, and his awareness of the water power being used may have given rise to his use of "animal spirits" flowing through nerves as the activating agent for human movement.

Descartes's first book was not published until after his death. Called *Le Monde,* it sought to cover all known aspects of science, from astronomy to zoology. In it, he elaborated a psychology based strictly on reflexes; that is, free will was eliminated. Further, he implied that there was no evidence of the existence of a human soul. The book was on the verge of publication in 1633, when Descartes learned of the sentence of life imprisonment imposed on Galileo. Now, Galileo's heresy had extended only to endorsing the Copernican astronomy, in which the earth revolved around the sun. The content of Descartes's book was substantially more heretical, and he decided that its publication could be hazardous to his health. The manuscript was stored and was published only after his death in 1650.

This development must be placed in its historical context. The neo-Platonists and the Christian fathers had related mental functions to a vital spirit or soul which was of different stuff from the body and obeyed different laws (if indeed it obeyed any). The *vitalist* philosophy, then, was one based on a vital force which controlled human behavior. The Greeks had debated this point; Democritus, for example, rejected the vital force notion. Aristotle had vacillated on the point; he followed Plato in assuming the existence of three "souls" and then reversed himself by characterizing soul as "function."

The important point is that the galaxy of scientists listed in Table 3.1 were undermining the vital force hypothesis. Francis Bacon, William Harvey, Luigi Galvani and Antonie van Leeuwenhoek were demonstrating the mechanical nature of bodily processes such as circulation of the blood, nerve firing and other physiological phenomena. The law of parsimony ("Ockham's razor") dictated that the vital force concept must be abandoned if a simpler explanation could replace it. Mechanism assumes that the human body functions like a machine; this eliminates the need for postulating a vital force.

At times, a mechanistic view of behavior is very tempting. A psychologist who is constantly being frustrated by the irrationality of neurotic clients, or of industrial executives to be counseled, or of schoolchildren needing help would no doubt like to believe that under all this confusion, there are some simple mechanical laws that will ultimately make all human behavior predictable. Mechanism may also be appealing because of the prestige of chemistry and physics. If people behaved as predictably as machines, we psychologists could also do great research, achieve marvelous insights, win Nobel prizes, and so on. Ironically, the physicists are now moving away from the mechanistic view of Newton to the fuzzy, unpredictable universe of quantum physics.

If Descartes could have foreseen the twentieth century, he might have been even more firmly convinced that mechanism was the correct solution. Millions of Americans arise at the same time, eat the same breakfasts, wend their standardized ways to workplaces, and perform rigidly defined movements for six or eight hours a day. They conform to socially specified roles, wear standardized clothing, applaud mechanized sports, and watch predictable television amusements. Truly, the case for mechanism is an easy one to make.

This was the Descartes of *Le Monde*. But Galileo's punishment made him cautious, and he decided that although animals were true automatons, and that much human behavior was mechanized, each human being also had a soul. This meant that in some respects, humans resembled the lower animals, but that in regard to thinking, reasoning, dreaming, and so on, humans were unique.

The Anthropocentric Predicament

In his scholarly analysis of Descartes's work, A. G. A. Balz (1952) charged the Frenchman with creating "the anthropocentric predicament." By this, Balz meant that Descartes was committed to seeing reality from the viewpoint of humans, ignoring that of other animals. Shall we say that psychology is the study of human functioning, ignoring that of the other species? This was the accepted doctrine of most of Descartes's followers until the rise of behaviorism, which rejected the anthropocentric position.

Balz explained Descartes's famous statement "I think, therefore I exist" as a way out of the anthropocentric predicament. Descartes was familiar with the classical criticisms of knowledge: The senses are easily deluded, authorities are untrustworthy, and experience is fallible (see Figure 3.1). But logic remains. "Whilst I thus wished to think that all was false," he wrote, "it was absolutely necessary that I, who thus thought, should be somewhat; and as I observed this truth, *I think, hence I am,* was so certain and of such evidence, that no ground of doubt could be capable of shaking it" (*Discourse on Method,* Pt. IV). This put Descartes in the interesting position of holding that his actions, such as walking, talking, and eating, might be illusory, but that his thinking could not be

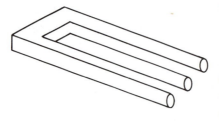

FIGURE 3.1   Sensory Information is Not Always Dependable.

The Greek skeptics had insisted that the senses were deceptive, that reality must be distinguished from appearance. Try to decide on the reality of this drawing.

illusory. Modern behaviorism reverses the relationship; thinking may be an illusion (only subvocal speech), but overt behavior cannot be argued away.

Balz asserted that this logical analysis evaded the anthropocentric predicament. By doubting his senses, and by doubting classical authority, Descartes reached a point at which reason was the only criterion of truth and reality. It is analogous, Balz (1952) claimed, to the procedures of science: "The scientist uses an elaborate system of controls, counter-balancing devices and procedures and means of error-cancellations" (p. 77). If we accept this interpretation, Descartes gave scientific psychology a push forward. The push was toward mathematics and measurement. His faith in logic required this: "Whether I am awake or asleep, two and three together always form five, and the square can never have more than four sides, and it does not seem possible that truths so clear and apparent can be suspected of any falsity or uncertainty" (*Philosophical Works*, vol. 1, p. 147). Descartes, then, was asserting that reality is not simply a matter of how events appear to the human eye; the real basis for knowledge is logical analysis and scientific reasoning.

As if he lacked confidence in his own logic, Descartes also incorporated an argument that God would not deceive him with regard to the sensed qualities of the external world. He conceded that God *could* have endowed him (Descartes) with delusory memories and imagined percepts so that his notion of reality would follow logically. But he was confident that God was not so malicious. Thus, ultimately, Descartes fell back on an appeal to a higher authority to confirm his belief in reality.

One unfortunate outcome of this intrapersonal debate about humans and animals was that the conclusion led Descartes to deny feelings and sensations to animals. They were mere machines. Thus, as J. Jaynes (1970) noted, Descartes had no qualms about dissecting animals without anesthesia and was "amused at their cries and yelps since these were nothing but hydraulic hisses and vibrations of machines" (p. 224).

Not all readers of Descartes agree. Margaret Washburn (1908/1917) held that Descartes had imputed sensory capacities, motives, and feelings to lower animals. The debate lingers on today; some scientists are reluctant to go along with Washburn; others find Jaynes's description of Descartes's views repulsive. Darwinians (see Chapter Eight) incline to the view that all living organisms form a continuum, from the ameba to the human being, with no sharp discontinuity at any point.

Dualism

For whatever reason, Descartes espoused the traditional conclusion, namely, that a human being has a (mechanistic) body and a (vitalistic) soul. This view accorded with the Hindu, Hebraic, and Greek traditions. The body was subject to the laws of physics; the soul was not. The uniquely human functions of thought and reason were attributes of the soul.

Further analysis of the problem makes us acutely aware of the dilemma. The body, having encountered an obstacle, cannot inform the soul, because the soul is unresponsive to mechanics; the soul, having devised a solution to the problem, cannot instruct the body about what movements are required, because the soul is immaterial and incapable of affecting a physical object. This is the classic dilemma of dualism.

It was necessary for Descartes to invent a communication device that would enable messages to move back and forth between body and soul. This device obviously had to be in the brain. But the brain is mainly composed of bilaterally symmetrical structures (left and right hemispheres, cerebellar structures, thalamic formations, and so on). Classical dogma, however, insisted that the soul must be *unitary*. By a curious leap of logic, Descartes concluded that the *pineal gland* would serve his purpose because it was not bilaterally symmetrical; hence, it could fit (in some fashion) with the unitary soul. Further, the gland is quite small; as Descartes wanted the soul to affect bodily tissue, small size was an asset. Finally, no one knew what else the pineal gland was good for, so assigning it this communicative role did not preempt some other physiological function.

Animal Spirits

The idea that some fluid flows through the nerves and affects thought or behavior goes back to the Greeks. Descartes was simply more explicit and less ambiguous in using this concept. He proposed that when a sensory receptor is stimulated, animal spirits travel along the nerve (a hollow tube, in his conception) to the brain and to the pineal gland. Similarly, effector organs were activated by animal spirits flowing out over the nerve pathways. The innate response patterns were designated as *reflexes* and were treated as the building blocks for more complex actions.

As the inflow of animal spirits reached the pineal gland, this organ could be tilted slightly in different directions and would present different aspects to the soul. This led the soul to generate an *idea* (e.g., of movement). The idea somehow tilted the pineal further, so that the animal spirits flowed into the motor nerves appropriate to this ideated movement. Insofar as reflexes were concerned, the whole process was mechanical; the pineal was not involved, and the soul made no decisions (see Balz, 1952, pp. 405–406).

Innate Ideas

Descartes specified that there were three degrees of cognitive activity: outer perception (inputs of information from physical objects); inner perception of representations of physical objects (e.g., memory images when the object was not present); and inner perception of pure ideas (e.g., mathematical abstractions and philosophical conceptions).

The physical versus mental dichotomy applied to these categories also. With regard to abstract ideas, Descartes held that "the mind can work independently of the brain; for clearly there can be no use of the brain for pure intelligence, but only for imagination and sensation" (Brett, 1962, p. 365). Although he called this "pure" intelligence a manifestation of innate ideas, he realized that there would be objections. He was not, he claimed, setting up a class of ideas that were uniquely different from the ideas based on sense impressions, but that differed only in their origin:

> I never wrote or concluded that the mind required innate ideas which were in some sort different from its faculty of thinking; but when I observed the existence in me of certain thoughts which proceeded, not from extraneous objects nor from the determination of my will, but solely from the faculty of thinking which is within me, then . . . I termed these innate. (1955, p. 442)

Emotions

In his book *The Passions of the Soul,* Descartes proposed that there were six basic emotions: wonder, love, hate, desire, joy, and sadness. But his dissection of the emotions makes them sound like cognitive functions. He wrote that love depended on expected pleasure and hate on expected injury or evil. He considered the brain the seat of the emotions (ending the traditional designation of the heart as the physical base for emotion). Emotions and actions became associated (as in J. B. Watson's conditioning experiments). The sight of an external threat elicited fear, which elicited escape; this was the traditional view (which was later opposed by William James).

Legacies of Descartes

History shows that we have two major legacies from René Descartes. The first is the problem of dualism, of finding a device for uniting a material, mechanical body to an unsubstantial soul. The assumption that two kinds of "stuff" exist—matter and soul—has been around since classic times. However, most of Descartes's predecessors had simply ignored the enigma of communication between these two aspects of human existence. Descartes brought the contradiction into the light and examined it.

Descartes's solution to the body–soul dichotomy is called *interactionism,* a solution that proposes that there is some special mechanism that can override or bypass the basic incompatibility of body and soul. This solution violates the principle of parsimony, in the sense that Descartes hypothesized the existence of a new mechanism not provided for in his original premises.

The most parsimonious solution to the body–soul dilemma is to abolish the assumption of two incompatible and different "substances." *Materialistic monism* asserts that only the physical is "real," that the alleged difference between physical and mental processes is a delusion, and that thinking, creativity, esthetics, and ethics must be reduced to purely physical terms. The theories of radical behaviorists like Watson and Weiss (see Chapter Nine) exemplify this solution. A second solution is *idealistic monism,* which asserts that the only "reality" is perceptual. Although there may be a physical world out there, all we can know is our perceptions. George Berkeley (see Chapter Four) defended this position. Taken to its extreme, this idea becomes *solipsism,* a worldview that holds that each person lives in a private universe not necessarily the same as the universes of other individuals. A third solution to the body–soul dichotomy is known as *double-aspect monism,* in which "reality" viewed from one aspect is physical, but viewed from a different perspective is mental.

In addition to these solutions to the body–mind or body–soul dilemma, there have been philosophical solutions that maintain the dualism but explain away the conflict over how incompatible substances can interact. Wilhelm Wundt (see Chapter Five) endorsed *psychophysical parallelism,* which postulates that physical events "cause" other physical events, and that mental phenomena determine later psychological events. *Epiphenomenalism* is a version of monism in which consciousness and mental states are treated as incidental to the ongoing physical processes, which are really decisive. The body can influence the mind, but the reverse is not true.

Many volumes have been written about this controversy, to little effect. Most American psychologists pragmatically adopt a kind of double-aspect monism, conceding that conscious phenomena are "real" and have consequences, but denying the assumption of a mind or a soul.

A second legacy of Descartes worth mentioning regards *method.* He advised the budding young philosopher-scientist to divide a complex problem into parts as small as possible, then to start with the simplest aspect and, when it was solved, to move on to the next most difficult.

The implicit sanction given to atomistic solutions has probably been a negative influence on theorizing since Descartes's time.

Whimsically, we might add a third, an offshoot of the pineal gland device. This is the ever-recurring tendency of psychologists to seek an anatomical locus for a psychological function; thus, we are told that the hippocampus is the seat of memory or that the amygdala is the seat of emotion. It is doubtful that such place theories have ever contributed to scientific progress, and in some instances, as in the case of lobotomies, they have simply led to hundreds of brain injuries with little gain in human welfare.

La Mettrie

Passions of the Soul was published in 1650, just before Descartes's death. It did not provoke an answer or expansion for a century. J. O. de La Mettrie (1709–1751) picked up the theory of the human being as a mechanism and in 1748 published *L'Homme Machine* (Man a Machine). The only significant difference from Descartes seems to have been that La Mettrie dispensed with the soul entirely, (as we believe Descartes intended), and treated human behavior as a complex of reflexes, thus anticipating the Russian and American behaviorists. Human beings differed from other animals only with respect to complexity; the basic mechanical principles held for all species of animals.

Brett (1962) claimed that La Mettrie was primarily a naturalist, who was engaged in describing human nature as an environmentally determined phenomenon. In this regard, he anticipated the omnipotent environment described by J. B. Watson and B. F. Skinner, capable of molding human actions into highly diverse patterns. His views were strictly materialistic and empiricist; as such, they may have contributed to the French Revolution.

Condillac

Etienne Bonnot, Abbé de Condillac (1715–1780), was another disciple of Descartes who merits brief consideration. Like La Mettrie, he disdained the metaphysical concept of a soul and proposed an aggressively materialist-mechanist psychology.

The influence of Descartes is clearly shown in his major works, *On the origin of Human Knowledge* (1746) and *Treatise on Sensations* (1754). He adopted the metaphor of the statue as Descartes had used it; however, Condillac proposed to show in more detail how "mental" functions could be deduced from a mechanical base. He postulated a statue endowed with only a single sensory receptor, the sense of smell. To show how

mental functions could develop, he envisioned steps more or less as follows: 1. The statue experiences an odor. As there are no competing
sensations, this one is of maximum clarity and provides us with the concept of focus of attention (E. B. Titchener later amplified this principle).

2. However, a later odor may be less intense; hence, the statue is aware
of differences among odors. If the new one is indeed less intense, the
statue develops a process of judging differences.

3. If the second sensation is followed by a recall of the first (as seems
necessary for comparison to occur), then the statue has acquired memory, the storage and retrieval of sensations. And so, by a few simple
stages, Condillac professed to have demonstrated how complex mental
functions could derive from the simplest of beginnings.

Later critics have sensed in this analysis an illicit violation of Condillac's own premise. He asserted that the statue was endowed with *no other*
mental functions than the sense of smell. Yet he smuggled in the ability
to recall a past sensation; a comparator function, for assessing differences; and a decision function, for making judgments of "more intense"
or "less intense." Such unstated and perhaps unconscious inconsistencies
are found in many theoretical presentations.

Note that Condillac also presented an excellent example of Descartes's
logical methodology, that is dividing the problem up into small parts. By
reducing the sensory channels to one, and by examining each complication beyond sensory experience successively, Condillac exemplified to
perfection the analytical mode of attack on a scientific problem. As later
chapters of this book will indicate, this legacy from the French mechanists is still a major source of tension among American psychologists.

Thomas Hobbes

If I were following a strictly chronological pattern, Thomas Hobbes (1588–
1679) should be discussed immediately after Descartes, as Hobbes' *Leviathan* was published in 1651, only one year after Descartes's *Passions of
the Soul*. Instead, I have chosen to describe the modifications of Cartesian
philosophy by La Mettrie and Condillac as an indication of the rise of a
French mechanistic school. The line of development from Descartes to
Condillac is quite clear. Placing Hobbes in the history of this period is
more debatable. Hobbes was a mechanist, but his approach to psychological problems was more sophisticated than that of La Mettrie and Condillac.

Hobbes oscillated between a devotion to empiricism (observe nature,
do not study authorities) and faith in logic and reason. At times he ridiculed the budding experimentalists in physics and chemistry: "They
preferred their eyes, ears, and finger-tips to their brains" (quoted by
Brett, 1962, p. 380). Yet he attempted to use Newtonian physics to ex-

plain psychological phenomena: "Desires and aversions are motions towards and motions away from objects . . . Even thinking itself was but motions in some internal substance in the head" (Brett, 1962, p. 381). Most historians classify him as an empiricist because of his concern with observing reality, but he actually relied on logic instead of data much of the time.

Whether Hobbes was consciously expanding on Descartes's ideas is not established. A loyal monarchist, he fled England after the execution of Charles I, and served as a tutor to the future Charles II in France for several years. It is thus plausible that his *Leviathan* was influenced by Descartes's *Le Monde* and *Passions of the Soul*.

The influence of Newton is apparent in his theory of sensation. "Our sense-organs were agitated by external motions without which there could be no sensation . . . The selectivity of perception was explained by suggesting that while the organ retains motion from one object, it cannot react to another." (Brett, p. 381). "All is body or body in motion" was one of his crisp phrases. Even imagination was a function of motion: "All Fancies are motions within us, reliques of those made in the Sense; And those motions that immediately succeeded one another in the sense, continue also together after sense" (Hobbes, 1651; see Herrnstein and Boring, 1965, p. 331). This statement echoes Aristotle, who had also described memories as motions within the body, and who had treated associations as following the sequence in which the original events occurred.

Hobbes knew that the mind can conjure up unlikely associations and get memories in the wrong order. He said that events cause this phenomenon also: the same object (say, a house) may be associated with weddings and funerals, with illness and health, and so these memories become jumbled. In sense (i.e., in real life), "to one and the same thing perceived, sometimes one thing, sometimes another succeedeth, it comes to pass in time, that in the Imagining of any thing, there is no certainty as to what we shall imagine next" (Hobbes, 1651; Herrnstein and Boring, 1965, p. 331). He also noted that imagining (e.g., dreaming) could be directed by desire, so that we imagine possible ways to satisfy a motive rather than merely reviving old memories. He did not, however, formulate a "motion theory" to account for this effect of desire on thought and memory.

Hobbes's theory of sensation was mechanistic. The qualities of sensations derive from differences in the rate and extensity of motions in the brain. An important deduction from this assumption is that the qualities of sensed objects cannot be inherent in the objects themselves. Color, odor, taste, and so on are functions of processes in the brain; the motions that give rise to them are related in an orderly way to the motions of the external objects, but this does not mean they are identical. The only *true* "reality" is composed of "atoms and the void," as proposed by

Democritus. Thus *perceived* reality is a function of motions in the brain.

Hobbes's theory of motivation was essentially one of pleasure and pain, but like Freud years later, he observed that infantile demands for immediate pleasure come to be modified as the individual foresees greater pain in the future. Thus, Hobbes argued that humans, at least intelligent humans, behaved so as to maximize pleasure and minimize pain *in the long run*. Today, this idea is known as Freud's reality principle.

Monism

Like La Mettrie and Condillac after him, Hobbes avoided Descartes's dualistic dilemma by espousing materialistic monism in a truly aggressive fashion. He found no evidence for the existence of a soul and hence had no need to hypothesize a way in which body and soul (or mind) could interact. Like the behaviorists of later centuries, he simply ignored the question of conscious awareness as a phenomenon of concern to psychologists.

Social Psychology

Hobbes can plausibly be labeled the founder of modern social psychology. His interest in this aspect of human behavior developed out of his political concerns. He was a confirmed monarchist and hence was traumatized by the execution of England's King Charles I. Human beings have an innate need for a ruler, someone to follow and òbey, according to Hobbes; without such an enforcer of social order, human life would be "solitary, nasty, brutish, and short." As Erich Fromm was to remind the West in *Escape from Freedom,* many humans become anxious and frightened when they have to make decisions for themselves. (Thus Fromm explained the support for Hitler and the Nazis.)

Hobbes viewed humans as inescapably selfish and greedy (following, no doubt, St. Paul and St. Augustine, whose views on human morality were gloomy); for Hobbes, social order became a matter of self-defense, meaning that each of us must be restrained from crimes against the other. Thus, Hobbes argued for an orderly society, and for the sacrifice of some freedom by the citizens in order to bolster the nobility and the monarchy.

Mechanism and Vitalism

The theorists described in this chapter bring us up to the beginning of the eighteenth century. They speculated about (but rarely collected data on) the role of bodily (physiological, mechanical) and mental (psychic, intangible) factors in human behavior. At this time, however, western

Europe was on the verge of a more observational, data-oriented development and an increased attention to the internal details of "mental" processes.

The philosophers described in this chapter exemplify a specific kind of philosophical approach: *mechanism.* Like a machine that can be disassembled into its component parts, human behavior can be disassembled into sensations, ideas, and responses. This property, the mechanists argued, proves that we do not need to assume any mental or spiritual force operating to hold these parts together.

Vitalists reject the mechanistic dogma. They point out that, once disassembled, the behavioral processes cannot be put back together. They hold that a key aspect of human life—the unity of personality and of mental experience—is lost in the analytic process of dissecting behavior into its component parts. The dead organism cannot be persuaded to resume functioning as it had while alive. There is a substantial difference between a live human being and a dead one, and where is the mechanist going to locate the difference?

It is interesting that the original drive against vitalism in favor of materialism or mechanism centered in France. Leonardo da Vinci and Galileo were Italian; Francis Bacon was English; Copernicus was Polish. Descartes, then, was the sole major French scholar of the seventeenth century (at least for our purposes), and he compromised between mechanism (animals have only reflexes) and vitalism (human beings have both mechanical responses and free will). Descartes kept vitalism alive by postulating a soul, a vital force animating the body, which without it would be merely a lump of clay. La Mettrie, Condillac, and Hobbes elaborated on the mechanistic side and dispensed with the mystical "vital force."

The mechanist–vitalist debate has waxed and waned over the years. In the late twentieth century, vitalism has almost disappeared, but mechanism is being modulated to account for some of the criticisms made by the vitalists. Principles of Gestalt and humanistic psychology, to be examined later, have tried to make mechanism more flexible and more compatible with observable phenomena.

CHAPTER 4

Britain: Empiricism and Rationalism

Whereas the French expanded on Descartes's radical ideas in the direction of materialism and mechanism, the British opted for an emphasis on empiricism, ignored the interaction problem, and restored the earlier practice of focusing on mental phenomena rather than behavior. The major contributions of eighteenth-century British philosophers lay in the area of breaking consciousness down into elementary experiences and then speculating about how to get the elements back together.

Descartes had proposed that humans had many "innate ideas," which presumably were the heritage of the soul. It was necessary, he speculated, for these ideas to be "activated" by experience; for example, one could have an innate idea of triangularity, but it would become conscious only when a person had seen one or more triangles. The difference is not trivial; even today, linguists are debating the point as it relates to the structure of language.

The British, beginning with John Locke, rejected the concept of innate ideas but held that the mind had a *capacity* for reflection, which made possible the transformation of specific ideas (experiences) into generalized abstractions. A subgroup called the Scottish school focused on this idea of capacity, which they called *faculty*, and laid the foundations for our contemporary research and practical applications in the field of individual differences.

Like most generalizations, this one has its exceptions. Not all British philosopher-psychologists defined their field as the study of consciousness. As I noted earlier, Thomas Hobbes is ideologically akin to the French mechanists. And the Scottish proponents of faculty psychology disagreed with John Locke, David Hume and David Hartley on empiricism (the Scots preferred a nativist-hereditarian approach to some problems which was rejected by the empiricists.) One of the perennial controversies still rampant in American psychology is this issue of the influence of heredity or of environment on behavior. One might speculate that the aggressive environmentalism of Locke, Hume and Hartley elicited a negative response from the faculty school.

Pinning nationalistic labels on these schools is also debatable. For instance, David Hume was Scottish, but he was strongly disliked by the more religious and nativist-oriented group of Reid, Stewart and Brown. And the Scots in turn received support from German rationalists such as Immanuel Kant and Gottfried Wilhelm Leibniz. The eighteenth century was thus a time of increased debate about human thinking and behavior, with the issues of environment versus heredity and sensation versus reasoning becoming more clearly defined than in earlier years.

John Locke

There is a kind of consensus among historians that John Locke (1632–1704) founded the tradition of British empiricism. A few argue for Thomas Hobbes to receive this title, but—as I have argued—Hobbes offered a philosophy more compatible with the French mechanists. Locke was not hostile to mechanism, but his ideas were not in harmony with those of Hobbes. For example, he accepted a dualism of body and mind and ascribed some cognitive powers to the mind. All information, he said, came through the senses, but this knowledge could be structured and rearranged by a process of reflection.

One also observes an echo of Descartes in much of Locke's writing. In his famous *Essay Concerning Human Understanding* (1690/1956) he described his basic orientation as follows:

> Every man being conscious to himself that he thinks; and that which his mind is applied about whilst thinking being the *ideas* that are there, it is past doubt that men have in their minds several ideas,—such as are those expressed by the words *whiteness, hardness, sweetness, thinking, motion, man, elephant, army, drunkenness,* and others: it is in the first place then to be inquired, *How does he come by them?* (Book II, Ch. 1, par. 1; 1690/1956, p. 121)

This quotation helps us to understand exactly what Locke meant by *idea.* The term includes sensory qualities (white, hard, and sweet), perceived objects (man and elephant), and abstractions (thinking, motion, and drunkenness). This definition of *idea* was fairly consistent through the nineteenth century; today, one tends to use *idea* only for abstractions. The broader usage was part of the empiricist theory; sensing, perceiving, and abstracting were all aspects of learning about the world.

Locke then propounded the conception of the mind as a blank page (tabula rasa), without innate ideas: "Let us then suppose the mind to be, as we say, white paper, void of all characters, without any ideas" (p. 121). This, too, was not a novel metaphor; Aristotle had written of the mind as a blank tablet ready for inscription. Locke also distinguished between the object and the perception of that object: "Whatsoever the mind perceives in itself, or is the immediate perception, thought, or understanding, that I call Idea; and the power to produce any idea in our mind, I call Quality of the subject wherein that power is." This distinction is important; the wavelength of light would correspond to a quality, but the color experience would constitute an idea. Conceding the existence of a material, external world, Locke needed to establish the relation to the inner world of consciousness.

The material world is the domain of physics. Galileo and Newton, towering intellectual figures of the immediate past, had argued that "reality" was composed of vibrating atoms; reality could be measured and understood in terms of physics. Locke proposed to distinguish among conscious qualities on the basis of the physical theory. *Primary* attributes were those directly linked to physics: awareness of mass, motion, duration, and number. *Secondary* attributes were those dependent on the organism: color, taste, smell, tone quality, and so on. The latter, he held, were determined by the receiving person, as physics indicated no measurable physical qualities directly parallel to these sensations.

In this respect, Locke was following Galileo. Galileo had written, "I think that if ears, tongues, and noses were removed, shapes and numbers and motions would remain, but not odors nor tastes nor sounds. The latter, I believe, are nothing more than names when separated from living beings" (quoted in Boas, 1961, p. 262).

Locke was well aware of the criticisms of the senses as sources of knowledge; these criticisms had been around since Aristotle. Illusions, hallucinations, misperceptions due to the physical situation, and misperceptions due to personal attributes argued against reliance on sensory input for knowledge. But we have no choice; there are no alternative sources of information. Almost without mentioning it, Locke had discarded the authoritarian position that reality is given by divine revelation or by rational deduction.

After distinguishing primary from secondary attributes, Locke proposed a distinction between simple and complex ideas. Simple attributes would include simple sensations but not the awareness of an object or a person. Simple ideas unite to form complex ideas, as of a person, a house, or an institution. Complex ideas manifest "attractive forces," which draw simple ideas into relationship and cement them together. The notion of an idea's being subject to an "attractive force" was obviously an attempt to draft Newton's gravitational hypothesis into service for psychology; "mutual attraction of masses" became "mutual attraction of ideas." This is an important theoretical issue, as most empiricists have preferred to rely on contiguity as the basic rule of combination. Do ideas have dynamic properties? The question is still debated today.

By assuming the existence of mind as distinct from body, and indeed as incapable of interacting with body (although he smuggled in some interactive processes illicitly), Locke created problems for himself with the question of causation. He seems to have postulated a *psychophysical parallelism*, in which physical causes have physical effects, and psychical causes have psychical effects. As the name implies, this theory of the body–mind relationship postulates independence of the physical from the psychical and the psychical from the physical. This solution to the problem of dualism encounters serious difficulties when applied to laboratory experiments (see p. 89). At any rate, Locke wrote of "finding that in that substance which we call wax, fluidity, which is a simple idea that was not in it before, is constantly produced by the application of a certain degree of heat we call the simple idea of heat, in relation to fluidity in wax, the cause of it, and fluidity the effect" (pp. 433–434). Note that he was careful to say that the *idea* of heat evokes the idea of fluidity; just as in the physical world, heat causes the melting of the wax.

Locke was not entirely consistent on this point. He wrote of "sensation, which is such an impression *or motion* made in some *part of the body*, as produces some perception in the understanding" (p. 139); the entire passage is in italics in the original; the italics here are added). Physicalism calls for the physical impression to take the form of motion; but Locke offered no hypothesis how a physical motion can induce perception.

Another inconsistency lies in Locke's deviation from his *tabula rasa* conception of the mind. He slipped in the notion that the mind has faculties, and that these can be modified: "So it (the mind) comes, by exercise, to improve its faculty of thinking" (p. 139). He also conceded that the mind, by reflecting on sensory input, could arrive at new ideas. Thus, he admitted that not every idea comes directly from experience, although he could argue that the reflection could not operate until experience provided the raw data for thinking.

Finally, Locke has been criticized for going at least partway back to Descartes's "innate idea," after having explicitly rejected it. His logic was very much that of Plato (see Figure 2.2 p. 30). Locke thought that by reflecting on sensations (impressions of objects), one can select some attribute and develop a complex idea that has the certainty of a mathematical proposition. Locke called such ideas *archetypes*. The archetype acquires its special status by virtue of the mathematical validation involved; thus, a circle is a continuous line covering 360 degrees, with every point on the line equidistant from some central point. Once this discovery has been made, the idea becomes independent of experience. However, the archetype did not exist before the discovery, and there is no mystical origin involved.

In an interesting leap of logic, Locke then used the archetype as a basis for a system of morals. In his view, an idea such as *integrity* or *altruism* had the same character as the circle; that is, it seemed to have validity independent of sensing. He appealed to the human need for *certainty* as a guide to behavior: "For the attaining of knowledge and certainty, it is requisite that we have determined (unchanging) ideas; and to make our knowledge real, it is requisite that the ideas answer (match) their archetypes . . . Nor will it be less true or certain because moral ideas are of our own making and naming" (Book IV, part IV). As Robinson (1981) commented, Locke's archetypes "come uncomfortably close to the rationalist's notion of innate, moral sensibility" (p. 223).

George Berkeley

The immediate successor to Locke in the development of philosophical psychology was George Berkeley (1685–1783). Late in life he was appointed Bishop of Cloyne, in Ireland, and so he is most often cited as "Bishop Berkeley." He differed from the other members of the empiricist school in that he was more religious, and also in that he rejected Locke's dualism in favor of *idealistic monism,* an epistemological doctrine which asserts that the only reality one can ever know is perceptual. There may be a physical world out there, but the world one knows is the world one perceives.

As a consequence of this emphasis on perceived reality, he found it necessary to reject Locke's distinction between primary and secondary qualities. (This distinction treated attributes directly correlated with physics as primary; these included shape, mass, number, and motion. The secondary qualities depended on the organism; for example, color, odor, taste and the like were secondary.) Berkeley's refusal to postulate a physical world required that he treat these as all in one category; there is no physical world to determine the primary attributes. As he commented, size is no more logically related to physical processes than is color (consider, for example, the change in apparent size of objects seen from a novel perspective, such as from a tall building).

Idealistic monism argues that we can be certain only of what we perceive. Hence, my "reality" may not correspond to yours. There may be an external world, but what we know depends on our senses (the empiricist essence). To the physical scientists who argue that their measurements are objective and independent of their senses, Berkeley would reply that physical measurements add nothing to human knowledge unless they are perceived by a human being. According to a familiar anecdote, Dr. Samuel Johnson, when told of Berkeley's theory, kicked a stone and said, "That's my answer to Bishop Berkeley." But Berkeley would have replied that what Johnson experienced in kicking the stone was sensory; there is no way of getting information except through the senses.

The theory that all reality is perceptual raises another problem: does the world exist when I am not observing it? Do objects vanish and reappear capriciously? How can I be sure that the automobile I am observing is the same one the salesman is observing? Some human beings find it disturbing to suppose that the world flickers into and out of existence according to their perceptions.

Berkeley adopted a religious solution to this problem. God is perceiving all of the world all of the time, thus objects do not appear and disappear in rhythm with mere human perceptions. God's all-embracing perception therefore maintains a stable universe, not subject to whimsical changes, and maintains also comparability, that is, the "reality" you see will be the same as what I see.

Many modern psychologists endorse one or another version of the theory that reality is perceptual. Gestalt theory, psychoanalytic theory, and humanistic psychology incorporate this theme in one way or another.

David Hume

Berkeley's idealism sets him apart from the other important members of the British empiricist movement. David Hume (1711–1776), who followed Berkeley as a major theorist in psychology, reinstated Locke's dualism in the sense of accepting the reality of the physical universe and the focus on consciousness as the primary datum for psychology.

Hume agreed with Berkeley on the error of separating primary from secondary attributes. However, he accepted the premise that there really is a world out there, independent of experience. Thus, he was back in the dualistic dilemma: How can mind be influenced by body, or body by mind? Hume's solution to this problem was to pretend it wasn't there. For him, the essential task of psychology was to analyze the content of consciousness: sensations, images, feelings, and ideas.

Hume is especially remembered for two contributions to the development of an empiricist system. One was to abolish the mind as an object of knowledge; the other was to reduce assumed cause–effect relationships to mere contiguity:

> We may observe, that what we call a *mind,* is nothing but a heap or collection of different perceptions, united together by certain relations, and suppos'd, though falsely, to be endow'd with a perfect simplicity and identity. Now as every perception is distinguishable from another, and may be consider'd as separately existent, it evidently follows, that there is no absurdity in separating any particular perception from the mind; that is, in breaking off all its relations, with that connected mass of perceptions, which constitute a thinking being. (1739, Bk. I, Pt. 4, Sec. 2)

> When I enter most intimately into what I call *myself*, I always stumble on some particular perception or other, of heat or cold, light or shade, love or hatred, pain or pleasure. I never can catch myself at any time without a perception, and never can observe anything but the perception. (Sec. 6)

Thus, the mind disappears as an entity and is reduced to a heap of separable perceptions, no one of which is a perception of the mind itself. Both soul and mind have now vanished.

Hume carried his skepticism to the extreme of questioning the assumption of *necessity* in cause–effect relationships. This is more of a problem in logic than in psychology, but it is relevant to his view that all one knows is the outcome of sensory input. Thus, one cannot *know* that A has caused B, and that a repetition of A must necessarily result in B. Hume wrote that "our experience in the past can be a proof of nothing for the future but upon a supposition that there is a resemblance between them (past and future)" (1955, p. xxvi). When an object, unsupported, falls to the ground, we are apt to say that this was a *necessary* consequence of the law of gravitation. Hume would argue that we have only our sensory knowledge, and we are really *assuming* a necessary connection when it cannot be proved to exist. The logical principle of cause and effect is an unsupported extrapolation of the observations of such events in the past. We can never be absolutely sure that sequences of yesterday will be repeated tomorrow.

Although most modern psychologies accept determinism, there is a tendency to agree with Hume at least to the point of warning against the *post hoc* fallacy. This is an error that logicians like to point out: B followed A, so it must have been caused by A. For example, if a sacrifice is followed by rain, the change in the weather must have been caused by the sacrifice. This inference process becomes especially important in some areas of personality, for example in an assumption that the criminal behavior of the child is caused by the rigorous discipline imposed by the father. (Note, for example, that the reverse is also often asserted: such behavior is due to excessively permissive parents.) The *post hoc* fallacy is an important one for all psychologists to remember. The phrase "necessary and sufficient" points to the rule that the truth of an hypothesis be accepted only if (1) B never occurs in the absence of A, and (2) in all cases in which A is present, B follows. Even if these conditions are fulfilled, caution is appropriate because there may be a hidden variable, C, which has not been detected in the past but may crop up in the future.

An interesting verbalism occurs in Hume that is probably relevant to nineteenth-century developments. This is his repeated references to "experiment," meaning only a "thought experiment": "We may, therefore, observe, as the first experiment to our present purpose, that upon the appearance of the picture of an absent friend our idea of him is evidently enlivened by the *resemblance*, and that every passion which that idea occasions, whether of joy or sorrow, acquires new force and vigor" (1955, p. 64). No one today would consider this an *experiment,* but the very introduction of the term may have suggested to later scholars the possibility of actually experimenting on mental processes.

Hume expanded more on the problems of memory and forgetting than had his predecessors. He noted mainly a loss of clarity and intensity when memory images are compared with present perceptions: "When we reflect on our past sentiments and affections, our thought is a faithful mirror, and copies its objects truly; but the colours which it employs are faint and dull, in comparison of those in which our original perceptions were clothed" (p. 299). Thus he showed no concern about errors of memory, distortions, and forgetting, which are today considered important phenomena for investigation.

Imagination was another topic to receive Hume's scrutiny, and to be analyzed into empiricist phenomena. Noting that one can dream of things never experienced, such as a dragon or an alien planet, he warned that "all this creative power of the mind amounts to no more than the faculty of compounding, transposing, augmenting, or diminishing the materials afforded us by the senses and experience" (1955, p. 27). Like all of Hume's other doctrines, this one is based solely on his own introspections; the idea of collecting evidence from others had not yet appeared as a potential tool.

Hume differed from Locke and Berkeley in the amount of attention he paid to motivation and emotion. He wrote of the "passions of the mind" as had Descartes, and he applied associationist thinking to the problem. Thus, for example, the idea of wealth might evoke a passion of anger and resentment (in the person deprived of wealth), just as the name of a loved one might activate the emotion of love. This section of his work did not involve any novel principles; he did not speculate on the dynamic role of passions in directing the sequence of ideas, nor did he speculate on unconscious emotional states.

Finally, we may note that Hume was the first to attach the label *experiment* to the analysis of imaginary situations. The procedure itself goes back to classical Greece; Socrates, for example, made use of hypothetical situations to draw out his respondent. When we read Hume on "experiment," therefore, we must keep in mind that he had no plan to use a laboratory or a rigorous procedure; he was proposing "thought experiments." This is the kind of armchair speculation so often criticized by modern psychologists. Hume also concerned himself with developing mathematical approaches to psychology and experimentation: "If we take in our hand any volume: of divinity or school metaphysics, for instance; let us ask, *Does it contain any abstract reasoning concerning quantity or number? No. Does it contain any experimental reasoning concerning matter of fact and existence?* No. Commit it then to the flames; for it can contain nothing but sophistry and illusion" (1955, p. 420). Clearly, Hume aligned himself with the "tough-minded" scientists of his time.

British Associationism

Locke, Berkeley, and Hume have traditionally been identified as the leading exponents of "British empiricism," whereas David Hartley, James Mill, and John Stuart Mill are named the leaders of "British associationism." There is not much basis for this distinction. The earlier triad wrote of association, although they did not explore the issue carefully; and the second triad assumed empiricism as a methodology and epistemology but elaborated on the way in which experience is analyzed and processed. One could plausibly call the set of six by either term without doing violence to the doctrines, of any one of them.

That being said, I should observe that with detailed consideration of the ways in which ideas become associated, we enter into the area that has most characterized twentieth-century American psychology. Today it is called *learning theory* or *behavior theory, classical conditioning,* or *operant conditioning;* there are sometimes advantages in inventing a new label for a phenomenon, but we should keep in mind that a change in the label does not mean a change in the event itself.

David Hartley

The first psychologist to build his entire system around the concept of association was David Hartley (1705–1757.) He resurrected the old Greek idea that all reality is movement. His concept of mental processes related every observable phenomenon to vibration, conceived of as a very rapid minuscule movement of a physical nature; "External objects impressed upon the senses occasion, first in the nerves upon which they are impressed, and then in the brain, vibrations of the small, and, as one may say, infinitesimal, medullary particles" (1749, Bk. I, Prop. 4.) These infinitesimally small vibrations he called "vibratiuncles." Two sensations become associated as their vibrations occur simultaneously in the nervous system; thus, the basic law of association is contiguity. The linkage of vibrations is directional; "if the Impressions A, B, C, be always made in the order of the Alphabet, B impressed alone will not raise *a,* but *c* only" (Bk. I, Prop. X).

The doctrine of vibration was manifestly an attempt to use the newly formed prestige of physics, specifically of Isaac Newton, to support the psychological speculation. Actually, there was no way in which Hartley could observe these vibratiuncles. He was perceptive when dealing with ideas and actions, but engaged in fruitless speculation about a hypothetical physiology underlying the sensations and ideas.

Hartley merits distinction for another contribution to the embryonic discipline of psychology. His predecessors had concentrated on consciousness, sensations, images, feelings, and so on. Hartley called attention to the fact that responses could also become associated with external stimuli, so that the recurrence of a physical stimulus might arouse the related response. This idea represents a major advance in theory. Descartes, of course, had written of automatic responses called *reflexes*, but he had assumed these to be controlled by the soul operating through the pineal gland. Hartley brought the response into the open as another item subject to the laws of association.

These laws included simultaneous pairing (as in Pavlov's conditioned-reflex model), successive pairing (as in Skinner's operant studies), the importance of repetition or frequency, and the formation of remote associations in successive sequences. Hartley held that, with repetition, an image could become as strong as a sensation. By the same process, a lack of repetition would be followed by loss of clarity (i.e., forgetting).

As might be expected, association was the process underlying the formation of complex ideas. Hartley wrote that "simple ideas of sensation must run into clusters and combinations, by associations; and that each of these will, at last, coalesce into one complex idea" (Bk. I, Prop. XII). Although this idea was not entirely novel, it set the stage for the debate over "mental physics" (James Mill) or "mental chemistry" (John Stuart Mill). In a longer perspective, it foretold the debate of structuralists and behaviorists against the Gestalt theorists regarding the organization of experience.

Another distinctive contribution of Hartley's was his treatment of feelings, that is, pleasure and unpleasantness. Moderate vibrations, he said, induce feelings of pleasure, but intense vibrations are likely to set off feelings of discomfort or pain. This principle obviously holds for many kinds of stimulation. He followed through on this proposal by discussing emotions as aggregates of simple ideas and feelings.

A subtle change in wording in Hartley's writings may be important in connection with later theoretical developments. Whereas his predecessors had confined themselves to discussing association as a fact (i.e., as an observable sequence of conscious experiences), Hartley introduced a dynamic element: prior sensations "get such a *power* over the corresponding ideas" that the occurrence of one, so to speak, compels the awareness of the other" (Bk. I, Prop. X).

James Mill

The pattern of associationist theory was pretty well set by Hartley. There are two remaining members of this school who deserve brief mention. These are James Mill (1773–1836) and his son, John Stuart Mill (1806–1873).

James Mill adopted more of Hume than had Hartley. He placed more stress on the mechanical aspects of association and less on the "power" of one idea to elicit another. His approach could be characterized as that of Newtonian physics; analyzing complex phenomena into simple elements, and treating the interactions of these elements in a purely objective way. Thus it is not surprising that his psychology is often characterized as "mental physics," or mechanics. The elements were labeled as "points of consciousness," and they were assumed to keep their separate identities even when embedded in large, complex ideas. One of Mill's passages will illustrate the argument: "Brick is one complex idea, mortar is another complex idea; these ideas, with ideas of position and quantity, compose my idea of a wall. My idea of a plank is a complex idea, my idea of a rafter is a complex idea, my idea of a nail is a complex idea. These, united with the same ideas of position and quantity, compose my duplex idea of a floor" (1869, Vol. 1, pp. 53–54). Note that a "duplex idea" is more comprehensive than a "complex idea": "In the same manner, my complex idea of glass, and wood, and others, compose my duplex idea of a window; and these duplex ideas, united together, compose my idea of a house, which is made up of various duplex ideas." It is not clear whether, if the individual does not know about the fireplace in the house, the idea of the house is somehow distorted. Presumably, as all associations of these ideas are mechanical, one simply plugs in the fireplace as another component of the "house."

The gradual transition from an emphasis on the acquisition of knowledge, i.e., empiricism, to the linking up of bits of knowledge, i.e., associationism, is summarized in Table 4.1. James Mill represented the logical culmination of this atomistic approach to the structure of human knowledge. His son, John Stuart Mill, introduced a striking new principle which foreshadows the transformation of associationist theory to gestalt theory.

John Stuart Mill

While James Mill had carried the analysis of associations to fine detail, he presented a picture of the mind as essentially passive, shaped by the environment. John Stuart Mill (1806–1873), while generally praising his father's insights, made it clear that human beings are actively involved in restructuring and rearranging the ideas provided by experience. A significant indicator of this revised emphasis is given by the metaphors each used; James Mill wrote of "mental physics"—perhaps more accurately, mental mechanics—while his son used the metaphor of "mental chemistry." The difference in the two metaphors is important. For the chemist, two substances which combine lose their identity and take on properties not manifested by each substance alone. Thus, hydrogen and oxygen, two gases, combine to form water, which is a liquid and has attributes such as a boiling point and a freezing point, which cannot be predicted from a knowledge of the component gases. John Stuart Mill

TABLE 4.1 Prominent Empiricists and Associationists

John Locke (1632–1704)	The mind is a blank slate; all knowledge derives from experience; primary and secondary qualities differ; illusions can be transcended by reflection.
George Berkeley (1685–1753)	Idealistic monism; the only reality is perception; thus, primary and secondary qualities do not differ.
David Hume (1711–1776)	Causality is only perceived succession; similarity and contrast reduce to mere contiguity; the "self" is no more than a bundle of perceptions, lacking unity.
David Hartley (1705–1757)	The central problem for psychology is the association of ideas; all ideas derive from experience; "vibrations of particles in nerves" constitute the physiological basis for consciousness.
James Mill (1773–1836)	"Mental physics"; a complex idea is no more than the sum of the simple ideas involved, and analysis reveals this atomistic structure.
John Stuart Mill (1806–1873)	"Mental chemistry"; a complex idea may have emergent properties not deducible from any of the component simple ideas.

followed his illustrious parent in most theories, but he recognized the transformation of properties that can occur in complex thinking.

Although the younger Mill agreed, on the whole, with the association theory of his father, he took a step in the direction of the Scottish school (see the next section). This was in conceding that the mind is active, not merely passive. It is active mainly in the sense proposed by Locke, (i.e., the passive reception of information is followed by active reflection on the material); thus, the identification of various animals might be followed by the mind's generating the abstract idea of a vertebrate. Further, this novel formulation has properties different from the sum of its parts—an idea that reached its culmination in Gestalt psychology.

Both Mills were interested in the relationship of psychology and economics, not in the sense of an impact of economic conditions on thinking—an issue of concern today—but in the sense of how the economic system grows out of mental processes. Thus Adam Smith's *Wealth of Nations* (1776) espoused the pleasure–pain theory of motivation, which is often referred to as *psychological hedonism;* as each person seeks to maximize his or her own pleasures and to minimize pains, the economy is based on individualism. Out of this Smith concocted the "invisible hand" of the market, which would automatically lead to fair treatment for everybody. J. S. Mill objected to this, arguing that psychological hedonism had to be supplemented by ethical hedonism, a term which means roughly that the goal of society is the greatest good for the greatest number of persons. Sigmund Freud would later take this concept and convert it into his "reality principle," as opposed to psychological hedonism, which Freud represented as the "pleasure principle." The link between Freud and J. S. Mill is closer than some historical instances of influence; Freud actually translated one of Mill's books into German.

The Scottish School

Although custom has led to my using the term *British empiricism* to refer to the views just summarized, from Locke to the Mills, accuracy might favor the term *English empiricism*. This would more appropriately distinguish it from the Scottish faculty psychology that originated in opposition to the extreme position adopted by Hume. In those days, the hostility of the Scots toward the English was rather high, and it is less than surprising that the scholars of the north would seek antithetical positions when faced with an English doctrine.

Thomas Reid

Thomas Reid (1710–1796) made it clear that he was stirred to action by Hume's *Enquiry* (1748). He rejected the extreme atomism and empiricism of Hume, as well as the implicit undercutting of religion. The Scottish philosophers were living in an atmosphere permeated by Calvinism; the Anglican church was considerably more tolerant of philosophical deviations. Reid set forth his replies to Hume in two books, *Inquiry into the Human Mind* (1749) and *Essays on the Intellectual Powers* (1785).

Reid made it clear that he would have none of Berkeley's subjective idealism or Hume's skepticism. Reality is there, and it is not merely an aggregate of sensory experiences in somebody's mind. Reid appealed to "common sense," which is not a very good guide to psychological theorizing; he did fairly well in avoiding the claim that reality is confirmed by the Scriptures. His religious bias is implied by his vigorous rejection of the Humean argument against the existence of a soul or mind or a self. He insisted that experiences are unified by the experiencing self, and, anticipating J. S. Mill, he treated this self as active in dissecting, merging, and transforming sensory inputs to develop complex ideas.

The important element of Reid's thinking, viewed from the perspective of modern American psychology, was his faculty theory. He postulated various mental "powers," such as "comparison" and "calculation," language and causality. Modern mental testers are accustomed to assuming that individuals differ with respect to numerical, spatial, and verbal reasoning, and these were, in the American literature of the late nineteenth century, called *faculties*.

Because Reid assumed that individuals differed with respect to these faculties, and that these differences showed up in various kinds of behavior, he replaced Locke's *tabula rasa* with an active mind that was not a mere victim of environmental inputs. Thus faculty psychology tended also to become a nativistic or hereditarian theory; where Locke and Hume would agree with Skinner that "the environment is everything," the Scots proclaimed that heredity is also important.

Dugald Stewart

Dugald Stewart (1753–1828) was a disciple of Reid's, and most historians treat him as a popularizer rather than a creative thinker. He has been criticized for such tautologies as "imitative behavior is due to an instinct of imitation," a definition that does not define. Stewart wrote well, and his texts were widely disseminated in the English-speaking world.

Thomas Brown

Thomas Brown (1778–1820) was a colleague of Stewart's and, according to some critics, a source of much of Stewart's success in his mission of popularizing faculty psychology. He is remembered, however, for ideas he set forth under his own name.

One of his innovations was calculated to bridge the gap between sensation and perception. Tradition had it that the odor of a rose was a sensation, hence, inside the person, but that the perception of the rose placed it out there in the external world. Brown proposed that the link was to be found in muscular sensations. Smelling the rose is not perceiving, but when one handles the rose, the muscular feedback sustains the judgment that this is a "real" object. In the twentieth century, this appeal to muscular activity became very prominent with the rise of behaviorism. In opposition to the skeptics, Brown held that our belief in the existence of a real world was largely based on these sensations of effort and manipulation.

The English associationists had agreed on a few primary laws of association: contiguity, similarity, and contrast. Hume had added cause and effect but later argued that this was no more than contiguity plus a subjective feeling of a "necessary" sequence. Brown proposed secondary laws of association, including the duration of the original sensations that had become associated, "liveliness," frequency, recency, and multiple connections with other ideas (i.e., a new experience that fits in with a cluster of ideas becomes associated quickly and endures longer than an isolated event.) Many of these "laws" of association have become targets of empirical research in today's laboratories.

Brown's most important contribution may have been in his substitution of "suggestion" for "association." He wrote that one idea suggests another, and he used Hartley's concept of the "attractive force" of an idea as an aspect of the "power of suggestion." This hypothesis of a dynamic aspect of associations later became important to Sigmund Freud and psychoanalytic theory.

Brown also objected to the fallacy of "nominalism," in effect, the assumption that because a phenomenon has a name, it must have a separate identity. Specifically, he opposed the belief that "consciousness" had some kind of existence independent of the contents of consciousness. Rather, consciousness is a name for a class of events: "There are not," he wrote, "sensations, thought, passions, *and also consciousness*, any more than there is *quadruped* or *animal*, as a separate being to be added to the wolves, tygers, elephants, and other living creatures" (1820/1970, p. 336). There is a recurring tendency in the history of psychology for writers to confuse the name of an object with its reality. The fact that there is a name for digestion does not mean that you can put digestion on a scale and weigh it. The same holds for perceiving, learning, desiring, and so on.

William Hamilton

Another important member of the Scottish school was *William Hamilton* (1788–1856). Hamilton is remembered today mainly for his concept of *redintegration*, referring to the reinstatement of the memory of a total experience when only one detail is physically present. The idea is of value primarily because it calls attention to the unity of experiences; that is, meeting a high school friend may remind one not only of activities with that friend, but also of others at the school, athletic events, dances, and so on. Redintegration, then, served to set up a new class of associations in which the part revives the whole, and thus it provides another element in the foundation of Gestalt psychology. An important derivative of the concept of redintegration is that memory operates more in the fashion of J. S. Mill's mental chemistry than James Mill's mental physics. The whole memory tends to hang together as a unit; it does not fall apart into simple ideas.

Influence of Faculty Psychology

Faculty psychology was subjected to severe criticism by contemporaries as well as by modern psychologists. Even before Reid's time, Locke had objected to explaining functions by faculties; when one said "the act of willing is due to a faculty of willing," the logic was circular and invalid. On the other hand, the Scots had a strong point in the phenomenon of individual differences. Two persons may announce a resolution to stop smoking, but one succeeds and the other fails. At this point, differences inside the organism may become important to an understanding of differences in action.

The Scots were widely taught in American colleges from about 1770 to 1830. Sahakian (1975) reported on textbooks used in various courses in the departments of philosophy and found Reid, Stewart, and Hamilton to be common sources of instruction.

The tradition of faculties of the mind persisted much longer. At the turn of the century, educational psychology often included a study of the "intellectual faculties"—the doctrine of formal discipline, for example, being based on faculty psychology. The theory led to the requirement of courses in Greek, Latin, and mathematics, on the grounds that these trained the intellectual faculties, which could then deal with any novel information. Empirical research, not surprisingly, demonstrated that this assumption was incorrect (see, e.g., Thorndike and Woodworth, 1901). Thus, practicing memorizing poetry did not improve a person's ability to memorize nonsense syllables, and there was no support for the idea that training improved the "faculty" in general. Later and more sophisticated research has shown that training does transfer, but not in the ways postulated by faculty theory.

Vitalism was not explicitly endorsed by the Scots. They were, of course, opposed to the mechanism of Condillac and La Mettrie, and to the aggressive atomism of Hume. The Scots perceived much of the associationist doctrine as mechanical, too, and criticized it accordingly. One common thread running through the Scottish school is a concern for the properties of the individual—and therefore, an acceptance of heredity and differences in human capacities. This is not the same as postulating a "vital force," but it does erode reliance exclusively on empiricism.

On the whole, the Scots were more accepting of a religious component of their psychology than the English empiricists and associationists.

There was also an acceptance of what Reid called "common sense" and what William James would later call "pragmatism," namely, recognizing that survival is one goal of life. In a critical response to Bishop Berkeley, which was less naive than that ascribed above to Samuel Johnson, Reid speculated on what would happen if he accepted Berkeley's version of the subjective nature of reality and the rejection of sensory evidence: "I resolve not to believe my senses. I break my nose against a post. . . . I step into a dirty kennel; and after twenty such wise and rational actions, I am taken up and clapped into a madhouse" (1970, p. 175). This argument, of course, pinpointed a weakness of the skepticist position regarding sensory data: it may look fine on paper, but it is not a safe guide to behavior. The problem persists today.

The Rationalists

Nationalistic rivalries should not be ignored in assessing the history of psychological concepts. John Stuart Mill commented, in one of his articles, that "The sceptre of Psychology has decidedly returned to this island." (Brett, 1962, p. 459). Certainly the most interesting speculations of the eighteenth century came from England and Scotland. However, interesting ideas were offered by Continental scholars, primarily in Germany, which cannot be ignored. Two of these figures, Gottfried Wilhelm Leibniz and Immanuel Kant, specifically ascribed their concern with philosophical psychology to the need to oppose some of the British theories. Table 4.2 summarizes the key ideas of the major figures of Scottish and German rationalism.

Leibniz

Gottfried Wilhelm Leibniz (1646–1716) reacted against the *Essay Concerning Human Understanding* (1690) by Locke. The contrast in their views

TABLE 4.2   Prominent Rationalists

Gottfried W. Leibniz (1646–1716)	The intellect was present (innate) before any sensory experiences; reality is composed of monads with both physical and mental aspects, which do not interact but run parallel; mental processes vary by tiny steps rather than by discontinuous jumps.
Thomas Reid (1710–1796)	Reality is physical; the mind or soul is unified and is active in seeking sensory input, analyzing it, and drawing inferences; the mind has "faculties," which may be greater in one person, less in another.
Immanuel Kant (1724–1804)	Reality exists but is unknowable; we know phenomena through the senses, but the data are categorized according to innate principles such as time and space.
Dugald Stewart (1753–1828)	Elaborate lists of human "faculties."
Thomas Brown (1778–1820)	One idea "suggests" another; mental operations are dynamic.
William Hamilton (1788–1856)	Memory is a process of redintegration; a part reinstates the whole experience.

is well summarized by the quote from Locke: "there is nothing in the intellect which was not previously in the senses"—and the reply by Leibniz, "except the intellect itself." In other words, Leibniz, like the Scots, was asserting that heredity was relevant, that sensory experiences did not process themselves, and that a simple mechanistic theory was a gross oversimplification. Leibniz is commonly called a *rationalist* because he stressed the capacity of the mind to reason, that is, to transform sensory experience into abstract ideas and theories that would guide action.

In a sense, Leibniz was also protesting the dualism of Descartes, who had separated body and soul and then had linked them through the pineal gland. Leibniz accepted the distinction—then rarely questioned—between mind and matter. Mental or psychical events constituted one order of reality; the physical was a totally separate realm, and no one could figure out a plausible interaction mechanism. Leibniz solved the difficulty in a mystical fashion by inventing a concept he called a "monad." This was a rather baffling concept that was both material and psychical; one is tempted to think of it as the same reality seen in different perspectives, but that is not what Leibniz meant by it. Every individual is a monad, and her or his physical activities are in exact synchrony with mental processes. They do not, however, interact; they coincide because of a preestablished harmony. Leibniz used the metaphor of two clocks wound up at the same time, and ticking away in perfect synchrony, but not influencing one another.

The metaphor leaves much to be desired. Leibniz was protesting specifically, Locke's formulation of the *tabula rasa,* the mind that is completely molded by experience. For Leibniz, the mind or soul was an active agent, taking in and processing information, not simply registering it. This seems to be contradictory to the preestablished harmony idea, which, in fact, resembles the Calvinist doctrine of predestination. Thus Leibniz's position may have made him attractive to the Scots, although none of them endorsed the monad as a philosophical or psychological concept. Certainly his theory favored an emphasis on heredity as a determinant of psychic processes.

Leibniz is known to mathematicians as a coinventor of the calculus, along with Isaac Newton. The point is relevant to psychology because it involves the principle of continuous variation; as Leibniz put it, "nature makes no leaps." This principle is found in various aspects of modern psychology; for example, in most of parametric statistics, the assumption of continuity is a necessary one, and it leads to odd conclusions like "The average American woman bears 2.2 children." As children come in units, the assumption of continuous variation is patently false. A similar problem arises in connection with learning theory; a substantial body of literature deals with the debate between the view that learning occurs by gradual increments and the view that one-trial learning or insight learning disproves the continuity theory.

The idea of continuity was important in Leibniz's thinking in another fashion. It is empirically clear that some stimuli do not elicit any conscious awareness, and at stimulus levels above a threshold, increasing stimuli lead to increasingly intense sensations. Leibniz thus evolved the theory that perceptions vary continuously on a scale from zero to some hypothetical maximum, but the important aspect for modern psychologists is that some stimuli give rise to psychic processes which are not conscious. Leibniz called these *"petites perceptions,"* little sensations that never become conscious. But they can influence behavior. Sigmund Freud was familiar with this concept and seized upon it as an essential element in his doctrine of the unconscious shaping of conscious events.

Kant

The other important figure in German philosophical psychology at this time was *Immanuel Kant* (1724–1804). Like Leibniz, Kant described himself as having been spurred into action by empiricist ideas. In Kant's case, it was the publication of Hume's *Enquiry Concerning Human Understanding* (1748) that "roused me from my dogmatic slumber."

Kant came very close to reinstating Plato's concept of "innate ideas." Like Leibniz, he denied that the mind was completely passive, and he suggested that certain very fundamental categories of mental life had to be innate. As an example, he examined the concept of time. Now, time cannot be directly experienced. One can observe an event in progress; one may daydream and suddenly realize that "time has passed"; and yet introspective study has never uncovered an experience of time as such. Therefore, Kant argued, time must be one of the basic categories that the mind brings to experience, and in terms of which experiences can be sorted into sequences or manipulated in other ways. The same analysis holds for space, which is never directly experienced; space is inferred from the perceived attributes of objects.

Kant differed from the Scottish faculty psychologists on the specific issue of faculties. He preached the unity of the soul, denying that any subdivisions were innate, and denying also that they could be acquired. One can support this unity, of course, by noting the unity of attention, the clustering of memories as those involving the person versus historical or fictional memories, and unity of the will. In this respect, Kant would have been distressed by the phenomena of multiple personalities, Freud's observations on the conflict between conscious and unconscious desires, and so on. He is easily recognizable as an ancestor of the Gestalt school of psychology.

Phrenology

One final variant in psychological thinking of this period deserves mention. This is the rise of phrenology, a doctrine relating to localization of functions in the brain. Its location in this chapter is dictated by its dependence on faculty psychology for an intellectual foundation.

Phrenology was founded by Franz Joseph Gall (1758–1828) and was popularized by Johann Kaspar Spurzheim (1776–1832). Gall was trained as an anatomist; and he observed that there were substantial variations among individuals with respect to the shape of the skull. Boring (1929) reported that, even as a schoolboy, Gall had been intrigued by the notion that he could detect differences in the anatomy of the heads of his playmates, and that some of these differences seemed to be related to their behavior. On the other hand, the idea may have germinated when he worked with inmates of jails and lunatic asylums; the notion that hereditary deformities characterized these unfortunate persons was held widely at the time. At any rate, Gall was collecting observations of physical deviations and their associated mental processes at the time when he became familiar with Dugald Stewart's theories and adopted the Scot's enumeration of mental "faculties" as the attributes he would link to anatomical features. Figure 4.1 shows the list of "faculties" and a phrenological chart of the skull showing the areas believed to be associated with them.

The "logic" of this association was that overdevelopment of a specific brain area would result in an outward bulge of the cranium; correspondingly, a deficit in the "faculty" would correspond to a depression in the skull. This hypothesis was laughed at by most nineteenth-century scientists on the grounds that the skull was too hard for the soft brain tissue to make any impression on the bony structure, and that there was no reason to expect the bony formation to move in to fill a gap if a cortical area were underdeveloped. It is one of history's little ironies that empirical evidence is accumulating to support the belief that the skull can be modified by the brain. Rats reared in an "enriched" environment have longer skulls than litter-mates reared under "normal" laboratory conditions. Further, paleoanthropologists are now studying depressions on the inner surface of the skull, seeking evidence that Broca's area (a cortical area involved in speech) developed at some point in hominid evolution and caused a change in the configuration of the skull.

Gall "validated" his theory by finding one or two persons who showed evidence of some distinctive personality attribute, and mapping their skulls for prominences and depressions. He then sought persons at the opposite extreme of the personality dimension and mapped their skulls. If some skull feature was found in the "high" group and was missing in

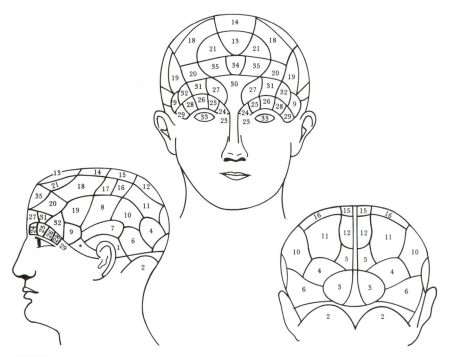

FIGURE 4.1   A Phrenological View of Human Attributes

According to Gall, human beings have some 35 affective and intellectual faculties. The numbers correspond to areas on the skull as shown in the drawings.

Affective Faculties

PROPENSITIES

? Desire to live
• Alimentiveness
1 Destructiveness
2 Amativeness
3 Philoprogenitive-
  ness
4 Adhesiveness
5 Inhabitiveness
6 Combativeness
7 Secretiveness
8 Acquisitiveness
9 Constructiveness

SENTIMENTS

10 Cautiousness
11 Approbative-
   ness
12 Self-Esteem
13 Benevolence
14 Reverence
15 Firmness
16 Conscien-
   tiousness
17 Hope
18 Marvelous-
   ness
19 Ideality
20 Mirthful-
   ness
21 Imitation

Intellectual Faculties

PERCEPTIVE

22 Individuality
23 Configuration
24 Size
25 Weight and
   Resistance
26 Coloring
27 Locality
28 Order
29 Calculation
30 Eventuality
31 Time
32 Tune
33 Language

REFLECTIVE

34 Comparison
35 Causality

(From Spurzheim, J. G. 1834. *Phrenology, or the Doctrine of Mental Phenomena.*)

the "low" group, Gall averred that these findings supported his theory.

This method is actually used today; that is, much of the research on personality characteristics utilizes the method of extreme groups. However, no one seeks to tie the data to skull formation. The major point of difference in modern research is that there is more concern with eliminating the prospect that random coincidences will give a spurious appearance of correlation. Thus Hermann Rorschach validated his inkblot personality measure by obtaining responses from institutionalized cases as well as from persons nominated by acquaintances as having the attribute being studied. A similar procedure was used by S. R. Hathaway and J. D. McKinley (1952) in developing the (MMPI) Minnesota Multiphasic Personality Inventory. The method, then, is useful, but Gall applied it carelessly.

Gall's logic with regard to the localization of functions also has its modern disciples. Research seeks centers for pleasure, for short-term memory, for aggression, and so on. Although the controversy over whether cerebral function is localized or is diffuse is not a major concern in American psychology, it recurs from time to time. It is tempting to hope that a little organ (like the pineal gland or the hippocampus) will provide a key to understanding the physiological basis of some mental process. Regrettably, we still will not know on what basis this connection operates.

Empiricism Versus Rationalism

In the eighteenth century, the major issues in psychological theorizing began to take on their modern forms. The debate over heredity versus environment still continues, as it did in the Locke–Leibniz and Hume–Kant debates. The controversy over the status of the "self" as a psychological structure in its own right, versus the "bundle-of-responses" hypothesis, also took shape. Atomism was also attacked by those favoring a holistic view of mental phenomena. The debate over the study of "mind in general" versus an emphasis on individual differences in mental functions appeared for the first time.

Let us sum up the empiricist–rationalist dispute. D. N. Robinson (1981) provided succinct definitions of the two conflicting theoretical positions. Empiricism, he asserted, can be defined by three propositions: *"the evidence of sense constitutes the primary data of all knowledge; . . . knowledge cannot exist unless this evidence has first been gathered; and . . . all subsequent intellectual processes must use this evidence and only this evidence in framing valid propositions about the real world"* (p. 205; italics in original).

This may be contrasted with the rationalist approach. Robinson proposed the following formulation: *"all knowledge is the result of a rational analysis of the evidence of the senses and . . . this very evidence cannot be gath-*

ered except by a rationally directing principle" (1981, p. 206; italics in original).

When the conflicting positions are juxtaposed in this way, it becomes apparent that the agreement was far greater than the debaters on either side were willing to admit. The rationalists conceded that evidence is gathered through the senses, by observation and experiment; the empiricists admitted that "intellectual processes" occur and that these are not identical with the evidence gathered. There was thus a different emphasis: the empiricist stressed sensory input; and the rationalist pointed to central processing. But the two are in no way mutually exclusive.

The associationists showed one remarkable gap in logic. They asserted that all knowledge comes through the senses, and that associations are based on the frequency of the pairing of two items. But there is *no* sensory basis for frequency. The data are clear; item pairs often repeated do become associated, and frequency of occurrence gives some pairs priority over others in the processing of information. But the fact of frequency cannot be an outcome of sensation alone. Frequency is computed within the organism as events are perceived as identical or similar to prior experiences. Even infants are known to be influenced by frequency, but not on the basis of a sensory input designated *frequency*.

A second point which remains to divide the empiricists from the rationalists in psychological research relates to logic or methodology. The advocates of what has pejoratively been called "dustbowl empiricism" argue against theory, proposing that data be gathered on almost every variable which may be relevant. But, the rationalist asks, What is relevant? It is not likely that any modern behaviorist will relate lever-pressing in the white rat to phases of the moon. The rationalist suspected that the empiricist had a concealed theory which defined what is relevant. It can easily be argued that an explicit theory can be tested and modified, whereas an unstated theory is not open to improvement. Thus it would seem that we need rationalists to construct theories and empiricists to test them.

CHAPTER 5

Germany: The Emergence of Scientific Psychology

It is something of a historical curiosity that scientific psychology, basically rooted in French mechanistic thinking and elaborated by the English empiricist-associationists and the Scottish rationalists, should first take form in Germany. This is not to deny the role of Leibniz and Kant, but to note that the important influences on the choice of problems and concepts came from other sources.

At the beginning of the nineteenth century, Germany was no more than a figure of speech. What is now called Germany (or East and West Germany) was a large group of principalities, sharing a common language but no governmental structure. Despite (or perhaps because of) this, the universities flourished and research burgeoned in Germany.

German Experimental Physiology

Experimental psychology emerged from experimental physiology. As was suggested in Figure 1.1, biology achieved independence from philosophy before psychology did, and the key events leading up to the recognition of psychology as a science occurred in laboratories of physiology.

Müller

Johannes Müller (1801–1858) studied both the physiology and the psychology of vision and prepared a *Handbook of Physiology* which not only summarized contemporary knowledge but also commented on future

trends. His first major contribution seems to have been in sensory physiology. A British physiologist, Sir Charles Bell, had discovered in 1811
that the motor and sensory nerves were not identical, and that each peripheral nerve could be separated into sensory and motor fibers. However, he leaped to the conclusion that different senses were mediated by
different fibers; he was correct, of course, in that the sensations are different. Müller took Bell's finding and clarified it: the nerves are identical, but the sensations are still different. Müller then made his faulty
leap; he decided that each sensory nerve carried a different *energy*. The
experimental data, of course, were limited to the fact that stimulating a
given sensory nerve led to its characteristic sensation, regardless of the
kind of stimulus. Thus pressing on the eyeball produces a visual sensation; an electrical stimulus to a taste bud produces a taste sensation; and
so on. (Today the differences in sensory quality are ascribed to the cortical terminus of the sensory nerve, not to any "energy.") This discovery
strengthened the hands of those philosophers who held that one does
not experience the "real" qualities out there in the environment, and
that something inside the body determines the sensory attributes of objects.

Helmholtz

Müller's *Handbook of Physiology* included many errors, at least as seen
from the twentieth century. For example, he treated the speed of the
nerve impulse as infinite, or at least as being so fast that it could not be
measured. *Hermann Ludwig Ferdinand von Helmholtz* (1821–1894) disproved this belief. He stimulated a person on the toe and measured the
time the person required to react; then he stimulated the same individual on the thigh and again took the response time. The first time was
uniformly longer than the second, and Helmholtz attributed this fact to
the extra route (toe to thigh). Measuring this distance and dividing it by
the reaction time, he was able to show that the impulse was fairly slow.
The obtained figures gave a speed of 150–300 feet per second.

Why was this considered a major contribution to understanding human behavior? The explanation is historical. In the past, philosophers
had speculated on the speed of thought and had argued (1) that it was
infinite and unmeasurable, or (2) that it matched the speed of light. There
was an odd confusion of the speed of thought with speed of "thinking
about" something. I can sit here in Michigan and think about a friend
walking on the Great Wall in China. Obviously my thinking is still in
Michigan; the content of the thought has changed, but not its location.
But this confusion seems to have led to the belief in the infinite speed
of thought. Now Helmholtz demonstrated that this speed is really quite
slow, and thinking became a phenomenon that—potentially, at least—
could be studied in the laboratory.

Helmholtz made another significant contribution to the embryonic science of psychology. Remember that Leibniz had, much earlier, proposed his theory of *"petites perceptions,"* sensations too weak to reach conscious awareness, but having an effect on behavior just the same. Helmholtz offered a theory of "unconscious inference," which, although by no means the same as the theory of Leibniz, added another argument for extending the domain called "psychology" beyond the fringes of consciousness. Historically, the overwhelming majority of philosophical speculation about human behavior had concentrated on conscious processes. Helmholtz noted that many acts are controlled unconsciously; for example, one can judge the distance from one house to the next without consciously identifying any sensory cues. While this supported the Leibniz thesis that some of behavior is unconscious, it does not depend on the idea of a sensory threshold.

It is not likely that Helmholtz had any conception of a system of unconscious emotions and impulses analogous to that later developed by Sigmund Freud. Nevertheless, the Helmholtz doctrine was put in imaginative terms: reaching conclusions without consciousness of the information being utilized was indicative of the "unconscious processes of association of ideas going on in the dark background of our memory." (1856/1924, III, p. 26.)

E. G. Boring (1950) speculated that this discovery by Helmholtz contributed to the rise of behaviorism. Although Descartes and La Mettrie had offered a conception of automatic, nonconscious behavior, they did not have any concrete evidence to support their hypotheses. Helmholtz demonstrated that an act of the mind could be independent of bodily response: "To separate the movement in time from the event of will which caused it was in a sense to separate the body from the mind, and almost from the personality or self" (Boring, 1950, p. 42). Whereas voluntary movement of the arm had been perceived as merely a part of the conscious decision to make this movement, the muscular action was now a distinct and separate event. From this insight to the decision to study *only* the physiological and bodily responses was a fairly easy step.

Helmholtz suffered the fate of many innovators: many scientists rejected his findings outright, and others discarded them as being irrelevant to the important concerns of physiology. It was only gradually that his research was recognized as being highly significant—perhaps, as suggested earlier, because his critics died off.

Weber

Ernest Heinrich Weber (1795–1878) introduced important new concepts and experimental findings in the field of sensory physiology. As early as 1834, he published some ingenious experiments on the sense of touch, and plausibly his book, *Der Tastsinn und das Gemeingefühl* (1846), could be called the first research monograph in experimental psychology. He distinguished three classes of skin sensations: pressure, temperature, and location. He also introduced the concept of the two-point limen, the minimum distance between two points on the skin at which they are sensed as two rather than one.

Important as these developments were, Weber's claim to fame rests elsewhere. He has been hailed in history texts as the first scientist ever to devise a quantitative measure of a psychical or mental process. This was the work which gave rise to the famous *Weber fraction.* The method involved placing weights on the skin of a blindfolded person. Weber then asked if a second weight was lighter, heavier, or the same as the first. He reported that a constant ratio or fraction represented the minimum change in the physical stimulus that could be detected by the observer; this fraction has come to be known as the *jnd* ("just noticeable difference"). For the weight observations, Weber reported that the ratio was 1:40; that is, if the first weight was 40 grams, an increase of 1 gram could be detected, but an increase of 0.5 grams could not; if the standard were 80 grams, the minimum weight to be judged "heavier" would be 82 grams. Later studies showed that visual brightness, auditory loudness, and other sensations obey the rule that the minimum perceptible difference is a constant fraction of the standard stimulus. The important aspect of Weber's work was that, for the first time, a measurable stimulus (weight) could be precisely related to a mental or psychical sensation; thus the "mind" could now be measured.

Fechner

The broader implications of Weber's work were recognized by *Gustav Theodor Fechner* (1801–1887). Unaware of Weber's work, Fechner began studying sensations on his own; when he saw Weber's 1846 monograph, he recognized its importance and began developing the implications. It was he who christened the constant ratio principle *Weber's Law,* although he formulated it more precisely. He showed, for example, that the changes in the physical stimulus increased on a logarithmic scale, whereas the sensations increased on a linear scale:

$$\text{sensation} = K \log \text{stimulus}$$

in which *sensation* refers to judgments of sensory intensity and K is a constant that varies from one modality to another (Fig. 5.1).

Although Fechner had a medical degree, he had specialized in physics rather than in biology. He was thus in a favorable position to see the importance of relating conscious sensations to quantitative physical measurements. He coined the term *psychophysics* to denominate what he saw as a new field of knowledge, the borderland between physics and mind.

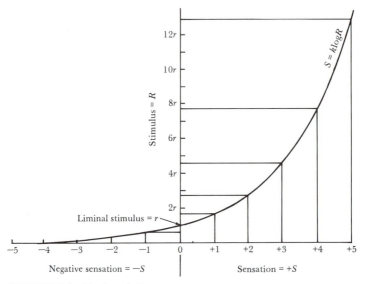

FIGURE 5.1   Fechner's Law

Fechner proposed the equation $S = k \log R$, when R is the physical energy of the stimulus, e.g., in decibels, and S is the reported sensation. The absolute threshold is the "liminal stimulus." Stimuli below this level may be presumed to set off some sensory process, but since this is not conscious, it is shown here as a negative sensation. Note also that for a given increase in the sensation, proportionately larger increases in R, the stimulus, are required.

He also worked out different psychophysical procedures that are still used.

Fechner is interesting to historians for another reason. He was among those Europeans who, in the nineteenth century, became intrigued by the philosophies of the Orient. Specifically, in a book called the *Zend-Avesta* in 1851, he proposed an "exact science of the functional relations or relations of dependency between body and mind" (Boring, 1950, p. 281). As the phrase suggests, his was a curious blend of physical science and mysticism. He held that plants and animals, as well as humans, were conscious in a limited sense. His view of reality could be characterized as a "double-aspect" theory in which the same event could be studied as a material object and also as a mental or psychic phenomenon.

The broad generalization derived by Fechner from his own work and that of Weber was that there are lawful relations between the world of physics and the world of psychology. Another important outcome was his demonstration that the method of introspection could be systematized and subjected to laboratory controls. Although the report of a sensation can still be said to be introspective, the meticulous control of the magnitude of the physical stimulus removed most of the uncertainty that plagued the armchair introspections of psychologists from St. Augustine to David Hume.

Neurologizing was not a major concern of Fechner. He did, at times, make explicit his belief that the lawful relationship between physical and psychical events carried with it a presumption of a lawful physiological process between the two. He wrote: "Sensation depends on stimulation; a stronger sensation depends on a stronger stimulus; the stimulus, however, causes sensation only via the intermediate action of some internal process of the body. To the extent that lawful relationships between sensation and stimulus can be found, they must include lawful relationships between the stimulus and this inner physical activity" (1860/1966, Vol. I, p. 3).

The continuity theory posed by Fechner assumed that, if measured changes in the stimulus induced a change in sensation, then a smaller change in the stimulus actually produced a change in the sensation that was too small to be noticed. This means that Fechner wanted a continuous sensation dimension, as against the stepwise function that resulted from the psychophysical experiment. It revived the Leibniz notion of *"petites perceptions,"* sensations too weak to become conscious; the continuity theory postulated that changes that were too small for the observer to report did nevertheless elicit unconscious changes in the sensation. This kind of reasoning is common in Western psychology, for example, in the learning theory of Clark Hull (see Chapter Ten). The assumption of a continuous change is also required by some statistical formulas.

It is obvious that Fechner was a major figure in the history of scientific or experimental psychology. Many scholars believe that, if he had not indulged in his extravagant speculations about mystical phenomena, he would have been identified as the founder of the new science. Instead, this recognition has gone to Wilhelm Wundt.

Wilhelm Wundt

The consensus among American psychologists is that the formal emergence of psychology as a science can be identified with the official recognition of Wundt's laboratory at Leipzig as a part of the university. There were other laboratories before this one (those of Helmholtz, Fechner, and even William James at Harvard), but none had official sanction.

Wilhelm Maximilian Wundt (1832–1920) was the son of a poor Lutheran minister; he was born in Neckerau, near Mannheim, and was educated mainly by a tutor, his father's assistant, until he was thirteen. He has been described as lonely and studious, spending much time in daydreaming. At nineteen he enrolled in the medical curriculum at the

Archives of the History of American Psychology

Wilhelm Wundt, first of the tough-minded psychologists
and an advocate of "pure" science

University of Tübingen, because he needed to prepare for a profession
in which he could be self-supporting. He qualified to become a practicing physician but never liked clinical work; he was fascinated by research
and showed considerable originality. He took his doctorate at Heidelberg in 1856 and almost immediately accepted an appointment as an
assistant to Hermann Helmholtz, whose reputation was already impressive. Wundt worked in the shadow of Helmholtz for eighteen years; he
expected to inherit the professorship at Heidelberg when Helmholtz
moved to Berlin and was traumatically disappointed when the post went
to someone else. Because each university had only one professor in
physiology, Wundt's prospects at Heidelberg were poor, and he accepted
a place at Zurich in the faculty of philosophy. A year later, the university
at Leipzig set up a second chair of philosophy (in these times, philosophers still covered a wide range of subject matter; hence philosophy was
exempt from the one-professor rule). Wundt was invited to fill the second post; he moved to Leipzig and remained there for forty-five years.

Only two years after the doctorate, Wundt published his first book, *Beiträge zur Theorie des Sinneswahrnehmung* ("Contributions to the Theory of Sensory Perception"). Although this book drew heavily on the work of Weber, Müller, and others, it contained some original work by Wundt. He cited Helmholtz's concept of "unconscious inference" as a phenomenon that was more than Weber's idea of a pure sensation. Primarily the book was an argument for laboratory research, although Wundt included some material forecasting his later interest in field study and social psychology.

Wundt's career became something of a model for bright young scholars for many years. They took their degrees in medicine or physiology, then found places in departments of philosophy. For years, there were no academic appointments identified as being in psychology. History records that Harvard University did not organize a department of psychology separate from the philosophy department until 1930, and many other universities, European and American, delayed even longer before recognizing the distinction.

G. Stanley Hall, who will be discussed later, was one of the first Americans to study with Wundt. He described the middle-aged professor as "a man of modest and rather unimpressive personality, of simple tastes and life, and untraveled . . . He has never been induced to attend any congress and avoids all public functions" (Hall, 1912, p. 312). This suggestion of a shy and inhibited personality is apparently correct only in part; Hall wrote further that Wundt "has always had a talent for making philosophical and psychological topics interesting and popular for students of medicine, theology, and even law, and his service in *stemming the tide of specialization* by attracting attention to the most humanistic fields has been very great" (p. 313; italics added). The argument over specialization continues even today; Hall approved of Wundt's efforts to resist narrow concentration on a single problem or discipline.

It was at Leipzig, in 1879, that Wundt established the *Psychologisches Institut,* an officially recognized unit within the structure of the University. There had been laboratories before in which data relevant to psychological problems had been collected, but the Leipzig Institute is the earliest recorded instance of official sanction for an Institute. For this reason, psychologists around the world cite 1879 as the birth date of scientific psychology.

Wundt on Methodology

The crucial change from armchair philosophy to scientific psychology was really one of method. Introspection had been the recognized way of studying mental processes since the time of St. Augustine. Wundt accepted introspection but insisted that it must operate under controlled conditions, those appropriate to the subject matter of psychology. "We must remember," he wrote, "that in every department of investigation, the experimental method takes on a special character, according to the nature of the facts investigated. In psychology we find that only those mental phenomena which are directly accessible to physical influences can be made the subject matter of experiment" (1892, p. 10).

His criticism of the armchair introspectors was forceful. Experiment, he asserted, is the means by which we may so control our mental processes "that the disturbing influence which the conditions of observation tend to exercise upon them is counteracted" (1892, p. 2). This quotation suggests a tendency to go beyond mere empiricism—that is, reliance on observation—to *operationism,* a requirement that concepts be defined by operations.

The "disturbing influence" to which he referred was the impact of surrounding sensory stimuli. Locke and the empiricists had done their introspective observations by sitting down quietly and reviewing some mental episode. Thus the content of introspection could be modified by incoming sensory stimuli and by the memory of events and ideas just preceding the episode, or occurring during the attempt at recall. In Wundt's approach, the experimental method involved putting the observer in a quiet, darkened room where an experimenter presented stimuli that the observer could not anticipate. Thus the influence of prior mental set and of current stimuli was reduced.

Wundt also stressed the training of introspective observers. Each observer was instructed to report only on sensations, and feelings and was critiqued by Wundt after each session until the reports eliminated all references to outside objects or persons. Thus he was limited to studying "mental phenomena . . . directly accessible to physical influences" (1892, p. 10). In a word, he was rounding out Fechner's view that the study of psychology was *psychophysics,* that is, the relation of the psyche to physical stimuli.

Wundt's Psychology

Wundt accepted the atomism of the British empiricists, as well as their assumption that psychology was the study of consciousness. He dropped the phrase "unconscious inference" in favor of "creative synthesis." From physics and physiology, he adopted the assumption that the task of the scientist is to seek *general* laws; he had studied individual differences when he was involved in the study of the "personal equation" of astronomers (Boring, 1929, p. 316), a problem involving the fact that astronomers had different reaction times to star transits and consequently got different values for the navigational tables that were essential in those days. This experience did not influence Wundt's conviction that individual differences were not a proper part of the new science of psychology. He proposed to study *mind,* not "minds."

Like his predecessors, Wundt accepted dualism as a basic philosophy. Body and mind were incommensurable, being different in their fundamental nature. Rather than going along with Descartes's interactionism (which involved the highly implausible role of the pineal gland), Wundt opted for a view known as *psychophysical parallelism,* the view that mental events and physical events ran in parallel but did not affect one another. He did not accept the Leibniz concept of the monad; he explicitly asserted that physical events could cause only physical effects, not mental effects.

This represents a curious blind spot in Wundt's thinking. His unique contribution to the emergence of a scientific psychology had been to impose laboratory controls, to exclude unwanted stimuli, and to have the experimenter apply stimuli so that the observer could not anticipate what was going to happen. But it is precisely this situation which demands that the physical sound, light, or other stimulus *determine* the mental event, the sensation. If the physical truly could not determine the mental event, the entire laboratory setup was nothing but hocus-pocus to confuse the outsider. And this, we know, was not true. The physical does determine the mental, and Wundt simply refused to admit it. Fortunately for modern psychology, Wundt's followers ignored psychophysical parallelism and clung to the scientific methodology.

Let us refer back to Figure 1.4. p. 12. This diagram indicates that in an ordinary situation, there are many incoming stimuli and many possible responses. The laboratory procedure deliberately reduces the number of incoming stimuli; this reduction is often called "impoverishing the environment." This simplification increases the probability that whatever happens will be a function of the stimulus used by the experimenter, although there will still be many unwanted stimuli operating. Wundt also impoverished the response side of that equation; he instructed his observers to report sensations and feelings but not objects or memories. Thus a major change from the speculative psychologies of the preceding centuries to the scientific version of today has been the restriction of stimuli and of responses in order to simplify the task of interpreting the results of the experiment.

The rigid training of Wundt's observers almost compelled reports that supported his theory. If the theory postulates sensations and feelings, and the observer is forbidden to report anything else, confirmation of the theory is guaranteed. Yet it must be noted that in no science is the naive observer tolerated; people who read X-ray photographs must be thoroughly trained, as must those nuclear physicists who read tracks on film to diagnose the kind of particle involved. And just as the cyclotron destroys the atom to permit study of its components, so Wundt's experiments interfered with the normal course of thought in order to seek for "pure" sensory experiences.

Psychology Studies Immediate Experience

Wundt distinguished between psychology and the other sciences on the basis of *immediate* versus *mediate* experience. The physicist does not study the sensation of red; she or he studies corpuscles (photons) or vibrations, waves of some kind that evoke color in the human observer. Thus the physicist is studying experience (visual evidence in diffraction patterns) independent of any specific observer, whereas the psychologist studies color only as the immediate experience of a specific person. A chemist may use a color experience (red or blue) to infer something about the acidity of a solution; acidity is inferred, not directly experienced. (It is worth noting that neither physics nor chemistry has any data source that means anything until it is experienced by a human being. A satellite in outer space may hold records, but until these are sent to earth and are interpreted by a scientist, they do not constitute data at all.)

This distinction gave Wundt his excuse for ruling *meaning* out of his experiments. Meaning, he held, is a matter of inference. Aristotle had noted the problem much earlier: "We speak of incidental objects of sense where, e.g., the white object which we see is the son of Diares; here 'being the son of Diares' is incidental to the directly visible white patch" (*De Anima*, Bk. II). The red you experience may, when linked with other sensations, give rise to the expectation that there is an apple out there; but this is an inference, not directly experienced. Gestalt psychologists, as we shall see, aggressively rejected this logic.

Wundt tried in this fashion to escape from Descartes's compulsive doubting, from Locke's distinction between primary and secondary qualities, and from Berkeley's subjective idealism. Unfortunately, Wundt did not solve the problem; at best, he pretended that it did not exist. On the positive side, he insisted that the conscious experience was *real,* regardless of its presumed relation to some external source of stimulation. A few years later, Sigmund Freud would be making this point even more vigorously; a dream, for example, is a real and significant event regardless of the absence of an external determinant.

Wundt clearly conceived of at least two levels of psychological operations, which we may, for convenience, call *sensation* and *image,* or *memory.* The process of *apperception* involves the emergence into consciousness of traces of earlier experiences; for example, the sight of an apple may evoke remembered gustatory and tactual qualities. Apperceiving can be affected by mental set and motivation. If one is engaged in problem solving, memory traces relevant to the task appear in consciousness. Drive states, such as hunger, also facilitate entry into the awareness of sensory residues related to food.

Apperception seems to have served many purposes for Wundt. A person does not have to spell out a visible word, letter by letter; the visual sensation elicits the pattern of the word, its auditory value, and so on. Conversely, apperceiving makes possible the analysis of the word into its component letters when this is necessary.

Attention is clearly involved somewhere here. For Wundt, attending seems to have been a response that brought certain sensory inputs into focus. Involuntary attention derived mainly from the intensity of the stimulation; voluntary attention resulted from learning about the sensory consequences that would probably follow some immediately present stimulus.

The studies on attending (or apperception) gave rise to one of the early controversies among scientific psychologists. Wundt devised experiments alleged to measure time for apperceiving, taking this form: the observer is told to press a key when a light flashes. In one series attention is directed to the onset of the stimulus: in a second series, the same person is directed to concentrate on responding as soon as possible. In Wundt's laboratory the difference consistently favored the motor instructions, and he interpreted this as meaning that the sensory set interposed an apperceptive phase (recalling that the light signalled key pressing), an intermediate step not required by response-directed instructions. Later investigators, notably J. M. Baldwin (see Chapter Eight) found that individuals differed; some gave faster responses under the motor set, some under the sensory set. Wundt's criticism was that obviously Baldwin had not trained his observers carefully.

Biological Basis for Psychology

Despite his medical training and his early researches in physiology, Wundt did not endorse efforts to reduce psychology to physiology. Indeed, Wundt (1904) pointed out that physiological research often depended on psychological data, as in reports of fatigue, pain, effort, and so on. "Practically everything that the physiologists tell us concerning the processes in the organs of sense and in the brain, is based upon determinate mental symptoms; so that psychology has long been recognized, explicitly or implicitly, as an indispensable auxiliary of physiological investigation." (p. 2). Wundt was thus at odds with those who later sought to reduce psychology to nerve firings and muscle twitches.

Wundt accepted the basic Darwinian thesis of the evolution of humans from other species, hence, the continuity of phylogeny. Although animals could not give introspective reports and hence could not provide the data Wundt held to be essential, he was willing to tolerate the study of animals interpreted in terms of the conscious experience that a human must have had if in that situation. In his *Lectures on Human and Animal Psychology* (1892), he held that psychologists can study "the nature and significance of those animal actions the conditions of whose origin lead us to refer them to mental processes similar to our own associations, and possibly even to our own processes of judgment and inference" (p. 340). In other words, having ruled mediate experience out of the psychological field, Wundt now slipped it back in as a way of justifying research on animal behavior.

This does not mean that Wundt was tolerant of the sentimental nonsense then being published about animals. He satirized the romanticized account of an ant funeral and suggested that a far simpler interpretation of the observation was available. Like C. Lloyd Morgan, he demanded the reduction of assumptions to an absolute minimum. When an ant was removed from the nest, kept for weeks, and then returned, the ant was "recognized" and accepted. Wundt suggested that a chemical sense identified all "natives," as opposed to the idea that the inhabitants recognized this specific individual.

Wundt was also one of the early social psychologists; in his later years, he published a huge, ten-volume *Völkerpsychologie* (which probably should be translated "folk psychology" instead of "social psychology"). It is a mixture of sociology, anthropology, history, myth, and legend. Although this work shows that he was much broader than his laboratory work indicated, it also raises questions about his critical analysis of evidence. It did, nonetheless, legitimize the study of social behavior by psychologists, and as early as 1924, a surprisingly consistent objective social psychology was published by Floyd H. Allport.

To provide a publication outlet for the voluminous research papers from the Leipzig laboratory, Wundt founded a journal. Curiously, he called it *Philosophische Studien* ("Studies in Philosophy"). He never quite resolved his own identity problem, alternating between the role of scientific psychologist and that of speculative philosopher.

Learning

Wundt's position with regard to learning was taken more or less verbatim from Locke and Hume. The association of ideas is based on contiguity in space and time. Any sensation may call up associated images.

Although learning was basically association by contiguity, Wundt postulated a "law of psychical fusion" providing that ideas often associated could fuse to produce a new experience in which the components could not be detected. Thus he sided with J. S. Mill rather than with James Mill in the argument over "mental chemistry" versus "mental physics."

Motivation

Wundt's ideas about motivation were not original. He simply repeated the hedonism of the British school: "Every motive is *a particular idea with an affective tone attaching to it*" (1896, p. 231; italics in original). This fore-shadows Kurt Lewin's notion of positive or negative valence, that is, an object's carrying with it an attraction or repulsion quality. Wundt was interested in the study of feelings and proposed a tridimensional theory postulating six feeling qualities: pleasant–unpleasant, tense–relaxed, and excited–depressed. Curiously, he sought physiological measures to confirm the differences among these six, despite his claim that the mental could not affect the physical. The search, however, was not successful.

Logical as he was, Wundt occasionally lapsed into an odd kind of anthropomorphism. Consider this statement on voluntary action: "But when the will has once discovered that its voluntary muscles enable it to do almost anything it wishes, it, and not the reflex, is master" (Wundt, 1896, p. 226). At about the same time, Sigmund Freud was writing about the id, the ego, and the superego, and also about the "censor" that prevented certain memories from rising into consciousness. Freud was criticized for anthropomorphizing, but Wundt was not.

Psychology as Pure Science

The exclusion of meaning from the realm of psychology led to a Wundtian psychology that was the ultimate in pure science. He did not exactly reject the idea that psychological data could be useful; he approved, for example, when the psychiatrist Emil Kraepelin used the word-association task in the diagnosis of mental illness. But, he noted, Kraepelin was a psychiatrist, not a psychologist. The latter, he held, should abstain from any applications of his discipline.

This puristic attitude led to friction with one of his best American students, J. McKeen Cattell. Cattell wanted to do a doctoral dissertation on the range of individual differences in reaction time under various conditions of stimulation. Wundt at first rejected the proposal, grumbling that it was "ganz Amerikanisch" ("typically American"). Eventually, Cattell wore down Wundt's resistance and opened a breach in the wall separating the study of mind-in-general from the study of minds as they actually exist.

Because of the dominance given to Wundt by the German academic system, and because of his own dominative personality, the work of the Leipzig laboratory focused on the analytical, atomistic study of sensations, images, and feelings. These contributions have been so thoroughly assimilated by general psychology that no one thinks of them, anymore, as triumphs of Wundt's theoretical system. When we consider the empirical vacuum into which Wundt moved, the achievements of his school are very impressive indeed.

The foregoing summary gives the generally accepted picture of Wundt's theoretical approach to psychology. But history changes; recently a revisionist movement has developed which seeks to show Wundt as more progressive and less restrictive in his theoretical and methodological convictions. A leader in this movement was Arthur Blumenthal (1975, 1980, 1985). Blumenthal did a thorough analysis of Wundt's writings, including some apparently ignored by earlier critics (e.g., Wundt's *Logik*, which, contrary to its title, contained much about psychological theory), and concluded that Wundt was less atomistic in his views than had been the consensus among historians of psychology. Blumenthal claimed that, far from seeking to reduce all mental life to elements such as sensations and feelings, Wundt recognized the complex character of mental processes. He even credits Wundt with anticipating the modern view of perceiving as a constructive process: "the individual's image of the world is . . . the product of constructive powers in the central control process." (1985, p. 28.) Unfortunately, it is possible by selective quotation to prove that Wundt was at heart a gestalt theorist, or an instinct theorist, or perhaps a cognitive behaviorist. William James once wrote of Wundt, "Cut him up like a worm and each fragment crawls"; that is, Wundt took different positions at different times. (So did James.) Thus it is difficult to say which is "the real Wilhelm Wundt." I incline to accept the traditional interpretation of Wundt's theory and methodology, but with the concession that new information and insights may modify that perception significantly.

Hermann Ebbinghaus

Although Wundt was beyond doubt the dominant figure in German psychology for thirty years, other German researchers should be listed as contributors to the development of American psychology. Particularly important was Hermann Ebbinghaus (1850–1909). Although not a student of Wundt, he was undoubtedly aware of the Leipzig program. By his own account, he was especially influenced by Fechner and his belief that mental processes could be studied by objective scientific procedures.

Ebbinghaus is best known for his innovation in the laboratory study of memory. Although the British empiricists noted that memory was important, they never considered the possibility that it might be open to quantitative study. Ebbinghaus speculated that the new laboratory methods could be applied to measurement of the speed of learning and the speed of forgetting, thus opening the whole field to quantitative investigation.

The methodological innovation we associate with Ebbinghaus is the nonsense syllable. When he considered having people memorize poetry or lists of words, he realized that some would probably be more familiar with the material than others; hence he could not know the zero point from which learning began. To eliminate meaning from the experiment, he devised the nonsense syllable (one vowel between two consonants), made up a list of all these combinations, then eliminated all the three-letter German words and items close to a meaningful word. He sorted the remainder into lists of varying lengths, put all the lists of the same length into a folder, and filed them away for future use. When he was ready to do an experiment, he opened a folder and took a list, recorded the number of repetitions required before he could recite it perfectly, and noted this information. A day or a week or a month later, he took out the same list and recorded the number of trials he required to relearn it to one perfect repetition. The reduction from the original learning was an index of retention, that is, of memory. This he called the "savings score"; it is still used in many studies on memory.

It is obvious that there were many wild uncontrolled variables in this procedure: Ebbinghaus had only one subject, himself; he did not record how many other lists he memorized between the original learning and relearning of one list; and he did not keep a record of how much he improved in learning *any* list as a result of his constant practice in this task. Nevertheless he established the "normal curve of forgetting," which is easily confirmed and is regularly reproduced in American textbooks.

Ebbinghaus confirmed the traditional laws of association formation: frequency and recency. He considered the hypothesis that associations are formed between one item and others remote from it (not just the immediately following syllable). Thus he made up new lists comprising the first, third, and fifth syllables (and so on) of the original learned list and found that remote associations do indeed speed up learning the new list. The association A–B was strongest, then A–C, and then A–D. The greater the separation in the original list, the less the saving when the modified list was learned.

Ebbinghaus also memorized poetry and found that essentially the same rules applied as in the nonsense learning. He also did the first truly long-term study; some twenty-two years after memorizing passages from Byron's *Don Juan*, he relearned them and showed that less time was required than for the original learning. This experiment has been repeated successfully by H. E. Burtt and others, and it lends support to Freud's dictum that the child never really forgets any experience completely.

Ebbinghaus also theorized about the varieties of memory. He suggested the existence of three types: (1) voluntary recall, as when a person remembers his or her birth date or home address; (2) involuntary (spontaneous) recall, as when one relaxes and finds in consciousness a memory of a vacation or a stressful incident when no attention has been directed to it; and (3) influence on the conscious process that does not itself become conscious. This final category is, of course, directly relevant to Freudian theory. One may fail to recall an event, yet make decisions which indicate that the memory is still there. "Most of these experiences," Ebbinghaus (1886) wrote, "remain concealed from consciousness and yet produce an effect which is significant and which authenticates their previous existence" (p. 2). Although this passage refers primarily to transfer of learning (e.g., past memories of French aid in the learning of Spanish), the generality of Ebbinghaus's finding makes it relevant to psychoanalytic theories.

Ebbinghaus is remembered mainly for his studies of remembering, but he contributed in other ways. For example, he devised the sentence-completion test, which is now widely used clinically. Ebbinghaus intended it as a device for detecting learned associations, and of course, it still has that function, but mostly in the context of finding repressed emotions. For example, a clinician may present a client with a sentence like "When I was a child, my mother used to punish me for————." The word written in indicates a probable link of the mother to some action of the child.

An interesting sidelight on Ebbinghaus's career is that his doctoral dissertation was on E. Von Hartmann's "philosophy of the unconscious." We know that Freud also read this book and may have been influenced by it. Thus experimental psychology and clinical psychology were closer together a century ago than they are today.

Hermann Rorschach

Like Ebbinghaus, Hermann Rorschach (1884–1922) was never a student of Wundt. Nonetheless, he accepted Wundt's fundamental assumption, that the proper study of psychology was conscious processes without regard to their meaning or their logical status. Rorschach's invention of the inkblot as a testing device fitted his purpose, just as the nonsense syllable had proved so useful to Ebbinghaus.

In his earliest work with inkblot protocols, Rorschach sought for "experience types," such as extraversive or introversive (he borrowed these terms from Carl Jung). He emphasized such details as whether the respondent was influenced more by form (F), color (C), texture (Fc), the whole blot (W), a large detail (D), or a small detail (d).

The method of validation used by Rorschach in his original studies left much to be desired. Because some impulsive psychotics simply gave color names as associations to the colored blots, he concluded that "C" responses indicated emotionality. Rorschach (1921/1942) wrote that "the most primary color (C) answers" were given by "epileptics, manics . . . or notoriously hot-headed and hyperaggressive and irresponsible 'normals' " (p. 33). Obviously the process of selecting criterion cases was, at best, careless. And it is not at all clear that the differences in response by criterion groups were statistically significant.

Rorschach devotees have since modified the approach to interpretation and have more meticulously validated certain scores. Psychoanalytic concepts have crept into protocol analysis, and the specific meaning of the response (in contrast to Rorschach's original intent) is now used by many practitioners. The influence of Gestalt thinking is also noticeable; most users of the Rorschach test insist that an isolated response can be interpreted only when placed in context with the other responses given to the blots. It is nonetheless of considerable historical interest that so many of the currently used procedures (psychophysics, nonsense-syllable learning, and projective testing) originated in this early historical period.

Why Germany?

Historians are interested not only in where a science began, but also in the reason for its developing there. Helmholtz, Weber, Fechner, Wundt, and Ebbinghaus—each a major figure in the history of scientific psychology—lived and worked in a small area called Germany. Yet the earliest speculations about a purely scientific approach to mental activity had been in France, and the basic principles of learning had been worked out by the British associationists. Why did Germany suddenly put these trends together in a formal and empirical way?

Ben-David and Collins (1966) offered an interpretation in terms of the Zeitgeist, the socioeconomic context in which these developments occurred. Medical research was flourishing, and physiology was a major component of this trend. Important figures like Helmholtz attracted many bright young people to their programs. But when these students completed their training, there was no place for them. The German university system provided only one professorship in a given science at each school. Because the leading physiologists were young and vigorous, the long wait for someone to retire was depressing. Further, the one department exempt from the single-professor rule was philosophy, which still covered so many diverse topics that specialization within the field was permitted. Now, again as part of the system, all of these promising young physiologists had a thorough grounding in philosophy. Thus, by studying "mental" problems like sensing and perceiving, they could qualify as professors of philosophy and continue their research on physiological psychology.

Ben-David and Collins describe this phenomenon as "role hybridization." The role of the physiologist and that of the philosopher merged to produce the physiological psychologist. Wundt set the pattern; when he failed to get the post vacated by Helmholtz, he went to Zurich and then to Leipzig as a philosopher, but with full freedom to continue his researches as long as he emphasized the psychological content of what he was doing.

The phenomenon is relevant to many recent developments in American psychology. Community psychology, for example, is a hybrid of clinical and social psychology; forensic psychology is a composite of criminology and psychology; the list is quite lengthy. Psychologically, we can say that motivation impels the individual to find a niche, a professional activity for which he or she has been trained; if no such niche is available, one tends to try to create one. Training provides the skills; society provides the problems that call for expertise.

CHAPTER 6

American Psychology Before Titchener: William James

American psychology developed out of the Greek tradition as it flowered in western Europe. Although most of the teachers of psychology in the American colonies were religious figures, who did not hesitate to introduce the Hebraic heritage into their doctrines, the effects did not last. By the time of Wundt's emergence in Germany, American teachings had settled into the same general pattern as was exemplified by the British associationists and the Scottish faculty psychologists.

The American colonies were not the intellectual deserts we sometimes imagine. Sahakian (1975) surveyed the history of higher education in the colonies, and found that new developments in philosophical psychology found their way across the Atlantic rather promptly. Psychological issues were being taught as early as the last half of the seventeenth century. The texts used included the major products of English empiricism and Scottish rationalism: Thomas Hobbes' *Human Nature*, George Berkeley's *New Theory of Vision*, René Descartes's *Discourse on Method*, David Hume's *Enquiry Concerning the Human Understanding*, and Thomas Reid's *Inquiry into the Human Mind*. Generally speaking, any important publication in Britain appeared in America within five years. Students may have been fewer in number, but the fare offered them generally was comparable to the materials available in Europe.

Sahakian identified four stages in the evolution of psychological thought and instruction in the American colonies and the first century of independence: (1) a period dominated by religious thought and moral philosophy (1640–1776); (2) a period dominated by the Scottish faculty psychology (1776–1886); (3) a very brief interval, which he called the

"American Renaissance", during which empirical data and methods became widely accepted; and (4) the era beginning with William James's masterpiece, *The Principles of Psychology* (1890) and extending to the present.

The dominance of the church in higher education before the American Revolution was compatible with the emphasis on moral philosophy and theological discussions of sin and guilt. The Calvinistic doctrine of predestination did not leave much room for a science of human behavior, and the French leanings toward mechanism were not popular. The emergence of the Scottish rationalists in the late eighteenth century offered a less religious orientation that was nonetheless compatible with the Puritanical background of the philosophical professors. It will be recalled that Thomas Reid's *Inquiry into the Human Mind* appeared in 1764; Dugald Stewart's *Elements of the Philosophy of the Human Mind* was first published in 1792 and had an American edition by 1821. The major topics were of the kind we now associate with cognitive psychology: perceiving, attending, reasoning, association (learning and memory), and imagination. Theological influences still dominated discussions of will and voluntary action. Motivation and emotion received little consideration. Classical education was defended as the proper training of the "faculties of the mind."

Developments toward a science of psychology, surprisingly, lagged only slightly behind those in Germany. John Dewey published his functionalist *Psychology* in 1886; Dewey was familiar with William James, and many of his ideas reflected this fact, despite James's laggard performance in putting his ideas into book form (many of his theories had, however, appeared in journal articles). Another significant milestone was the publication of George Trumbull Ladd's (1842–1921) *Elements of Physiological Psychology* (1891). Ladd had had virtually no laboratory experience; nevertheless he did a competent job of reporting on the developments in Germany.

All historians interested in American psychology agree that its status as an independent, empirical science should date from the publication of William James's classic two-volume *Principles of Psychology.* It still merits careful examination.

A familiar comment about William James and his brother is that Henry James was a novelist who wrote like a psychologist and William was a psychologist who wrote like a novelist. Although scholarly tradition today frowns on the kind of writing that we so enjoy in William James, it is unfair to suggest that he was writing fiction. He simply had a flair for vivid examples and tart phrases (directed at his critics), which greatly deserves revival in modern psychology.

William James (1842–1910) was born into a wealthy family and had ample freedom to explore, to learn, and to write. His grandfather acquired a fortune in building the Erie Canal; his father lost a leg in an accident and became a recluse with a strong interest in spiritualism and other speculative movements. The family traveled extensively in Europe, and it is certain that William James was well-informed about the work of Fechner, Helmholtz, Wundt, and others.

James seems to have been sickly (perhaps psychosomatically, according to some accounts). He had little formal education until he was admitted to Harvard in 1861; even then, he progressed slowly because of his limited energy. One of his chemistry professors described James as having to go and lie down in the middle of an experiment. He was excused from military service for health reasons.

In 1865, James went with the noted naturalist Louis Agassiz to South America to study and collect tropical flora and fauna. Here he contracted an obscure tropical disease and returned to the United States in a feeble condition. He finally completed his M.D. degree in 1869, still in poor health; but in 1872, he read a book by the French philosopher C. B. Renouvier, asserting the curative power of will. James was enthusiastic about the book, followed its prescriptions, and according to his father and brother, made a fantastic recovery.

Gardner Murphy (1968) observed that the credit for James's recovery may not have been entirely due to Renouvier. The year 1872 also marked his first appointment to a part-time post at Harvard. For whatever reason, he recovered from most of his aches and pains, although he was never truly robust.

James had visited Wundt's laboratory as well as several others in Germany. In France, he had visited Charcot, as did Sigmund Freud at about the same time, and he was intrigued by the work of Pierre Janet on unconscious systems within the personality. It is clear from the *Principles* that he found the French school, which based its work on clinical observation of the abnormal, more congenial than the rigorous but "trivial" laboratory investigations at Leipzig. He made his poor opinions of the Germans clear in many of his publications; James wrote of Fechner that "The 'exactness' of the theory of sensibility . . . consists in the *supposed* fact that it gives the means of representing sensations by numbers." (1890, I, 537; italics added). Regarding the exhaustive laboratory studies on sensation and reaction time, he said that they could not have been done in any country "whose natives could be bored." He did not anticipate that thousands of student hours would be used up in American laboratories in memorizing nonsense syllables.

Some James enthusiasts identify him as having founded the first laboratory in experimental psychology. James (1895) wrote:

> I, myself, "founded" the instruction in experimental psychology at Harvard in 1874–5, or 1876, I forget which. For a long series of years the laboratory was in two rooms of the Scientific School building, which at last became choked with apparatus . . . I then, in 1890, . . . raised several

> thousand dollars, fitted up Dane Hall, and introduced laboratory exercises as a regular part of the undergraduate psychology course. (p. 626)

This reminiscence played a role in the argument between supporters of G. Stanley Hall and supporters of James, but the vagueness about the timing of the first laboratory undermines the claim of James's priority. (It should be added that Wundt had also had an informal laboratory in his home before the funding of the Institute at Leipzig.)

James wanted a laboratory for instructional purposes, but he did not use it—and apparently no students did—as a research facility. By temperament, he was more of an armchair introspectionist, inclined to look within himself to find answers to psychological questions. Although intellectually aware of the superiority of experimental procedures, he never adopted them for his own purposes. He was a fascinating combination of the speculative philosopher and the down-to-earth pragmatist, whom Wundt would have characterized as *"ganz Amerikanisch."*

In 1878, James signed a contract to write a textbook in psychology. This fact suggests that the study of psychology was expanding, and that publishers saw a prospective market for texts and wished to have a purely American product to compete with the available British texts. But James's book did not appear until 1890; in the meantime, he wrote many essays, which later appeared as chapters in the book. It is probable that this segmented mode of operation accounts for much of the inner contradiction one finds in *The Principles of Psychology;* James found it easy to make the assumptions necessary for coping with one topic, and to forget these by the time he tackled another.

The book was a tremendous success. It shaped the form of introductory textbooks in psychology (in America, at least) for the next twenty-five years.

Psychology According to James

The first impression one receives from the *Principles* is that James had rejected the Cartesian legacy of doubt. Where British scholars had accepted the thesis that sensory information is illusory and therefore an inadequate guide to action, James came out firmly for Reid's "common-sense" view that there is a real world out there, that the senses put us in touch with that world, and that we must act on the basis of our sensory information. This view reflects a personal desire for a firm footing in reality; James wrote to Charles William Eliot, president of Harvard, that "my strongest moral and intellectual craving is for some stable reality to lean upon" (1920). Thus he chose the position of "naive realism," rejecting the historical legacy of doubt and distrust of the senses.

It might be thought that this would lead him to applaud the meticu-

William James, model of a "tender-minded" but perceptive and pragmatic psychologist

lous work of the Germans on sensation. Not so. He wrote almost contemptuously of "brass-instrument psychology." He often pounced on some fairly complex report of an experiment and satirized it. For example, James quoted from Wundt (1880) on the localization of sensory experiences in space:

> In the eye, space-perception has certain constant peculiarities which prove that no single optical sensation by itself possesses the extensive form, but that everywhere in our perception of space, heterogeneous feelings combine. If we simply suppose that luminous sensations *per se* feel extensive, our supposition is shattered by that influence of movement in vision which is so clearly to be traced in many normal errors in the measurement of the field of view. (Vol. 2, p. 457)

James (1890) quoted even more of this analysis, then wielded the hammer: "Now let no modest reader think that if this sounds obscure to him

Archives of the History of American Psychology

it is because he does not know the full content. Really it is quite the reverse; *all* the virtue of the phrase lies in its mere sound and skin. . . . Wundt's theory is the flimsiest thing in the world. It starts by an untrue assumption, and then corrects it by an unmeaning phrase" (Vol. 2, pp. 276–278).

The Analysis of Consciousness

James's distaste for Wundt probably started with his rejection of the analytical, atomistic approach that reduced all conscious experience to sensations and feelings. He insisted on a holistic approach; he charged that the analytic approach destroyed what it was calculated to investigate.

> Consciousness does not appear to itself to be chopped up into bits. Such words as "chain" or "train" do not describe it fitly as it presents itself in the first instance. It is nothing jointed; it flows. A "river" or a "stream" are the metaphors by which it is most naturally described. *In talking of it hereafter, let us call it the stream of thought, of consciousness, or of subjective life.* (Vol. 1, p. 239; all italics in quotes from James are in the original)

And again:

> The fringe, as I use the word . . . is part of the *object cognized,*—substantive *qualities* and *things* appearing to the mind in a *fringe of relations.* Some parts—the transitive parts—of our stream of thought cognize the relations rather than the things; but both the transitive and the substantive parts form one continuous stream. (Vol. 1, p. 258)

Inevitably one thinks of Heraclitus and the river that is constantly changing so that if one steps in it a second time, it is not the same river.

There are pitfalls in this path, and James recognized them. He conceded that one had to divide up the stream of consciousness into episodes in order to deal with a single event. His defense of this division is superficial; he relied heavily on "common sense," or the awareness that one episode had ended and another had begun. But this criterion is arbitrary and subjective. A psychologist observing children has a problem: Did the fight begin with the first blow, or with name calling, or with an approach to a desired object? Laboratory experimenters can control the onset of an episode; field observers cannot.

James differed aggressively with Wundt on the topic of meaning; Wundt had tried to exclude meaning from all introspective reports. He had insisted on a report that gave only sensory elements, not the objects that were inferred as giving rise to these sensations. (E. B. Titchener would later call this intrusion of the "real" object the "stimulus error.") James opposed Wundt categorically; the elements, James held, were artifacts of the experimenter's instructions, and he coined the term *psychologist's fallacy* to label the phenomenon.

In James's view, the object was directly given in consciousness, although it was not clear how the object got there. He held that the elements reported by Wundt were induced by the experiment's instructions, not by the stimulus input—hence the term *psychologist's fallacy*. According to Wundt, the elements were there first; according to James, it was the theory that led the observer to report elementary sensations. (An analogous point is the question raised by some critics of modern atomic physics, that the mesons, gluons, and quarks are experimental artifacts rather than natural phenomena.)

Similarly, James attacked Fechner's *Elemente der Psychophysik:* "Fechner's book was the starting point of a new department of literature, which it would perhaps be impossible to match for the qualities of thoroughness and subtlety, but of which, in the humble opinion of the present writer, the proper outcome is just *nothing*" (Vol. 1, p. 534). James was, of course, anything but humble; it is equally obvious that he did not grasp the far-reaching implications of Fechner's contribution. One suspects that at least one element in James's preeminent status in early American psychology was the extent to which he satirized the new German school and bolstered the feelings of security and self-confidence of American colleagues who had not had the good fortune to study in Germany.

Unconscious Processes

James's attitude toward the phenomenon of an unconscious process affecting thought and behavior was also inconsistent. On the one hand, he clung to his definition of psychology as the study of conscious processes; of the search for Helmholtz's unconscious inferences, he wrote, "If we find them, they are *conscious;* and when we do not find them, they are not mental states" (1890, 1, p. 165). And yet James could write that "we know more than we can say. . . . Most of our knowledge is at all times *potential.* We act in accordance with the whole drift of what we have learned, but few items rise into consciousness at the time" (Vol. 1, p. 167). It could easily be argued that if items "rise" into consciousness, they must have had an existence of some kind before that moment.

James was familiar with the work of Charcot, Janet, and the other French students of unconscious phenomena, and it is surprising that he did not simply accept their formulation on this point. He was, perhaps, torn between a desire for consistency (in stressing consciousness) and his desire for accuracy (which required a recognition of unconscious phenomena).

The Unity of Perception

James's attack on the Germans and the British associationists centered on the fragmented, atomized nature of their version of perception. In a popular analysis of the idea "The pack of cards is on the table," he insisted that James Mill was wrong; the mind cannot separate the idea of cards and the idea of table from the unified awareness of "the-pack-of-cards-is-on-the-table." (1890, 2, 279). This seems to have foreshadowed the forthcoming development of Gestalt theory.

The unity of perception, in turn, is supported by James's concept of the unity of self. In this respect, he took a view more or less resembling that of Leibniz. The self is a real object of thought, and in turn, it really unites diverse perceptions. "My" memories have a different status in consciousness from memories of what others have taught me. I experience myself as the same person known by my name last year, although changes have occurred. Yet James admitted that, like Hume, he could never get an introspective observation of himself in action: "Whenever my introspective glance succeeds in turning round quickly enough to catch one of these manifestations of spontaneity in the act, all it can ever feel distinctly is some bodily processes, for the most part taking place within the head" (Vol. 1, p. 300). He differentiated between the self as active knower and the self as perceived and remembered; this latter concept resembles the idea of *self-image* as developed later by Rogers, Kelly, Allport, and other "humanistic" psychologists (see Chapter Seventeen).

Responses

Whereas Wundt and Fechner had virtually ignored the place of the response in a systematic psychology, James recognized that a complete account of human behavior and experience would have to pay some attention to overt responses. James distinguished between reflexes and voluntary behavior. A voluntary response, James proposed, was one in which the idea of the act preceded the act itself. But, if there were no innate ideas—as James held—how could he introduce the idea of a movement? James fell back on innate reflexes to avoid innate ideas: once a reflex has occurred, the mind adds to its collection of ideas the idea of making that movement. "When a particular movement, having once occurred in a random, reflex, or involuntary way, has left an image of itself in the memory, then the movement can be desired again, proposed as an end, and deliberately willed. But it is impossible to see how it could be willed before." (1890, 2, p. 487). This formulation is comparable to those of Max F. Meyer and John B. Watson (Chapter Nine) in which reflex movements become organized into complex adaptive habits.

James also anticipated the behaviorists in his concept of the chaining of responses. Figure 6.1 shows how James introduced the concept that kinesthetic feedback from one response becomes the stimulus for the next step in the chain. He connected this with his "stream-of-consciousness" idea by speculating that in the formation of a chain, conscious reflection is involved in the selection of the "next" response from various

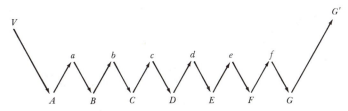

FIGURE 6.1 James's Conception of Response Chaining

James developed the use of kinesthetic stimuli as cues for successive movements in a complex habit. *V* designates an impulse to start an act; *A, B, C, . . .* , are muscular contractions, and *a, b, c, . . .* , kinesthetic sensations from the contractions. *G'* indicates the goal of the act. After practice, the whole series can run off mechanically. (*James, 1890, 1, Fig. 24, p. 116*).

possibilities, but that after practice, the conscious evaluation drops out and the whole act sequence runs off without conscious awareness.

Neurologizing

James obviously felt a compulsion to show how learning such a chained sequence of movements might be treated neurologically. In fact, out of some fourteen hundred pages in the 1890 *Principles,* only about a hundred deal directly with speculation about the nervous system, but there are also frequent digressions in the midst of discussions of mental phenomena. Most of these ruminations sound terribly naive today, not to mention their irrelevance to a psychology based mostly on consciousness. It is possible that James's pragmatism—his concern with "common sense" and practical considerations—impelled him to examine the possible neurological explanations for thought and action.

James ultimately adopted an interactionist position on the question of how brain and mind are related. After considering the functions of subcortical brain structures, he concluded that "*the cortex is the sole organ of consciousness in man.*" (1890, 1, p. 66). He recounted the conceptual problems of converting a physical event, a neural impulse, into a psychical event, an idea, plan, or fantasy. However, he noted that in the darkness of metaphysical criticism, "all causes are obscure."

Learning

James endorsed a neural pathway theory of learning. "*Memory being thus altogether conditioned on brain-paths, its excellence in a given individual will depend partly on the number and partly on the persistence of these paths*" (Vol.

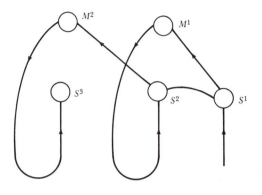

FIGURE 6.2   Theory of Neural Drainage as a Correlate of Learning

James proposed that learning involved forming a "path" in the central nervous system. *(James, 1890, 2, p. 591)*

1, p. 659). The first desideratum is a "tenacious" memory, that is, "a high degree of this physiological retentiveness." However, in middle life we begin to lose pathways about as fast as we form new ones, and in old age no new acquisitions occur and losses continue. Frequency is a major determinant of retention: *"The more other facts a fact is associated with in the mind, the better possession of it our memory retains"* (1890, Vol. 1, p. 662). He adopted from faculty psychology the notion that one idea acquires the "power" to call up another: "every fact is retained by the combined suggestive power of all the other facts in the system." (Vol. 1, p. 663).

The speculative neurology included a theory of "neural drainage" which bears a startling resemblance to Descartes's theory of "animal spirits". Figure 6.2 shows how he related the theory to the case of a burnt child dreading a flame. "The sight of the flame stimulates the cortical centre S^1 which discharges by an instinctive reflex path into the centre M^1 for the grasping movement. This movement produces the feeling of burn, as its effects come back to the centre S^2 and this centre . . . discharges into M^2, the centre for withdrawing the hand. The movement of withdrawal stimulates the centre S^3 . . . the last thing that happens. Now the next time the child sees the candle, the cortex is in possession of the secondary paths . . . S^2, having been stimulated immediately after S^1, drained the latter, and now S^1 discharges into S^2 before the discharge of M^1 has had time to occur . . ." (1890, 2, p. 591).

The general principle of the neural basis of learning was stated as follows: *"Each discharge from a sensory cell in the forward direction* (i.e., toward a motor cell) *tends to drain the cells lying behind the discharging one of whatever tension they may possess"* (Vol. 2, p. 584). If, on a later occasion, the rearward cells are independently excited, the *"path . . . will tend to carry off their activity in the same direction so as to excite the forward cell, and will deepen itself more and more every time it is used."* (Vol. 2, pp. 584–585). Note the absent-minded use of a metaphor in the word "deepen"; neural drainage does not imply a deepening path, but this figure of speech was common at the time.

Habit

As the preceding quotation indicates, James thought of habit as the overt manifestation of a well-worn pathway in the nervous system. Thus he was striving for a physiologically based psychology. However, he placed his emphasis on the psychological and social importance of habits. His famous metaphor of the flywheel occurs in the following passage:

> Habit is thus the enormous fly-wheel of society, its most precious conservative agent. It alone is what keeps us all within the bounds of ordinance. . . . At the age of twenty-five you see the professional mannerism settling down on the young commercial traveller, on the young doctor, on the young minister. . . . You see the little lines of cleavage running through the character, the tricks of thought, the prejudices . . . by the age of thirty, the character has set like plaster, and will never soften again. (1890, Vol. 1, 121–122)

Thus James tied his individual psychology into a theory of social roles and images.

The term *conservative* in the first sentence of the quotation is not accidental; included in James's list of the virtues of habit is "It keeps different social strata from mixing." Being born into a wealthy family may have had an effect on narrowing James's views in some ways while widening them in others.

Emotions

James formulated his radical theory of the emotions in an article published in the journal *Mind* in 1884, which later formed most of Chapter 25 of the *Principles*. He argued that the traditional views of emotion, such as that of Descartes, had the true sequence of events inverted. The usual theory was that we see a strange animal, are afraid, and run; James proposed that we see the animal, run, and then feel fear. The emotion, then, as a conscious experience, is a composite of the sensations from the muscular activities and the visceral responses that are associated with escape. J. B. Watson, not surprisingly, would later find this to be a useful approach and would repeat it in his theorizing, although unkindly attacking James at the same time.

James (1890) buttressed his argument in favor of the response theory of emotion by an adaptation of Wundt's logic in a similar situation: "I now proceed to urge the vital point of my whole theory, which is this: *If we fancy some strong emotion, and then try to abstract from our consciousness of it all the feelings of its bodily symptoms, we find that we have nothing left behind*" (Vol. 2, p. 451). Having criticized the analytical introspectionists, he now endorsed their procedures.

Motivation

For James, basic motivation derived from the instincts. In this respect, he was in accord with the Darwinian thesis (which was just attaining widespread acceptance) that any species, to survive, must inherit some response tendencies that will increase the chances of contacting the substances essential for life. He was realistic, however, in rejecting the view that humans are limited to the instincts observable in the other primates. If humankind represents a new species, it is plausible that this species will also manifest new instincts. James's listing is quite extensive: vocalization, imitation, pugnacity, rivalry, love and jealousy, sympathy, acquisitiveness, kleptomania, play, constructiveness, and several others. His indebtedness to the Scottish school in this respect is obvious.

However, James improved on the Scots in his handling of the instinct question. In the first place, he emphasized the flexibility and adaptability of each instinctive tendency. No animal goes on mechanically responding without change to a given environmental stimulus: *"Every instinctive act, in an animal with memory, must cease to be 'blind' after being once repeated"* (Vol. 2, p. 390). Thus an instinct theory need not imply an automaton theory of behavior. Learning how to satisfy instinctual needs is a significant feature of behavior.

A second improvement on traditional instinct theory was James's recognition that instincts are not necessarily compatible with one another. Humans may have instincts that contradict each other (Vol. 1, p. 393). Unlike those who explained human flexibility by suggesting that humans had *few* instinctual patterns, James (2, p. 392) argued that conflicts result from a *surplus* of them; the human being *"has so many that they block each other's path"* (2, p. 393). Thus we observe James anticipating Freud and his dynamic psychology based on conflicting instinctual impulses.

Anyone who pontificated on so many aspects of psychology can be quoted on both sides of controversial issues. Ardrey (1966, p. 262), for example, quoted James as endorsing an instinctual basis for war: "Our ancestors have bred pugnacity into our bone and marrow, and thousands of years of peace won't breed it out of us" (William James, 1910.) But the context of the quotation is that humanity is not doomed to eternal warfare; there are peaceful outlets for this assumed instinctual impulse. James asserted that an instinct was blind only until one single act based on it had occurred; after that, the environment played its part in shaping and directing the behavior that might be energized by that instinct.

The Will

James introduced a concept of "will" that differed markedly from that of the moralistic psychologists of the early colonial period. He suggested that will be considered a combination of motive and percept; if one has a desire but perceives the attainment of this desire to be impossible, we should speak of a "wish," but if the end is seen as being within one's power, we should speak of "will." Note that this does not coincide with the Victorian concept of willpower as a moral virtue. It is somewhat nearer to J. B. Rotter's conception of "internal fate control," an expectancy that effort will lead to the attainment of a desired goal (see Chapter 18).

James used his chapter in the *Principles* on "the will" to discuss decision making and was one of the first to treat it as a psychological rather than a spiritual matter. He emphasized that decisions derive from choosing between alternatives, not from the activities of a homunculus, a little person somewhere in one's head who prods one hither and yon. To a modern reader, the most interesting of James's classes of decisions is "the dreary resignation for the sake of austere and naked duty of all sorts of rich, mundane delights"; this sounds remarkably like Freud's "reality principle," with its insistence that one abandon the immediate pleasures of the flesh in favor of long-term gratifications, or Plato's endorsement of "intellectual" pleasures.

Temperament

The broad sweep of James's conception of psychology is shown by his inclusion of temperament as a proper topic. I noted in Chapter 1 his classification of people as "tender-minded" or "tough-minded" and his use of this theory in categorizing some of his fellow psychologists. The traits he attributed to the tender-minded group included idealism, rationalism, religious conviction, and belief in free will; to the tough-minded he assigned empiricism, materialism, skepticism, and determinism. As shown in Coan's research (p. 19), contemporary psychologists respond to questions in very much the pattern predicted by James.

The inclusion of temperament as a legitimate topic for scientific psychology was another manifestation of James's rejection of Wundtian theory. Facing Wundt's stubborn denial of the relevance of individual differences and his insistence that psychology should study only the content of consciousness, not the adaptive utility of consciousness, James staked out a claim to an important area of investigation, richly explored by later American psychologists. But he did not choose to extrapolate this study of temperament to the areas of vocational choice and occupational counseling. In general, he showed little interest in applied work. He did not rule it out of pure psychology, as Wundt had; probably, despite his commitment to pragmatism, applied work simply did not appeal to him.

Contemporary Views of James

Walter B. Pillsbury, a student of Titchener but not a devotee, recorded a contemporary view of James and his magnum opus. Commenting on the *Principles,* Pillsbury (1929) wrote:

It is valuable rather for the brilliancy of its parts than for the presentation of a system. In a famous letter to Stumpf (a German critic of Wundt), James criticizes Wundt's system, or lack of system, in the words: 'Cut him up like a worm and each fragment crawls; there is no *noeud vital* in his system, so that you can't kill him all at once.' The same statement may be applied to James' own presentation. (pp. 238–239)

And Pillsbury provided us with one of those trivial bits of information that get lost as the years go by: "Each chapter (of the *Principles*) was written as a separate contribution and often it was published before it appeared in the book" (1929, p. 239). This information helps us to understand how James could be so inconsistent; as he concentrated on a specific problem, he made the assumptions most appropriate for that topic, without checking for consistency across chapters. And this method of working may, in turn, account for R. B. MacLeod's (1979) tart phrase for James, that he could be "all things to all men" (p. v). James spread his net widely, shaped the pattern of psychology texts for years to come, asked shrewd questions, and offered answers; but he did not construct a unified theory to tie together his speculations on these varied topics.

The high status of James in American psychology at the turn of the century is attested to not only by historians like Pillsbury, but also by today's judges. Coan (1973) asked forty-two prominent psychologists to give their judgments on the dominant figures in the discipline, by decades, beginning with 1880. For the first decade (1880–1889), the top-rated figures were Wundt, James, Helmholtz, Ebbinghaus, and Fechner. For the next decade (1890–1899) the top five were James, Wundt, Dewey, Titchener, and Freud. But for the decades after 1900, James was no longer judged to be a major influence on psychology.

CHAPTER 7

Titchener and Structuralism

William James had belabored Wundtian psychology in his numerous articles and in his *Principles of Psychology* (1890). Very shortly, he found himself faced with an invasion of Wundtians into American psychology. E. B. Titchener, the most prominent of these, arrived in 1892 to take charge of the laboratory at Cornell University. Hugo Münsterberg arrived in the same year, by invitation of James, to supervise the Harvard laboratory. It must be noted that James probably invited Münsterberg precisely because he, although he had been trained by Wundt, had broken with the atomistic introspectionism that James opposed so vigorously.

In the minds of many psychologists, Wundt and Titchener were twins, spokespersons for what is basically the same brand of psychology. In fact, it is not unusual to hear it said that Titchener merely took Wundt's ideas and purified or perfected them. This is not really fair to either man. Wundt laid down the strictures with regard to the prescriptions for psychological science: The subject matter is consciousness, the field is the study of mind in general, and the goal is to identify elements and their relations. He also defined the acceptable method: controlled introspection. However, as Chapter Five indicated, Wundt was flexible on many theoretical issues, and he made many exceptions to his rules; for example, disregarding the consciousness restriction, he wrote about human *and animal* psychology, and he collected observations of social behavior that did not involve introspection. Titchener was a systematizer, a more rigorous thinker and more consistent in his practices. In contrast to James, he avoided pragmatism and espoused a "pure" science of psychology. Although he never achieved the status of being the acknowledged leader of American psychology, he had a major influence on theoretical developments and on psychological training.

Edward Bradford Titchener

E. B. Titchener (1867–1927) was born into a poor family in the south of England. His academic brilliance won him a scholarship to Malvern College, which is the source of one familiar anecdote about him. It seems that James Russell Lowell, the American poet who was also U.S. Ambassador to Britain, had agreed to hand out the academic prizes at Malvern at the end of the school year. After young Titchener had collected several of these, Lowell found his name on still another and unkindly remarked, "I am tired of seeing you, Mr. Titchener." This evidently did not crush the youth; he won a scholarship to Brasenose College, one of the units of Oxford University, where he received his B.A. degree in 1890.

Most of Titchener's undergraduate study was in philosophy (Oxford did not recognize psychology as an independent discipline until 1930). From Locke and Hume it was an easy transition to Wilhelm Wundt, and Titchener arranged to enroll at Leipzig for graduate study, receiving his Ph.D. in the exceptionally short time of two years. It is recorded that even before going to Germany, he had translated into English the third edition of Wundt's *Physiologische Psychologie,* and he took the translation with him to Leipzig, where he was distressed to learn that a fourth edition was almost complete. Plugging away, Titchener translated the fourth, only to find that a fifth edition was in preparation. After coming to America, he translated other books of Wundt's prolific output; these were successfully published.

Titchener found a congenial set of graduate students in Leipzig, which was still a major center of training in psychology, although competing institutes had been established by 1890. He was particularly fortunate to become friendly with Frank Angell, who arranged for the young Englishman to become professor of psychology at Cornell University in 1892.

Given the attitude expressed by William James toward Wundt and the "German" school, it should be no surprise that Titchener became involved in professional debate as soon as he arrived in the United States. As Boring (1950) put it, "the American and German psychologists of that day felt that they were engaged in a battle to bring old territory under a new authority" (p. 412). Titchener made an important contribution to this effort by translating and publishing several German texts, and of course, he wrote a number to express his own ideas. However, he was never entirely accepted by—nor did he accept—the American psychological community. He joined the American Psychological Association when G. S. Hall organized it in 1892, but he was never honored by being elected president. And his "pure" psychology never became the dominant theme in American psychological activity; pragmatism and James and the functionalists carried the day. Despite these defeats, he did have an important place in the development of the new discipline in America.

That place, as he saw it, was to defend a "pure" scientific psychology against the fallacies of pragmatism, functionalism, and vitalism. In an entertaining military metaphor, R. B. Evans (1972) described the activities of the structuralists:

> Titchener served much as a commander-in-chief and tactician. It was he who held the total battle-plan against "the enemy" and it was he who set the direction and timing of attack. The Cornell faculty served as field generals in charge of implementing directives . . . seeing to the training and activities of the graduate students who were, of course, the troops . . . these troops would assault one adversary, perhaps Würzburg, and then another, perhaps Act psychology. (p. 168)

It is more than a little amusing that both Lundin (1975) and Marx and Hillix (1973) buttressed their claim that Titchener was "Germanic" by citing the fact that he wore a full beard. Perhaps these historians had never seen portraits of William James or of G. Stanley Hall, both stubbornly American and both sporting bushy facial hair. Is it possible that some prejudice against Germanic psychologists persists in America?

The Method of Psychology

Titchener wholeheartedly adopted Wundt's dictum that introspection was the sole method to be used in a scientific psychology. The task of the psychologist was to establish laws relating to the *content* of consciousness. Content, however, was not to be confused with *meaning*. This distinction is fundamental to structuralist theorizing, so an illustration is in order. Consider the following passage: "If I chance to be reflecting on the progress of science, there is likely to arise before my mind's eye a scene familiar to my childhood,—the flow of the incoming tide over a broad extent of sandy shore" (Titchener, 1909, p. 3). Thus the meaning (progress of science) is carried by a conscious content, the image of the incoming tide.

Titchener used many such images in his writings; as he once commented to himself, "My mind, as I shall presently show in more detail, is prone to imagery" (1909, p. 3). By contrast, it has been said of John B. Watson that his imagery was very poor and that he therefore found it difficult to believe the introspective reports of the structuralists and was thus impelled to rebel against introspection.

Actually, Titchener deviated from his own theory by using the "incoming tide" as conscious content. In his research, he insisted that his observers limit themselves to a description of experience; thus, instead of reporting the flow of the tide, he should have reported a patch of

Archives of the History of American Psychology

E. B. Titchener, founder of a tough-minded structuralist psychology

blue that spread over more of the conscious field, which was preponderantly of a yellowish-brown hue. In practice, of course, it is very difficult to identify conscious content without using the names of common objects or scenes.

Introspection has its disadvantages. It cannot be used with animals, nor with very young children. Also, it would be untrustworthy if used with abnormal personalities. Thus, structuralist psychology was the psychology of the *normal adult* human being. Further, it was a purely sensory psychology. Observers were taught that they must limit their reports to sensations, images, and feelings. Such instructions drastically limited the terrain to be covered by introspective research.

There is another important disadvantage to introspection. This is that, as when the physicist studies the electron, introspection interferes with the phenomenon being investigated. Titchener faced up to this paradox and tried to cope with it. First, he conceded, "If you try to report the changes in consciousness, while these changes are in progress, you interfere with consciousness" (1911, p. 177); and tacitly agreeing with James and his metaphorical "stream of consciousness," Titchener granted that "consciousness is a flow, a process, and if we divide it up, we run the risk of missing certain intermediate links" (1911, p. 179).

Against these arguments he proposed the thesis that one can repeat the same introspective experiment, so that conscious material missed on one trial may turn up on another (forgetting Heraclitus' dictum that no one has exactly the same experience twice). He even admitted the possibility of questioning the observer about an experience, although Wundt had criticized this procedure.

Titchener realized that emotional experiences particularly susceptible to being destroyed by the effort at introspection: "Cool consideration of an emotion is fatal to its very existence; your anger disappears . . . as you examine it" (1911, pp. 177–178). He proposed the replacement of introspection by retrospection; allow the emotional state to run its course, then try to recall the various conscious phenomena that occurred.

Physics and Psychology

Titchener was well aware that Fechner's psychophysics was based on relating a series of physical stimuli to a series of conscious sensations. The question then arises: In what way does psychology differ from physics? Wundt and Titchener identified the difference as follows: Physics is the study of *mediate* experience, whereas psychology is the study of *immediate* experience. Or stated another way: Psychology is the study of events *dependent* on an observer, whereas physics is the study of events *independent* of an observer.

Consider Figure 7.1. This is interesting primarily because it shows how the Wundtians went about testing hypotheses. The Greeks had known about the illusion now called the "Müller-Lyer" illusion, on the left in the figure. One hypothesis was that the arrowheads (C–D) induced a mental orientation of compressing the line, while the reversed arrowheads (A–B) suggested expansion. To test this hypothesis, Ebbinghaus (1908) devised the figures on the right. Here, if any unconscious "force" is operative, the two birds at the top will be seen as getting closer together, and those below will be seen as drawing farther apart. As any observer can see, the prediction was not confirmed. Whatever the Müller-Lyer illusion depends on, it is not an unconscious assumption of reducing or increasing distance. Psychologists in the Wundt-Titchener tradition were ingenious in devising these variations in stimulus material as tests of hypotheses.

Now let us return to the physicist. The physicist lays a ruler down by the lines A–B and C–D and concludes that they are equal although they do not appear to be equal. Similarly, he finds that the distances between the birds' heads are equal but the *appearance* of inequality persists. Thus,

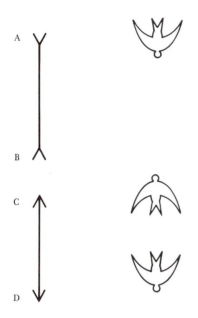

FIGURE 7.1 A Test of the Theory of the Müller-Lyer Illusion

On the left is the traditional Müller-Lyer figure in which the distance A–B is regularly judged greater than C–D. One theory was that the mind was sensitive to "forces" expanding A–B and compressing C–D. Ebbinghaus therefore devised the figure on the right in which these hypothetical forces would be compressing A–B and expanding C–D. As is readily visible, the demonstration rejects the theory.

if we rely on the report of an observer, the distances are not equal; but if we interpose a measuring device, the distances are equal. Thus, in *immediate* experience, the differences are real; in *mediate* experience (using measuring devices) the differences are not real. This problem of appearance versus reality will recur often in our exploration of psychological theorizing.

Why Structuralism

Wundt never applied the term "structuralism" to his variety of psychology, and Titchener seems to have adopted the term in the course of a polemic against functionalism (see Chapter Eight). He asserted that his version of psychology (the only "true" psychology, of course) corresponded to the stage of taxonomy in biology. The taxonomist was concerned with identifying all the different species of fauna and flora, and identifying them descriptively. Taxonomy does not concern itself with function.

Titchener's aim, therefore, was to give as complete a description as possible of the contents of consciousness, a task which included dividing conscious events into their smallest component parts. Thus, one's experience of an apple could include a circular shape, a reddish color, a waxy feel, a crunchy texture, a characteristic odor and taste, etc. The structuralist study of an apple might provide an extensive description of sensory attributes without ever mentioning the fact that it is good to eat.

Titchener, having decided that the elements of conscious experience were sensations, images, and feelings, trained his graduate students (who served in each other's experiments) to adhere rigidly to reports in these terms. As a dominant and forceful teacher, he required compliance with the theoretical assumptions. It is no surprise, then, that the Cornell laboratories turned out only reports confirming the structuralist position. As I shall note later, adherents of almost every known psychological theory commit the same sin against the pure search for knowledge; they simply do not publish studies contradicting their theories.

Sensations

The area of psychology that the structuralists took as their domain, and which they exploited thoroughly, is the area of sensation. Fechner's great breakthrough had been the establishment of the law that a sensory experience is a function of the logarithm of the physical stimulus. This principle, which was at that time taken as proving that psychic and physical data could be related by mathematical formulas, was extended in many directions. Difference thresholds patterned on Weber's work were computed for most sensory modalities. Contrast effects were also studied, as were summation of stimuli and masking effects of stimuli. Thus, Titchener (1896) used the j.n.d. (just noticeable difference) for visual sensations to compute that one could experience 32,820 distinct and identifiable visual sensations. However, he allotted only one sensation intensity to the sex organs, and this—in the light of modern treatments of sexuality—must have been a gross underestimate.

Titchener defined his field so narrowly, and the acceptable methods so precisely, that his students soon tested and recorded most of the important hypotheses about sensation. A comparison of a textbook such as Titchener's *Primer of Psychology* (1918) with a 1980s elementary text will show that, as regards sensory processes, there have not been any major changes over the years. This is not true of any other topic in the Titchener book.

It was possible for Titchener to list ten or more "laws" of psychology that had been confirmed empirically (Titchener, 1911, 1918). These were statements of "a regularity, an unbroken uniformity, of some aspects of experience" (1911, p. 5). Many of these laws appear to be models of precise statement. Consider his passage delineating the law of sensory contrast:

> Every patch of light and colour in the field of vision affects and is affected by all the rest in certain definite ways. The principal laws of contrast . . . are as follows: (1) the contrast effect is always in the direction of greatest opposition; a yellow makes its surrounding bluish, a black makes its surroundings light. (2) The nearer together the contrasting surfaces, the greater is the contrast effect. . . . (3) The contrast effect is enhanced by the elim-

ination of contours or boundary lines.—There are two further laws of colour contrast: (4) that the effect is greatest when there is no simultaneous
light contrast; and (5) that the effect increases with increase in saturation
of the inducing colour. (1911, p. 76)

Sensations were described in terms of their *attributes*. *Quality* referred
to sensory modality (e.g., visual, auditory, kinesthetic, tactual, etc.) and
also to variations within a sense organ, such as hue, brightness, bass and
treble, salty and sweet. Some individuals reported synesthesia, a linking
of two qualities; for example, a bass tone was associated with dark coloring, treble with a bright red. In addition to quality, Titchener enumerated *intensity* (loud vs. soft), *extensity* (spatial distribution), *duration* over
time, and *vividness*. He warned against confusing intensity with vividness,
commenting that a mother listening for a baby's cry may experience the
sound vividly although it is low in intensity.

Attention was also defined in terms of sensory attributes. When a sensation becomes brighter, clearer, or more detailed in the absence of a
change in the physical stimulus, we say that attention has become focused on the source of the sensation. Titchener avoided any discussion
of attending as a form of *response;* for him, the change in consciousness
was the sole criterion.

Images

In a psychology derived so obviously from British empiricism, images
necessarily played an important role. They made up the context of a
specific sensory input, relating it to past experiences, and thus to meaning.

An important debate among the structuralists was whether the image
was a separate phenomenon or merely the neural trace from prior sensation. Titchener pointed out that the image has its own character; for
example, a sensation, if long-lasting, gives rise to a *negative* afterimage;
however, if you recall a memory image of a vividly colored scene, you
will not experience a negative afterimage. The memory image, then, is
not a mere facsimile of the original sensation.

This raises an interesting question: Can a trained observer differentiate between a sensation and an image? In daily life, this is easy: the
sensation has a physical energy source that affects a sensory surface.
However, Perky (1910) devised an ingenious experiment to reduce these
environmental cues. She placed her observer in a dark room with a
translucent screen on which pictures could be projected from behind.
The observers were asked to rate the clarity and intensity of the pictures,
and they were occasionally given a blank slide with the request to image
the earlier picture. By gradually reducing the light intensity, Perky was
able to reach a point at which the observers could not distinguish whether

the picture was objectively present. For Titchener, this experiment was convincing evidence that sensation and image were psychologically interchangeable as experience, but physiologically different (there was no negative afterimage from the memory image.)

Learning

Titchener liked William James's description of the infant's consciousness as a "blooming, buzzing confusion," as it fitted his theory that sensations, as such, acquire meaning only over time by association. Similarly, he approved of the work of Ebbinghaus on the learning of nonsense syllables. These, he wrote, constituted "pure perceptions, sights and sounds that had no meaning and no associates" (1911, p. 380); he went so far as to hail the nonsense syllable as "the most considerable advance . . . since the time of Aristotle" (1911, p. 381). He perceived the elimination of meaning as an approach to true elementary conscious experience.

Titchener called attention to an aspect of the Ebbinghaus experiment that still concerns students of learning. The learner faced with a list of nonsense syllables has two tasks: to learn the individual syllables, and to learn the linkages that establish the sequence within the list. Titchener proposed that we use the term *impression* for the degree of learning of the syllable itself and the term *association* for the learning that determines the sequence in which impressions are verbalized (1911, p. 383). His predecessors would probably have discarded the notion of *impression* as being synonymous with the formation of an idea, but in terms of modern analysis, and especially in terms of motor learning, the response itself and its place in a sequence are clearly *separate* if not *independent* phenomena.

Meaning: The Core–Context Theory

For Titchener, a sensation had no meaning; it was simply a fact of experience. Consider the bird watcher, who may see a flash of red and say, "I think it was a cardinal." This statement goes beyond the sensation itself. It draws on past experience, mainly on images associated with the focal sensation. Thus Titchener (1910) wrote:

> Perceptions are selected groups of sensations, in which images are incorporated as an integral part of the whole process. But that is not all: the essential thing about them has still to be named: and it is this,—that perceptions have meaning. *No sensation means;* a sensation simply goes on in various attributive ways, intensively, clearly, spatially, and so forth. *All perceptions mean. . . .* Meaning, psychologically, is always context; one mental process is the meaning of another mental process if it is that other's con-

text . . . Originally, the situation is physical, external; and, originally, meaning is kinaesthesis; the organism faces the situation by some bodily attitude. . . . . For ourselves, the situation may be either external or internal, either a group of adequate stimuli or a constellation of ideas; image has now supervened upon sensation, and meaning can be carried in imaginal terms. (p. 367)

Meaning, then, is perceiving, and perceiving is constituted of a core sensation (the immediate focal experience) plus context (the associated images derived from past experience). Titchener often seemed unhappy with this inclusion of meaning in psychology; like Wundt, he preferred to shunt the problem of learning and meaning over to logic and the natural sciences. However, he bowed to tradition to the extent of endorsing the principles of association that had been enunciated by Locke and his successors.

The Stimulus Error

Titchener explained that his concern over the confusion of immediate experience with meaning was to prevent his observers from committing the "stimulus error." Quite simply this involves reading more into the stimulus than is given, for example, when a red circle is seen as an apple. This is a phenomenon closely related to the "attribution theory" research, in which people project their own beliefs into the behavior of another person. A similar phenomenon occurs when an experimental student tries to guess what the purpose of the experimenter is and then tries to produce that result (or, sometimes, the opposite). The applicability of the phenomenon to other psychological theories will be noted in later chapters.

Association

Learning was a process of formation of associations, and the major laws were those of frequency and recency, or contiguity, as Titchener's predecessors had labeled it. These associations may be across modalities; for example, in discussing thinking, Titchener (1909) approximated Watson's later hypothesis of subvocal speech: "There are occasions when my voice rings out clear in the mental ear and my throat feels stiff as if with much talking" (p. 9). It would appear, therefore, that the learning of nonsense syllables is a matter of associating visual sensory experiences with the kinesthetic and auditory images associated with responding. As Titchener (1911) summed it up, "whenever a sensory or imaginal process occurs in consciousness, there are likely to appear with it (of course, in imaginal terms) all those sensory and imaginal processes which occurred together with it in any earlier conscious present. This we may term the law of association" (p. 378).

Response

Given his narrow definition of psychology, one would not expect much discussion of response functions in Titchener. He referred somewhat cautiously to J. M. Baldwin's "law of dynamogenesis," an idea asserting that "every conscious experience has its associated motor outlet." Although Titchener expressed doubts about the validity of this principle, he obviously thought it should be considered. His observers were continually reporting kinesthetic sensations, of movement or of muscle tension, when describing their experiences, notably, in reporting on problem solving.

The discovery of REM sleep (rapid eye movement episodes during sleep) would no doubt have pleased Titchener. Because eye movements are very frequent, they can become associated with and thus cues for recalling visual and other experiences. A person looking at a picture, for example, shows a characteristic pattern of fixations. It would seem plausible, therefore, that if, in sleep, the eye movements replicated those of some waking experience, the visual images of that occasion would be recalled.

Research Methodology

Because introspection was the method of choice in Titchenerian psychology, training observers became crucial. Nowadays, psychologists devise experiments in which the subject need not know what is to be observed; indeed, elaborate deceptions are often used to mislead the subject with regard to what is sought. In structuralist work, the opposite was true. Only well-trained observers were considered competent to report on their conscious experiences. (An analogy: Some critics have suggested that psychoanalysis takes so long because the analyst has to train the patient to identify certain cues—images, dreams, and so on—and then to verbalize them.)

A hazard in this emphasis on training is that the observer will report only what is considered acceptable and will not mention other items that may be important. P. T. Young (1927) reported an observation that will illustrate the dilemma. Working at Cornell, Young persuaded three of his colleagues to report on their affective experiences. Two of the three were trained in Titchenerian approach, but one was a behaviorist (Young did not explain how such a person was found at Cornell). In reporting on his feelings, the behaviorist commented, "The instruction asks me to watch for organic sensations. *That means* that I have a tendency to respond to various conditions in the abdomen which are present all the time but to which I don't ordinarily respond" (Young, 1927, p. 181; italics added). It would seem that this is a clear case of the experimenter's determining the outcome. The instructions had the effect of facilitating a report that would not have been given in the absence of the instructions—William James's "psychologists' fallacy."

This raises the question: is introspection inevitably tainted with subjective bias? Certainly this is a possibility. Wundt and Titchener made a practice of criticizing their opponents, such as Külpe and Stumpf, by charging that their observers were untrained, or poorly trained. (As some of them had been trained by Wundt himself, the charge is puzzling.)

Introspection is necessarily retrospection. It is quite literally impossible to have an experience and *simultaneously* to examine that experience. That is William James's problem of the self as knower and the self as known. Thus, Titchener had to instruct his observers to *recall* or relive the experience, this time analyzing its components.

Introspection also *modifies* the remembered experience. It is a familiar phenomenon, when one asks an angry person to report on his or her sensations of muscle tension, heart beat, respiration, and so on, that almost at once, the felt anger disappears. The process of observing modifies the experience. This is a problem in contemporary research that uses what we now call *self-monitoring,* in order to avoid that obsolete term *introspection.* The process of monitoring modifies what is being monitored.

Titchener had a passion for experimental control. His idea of proper research methodology included training the observer, excluding distracting stimuli, immediately recording the response, and making precise time measures if possible. In many ways, it was an admirable model to be imitated by later psychologists. Titchener (1911) wrote:

> An experiment is an observation that can be repeated, isolated, and varied. . . . The more strictly you can *isolate* an observation, the easier does your task of observation become, and the less danger there is of your being led astray by irrelevant circumstances. . . . The more widely you can *vary* an observation, the more clearly will the uniformity of experience stand out, and the better your chance of discovering laws. (p. 20)

Obviously the task of being an observer in a Titchenerian experiment was rather demanding. For the most part, the structuralists used each other as observers. Efforts to use naive subjects (undergraduates) raised difficulties: the less-trained individuals would not follow—and probably did not understand—the instructions. Titchener's frustrations in attempts to widen the range of subjects by bringing in naive undergraduates are reflected in the following remarks relative to an experiment using nonsense syllables as stimuli: "In most psychological experiments, the novice is likely to do anything other than what is required of him; he will search for meanings (in the nonsense syllables), stress the position of syllables, mark the rhythm, shift his imagery" (p. 382). Titchener might well have learned a lesson from this, namely, that human beings have creative potentials and may respond to stimulus attributes of which the experimenter is not aware. The experimental design uses impoverished stimuli and impoverished response alternatives; the human subject often declines to accept this rigid straitjacket. (It should be added that behaviorists try to impose comparable constraints; this issue will be examined later.)

Not even intensive training can eliminate conflicts over introspective data. Boring (1946) provided an amusing anecdote to illustrate this problem. The scene was a meeting of Titchener's "purely scientific" experimental psychologists. "Titchener, after a hot debate with [E. B.] Holt, exclaimed: 'You can see that green is neither yellowish nor bluish!' And Holt replied: 'On the contrary, it is obvious that a green is that yellow-blue which is just exactly as blue as it is yellow' " (p. 176). What was obvious to one was not at all obvious to the other.

The Study of Illusions

Given this concern over sensory inputs, and particularly over errors in perceiving, it is not surprising that the structuralists did many investigations on common illusions. Their method has been illustrated in Figure 7.1. The figure showed a device of Ebbinghaus which tested a theory of perceptual dynamics of the illusion. Many other instances could be cited. The whole Wundt-Titchener tradition was organized around the relation between physical stimuli and conscious experiences. Illusions provided a particularly useful tool for investigating this area because the stimulus and the experience were so obviously in contradiction.

Perceptual Conflict

The rigorous training that Wundt and Titchener imposed on their graduate students sometimes paid dividends in an unexpected way. Of the serendipitous discoveries made, I shall mention only one: the phenomenon of loss of clarity in a percept as a consequence of perceptual conflict. G. M. Stratton (1897), who had studied with Wundt at Leipzig, did an investigation that involved wearing inverting lenses for a week. These lenses caused him to "see" objects below him as being above him, and vice versa. Naturally he often saw his hands and arms in this unnatural position, but not the parts of his body that were clothed. After the experiment, when he had discarded the lenses and was taking a bath, he commented that "the old representation of those parts of my body which I had so frequently seen . . . during the experiment was decidedly less vivid, the outline more blurred, the color paler, grayer, more 'washed out' than of the parts which had never come within the limits of the visual field" (quoted by Herrnstein and Boring, 1965, p. 106). Clearly, the loss of clarity was a consequence of conflict between the percept developed during the experiment and that of "normal" vision, whereas the expected clarity was experienced for those parts not seen during the experiment and hence not trapped into a conflict of perceptions. This observation can be compared with the later work on approach-avoidance of Neal Miller and of Kurt Lewin.

Temperament

Titchener supported Wundt's position that individual differences were not a proper part of psychological research. He did, however, venture in one of his later books (1918) to include almost two pages on "temperament." He adopted the scheme used by the Greek physician Galen but integrated it into his own schema by using strength of feelings and speed of association as dimensions. Using two levels of each, he generated a fourfold classification of temperaments as follows:

	Quick Thought	*Slow Thought*
Strong affection:	Choleric	Melancholic
Weak affection:	Sanguine	Phlegmatic

He must have recognized quickly that this was *faux pas;* he dropped the subject and did not mention it again. However, this table has been used as a starting point (not a formal theory of temperament) by contemporary psychologists, notably R. B. Cattell (1950), H. J. Eysenck (1947), and R. Stagner (1974).

Neurologizing

Titchener showed, on the whole, good judgment by avoiding discussion of how the activity of the nervous system fits into the processes of sensing, perceiving, and associating. In this caution, he might have been reacting to some of the bizarre speculations of William James on how the brain functions. Titchener used the telephone-exchange metaphor in some of his theorizing, but he recognized its weakness as an analogy for the workings of the human nervous system.

Titchener was criticized by John Dewey (1896) for making the reflex the unit of physical action. Whether this was justified by some of Titchener's early writings is unclear. Certainly, by 1911, Titchener had explicitly rejected the reflex as a fundamental unit: "The assumption that the reflex arc is the unit of nerve-function evidently makes the brain nothing more, in principle, than a mass of superposed reflex arcs . . . the office of the brain is to receive, to couple up, and to send out. But this view, that the nervous system is . . . . a sort of glorified telephone exchange, is in the author's opinion wholly inadequate to explain the phenomena of mind" (p. 489). Contemporary psychologists would surely applaud this judgment about the reflex arc theory, adding *sotto voce* that Titchener's version of psychology and his view of "the phenomena of mind" would seem admirably adapted to just such a view of the brain.

Placing Titchener in History

Students sometimes ask why the structuralism preached by Wundt and Titchener is given so much attention in the history of American psychology. The reason is that these theoreticians provided the indispensable bridge from the empiricist philosophical psychology of Locke and Hume to the modern scientific psychologies of behaviorism, Gestalt psychology, and psychoanalysis, which share a common trait: each is a rebellion against one or another facet of structuralism. Speaking in dialectical terms, we could say that structuralism carried within its corpus of theory the seeds of its own destruction.

A first major contribution of Wundt and Titchener to modern scientific psychology was their obsession with research methodology. Rebelling against the facile armchair introspection practiced by their predecessors, not excluding William James, they laid down rigorous criteria for investigations of mental processes. They sought to demonstrate that scientific methodology could cope with these. It seems fair to say that in a strictly formal sense, Titchener was the intellectual ancestor of Clark Hull and B. F. Skinner as much as of the group I have called the neo-structuralists.

In the second place, many of the basic assumptions of modern psychology could not be taken for granted before 1879. One need only remember the debate between Locke and his critics over the "primary" and "secondary" attributes of objects to realize that the field of sensory psychology had to be explored carefully.

Many of these assumptions are important today. The principle of contrast, for example, forms a backdrop for much attitude research; it is also relevant to much of the work on opponent-process phenomena in dynamics as well as the work on perceiving. The principle of just noticeable differences appears both in attitude study and in Hull's theory of learning. The research on habituation to repetitive stimulation is directly relevant to Harry Helson's work on adaptation level; it is of interest to industrial psychologists investigating the effects of highly repetitive jobs on the worker, and in learning theory, to the phenomenon of reactive inhibition.

Finally, structuralist theory and methodology probably speeded the process of acceptance, in the scientific community, of psychology as an independent discipline. This was accomplished by splitting psychological problems into their tiniest parts, as in physics, and by probing the effect of systematic variations along one or more parameters (e.g., intensity of stimulation, duration, summation). The insistence of the structuralists on careful training of observers fitted the experience of other scientists. And the laboratory controls of irrelevant variables, with the severe limitation of response alternatives, was in the pattern approved by physics and chemistry as devices for improving the accuracy of observations, as well as the precision of interpretations.

Although these contributions were generally recognized by other psychologists, they did not guarantee Titchener the national prestige he might have received in a more philosophical climate such as that of Germany in the early 1900s. The intellectual tradition in Germany was receptive to the fine analysis of logical points having little relevance to everyday problems. The atmosphere in the United States was pragmatic. Even today, politicians delight in ridiculing the concern of academics with remote, artificial problems; the tactic seems to win many votes. William James, the great representative of pragmatism, could write of Titchener's theoretical system that "The 'function' of Titchener's 'scientific' psychology (which, 'structurally' considered, is a pure will-of-the-wisp) is to keep the laboratory instruments going, and to provide platforms for certain professors" (quoted in Perry, 1934, Vol. 2, p. 123).

Criticisms of Structuralism

Other psychologists treated Titchener with greater respect than did James, and they deigned to apply logic instead of ridicule to the tenets of structuralism. One of the criticisms most widely voiced related to the definition of the discipline. Structuralist thinking excluded the study of animals, of children, and of abnormal personalities, as these subjects could not participate in the formal introspection that was the primary research tool.

Another criticism leveled at the structuralists is that many of their claims were exaggerated. Titchener wrote of the absolute threshold, the differential threshold, negative adaptation, afterimages, just noticeable differences, sensory qualities, and so on as if these were fixed values. Yet his own studies revealed practice effects, fatigue effects, motivational influences, and other variables that modified the various thresholds. The work on sensory stimuli and conscious experiences was valuable, but it was oversold by Titchener and by some of his students.

Finally, it is important to note the criticism that this doctrine of the structure of consciousness was missing the most important feature of sensory psychology, namely, how it helps the individual to adapt to his or her environment. The functionalists asked the question: How does consciousness function in the struggle for survival? To which Titchener would have replied, "We have to know about the basic structure of conscious awareness before trying to identify functions."

Neither Wundt nor Titchener would have heeded the criticism that their work was impractical. They might have regarded this assertion as praise; they explicitly chose careers as "pure scientists," just as many physicists and chemists also boast that what they are doing is remote from practical application. The structuralist might also counterattack with the observation that teaching flatworms to turn left or right in a T maze can be criticized as sterile, artificial, and unrelated to any considerations of practical affairs. Much of the essence of science is found in the artificiality of the settings within which knowledge is obtained. There are still important questions, for example, about the validity of extrapolating laboratory studies of learning to the procedures of clinicians using behavior modification techniques.

The critiques of structuralism led to the posing of alternative theories of psychology. The behaviorists rejected the idea of consciousness as a focus but kept the analytical, atomistic logic of Titchener. The Gestalt theorists kept the focus on consciousness but rejected the atomistic approach. And psychoanalysis went even further, insisting on the supplementation of consciousness by unconscious processes, and limiting atomism to what might be called functional units as opposed to theoretical units. Thus, even in the process of being rejected, structuralism played its part in the development of modern psychological theories.

Students of Titchener

Titchener presided over the doctoral researches of fifty-four graduate students during his long tenure at Cornell. Many of these psychologists became leaders in the field. Margaret Washburn, Edwin G. Boring, Madison Bentley, and Walter B. Pillsbury were the most honored, each being elected to the presidency of the American Psychological Association (APA).

Titchener's students illustrate, to a greater or lesser degree, how a system of psychology can be modified by gradual steps until it becomes indistinguishable from, or is easy to merge with, a rival systematic conception. Titchener attacked both functionalism and behaviorism fluently, yet his students adopted amendments to his theory which moved them ever closer to these alternative theories about human psychology.

Margaret Floy Washburn

It speaks well for Titchener's freedom from antifeminine prejudice that his first—and some say his brightest—doctoral candidate at Cornell was Margaret Floy Washburn (1871–1939). Receiving her Ph.D. in 1894, she went on to an impressive career in research and theorizing. Despite her mentor's objections, she plunged into research on animal behavior, devising some clever procedures, and publishing one of the best early books in this area (*The Animal Mind,* 1908, 1917). She found that the path of a woman seeking a career in science was not a comfortable one. (Her first job after the Ph.D. was as a dormitory counselor for female students!) She did eventually obtain an appointment to the psychology faculty at the University of Cincinnati, and then at Vassar College, where she moved up to head the psychology department before retiring in 1937. She was elected president of APA in 1921.

One of Washburn's animal studies is interesting for the theoretical approach she used in interpreting the results. Washburn and Abbot (1912) trained rabbits to push open a door with a red paper on it in order to get food, and to avoid the door covered with gray paper because that door was always bolted. Washburn (1917) wrote, "The gray stimulus acquired a tendency to lose its motor effect because the movements to which it gave rise were useless" (p. 267). Modern behaviorists would quibble about words like *tendency* and *useless* but would nevertheless recognize this as the principle of extinction of nonreinforced responses.

Washburn, like James, was interested in Asian philosophy. In *The Animal Mind* (1917) we find this interesting comment: "When a process purely centrally excited holds the field and makes the individual deaf and blind to powerful external stimuli pouring in upon his sense organs, then he is *superior to the immediate environment* at least" (p. 322; italics added). Thus Washburn recognized one limit imposed on Titchener's doctrine of the primacy of the physical stimulus in inducing conscious experience. And, of course, the idea of rising above environmental stresses by refusing to perceive them was a major theme of Hindu philosophy.

Washburn showed a clear desire to bridge the gap between Titchener's structuralism and the emerging behavioristic movement led by Max Meyer and John B. Watson. In her most important theoretical contribution, *Movement and Mental Imagery* (1916), she offered some ingenious bridges between the realm of overt responses and the realm of conscious experience. She proposed a principle that consciousness is at a peak when conflicting response tendencies are about equally strong. She even went so far as to concede that "all association is association between movements" (p. 34). In this, she may have been giving too much ground to Watson.

Washburn (1916) posed the theory of response conflict and consciousness in neurological terms:

> Whenever a motor pathway is at the same time excited by a sensory pathway and partially inhibited by an antagonistic motor excitation, a process occurs in all sensory pathways connected with the motor pathway by low synaptic resistances, including the sensory pathway that is exciting the motor pathway in question. This process is accompanied by consciousness. When it occurs in a sensory pathway that is being excited by an outside stimulus, it gives rise to the type of consciousness that we call a peripher-

Archives of the History of American Psychology

Margaret Floy Washburn, a brilliant student of Titchener
who strove for the reunion of structural and functional
psychology

ally excited sensation. When it occurs in a sensory pathway that has no
outside excitation, it gives rise to the type of consciousness that we call a
centrally excited sensation or a mental image. (pp. 30–31)

In a way, this is no more than Titchener's distinction between sensation
and image; however, the introduction of an inhibiting factor (a competing response tendency) is relevant to Washburn's hypothesis that consciousness is at a maximum when there is external stimulation tending
to set off mutually incompatible responses.

Washburn also accepted a thesis which had already been proposed by
Watson, that there is no learning without a response. "No associative
reaction can take place," she wrote, "because *associative activity requires the
actual performance of a motor response*" (1916, p. 36; italics added). She did
not speculate on just what aspect of the process prevented learning; later

writers would, of course, explore the role of feedback as a determinant of learning and retention.

Another interesting contribution was her distinction between two kinds of inhibitory processes in learning. One she called "generative inhibition"; this operated in a forward direction (i.e., learning an association such as A–B would interfere with later learning A–C), which would be recognized as "proactive inhibition" in later years. A second inhibitory process she called "effectual inhibition"; this would result if the person, having learned A–B and A–C, is then presented with Stimulus A. As B and C are both associates of A, the tendency for each response will be activated, and the two tendencies will interfere with each other (1916, p. 123). The latter phenomenon is often called *retroactive inhibition* or *response competition* because later learning blocks the arousal of a response learned earlier.

Meanwhile, German psychologists were rebelling against Wundt's severe constraints on the kind of phenomena to be classified as "psychology." Introspective observations were being collected on problem solving, abstraction, and controlled association. Washburn proposed that the results of these studies could be fitted into a structuralist framework that would make use of the muscular sensations and kinesthetic images often reported by observers. She suggested that, when the experimenter instructs the observer to "give an example of this general class" (flowers, for example), the observer makes certain muscular responses, adopting a mental set to search memory images for the correct response. These muscular tensions give rise to sensations, and these, in turn, can provide the "context" (in Titchener's terms) for the stimulus word. Thus, the kinesthetic pattern may be compatible with a response such as "daisy" but may block an incorrect response such as "window." Külpe and other German psychologists of the so-called Würzburg school had called this mental set a *determining tendency;* Washburn's 1916 rephrasing of the phenomenon made it possible for her to fit these experiments into Titchener's "core-context" theory of meaning (1916, pp. 151–153).

Walter Bowers Pillsbury

Walter B. Pillsbury (1872–1960), another Titchener student (Ph.D., 1896), disagreed with Washburn. He conceded that movements must also be considered important data for the psychologist, but he rejected the idea that all of consciousness could be reduced to movement. (Washburn claimed that she had had no intention of going as far as Pillsbury said she had.) As John B. Watson was to assert, shortly thereafter, the introspectionists often disagreed with each other.

Pillsbury's more important claim to fame lies in his expansion of the scope of psychology. He wrote a book on *The Psychology of Reasoning* (1910), two textbooks, and the first American *History of Psychology* (1929).

Most significant was his development of social psychology. In *The Psychology of Nationality and Internationalism* (1919), he took issue with Gustave LeBon and others who had endorsed a "group mind" concept. This, he argued, could serve only as a metaphor, not as a realistic concept. "It must also be remembered," he wrote, "that the nation always exists merely *in the individuals who compose it,* even when they regard it as an independent entity, and furthermore, that it exists for the individuals, not the individuals for it" (1919, p. 247, italics added). Thus he struck out at the Hegelian (and Marxist) notion of the nation as a superorganism, entitled to control and subordinate the welfare of individual persons.

Pillsbury probably should be classified as a functionalist (see Chapter 8); he certainly was no structuralist. His texts were influential in the early part of this century, and his insistence on the individual as the irreducible unit of a social group or an institution undoubtedly influenced the development of social psychology, notably the work of Floyd H. Allport, who would later adapt Watsonian behaviorism as a foundation for social psychology. On the other hand, we can only be astonished that he allowed his mentor, Titchener, only 4 pages out of 315 in his *History of Psychology,* and that he did not find it possible even to mention Margaret F. Washburn or Mary W. Calkins, brilliant contemporaries, in his book. As I have noted, every historian brings his or her own biases to the task of chronicling the development of a science.

Edwin Garrigues Boring

Probably the best-known of Titchener's students (Ph.D., 1914) in the present population of psychologists is E. G. Boring (1886–1968), whose *History of Experimental Psychology* (1929, 1950) has been widely studied. Like Washburn, Boring at first adopted structuralism completely, then gradually edged away. Unlike her, he developed no original ideas to adapt structuralism to the rising tide of behaviorism; instead, he became an eclectic, citing whatever explanation seemed appropriate to a bit of research rather than seeking for internal consistency in his opinions.

He did make one valiant effort to preserve most of structuralism by abandoning the philsophical dualism which characterized both Wundt and Titchener. His book *The Physical Dimensions of Consciousness* (1933, 1963) amounted to treating sensations, images, and feelings as *responses* having a physical basis comparable to the muscle action used in pressing a lever. We do not, he argued, worry about just which muscle is involved when we deal with escaping from a puzzle box, and we need not fret about specific cortical cells when dealing with the class of responses traditionally called "mental." On this basis, all of the experimental data collected in structuralist-designed research could be salvaged; and indeed, most of this material has quietly slipped into the category of "everybody knows that . . ." without being credited to Titchener or his theories.

Boring's purpose was to dissociate the study of sensory and other conscious phenomena from the dualistic assumption that the physical cannot affect the mental, and vice versa. By adopting the slogan, "Phenomena exist for science only as they are reported," Boring held that he was dealing with verbal reports in the same objective fashion as Watson dealt with records of rats running a maze. In a way, Boring contributed to the development of an offshoot of behaviorism that can be called *neobehaviorism* (Chapter Eighteen) because it rejects Watson's arbitrary denial of consciousness in favor of treating conscious experiences as responses.

Other Titchener Students

Many others of Titchener's doctoral students have left important records behind them. Madison Bentley (Ph.D., 1899) was another of those who clung to the structuralist tradition when people like Washburn and Pillsbury were forsaking it in favor of functionalism or behaviorism. Joy Paul Guilford (a Cornell Ph.D. of 1927 under K. M. Dallenbach) likewise abandoned structuralism, moving instead into quantitative methods and the structure of intellect, a quasi-Galtonian approach that has influenced much of current research on questions of independent mental abilities and their relevance to behaviors such as problem solving. Both were honored by election to the presidency of the American Psychological Association.

Lillian Gilbreth

One person who was not a Titchener student should be mentioned here. Lillian Gilbreth (1878–1972) took her doctorate at Brown University and started her professional life with a structuralist bent. However, she was married to Frank Gilbreth, who was an engineer involved in the construction industry. Lillian brought to their collaboration the laboratory skills one would expect, as well as the analytical, atomistic style of thinking of the Titchener school. Thus the Gilbreths pioneered in the variety of time-and-motion study which involved breaking each task, such as laying a brick on a wall, into separate movements of fingers, hands, wrists, and arms, timing each, and trying to fit them back together into the optimum pattern for efficiency without fatigue. Similar work was under way by Frederick W. Taylor, a nonpsychologist. Both he and the Gilbreths urged piecework and careful structuring of the task so that all workers did exactly the same thing; however, Taylor encountered bitter opposition from unions and even from some employers. The Gilbreths apparently fared much better. Bartle (1984), in an appreciative note on Lillian Gilbreth's work, commented that the Gilbreths "enjoyed better cooperation from the workers, union, and management than did the

'Father of Scientific Management' [Frederick W. Taylor]" (p. 2). Bartle attributed this success to Dr. Gilbreth's training in psychology and her interest in the health and welfare of the workers. Bartle also noted that Lillian Gilbreth is so far the only psychologist ever honored by a U.S. Postal Service commemorative stamp! (February 24, 1984).

Titchener: A Summing Up

Although Titchener is recognized as an important figure in the history of psychological theorizing in America, he could not at any time be said to have dominated the field. In Coan's (1979) study, he ranked among the top five psychologists only for the decade 1890–1899.

The most important factor was probably that intangible yet pervasive influence called the Zeitgeist. America did not have the background of philosophizing that was so strong in Germany; on the contrary, even the academic world was affected by an intense pragmatism. In one of William James's telling phrases, "Truth is the cash value of an idea." Structuralism was not a theory that could be turned to cash.

Titchener was, however, to some extent the maker of his own difficulties. He isolated himself from the majority of American psychologists; although he joined G. S. Hall's newly founded American Psychological Association, he rarely participated and was once dropped for nonpayment of dues. As a substitute, he formed a small group of "pure" experimentalists, introspectionists like himself; in effect, he retired into his Fortress Cornell and pulled up the drawbridge.

Despite this isolationist tendency, Titchener lent his name to various projects that held little to interest him. Thus he accepted membership on the board of directors of J. M. Cattell's *Psychological Corporation* when it was founded in 1919, although he never participated in any applied research. He also accepted the editorship of the *American Journal of Psychology* in 1921, where he fostered the publication of papers with a structuralist tendency.

Boring's epitaph for Titchener and structuralism has been widely quoted: "Somehow Titchenerism in America had been sustained by his magnificent personality. With his death it suddenly collapsed, dwindling rapidly from the status of a vital faith in the importance of consciousness to the equally essential but wholly inglorious state of having been an unavoidable phase of historical development" (1950, p. 420).

Boring's adjective *inglorious* is too extreme. Today we find a resurgence of concern with consciousness: there are least two psychological journals specifically devoted to research on imagery. Much of current information-processing work looks like a logical extension of studies from the laboratories at Leipzig and Cornell. Structuralism was indeed unavoidable as the formal transition from British empiricism to modern psychology; and in strict dialectical fashion, it evoked behaviorism and Gestalt as countertendencies. This is not an "inglorious" record.

Practical Implications

Theories of psychology are not simply interesting intellectual exercises. They also have practical consequences. Although this book is not a text in applied psychology, or even a history of applications, I believe it is proper to point out some of the areas within which a given system has been useful (or even, on rare occasions, harmful). At any rate, every approach to human psychology impinges to some degree on human activities outside the laboratory, and a brief comment on these interrelations may be helpful.

Let me first refute William James's caustic comment that the structuralists' elaborate experimental designs were useful only to provide more jobs for structuralist psychologists. This was an unfair blow, and indeed it glossed over James's own contribution to the development of laboratories. His laboratory was, of course, used mainly for teaching, but the research laboratories of Titchener, Bentley, Boring, and other structuralists ground out substantial amounts of data. Many of these researches led to practical knowledge about sensory processes that has been useful in applications from human engineering laboratories to textile manufacturing and interior decorating.

Indirectly, structuralist psychology provided a foundation for the extensive work in aptitude testing, employee selection, and similar applied fields. Joseph Tiffin, a distinguished industrial psychologist, told in his autobiography of solving a problem in a steel mill during World War II by the use of psychophysical methods (see Stagner, 1981). Wundt himself worked on an individual-differences problem early in his career—the study of disagreements among astronomers in recording star transits. Because of the great importance of star tables to navigation, this work was "applied" in the best sense of that word. Of course, Wundt then proceeded to reverse the logic involved and to turn his skills to a search for laws of "mind in general," but his student, J. McKeen Cattell, introduced these methods to American colleges (for student admissions) and to American industry (for employee selection). Hugo Münsterberg, a rebellious Wundt product, improved markedly on Cattell's methods, mainly by keeping his test procedures closer to real life (see Chapter Eight).

Titchener contributed substantially to the development of American psychology. His emphasis on careful experimental design and the control of irrelevant variables had the effect of moving psychology farther from the anecdotal procedures of the British empiricists into the mainstream of modern science. His concept of the *stimulus error* has given rise to a line of research called *attribution theory,* in which qualities perceived in a person or a situation are actually being projected by the observer. Titchener taught his observers to distinguish between the immediate experience and the external object that might have given rise to that experience. Modern investigators are trying to determine the cues that actually emanate from the stimulus as opposed to the characteristics stored in the observer's memory and misperceived as inhering in the external situation. These studies, in turn, have given rise to investigations of how juries perceive evidence of guilt in criminal trials, and of similar concrete everyday events. The psychologists working in these areas would hoot at the idea that their work was rooted in structuralist doctrine, but the logic of development indicates that Titchener contributed substantially to the body of theory and methodology underlying these recent innovations.

Wundt and Titchener: A Reevaluation

The tradition in histories of psychology has been that Titchener was a Wundt devotee who simply purified Wundt's psychology. T. H. Leahey (1981) took issue with this identification. He accumulated a number of quotations, mostly from Wundt, showing that the German was much broader and more flexible than had been generally recognized. Leahey found evidence that Wundt anticipated some of the modern ideas of cognitive psychology, so that he was much closer to the Würzburg school than he is customarily thought to have been.

This does not prove that Leahey was right and that the consensus among historians is wrong. Leahey did offer an intriguing hypothesis to explain the tradition. Assuming that most of the historians have been behavioristically biased, he suggested that they had got so far away from both Wundt and Titchener that they could no longer see differences in theories and methods. This is a common enough phenomenon in social psychology; persons far from the position endorsed by the judge are seen as being similar, but judges see many differences among persons close to their preferred stance.

Another possible explanation for an error in judgment by American psychologists involves the "Germanic" stereotype. William James did not try to conceal his dislike for the German tradition as represented by Wundt in Europe and Titchener in America. This view was widely shared; John B. Watson, for example, occasionally fired off a barbed remark about the German invasion of American psychology. It may be that the similarities of Wundt and Titchener were exaggerated because of this common attribution.

CHAPTER 8

Functionalism

Despite Titchener's great personal prestige, structuralism never dominated American psychology. It was none the less important, if only in the sense that the behaviorist and Gestalt theories arose as rebellions against structuralist doctrine. Actually, during his lifetime Titchener contended more against "functionalist" psychology than against any other variety; this school predated Titchener's immigration to the United States. William James was the first great exponent of a functional psychology here, and the James–Titchener polemics were sometimes harsh.

In a curious way, Titchener shaped the functionalist movement, or at least defined it. Responding to criticisms of his theory, he wrote, "Introspection, from the structural standpoint, is observation of an *Is;* introspection, from the functional standpoint, is observation of an *Is-for.*" (1899, p. 291). Thus one might write a description of a hammer in structural terms without ever mentioning that it is handy for driving nails into wood.

Structuralism, Titchener wrote, is concerned with "real things," by which he meant not physical objects but real conscious experiences, denuded of logic and meaning. These real experiences were sensations, images, and feelings—abstractions, he conceded, but abstracted from an observable reality. The functionalist concept of "process" or "adaptation" is also an abstraction, but abstracted from a world of physical objects and logical meanings. "The phrase 'association of ideas,'" Titchener (1898) wrote, "may denote either the structural complex, the associated sensation group, or the functional process of recognition and recall" (p. 451).

Perhaps it was left to Titchener to define a theory he opposed—functionalism—because the functionalists were not much interested in defining their science. They were going about the business of gathering data and applying their ideas in various ways. Functionalism never did coalesce sufficiently to have a recognized spokesperson or an agreed-upon set of hypotheses.

Of the historical ideas sketched earlier in this book, functionalism most resembles faculty psychology. This is appropriate, because structuralism was the obvious descendant of British empiricism. Titchener criticized his opponents for making memory a "faculty"; he said it should be regarded as a function of the "psychophysical organism." Although the remark is true, it seems odd coming from Titchener, who had little to say about the organism at any time.

The study of the organism had, up to this time, been the province of biology, and developments within biological science became major influences on functionalist psychology. The two major figures in this relationship were Charles Darwin and Francis Galton.

Darwin and Galton

Two talented Englishmen provided the basic intellectual underpinnings for functionalism. Charles Darwin's revolutionary book *The Origin of Species* (1859) postulated that living organisms must adapt to the demands of the environment or suffer extinction. In psychological terms, this postulate meant that every psychological function must be evaluated in terms of how it relates to the survival of the individual or of the species.

Darwinian theory is inextricably tied to the study of individual differences. Every species shows a range of variation—in size, in strength, in cunning, and in temperament. One such variation may be beneficial in that it maximizes the probability of survival; another may be harmful, contributing to the 'early death and elimination of offspring receiving that genetically determined characteristic.

It must be understood that Darwin's phrase "the survival of the fittest" is a tautology. What it means is that the survivors are those who survive. It is by no means certain that the survivors will be "best" at anything but survival. Furthermore, Darwin was explicit in rejecting the view that adaptation was a conscious or purposeful process. A bird does not develop talons for the purpose of seizing prey, but those birds who inherit longer, stronger claws survive and have more offspring than those without this variation. The same, Darwin speculated, holds for mental processes.

The theoretical implication of this principle relates to the problem of the continuity or discontinuity of species. Continuity theory holds that the human being has no unique attributes but differs in degree from the other primates, or from animals in general. Discontinuity theory holds that humankind is a unique and distinctive phenomenon with attributes (such as a soul) that cannot be demonstrated in the "lower" animals. Although this latter view sounds like "creationism," a more scientific term is *species-specific behavior*. Baby chicks inherit a specific tendency to peck at visible objects; puppies do not, but they do have a sucking reflex. People may possess species-specific attributes remote from the concept of soul. We have been familiar with this controversy ever since Descartes; it is by no means resolved.

In some respects, all sciences accept the continuity theory. Physiology and anatomy are built on the continuity hypothesis. Even biochemistry contributes impressive evidence of the similarities of species. Nonetheless, there are gaps between species, by definition. Hence, one psychologist may rely on the *similarity* of white rats and college sophomores, whereas another emphasizes the differences. In a rough way, we can characterize behaviorism as favoring continuity, and humanistic psychology as stressing the unique attributes of *Homo sapiens.*

Francis Galton, a cousin of Darwin, had an even more direct impact on the development of psychology as a science. He became an enthusiastic propagandist for Darwinism, as well as a researcher seeking evidence to support it. Galton hypothesized that individual variations enhance the probability of species survival (or extinction). It should be possible to trace these and to relate them to the success of the individual, which, in turn, means more surviving offspring and a large hereditary contribution to later generations. Such contributions may be physical or mental. Galton thus saw a major task of psychology as being the identification of variations in important human attributes, the measurement of these variations, and the establishment of their relevance to human survival.

One obvious variation in human attributes is sensory acuity. Galton studied many individuals with tests of vision and audition. One of his ingenious inventions was the Galton whistle, a device that can be tuned to a pitch near or beyond the upper threshold of human hearing. A somewhat sadistic attitude is revealed in his account of how he first used it: "It is an only too amusing experiment to test a party of persons of various ages, including some rather elderly and self-satisfied personages. They are indignant at being thought deficient in the power of hearing, yet the experiment quickly shows that they are absolutely deaf to shrill notes which the younger persons hear acutely, and they commonly betray much dislike to the discovery" (quoted by Dennis, 1948, p. 277). Today we find that loss of hearing acuity is associated with aging and also with exposure to loud noises, as in some factories, among rock musicians, and in some military services.

Galton also developed a speed-of-association task that was picked up and used extensively at Leipzig. He initiated that dubious gift to social science, the questionnaire, and made surveys of such mental functions as visual imagery. G. Stanley Hall later adapted the questionnaire to the study of children's development, and of course, American social psychology and industrial psychology use it extensively.

Galton's first major publication in this area was *Hereditary Genius* (1869). He studied various eminent persons in western Europe and demonstrated that they came from eminent families; the likelihood that an em-

Archives of the History of American Psychology

Francis Galton, aristocratic advocate of nativism and eugenics; innovator in statistics and research on individual differences

inent person would have eminent relatives was significantly above chance expectancy. The method, of course, is full of fallacies: it ignores the environmental influence—being reared in an affluent family is far different from growing up in a sheep-herder's cottage; and the child of an eminent person gets an initial job halfway up the ladder to success as compared with the farmer's child.

Galton's later work was more scientific. He began measuring the speed of reaction in various tasks, the speed of problem solving, the clarity of reported imagery, and so on. He applied mathematics to the determination of differences from chance. He set up laboratory booths at county fairs and similar meeting places where he encouraged people to take his tests, thereby collecting mounds of data for analysis. He told of walking the London streets estimating the length of noses, keeping a counter in his pocket on which he recorded (1) longer than normal, (2) normal, and (3) shorter than normal—highly subjective but more advanced than the then-current anthropometric procedures.

Another innovation was Galton's study of the predictive validity of tests. He collected data on the examination scores of hundreds of Englishmen joining the Indian Civil Service; he then got their salaries twenty years later. He was able to demonstrate that those with superior test performance in 1861 were ranked higher than their lower-scoring colleagues in 1881. (A later reworking of his data showed the correlation to be only + .26, but when we consider the influences of family connections, seniority rules, and other factors independent of ability, this correlation seems reasonably high.)

Wundt and Titchener had opted for a psychology of the "mind in general"; Galton advocated the study of individual minds. American psychologists still represent these two choices in large numbers.

Granville Stanley Hall

A rival of William James for the post of dean of American psychologists at the turn of the century was Granville Stanley Hall (1844–1924). Although he was not a theoretician, Hall deserves to be classed with the functionalists and to be recognized as an important figure in history.

Hall was an ardent disciple of Darwin and Galton. He received his Ph.D. degree from William James at Harvard in 1878 but later became estranged from James. Opinions differ about whether this estrangement was an Oedipal reaction or sibling rivalry—probably the latter; the consensus seems to be that Hall was extremely ambitious and prestige-motivated; thus he maneuvered to advance his own status, in part by depreciating the importance of James. (We are told by one of his colleagues that he shortened his professional name to G. Stanley Hall because *Granville* sounded pompous, but this story does not fit with his typical behavior and should be discounted. At any rate, he is always listed in bibliographies as G. Stanley Hall.)

Hall's doctoral research was in the Wundtian tradition of physiological psychology; it dealt with the role of muscular sensations in the perception of visual space. He tied this topic to Darwinism by arguing that psychic evolution involved the gradual transformation of muscle fibers into nerve fibers; this view, apparently of some importance in the nineteenth century, has now been abandoned.

Biography

Unlike James, Hall was born into a poor family. He did not take kindly to farm life, and in adolescence (with support from his mother, but opposition from his father), he decided to study for the ministry. As an undergraduate, he was intrigued by John Stuart Mill; he also won many scholastic honors. He then studied at Union Theological Seminary, where he did well in philosophy but poorly in theology. According to one anecdote, Hall was required to preach a trial sermon near graduation time; after hearing it, the president of the seminary declined to criticize the sermon but dropped on his knees to pray for Hall's soul.

Realizing that his forte was philosophy, Hall went to Germany (1868–1871), where he studied both philosophy and physiology, a combination that we know carried high prestige in Germany at the time. On his return to America, he was appointed to the faculty at Antioch College, where he taught, at different times, English, modern languages, and philosophy!

It was the appearance of Wundt's *Physiologische Psychologie* in 1874 that led to Hall's decision to become a psychologist. He immediately started planning to go to Leipzig, but finances interfered. He got a minor appointment at Harvard, which enabled him to study with William James for his doctorate. He had saved some money and left for Germany immediately after earning the degree. In Germany he met Fechner and became Wundt's first student from America.

Back home, he obtained an appointment at Johns Hopkins University, a new institution devoted entirely to graduate study. Here he found a group of young men who later played important roles in the explosive growth of American psychology. The most notable were John Dewey, who later became a spokesperson for functionalism, and J. McKeen Cattell, who initiated testing for college students and for industry. Hall founded a laboratory of psychology at Hopkins and, with typical effrontery, announced that it was the first in the United States. For this, James tartly scolded him, noting that Hall had studied in the Harvard laboratory years earlier.

In 1888, Hall was invited to become president of Clark University, another new institution. In this capacity, he encouraged instruction and research in psychology, actually teaching while handling his administrative duties. For a twentieth-anniversary celebration of the university's founding, he invited Sigmund Freud, C. G. Jung, and other pychoanalysts to lecture at Clark; Freud was tremendously grateful, characterizing this as the first official recognition of his contributions. William James, Titchener, Cattell, and others were invited and enthusiastic. It was on this occasion that James made his famous endorsement of psychoanalysis. W. S. Sahakian (1975) wrote, "Freud left pleased with James' words of parting, with his arms around Freud's shoulder, 'the future of psychology belongs to your work'" (p. 253). We must assume that by this time, James had modified his earlier resistance to the inclusion of unconscious processes as part of psychology.

Hall's enthusiasm for Freud continued after the 1909 symposium. In 1920, he wrote a preface to Freud's *General Introduction to Psychoanalysis* in which he hailed Freud as "the most original and creative mind in psychology of our generation."

Hall was an organizer, an entrepreneur. He initiated the organization of the American Psychological Association (APA) in 1892, inviting some of his friends and acquaintances to meet at Clark University for this purpose. He contrived things so that neither James nor Titchener attended; Hall was elected president by the twenty-six people who were present. (By way of contrast, in 1986, the APA listed some 63,146 fellows, members, and associates, and this is by no means the total of American psychologists, who probably added up to 90,000 for the entire country at that time.) Hall also founded the first American journal devoted exclusively to psychology; the *American Journal of Psychology* got off the ground in 1887.

Hall's Psychology

Although Hall was influenced by Fechner and Wundt, he could not accept their narrow definition of psychology. He felt, for example, that the study of children was of great importance, but obviously they could not provide the rigorous introspective reports demanded by structuralism.

He was enthusiastic about Darwin and argued for the genetic approach to psychology, including both individual development and species development. In his Darwinism, he was—as of that period—taking a stand very unpopular in America, just as his sponsorship of Freud exposed him to criticism because of Freud's emphasis on sex.

Hall devoted most of his professional life to developmental psychology. He published books on children (1893), on adolescence (1904), on youth (1906), and on old age (1922). He formulated a plan for compiling empirical data on the developmental changes in children's behavior, which was later carried to completion by his student Arnold Gesell (1880–1961). Gesell's behavioral atlas revealed remarkable uniformities in the appearance of certain behaviors; although his work has been criticized for using only white middle-class subjects, his data strongly suggest that many motor activities resemble the unfolding of inherited patterns rather than learning. The observations show, for example, that crawling appears considerably in advance of walking, yet it is most improbable that the child has observed adults crawling and has imitated them.

There is less theorizing in Hall's writings than in those of William James or John Dewey. He is remembered for his arguments in favor of what he called the "recapitulation theory," namely, that each individual child recapitulates in capsule form the historical evolution of the human race. Thus, in a two-volume work entitled *Adolescence: Its Psychology, and Its Relations to Physiology, Anthropology, Sociology, Sex, Crime, Religion, and Education* (1904), he suggested that adolescents like hunting and fishing or cowboy–Indian games because these represented stages in racial development. Somewhat like C. G. Jung, Hall asserted that there is a "general psychonomic law which assumes that we are influenced in our deeper, more temperamental dispositions by the life-habits and codes of conduct of we know not what unnumbered hosts of ancestors" (cited in Lowry, 1982, p. 105). Although this may purport to be an evolutionary view of psychology, it directly contradicts Darwin's thesis that only variations in innate structure or function can be involved in the evolutionary modification of species. Hall's view implies a Lamarckian conception of inheriting acquired attributes, a theory generally abandoned today.

Hall was in advance of his time in trying to carve out a niche for the psychology of aging. In his last book, *Senescence* (1922), he proposed that psychologists begin studying the assumed decline in mental performances associated with later life. Although this plea was not immediately successful, the last half of the twentieth century has seen a tremendous expansion of research and theorizing on the aging process. The concept of *functional age*—that some persons function at a level younger than their years would predict, whereas others lose skills and memories faster than expected—has particularly led to evidence that senescence is not a uniform process. In a given individual, one function may decline, another may remain unchanged from earlier norms, and still another may actually improve after the age of sixty or seventy.

Hall was eclectic in his approach; he did not hesitate to lift ideas from James, Münsterberg, Freud, and others as he found them convenient. However, he did not find much, if anything, useful in the work of Wundt and Titchener.

Hall's Students

Although Hall's students did not pile up professional honors as impressively as did Titchener's, they occupied respected places in American psychology. The most prestigious was John Dewey (Ph.D., 1884); J. M. Cattell was a student, although he took his degree at Leipzig. Another less well-known psychologist was Joseph Jastrow (Ph.D., 1886), who wrote in his autobiography that his was the first Hopkins degree specifically in psychology, Dewey's having been in philosophy.

One of Hall's students whose status is rising after decades of neglect is Florence Mateer (Ph.D., 1916). Mateer (1887–1961) did her doctoral research on conditioned responses in infants (years before John B. Watson), repeating Russian work by Krasnogorskii. In 1918, she published *Child Behavior*, which gave more information about her work. To establish a conditioned sucking response, she sounded a bell and then placed a nipple in the baby's mouth. However, to obviate the influence of visual cues, she first placed a soft bandage over the baby's eyes. Within a few repetitions, she found that sucking movements occurred as soon as the bandage touched the face. This experimental procedure had become the conditioned stimulus (a reminder that it is not easy to be sure which stimuli are eliciting learned behavior).

Hugo Münsterberg

Functionalists inevitably gravitated into applied psychology. One of the earliest and most successful of these was Hugo Münsterberg (1863–1916). He took his doctorate in 1885 under Wundt and was brought to Harvard in 1892 to supervise the laboratory. Danish-born but a longtime resident of Germany, Münsterberg resembled J. McKeen Cattell in his concern with individual differences, in contrast to Wundt's quest for universal laws. Also like Cattell, Münsterberg clashed with Wundt over a doctoral dissertation. As Pillsbury summarized the sequence of events, "In those early years Wundt believed that man was directly conscious of the discharge of motor energy to a muscle, that when a man moved a muscle he was aware of the motor nerve-current before it left the cortex, and that this constituted the consciousness of will" (p. 249). Münsterberg had the audacity to argue against Wundt that "everything favored the view that all appreciation of movement arose from the stimulation of the sensory nerves in the muscles while the movement was being executed. He presented his results as a dissertation for his degree and Wundt refused to accept it" (Pillsbury, 1929, p. 249).

After Münsterberg obtained his degree by submitting a noncontroversial dissertation, he reverted to his view that awareness of movement was peripheral, not central. But as Pillsbury commented, "the vanity of controversy" operated in such a way that Wundt later adopted Münsterberg's peripheralist position, and Münsterberg began arguing for Wundt's earlier "centralist" view of the phenomenon. It is interesting to add that contemporary research seems to lend support to the centralist theory, namely, that awareness accompanies the activation of motor cortex nuclei before any muscular contraction—that there can be, in short, consciousness of cortical events in the absence of afferent impulses from peripheral sense organs.

Münsterberg was an ingenious experimenter. For instance, he was not content with descriptive reports on the vividness of sensations; he devised experiments that indicated that vividness was increased by making a *motor response* to the stimulus. This work may have influenced Margaret Washburn in her efforts at reconciling structuralism with behaviorism.

Münsterberg developed what he called an "action theory" of psychology which proposed the study of functional units of behavior rather than consciousness alone. By emphasizing that stimulus, association, and response were integrated into a single action pattern, he supported John Dewey (who had proposed a similar unit but called it a "coordination"). It is probable that James invited Münsterberg to join the Harvard faculty because of his rejection of Wundt. James, never an experimentalist, wanted someone to run the teaching laboratory and was disappointed when Münsterberg, after a few years, began devoting all of his efforts to his applied projects. To replace him, James brought in Herbert Sidney Langfeld, who had been trained by Carl Stumpf, another critic of Wundt.

Münsterberg and Titchener both arrived in the United States in 1892. It is possible that this coincidence prevented Titchener from getting the acclaim he felt was his due. The prestige of a Leipzig doctorate was diffused rather than concentrated at Cornell. Besides, Münsterberg had the advantage of being sponsored by James, already recognized as a major contributor to the new science of psychology.

Münsterberg's status grew rapidly. The American Zeitgeist favored practical contributions. He published an amazing variety of applied texts: *On the Witness Stand* (1908), *Psychotherapy* (1909), *Psychology and the Teacher* (1910), *Psychology and Industrial Efficiency* (1911), and *Psychology and Social Sanity* (1914). He speculated about the use of blood pressure as a lie detection device. He became an object of personal attacks in the period just before our entry into World War I because of his public defense of German war aims; his death in 1916 probably saved him from the treatment accorded J. McKeen Cattell in 1917 (discussed in the next section).

When he began his pioneer research on the selection of street-car motormen, Münsterberg adapted the reaction-time experiment to use meaningful stimuli instead of lights and sounds. Thus he might have figures representing a horse-drawn carriage, a pedestrian, a child on a bicycle, and so on. The job applicant had to size up the situation and respond quickly to a threatened accident. Münsterberg claimed that the motormen selected by his method had dramatically fewer accidents than those chosen by interview.

Münsterberg's views were compatible with those of the rising behaviorist school, and it is interesting to note that Floyd H. Allport, one of his students, wrote the first behaviorist text in social psychology (1924).

Like Hall, Münsterberg contributed to the popularization of psychology. He imitated Galton's practice of setting up booths and demonstrations at fairs and inviting people to test themselves; with Joseph Jastrow, he arranged for such a display at the Chicago World's Fair in 1893. Limited in his influence on the development of theory, he was a major factor in the growth of applied psychology. He was elected to the presidency of APA in 1898.

James McKeen Cattell

Yet another Wundt doctoral student who deviated into functionalism was James McKeen Cattell (1860–1944). Cattell shared with Münsterberg an enthusiasm for applications of psychology and a keen interest in measuring individual differences in the psychological functions that might be relevant to solving practical problems. But he was also an enthusiast about the use of quantitative methods in psychology. Thus he had links to both the "tender-minded" and the "tough-minded" psychologists.

Cattell was born in 1860 to an intellectual family; his father was president of Lafayette College for twenty years. The son received his B.A. from Lafayette in 1880. He then followed the common pattern of migrating to Germany, where he studied with Lotze at Göttingen and with Wundt at Leipzig. He then spent a semester at Johns Hopkins and, as Boring (1950) puts it, "was a student of Hall's by accident." Just why Boring used this phrase is not clear.

In 1883, Cattell returned to Leipzig and Wundt. It was at this time that he is alleged to have approached Wundt and announced, "Herr Professor, you need an assistant. I shall be your assistant." To this, the story goes, Wundt grunted "ganz Amerikanisch," but Cattell had his way and worked with Wundt for three years, receiving his doctorate in 1886. He was very prolific, publishing articles in the *Philosophische Studien,* Wundt's journal; in *Mind,* an English periodical; and in *Brain,* an American journal. He was taken with the reaction-time experiment, which Wundt perceived as an instrument for deriving universal laws and Cattell viewed as a device for comparing individuals on differing mental tasks. He proposed a doctoral topic dealing with individual differences. Wundt again commented "ganz Amerikanisch", but again, Cattell had his way and earned his doctorate with a dissertation on differences in reaction time.

After receiving his degree, Cattell had the good fortune to spend a few months at Cambridge University and to work with Francis Galton. It is clear that his interest in measurement preceded this visit, but he later stated that he learned much from Galton. He was invited back to the United States to become professor of psychology at the University of Pennsylvania, where he also founded a psychology laboratory (1887), but he stayed only two years, going to Columbia University in 1890.

Like Hall, Cattell starred as an organizer and an administrator. He founded the *Psychological Review* with J. M. Baldwin in 1894; later he started a journal called *Popular Science Monthly,* sold it, and replaced it with *Scientific Monthly.* He initiated the publication of *American Men of Science* (although it included women; it is now called *American Men and Women of Science.*)

Cattell is not noted for contributions to theory. Boring (1950) mentioned the shift in Cattell's work on sensory discrimination from reliance on the just noticeable difference to the use of the probable error of a judgment. "The functional formula," wrote Boring, "assumes that the subject is trying to discriminate every difference and failing only when it is too small. Hence it treats of the size of the average error instead of the magnitude of the just noticeable difference" (p. 534).

Like Münsterberg, Cattell suffered anti-German feelings during World

War I. He was a vigorous pacifist, and emotional critics could not distinguish his pacifism from pro-German activism. He was fired from Columbia University in 1917 and sued the university officials for libel; he won an award of $40,000 but he did not win reinstatement to the faculty. After examining the records on behalf of the American Association of University Professors as part of a study of academic freedom cases, Gruber (1972) suggested that Cattell's personality may have been a factor in his discharge. Gruber described him as "a difficult man to get along with . . . 'ungentlemanly,' 'irretrievably nasty,' and 'lacking in decency' " (p. 300). Unfortunately, such descriptive terms may reflect the personality of the critic more than that of the victim. Other observers did not find these attributes in Cattell's personality.

After World War I, in 1921, Cattell took the lead in organizing the Psychological Corporation. The war had won kudos for psychology in the mental testing program and the improved placement of soldiers in the units where they could be most useful. But there were charlatans about who promised to solve all industrial problems with a testing program that often used instruments of low reliability and undetermined validity. The Psychological Corporation was dedicated to developing better tests and to imposing ethical controls on their use. Stock ownership was limited to members of the American Psychological Association. Astonishingly, E. B. Titchener allowed his name to be added to the list of directors, although it is unlikely that he ever took an active part in the board's deliberations. The corporation was eventually sold to a commercial publisher, but it still operates very much as an independent enterprise.

Contributions to Psychology

Although he had little to say about theory, Cattell's contributions to research were not insignificant. One of his early studies demonstrated that the intensity of a stimulus was a major determinant of reaction time. He verified this finding for vision, hearing, and pain due to electric shock. In the area of word associations, he found (as predicted) that even for fluent bilingual subjects, the presentation of a word in the native tongue gave faster associations that if the later-acquired language was used. This implied that there was an additional psychic process, translation, which was measured by the increased latency of response; this in turn suggested that the subtraction of simple from complex reaction time could be used to measure the speed of the additional process. Such an assumption is involved in much contemporary work on "information processing."

A fallacy of the subtraction method was demonstrated by Cattell in a charmingly simple experiment. He asked subjects to name letters as they appeared in succession through a slit in a screen. He got the average naming time (about 0.5 seconds) when only one letter was visible at a time. If, however, the slot was widened, so that a second letter became visible while the first was being named, the mean time per letter decreased by some 0.025 seconds. Further widening, to three letters, led to another decrease in mean time of 0.016 seconds, with four letters visible, the decrease in time was 0.01 seconds, and with five letters, there was another decrease, but of only 0.005 seconds. Clearly, Cattell reasoned, parallel processing was going on; a search for the name of the later letter was going on while the name of the earlier letter was being voiced. This experiment is important because it shows that subtraction cannot give the exact time required for the additional process; it is strange that experimenters in the 1980s were still relying on this logic, which Cattell undermined in 1886 (see Chapter Nineteen).

Cattell demonstrated that forward associations are more potent than backward associations. Ebbinghaus, it will be recalled, had demonstrated that remote associations could still facilitate learning, but he had tested these only in the forward direction. Cattell found, for example, that if a person is asked to name the month preceding April, the response is slower than for the month following April. In this research, he also laid the foundation for the use of association times as a clinical diagnostic tool, commenting that these associations "lay bare the mental life in a way that is startling and not always gratifying." Later, C. G. Jung (1904/ 1918) would develop the method in more detail; the well-known Kent–Rosanoff tables were also developed from Cattell's beginnings.

In these reaction-time and association-time experiments, Cattell eschewed any use of introspection. Indeed, in typical functionalist style, he insisted that his procedure was more scientific than that of Wundt: "Most of the research work that has been done by me or in my laboratory is nearly as independent of introspection as work in physics or zoology" (Boring, 1950, p. 538).

It has been said of Cattell's psychology that "It is a psychology of human *capacity*" (Boring, 1950, p. 539). Historically we can trace this approach to the Scottish faculty school, but Cattell was interested in determining capacities by means of objective tests rather than in hypothesizing their existence from the observation of social activities or from *a priori* speculation. He initiated a rather elaborate testing program for entering freshmen at Columbia and was disappointed when the performances did not correlate well with each other or with academic success. Nonetheless, it was an attempt to apply the theory of functional psychology to a concrete problem, and it spawned the vast expansion of testing in America. He was chosen president of APA in 1895.

As Cattell's work on testing was atheoretical, it is not necessary to say more about it here. It differed, of course, from the work of Alfred Binet in France and C. E. Spearman in England, each of whom theorized that "intelligence" was a single factor, a general quality of the organism, underlying performance on psychological tests, and also from the work of

L. L. Thurstone, whose theory proposed the existence of relatively independent "primary mental abilities." Because these theories do not interlock well with general theoretical psychology, they will be explored separately (see Chapter Twenty).

John Dewey

One of the early spokespersons for functionalism was John Dewey (1859–1952). As I have already noted, Dewey beat James in the race for an American textbook that would reflect this kind of orientation. He differed from most of his generation of psychologists in having no direct training in Germany. Having been a student of G. Stanley Hall at Hopkins, he was imbued with a functionalist approach; Hall had already abandoned the strict Wundtian view to which he had been exposed at Leipzig.

Dewey was also influenced by C. S. Peirce, the founder of "pragmatism" as a philosophical doctrine. Peirce is remembered particularly for his definition of meaning: "What a thing means is simply what habits it involves" (1878, p. 286). This, of course, has elements in common with Titchener's "core-context" theory but shifts the focus from sensory consciousness to responses.

Dewey's claim to being a "founder" of functionalism rests on an article, "The Reflex Arc Concept in Psychology" (1896). Its place in history depends on the fact that it challenged atomistic conceptions of human conduct. Oddly enough, Dewey did not specify just whose conception of a "reflex arc" he was denouncing, and today's reader may find the article puzzling. Boring (1950) stated that Dewey was really attacking Titchener (Titchener had said relatively little about behavior, but he had used the reflex concept), and that, as a reply to Dewey, Titchener (1898) had offered the assertion that psychologists must develop a clear taxonomy of events and actions. Sometimes the real issue in a debate becomes unclear as observers forget the context within which the debate occurred.

Dewey's article echoed some of Münsterberg's theorizing. Dewey called his functional unit "a coordination," a term devised, apparently, to sound distinctive and to emphasize the internal unity of the person. A coordination is a stimulus–response unit, not a chain of separable events. Dewey wrote that "the reflex arc idea, as commonly employed, is defective in that it assumes sensory stimulus and motor response as distinct physical existences, while in reality they are always inside a coordination and have their significance purely from the part played in maintaining or reconstituting the coordination" (quoted in Dennis, 1948, p. 357). And similarly, "stimulus and response are not distinctions of existence, but teleological distinctions, that is, distinctions of function" (p. 361). A coordination, then, is an integrative unit based on the functional significance of seeing and behaving; the separation between stimulus and response is seen as both arbitrary and unrealistic. Although couched in terms of movement, this has a notable similarity to the criticisms offered by Gestalt theory against both structuralism and behaviorism. It also spells out the nuclear concept that identifies the slim thread uniting the "functionalists" as a recognizable tendency in American psychology, that is, an emphasis on adaptive response, not on consciousness.

A coordination either is a habit or will become one. The Dewey conception, which is reasonably representative of all functionalists, is that habit is a way of adapting to the environment. It must therefore be flexible because the environment often changes. A rigid reflex system would not have survival value in such a world. Dewey argued against what he called a reflex, but his logic would hold for any highly rigid stimulus–response connection. He wrote, "The essence of habit is acquired predisposition to ways or modes of response, not to particular acts" (1922, p. 42). Behaviorism, particularly in its early form, endorsed the more specific, rigid stimulus–response connection as its central concept.

James Rowland Angell

Probably the best theoretician in the functionalist group was James Rowland Angell (1869–1949). A student of William James, he also spent some time in Germany, presumably sampling different universities; he has been variously described as a student at Würzburg (Murphy, 1941, p. 230), at Berlin (Sahakian, 1975, p. 364), and at Halle (Schultz, 1981, p. 164). This would not be unusual; students regularly flitted from one university or institute to another. Completion of an original research project and "defense of the thesis" were the major hurdles to a doctoral degree. It was alleged by Schultz (1981, p. 164) that Angell submitted a dissertation at Halle, but his German was so poor that he would have been required to rewrite it, and he returned to America instead.

Angell was born into an academic family. His grandfather had been president of Brown University; his father was president of the University of Vermont and later, of the University of Michigan. Angell studied with John Dewey at Michigan, and at Harvard with William James. He received a Harvard M.A. in 1892, having earned one at Michigan in 1891. He taught at the University of Minnesota and then moved to join Dewey at the University of Chicago, where he remained until 1921. He left Chicago to become president of Yale University. He was elected president of the APA in 1906.

Angell's Contributions

Although it cannot be argued that Angell founded functionalist psychology, he gave it form and theoretical sophistication. More philosophically oriented than Cattell, and less active in research, he contributed mainly by defending the functionalist position against its critics. His introductory textbook, *Psychology* (1904), was a great success and undoubtedly influenced many young people who were being attracted to the field. His best formal paper is his presidential address to the APA, "The Province of Functional Psychology" (1907).

Angell proposed three interrelated conceptions of a functional psychology:

> We have to consider (1) functionalism conceived as the psychology of mental operations in contrast to the psychology of mental elements; or, expressed otherwise, the psychology of the how and why of consciousness as distinguished from the psychology of the what of consciousness. We have (2) the functionalism which deals with the problem of mind conceived as primarily engaged in mediating between the environment and the needs of the organism. This is the psychology of the fundamental utilities of consciousness; (3) and lastly, we have functionalism described as psychophysical psychology, that is the psychology which constantly recognizes and insists upon the essential significance of the mind-body relationship for any just and comprehensive appreciation of mental life itself. (Quoted in Hilgard, 1978, p. 99)

Angell noted that these three aspects of functionalism were sharply different from Titchener's structuralism. Titchener's version of psychology was essentially static and analytical; functionalist doctrine is represented as being dynamic and integrative. Angell accused the structuralists of isolating themselves from the rest of psychology; the process of setting up a specialty means exaggerating the differences from neighboring sciences (see Chapter One).

One gathers from reading Angell that controversy in those days was, to say the least, vituperative: "when the critics of functionalism wish to be particularly unpleasant, they refer to it as a bastard offspring of the faculty psychology masquerading in biological plumage" (quoted in Hilgard, 1978, p. 83).

In a conciliatory vein, Angell proposed the view that every mental event "can be treated from either point of view," that is, structural or functional. However, he made it clear that in his opinion the structural approach offered little of value. He compared it to the biologist's teasing apart the muscle fibers of a specimen, after which, of course, it can no longer function as a muscle.

Angell paid his respects to William James, repeating the James criticism of structuralist research as committing the "psychologist's fallacy" of analyzing a conscious experience into sensations, images, and feelings, and then supposing that they are present in the original experience. He likewise adopted Dewey's concept of coordination as a complex act relating stimulus to response rather than separating them.

The treatment of consciousness as synonymous with adaptive reactions to novel situations seems insightful. Like Washburn, Angell called attention to the fact that self-consciousness is clearest when one is solving a problem involving choice; when habits become routinized, consciousness wanes and disappears. Although not using the term, he came very close to the idea that consciousness may be a species-specific form of behavior that is a major factor in the survival of the species *Homo sapiens*.

One more constructive feature of this article should be noted. This is Angell's idea that "the mind–body relation" can be treated as "a methodological distinction rather than a metaphysically existential one" (quoted in Hilgard, 1978, p. 97). If one adopts a monistic hypothesis that there is only one kind of "stuff" in the universe, then some of the phenomena can be analyzed in a physicalistic fashion, and other data in a mentalistic or psychological mode. This logic eliminates the Cartesian dilemma of the interaction between incompatibles that bothers every dualistic philosophy. In a sense, Angell accused his functionalist colleague Mary Whiton Calkins of the dualistic error; he complained of her "refusing to allow the self to have a body, save as a kind of conventional biological ornament" (quoted in Hilgard, 1978, p. 96).

There were several other functionalist psychologists who would merit attention here if more space were available. Harvey A. Carr was an active proponent of the functionalist doctrine, and John A. McGeoch expanded significantly on the phenomena of learning in this theoretical vein. However, none of them did as well as Angell in expounding a specific formulation of functionalism's "vague intentions" (Angell's phrase), and tying it to specific principles and tactics.

James Mark Baldwin

In recent years, there has been a noticeable increase in interest in the contributions to American psychology of James Mark Baldwin (1861–1934). Baldwin, who was elected president of the American Psychological Association in 1897, was influential in the area of developmental psychology that had been opened up by G. Stanley Hall; like Hall, Baldwin toyed with the idea that individual development recapitulated racial and cultural evolution. His book *Mental Development in the Child and the Race* (1895) relied heavily on his observations of his own children. J. M. Broughton (1981) called attention to the fact that it was Baldwin, and not Piaget, who introduced the concepts of assimilation and accommodation into the study of psychology.

Broughton considered Baldwin a functionalist who never accepted that label. Broughton (1981) wrote that Baldwin found a place for consciousness in his theorizing: "Mind was a psychophysical system relating organism and environment, but with a structure represented by consciousness" (p. 399). Baldwin also offered a "law of mental dynamogenesis": that each sensory input carries with it an implicit motor significance, that is, a reflex, as the reflex had been conceptualized by William James. Titchener toyed with the dynamogenesis idea but eventually rejected it, and much of Gestalt theorizing sounds as if a comparable principle were operative (e.g., when a perception carries with it a "demand character" for some type of action).

Baldwin also set the stage for explorations of social psychology. His major concepts in this connection were suggestion and imitation. That is, parents and other adults suggest certain ways of perceiving the environment, and of appropriate associations of ideas; the child also imitates the behavior of parents and others in defined social roles, thus acquiring the patina of civilization. Baldwin anticipated F. H. Allport by proposing the "circular reflex" as the basic process in the acquisition of spoken language by the child.

Broughton (1981) cited evidence that Baldwin had considerable influence on his American colleagues and also on Piaget and other Europeans who studied children. He did not, however, explain why Baldwin became virtually invisible for decades and why he has only recently come into professional view. Further research on Baldwin's career and ideas may reveal answers to these questions. His discharge from Johns Hopkins over a "sex scandal" may have been relevant.

Mary Whiton Calkins

Another brilliant psychologist who has been unduly neglected was Mary Whiton Calkins (1863–1930). A victim of sex discrimination, she studied psychology under William James but was not allowed to register for a degree. James certified that she had met all of the requirements, but the Harvard University authorities firmly refused to grant her a Ph.D. She was later offered a doctorate through Radcliffe College (a unit within Harvard), but she turned it down.

In theoretical psychology, she contributed mainly to the field of personality theory and self-psychology. Titchener took a position with regard to the self which resembled that of David Hume; Hume thought that although we talk about the self, we cannot observe it introspectively, and it is thus not a part of scientific psychology. Calkins adopted a different style in introspection, which is sometimes called *naive realism,* or *phenomenology,* in which meanings as well as sensory elements play a part. Her argument resembles that of Descartes. Calkins (1921) wrote, "Because I am directly conscious of a unique, a relatively persisting self in relation to its environment, therefore I assert the existence of a self and scientifically study its constituents and relations" (p. 278). And she quoted with approval another psychologist, S. Witasek: " 'Psychic facts belong to

Archives of the History of American Psychology

Mary Whiton Calkins, creative innovator of a "self" theory of psychology

individuals; a feeling, for example, is either mine or somebody else's' "
(Calkins, 1921, p. 278). This experience of belongingness was also being
stressed at that time by the rising Gestalt school in Germany, and we
know that Calkins was familiar with the doctrine.

Calkins (1921) accused Titchener and the structuralists of inconsistency. She said that they implicitly assumed the existence of a self while
overtly denying its existence "when they describe consciousness in such
words as 'I attend to a color,' . . . and still more when they mark off
certain experiences as peculiarly personal; that is, as especially related to
myself" (p. 279).

This humanistic orientation was carried through logically in Calkins's
self-psychology (1921): "As a merely perceiving self I am bound to this
desk, this loom, this plot of ground; but as a remembering self I am
hampered neither by 'now' nor by 'then.' I go beyond my own actual
experience, I see visions, I dream dreams" (p. 126). Clearly the psychol-

ogy she espoused reached far beyond the narrow scope of structuralism.

Aside from her work on the psychology of self, Calkins was active in laboratory work. She devised the paired-associates learning experiment and published research using it (Calkins, 1894). She received high praise from her professors: Münsterberg, who was not noted for saying kind things about students, wrote that "she is the strongest student of all who have worked in this laboratory in these three years. . . . [she is] one of the strongest professors of psychology in this country" (quoted in Furumoto, 1979). This comment was written in 1894, when the psychology faculty was still trying to induce the Harvard University authorities to award the doctorate she had earned. The university turned down these pleas and, as late as 1927, rejected the recommendation of a panel of distinguished psychologists that she be given her degree. Prejudices die hard.

Calkins, like Cattell, was strongly opposed to war. She echoed her mentor, William James, whose article on the "moral equivalent of war" had proposed substitute outlets for a supposed instinct of pugnacity. Although she accepted the hypothesis that such an instinct occurs in human beings, she denied the inference that war was inevitable. She showed a very modern way of thinking in her proposals for diminishing frustrations and for increasing substitute outlets for aggression. Some of her ideas can be found in the Yale book (Dollard et al., 1939: *Frustration and Aggression*). Calkins was also a feminist, but not much of her energy was devoted to fighting discrimination against females; she targeted war and international relations as her area of concern.

Robert Sessions Woodworth

The psychologists listed so far in this chapter considered themselves functionalists or at least accepted that label. Two later psychologists seem to fit this pattern as well, although they classified themselves differently. Robert Sessions Woodworth considered himself a "dynamic psychologist," and Edward Lee Thorndike called himself a "connectionist." In all major details, I think they qualify as functionalists.

Woodworth (1869–1962) attended Harvard University and studied with William James but elected to transfer to Columbia University and took his doctorate with Cattell in 1899. He was the first American psychologist to make motivation a central concept in his theory of psychology. At one time, he even proposed that psychology be called *motivology*. His was not a complex theory of instincts comparable to that being developed at the time by Sigmund Freud; rather, he was interested in the goals that people strive for and the way in which these goals become integrated with habits. He proposed that "mechanisms become drives" (1918), meaning that a habit, if it leads regularly to goal achievement, will acquire dynamic attributes of its own and will continue functioning in the absence of the needs for which it was originally developed.

Woodworth toyed with the idea of mastery of the environment as a kind of generalized motive; he described it as "the tendency to deal with the environment as a primary drive, and indeed as *the* primary drive in behavior" (1918, p. 133). At about this time, Alfred Adler (see Chapter Fifteen) was formulating his concept of mastery as the fundamental motive in human behavior.

Woodworth spent a year in Würzburg with Külpe (see Chapter Five), a forerunner of the Gestalt theorists, and he came back convinced of the importance of "imageless thought." This was, of course, antithetical to the ideas of Wundt and Titchener but was compatible with the ideas of the functionalists.

The men whom Woodworth especially *disliked* in American psychology were Titchener, John B. Watson, and Hugo Münsterberg. Woodworth objected to the limited view of psychology expressed by Titchener (sensory consciousness) and by Watson (muscular movement), arguing that psychology embraced both sensory input and response output. The reason for his dislike for Münsterberg is less obvious. Boring (1950) quoted Woodworth as rejecting Münsterberg because of an alleged statement by Münsterberg that "a scientific psychology could never envisage real life" (p. 565)—but this statement is not even typical of Münsterberg, who spent many years applying psychological theories to real-life problems.

Both Titchener and Watson used the formula $S-R$, that is, a stimulus leads to a response. Woodworth held out for a formula $S-O-R$, meaning that a stimulus affects an organism, and that the two jointly produce the response. This view was sketched earlier. Woodworth also brought in a Darwinian argument: Behavior must have survival value, and this means survival of the organism. Like other functionalists, Woodworth emphasized flexibility of adaptation as opposed to rigid reflex behavior.

Woodworth sponsored another interesting concept in the field of memory: the schema. The term has a close kinship with attitude and mental set. An event, he said, is stored in memory in the form of a skeleton or outline. Trivial details may be lost completely, and in some instances, details are added to make the memory more "typical." This view of remembering as an active process subject to distortions broke with the British associationist tradition and leaned toward Freud's idea that memories express unconscious emotional impulses (See Bartlett, p. 437).

Boring (1950), a historian of high status, held that from World War I to the rise of Clark Hull, Woodworth was the dean of American psychology. This point could be debated, but there is no question that Woodworth was respected and influential. He was honored by election to the presidency of the APA in 1914. However, he did not make Coan's (1979, p. 81) list of the "top five" in psychology in any decade.

Edward Lee Thorndike

Edward Lee Thorndike (1874–1949) also attained substantial eminence in American psychology. He never called himself a functionalist and preferred the label *connectionist* for his variety of psychology. He meant that, like the British associationists, his interpretation of psychological data leaned heavily on the learning and remembering of associated events. (He rejected Titchener's ejection from psychology of all meaningful material.)

Thorndike is remembered mainly for his discussion of learning as being dependent on the "law of effect" and the "law of exercise." The principle of exercise turned out to be nothing more than the familiar associationist principle of frequency of contiguity in space and time. The "law of effect" introduced the problem of reinforcement as a factor in learning, an aspect long ignored by his predecessors. Thorndike asserted that "satisfying effects" stamped in learning of new responses, and that "annoying effects" prevented learning. This grew into the principle of reinforcement, but the introspective implications of *satisfy* and *annoy* caused the behaviorists to switch to the terms "positive" and "negative" reinforcers, and the Gestalt psychologists to endorse the terms positive and negative valences.

Thorndike, prompted by Gestalt critiques of his mechanistic view of associative connections, initiated a novel line of research that unintentionally gave the Gestalt approach some support. This related to the principle of contiguity. The hypothesis was that if two items frequently occur together, they will become associated. Thorndike had subjects memorize pairs of sentences. He found that if one word in a sentence was presented, the next word in that sentence was regularly supplied. However, if the stimulus was the *last* word in the first sentence, virtually no one responded with the *first* word of the second sentence. The words in one sentence hung together as a configuration, or Gestalt (Thorndike did not use the word *Gestalt*), and there was no associative link to the first word of the next sentence. Mere contiguity, then, was by no means adequate as an explanatory principle. Regrettably, Thorndike has been remembered more for the "law of effect" than for his ingenious study of the inadequacy of the classical principles of association. His defenders argue that Thorndike's *satisfier* was not defined solely as pleasure, and that *annoyer* was not defined as unpleasantness. Each was treated operationally as eliciting a continued approach to the incentive, or as continued avoidance of the learning situation. This does not help much; in such a definition, a satisfier is something that facilitates learning, and an annoyer is something that interferes with learning. But this is what

Thorndike wanted to explain. His "law of effect," then, turned into a tautology.

Thorndike was a student of Cattell, and he taught for many years at Columbia University. He was president of APA in 1912 and was ranked by Coan (1959) as one of the top five figures in psychology for three decades (1900–1929).

Functionalism: A Summing Up

The need for a professional identity and a defined territory pressed Wundt and Titchener to delineate a rigid view of "scientific psychology." In rebelling against that constriction, the functionalists drew together, though with far less unanimity of interpretation than the followers of Titchener. The very pragmatism that the functionalists used as a symbol of group identity was also a license for individual diversity; "truth" was "what worked," and given the variety of the study environments—laboratory, field, school, and industry—it was inevitable that some principles that seemed to work well in one context might contradict those that had been successful elsewhere. It is even arguable that this is as it should be; the "laws" of psychology may always be situation-specific. Certainly this position has been aggressively promoted by K. J. Gergen (1985) as well as by others sharing this view.

Rigidity can create an impulse toward flexibility, and too much flexibility can prod some members of a discipline to reassert a tighter theoretical framework. Thus, we should regard, at least in part, the theoretical systems of Clark L. Hull, Kurt Lewin, and Sigmund Freud as a rebellion against functionalism. We could also speculate that the real rebellion was against structuralism, and that functionalism was merely a way station on the road to behaviorism. Washburn, Dewey, and Angell can all be viewed as trying to unite the study of consciousness with the study of behavior.

Modern psychology has a clear-cut legacy from structuralism. The simple theoretical structure mapped out a set of problems in sensory consciousness and, in a few decades, exhausted the field. Most of the interesting problems faced by the structuralists have been solved, and the body of our knowledge in this area derives from structuralist research.

Functionalism left no such legacy. Perhaps it would be best to say that, like William James, who was so good at asking penetrating questions, the functionalists were good at identifying problems. Among these, it is appropriate to mention dynamics and the nature–nurture controversy. Dynamics had been virtually ignored by Titchener; the functionalists faced up to it but did not make much progress. They did, however, point to the evolutionary significance of instinct: an organism that inherited impulses of an antisurvival nature would not survive. One criterion of a valid instinct, then, would have to be survival value. The behaviorists and the psychoanalysts accepted this dictum; the former stressed the instinctual needs for the survival of the individual, whereas the Freudians emphasized the survival of the species.

The problem of heredity and environment is clearly linked to instinct but goes beyond it. The emphasis on individual differences compelled psychologists to ask the question: Where do these differences originate? One possible answer is hereditary capacity; the other is environmental opportunity or handicap. An offshoot of the problem is the structure of intellect; that is, if individuals differ in performance, is this difference due to the inheritance of a general cognitive superiority, or to the inheritance of specific talents (the readiness to acquire some skills more rapidly than others)? Environmentalists do not face this problem; variations in specific areas are attributed to variations in childhood opportunities and to the motivation to acquire relevant habits and skills. Thus we see the shape of modern psychology emerging from the "vague intentions" of the functionalists.

CHAPTER 9

Early Behaviorism

One of the principles governing the association of ideas, according to the British empiricist-associationists, is *contrast.* A presentation of one idea tends to evoke an association opposite (in some sense) to the first. In logic, a similar principle is dialectics: one proposition tends to generate its opposite. Colloquially, this idea has been enshrined in academic circles in the epigram "A college professor is a person who thinks otherwise."

A dialectical approach may help us to develop a meaningful framework for classifying the different approaches to psychological theory. Historically, we have seen that the dominant trend in Western psychology up to the middle of the nineteenth century was epitomized by British empiricism and associationism. This was a tradition of introspection, of reflection, of the association of ideas by simple linkages, of the motivation to seek pleasure and to avoid pain. When Wilhelm Wundt set out to transform this armchair psychology into a laboratory science, he assumed that psychology should be the study of consciousness. His student E. B. Titchener took the carelessly assembled materials of Wundt's psychology and transformed them into an elaborate set of prescriptions defining the boundaries of the new psychology.

Thereafter some psychologists reacted negatively to Titchener and posed alternate solutions. This opposition was not necessarily a point-by-point rejection of everything that the structuralists wrote. Rather, some critics seized on one component of the theory and rejected it, although accepting the remainder. Some rejected elementarism. Others objected to the study of consciousness. And still others sought to modify the study of consciousness, making room for the study of responses.

The functionalists, prodded by Titchener, became more self-conscious about their postulates. Definitions of "psychology" took shape as the polemics proliferated. By 1910, there were two psychologies in America, with only a modest overlap.

In the next decade, another rebellious movement, behaviorism, took form. John B. Watson's definition of the new religion opposed Titchener and structuralism and then quickly excluded the functionalists. Watson proposed prescriptions defining psychology that did not coincide with the boundaries stated by Titchener or by Angell. Watson retained an atomistic or elementaristic approach but banished consciousness from his variety of psychology.

In constructing this progression in the study of psychological theories, I have had the most difficulty with psychoanalysis. Freud may not have known about Titchener—and certainly did not care about him. On the other hand, Freud was well informed about British associationism; one of his publications was a German translation of a book by John Stuart Mill. Furthermore, Freud expressed his negative view of Wundt in no uncertain terms. It is not unreasonable to say that psychoanalytic theory, too, can be seen as an antithesis to Titchener's work. This figure of speech will be elaborated later; the first overt rebellion was behaviorism.

The Roots of Behaviorism

About the relation of Watson's new psychology to structuralism there can be no question. John B. Watson made his bow on the stage of psychological theorizing with explicit opposition to introspection and to the concept of consciousness. Much of his opposition applied as well to functionalism. In his doctoral research, under J. R. Angell, Watson was required not only to observe the behavior of his rats; he also had to speculate about their mental processes. His doctoral dissertation (in 1903) was entitled *Animal Education: The Psychical Development of the White Rat.* He resented this requirement and, as soon as his doctoral degree was safely in hand, he began a counterattack. By 1913, he was sure enough of his footing to publish what some call the behaviorist manifesto: *Psychology as the Behaviorist Views It.* He received some heckling on the implication that he was *the* sole behaviorist; in 1919, he yielded and titled his first textbook *Psychology from the Standpoint of a Behaviorist.* His message was well received: by 1915, he had been elected president of the APA when he was only thirty-seven years old.

This brief sketch makes it sound as if behaviorism, like Athena, sprang full grown into the world. This is obviously not true. I have indicated the importance of the French mechanists, especially Condillac and La Mettrie, who described behavior without recourse to soul or mind. Less well known, but of greater importance, was the Russian background.

The Russian Antecedents of Behaviorism

Czarist Russia provided some of the ideological ancestors of behaviorism. The following account, while necessarily brief, will indicate some of Watson's intellectual sources.

Ivan Mikhailovich Sechenov

Sechenov (1829–1905) was originally trained as an engineer, but as a young man, he developed an interest in psychology. He went to Germany and studied with Helmholtz, Johannes Müller, and others of the physiological psychology school.

Sechenov's first and most important book was *Reflexes of the Brain* (1863/ 1965). In it, he propounded the view that "all acts of conscious or unconscious life are reflexes." Although he was ostensibly discussing the brain, he anticipated Watson by focusing on responses. *"All the external manifestations of brain activity,"* he wrote, "can be attributed to muscular movement (1863/1965, pp. 3–4; italics in original). Thus his speculative neurology was transformed into an objective observation of muscular actions.

Sechenov's approach was analytical in the style of Descartes: *"All psychical acts without exception, if they are not complicated by elements of emotion . . . are developed by means of reflexes. Hence, all conscious movements (usually called voluntary), inasmuch as they arise from these acts, are reflex, in the strictest sense of this word"* (quoted in Herrnstein and Boring, 1965, p. 317; italics in original). And his environmentalism was as thorough-going as that of John Locke: *"The initial cause of all behavior lies, not in thought, but in external sensory stimulation, without which no thought is possible"* (Herrnstein and Boring, 1965, p. 321; italics in original).

Vladimir Mikhailovitch Bekhterev

Bekhterev (1867–1927) founded the first laboratory of experimental psychology in Russia in 1886. He had studied in France, with Charcot and DuBois-Reymond, and also in Leipzig with Wundt. He is also noted for founding the first research journal with the phrase "experimental psychology" in the title. Wundt, it will be remembered, had founded an earlier journal but called it *Philosophische Studien.*

Bekhterev broke with Wundt over the question of introspection as the only valid method for psychology. Instead, he argued for a focus on behavior as the proper methodology. His first book in psychology, *Objective Psychology,* was published in Russian in 1907, but no translation into a Western language was available until 1913. Watson recorded that he encountered the French translation in 1914 and immediately seized on the reflex as the appropriate unit for his analysis of behavior. According to Hilgard and Marquis (1961), "During the winter of 1914–1915, Watson's seminar at the Johns Hopkins University was devoted to the translation and discussion of the French edition of Bekhterev's (1913) book" (p. 24). This is a little puzzling in that Watson consistently used the spelling *Bechterew* of the author's name, which is the German transliteration of the Cyrillic alphabet. However, in those days, graduate students were required to read French and German, and both editions may have been used.

Although Bekhterev was in most respects a follower of Sechenov, he expanded psychology somewhat from Sechenov's restricted view. For example, Bekhterev conceded that both external and internal stimuli were involved in learning, inhibition, generalization, and extinction. He also wrote of conditioning, but focused on motor reflexes such as lifting the foot to an electric shock, and this is the model that Watson used exclusively in his presidential address to APA (Watson, 1916). Ivan Pavlov's work on the conditioned salivary reflex had barely been mentioned in the American literature at that time; it was 1927 before any major book of Pavlov's became available in English.

Oddly enough, Bekhterev also tossed in a bit of Lamarckian biology. He speculated that man "is a product both of the past life of his ancestors (racial experience) and of his own past individual experience."

Ivan Petrovich Pavlov

Pavlov (1849–1936) is the best known of the Russian psychologists, or reflexologists. His first career was in the study of digestion, for which he won a Nobel Prize in 1904. While working on the digestive juices in the dog, he observed that the flow often increased as if food had been taken in. Pavlov correctly identified these as evidences of learning. When he decided to explore the learning process, he switched to the salivary reflex because it was so much easier to tap and measure. At first, he called the conditioned reflex a "psychical" reflex; later he became annoyed by this term and fined his laboratory workers five kopeks if they used it.

To collect his data, Pavlov made a small opening in the dog's cheek and inserted a cannula through which drops of saliva could be conducted to the outside, where they fell into a measuring gauge. Time from the signal was recorded automatically so that the duration of the response, as well as the total secretion, could be investigated.

The basic model was association by contiguity. The experimenter rang a bell and then placed some meat powder in the dog's mouth. After a few combinations of these stimuli saliva flowed at the sound of the bell. This was the conditioned reflex (CR). If the bell was sounded several times without food, salivation would decrease and then stop. Pavlov called this *extinction*. If the bell alone produced food, but the bell plus a light did *not* produce food, the animal soon stopped secreting in response to the combination; this Pavlov called *conditioned inhibition*. If a tone of 512 Hertz was used as the food stimulus, a tone of 256 Hertz would produce a smaller amount of saliva, and a tone of 128 Hertz would produce virtually none. This spread of response to a similar stimulus Pavlov labeled *stimulus generalization*.

Time relations were also investigated. The earliest experiments presented the conditioned stimulus just before (or simultaneously with) the unconditioned stimulus (food). Pavlov established delayed CRs by starting the conditioned stimulus (CS) some seconds before food, and by gradually lengthening the interval. *Trace* reflexes involved ending the CS before the food was presented. Pavlov also tried to establish a backward CR (food before the CS), but this effort was a failure, much as Thorndike (p. 159) had failed to get backward associations.

The empirical findings of the Pavlov laboratory fill volumes. I am concerned here with his theoretical interpretations, as these were carried over into American behaviorism. He started with the Descartes version of a reflex (1927, p. 6) and analyzed all complex behavior into reflex units. Thus he had essentially an atomistic theory like Titchener's. He also assumed that these reflexes could be glued together, somewhat as in James Mill's "mental mechanics," so that the execution of one reflex became the stimulus for the next. Contiguity and frequency were the two agents which held the pieces together.

Pavlov's neurology was highly speculative. Essentially he postulated a cerebral cortex laid out like tiles on a bathroom floor; a given stimulus would activate a specific one of these centers. When one center was activated, neighboring cells would be *inhibited,* and this inhibition could be accentuated by the extinguishing of responses to nearby stimuli. If the animal were faced with an impossible task (e.g., salivating to a circle but inhibiting response to an ellipse of 9:10 ratio), the animal would break down, bite the harness, shiver, bark, and howl. Pavlov attributed such "neuroses" to incompatible waves of excitation and inhibition in the cortex. It is an interesting exercise to compare his description with that of Dollard & Miller (p. 213), Kurt Lewin (p. 278), and Sigmund Freud (p. 301).

Signal systems is the term devised by Pavlov for fitting his observations into a Darwinian framework. He wrote that "under natural conditions the normal animal must respond not only to stimuli which themselves bring immediate benefit or harm, but also to other physical or chemical agencies—waves of sound, light, and the like—which in themselves only *signal* the approach of these stimuli" (1927/1960, p. 14). These signals of imminent food or imminent danger constituted a *primary signal system.* He also postulated the existence of a *secondary signal system;* he conceived of this as an outgrowth of secondary conditioning, in which a signal *for a signal* provided the CS. The secondary system is of limited interest in animal behavior, but when Pavlov wanted to speculate about human learning, he laid great stress on the role of the secondary signals.

Psychological atomism was a major assumption in Pavlov's theory. He proposed to analyze all behavior into simple stimulus–response connections:

> An external or internal stimulus falls on some one or other nervous receptor and gives rise to a nervous impulse; this nervous impulse is transmitted

along nerve fibers to the central nervous system, and here, on account of existing nervous connections (reflexes), it gives rise to a fresh impulse which passes along outgoing nerve fibers to the active organ, where it excites a special activity of the cellular structures. Thus a stimulus appears to be connected of necessity with a definite response, as cause with effect. (1927/ 1960, p. 7)

Pavlov's methodology was designed to insure that a single stimulus would be linked to a single response; the procedure limited the incoming stimuli (soundproof, light-controlled room; the experimenter was in a different room communicating by mechanical signals only to the experimental animal). Like Wundt and Titchener, Pavlov wanted to be sure just which stimuli were effective.

There is a good deal of evidence that Pavlov's strategy did not work. Animals can learn to respond to the experimental conditions in ways not contemplated by the psychologist. As in Florence Mateer's studies of infants (p. 145), the experimental setting itself can come to control behavior. Herbert Liddell, an American psychologist who worked for some time in Pavlov's laboratory, told of a dog conditioned to salivate when a metronome beat was accelerating, but not when it was slowing down. One day, when the dog was not in harness but the metronome was ticking (and slowing down), the animal ran to the metronome and pushed it with his nose, seeming to try to speed it up (cited in Hothersall, 1984, p. 358). Back in his laboratory at Cornell University, Liddell performed an amusing experiment with a sheep to demonstrate the point. The sheep, in harness, heard a bell, followed by shock to a forefoot. In a short time, the animal would lift her foot as soon as the bell sounded. Now Liddell turned the sheep upside down so that her head, not her foot, rested on the metal shock plate. When the bell sounded, she lifted her head off the plate but *did not flex the leg* (Liddell, *et al.*, 1934). Clearly, what had been learned was much more complex than a simple bell–leg flexion connection.

Pavlov derived many generalizations from his experiments and interpreted them in neurological terms. For example, he noted that activation of a specific cortical area—for example, cells representing the skin on the right shoulder—would induce an inhibitory process in the cortical cells immediately surrounding this activation. Thus he inferred that the cortex can be considered a mosaic, or set of tiny areas, and that these affect each other in the living organism. He concluded that "The cerebral cortex can accordingly be represented as an exceedingly rich mosaic, or as an extremely complicated 'switchboard.' " (1927/1960, p. 219). The mosaic metaphor is descriptive, the switchboard is an analog for the function of connecting stimulus to response. Neither represents an empirical observation.

Pavlov (1927/1960) also propounded an equilibrium theory of behavior that has been largely neglected by American psychologists: "Every material system can exist as an entity only so long as its internal forces, attraction, cohesion, etc., balance the external forces acting upon it. . . . Being a definite circumscribed material system, it (the organism) can only continue to exist so long as it is in continuous equilibrium with the forces external to it" (p. 8). Thus Pavlov conceded a determinative role for internal states and stimuli that has been ignored in later behavioristic theorizing.

Max F. Meyer

Although John B. Watson is commonly cited as the founder of behaviorism, Max F. Meyer (1873–1967) had a legitimate claim to the title. Meyer got his doctorate in Berlin under Carl Stumpf, a rival of Wundt, and under Max Planck, the famous physicist. It is likely that Meyer's training in physics contributed to his widely cited research on hearing (which was also a major interest in Stumpf's laboratory) and probably nudged him toward his theoretical endorsement of an objective approach to psychological phenomena. We shall see this tendency exaggerated in A. P. Weiss, Meyer's most distinguished student. Meyer's first book, *Fundamental Laws of Human Behavior* (1911), clearly antedated Watson's earliest formulation (1913). On the other hand, we know that Watson was making speeches about an objective approach before his 1913 manifesto. It is quite likely that some of his ideas were influenced by Meyer.

Meyer's psychology was a curious blend of behavioral observation and speculative neurology. It is a nerve-ending source of surprise that psychologists who write so firmly about psychology's limiting itself to observable data should then indulge in flights of fancy about the unobservable that may be going on somewhere inside the cerebrum.

In a second book, *The Psychology of the Other One* (1921, 1922), Meyer developed more elaborately the idea that the only scientific psychology is one that eschews introspection and concentrates on understanding the actions of the "other" person. Although this book appeared well after Watson had staked out his position as an objective psychologist, Meyer did not mention Watson at all (nor did Watson ever acknowledge the existence of Meyer's theorizing).

Meyer's view of learning was a strict connectionism, but it was marred by his reliance on the theory of "neural drainage," the notion that excitation aroused in one cortical area may be "drained" into another if the two are simultaneously active (compare p. 108). Meyer could have got this idea from William James, but it is more probably derived from the writings of J. Von Uexkull, a brilliant speculative biologist. The assumption, of course, was that repeated "drainages" carved a pathway that would then provide the neural basis for a habit.

Dr. Robert S. Daniel, Department of Psychology, University of Missouri, Columbia, Missouri

Max F. Meyer, the first systematic behaviorist in America.

Some of Meyer's neurology was even more startling. He wrote of geometrical designs in the grouping of atoms in the central nervous system (1922, p. 137) and evolved a kind of Pythagorean magic-number series for preferential linkages of some stimuli with others: "A neuron accommodating, so to speak, a group of 30 [atoms], may also readily accommodate a group of 45 atoms—perhaps on account of the same factor (15) existing in both numbers" (1922, pp. 137–138). How "objective" this explanation of behavior is!

On the other hand, there are many modern ideas in Meyer's writings. He was impressed by the process of learning motor skills, which was being investigated by functionalists influenced by Cattell and Thorndike. He noted that many random movements are made at first, and that slowly the nonessential motions drop out to leave the skilled performance in relatively pure form. This is essentially the view later propounded by Watson; Meyer (1922) referred to it as "motor condensation" (p. 120). He also identified the kind of learning in which one reflex replaces another, and he anticipated Watson in treating thinking as "internal language." He proposed that the muscular contractions of talking to oneself may become too weak to produce audible sound and yet may integrate movements (representative of ideas) into a conclusion. He even extrapolated this process to the point of speculating that mere activation of the appropriate neural circuits in the brain, without any efferent activation, might effectively reproduce speech processes and thus initiate thinking. Although Meyer may not have known of Pavlov's work, he hit on a formulation of language learning based on conditioning, describing step by step the stages that are now familiarly credited to F. H. Allport (1924); see Figure 9.2, p. 189.

Meyer (1922) sided with Wundt and Titchener on the question of general laws versus individual differences: "The psychologist is interested only in the fundamental laws of the Other-One's life, not in the special form which these laws take when applied to particular historical, geographical or ethnological conditions" (p. 9).

Meyer formulated the term *sensory condensation* to label a process by which a part of a total situation could reinstate a memory of the entire situation as originally perceived. This appears to be a new label for what William Hamilton had earlier called "redintegration" (p. 71). Meyer, of course, did not treat this as a revived *consciousness* of the original event; it was only a reinstatement of the total *response* to that occurrence.

Meyer also examined the phenomenon of inhibition. Using the same example employed by William James (the burnt child avoiding the fire), Meyer conceptualized inhibition as the deflection of a nervous impulse from its expected outlet to a different motor response (a solution very similar to that earlier devised by Freud in his *Scientific Project,* see Chapter Fourteen). Meyer speculated that the flame as a visual stimulus elicits only a weak nervous process, whereas the flame as heat releases a powerful impulse. On later occasions, "the stronger nervous process would sufficiently deflect the flux of the weaker nervous process" (1922, p. 95). It may be that Meyer was groping for a conditioned-reflex interpretation of the phenomenon; the statement is not clear. He also advocated close observation of the development of the behavior of the child, anticipating Watson's work on the emotions.

Contemporary Assessment of Meyer

Pillsbury's *History of Psychology* (1929) gave priority to Meyer as the founder of behaviorism: "The first man to write a completely behavioristic explanation of human action was Max Meyer . . . in *The Fundamental Laws of Human Behavior,* published in 1911. In this work all psychology is restricted to a discussion of action, and action is explained as primarily reflex, with such variations as would occur owing to inaccuracy in the physiological adjustment" (p. 290). Further, Pillsbury commented, "Meyer insists that all the functions ordinarily studied by introspection and stated in terms of consciousness may just as well be described in terms of movement and nervous processes, and science would gain in clearness by the change" (p. 291).

The Missouri Sex Scandal

Like Freud, Meyer was a victim of the puritanical attitudes of that era regarding sex. In what seems to have been a purely accidental manner, Meyer offered some help to a student and became the victim of a "sex scandal" at the University of Missouri. At the time, O. Hobart Mowrer, a graduate student in a sociology course, did a questionnaire study of "economic aspects of women" and asked coeds a number of questions, three of which dealt with premarital sex. Meyer was involved only to the extent of making some suggestions on wording and allowing Mowrer to use envelopes from the department of psychology. When news of this "sex study" reached the St. Louis newspapers, they made a great scandal out of it. The sociologist was fired, and Meyer was suspended for a year without pay, but Mowrer survived and later became president of the American Psychological Association.

John Broadus Watson

The name virtually synonymous with behaviorism is, of course, John Broadus Watson (1878–1958). Watson was a charismatic character, aggressive and forceful in his presentation of his ideas. As has already been intimated, some of these may have been borrowed from the Russians and from Meyer, but Watson popularized them and cleared the way for behaviorism to become the dominant psychology in America for half a century.

Biography

Watson was born near Greenville, South Carolina, in 1878 and was married in 1903 to Mary Ickes, the sister of Harold Ickes who was later to be an important figure in national politics. Watson described himself as "lazy, somewhat insubordinate, and, so far as I know, I never made above a passing grade" in the Greenville schools (Murchison, 1936, p. 271). His aggressive pattern showed up early; he was arrested at least twice, once for fighting, and once for shooting off firearms inside the city limits.

A rebellious pattern was also manifested early: "Professor Moore . . .

said that, if a man ever handed in a paper backwards, he would flunk him. . . . By some strange streak of luck, I handed in my final paper in Civics backwards. He kept his word" (Murchison, 1936, p. 272).

Although his parents had expressed the hope that he would enter the ministry, Watson decided to enroll in the University of Chicago to study philosophy. He soon found Dewey, Angell, and the other psychologists and switched to that specialty. He introduced an amusing sidelight on academic politics in his autobiography; he wanted to do his doctoral research under Jacques Loeb, a famous biologist, but "Neither Angell nor Donaldson in those days felt that Loeb was a very 'safe' man for a green Ph.D. candidate," so Watson was pressured to do his research under Angell on the increasing complexity of behavior in the white rat as correlated with medullation of the central nervous system.

Watson devised sundry tasks for his rats, determined the age at which the average animal could solve the task, and then examined the central nervous system to correlate the process of medullation of fibers with sudden increases in ability to deal with complicated problems. As D. Cohen (1979) noted, much of this was trial-and-error on Watson's part; there was no generally accepted model of animal behavior he could follow. Watson wrote that he enjoyed working with the rats, but Cohen (1979) commented, "he did not have to construct elaborate analogies about what humans who behaved in the same kind of way might be introspecting" (pp. 31–32).

Watson's thesis, *Animal Education,* was judged to be so outstanding that Henry Donaldson, the neurologist who supervised the histological work, lent him $350 to have it published. It was a long-term loan; according to Cohen it was repaid only after twenty years.

Angell was also enthusiastic in his praise of Watson the graduate student, although his feelings cooled with the campaign Watson later mounted for behaviorism, "which my student and assistant developed in such an extravagant manner" (Angell, 1936, p. 26). Angell also deprecated "the excesses of behaviorism as a cult," a charge echoed by Edna Heidbreder (1933) in her history of psychology. Nevertheless, Watson acknowledged Angell's helpful attitude, and it would not be realistic to ascribe Watson's theorizing to an Oedipal hostility to Angell. The explanation may still have been personal, but in a different vein. It was the custom at Chicago (as everywhere) for graduate students to serve as observers in one another's research. Watson was often asked to introspect about his imagery and conscious states and found this very frustrating. According to those who knew him, his imagery was quite poor. His own comment was "I hated to serve as a subject. I didn't like the stuffy, artificial instructions given to subjects. I always was uncomfortable and acted unnaturally" (Murchison, 1936, p. 276).

In 1908, he moved from the University of Chicago to Johns Hopkins University, still an important center of psychological training despite Hall's departure some years earlier. Watson enjoyed working with Adolf Meyer, a psychiatrist with a decidedly objective slant, and with a brilliant graduate student, Karl S. Lashley. Watson credited Lashley with coining the term *conditioned emotional reflex* to refer to Watson's experiments on learned fears in infants. Lashley also accompanied him on a summer trip to the Dry Tortugas to study instinctual and learned behavior in noddy and sooty terns (Watson, 1909). The project involved testing the limits of genetically determined behavior in newly hatched chicks and the ease of modifying these responses through learning. H. F. Harlow (1969) deplored the premature ending of the study; he felt that if Watson had pursued these experiments, he would have accepted the importance of instincts and would have avoided the excesses of environmentalism that followed his rejection of innate patterns. Harlow noted that, according to Lashley, the expedition ended because they ran out of cigarettes and whiskey; this shortage, Harlow speculated, had a deplorable effect on the history of psychology.

Watson interpreted his study of the terns as validating the empirical approach (direct observation as opposed to armchair speculation). He had planned the research to identify hereditary and learned components in the behavior of chicks from the time of hatching until they functioned independently of their parents:

> In order to understand more thoroughly the relation between what was habit and what was hereditary . . . I took the young birds and reared them. In this way I was able to study the order of appearance of hereditary adjustments and their complexity and later the beginnings of habit formation. My efforts at determining the stimuli which called forth such adjustments were crude indeed. Consequently my attempts to control behavior . . . did not meet with much success. (1914, p. 90)

It seems clear that some hereditary behaviors were identified; yet in later years, Watson espoused an aggressive environmentalism that completely ignored these innate components.

During World War I, Watson was in the Aviation Medical Corps, working on the effects of oxygen deprivation (planes were not pressurized in those days). Many trainees were flunking out of the pilot-training program, and the U.S. Army set up a task force to investigate the causes. According to Watson, this group involved an obstetrician, a pediatrician, and an otologist. Not a single person (psychiatrist or psychologist) specializing in human behavior was on the task force, Watson wryly noted.

Another outcome of the war was Watson's concern with sex. He was impressed by the high rate of venereal diseases among the troops and speculated about the intensity of the sex drive. He was already acquainted with some of Freud's writings; in his autobiography, Watson mentioned reading Freud beginning about 1910. By 1917, Watson was firmly con-

Archives of the History of American Psychology

John B. Watson, an aggressive propagandist for a behavioristic psychology

vinced that sex was an important but neglected area of psychology. At
the end of the war, he returned to Johns Hopkins and enlisted a female
graduate student, Rosalie Rayner, to do experimental studies of physiological changes during sexual intercourse. The records of bodily responses were duly recorded on kymographic tape. Unfortunately for the
history of science, Watson's wife discovered the project and got the boxes
of recordings, which were presented as evidence in her suit for divorce.
After she won the case, she burned the records. McConnell (1983) considered this a major blow to the advancement of scientific knowledge,
but the gap has been adequately filled by the more sophisticated researches of Masters and Johnson (1966).

It can be considered evidence that human beings do not learn from
examples that Watson replicated the behavior of J. M. Baldwin, who had
induced him to move to Johns Hopkins University and had been forced
out over his sexual nonconformity. Watson's reading of Freud evidently
did not immunize him against the power and irrationality of the sex
drive.

After a short period of unemployment, Watson was invited to join an advertising firm and became financially quite successful. Incidentally, E. B. Titchener, with whom Watson had indulged in raucous polemics, was one of the psychologists who wrote letters of recommendation and provided encouragement at this time.

Watson never did any further research, but he continued to give lectures and to propagandize for behavioristic ideas. He married Rosalie Rayner, who later wrote a magazine article, "I Was the Mother of a Behaviorist's Sons" (1930). They shared credit for the preparation of the book *Psychological Care of Infant and Child* (1928), which prescribed a rigidly scheduled, impersonal way of dealing with infants that is now viewed with horror by child psychologists. Watson engaged in public debates with Wolfgang Köhler, a leading spokesperson for Gestalt theory, and with William McDougall, who emphasized instinct theory, as opposed to Watson's brash environmentalism.

Watson's election as president of the APA in 1915, when he was only thirty-seven, attests to his prestige in academic psychology. After the Johns Hopkins affair, he fell in the esteem of his colleagues, but in time their feelings mellowed. He was given an unusual honor by the APA in 1958, shortly before his death; he was awarded a gold medal for distinguished contributions to the science of psychology (Schultz, 1981, p. 207.)

Psychology According to Watson

Watson self-consciously set out to revolutionize American psychology. Although he had been giving lectures favoring an objective alternative to structuralism (and the introspective component of functionalism) for some years, the landmark year for the foundation of behaviorism as a theory is 1913. In that year, he published an article entitled "Psychology as the Behaviorist Views It," which is often referred to as the behaviorist manifesto. The opening sentence read, "Psychology as the behaviorist views it is a purely objective experimental branch of natural science. Its theoretical goal is the prediction and control of behavior. Introspection forms no essential part of its methods" (1913, p. 158). The article set off extensive debate and controversy.

There is a curiously rebellious tone in much of the article, enough to justify the suspicion that Watson's emotions played a significant role in his decision to attack the established doctrines of American psychologists. He wrote, "Should human psychologists fail to look with favor *upon our overtures* and refuse to modify their position, the behaviorists will be driven to using human beings as subjects and to employ methods of investigation which are exactly comparable to those now employed in the animal work" (1913, p. 159; italics added). This suggests, first, that Watson was taking the role of spokesperson for the animal researchers, perceived as opposing the human psychologists, and second, that the animal psychologists felt somehow excluded, having made overtures and being rejected. Watson was inviting psychologists to choose sides for an inevitable clash.

Actually, the points made in the "manifesto" were radical only with respect to introspection. In simplified form, the argument ran as follows: (1) introspection is not and should not be the preferred method of psychological research—in fact, it should be abandoned; (2) there is no need to translate behavioral observations into "conscious" states; (3) it is pointless to speculate about the place in evolutionary theory for consciousness—the problem is irrelevant; (4) psychologists have been explaining contradictory results in research by blaming the training of observers, when they should be examining their experimental designs; and (5) the body–mind controversy is obsolete—we should adopt a materialistic monism. Of these, Point 4 probably had the most salutary effect on the progress of scientific psychology; the two decades after this 1913 essay were marked by important progress in improving research designs and procedures.

G. Murphy (1949) commented that even in his presidential address to the APA in 1915, Watson was still attacking introspection without offering a suitable alternative. Watson described, in that address, the use of a motor conditioned reflex in the study of sensory discrimination. A finger response was conditioned to a colored stimulus, and then negative stimuli (not reinforced by shock) were introduced. "The differential reaction," Watson (1916) wrote, "can be so highly perfected that it becomes possible to use it with great accuracy in determining difference limens on human subjects" (p. 100).

W. S. Sahakian (1975) suggested the possibility that Watson's manifesto got more attention within the profession because Titchener attacked it: "By attacking he dignified behaviorism by centering the attention of the entire community of psychologists on this budding school of thought, instead of permitting it to go unnoticed" (p. 369). This seems improbable. The trend away from structuralism, and from the concern of the functionalists with conscious components of behavior, was too strong. At most, Titchener may have accelerated the movement by a few years.

Determinism

Having discarded the problem of psychical causation and mind–body interactions, Watson (1924) could adopt a simple and rigid materialistic determinism: "There must be an *invariable* group of antecedents serving as 'cause' of the act" (p. 5). However, forgetting his own studies of the terns, as well as his observations of the innate reflexes of human neonates, he extrapolated this assumption of rigid cause–effect determinism to an extravagant environmental determinism. His ideas echoed those of

John Locke, whose conception of the mind as a *tabula rasa,* a blank slate on which the environment could write freely, was widely discussed in American philosophy classes, of which Watson took many.

The most exuberant of Watson's statements on the dominance of the environment is found in his book *Behaviorism* (1930): "Give me a dozen healthy infants, well-formed, and my own specified world to bring them up in and I'll guarantee to take any one at random and train him to become any type of specialist I might select—doctor, lawyer, artist, merchant-chief and yes, even beggar-man and thief, regardless of his talents, penchants, tendencies, abilities, vocations, and race of his ancestors" (p. 104). The inclusion of race is particularly striking, for Watson made no secret of his anti-Negro feelings, a typical outcome of the kind of community in which he grew up. The statement as a whole, he admitted, went beyond the evidence; but his environmental bias is hardly debatable.

His conception of instinct merely serves to illustrate more clearly the downgrading of heredity. The "instincts" he listed included such items as yawning, grasping, the Babinski reflex, spreading and closing the fingers, leg and arm movements, sucking, blinking, and crawling. These fragments of behavior are the raw material to be integrated through the process of learning.

Learning

Watson conceptualized learning largely as being a matter of selection and sequencing. Sensory stimuli elicit the reflex movements previously cited; some are retained and others eliminated. "We can define habit," Watson (1924) wrote, "as a complex system of reflexes which functions in a serial order when the child or adult is confronted by the appropriate situation" (p. 294). He implied that the sensory stimulus disturbed some kind of equilibrium or adjusted state: "In observing the 120-day infant we saw that instinctive factors came into play as soon as it was faced by a situation to which it was not adjusted" (p. 303). Similarly, the random series of movements terminated when that adjustment was restored.

Watson's theory of learning, as it had developed in his first textbook (1919), placed the major emphasis on contiguity. Reinforcement was not recognized as inherent in the use of either food or electric shock as unconditioned stimuli. Thus major attention was given to time relations, frequency of repetition, massed practice versus distributed trials in learning, and so on. Chaining was proposed as a way of linking simple reflexes into complex habits. Watson also seemed to adopt (without credit) the phenomenon that Max Meyer had called "motor condensation," that is, the dropping out of unnecessary movements from a myriad of random movements. The major explanatory concepts are these in this selection process:

1. *Recency.* The successful group of movements is always the last one to appear before the series stops, as adjustment is achieved.
2. *Frequency.* The successful movement is sure to occur at least once on every trial; hence ultimately, frequency will pile up to make this the preferred response.
3. *Reinforcement.* Any act that brings food, water, relief from pain, and so on will result in "heightened metabolism," which "fortifies" the neural process associated with the successful act.
4. *Emphasis.* The successful act is often an emotion-producing one, with possible effects due to hormones, for example, strengthening the neural connection.

Watson did not use either "reward" or "reinforcement" as a theoretical concept. He did, however, come down strongly against the use of punishment with children, primarily because close contiguity of misbehavior and punishment is hard to achieve, and also because punishment is likely to become associated with the parent, thus engendering hostile attitudes that negatively affect future learning from the parent.

Watson described the linkage of reflexes into series as depending on the functioning of kinesthetic sensations as connectors. That is, the feedback from the first movement in a sequence becomes the cue for the second movement, the kinesthetic sensation from the second movement cues the third, and so on (Figure 9.1). Watson apparently did not use the term *chain reflex,* but this seems to be an appropriate label for the complex act as he conceived of it as developing. The concept was borrowed from William James (see p. 107) with no acknowledgment—as was typical for Watson.

It is clear that he conceived of the conditioned reflex as being simpler than habit. The differentiation seems to be based on the fact that conditioning can take place in one trial (Watson, 1930, p. 209), whereas habits require "the stamping in of the successful movement" and "stamping out of unsuccessful movements." The wording here is curious, inasmuch as it is a quotation from Thorndike, whose approach Watson had criticized. It is possible that the essential controversy was over the use of the terms *satisfiers* and *annoyers* by Thorndike to identify positive and negative reinforcers; these terms have a subjective connotation which would have been aversive to Watson.

Watson was not unwilling to cite structuralist research where it could be reinterpreted to fit his approach. For example, he analyzed the experiment by Stratton (1897) with inverting lenses (see page 125) as a case of learning new responses: "Walking and movements of the hands with open eyes were extremely awkward. . . . When the subject reacted to objects with eyes closed the old habits reasserted themselves and the reactions were made correctly" (Watson, 1924, p. 433).

Watson perceptively related the disturbance of Stratton's adjustments

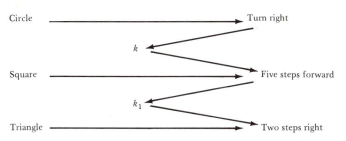

FIGURE 9.1   Response Chaining according to Watson

Watson (1930, p. 209, p. 219) described linking of specific responses into a firm sequence; the muscular activity elicited by the first cue becomes an adequate stimulus for the later movements.

to the problem of personality maladjustment. In this, he may have been influenced by Pavlov's experiments on neurosis in animals (produced by the presentation of stimuli conditioned to opposite reactions), which were known in this country by the time Watson wrote his textbook. In fact, Watson mentioned that Lashley had replicated some of Pavlov's studies, although he did not specify the neurosis research.

Complex Learning

In his 1924 book, Watson expanded on his treatment of complex learning processes. He assumed that these could be handled on the basis of a variety of random movements from which the correct responses could be selected:

> When put in front of a problem the solution to which cannot be effected by an immediate instinctive act or by one belonging to his past habit acquisitions, the whole organism begins to work in each and every part but without working together. Not only are the arms, legs and trunk active, but the heart, stomach, lungs and glands as well. . . . On each succeeding attempt . . . some of these part reactions fall together in such a way as to facilitate succeeding movements. (pp. 314–315)

Because the components of the final integrated response are always in the total activity, whereas the unnecessary components vary from trial to trial, *frequency* results in the retention of the essentials, the other responses being eliminated. Thus Watson's formulation bears an obvious kinship to Meyer's "motor condensation," in which irrelevant motions drop out and those leading most directly to success are preserved. It is interesting that neither Meyer nor Watson assigned any role to reinforcement or goal achievement, although Thorndike's studies on the law of effect were well known at the time.

Emotions

In the course of his explorations of the infant's reflex endowment, Watson also examined some responses that he labeled "emotions" rather than reflexes, although he seemed to view them as belonging to the same category. He concluded that the neonate has three emotional patterns, which he labeled "fear," induced by loud sounds and falling, or loss of support; "rage," induced by the restraint of movements of the arms and legs; and "love," induced by stroking the erogenous zones: lips, nipples, and genitals. Watson validated his judgment that these were different response patterns by having obstetrical and pediatric nurses watch as he applied the appropriate stimuli, and they agreed with his verbal labels.

The crucial pair, of course, were anger and fear, as the love response (cooling, gurgling, and relaxation) was clearly different from the responses to the two "unpleasant" states. Mandel Sherman (1927) sought to ascertain whether fear and rage could really be distinguished by observers. He repeated Watson's stimuli (loud sounds, falling, and restraint) and filmed both the stimulus and the response. When his judges (pediatric and obstetrical nurses) saw the entire film, they agreed with Watson's labels for fear and rage; but when Sherman showed the response without the stimulus, the labels were applied at random. In other words, judges based their labels of the responses on their awareness of which stimulus had been applied.

This is actually a behavioristic version of Titchener's "stimulus error." (see p. 122). Titchener had warned his observers not to allow incidental information (the nature of the stimulus object) to influence their reports of conscious experiences. Obviously, when Sherman's nurses saw both the stimulus applied and the infant's response, their expectations determined the label they attached to the infant's behavior. When this information was not available, they could not discriminate between the two alleged response patterns. This finding is also relevant to current speculations about the concept of emotion as a form of social communication; that is, the situation is evaluated as one in which anger would be appropriate, and the person behaves in a way that communicates, "I am angry." (For a further amplification of this idea, see Averill, 1982.)

The Story of Little Albert

Of course, Watson wanted to demonstrate the conditioning of emotions. Choosing fear as the simplest case, he explored possible stimuli. He found that most of the traditional fears of children (e.g., snakes, fire, and the dark) did not elicit any fear response in the infants at the Johns Hopkins Hospital. Only a loud noise or the loss of support (falling) elicited the "fear" pattern. He decided to try to condition this fear to the sight of an animal.

Albert was the eleven-months old child of a woman who worked in the hospital. Unsuspectingly, she gave Watson permission to study the infant's reactions. Albert showed no anxiety when a white rat was presented; he reached for and stroked the animal. Watson then arranged for several paired presentations of a loud sound immediately following the appearance of the white rat. Soon Albert reacted to sight of the rat by turning away and crying, and Watson concluded that the animal had become a conditioned stimulus for fear. This case has been described as a basic fact of the psychology of emotion for some sixty years.

F. Samelson (1980) examined the publications dealing with "Little Albert." He found that Watson gave differing descriptions of his procedure in various published reports; however, none of these deviations seemed adequate to cast doubt on Watson's conclusion. More damning was an observation that Samelson turned up in an article (Watson and Rayner, 1920) about the filming of Albert's "conditioned fear." Whenever Albert was upset, he would "continually thrust his thumb into his mouth [thus becoming] impervious to the stimuli producing fear. Again and again [while making the movie] we had to remove the thumb from his mouth before the conditioned response could be obtained" (p. 13). It is thus impossible to decide whether the crying was due to fear of the rat or to annoyance at having the thumb removed.

The crucial theoretical point is that Watson never claimed that Albert had developed a *conditioned response* of *putting his thumb in his mouth.* Yet this was Albert's immediate response to the presence of the animal. Watson preferred to speak of a conditioned fear, but it might be more accurate to say that Albert had acquired a conditioned anxiety state that was relieved by thumb sucking. At the very least, Little Albert proved that the initial response is not the *only* response conditioned to a novel stimulus. The issue becomes relevant when we consider theories of behavior modification (in Chapter Twenty-one).

Language and Thinking

Watson offered a potentially useful distinction between *vocal* habits and *language* habits. The former are simply conditioned reflexes; the child vocalizes and the presence of external stimuli may be enough to form associations such that the stimulus cues the vocal behavior. This is not genuine language: "Vocal acts or habits, however numerous they may be, do not become *language* habits until they become associated with arm, hand and leg activities and substitutable for them" (Watson, 1924, p. 340; italics added). This means that what linguists call a *symbolic function* must develop if true language is to appear. Chopping down a tree is a physical act; planning the work, or reflecting on the consequences of a deforestation, must be based on the use of words as symbols for reality. In an intriguing speculation about ancient history, Jaynes (1976) echoed Watson by suggesting that language developed as a means of social control: If the chief ordered some men to go out and repair an irrigation ditch, his presence might have been necessary to keep them at work. When they learned to talk to themselves, and so to reinstate the chief's orders, they could keep on the job for the time required.

Watson held that verbalization soon became implicit, that is, inaudible. Some individuals, of course, seem never to reach this level of linguistic functioning; they mouth words as they read, and facial movements can be observed as the person wrestles with a problem of some kind. For most persons, the observable movements drop out when they are no longer necessary, as in Meyer's concept of "motor condensation"; implicit speech is an efficiency measure: "In the acquisition of general bodily acts of skill we have found . . . that every short-cut possible which would abbreviate action and increase speed and skill is finally hit upon by the individual in a trial and error way" (Watson, 1924, p. 344). The use of words to designate and eventually to represent objects is a social process, but language acts learned under stimulation from adults and peers may continue to function in the absence of these other persons.

Although Watson (1924) urged (and attempted) experiments to measure the laryngeal and other movements associated with speech, he protected himself from negative findings by warning that "it is possible that they would be so abbreviated, short-circuited and economized that they would be unrecognizable" (p. 344). This is a kind of parallel with Titchener's defense that if the findings do not fit, it may be because the observer did not know how or where to look.

The use of language as symbol raises the question of meaning. If the verbal responses may become so distorted, so remote from audible speech, in what respect can they function to provide meanings for objects or actions? Watson (1924) evolved a theory which resembles Titchener's "core-context" theory: *"Determine all of the organized responses a given object can call forth in a given individual, and you have exhausted all possible 'meanings' of that object for that individual"* (p. 355; italics in original). Thus the meaning of a knife would comprise all of the verbal and gestural responses it evokes, presumably including some Freudian symbolism. In fact, Watson explicitly referred to daydreaming and rehearsal of memories in this connection.

The identification of thinking with subvocal speech is found in Max Meyer, as also in B. F. Skinner. It is, one may argue, an optimistic perspective, as compared with that of the pessimists such as Montesquieu, who remarked that "The less men think, the more they talk." Obviously the behaviorist can work out a solution to Montesquieu's paradox, but it is not entirely convincing.

Neurologizing

Watson, like so many of his predecessors, allotted a large part of his introductory book on psychology to the nervous system, the endocrine glands, and the musculature. In his best textbook (1924), he devoted 166 pages out of 448 to physiology, including the nervous system; much of the material included had no established relevance to behavior studies. Apparently it was included to strengthen the image of psychology as a "science." (Cynically one might comment that today this space is occupied by discussions of computers, which are for the most part irrelevant to the study of behavior but make psychology seem more scientific.) Oddly enough, Watson himself was at times conscious of this logical paradox, confessing that such neurological speculations were futile: "What possible good does it do when discussing bricklaying or subvocal arithmetic to guess at what goes on in the synapse, in the efferent or afferent leg of the reflex arc or in the muscle itself?" (1924, p. 372). One of Watson's successors, B. F. Skinner, took this counsel seriously and refused to hypothesize anything about processes going on inside the organism. Watson could not quite take this step, even though he perceived it as necessary. He did reject one speculation current in his day, namely, that the synapse could be made more permeable or more resistant by the expansion or contraction of the neurons themselves. Today the debate centers on neurotransmitters, but it is equally remote from what the organism does in relation to its environment.

Applications of Psychology

Watson's aggressive environmentalism predisposed him to be interested in the applications of psychological knowledge to the conditions of life; it is obvious that, if all our mental troubles are due to the environment, the least we can do is try to improve the situation. Some of Watson's suggested applications are held in low repute today; his ideas of child rearing hint of the robotized treatment of babies in Aldous Huxley's *Brave New World*. He opposed kissing, cuddling, and similar manifestations of affection; the father should shake hands with his little son, not hug him, and so on.

On the other hand, he complained of the harm done to children by factory jobs. He wrote that "in the cotton mills of the South, children from fourteen years of age and on are taught to run one loom. As they grow older and become more adept in their work they are given more and more looms to manage . . . the larger the number of separate operations the individual can conduct simultaneously and efficiently the greater is the advantage to the manufacturer . . . it may be extremely detrimental to the organization of the individual himself" (1924, pp. 313–314). Although Watson wrote this in the context of "splitting" of the personality in response to the division of attention across several machines, this speculation is quite compatible with masses of empirical data that show that assembly-line jobs are associated with a variety of personality disturbances.

In another connection, Watson quoted extensively from Frederick W. Taylor about the introduction of improved work methods (1924, pp. 377–378). However, he omitted any credit to Taylor. This omission was probably due to carelessness rather than to a desire to dissociate himself from Taylor, as Watson regularly lifted ideas from other psychologists without any acknowledgment.

In cooperation with a graduate student, John J. B. Morgan, Watson worked out (shortly after reading Bekhterev) a program of research on psychopathology, using the conditioned-reflex methodology as the major tool. Watson's participation ended with his divorce, but Morgan went on to produce an excellent volume, *The Psychology of the Unadjusted School Child* (1924), applying behavioristic concepts to personality development and pathology. After World War II, a whole movement called *behavior modification* applied concepts from Watson, Morgan, Pavlov, Hull, and Skinner to traditional clinical problems. This development will be examined in Chapter Twenty-one.

An early example of this work is that of Edmund Jacobson, whose "progressive relaxation" involved learning to inhibit maladaptive responses by deep relaxation of the muscles involved in "neurotic" behavior. Watson praised Jacobson's work as evidence of the utility of the behaviorist approach; there is some evidence that Jacobson would have been just as happy if Watson had ignored his work (see McGuigan, 1986).

Watson and the Zeitgeist

The success or failure of a new theoretical approach may depend on how well it fits with the Zeitgeist, the social-political-economic environment within which the new ideas were generated. Watson has been a favorite example of the Zeitgeist theory.

I have noted the vigorous pragmatism of nineteenth-century America and the advantage it gave to William James in his arguments with the Wundt–Titchener school. This pragmatism also was a major factor in the amazing spread of behavioristic thinking into child rearing, industrial practices, and social psychology. Watson exploited this attitude, and he poked fun at the introspectionists, especially Titchener, for their remoteness from real problems.

Watson's ideas reached the public eye just after the close of World War I. Flushed with success, Americans believed that all problems could be solved with enough effort. Watson's psychology seemed to say: Do something! Although his disregard for heredity set him against some prejudices, such as those against blacks and Greeks and Italians, his lusty environmentalism encouraged those researchers who thought that society could be rearranged to provide equal opportunity for everyone.

David Bakan (1966) held that Watson's success was due to the rapid industrialization of the United States around the turn of the century and to the war effort. Behaviorism was adopted by management, Bakan suggested, because the new factory system, into which thousands of farm workers were being integrated, required individuals who would do as they were told, without thinking. A response psychology filled this need; an introspective psychology did not. Bakan unintentionally revealed one of the hazards of a Zeitgeist interpretation when he attributed Watson's espousal of Darwinism to Watson's childhood on a South Carolina farm. Now it is true that there are animals on a farm, and Watson seems to have enjoyed working with them; but Bakan was unaware of the intensely Fundamentalist Christianity of rural South Carolina, which still spawns attacks on Darwin. In fact, it may have been Watson's *rejection* of this component of his childhood that led him to endorse Darwin. The moral is: Be sure you know your Zeitgeist before you use it as an explanatory concept.

Albert Paul Weiss

Overshadowed by Watson's publicity, Albert Paul Weiss (1897–1931) has been ill-treated in psychological history. He was much more sophisticated than Watson, at least in the sense of intellectual and philosophical background, and he wrote a more concise and systematized theory of behaviorism than did Watson.

Weiss reversed the tradition in which Americans went to Germany for study, then returned to practice their skills. He was born in Germany but came to this country as a child (not for study). As things worked out, he enrolled as a graduate student at the University of Missouri and came under the influence of Max Meyer, who had trained with Carl Stumpf and Max Planck. Weiss absorbed both of these guiding influences, along with Meyer's rejection of introspection.

He shared Watson's exuberant expectations with regard to the importance of behaviorism. "Behaviorism," he wrote, "claims to render a *more* complete and *more* scientific account of the totality of human achievement *without* the conception of consciousness than traditional psychology is able to render *with* it" (1929, p. vii; italics in original).

Weiss came down firmly in favor of materialistic monism, asserting the point more clearly than Watson. Weiss (1929) wrote, "The *Individual* on the basis of physical monism, is to be regarded as a locus in this movement continuum, and a function (in the mathematical sense) of the changes that are occurring in all other electron-proton aggregates. A human movement is a cross-section of this locus at a given time, is the *effect* of antecedent changes, and the *cause* of subsequent changes" (p. 57; italics in original). So far, so good. But our knowledge of the universe is inside the individual: "The locus of the *cosmic* movement continuum is in the sensori-motor system of the individual, (hence) its properties will depend upon sensori-motor organization, and the properties of the movement continuum can thus only be described as functions of, or in terms of, human responses" (1929, pp. 57–58). So the world is composed of electron–proton aggregates, but our knowledge of it is composed of sensorimotor activities.

Behaviorism, then, is defined as "the science that studies the origin and development of those bodily movements (responses) of the individual which establish his status in the social organization of which he is a member" (1929, p. 143). By *status,* Weiss means here much more than whether people look up to and admire a person. One's status includes one's ability to speak and to read, to calculate and to drive a car; in other words, the psychological relevance of any movement of any part of the body is determined by its relation to other human beings.

This leads us to what may well be Weiss's most important contribution to psychological theory: his distinction between *biophysical* and *biosocial* responses. *Biophysical* refers to the sensory-cerebral-effector mechanisms; thus, movement of your arm as studied by a physiologist would be composed of stimulation, connection, and effector action. But if the movement of your arm brings your fist into contact with my nose, the event becomes a *biosocial* response. Similarly, my thinking might be viewed merely as minimal movements of throat and larynx (biophysical); but it may eventuate in movements that shut down an automobile factory (a biosocial response.)

It is obvious that all biosocial responses must also be biophysical, but that the reverse is not true. Sneezing, coughing, blinking, and so on, which made up Watson's raw material for complex movements, have no biosocial significance and thus disappear from Weiss's version of behaviorism. The utility of the biosocial category lies in the fact that variable movements may have the same function and may thus be classified as different forms of the same response. If I decide to visit a friend in Chicago, I may walk, ride a bicycle, or take a plane. Biophysically these are different; biosocially they are the same.

Weiss's analysis of learning is essentially that of Meyer and of Watson; that is, Weiss placed emphasis on the generation of random movements, the selection of some as successful, and the dropping out of others as irrelevant. He ignored reinforcement as a factor in selection of responses. Indeed, he handled the whole topic of motivation in an unrealistic way. He said that motivation is shown when one continues an activity instead of abandoning it; like so many definitions, this is simply a tautology. It offers no conception of either the innate or the external conditions that may determine the persistence of an activity focused on a certain stimulus (goal), such as hunger and food.

One advantage of reading Weiss is that he stated matters so explicitly that certain problems become highly visible. He had ruled out introspection as a method for psychology. His criterion of a response, therefore, required an external observer. Consider his treatment of color discrimination: "Since science itself is a social phenomenon, *differentiating* can only mean that *two* different sets of movements have been made: (1) a subject has said, e.g., 'this is red,—this is green,' and (2) an observer has recorded the movements of the subject" (1929, p. 214). But consider: Weiss really should have another observer to record the fact that the first observer did record what the subject said, and a third observer to record that the second had recorded what the first observer had done; in other words, once Weiss had rejected the verbal report of the initial subject in favor of a record made by an outsider, he needed confirmation of the observer by another observer and so on, *ad infinitum.* In general, the physical sciences evade this paradox by recording data in such a form that they can be examined independently by two or more observers; however, this method does not eliminate controversy, as when one physicist claims to have found proof of the occurrence of a magnetic monopole, but others look at the same trace and reject the interpretation. Weiss could have done the same; he could have recorded the subject's words ("This is red") and allowed independent observers to debate whether the response corresponded to the presence of a certain wavelength of light. People do make false statements, so one need not accept introspective reports at face value, but there are various ways of coping with the problem. Freud offered a variety of techniques for hunting what he considered to be the truth behind an introspective report.

I have suggested that Weiss's most significant contribution was his distinction between biophysical and biosocial responses. The importance of this latter concept may be found in its numerous applications by later psychologists; for example, E. Goffman (1959) described the process of self-presentation, the ways in which individuals learn to act so as to communicate subtly to others in search of cooperation, affection, or status; and Emler (1984) worked on "reputation management" as a factor in varieties of delinquent behavior.

Floyd H. Allport

Although Watson and Weiss had noted that social stimuli influenced the behavior of children and adults, they had not exploited this field. The earliest theorist to develop a detailed application of behaviorist theory to social psychology seems to have been Floyd H. Allport (1890–   ), whose textbook *Social Psychology* (1924) became a landmark in the systematic application of a theoretical view to an applied area.

Allport took his doctorate at Harvard under Münsterberg, whose theorizing (see Chapter Eight) deviated from Wundt's toward a kind of functionalism or an "act psychology." Allport took this tendency one step further and adopted a strictly Watsonian behaviorism.

Like Watson, Allport emphasized the production of random responses, reflexes, and "emotions," followed by the selection of some responses and the elimination of others. This is not especially different from the point made by William James (1890) that "an instinct is blind only on the first contact with reality" (Vol. II, p. 389). Allport deviated from Watson only in his concentration on the role of social stimuli in learning, and on the acquisition of response patterns of a social nature.

Naturally this tends to limit social psychology to events occurring inside the individual. Allport's (1924) definition of social psychology emphasizes biology: "Social behavior comprises the stimulations and reactions arising between an individual and the *social* portion of his environment. . . . The significance of social behavior is exactly the same as that of nonsocial, namely, the correction of the individual's biological maladjustment to his environment" (p. 3). Thus a family is not a group phenomenon; it is interesting only as a set of stimuli modifying the learned behavior of its members, considered one at a time.

A crucial aspect of social learning is, of course, the acquisition of language. Here Allport adhered strictly to Watson, starting with the babbling reflex of the infant (see Figure 9.2). Before the "neural traces" of sound *production* have faded, the auditory afferents activate the auditory cortex, and the simultaneity of these neural events insures the formation of a connection between them. The sound "da" can now trigger the vocalization "da." This means that the imitation of adult sounds has become possible. Through contiguity, the vocalization becomes associated with visual objects, which thus acquire names. In Allport's formulation, reinforcement is ignored as an effective variable. The whole process is treated like the formation of a telephone connection, as a purely mechanical process. Contiguity (frequency and recency) and emphasis (intensity of stimulation) are the major explanatory principles invoked. The question of motivation as a factor in the acquisition of language is also ignored.

Allport's "circular reflex" hypothesis, which leans heavily on the child's imitating adult sounds, was probably suggested by J. M. Baldwin's (1895) analysis of this phenomenon. Baldwin had emphasized "conscious imitation"; Allport, because of his behavioristic bias, dropped the word *conscious,* probably wisely. The transmission of regional accents and other speech patterns almost certainly depends on unconscious imitation by the child of parental and peer-group sounds. On the other hand, Allport was probably wrong in disregarding the role of motivation and reinforcement; certainly parents and teachers correct nonconformist pronunciation, and playmates will ridicule nonconforming speech.

Allport took over from George Herbert Mead the concept of social role. The sociologists had long stressed the uniformities of social behavior, as in the relations of employer and employee, police officer and citizen, priest and parishioner. Children acquire these role behaviors (ac-

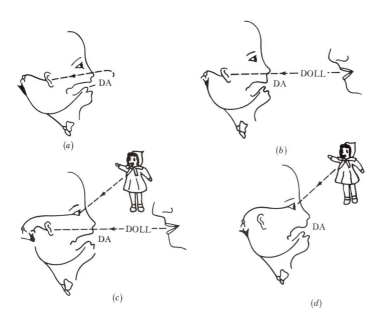

FIGURE 9.2   Acquisition of Language according to Allport

Imitation of adult sounds must precede acquisition of meanings. *(a)* Child
acquires circular reflex; *(b)* adult sound sets off vocalization learned at *(a)*.
Sign functions represent true language: *(c)* simultaneous presentation of
object and adult name makes possible *(d)* the elicitation of sound by the
object alone. *(Redrawn from Allport, 1924)*

cording to Allport) in the same way as speech, by imitation and observation. Allport discovered a phenomenon that he called a "J curve," that
is, a distribution of behaviors piled up at one end of a continuum and
tapering off sharply. Consider, for example, motorists approaching a
stop sign. An overwhelming majority come to a complete stop; a few
may make a "rolling stop"; and very few drive past without slowing.
Allport considered this kind of distribution indicative of social coercion
or conformity, in contrast to distributions of ability or personality traits,
which conform more closely to the normal bell-shaped distribution curve.
Although Allport did not speculate on the variables distinguishing learnings that produced a J curve from those producing a normal curve, it is
plausible to suggest that J curves develop where a highly uniform consensus exists in the child's environment with regard to specified behavior
(e.g., sexual or aggressive acts), whereas normal curves of distribution
are found where many variables operate at cross-purposes, as in the formation of a gregarious tendency.

Given his perspective that all of social psychology is contained within

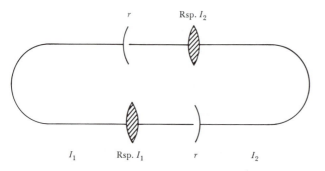

FIGURE 9.3   Allport's Conception of a Reciprocal Social Interaction

Individual one (I_1) emits response I_1, affecting a receptor of I_2 who then emits a response I_2, and so on. This illustrates the theorist's effort to eliminate all but indispensable details from a concept; often the outcome is loss of meaning.   *(Redrawn from Allport, 1924, p. 150)*

the skin (i.e., psychology is concerned solely with the behavior of individuals), it is natural that Allport would deny the status of independent reality to social institutions. Rather, an institution exists only as a verbal symbol in the behavioral repertoires of its members or observers. An institution, he wrote, "is not a tangible thing, but a conceptual relationship of things. The notion of an institution is, in some ways, like the notion of a triangle . . . the triangle itself is not substantial; it is a conceptual relationship" (1924, p. 13). Thus Plato's ideal triangle reappeared in behavioristic camouflage.

As the language example (Figure 9.2) shows, Allport knew that social psychology depended on the interaction of two or more persons. He described "reciprocal social behavior," in which the act of one person becomes the stimulus for the act of another. Figure 9.3 reproduces the illustration that accompanied this concept. It is amusing that he carried over the use of symbols from individual psychology; thus, r = a receptor, and the spindle-shaped element represents a muscle cell, the traditional way of diagramming a response.

There are still a few American social psychologists who cling to this stripped-down, mechanistic social psychology. For the most part, it has been replaced by a Gestalt-phenomenological orientation such as that offered by S. E. Asch (1952) or Kurt Lewin (1951).

Edwin Ray Guthrie

Another behaviorist author was Edwin Ray Guthrie (1886–1959). Less a popularizer than Watson, and less systematic than Clark Hull, Guthrie had some devoted followers at one time, but they have generally disappeared. Guthrie is classified with Meyer, Watson, and Weiss on the basis of his reliance on contiguity and the minimization of reinforcement as explanatory factors in learning. In a rough fashion, he can be characterized as a John Locke who switched from associations of ideas to associations of responses, while clinging to the basic principles of contiguity, frequency, recency, and intensity as determinants of associations.

Behavior, Guthrie held, is a function of environmental stimulation. If food is available, an animal will exert effort (emit responses) to try to obtain it. Many movements will be made in this effort, and the successful responses will be learned. Success, however, is not defined as getting the food; it is rather the *ending* of the activity sequence: the last act is the one learned and remembered. The food has functioned to terminate the response sequence; recency, then, is the principle accounting for its preferred occurrence on a later trial.

A novel feature of Guthrie's theory was that learning of an S-R association occurs in one trial. To account for the gradual perfection of a complex performance, he postulated that the animal may be learning a large number of S-R elements, perhaps only one of them being acquired on a given repetition of the task. Guthrie concentrated on complex performances, such as the behavior of cats escaping from a puzzle box to obtain food (Guthrie and Horton, 1946). This research was characterized by an interesting methodological advance; pictures of the animal's behavior were preserved for study, whereas earlier research relied on observers' notes. The pictures revealed that a given animal might repeat the same solution many times; other animals, however, adopted different specific movements (to paraphrase Weiss, the biophysical responses were different, but the biosocial response was the same).

Guthrie (1952) admitted that there were problems in his formulation that "a combination of stimuli which has accompanied a movement will on its recurrence tend to be followed by that movement" (p. 23). And in a very perceptive sentence, he reminded us that "It is very hard to be sure just what stimulus is primarily responsible for any response" (1938, p. 36). For this reason, experimental psychologists try to restrict the stimulus situation so that only one input varies. If varying a single stimulus changes the response, an antecedent-consequent relationship can be inferred.

Guthrie's explanation of forgetting relied heavily on interference. Strictly speaking, we do not forget an S-R connection, once it is formed, but a new one may displace it. This is what the functionalists called *retroactive inhibition*. The phenomenon will seem more interesting when we consider behavioristic efforts to deal with some Freudian concepts, such as repression.

Guthrie and his students developed empirical evidence casting doubt on the role of reinforcement in learning. Sheffield and Roby (1950) demonstrated that rats would learn a task for a reward of saccharin-sweetened water. As such a drink has no survival value, theories of homeostatic tension-reduction become questionable. An even more star-tling study was that of Sheffield, Wulff, and Backer (1951), who discovered that if a male rat runs to a goal box containing a female in heat, the male learns the maze even if not allowed to copulate. As behaviorists dislike such subjective concepts as *hope* or *expectancy*, they find such data a bit baffling.

Guthrie was, however, willing to use the concept of *voluntary acts* as part of human behavior; he limited the idea to a narrow set of circumstances in which a person had a choice between two courses of action and carried on an internal dialogue about the costs and benefits of each. The "voluntary" element depended on identifying the preferable act and carrying it out. No "willpower" or other special faculty was involved. This account resembles that of Margaret F. Washburn (see Chapter 7), but in her case, the balancing of consequences was conscious and involved images of potential outcomes.

In a passage reminiscent of David Hume, Guthrie wrote of the self as a "system of habits" (Hume had called it an "aggregate of perceptions"). This view of the self is still widely held among American psychologists.

Motivation was not systematically examined by Guthrie. "Intense or prolonged stimuli" were invoked to explain the activation of responses and persistence in goal-seeking behavior. The survival value of such behavior was not explored. In these respects, Guthrie was a true follower of Locke and Hume.

The disadvantage of neglecting these dynamic factors becomes apparent if we look at the problem of extinction. Guthrie knew that if a given S-R unit repeatedly failed to lead to a goal, presentation of the stimulus would not be followed by the response. Because he believed that the reinforcement was not essential for learning, this was unsettling. Guthrie dealt with the apparent paradox by proposing that the reward kept the animal from engaging in behavior patterns that would "break up" the newly learned act. Extinction, then, involved random activities that could interfere with the prior learned habit; such activities result in loss of performance.

Graydon LaVerne Freeman

One further figure merits brief mention as part of the early behaviorist movement. We know that motivation was largely ignored by this group. Watson, for example, referred more or less incidentally to primary drives such as hunger and thirst, but without explicitly tying them to the learning process. Weiss had assigned to motivation a role rather like that of Guthrie; that is, a motive is a behavioral process that operates to exclude distracting stimuli and to maintain responding to the stimulus problem.

An effort to correct this deficiency was made by G. L. Freeman

(1903–   ) in his *Energetics of Human Behavior* (1948). As would seem necessary in an avowedly materialistic, physicalistic theory, Freeman laid heavy emphasis on physiology as the source of motivation. The theory is built around the concept of homeostasis; he postulated a large number of biological equilibria, maintenance of which is indispensable to survival, including glucose in the blood stream, osmotic pressure of blood, body temperature, and various ion interchanges. By heredity, humans are so constituted that the disturbance of any one of these essential steady states triggers a mobilization of energy and random activities that persist until the equilibrium is restored.

All of this is set in a context of aggressive materialism. There are no relevant conscious states. At present, Freeman conceded, it may be necessary to use a "consciousness" vocabulary to identify some phenomena, but in the long run, it is the motor activity accompanying conscious states that plays the crucial role in behavior. Thus consciousness becomes a kind of epiphenomenon, an irrelevant accompaniment of a physiological function.

Like Weiss, Freeman appealed to the prestige of physics to make his theorizing seem more "scientific." "Energy transformations," he wrote, "can, of course, be considered as occurring in any number of orders or systems—from atomic physics to the cosmos, from the single cell to the combined action of all living things. . . . When the behavior of the organism is taken as a whole, its basic field of energy transformation is *limited by the skin*" (1948, p. 35). This is a vivid picture, but one wonders how to get from the skin to the cosmos.

Freeman was explicitly Darwinian. He described homeostasis as essential for survival; species that failed in this regard become extinct. Steady states also become the basis for recognizing threats; a danger of any deficit, such as a food shortage, releases the same energy as an actual state of hunger. This response is, of course, a simple matter of conditioning.

Freeman was able to offer some concrete notions about the physiological basis of energy mobilization. Writing two decades after Watson and Weiss, he had much more information on the autonomic nervous system and the endocrine glands than was available to his predecessors. Freeman was also able to use these autonomic response patterns as mediating links in his behavioral analysis. Watson had written of conditioning a global fear response; Freeman described the conditioning of heart rate, blood pressure change, the galvanic skin reflex, and so on, to a fear stimulus.

The occurrence of a disturbance of a steady state, or the presence of a stimulus that signals the approach of such a disturbance, sets off these physiological responses. As a measure of the intensity of the motivational state, Freeman proposed what he called an "arousal index." This was a measure of "the extent to which the organism (in whole or in part) is aroused by stimulation" (1948, p. 101). As measures of this arousal, he proposed "the percentage increment in total energy mobilization to a typical startle stimulus" (i.e., using prior measures as baselines for comparisons.) "Every stimulus," he wrote, "sets up a series of organic processes. Some of these are excitatory, catabolic, tearing down reserve energies. Others are relaxing, anabolic, rebuilding the prestimulus level of metabolic balance" (p. 104). These measures include blood pressure, heart rate, the galvanic skin reflex, and other indices of autonomic nervous system activity.

Paralleling his studies of the arousal index, Freeman also attempted to measure the "discharge index," a composite of indicators of the restoration of homeostatic equilibrium. These largely involved the same autonomic functions as the arousal index. Finally, Freeman proposed the computation of a "recovery quotient," which would indicate a residual tension (not all of the arousal having been discharged) or a complete restoration of equilibrium. Associated with this measure was an index of focal energy to background energy; this would be relevant, for example, if an individual engaged in restless, meaningless activities (background) instead of focusing effort on the current problem. Although Freeman did not mention Sigmund Freud anywhere in his book, it seems apparent that these homeostatic response measures offer potential objective indicators of some of the phenomena Freud identified (e.g., "dammed-up libido").

Another important concept introduced by Freeman is that of optimal level of stimulation or arousal. Because the satisfaction of a motive typically leads to relaxation (discharge of tension), and because Freeman's experiments indicated that stimulation applied during a state of relaxation induced less vigorous response (less arousal), it follows that there is some optimal level between excessive relaxation and excessive undischarged tension. The latter condition would exist when the organism is faced with repeated threats that prevent tension discharge and homeostatic recovery. Hans Selye (1956) reported experiments in which repeated stresses led to the exhaustion and death of laboratory animals.

A related problem is the hierarchy of motives. In the physiological realm explored by Freeman, we know that need for oxygen will dominate all other deficiencies; need for water typically is second, pain third, food fourth, and so on. But how does the organism know which of the various threats must take priority? At best, Freeman could offer a vaguely defined sensory system prewired to order these priorities. At the level of social motives (ethics, religion, ambition, and ego expansion), Freeman could only refer to learning and to accidents of the individual biography.

A kind of validation of Freeman's concepts was reported by Albert Ax and J. L. Bamford (1968). They compared the autonomic response to electric shock with the response to a bell that signaled electric shock. Three groups were tested; normal controls, schizophrenics, and Job Corps trainees. The normals showed as strong a response to the signal as to the shock itself; however, the schizophrenics never got to the point where the physiological response to the bell equaled the response to the shock itself. Most interesting was the fact that instructor ratings of the motivation of Job Corps trainees predicted the anxiety response; those trainees judged highly motivated resembled the normals; those judged unmotivated resembled the schizophrenics. It appears that anxiety is a key concept in understanding human motivation. (See Chapters 14–16.) Elaborations of these homeostatic principles have been published by R. Stagner (1977) and S. B. Brent (1978). These principles offer promise of linking physiological psychology with values and aspirations.

What Is a Stimulus?

Is it correct, as in the Ax and Bamford study, to speak of the physical stimulus—the bell—or is the real stimulus the threat of electric shock? This question has its roots in Titchener's warning about the stimulus error. Titchener wanted his observers to give a "pure sensation" report, without including the apperception, that is, the meaning of the stimulus. Behaviorists have leaned in the same direction; they focus on the physical qualities of the stimulus (e.g., the sound vibrations of the bell) rather than recognizing that the stimulus now carries with it an important meaning: Trouble is coming.

Gestalt and phenomenological theories treat the stimulus as a complex phenomenon, including meaning as well as physical attributes. This approach has the advantage of corresponding more to patterns of daily behavior; it has the disadvantage that a stimulus is no longer the same for two or more persons, because each individual will associate diverse responses or meanings with the stimulus.

The definition of a stimulus has implications for research design. Experimentalists try to maximize the control of behavior by excluding almost all stimuli except the focal stimulus; thus we say that control leads to impoverishing the environment. At times, this method leads to a sterile outcome in the sense that behavior in nonlaboratory situations cannot be predicted from laboratory data. This is one of the reasons for the developing schism in American psychology between the experimentalists and the humanists. The question is one of research strategy: Do we opt for rigor by impoverishing the experimental environment, or do we opt for relevance by studying behavior in the messy, complicated situation outside the laboratory?

What Is a Response?

Aside from Weiss, early behaviorists did not concern themselves with defining the response. Pavlov had it easy; he limited himself to the salivary response, which could be measured, timed, and analyzed without

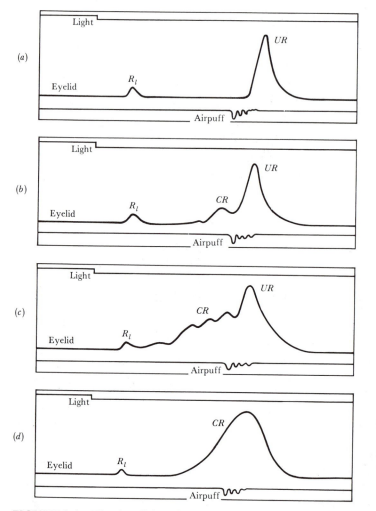

FIGURE 9.4   The Conditioned Response is not a Replica of the Unconditioned Response

In these records of stages in the development of a CR of eye blink to a
puff of air, the anticipatory response (CR) is not a case of attaching the
unconditioned response (UR) to a novel stimulus (Light). The records are
for a single human subject.   (*Redrawn from Hilgard, 1936, by permission of
author and the American Psychological Association*)

any confusion with other activities. But in the study of mazes and puzzle
boxes, not to mention mathematics and chemistry, the question is more
demanding. Guthrie found that cats varied in the movements they used
to solve the puzzle box, but each individual cat tended to use the same

stereotyped movement each time. Thus he leaned to Weiss's concept of the biophysical response: a specific stimulus–neuron–response link.

Microscopic studies of human behavior reveal the problem. E. R. Hilgard (1936) studied the conditioned eye blink in human subjects. The record of one individual is shown in Figure 9.4. The unconditioned response (UR) is easily identified at Stage A. However, as learning proceeds, a new response forms, anticipating the US (unconditioned stimulus—in this case, a puff of air). Ultimately, in Stages C and D, a totally new response has developed, which cannot in any sense be considered simply the UR to the air puff.

The same problem was highlighted by Watson's study of Little Albert. When Albert saw the white rat, he stuck his thumb in his mouth. When it was removed, he began crying and crawled away. Which was the conditioned response: The thumb or the cry?

Even trickier questions arise when we consider social psychology and cognitive psychology. When a person circles "yes" on an attitude scale, is the response that of moving a pencil in a circle, or is it the central response of accepting the opinion statement? When a person writes "I" (for image) in a study of imagery, is the response one of marking on paper, or is the response a conscious image? These are questions that are often ignored, but they are relevant if we are to build a comprehensive theory of human behavior and experience.

These two enigmas—*stimulus* and *response*—were not dealt with very successfully by the early behaviorists. But behavior theory has been revised in a more complex form by Clark Hull and in radically new contexts by B. F. Skinner. The following chapters will examine their contributions.

CHAPTER 10

Behaviorism at Maturity: Clark Hull

The growth and development of a psychological theory may be viewed as a parallel to the development of a human individual. The simple evolves into the complex, incongruities and inconsistencies are identified and rejected, criticisms are countered, and at times, new possibilities are recognized and exploited. Behaviorism can be examined in this perspective. The first quarter of the twentieth century spawned a rebellious movement, rich with critiques of structuralism and functionalism, and rather short on new concepts and principles. It was self-consciously Darwinian and biological, but much of the biology was pure speculation.

The behaviorism of Meyer, Watson, and Weiss was largely a replay of British associationism, with the word *idea* replaced by *response*. The essential feature was connectionism, and in these early theories, even the importance of reinforcement was unrecognized; everything was contiguity. Taking a tip from the structuralists with their constant reports of kinesthetic sensations in complex cognitive processes, the behaviorists proposed that implicit movements could provide the links between successive overt movements. The key metaphor for all of these early theories was the telephone switchboard, itself a recent development, but an appropriate one for a connectionist psychology.

Mature behaviorism differed in two major respects from these earlier versions. First, it recognized that the simplistic chain-reflex formulation is inadequate to deal with human behavior, and probably with animal behavior as well. Second, it put the phenomenon of reinforcement at center stage, and interpretations of empirical data concentrated on that aspect of the situation. The two psychologists to be examined in this connection are Clark L. Hull, who recognized the role of reinforcement but attended to a variety of other complicating variables in human behavior; and B. F. Skinner (see Chapter Eleven), who offered a detailed

examination of reinforcement and schedules of reinforcement, while ignoring some of the variables stressed by Hull. However, each was thoroughly behavioristic at both the descriptive and the methodological levels. At times, each seemed to discard consciousness as being irrelevant to
psychology; at times, each let consciousness sneak back in. In Chapter
Eighteen, I shall describe neobehaviorism, which is characterized by a
frank treatment of conscious states as forms of response.

Clark Leonard Hull

The individual who would have been chosen by most American psychologists as the outstanding member of the profession in the 1930–1950
period was Clark Leonard Hull (1884–1952). He was rated in the top
five in Coan's (1959) study for both of these decades.

Hull was unusual in the respect that he really had three different careers in psychology. His first ten years were devoted to statistics and
aptitude testing; a shorter period, to hypnosis and suggestibility; and the
last two decades of his life, to learning and behavior theory. Although
Hull claimed that he could demonstrate common threads running through
these researches and publications, this sketch will be limited to his behavior theory.

Biography

Hull did not have the fortune to be born into a wealthy family, as did
William James, but in several ways, their background was similar. James
had a sickly childhood; Hull developed polio when he was twenty-four.
Hull also had a serious case of typhoid fever. Both Hull and James illustrate Alfred Adler's theory: They overcame these handicaps and demonstrated great cognitive skills and tenacity in pursuing their ideas.

Hull was born into a very poor family in New York State and had only
a very spotty education because he was so often kept out of school to
help on the family farm. The family was never prosperous and was forced
to move several times. Hull was virtually self-educated until the family
moved to Michigan and he enrolled in Alma Academy, a preparatory
school associated with Alma College. In his autobiography (Boring et al.,
1952), he described how he designed a steel brace for his paralyzed leg,
which his brother fabricated in a local blacksmith shop. At this time,
Hull became aware that he had a talent for mathematics and philosophy.

Like James, Hull reported that reading a single book decided him on
a career in psychology; it was none other than James's *Principles of Psychology.* Hull had toyed with the idea of becoming a Unitarian minister
but decided that too many intellectual constraints would be imposed on
him in that role. He therefore opted for graduate school at the Univer-

Archives of the History of American Psychology

Clark L. Hull, developer of the hypothetico-deductive
method and of the application of formal logic to
psychology

sity of Wisconsin. Among his mentors were Joseph Jastrow, a Stanley
Hall student; Daniel Starch, who is best known for his work in advertising; and V. A. C. Henmon, a Cattell Ph.D. who had taken an active role
in the mental testing program in the army during World War I. Hull's
doctoral dissertation was an excellent study of concept formation, modeled on the Ebbinghaus studies of memory; Hull used Chinese ideo-
graphic characters as stimuli and nonsense syllables as names for these,
thus minimizing the role of past experience and presumably tapping the
learning–cognizing progress at its earliest stage.

Hull carried on some of Henmon's work and taught statistics as well
as mental test construction. He built a correlation machine, a primitive
computer; data could be punched on rolls of paper tape and run through
the machine, which dutifully produced Pearson product–moment correlation coefficients. The outcome of this work was Hull's book *Aptitude
Testing* (1928). His second specialty, hypnosis and suggestion, was probably influenced by Jastrow, who had published on these topics. Hull's
book, *Hypnosis and Suggestibility* (1933), reported a mass of empirical data
on problems that had formerly been purely matters of speculation.

In 1929, Yale University received a large endowment for the establishment of an Institute of Human Relations. J. R. Angell, who had supervised J. B. Watson's dissertation, was president of the University and he
invited Hull to become a member of the senior staff. Between 1929 and
1952, Hull and his students dazzled the psychological community with
research reports, books, mimeographed papers on the mathematics of

behavior, and so on. Even before this tide had reached full flood, Hull was honored by election to the presidency of the APA.

N. Guttman (1977) estimated that in 1940, only about 4 percent of the papers published on learning (in the *Journal of Experimental Psychology*) were "Hullian" in orientation; by 1950, this percentage had jumped to 37 and held at a fairly high level (24 percent) in 1960. By 1970, however, the figure had fallen back to 4 percent. This, incidentally, is a common observation in science: a new theory, concept, or method evokes interest and experimentation, then gradually recedes into the background.

Hull was characterized by "behavioristic" thinking throughout his professional career, but he confessed in his autobiography (1952) that he was disturbed by the "semi-fanatical ardor" of some Watsonian enthusiasts. He noted also a period of interest in Gestalt theory; he tried to wangle a fellowship to study with Kurt Koffka in Germany. Failing this, he arranged for Koffka to receive an appointment as a visiting professor at Wisconsin. He was impressed by Koffka's "personal charm" but was annoyed that Koffka spent more time attacking behaviorism than he did expounding Gestalt principles and experiments. Ultimately Hull concluded that Watson had done a poor job of formulating and defending behaviorist theory, and he set himself the task of improving on the Watsonian version.

Psychology According to Hull

Despite his early work on individual differences, Hull's real devotion was to nomothetic psychology, that is, the development of universal laws of behavior. He wrote that his work was focused on "the determination of the quantitative laws of behavior and their deductive systematization" (Boring et al., 1952, p. 154). Thus he followed the tradition of Fechner, Wundt, and Titchener, as well as of Watson and Weiss.

The nearest to a complete and definitive statement of Hull's views is given in *Principles of Behavior* (1943). In many respects, it is a model of formal logic applied to psychological problems. Hull identified certain postulates (theoretical presuppositions), then deduced corollaries, that is, predictions of what should happen if a given variable were changed systematically. Many of the corollaries were tested in the Yale laboratories and generally led to confirmation of the theory. Regrettably, not all replications outside the Yale context were successful; there is a problem in having theories tested by their authors, as negative results may be discarded and only positive findings published. (Critics of a specific theory may, of course, make the opposite error.)

Hull published two revisions of his system: *Essentials of Behavior* (1951) was a skeleton version of the 1943 book, and *A Behavior System* (1952) offered some revisions but was uncompleted because of Hull's death in that year.

Hull admitted that one does not *prove* the accuracy of any psychological theory; all one can hope for is to increase the *probability* that the basic structure is sound. On the whole, Hull's system has held up surprisingly well.

Darwinism

Hull started with a biological bias and a firm belief in the Darwinian approach to behavior. His Postulate 3 is clear: *"Organisms at birth possess receptor effector connections (sUr) which, under combined stimulation (S) and drive (D), have the potentiality of evoking a hierarchy of responses that either individually or in combination are more likely to terminate the need than would be a random selection from the reaction potentials resulting from other stimulus and drive combinations"* (1943, p. 66; italics in original). Natural selection has eliminated those species in which such receptor–effector connections were not innate. Each organism must be receptive to stimuli that may signal reduction of need and must have innate response tendencies likely to contact those stimuli. This is about the extent of Hull's concern with heredity; from this point on, all is environment.

Like Darwin, Hull assumed a continuity of behavioral functions on the evolutionary scale. Unlike Darwin, he ignored the possibility of species-specific behaviors. Most of Hull's corollaries were written in terms applicable either to human or to animal behavior.

Neurologizing

Despite this foundation in biology, Hull did not imitate his predecessors in speculative neurologizing. Behavior was seen as "molar," that is, as being composed of adaptive acts, not nerve impulses and muscle twitches. Like Wundt, Hull thought psychology might help the physiologists rather than vice versa; the study of behavior, he wrote, may "aid in the development of an adequate neurophysiology" (1943, p. 20).

Intervening Variables

A crucial phase of Hull's theorizing, and the point on which he has been attacked by other behaviorists, was his use of *intervening variables*. Where Watson and Weiss had been content to say that connections were formed between stimulus and response, Hull sought to explicate both the nature of the connection and other intraorganismic variables affecting the transformation of a connection into appropriate performance.

The key concept was what he called "habit strength," represented in his symbolic language by the term sHr. This is the hypothetical link between the stimulus trace (s) and the overt response (R). The physical stimulus (S) gives rise to a stimulus trace (s)—this is the closest Hull came to neurological speculation—and the slow decay of s makes possible its overlap with the neural activity of responding so that a linkage depends on contiguity. Like Guthrie, Hull assumed that a given sHr was formed in a single repetition; however, it might not be manifested in behavior because of interference, competition of other sHr linkages, and so on. This broader context made Hull's a true theory of behavior, not simply of learning.

The sensory area actually got very short shrift in Hull's system. Perhaps because the structuralists had explored the field so thoroughly, Hull wrote in his book without elaboration about such phenomena as summation of stimuli, the Weber–Fechner ratio defining a perceived difference in stimulation, and so on. Hull postulated a certain degree of interaction of simultaneous stimuli, thus allowing for sHr units geared to complex stimuli, as opposed to the prior emphasis on a single stimulus, as in Pavlov's and Watson's experiments.

A given S may become associated with several Rs. However, the habit strength varies for the different sHr connections formed, and there thus develops a *hierarchy of responses* that differ in probability of occurrence. The most probable response is the one at the top of this hierarchy, and less likely responses appear at the lower levels. An individual annoyed by a fly may first brush it away, then try to swat it, then use insect spray, and finally get up and go indoors. Hull observed that such flexibility had survival value. This was no novelty; Meyer and Watson had said the same. What Hull added was the notion that the succession of responses was not random. Within a person's behavior repertoire, there existed a rank order of sHr units, that when s appeared, the highest-ranking r would be emitted. If s persisted, successively lower-ranking responses would appear.

It is also possible to draw information from a hierarchy for a population of individuals, as in the Kent–Rosanoff tables for frequency of association. These tables, which give the probabilities with which different response words will be emitted to a specific stimulus word, are useful in clinical work. To the stimulus word *mother,* a high probability response is *love.* If a person replies to *mother* with *spider,* a very low-probability response, a clinical psychologist will suspect some oddity in the personality of the respondent. We are reminded of the finding of Ebbinghaus that pairs of words close together will form "stronger" associative connections than words separated in space or time. The acquisition of the individual words is, in some respect, a different process from the acquisition of connections between words.

Hull believed that any given stimulus–response $(S-R)$ connection (sHr) was formed in a single trial. However, the connection could accumulate units of *habit strength* through repetition and reinforcement. The term *strength,* unfortunately, was never precisely defined. Hull suggested that latency was a measure; this would mean that a strong habit would function *faster* than a weak one. Unfortunately for the theory, research did not always confirm this prediction. Similarly, Hull proposed resistance to extinction as a measure, and it, too, came off poorly in an experimental test. Worst of all, latency and resistance to extinction did not correlate well with each other.

Probability of occurrence seems relatively unambiguous as an index of habit strength. A person whose car refuses to start will try possible responses (ways of correlating the malfunction) in a certain sequence. For a given person, this sequence is likely to remain constant over time. However, extraneous stimuli, such as temperature or humidity, may prompt trying an alternative immediately that would normally occur later. Finally, we must note that the hierarchy of responses may be affected by fatigue, motivation, selective attention, and immediately prior activities. Thus the status of the rank order of responses in a hierarchy is never fixed. Nonetheless, most psychologists perceive the hierarchy concept as constituting a significant advance over random trial-and-error and chaining, concepts used by Watson and his colleagues.

Reinforcement

A second advance by Hull over Watson was in the use of reinforcement as a variable. For the contiguity theorists, food or another reward served mainly to keep the organism on the job, trying to solve the problem, whatever it was. Hull proposed that reinforcement was the major determinant of habit strength. Obviously this did not rule out contiguity; the stimulus, the response, and the reinforcement had to occur close together in space and in time, at least in the early phases of learning.

What constitutes a reinforcement? Working with animals, Hull identified a *positive* reinforcer as anything *reducing* tension. Hunger, for example, induces tension, and food reduces it. Thirst, sex, and escape from pain can be used in this model. In Hull's 1943 book, the number of reinforcing experiences was decisive: "The increments (of habit strength) summate in a manner that yields a combined habit strength . . . which is a simple positive growth function of the number of reinforcements" (p. 178). This formula worked well in animal studies; it sometimes encountered difficulties with human subjects. Sheer repetition may not be a problem with white rats, but human beings become bored, and repetition can sometimes become aversive.

The problem of motivation is obviously intertwined with reinforcement. However, Hull had no desire to imitate the Freudian analysis of human motivation, which had swept across the Atlantic before Hull received his doctorate. Further, he wanted an approach that denied any difference between his animal subjects and human beings. His solution was the concept of *drive (D)*. It was an abstraction from hunger, thirst, and other tensions. An increase in D led to increased responding—as in

Watson's random trial-and-error behavior—and a decrease in D consti-tuted reinforcement. D had an interesting property beyond its role as the substructure of reinforcements, however. Given a particular habit *(sHr)*, an increase in D would make this response more energetic. It would also increase the flow of responses. Many a response that was below a threshold of habit strength would be pushed above it by increased drive. Thus, under high drive, a person would try a far wider range of re-sponses than if drive were low. D operated as a multiplier, not an addi-tion. The logic was simple: if D were zero, there would be no response. Hull therefore concluded that no learning could occur in the absence of D. However, the strength of D in an initial learning trial did not affect the speed of learning.

In a later version of his theory, Hull (1952) added another reinforce-ment variable: incentive *(K)*. *Incentive* refers to the specific drive-reduc-ing object involved in a task. Thus rats would learn faster for a reward of sunflower seeds (preferred) than for dog chow (nonpreferred). The value of different incentives varies widely in human learning; Hull did not attempt a solution to this perennial problem.

Another modification of the theory involved the recognition of *secon-dary* reinforcers. Hull had hoped to get by with primary drives (physio-logical states and homeostatic disturbances) and primary reinforcements, but even the animal subjects behaved in such a way as to require expan-sion of the theory. Pavlov had demonstrated secondary conditioned re-sponses, for example, when stimulus C is paired with B, and B with A, but not C with A. Thus a buzzer could become a stimulus for salivation when it was paired with a winking light, which, in turn, had been paired with food. Hull added secondary drive to his conceptual armory, using mostly negative stimuli, signals of pain, and signals of signals of pain. Given the secondary drive, a secondary reinforcement is a natural con-sequence. In human behavior, most rewards are secondary in nature; a good report card, or a diploma bearing the letters *Ph.D.* does not reduce physiological tension, but it symbolizes tension-reducing states.

Inhibition

Hull's original purpose was to develop a comprehensive theory of learn-ing. However, this grew into the task of formulating a theory of behav-ior. Behavior theory must take account of more variables than does learning theory. One such item has already been mentioned: drive af-fects learning and also influences performance. A person may have learned calculus but may ignore an invitation to solve a calculus problem because of lack of motivation or because the extant motives impel him or her to do something else.

A second such factor is inhibition. Hull speculated that there were two kinds of inhibition: *reactive* inhibition and *conditioned* inhibition. Reactive inhibition is a primary state which is built up by responding; that is, if R_a is emitted now, there will be some resistance to making the same response immediately afterward. This inhibitory state can build up until the person refuses to continue with the task. Industrial psychologists speculate that reactive inhibition may account for the job dissatisfaction felt by workers on highly repetitive jobs. Being an experimentalist, Hull was more interested in the fact that this concept helped explain variation in responses, the "random" activity (changes in response) associated with learning a new task. Reactive inhibition also served as an explanation for the superiority of distributed over massed practice in learning. If practice is spaced out over hours or days, the reactive inhibition is alleged to dissipate, whereas massed repetitions build up inhibition.

Conditioned inhibition is *learned* inhibition. For instance, if reactive inhibition is regularly built up in a certain context, the appearance of that context will at once evoke inhibition. An inhibitory state can also be conditioned to other stimuli; if sex play is associated with punishment, later mention of sex can elicit an inhibitory response. For Hull, inhibition was a response in the same way that running a maze or pecking at a lighted disk was a response.

One problem with this analysis is that massing of extinction trials works faster than distributing them. If the inhibitory state obeys response laws, distributed extinction trials should give faster elimination of the undesired response. C. E. Osgood (1953) suggested that fatigue in the massed-practice extinctions might speed up the inhibition of the response being eliminated.

A more efficient way of eliminating an undesired response is to replace it with a conflicting response. If a rat has been trained to press a treadle for food, the experimenter can eliminate the habit by training the rat in a new response, such as biting the treadle. This is a version of Hullian theory that contributed to the development of behavior modification (see Chapter Twenty-one).

Mediating Responses

Behavioristic theories uniformly seek to replace "ideas" with "responses" in the process of association. This trend goes back to Max Meyer and Watson; even earlier, Margaret Washburn (1916) had proposed a concept of linking one response to another. The conceptual change involved is that one replaces *implicit, unobservable* conscious states with *implicit, unobservable* responses.

Hull's version of the mediating response emphasized fractional implicit movements. For example, a rat running a maze gets food as a reinforcement. The food elicits biting, chewing, and swallowing responses. The mediating-response theory assumed that fractional biting, chewing, and swallowing responses, too weak to be observed, could persist through the maze-learning performance and so link the overt actions necessary to cope with the task. (Compare Watson's version, Figure 9.1). Hull referred to these as "fractional anticipatory goal responses."

Other implicit responses can also serve linking purposes. An obvious variety is verbal. When learning to operate a new machine, one is likely to verbalize the instructions aloud, but shortly the overt verbalizations disappear. Introspective reports may nevertheless show that one may think "twist to the left" without saying it aloud. Hull called such responses *mediating* responses because they helped to keep the sequence of movements unbroken and in proper order.

R. G. Triplet (1982) examined the mediating response from the viewpoint of linking Hull's hypnosis research to his learning theory work. In his early work, Hull had used the concept of *ideomotor action* as an intervening variable between the hypnotist's suggestion and the overt action. This concept seems to correspond to the mediating response, r, in the later work. According to Hull's formula, a physical stimulus leads to an internal process, the stimulus trace; this evokes a mediating response, an implicit state that seems to involve a blueprint of the act and, finally, the overt response. Although some behaviorists decline to speculate about such inner states, Hull's concept fits with the writings of Watson and Weiss; more of interest is its echo in some of the writings of the psychologists called *neobehaviorists* (Chapter Eighteen).

Generalization

Pavlov had demonstrated stimulus generalization; for example, a conditioned reflex (CR) to a touch on the dog's shoulder would be given in a weaker form to a point a few inches back, but not to a touch on the right knee. Generalization is a process of treating incoming stimuli, and it probably follows the distribution of just noticeable differences; that is, a novel stimulus just one jnd from the original conditioned stimulus (CS) will elicit a fairly strong response, but one that differs by three or four jnd units will elicit little or no response.

Hull took over this concept from Pavlov, but without much elaboration. On the whole, Hull's psychology is a response psychology (which is why it is classed as behavioristic), and the stimulus side is relatively undeveloped. He did point out that some experimental failures were due to contextual stimuli; for example, a change in the laboratory equipment might set off exploratory responses instead of the trained response.

Human behavior introduces other complications. Robert Leeper (1944) described an amusing episode when a student tried to replicate a Yale experiment. The procedure called for memorizing paired associates, for example, *red–mountain.* On a memory test, the stimulus word was changed slightly, perhaps to *pink.* Some learners gave *mountain* as the response to *pink,* but others said that *pink* was not the original stimulus word and so they could not respond. "Generalization" from red to pink would work for some college students but not for others.

Purposive Behavior

If the brain is an automatic switchboard, and if connections are made as mechanically as the theory prescribes, how can a human or an animal pursue a purposive course of action? This debate has a long history. In the nineteenth century, complex animal behaviors were ascribed to instincts, which implied an ability to foresee future needs. Birds, for example, built nests, incubated eggs, and fed nestlings. Most of these acts are not under immediate stimulus control, and observers felt that some kind of innate understanding of future developments was essential to explain the behavior. Later investigators identified specific stimulus influences, as well as hormonal determinants, and the term *instinct* fell into disrepute. Nowadays the term *species-specific behavior* is often invoked to slip an "instinct" back into the explanation of behavior.

Hull admired the discussion of purpose given by A. P. Weiss and quoted it in his presidential address to the APA (Hull, 1937):

> We may best visualize this relationship between the responses that make up the so-called purposive behavior category by the raindrop analogy. We may start with the assumption that every drop of rain in someway or other gets to the ocean . . . we may say that it is the *purpose* of every drop of rain to get to the ocean. . . . Falling from the cloud it may strike the leaf of a tree, and drop from one leaf to another, until it reaches the ground. From here it may pass under or on the surface of the soil to a rill, then to a brook, river, and finally to the sea. Each stage, each fall from one leaf to the next, may be designated as a *means* toward the final end, the sea. . . . Human behavior is merely a complication of the same factors. (Weiss, 1929, pp. 373–374)

Weiss and Hull agreed that human behavior involves a far wider set of variables than gravitation, but in principle, they held that examples of so-called "purpose" in human life were no more than acting out of deterministic stimulus–response connections. If determinism as a scientific philosophy is taken seriously, then the terminus of a planned course of action (e.g., earning a Ph.D. in psychology) is the inevitable outcome of various stimuli and pressures on the individual.

Mathematicizing

Hull was good at mathematics, and he became intrigued by the idea of working out precise functional relations in equation form, with the computation of constants based on experimental data. Thus, for example,

$$sEr + s_1 + S_DHr \times \frac{\dot{D} + D}{\dot{D} + M_D}$$

(translated as: The effective reaction potential equals the external stimulus plus the drive stimuli associated with this habit multiplied by the sum of the dominant drive plus the sum of the nondominant drives active at the moment, divided by the sum of the nondominant drives plus the physiological maximum drive possible to the organism). All of this is, of course, perfectly simple and obvious—or was to Hull, at least—but it has very little to do with any possible predictions of behavior.

Hull coined several new terms: *hab* for habit strength, *mot* as a unit of drive strength, and so on. Thus, *hab* is defined as a function of the number of reinforced repetitions that can be converted into *hab* values by calculating a logarithmic function of maximum drive. In a table (1943, p. 115), Hull computed *hab* values for a hypothetical habit that received an increment of 10 on the first repetition, 9 on the second, 5.9049 on the fifth, and 1.3509 on the twentieth. When these are summed successively, we get a typical learning curve with negative acceleration, whereupon Hull obviously considered his computations to be validated.

As Charles Osgood (1953) pointed out, the concept of habit strength makes intuitive sense, because observationally we know that some habits are more persistent and resistant to change than others. However, when proposed measures of habit strength are intercorrelated, the figures are too low to justify the assumption that habit strength is a unitary function. Correlations of response frequency, response latency, and response amplitude ranged from .15 to .94, most being around .50. Such figures demonstrate that we do not yet have a valid operational measure of Hull's version of habit strength.

Calculations such as those just cited assume that learning is a smooth, continuing process with equal increments even when these are fractional. Hull recognized the logical difficulty here and reminded his readers that *hab* is probably not divisible. Learning either adds one *hab* or it does not. Thus the smooth curve resulting from Hull's equation is misleading. Later critics have speculated that most of the computations are fantasies, although the logic of many of Hull's concepts is sound.

The Metaphor

Hull avoided metaphorical analogies as much as possible. However, he occasionally found it convenient to use the telephone switchboard as a hypothetical model. "For the most part," he wrote, "neural impulses flow to the brain, which acts as a kind of automatic switchboard mediating their efferent flow *(r)* to the effectors in such a way as to evoke response *(R)*" (1943, pp. 384–385). If we substituted the pineal gland for the switchboard, this statement would fit the logic of Descartes. The French-man would have designated the soul as the agency making decisions among alternate responses; Hull would presumably say that the switchboard is not really automatic, but that neural traces can deflect the neural impulse to a new response pattern.

Summary

Osgood (1953), a Yale Ph.D. but not a Hull student, prepared a diagram that summarizes the interrelations of elements of the Hullian system as sketched in the preceding pages (Figure 10.1). It should be read from the top down, with an implication of successive steps, although many of the intervening variables must be presumed to act simultaneously. The diagram gives the essential steps from the occurrence of a physical stimulus (S) to the occurrence of an overt response (R) and the contact with the goal object (G). As the diagram indicates, most of Hull's intervening variables, the theoretical constructs of the system, are anchored to observable phenomena. These observables are circled in the diagram; for instance, Cd (drive conditions) is indexed by the number of hours of food deprivation, water deprivation, or sex deprivation, as a way of determining how "strong" the relevant drive is. The only error in this chart seems to be that of treating (sOr) as an observable; this was conceived of by Hull as an implicit and essentially unpredictable factor that ironed out errors in predictions. Some critics referred to it as a "fudge" factor. On the bottom line, P refers to the observed probability of occurrence (which is dubious, as the rest of the chart claims to deal with a single response, hence probability cannot be determined); (stn) is response latency, and n is the number of trials without reinforcement required to induce extinction. It is relevant to note that experimental studies have shown correlations between response latency and response magnitude of only $+.27$ (Campbell and Hilgard, 1936) for the conditioned knee-jerk. Using the conditioned eye-blink, A. A. Campbell (1938) got a correlation between latency and magnitude of only $+.15$. The validity of the theoretical construct of "habit strength" was thus thrown into question. Although this might seem to undermine the entire Hullian theory, it has not done so, mainly because there is a kind of logical compulsion to develop some concept such as habit strength. Learning, after all, does take place, and we need some verbal label to identify the *degree* to which it has been accomplished. Measuring the "strength" of the habit, however, has proved to be very tricky indeed.

It is obvious that Hull attempted to cover most of the contingencies involved in predicting human behavior. Most of the theory is couched in deterministic terms. However, the introduction of oscillation (O) seems to be a confession that random or unexplainable variables make perfect prediction impossible, at least at present.

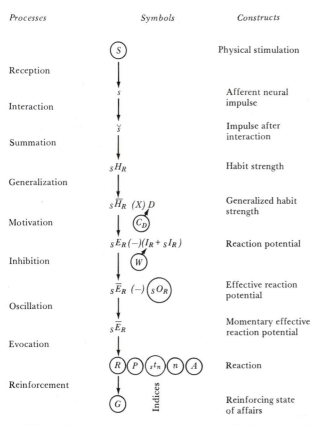

Processes	Symbols	Constructs

Reception — Physical stimulation (S)

Interaction — Afferent neural impulse (s)

Summation — Impulse after interaction ($\breve{s}$)

Generalization — Habit strength ($_sH_R$)

Motivation — Generalized habit strength ($_s\overline{H}_R\ (X)\ D$), (C_D)

Inhibition — Reaction potential ($_sE_R(-)(I_R + _sI_R)$), (W)

Oscillation — Effective reaction potential ($_s\overline{E}_R\ (-)(_sO_R)$)

Evocation — Momentary effective reaction potential ($_s\overline{\overline{E}}_R$)

Reinforcement — Reaction (R)(P)($_st_n$)(n)(A), Indices

Reinforcing state of affairs (G)

FIGURE 10.1   Osgood's Summary of Hull's Behavior Theory

See text for interpretation.   *(From Osgood, 1953, Figure 136, p. 374, re-printed by permission of Oxford University Press.)*

Most critics would agree that Hull accomplished a formidable task in developing his postulates and corollaries to cover so many contingencies. The theory is a model of what Hull called his "hypothetico-deductive method." It is the most sophisticated theoretical analysis available in the rubric of consistent behaviorism.

The Hullians

Hull was fortunate in attracting to his institute at Yale a covey of brilliant young graduate students as well as a few talented postdoctoral research associates. Space does not permit a detailed listing of these people and their contributions, but the following individuals are important enough to the history of psychology to require inclusion here.

Kenneth W. Spence (1907–1967) received his doctorate at Yale in 1933. He was occasionally described as "more Hullian than Hull" (just as Titchener had been more Wundtian than Wundt). By this, his colleagues intended to say that Spence was even more meticulous than his mentor with respect to the postulates and deductions involved in the theory and was also a careful, innovative experimenter.

One of Spence's more exciting investigations dealt with an issue of considerable theoretical importance. The Gestalt psychologists (see Chapter Twelve) had published reports of relativistic discrimination learning, learning that could not be tied to a specific stimulus but only to the relationship between pairs of stimuli. For example, hens were trained to peck for grain on a dark gray and a medium gray card; the grains on the dark gray were glued down, but those on the medium card were edible. Soon all the hens pecked only at the medium card. Now the psychologist changed the cards, removing the dark gray and pairing the medium with a light gray. Because the medium card had been a positive stimulus, it should follow from S-R theory that the birds would continue to peck at the medium card. But no; most of them switched immediately to peck at the light card; and the interpretation was that the hen had learned that the lighter card was positive. This would have conflicted with Hull's formulation.

Spence analyzed the problem by using hypothetical excitatory and inhibitory gradients (assumed generalization around the positive stimulus, excitatory, and the negative stimulus, inhibitory). By assuming that the excitatory gradiant covered a wider range, he was able to compute predictions that in certain areas, the animal would choose the relational stimulus but, in others, the absolute stimulus. Interestingly, one of Spence's students, Margaret Kuenne (1946), found that his deductions held for children under the age of four but did not work for older children. This does not justify the conclusion proposed by critics of Hullian theory that it was revelant only for animals and young children. A more judicious conclusion would be that the Gestalt prediction holds in some cases and the behavioristic prediction in others, but we do not yet have a clear indication as to which set of variables determines this outcome.

Spence differed from Hull on two points. One was that Spence placed great significance on *K,* the incentive or goal involved in a learning task. Hull did not introduce this concept until his last book, *A Behavior System,* and may have done so under Spence's prodding. A second difference was that Spence leaned somewhat more toward Guthrie's position of a pure contiguity theory than did Hull. For Hull, a learning trial was a *reinforced* trial, whereas for Spence, a trial in which CS and UR occurred together, regardless of reinforcement, was the significant unit of learning. Like Guthrie, Spence often wrote as if the only role of the reinforcing stimulus was to keep the organism in the learning situation.

Ernest R. Hilgard (1904–   ) received his doctorate at Yale, but instead of Hull, his thesis adviser was W. R. Miles. None the less, he participated in Hull's seminars on learning theory and adopted a theoretical outlook which was preponderantly Hullian. His career paralleled that of Hull in two areas: learning and hypnosis; but Hilgard took them in reverse order from Hull.

The fact that he was not directly under Hull's influence may have made him more objective in his assessment of the success of Hull's system. He noted that Hull had proposed 110 corollaries to his postulates which predicted specifiable research findings. Empirical data were found relevant to 71 of these. Hilgard (1940) concluded that 55% were successful, 28% ambiguous, and 17% unsuccessful. This is not a bad record, and one wonders why Hilgard concluded of Hull's (1943) book that "the actual influence of the book was minimal" (1987, p. 188). Other data suggest that the influence of the book was substantial. I must none the less note that tests of predictions made by a theorist or his/her adherents tend to be biased toward confirmation, while tests by critics may be biased toward rejection.

Since this history is focused primarily on theoretical issues, neither the work on hypnosis of Hull or of Hilgard will be described. At best they make clear the principle that much of human behavior cannot be categorized as conscious—in accordance with the views of Locke, James, Titchener, and others. Introspection simply does not reveal some of the goings-on in individuals. Structuralism and Gestalt thus have difficulty in assimilating data on hypnosis. Psychoanalysis, of course, took off from the hypnotic work of Charcot and Bernheim, and the researches of Hull and Hilgard have not modified any insights from the French psychiatrists. Some of Hilgard's work indicates that the segregation of specific items in the "unconscious" is only partial, but we do not have firm information about the variables which account for the availability (or non-availability) of some materials to conscious report.

Neal E. Miller (1909–   ) received his doctorate at Yale in 1935. His doctoral adviser was W. R. Miles, but he participated in Hull's seminars and adopted much of Hullian theory. One of the most prolific writers of the Yale school, he collaborated with John Dollard (Ph.D., Chicago, 1931), a member of the Institute staff, on two important books: *Social Learning and Imitation* (1941), in which the concept of imitative behavior was rescued from oblivion and shown to be both useful and valid; and *Personality and Psychotherapy* (1950) which translated important Freudian concepts into behavioristic terms and reported on a variety of studies testing hypotheses derived from psychoanalytic theory. This latter book has been very influential both in the area of personality theory and research and in the development of behavior modification procedures.

The key concept in the translation of Freud's ideas was the approach–withdrawal gradient. As Freud had focused his attention on conflict as the basic process in personality development, the appropriate behavior-

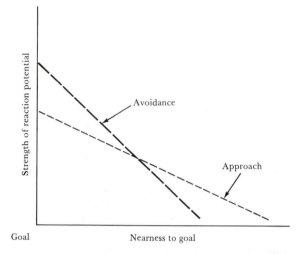

FIGURE 10.2   Hullian Analysis of Behavioral Conflict

The theory holds (1) that the strength of a behavioral tendency increases with nearness to the goal, and (2) that the avoidance gradient increases more rapidly than the approach gradient.

istic analogue was the conflict of responses. As Figure 10.2 indicates, the behavioristic approach lends itself to quantification in a way impossible in the Freudian version (see Chapter Fourteen). The theoretical propositions underlying Figure 10.2 are (in abbreviated form) as follows: (1) the tendency to approach a goal is stronger as the organism nears it; (2) the tendency to avoid a feared stimulus is stronger as the organism nears it; (3) *the strength of avoidance increases more rapidly with nearness than does that of approach;* and (4) the strength of the approach and avoidance tendencies varies with the strength of the drive on which they are based (Dollard and Miller, 1950, pp. 352–353). The third, italicized proposition is the key to the vacillating behavior so often associated with conflict. It must be noted, however, that because the approach behavior is based on a positive goal such as food or sex and on the avoidance on pain, a very strong positive motive will overcome the aversive tendency. In contrast, an intensely painful experience may raise the avoidance gradient so high that no vacillation occurs. Other aspects of this kind of analysis will be explored in connection with the theory of Kurt Lewin (Chapter Thirteen).

In addition to the books on social learning and on psychotherapy, Dollard and Miller were collaborators with other Hullians on an important book that overlaps general, social, and clinical areas: *Frustration and Aggression* (1936); by John Dollard, Leonard Doob, N. E. Miller, O. H. Mowrer, and R. R. Sears. Primarily begun as a project to explore Freud's hypotheses about aggression (before his proposal of a death instinct), the book expanded to cover crime, lynching, fascism, communism, and other social topics.

Freud's view, of course, had centered on the blocking of libidinal (pleasure-seeking or sexual) impulses by the social environment or by moral training, and on the aggressive behaviors often triggered in such incidents. The Hullians relied more on the physiological drives, such as hunger and thirst, plus escape from pain. *Frustration and Aggression* has been widely cited and widely used as a basic text in programs dealing with social and clinical psychology. It has also been elaborated on for application to industrial psychology (see Stagner, 1956; Stagner and Rosen, 1965). It has been so widely accepted that many psychologists will say, "Such aggression proves there was a serious frustration even if we don't know what it was." This logic is not recommended; evidence for the frustration must be developed before this statement is defensible.

Dollard and Miller's three books contributed significantly to the development of what I have labeled *neobehaviorism*, notably the writings of Julian B. Rotter and Albert Bandura (see Chapter Eighteen).

Carl Iver Hovland (1912–1961) earned his doctorate at Yale in 1936 and joined the staff immediately, developing a specialty in social communication and attitude change. Although the communication and persuasion studies of attitude change were ingenious, they made less use of the Hullian learning theory than might have been expected. Attitudes are learned, and changes are also learned. One might have hoped for a more extensive use of Hullian postulates in the program; nonetheless, it made important contributions to social psychology.

One of Hovland's doctoral students was *Charles Egerton Osgood (1916–)*. Osgood was exceptionally familiar with the Hullian system but felt no personal identification with it; this may account for his perceptive discussion in his major book, *Method and Theory in Experimental Psychology* (1953). His summary diagram (Figure 10.1) has served a valuable purpose in relating the various concepts to the flow of the learning process in a meaningful way. Osgood has also made major contributions to the study of language with his semantic differential, a device for measuring the affective meanings of a concept. He has consistently found across worldwide samples that there are three affective dimensions of meaning: evaluation, potency, and activity. One naturally thinks of Wundt and his tridimensional theory of feelings, although the parallel is considerably less than perfect.

Frederick D. Sheffield (1914–) had been an undergraduate student with E. R. Guthrie before doing graduate study with Hull. This may account for his critical view of Hullian thinking and for some ingenious experiments questioning the role of reinforcement as opposed to pure contiguity. In his doctoral research, Sheffield tested the drive-reduction hypothesis by using saccharine-sweetened water as a goal; the animals, motivated by hunger, learned tasks rapidly, yet saccharin cannot possibly reduce the glucose deficit underlying hunger. In a later study, even more ingenious, F. D. Sheffield with J. J. Wulff, and R. Backer (1951), required male rats to run a maze with a female in heat as the goal object. However, the male was allowed only to mount the female before being removed without copulating. The males learned and improved in speed despite the absence of drive reduction.

Orval Hobart Mowrer

Mowrer (1907–1982) survived the "sex scandal" at the University of Missouri (page 171) and went to Johns Hopkins University to take his doctorate with Knight Dunlap. He then went to Yale as a research associate with Hull and did some work on animal learning, studying the mynah bird, which can be trained to imitate human speech within limits. One of Mowrer's conclusions (which seems hard to fit into a Hullian framework) was that the bird must develop some affection for the trainer before the imitative conditioning is effective. Food rewards alone did not produce the desired effect.

Mowrer also attracted considerable attention with his "two-factor learning theory" (1956). This theory affirmed a difference between classical conditioning (à la Pavlov) and instrumental learning, as in the typical experiment by Watson, Thorndike or Hull. Essentially, Mowrer held that "sign learning" followed the Pavlov model; one stimulus became a signal or sign that another would follow, and the organism responded in anticipation of the record stimulus. This model is particularly useful in cases of pain–anxiety learning. Mowrer hypothesized that when a signal is followed by pain, any recurrence of the signal would elicit anxiety. The mechanism involved would be conditioning of heart rate, blood pressure and other reflex visceral activities to the warning signal. This formulation, incidentally, stands in opposition to William James's theory of fear as it is usually stated: "we are afraid because we run." Actually, James included visceral responses in his concept of action preceding conscious feeling of fear, so the difference in Mowrer's approach becomes unimportant.

Mowrer is another example of a personality affecting theorizing. He was a lifelong victim of severe depressions, two sufficiently incapacitating to require hospitalization. He entered psychotherapy twice without much relief, but became interested in the problem and developed his own approach to therapy which involved confession and catharsis. It does not seem far-fetched to assume that his obsession with guilt, the conviction that we are all guilty, was a function of his repeated depressive attacks, during which a wide variety of persons and situations were seen as symbols of guilt.

Mowrer's "two-factor theory" extended from the signal function of conditioned fear or anxiety to responses seeking to escape the threat.

Anxiety, he speculated, would release a number of random responses in an attempt to escape the impending danger. Successful acts would be reinforced by anxiety reduction. Thus, his concept of "instrumental learning," or complex habit formation, resembled the pattern Watson had called trial and error, and Hull had treated as sHr formation. Skinner's development of a similar distinction will be reviewed in the next chapter.

Criticisms of Hull

Some critical comments have been inserted in this discussion, where it seemed that empirical data relevant to a specific proposition should be cited. Hull has been criticized on more general grounds. Specifically, he is charged with analyzing complex behavior into minute elements, much as Titchener had analyzed consciousness into elements. Although Hull's concept of habit hierarchy offered an approach to the development of higher-order, more complex behaviors, it is true that the thrust of the theory is toward an analytical approach. Ultimately, according to Hull, we should be able to find a single stimulus attached to a single response, regardless of the vicissitudes outlined in Figure 10.1. Gestalt psychologists have objected more specifically to Hull's treatment of the stimulus side of his equations; this issue will be examined in Chapter Twelve.

Criticisms by other behaviorists, notably Skinner, have focused on the intellectual machinery of the system. Hull's reliance on intervening variables (an idea he borrowed from E. C. Tolman) is opposed on the ground that they are not open to direct observation. Hull replied that each intervening variable was anchored to observables (the items circled in Figure 10.1). The answer is a shade less than satisfactory; the relation of the intervening to the overt variable is sometimes tenuous and in some instances has not held up in crucial experiments.

Hull has played an important role in the development of American psychology, in part because he stated his ideas very clearly and made no concessions to opponents. He has provided an excellent target for the "humanistic psychologists" (Chapter Seventeen) who have charged him with fragmenting human behavior, destroying individuality, and generally depersonalizing psychology; like Wundt, Hull sought universal laws, not the understanding of specific individuals. Hull is thus at the crux of the debate between "tough-minded" experimentalists and "tender-minded" humanists, a debate which has a lengthy past and will probably have an equally lengthy future.

Some indication of the impact of the Hullian tradition on American psychology can be gleaned from the fact that five of the adherents to Hullian ideas (Hilgard, Miller, Mowrer, Osgood, and Spence) were elected to the presidency of the American Psychological Association. All five also received "distinguished scientific contribution" awards from the association. Hull and his ideas dominated experimental psychology in America for most of two decades. They did not, however, have much of an impact on industrial, social, or clinical psychology. The work of Dollard and Miller (1950) undoubtedly contributed to the development of the objectivistic versions of psychotherapy, generally lumped together as behavior modification. However, the major impulse in that area came from B. F. Skinner.

A Note on Artificial Languages

In the preceding pages, I have used Hull's symbolic language to identify his theoretical constructs, instead of labeling them verbally. The reason is that Hull invented these concepts (such as sHr) in order to avoid the clutter of traditional usages that blur the meaning of a popular term such as *habit*. Any term from everyday language carries a cargo of surplus meanings; Hull avoided criticism by inventing the new vocabulary.

The logic here is similar to that of Titchener and Ebbinghaus in trying to exclude meaning, or the effects of past experience. Titchener wanted to get pure sensory data without reference to objects; Ebbinghaus wanted to study learning without the disturbing influence of prior experience with the stimulus material used.

The idea is not novel; philosophers have traditionally invented their own vocabularies to insure that a term would not carry connotations contradictory to the intent of the theorist. E. C. Tolman (1932) actually preceded Hull in this respect; his theory made use of a whole range of neologisms, words invented so that they did not carry any confusing associations. Kurt Lewin used symbolic diagrams for the same purpose. Although he used labels from popular speech, Lewin's diagrams pinned down a specific meaning that he wished to convey.

Sigmund Freud, of course, has been most often criticized for his use of esoteric terminology. In his attempt to communicate his abstruse theories, he resorted to names for functions that sounded like personifications: the id, ego, and superego; the censor; the demon; and so on. The unfortunate outcome was that much of his theorizing suggested little people inside the head pushing and pulling the person to and fro. Freud had no such intention, but his use of personified labels contributed to misunderstandings. It is interesting that researchers in information processing have not learned form Freud's troubles; they regularly use terms like *encoder* and *comparator* (Chapter Nineteen).

Truly, the way of the theorist is thorny. If labels for theoretical constructs are taken from daily speech, they will be subject to attack as not agreeing with traditional meanings. If, on the other hand, the theorist invents an artificial vocabulary, he can be charged with hiding his ideas behind a cloud of unfamiliar labels.

CHAPTER 11

Behaviorism at Maturity: B. F. Skinner

The term *behaviorism* covers a multitude of doctrines. All behaviorists share a few articles of faith; the principal one is that the proper study of psychologists is behavior and not consciousness. We can distinguish at least three varieties of behaviorism: metaphysical, as in the case of A. P. Weiss and his aggressive advocacy of a materialistic monism; methodological, a shared belief in defining research so that only responses that can be recorded by independent observers will be considered acceptable data (this class has a wide range, including Tolman and Guthrie as well as Hull and Skinner); and descriptive behaviorism, which confines itself to describing behavior as observed, with no effort to link observations to hypothetical intraorganismic processes (Guthrie and Skinner).

The lines of development from La Mettrie and James Mill to Bekherev and Pavlov, and from them to Meyer, Watson, and Weiss, leads directly to Clark Hull. The placement of Skinner is more difficult. In the tradition of British empiricism, he comes closest to David Hume. Hume, it will be remembered, denied any unity to the person; the "mind" was composed of a snowstorm of isolated, independent perceptions. For Skinner, it appears that behavior is fragmented, unconnected, lacking unity or consistency except as consistency holds for specific responses. Skinner also resembled Hume in that he evoked enthusiastic support from some and vigorous dissent from others.

Psychology according to Hull, as it was summarized in Chapter Ten, occupied center stage in American psychology during the late 1930s and on into the 1950s. This does not mean that functionalism disappeared; it does mean that theoretical arguments and "crucial" experiments took off from propositions in Hull's writings as opposed to those of William James or E. L. Thorndike or G. Stanley Hall. The Hullian era waned in the 1950s as a new approach became the focus of debate and investigation. This was the radical behaviorism of B. F. Skinner.

Biography

Burrhus Frederick Skinner (1904–   ) was born into a middle-class Pennsylvania family. He did not have the wealthy background of William James nor the poverty of Hull. His childhood seems to have been uneventful. He did not elect to study psychology early in life; in fact, he did an undergraduate major in English at Hamilton College, and for some years, he sought to establish himself as a writer. Despite his unquestioned verbal facility, he had difficulty in finding a secure niche or even in paying all of his own living expenses.

The turning point seems to have occurred in 1928, when he picked up a copy of Pavlov's *Conditioned Reflexes* and found himself drawn to a career in scientific psychology. Within a short time, he had enrolled at Harvard University, earning an M.A. in 1930 and a Ph.D. in 1931. He was assigned to E. G. Boring as his dissertation adviser, a choice that was emotionally unfortunate but intellectually irrelevant. Boring, at that time still a devotee of Titchener, cannot have found Skinner's bumptious behaviorism acceptable, and Skinner clearly rejected Boring's approval of introspectionism.

According to an early volume in his series of autobiographical books, Skinner was a hard-working, deeply committed student in graduate school: "I would rise at six, study until breakfast, go to classes, laboratories, and libraries with no more than fifteen minutes unscheduled during the day, study until exactly nine o'clock at night and go to bed. I saw no movies or plays, seldom went to concerts, had scarcely any dates and read nothing but psychology and physiology" (1976, p. 398).

This schedule sounds very impressive but is less so when we read what Skinner had to say several years later: "I was recalling a pose rather than the life I actually led" (1979, p. 5). This admission raises intriguing questions, not only about which was the real Skinner, but also about the validity of autobiographies in general, if so methodical a searcher after facts as Skinner could publish so misleading a self-description. As Sigmund Freud pointed out, memory distortions can lead us to report with conviction events that never happened in an objective sense.

There is more agreement with regard to Skinner's relations with the faculty at Harvard. Skinner (1983) commented, "In graduate school I had the advantage of scarcely being taught at all" (p. 25). Alongside this one places Boring's (1950) remark that Skinner "has a 1931 Ph.D. from Harvard, but he owes little to Harvard psychologists" (p. 650). It would appear that Skinner's prior learning (from Pavlov) prevented further learning in some areas of psychology.

Skinner (1979) recorded only one incident of explicit conflict with Boring: "I was already well along in my work on changes in rate of eating and had written two short papers on drive and reflex strength [concepts Skinner later eschewed]. I combined these with my paper on

B. F. Skinner

B. F. Skinner, a consistently descriptive behaviorist who introduced single-organism study

the reflex and submitted them as a thesis to Professor Boring. . . . He was bothered by my selective use of history . . . he suggested an alternative outline. I felt that he had missed my point, and I resubmitted the thesis without change" (p. 399).

Boring tolerated the stubbornness and appointed an examining committee but did not include himself on it, and Skinner was approved for the doctorate. A possible incidental effect may be noted: in the widely used book of readings in psychology edited by Herrnstein and Boring, no article by Skinner is included.

Although Skinner's treatment of learning relies heavily on the concept of positive reinforcement, his career raises questions about its accuracy. During his early years in the profession, he was considered an odd character by many colleagues. Two factors contributed to this perception: first he differed from orthodox opinion in holding that one could do meaningful research on a single organism, as opposed to the current fixation on numbers of cases and statistical manipulation of the data; and second, he declined to speculate about what might happen inside the organism as learning took place. He won on the first point, and the second may be called a draw. Certainly his status rose rapidly after *The Behavior of Organisms* was published in 1938. In 1949, he was elected president of the Midwestern Psychological Association, and as his presidential address, he read the paper "Are Theories of Learning Necessary?" As expected, the answer was "no." In 1958, he received the APA award for distinguished scientific contributions, and in 1968, the National Medal of Science, the Federal Government's highest award for achievements in science (an award rarely given to a psychologist).

A vindication of his early inclination toward a literary career came in 1948 with the publication of his novel, *Walden Two,* a combination of Henry David Thoreau's naturalism with sophisticated techniques of behavior control. The novel has had very wide exposure, both among the general public and in college classes; many professors of psychology have adopted it for required reading, in some cases to praise it and, in others, to warn against the ideology presented.

Like Watson, Skinner has attracted an enthusiastic following that sometimes has the attributes of a cult. The group has its own journal, the *Journal of the Experimental Analysis of Behavior,* and is organized as a division of the American Psychological Association with more than 1300 members in 1986. It has also played a major role in the development of the clinical applications of psychology by way of behavior modification.

Skinner's Contributions

Because Skinner insistently denied that he had a theory, or that theories were necessary, I can hardly write about "psychology according to Skinner." He has, however, made important contributions to the science of psychology, and in the view of his colleagues, these add up to a theoretical perspective if not a system.

Type S and Type R Behaviors Perhaps the earliest manifestation of Skinner's talent for conceptualizing behavioral phenomena came with his distinction between the stimulus-controlled reflexes studied by Pavlov and the organism-controlled behavior studied by Thorndike. In 1938, Skinner proposed that automatic reflexes like the salivary reflex be called *Type S,* and responses emitted by the organism in the absence of an identifiable external stimulus be called *Type R.* The former is under the control of the experimenter, who can elicit it more or less at will. The latter is not under external control and is presumed to be initiated by internal stimuli (about which Skinner refused to speculate).

The importance of this conceptual advance quickly became obvious.

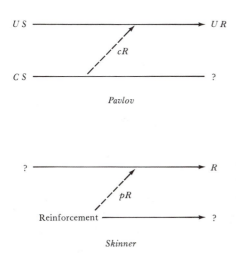

Pavlov

Skinner

FIGURE 11.1 Conditioning according to Pavlov and to Skinner

Pavlov believed that his procedure simply substituted a new stimulus (CS) for an innate or earlier-learned stimulus (US). Skinner's operant conditioning involved reinforcing a response "emitted" by the organism in the absence of an identifiable stimulus.

Watson had lumped automatic reflexes and random behavior into a single category. But experiments using the automatic reflex did not help much with the understanding of complex behavior. Efforts to explain language, occupational skills, or other day-to-day activities were unconvincing. Skinner noted that citizens do not go around placing food in the mouths of others, or applying electric shocks to elicit walking or other motor activity. As suggested in Figure 11.1, the Pavlovian formula for learning emphasizes the replacement of an unconditioned stimulus by a conditioned stimulus, whereas Skinner's Type R stresses an increase in the probability of a response to an indeterminate stimulus.

Skinner called this Type R response an "operant" because it operated on the environment. This usage has puzzled many psychologists because elsewhere he claimed that "the organism does not act upon the environment; the environment acts upon the organism." This contradiction will be explored later. Skinner's method for studying an operant called for watching until his experimental subject (animal or human) made a movement more or less resembling the one Skinner wished to modify. A positive reinforcer would then be supplied, and the consequence was an increase in the frequency of that response. Later the experimenter might withhold the reinforcer until the response approximated the "shape" desired. For this reason Skinner, called his method "shaping" the response. Thus, he was able to teach a pigeon to play Ping-Pong by reinforcing, first, any peck in the direction of the ball, later any peck striking the ball, then any peck knocking it in the desired direction. Shaping, then, has a marked similarity to the procedure parents use in teaching a small child a skill such as riding a two-wheel bike.

We can say, then, that Type S experimentation follows the Wundtian tradition of tight experimental control, whereas Type R experimentation involves control by the modification of consequences. This does not mean that Skinner abandoned the idea of experimenter control; he impoverished the environment by eliminating as many cues as possible, maximizing the probability that the organism would be stimulated by (and only by) the significant stimulus.

Hull had used the probability of a response as one of his criteria of habit strength. Skinner avoided the abstract term, but used probability of occurrence as his chief criterion of learning.

Defining a Response At first glance, it may seem that Skinner had adopted Weiss's biophysical response as his unit, at least in the sense of a response by a specific effector mechanism. In fact, Skinner quickly learned that the animal might press a lever with a forepaw or a shoulder, by sitting on it, by pushing it with the nose, and so on. He did not find Guthrie's highly predictable repetition of successful acts. For this reason, he adopted as a criterion the *observer's judgment* that the response had achieved the same objective, that is, the same impact on the environment. From his data, Skinner inferred that we reinforce not a response, but a *class* of responses: "The word 'operant' will be used to describe this class. The term emphasizes the fact that the behavior *operates* on the environment to generate consequences" (1953, p. 65). Clearly Skinner had shifted to Weiss's "biosocial" response: a response is "the same" if it has the same environmental significance. He thus avoided the problems associated with the traditional "one receptor, one connector, one effector" paradigm that had characterized his predecessors.

Reinforcement The definition of *operant* just quoted serves to point up Skinner's major contribution to learning theory, namely, his emphasis on the importance of the consequences of behavior. In Pavlov's and Guthrie's views, the mere contiguity of a stimulus and a response explained their linkage. Watson and Weiss paid little attention to the role of reward and punishment. Thorndike, however, had built his "connectionism" on his law of effect, that is, of consequences. Hull and Skinner resemble each other in combining contiguity with consequences to develop a more complex and more realistic view of learning than their predecessors.

Skinner's view of reinforcement is disarming in its simplicity: "As the term is used here, . . . *the only defining characteristic of a reinforcing stimulus is that it reinforces*" (1953, p. 72; italics added). This is a tautology, as so many "definitions" are. The circular definition makes possible such exuberant pronouncements as that of R. W. Lundin (1979) praising "The importance of reinforcement as the basic principle. . . . *In all instances it works*" (1979, p. 218; italics added). Because, by Skinner's definition, a stimulus that does not reinforce is not a reinforcer, it is hard to see how

Lundin could miss. We simply define all failed reinforcers as nonreinforcers.

Skinner's strategy in avoiding a noncircular definition is defensible. Hull's equation of primary reinforcement with drive reduction had been shown to have numerous exceptions. Definitions based on other biological considerations would have required abandonment of Skinner's principle that he dealt only with inputs and outputs, with no speculation about internal processing. Sometimes it is safer to retreat to a tautological definition that, though uninformative, cannot be disproved.

Positive reinforcers were defined as those that, if presented following a response, increase the probability that the response will recur. *Negative reinforcers* were defined as those that, when *removed,* increase the probability of the relevant response. If a loud noise is turned off when a person lifts his hand from his lap, in a short time the frequency of hand lifting will increase markedly. However, this method has obvious disadvantages; at what time can one resume the annoying stimulus without its being perceived as punishment? Skinner wisely recommended the maximum possible use of *positive* reinforcers.

Skinner also deserves credit for his rejection of punishment as a device for controlling learning. Punishment may involve the removal of a positive stimulus or the imposition of a negative, aversive stimulus. Like Hull, Skinner conceded that punishment might, on occasion, accelerate learning; unlike Hull, he pointed out that it often serves to reinforce *undesirable* responses. Thus a parent who punishes disapproved behavior may induce anger responses directed at the parent. These, as the psychoanalysts tell us, may damage both the parent–child relationship and the personality of the child.

Schedules of Reinforcement   Much Skinnerian research was directed at the discovery of functional relationships between the schedule on which reinforcements are supplied and the subsequent behavior of the organism. Reinforcers may be supplied on every trial, on some trials but not others, after specified time intervals, or after some arbitrary number of responses.

Continuous positive reinforcement means that every response approved by the experimenter is rewarded. This procedure results in the fastest learning—and if the rewards are stopped, the fastest extinction. *Fixed-interval* schedules may mean that a reward is available every fifteen seconds or every minute. Paychecks are issued at fixed intervals. Lengthy intervals run the risk of response extinction; a year-end bonus is not effective with many workers because the response (working efficiently) is separated excessively from the reinforcement. *Variable-interval* schedules lead to slower learning than continuous reinforcement, but this procedure generates a learned response remarkably resistant to extinction.

To use a concept alien to Skinner, we may say that if continuous rein-forcement stops, the person quickly abandons the *expectancy* that reward will follow; but when many trials have gone without reward, only to have positive reinforcements reappear, one may continue to respond in the absence of reinforcement.

Ratio schedules reward a fixed percentage of responses. In some experiments, a pigeon has been trained with a reward on every other response, then on every fifth response, on every tenth response, and so on. *Variable-ratio* schedules may be contrived so that on the average, every tenth response is reinforced, but this may mean a reward after eight and then after twelve, or even fifteen, responses. Variable-ratio schedules seem to produce associations highly resistant to extinction; we note that slot machines operate on a variable-ratio payoff, thus inducing a maximum number of plays before the player extinguishes that response.

Skinner did not speculate on explanations for these differences. Titchener would probably have focused on sensitivity to time intervals and muscle sensations as cues governing the continuation of responses. Phenomenologists would call the success of interval and ratio schedules evidence of "expectancy" that a reinforcement will be forthcoming.

"Backward Associations?" Ebbinghaus and others tried to establish "backward associations," that is, learning in which A is followed by B, but a link so that B elicits A is formed. Their results were uniformly negative. It is virtually impossible to establish a backward association in animals, and humans probably show it only when they have rehearsed it playfully. Skinner knew this and recognized the implied backward association in his assertion that the consequences of an act change the probability of that act. Time does not run backward. We cannot, he admitted, reinforce a response when it has already ended: "We can only predict that *similar* responses will occur in the future. The unit of a predictive science is therefore not a response but a class of responses" (1953, pp. 64–65). As was indicated in the description of Skinner's procedure, the experimenter's judgment is the criterion for admitting this present response to the "class of responses" being reinforced. In this way, Skinner's operations resemble those of teachers grading children's examination papers or of supervisors evaluating the performance of subordinate workers. We reward those responses that fit a criterion, but the criterion is rarely objective; far more often, it is an image in the mind of the judge. Skinner avoided taking a position on just what went on inside the experimenter while teaching a pigeon to walk a figure 8. Skinner was of course, consistent; he would not speculate about the pigeon either.

Inner Functions as Explanations Skinner supported his position persuasively. We do not, he argued, "explain" behavior by appealing to inner constructs. To explain smoking behavior in terms of a "habit of smoking" is tautological. He would account for smoking in terms of the positive reinforcements received in the past, from the nicotine, and also from motor activity, pose before peers, and so forth.

Skinner held that we do not clarify anything when we say, "He ate because he was hungry." How do we know he was hungry? Because he ate. The point may be exceptionally apt as we learn more about bulimia (compulsive eating and purging). Persons afflicted with this problem report eating excessively when they do not feel hungry at all.

Skinner may have adopted this position because he was aware of the problems facing some of Hull's predictions, for example, that hours of deprivation of food determined the strength of the hunger drive. At the least, Skinner made speculative psychologists aware of the pitfalls to be avoided. On the other hand, Skinner's resolutely external view of behavior is unsatisfactory to many psychologists. An example can be taken from Skinner's autobiography. Remember that Skinner said he did not know what caused an operant to occur. In his autobiography (1979), he told of afternoons during his high-school days when he visited a girl friend to talk about sex. He was allowed to stroke her thigh ("3 inches above the knee,") but no farther (p. 168). Skinner would undoubtedly call this stroking an operant. Freud would ascribe its origin to the libido, the sexual instinct, and in this context, the impulse seems relevant to an understanding of the behavior.

"Strength" of Reinforcers   Hull eventually felt compelled to add K (incentive value) to his formula because behavior may be modified not only by the strength of the drive, but also by the kind of goal object offered. Rats will learn faster for preferred than for nonpreferred foods. Skinner did not opt for Hull's formal terminology, but he recognized differences in inner states as affecting reinforcers. Thus, he wrote, "when strong reinforcers are no longer effective, lesser reinforcers take over. . . . Sexual behavior, therefore, takes a prominent place in leisure" (1971, p. 178). Lest this be misunderstood, let me note that Skinner recognized sex as a powerful reinforcer. What he seems to have meant is that hunger and escape from pain (which "motivate" work behavior) can take precedence at first; when these motives have been satiated, sex may take over. For some individuals, obviously, sex may dominate over other kinds of activities.

Skinner was trying to deal with the phenomena of drive satiation and the hierarchy of motives; it is obvious that his refusal to recognize internal states hampered his effort. He could not talk about satiation because that is an intervening variable. And he could not deal with ambitions, aspirations, or phobias except by saying that the individual emitted a large number of responses that appeared to an observer to be related to some external goal.

Secondary Reinforcers   Skinner adopted the term *secondary reinforcement* from Hull but modified its meaning. An experimenter who wishes to bring an operant under *stimulus control* (i.e., to establish a habit so that the new stimulus will dependably elicit the operant) may set up a schedule so that reinforcement is given only when a specific stimulus is present (e.g., a pigeon gets grain for pecking a disc when the disc is illuminated in red, but not when it is white or green or blue). Soon the red illumination (for example) will trigger responding. At this point, the response is under the experimenter's control because the experimenter turns on the lights. However, the red light can also function as a reward; within limits, the experimenter can "strengthen" other responses by following them with the red light. As Pavlov and Hull found, one must not overdo such secondary training, or the stimulus will lose both its signal value and its reward value.

The design of the stimulus control experiment also makes possible the study of *sensory discrimination* in animals. Suppose that in the foregoing experiment, we used a large pink placard over the food dish and rewarded pecking when it was present. When this begins to function as a positive stimulus to pecking, we can present a brilliant red card but not reinforce it. It will soon function as an inhibitory stimulus. The red card can then be modified gradually toward the pink, until a point is found at which the bird can no longer distinguish the positive from the negative stimulus. In this way, one can determine a just noticeable difference (jnd) for animals. (Pavlov and Watson, of course, had demonstrated the same point earlier.)

Extinction   Skinner defined extinction operationally, as the cessation of responding when no reinforcements had been provided for a sufficient time interval. He did not explicitly include any inner state, but most psychologists assume that some inner process has changed. Extinction is Skinner's main approach to forgetting, as for the functionalists a conflicting response had been the major explanation of forgetting. There is some reason to speculate that memory traces endure indefinitely if no competing response is introduced; although extinguishing one response does not replace it with another act, it may activate an inhibitory response. There is ample evidence that Skinner's "extinction" often matches Hull's "conditioned inhibition" (see, e.g., the case of Helen, Chapter 21).

Feedback as Reinforcer   Sometimes Skinner used the term *reinforcement* as an equivalent to *feedback.* Thus, in describing a child learning to throw a baseball, he commented, "These responses (of throwing) are differentially reinforced by the fact that, when so released, the ball covers a considerable distance" (1953, p. 95). Unlike Thorndike, who would have ascribed improvement to a feeling of satisfaction, Skinner would point only to the perceived distance that the ball traveled.

And this is another worthwhile element in Skinner's psychology. Before his day, the role of feedback had been limited to kinesthetic sensations deriving from muscular movement as an act was executed. Skinner said the purpose of behavior was to change the environment or the relation of the organism to the environment; so, hitting the ball with a tennis racket and watching it sail over the net constitutes a significant feedback, that is, information regarding the success of the action. The importance of feedback is shown by the extensive use made in recent years of false feedback to experimental subjects. A person may be encouraged (or discouraged) by reports indicating improvement of performance or poor performance.

Immediacy of Reinforcement Feedback should, if possible, be immediate. A student who writes a paper wants to get a report on it soon. Industrial workers also crave prompt information on "How am I doing?" American industry has not learned to use Skinner's ideas efficiently.

By the same logic, the individual should receive a reward as quickly as possible after performing. In the laboratory, it is clear that prompt reinforcement speeds up learning, as compared with delayed reinforcement. However, as was noted earlier, the persistence of the response over time will be facilitated by the introduction of longer and longer delays before the reinforcement is supplied. This phenomenon has important industrial implications, aside from its obvious relevance to child socialization. Freud (see Chapter Fourteen) considered the demand for immediate gratification a feature of the infantile personality, a demand that should have been more or less abandoned by adulthood. Unfortunately, many of Skinner's followers have attempted to work in industry using the principle of immediate reinforcement. The method often gives quick encouraging results, followed by disappointment later. As regards executive decision-making, a case can be made that an insistence on immediate gratification (e.g., quick bonuses for profitable operation) may lead to long-term catastrophe, as in the success of Japanese-style management compared to American policies (Stagner, 1984). Skinner himself recognized this danger explicitly in *Walden Two;* children were to receive prompt gratification in infancy but to be subjected to progressively longer delays as they matured.

Darwinism Skinner accepted the continuity hypothesis (that human and animal share common heredity and behavior patterns). He noted that the widely recognized powerful reinforcers were those having survival value. He commented that humans are generally receptive to reinforcers such as sugar, salt, and sex. A species of animal that did not respond favorably to such stimuli would have limited prospects for survival. Specifically, Skinner wrote that "competition for a mate tends to select the more skillful and powerful members of a species, but it also selects those more susceptible to sexual reinforcement" (1974, p. 47). But he was unwilling to take the next step: hypothesizing a sexual instinct, or even a food-seeking instinct.

In his novel, *Walden Two,* Skinner advocated the consistent use of positive reinforcement and the avoidance of punishment, both ideas widely approved by child psychologists. He did, however, recognize that adults cannot expect to get positive inputs all the time; some events are painful or unpleasant. The visitor to Walden, Professor Burris, asks how the society goes about building frustration tolerance so that an unpleasant experience will not be demoralizing. Frazier, his guide, replies, "Oh, for example, by having the children 'take' a more and more painful shock, or drink cocoa with less and less sugar in it until a bitter concoction can be savored without a bitter face" (p. 99). Frazier does not go into the question of pressure on the child to "take a shock" or to drink the bitter cocoa.

Another example: "A group of children arrive home after a long walk, tired and hungry. They're expecting supper; they find, instead, that it's time for a lesson in self-control: they must stand for five minutes in front of steaming bowls of soup" (Skinner, 1948, p. 99). It is only fair to add that the children are given suggestions on how to delay without too much suffering, for example, by making jokes.

Skinner seemed incapable of understanding the criticisms made of *Walden Two,* especially those centering on "who will control the controllers?" Skinner, being himself a mild, democratic individual, could not conceive of controllers taking over such a society and conditioning the children as George Orwell had described the process in *1984,* or as Aldous Huxley had pictured it in *Brave New World.* It would be most astonishing if no controller decided to arrange matters to maximize his or her power, luxuries, and personal security. These, too, are powerful reinforcers, and if the children were properly indoctrinated, they would perceive this state of affairs as right and proper, and perhaps even as ordained by heaven. More could be said about *Walden Two;* the foregoing will indicate some of the critical remarks it elicited from psychologists.

Language and Cognition   Skinner's position on the acquisition of language is hardly distinguishable from that of Floyd Allport (see Chapter Nine.) The only difference is in Skinner's recognition of the role of reinforcement; Allport had relied entirely on contiguity to explain learning. Parents and other adults reward the infant in various ways for emitting recognizable words. Much of this process also involves unconscious imitation of the adult vocalization; this is the way local dialects and jargon are transmitted. The effect of the reinforcement spreads to these imitative responses.

As the child matures, it becomes obvious that, instead of speaking aloud, silent speech will be rewarded (e.g., in church or some other situation where sound is disapproved). In school, the teacher may reward silent verbalization (e.g., "mental arithmetic"). Gradually most of us learn to inhibit audible speech, but Skinner would argue, the muscular activities are still there, only quite restrained. He thus continued the tradition set by Meyer and Watson.

Skinner did not deal systematically with this issue of implicit speech. It presented problems because of his refusal to hypothesize about unobservable events, processes inside the organism. Basically, he decided to ignore the question and to deal with language as if it were invariably a response (explicit or implicit.) He did not even choose to adopt a special term for the implicit movements; L. E. Homme (1965) had proposed the term *coverant* to label a covert operant, but neither Skinner nor any of his followers adopted it.

The Chomsky Debate   Noam Chomsky, a noted linguist, reviewed Skinner's book *Verbal Behavior* (1957). Skinner had set forth the operant-conditioning view of behavior as a complete explanation of the acquisition of language. Chomsky (1959) attacked the book on the following grounds : (1) the environments used in Skinner's experiments were so narrowly restricted that generalization from them to the everyday world is impossible; (2) Skinner ignored the evidence for innate limitations on language, in the form of "pre-wired" patterns such as subject-verb-object, and the concept of "deep structure" in spoken and written sentences; (3) the theory offered no consideration of the child's curiosity, spontaneity, and creativity as these affect language development; (4) the theory shifted from reinforcement to "self-reinforcement" without justification; and (5) the theory failed to consider existing evidence on language acquisition.

Chomsky cited such phenomena as the early acquisition of rules by young children. A child may say "She *singed* a song," which is almost certainly not an imitation of an adult, nor a response that has been reinforced by an adult. Rather the youngster has formed the generalization that the past of an action is indicated by the ending *-ed*. Grammatical sentence structure is also acquired without any specific reinforcement. Chomsky held that it is necessary to assume some kind of inherited pattern, a "pre-wiring" of the language apparatus so that certain patterns are easy to learn and others almost impossible.

H. S. Terrace, a Skinner student, did a four-year study of language learning in a chimpanzee. To make it clear just what he sought to achieve, he called the animal "Nim Chimpsky." No one was surprised when he reported that the experiment disproved Chomsky's theses about language acquisition. A detailed report was published as *Nim* (1979).

The Role of Consciousness   Skinner never denied that such a phenomenon as consciousness can be identified and described. What he resisted was the notion that consciousness determines speech or behavior. It would seem that there is a problem here with respect, for example, to lying. One who sells used cars may know that a vehicle on the lot is defective, but praises it nonetheless. Did someone reinforce this person for falsifying reports, or did it appear that a truthful account would mean no sale and no commission?

In the verbal conditioning experiment, consciousness is not supposed to play a role. L. D. De Nike and C. D. Spielberger (1963) had students choose singular or plural nouns to complete sentences. To plurals, the experimenter said, "Good" or some equivalent. Statistically, the treatment worked; there was a significant increase in plurals. But when the subjects were asked what the purpose of the task was, five of the thirty-two subjects said that they had seen that plurals were being rewarded. Figure 11.2 shows what happened to the data when these five were separated from the others. All of the "statistically significant" change was due to these subjects; the "unaware" group had behaved exactly as the controls did. (It should be noted that in some experiments, consciousness seems not to have been involved, but at least some of the successful studies of operant conditioning are open to this criticism.)

Skinner also postulated that many language interactions are reinforced without consciousness on either part. Thus a speaker may say, "Step aside" in such a way as to create mild anxiety in the listener (Figure 11.3). The listener may say something mild like "Of course" and step aside. The speaker then says, "Thanks," and the relief of anxiety reinforces the verbal-behavioral response.

Remembering   Skinner's treatment of "remembering" is not clear. "A name may remind us," he wrote, "of a person in the sense that we now see him. This does not mean conjuring up a copy of the person which we can then look at; it simply means behaving as we behaved in his presence upon some other occasion. There was no copy of his visual appearance inside us then, as there is none now. The incidental stimulus does not send us off in search of a stored copy, which we perceive anew when we find it" (1974, p. 109). This seems very odd. If I am reminded of a professor who lectured to me fifty years ago, I do not start taking notes on her lecture. I speculate about where she is now and what she may be doing—definitely not the way I behaved in her class.

In rejecting the concept of *search*, Skinner also seems to have been discounting the value of a volume of "information-processing" research in which the "search" function has seemed unquestionable as a measurable phenomenon. Finally, he failed to take account of errors of remembering, as when an eye witness testifies to a crime, or a therapy patient gives an inaccurate account of an incident that occurred twenty years ago. Indeed, Skinner's position would undermine the traditional distinc-

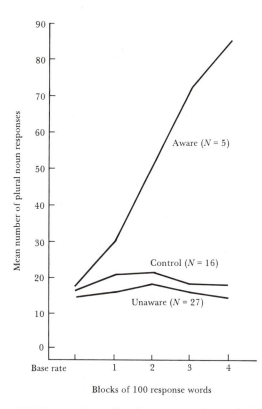

FIGURE 11.2   Role of Awareness in Verbal Conditioning

The subjects who heard "Good" after certain verbal responses showed a significant increase in the class of responses being rewarded. However, when the five persons who had spotted the purpose of the experiment were separated out, the other reinforced subjects did not differ from the control group.   *(From DeNike & Spielberger, 1963, Fig. 2, p. 342)*

tion between sensation and image, that is, the presence or absence of a physical stimulus.

Personality   Skinner has not published any full-scale discussion of how his approach deals with the problem of personality. He would presumably agree with Bandura, Mischel, and others (see Chapter Eighteen) who treat personality as simply a collection of S-R units. Skinner did propose that "A self may refer to a common *mode of action. . . .* On the other hand, a personality may be tied to a particular type of occasion—when a system of responses is organized around a given *discriminative stimulus.* Types of behavior which are effective in achieving reinforce-

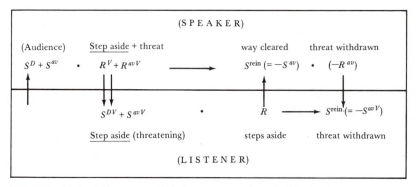

FIGURE 11.3   Skinner on Reinforcement of Verbal Behavior

Skinner proposed that we acquire verbal habits through reinforcement.
In this sequence, S^D = a directive stimulus; S^{av} = an aversive stimulus;
R^V = a verbal response; R^{avV} = an aversive verbal response (mild
threat); S^{rein} = a reinforcing stimulus (reduction of anxiety).   *(From B. F.
Skinner, (C) 1957, p. 39, reprinted by permission of Prentice-Hall, Inc., Englewood Cliffs, New Jersey.)*

ment upon occasion *A* are held together and distinguished from those
effective upon occasion *B*" (1953, p. 285). Thus, one person may approach groups and mingle with them, expecting reinforcement; another
avoids groups, expecting nonreinforcement. One is said to be sociable;
the other, seclusive. Thus, a hierarchical response structure may come
into existence (this is not Skinner's idea) that would lead to a prediction
about future behavior in groups.

Personality and Conditioning   Skinner continually insisted that positive
reinforcement was a universal principle, although he did not reach Lundin's confident "It always works." What Skinner did not take into account was variation in the personality of the person being subjected to
conditioning. E. O. Timmons and C. D. Noblin (1963) gave the "Blacky
Test," a projective test based on Freudian categories, to college males
and selected fifteen "oral" personalities and fifteen "anal" types. When
they were subjected to the verbal conditioning experiment, the orals
formed the verbal set demanded by the experimental design. The anals,
however, showed no signs of conditioning; indeed, several showed *reverse* conditioning (e.g., giving more singular nouns when the reinforcement was for plurals). It is probably that the anals became conscious of
the influence attempt and deliberately gave a nonconforming response.
    Skinner has occasionally lapsed into giving practical advice; for ex-
ample, he has recently (1983) written about how the elderly person can

avoid any detrimental consequences in terms of memory loss or in terms of disapproved habits. For the latter, he recommended "engaging energetically in some other response." This advice is puzzling, inasmuch as he had postulated that "the individual is nothing, the environment is everything." If the impact is all from environment to person, there is no room for the free will required to engage voluntarily in any activity. *Beyond Freedom and Dignity* (1971) made this point quite explicitly.

But individual differences continue to foul up universal laws. To quote from a critical review of the literature on operant conditioning, "For many persons, it is highly reinforcing to be resistant to attempts to alter their behavior and highly aversive to succumb to external control. . . . The person conducting the [behavior modification] program may not be able to find any consequence strong enough to compete with the individual's desire to remain unchanged" (Stolz, S. B., L. A. Wienckowski, and B. S. Brown, 1975, p. 1037). What this passage seems to say is that it is reinforcing to some people not to be reinforced, or, perhaps, that it is reinforcing to some individuals to reject preferred reinforcements.

Skinner's rigidly objective approach to motivation has also caused errors in prediction. His criterion of hunger, for example, was hours of food deprivation, or percentage of weight loss. He kept his pigeons hungry by maintaining them at 90 percent of normal body weight. This procedure works well for pigeons, but consider the case of a young woman who decides to lose 10 percent of her weight. When the scales tell her she has succeeded, she goes out in triumph, *not to eat* but to buy a new wardrobe.

In a sense, the same problem applies to Skinner himself. Who reinforced Skinner? Did somebody feed him candies as he typed the content of his books? Did his birds reinforce him for devising new and ingenious experiments? Given a theory based almost exclusively on reinforcement, and excising all considerations of internal processes, how could Skinner explain his own performance? The question does not detract from his successes, but only from the logic of his writings.

Applications of Skinnerian Ideas

Because Skinner has emphasized studying behavior and deciding precisely what act or movement one wishes to change, his approach has spurred a remarkable amount of practical application. In industrial psychology, for example, many training programs are built around vague instructions like "Don't waste materials" and "Take care of your machine." Skinnerians moving into this area have taught supervisors to provide specifics: "Put metal into the machine this way"; "Listen for odd noises from your equipment"; "Sprinkle sawdust on oil spills." The result has been a marked increase in efficiency of operation. "Reinforce specific behaviors; don't deal in generalities" is the message.

The same tactic has been useful in the schools. Skinner criticized many teaching programs because the teacher did not point explicitly to the fact or principle to be learned. An outcome of this approach was the "teaching machine." It presented simple statements and alternative answers as in a multiple-choice examination. Thus an item might be "Columbus discovered the West Indies in (a) 1066; (b) 1492; (c) 1776; (d) Columbus really discovered the East Indies." The student who marks the wrong answer is required to reread the related material and take the test again. Computerized versions tell the pupil the correct answer, and they identify incorrect answers if these are chosen. Teaching machines are useful if and only if very great care goes into the preparation of the program. Each frame must build on the previous one and lead to the next one. This seems to be an excellent idea, with the caution that excessive analysis may fragment learning.

Industrial Applications

Industrial applications of Skinner's ideas on reinforcement schedules have been devised by various psychologists in industry. An especially ingenious experimenter has been Gary Latham. Working with crews planting tree seedlings in reforestation programs in the Pacific Northwest, Latham has been able to show improved work efficiency by using Skinnerian reinforcement scheduling.

One of Latham's studies, however, pointed out a caution needed in interpreting the results. With one production crew, Latham decided to try a VR (variable-ratio) schedule in rewards. At the end of the day, the supervisor would throw dice to decide how the production bonus was to be distributed for that day. The result was a *decline* in output, instead of the expected increase. Investigation revealed that this crew was composed mainly of fundamentalist Christians who considered gambling a sin. Thus they were annoyed by the introduction of a chance factor into the bonus plan (Yukl and Latham, 1975, p. 297). What will be a reinforcer for a particular person depends on how the reinforcer is perceived.

The Token Economy

Finally, we may mention the token economy, an educational-social application of Skinner's ideas. In a home for retarded children, for example, it has been shown that if a child is rewarded for a specific behavior (e.g., making the bed or putting clothes away neatly) with tokens that can be exchanged for candy or for TV time, so-called deeply retarded children can learn many skills formerly considered beyond them. For these handicapped youngsters, most of the research reports have been very positive.

The outcomes in groups of normal children are less clear. F. M. Levine and G. Fasnacht (1974) warned that "token economies may lead to token learning"; that is, when the tokens stop, the learning effects disappear. Skinner, of course, would argue that token rewards should not stop abruptly but should be phased out so that the child learns to "expect" some nonreinforced trials.

Another criticism of use of the token reward system to foster school learning comes from Edward Deci and his students, whose investigations indicate that providing an external reward for an act reduces any intrinsic, intrapersonal motive to carry out that action. Thus, a child who willingly washes the family car without pay may stop this voluntary action unless paid to do it. The self-generated motives are easily replaced by extrinsic rewards; as these are not likely to persist outside school, the net result is not socially desirable.

Skinnerism as a Cult

John B. Watson was criticized by his contemporaries on the ground that his followers created a kind of behavioristic cult. To some extent, the same has been true of Skinner. His students have become keenly devoted to him and defend him with enthusiasm. I mentioned earlier Lundin's exuberant "Positive reinforcement always works" and Herbert Terrace's naming the ape in his language study "Nim Chimpsky" as a jibe at Noam Chomsky. The Skinnerians have formed their own division within the American Psychological Association; in 1986, it had over 1300 members. They have also founded their own journal, the *Journal for the Experimental Analysis of Behavior*, which publishes mainly operant-conditioning studies.

The homogeneity of the beliefs of Skinnerians provided an opportunity to M. J. Mahoney (1977) to study the effect of theoretical conviction on the acceptance of articles for publication. He sent to members of the editorial board of the *Journal* (all, naturally, favorable to Skinner) drafts of an alleged research paper. Although the introduction and the method were identical for all, one third of the board members got a version supporting Skinner's views; one third got a version rejecting Skinner's alleged prediction; and one third got an ambiguous draft. The version favorable to Skinner got mostly recommendations for publication; that opposed was almost universally rejected; the third version fell between. One especially intriguing datum was that for the pro-Skinner paper, the rating on methodology was very high (4.2 out of 5), yet the identical methodology was depreciated when the results opposed Skinner (2.4 out of 5). This finding, incidentally, confirms a Gestalt prediction that an

overall pro or con attitude changes the perception of parts of the Gestalt. I should add that Mahoney explicitly generalized this biased rating
conclusion to *all* editors; a paper contravening the editor's established
theoretical stance is usually doomed to rejection.

Lundin (1979, p. 205) enumerated Skinner's honors: APA's Distinguished Contribution Award, the National Medal of Science Award, the
APA Gold Medal Award, and so on. These awards demonstrate the respect in which Skinner has been held. The interesting aspect is that although Lundin reported on dozens of other eminent psychologists, he
gave this summary of awards *only* for Skinner.

Hull and Skinner: Some Comparisons

Both Hull and Skinner fall clearly into the "tough-minded" category of
psychologists. Each was objective in research, planning his studies so that
clearly determinable stimuli were manipulated to establish links to readily observable responses. Each used laboratory procedures that minimized the possibility that subjective bias would affect the data. Each endorsed the Darwinian thesis that behavior is directed toward survival.
This acceptance of some kind of genetic mechanism operating in obscu-
rity did not lead either of them to speculate about innate differences in
capacity or in behavioral repertoire. Skinner resembled Watson in his
exaggerated environmentalism; Hull took the same position, but less aggressively.

Aside from such resemblances—all of which are, by definition, a part
of behaviorism—there are interesting differences. Hull's theoretical system appears to be elegant and sophisticated, at least on first contact. He
certainly recognized and attempted to write into his equations factors
that Skinner simply ignored. Their most obvious point of difference was
on the role of inhibition. Skinner treated inhibition mainly as extinction,
with an occasional allusion to conflicting responses. Hull was more per-
spicacious in proposing that inhibition may itself be a response, and that
negative consequences may increase the probability of an inhibitory response.

Skinner conceded that the control of behavior may be aversive, but he
offered only a slight explanation of the definition of *aversive*. Because he
defined *reinforcer* as "anything that reinforces," one may assume that
aversive means "anything that sets off avoidance reactions." Hull did not
discuss the issue of control, primarily because he was not setting his theory in the expansive social context that Skinner found attractive—in *Walden
Two* and also in *Beyond Freedom and Dignity*. It is easier to criticize Hull
on theoretical grounds precisely because he spelled out his theory in
detail; it is easier to criticize Skinner on social implications because he
did not hesitate to extrapolate his laboratory findings to larger issues.

Hull was more attentive to the problem of motivation. He explicitly incorporated "drive" into his explanation of behavior, and homeostatic restoration of equilibrium into his conception of reinforcement. The fact that the homeostatic formula does not always work out satisfactorily gave him a problem, but at least, he attempted to conceptualize the process of reinforcement in more abstract terms than did Skinner.

Both founded their theories on animal studies. Neither was very successful in extrapolating to human behavior. Skinner's pigeons never complained about being trained to walk a figure 8; automobile workers may rebel at restrictive work movements and oppressive supervision. But neither Hull nor Skinner found any place for ambitions and aspirations as determinants of behavior. "Humanistic" psychologists reject both of these theorists on those grounds.

Finally, both theories were atomistic; they called for analyzing complex behaviors into specific S-R units. Putting the units together into integrated patterns was glossed over by both. Hull's theory has a marginal advantage in the concept of a response hierarchy, which gives a clue to response interactions and to the behavioral consequences of frustration.

Skinner has one obvious advantage over Hull in his relationship to social psychology. Although his treatment of language learning has been criticized, his emphasis on the "reinforcement community" should remind psychologists in general that psychological functions are profoundly modified by societal controls. Among the Navajo Indians, there is only one word that covers the range of colors generally labeled *blue* and *green*. Furthermore, when speakers of this language and no other are tested with color chips, they mix blues and greens despite instructions to separate the chips by appearance. The basic sensory modality, as defined by Titchener, has been altered by social reinforcement.

The respect accorded Hull by his colleagues is indicated by his rank at the top of the five "eminent" psychologists identified by Coan (1979, p. 81) for the decades 1930–1939 and 1940–1949. The increasing prestige of Skinner is also apparent; in 1940–1949 he placed third in these rankings, and first in 1950–1959. It is noteworthy, however, that two Hullians (Miller and Spence) replaced their mentor in the top five for 1950–1959.

CHAPTER 12

Gestalt Theory

The functionalists and behaviorists rebelled against the Wundt–Titchener conception of psychology, but for different reasons. Functionalists objected to the atomism of the structuralist theory, and also to its exclusion of research on children, animals, and abnormal individuals. Behaviorists denounced the limitation of psychology to conscious phenomena, and overreacted by discarding the concept entirely.

Still another variety of rebellion against structuralism developed in the form of Gestalt theory. The crucial feature here was the atomistic analysis of consciousness into arbitrarily defined elements. Gestalt theorists accepted a major emphasis on consciousness but stressed the presence of organized wholes that did not depend on the formation of associative links between elementary sensations. Within a few years, they had also moved to include behavior as a legitimate datum for the psychologist, applying the same principle of organization to responses as to conscious states.

Gestalt theory had its origins in Germany at about the time Watson and Meyer were publishing the earliest behavioristic formulations. Meyer's first book came in 1911; Watson's Columbia lecture came in 1912 and his "manifesto" in 1913. A similar landmark in the history of Gestalt is 1910, when Max Wertheimer began his ingenious experiments on apparent movement. Before I describe these, it will be appropriate to note some of the predecessors of Wertheimer and their influences on the new theory.

Predecessors of Gestalt

The place of *Immanuel Kant* (1724–1804) in the history of philosophy is well known. His rationalist approach also had an important influence on psychology, specifically on Gestalt theory. He proposed that the human organism comes equipped with some innate capacities (in contrast to the Lockean *tabula rasa*); among these are awareness of space and of time, neither of which can be ascribed to pure sensation. Time, particularly, resists an empiricist approach; *frequency,* so beloved of the associationists, is not given in any sensation but only as the individual "adds up" the occurrences of specific experiences.

Within the tradition of scientific as opposed to speculative psychology, an important early figure was *Christian von Ehrenfels* (1859–1932). He used the German term *Gestalt* to identify the form quality or organization of an experience. Ehrenfels pointed out that one can play a melody in one key, then transpose it to another. Now every individual note is changed, yet the listener immediately identifies it as the same tune. As Ehrenfels (1932) wrote, "If the melody were *nothing else than the sum of the notes,* different melodies would have to be produced, because different groups of notes are here involved" (p. 521; italics added). Thus a principle different from association must be invoked; he called this principle "Gestalt quality." It meant that the pattern of organization could be consciously perceived even if all the elements were changed; this would of course be impossible under structuralist theory.

This point is the source of the oft-quoted Gestalt argument that "The whole is different from the sum of its parts." Early discussions put this principle as "The whole is *greater* than the sum of its parts"; the fallacy quickly became apparent, and all recent Gestalt literature merely asserts that the whole is different from the parts.

Carl Stumpf (1848–1936) was intrigued by the Ehrenfels paper, perhaps in part because he was an accomplished musician. In his studies of musical phenomena, Stumpf noted that if two pure tones are sounded together, they often give rise to a new experience distinctively different from the separate components. Wundt attacked this report, asserting that the finding could only have occurred if the observers were "improperly trained." This comment seems to mean that the criterion of proper training was finding data to confirm Wundt's theory. At any rate, Stumpf fought Wundt in bitter polemics, and his attitude toward Wundt undoubtedly influenced Stumpf's students to be critical of the whole Leipzig school.

Stumpf was a close associate of Edmund Husserl (1859–1938), who was a student under Stumpf, later a friend and colleague. Husserl's name is associated with the rise in Europe of phenomenology (which will be discussed later). Husserl fostered a kind of introspection that accepted the directly perceived object as a real experience, in contrast to Wundt, who insisted that the only unanalyzable experiences were sensations and feelings. Many of Husserl's successors extended his phenomenology to *solipsism,* the belief espoused by Bishop Berkeley that the only *real* world is the world as perceived, denying the "reality" of physics and chemistry. Stumpf did not go so far, but asserted the legitimacy of studying perceptions of houses, trees, and mountains, as opposed to colors and brightnesses.

For some years, Stumpf held the professorship in philosophical psychology at the University of Würzburg, which later gave rise to a school of psychology competing with that at Leipzig. The "Würzburg" school had certain obvious similarities to the functionalists in America; the theoretical position differed significantly from that of Wundt but did not break completely with the old master. This break came as the Würzburg trend gave rise to the new rebellion; Gestalt theory.

Külpe and the Würzburg School

Oswald Külpe (1862–1915) was a student of Wundt's; in fact, he took the assistantship first held by J. McKeen Cattell. At first, Külpe's relations with Wundt were cordial, and his earliest book (1893) was systematic structuralism. He joined Stumpf at Würzburg, and they attracted some brilliant students; some cynical historians have judged that Külpe's place in history was the outcome of his students' researches, not of his own originality.

One of Külpe's early experiments will show how he began moving away from Wundt. He showed observers nonsense syllables printed in various colors and patterns. Later he asked them to describe the cards. Some reported the variations in color; others mentioned the number of syllables; others described the pattern. Because all of the "sensations" must have been the same, Külpe inferred that what one experiences depends on a mental set or attitude; if the individual focuses on one aspect, the other sensory inputs might as well be absent. Although this finding was not completely incompatible with Wundt's theory, it was difficult to explain in structuralist terms.

Later Külpe and his students began work on the higher mental processes: decision, judgment, and problem solving. The method was still introspection under rigid controls, but the results were in conflict with Wundtian theory. An observer was asked, "What is harder than glass?" He answered, "Diamonds." Then, introspecting, the observer insisted that he had not experienced a visual or even a kinesthetic sensation; the answer was just there, with no sensory accompaniment. Again Wundt asserted that the observers had not been properly trained. However, the term *imageless thought* soon became popular in the literature, to identify this kind of judgment or decision without any accompaniment of a sensory nature.

Another major concept developed at Würzburg was the *Bewusstseinslage*, or conscious attitude. Today the term *mental set* would be used. Watt, a Külpe student investigating word associations, divided the judgment process into four stages: (1) preparation for observation; (2) reception of the stimulus; (3) search for a reaction word; and (4) appearance in consciousness of the reaction word. When Watt instructed an observer to be especially attentive to one of these stages, he got—not surprisingly—richer detail about that stage. Thus the conscious attitude had a great deal to do with the introspective report.

Similarly, *Karl Bühler* (1869–1963) further modified the classical experiment to permit detailed questioning of the observer after the first introspective report. For the most part, he got no sensory material out of judgments on abstract propositions; occasionally there was a report of muscle tension or a feeling of strain in the throat. This report may be relevant to Watson's thesis that thinking is subvocal talking.

Another Stumpf product, one who, like Külpe, broke in a limited degree with the Wundtian tradition, was *Herbert S. Langfeld* (1879–1958). Langfeld began his professional life focusing on introspective research, although without the theoretical rigidity that characterized Titchener, no doubt because Stumpf had made him aware of some of the difficulties in that orientation. Langfeld received his doctorate at Würzburg in 1909 and joined the Harvard University faculty in 1910. Here, as Münsterberg began to neglect the laboratory for his applied activities, James appointed Langfeld to take charge of the laboratory work in 1917. In 1924, he moved to Princeton University and remained there until retirement.

In his later years, like Margaret Washburn, Langfeld moved partway toward a functionalist position; he conceded that psychology should study overt responses as well as conscious states. In his presidential address to the American Psychological Association in 1930, Langfeld revived the Münsterberg hypothesis that consciousness of voluntary action might have as its psychological base the efferent impulse going from the cortex toward a muscle, before actual movement began. At the time, neurologists considered this impossible, but recent research indicates that it may be correct.

The Würzburg school has been largely ignored by recent historians. It merits careful consideration because it introduced the notion of unconscious processes into the laboratory side of psychology, as Freud had just brought them into the clinical side. The study of attitudes provided a transition from the pure structuralism of Titchener to the now-emerging theory of Gestalt. Present-day research on information processing has revived both the ideas and the methods of Würzburg.

Max Wertheimer

The founder of Gestalt theory in its contemporary form was Max Wertheimer (1880–1943). Himself a student of Külpe and of Stumpf, he did not question the premise that psychology was the study of consciousness. However, it is probable that he absorbed from them some doubts about the legitimacy of Wundt's claims for analytical introspec-

Archives of the History of American Psychology

Max Wertheimer, founder of Gestalt theory and opponent of single stimulus–single response research

tion. Wertheimer endorsed a phenomenological approach to science, that
is, the idea that scientific psychology deals with the real experience of
the observer as it appears in consciousness, without dissection into elements that may be creatures of the theory (James's "psychologist's fallacy").

The official date for the founding of Gestalt theory is 1910. In that
year Wertheimer was experimenting with a stroboscope, a device that
permits different visual stimuli to be presented at very short time intervals. He found that when he looked at a vertical line, then at a horizontal
line of the same length, with an interval of only 0.02 seconds, he saw the
line "fall" from the vertical to the horizontal.

Wertheimer enlisted two younger psychologists, both Stumpf pro-
tégés, Kurt Koffka and Wolfgang Köhler. They conducted an elaborate

series of experiments on the "apparent movement" experience, which Wertheimer christened the "phi phenomenon." These experiences contradicted orthodox structuralism; there was no point-to-point correspondence of stimulus to sensation; indeed, part of the visual experience could not have been elicited by a stimulus at all, as the line did not physically move. In 1912, Wertheimer published the first data and interpretations, insisting that the experience depended on the Gestalt, the configuration, rather than on elemental stimuli. Wertheimer criticized Wundt for trying to explain sensory experiences "from below," in terms of elements, whereas perceiving the real world demanded an explanation "from above": the Gestalt came first. He once offered a *reductio ad absurdum* of the structuralist approach as follows: "I stand at the window and I see a house, trees, sky. I could now on theoretical grounds try to count them and could say: There are . . . 327 brightnesses (and hues). (Do I have '327'? No: sky, house, trees") (quoted in Boring, 1950, p. 607). Wertheimer reversed Titchener's methodological dictum: in his view the observer's task was to describe *experienced objects*, not to describe experience.

Wertheimer did not write a great deal, exercising his influence more through seminars and direct conversation. Koffka, the most prolific of the group, also tried to be its synthesizer; his *Principles of Gestalt Psychology* (1935) is still regarded by some psychologists as the oracle of last resort on what Gestalt is all about. Köhler enjoyed the role of polemicist, debating with Watson and writing scathing accounts of both structuralism and behaviorism. However, as with most new movements, all three men spent too much time on the attack (cf. Hull's reaction to Koffka in Chapter Ten, p. 201).

Gestalt psychology came to America courtesy of Adolf Hitler. Wertheimer and Koffka were Jewish, and Koffka, at least, was farsighted enough to leave Germany in 1927. He had previously held visiting appointments at Cornell University (1924–1925) and the University of Wisconsin (1926–1927); in 1927, he accepted a permanent appointment at Smith College. Wertheimer stayed in Europe until 1933 but was outside Germany when notified that he had lost his university appointment in the purge of Jews. Köhler could have remained, but became angry when the Nazis interfered with his direction of the Institute of Psychology in Berlin. Köhler obtained an appointment at Swarthmore College, and Wertheimer was welcomed by a school set up primarily for the benefit of refugee scholars, the New School for Social Research, in New York City. He remained there until his death in 1943. His most important publication is *Productive Thinking* (1945) an innovative approach to reasoning and problem solving utilizing the basic principles of Gestalt. His style has been described as intuitive rather than rigorously logical; he would have been skeptical of the elaborate system of postulates and corollaries offered by Hull.

Wolfgang Köhler

Wolfgang Köhler (1887–1967) was born of a Prussian family in what is now known as Estonia, a part of the USSR. Like Wertheimer, he got his advanced training in psychology under Carl Stumpf, but he was also influenced by the great physicist Max Planck. His affection for Planck and his desire to emulate Planck's contributions to field theory in physics undoubtedly shaped much of his career.

A tall, handsome man, Köhler had a charming manner and at the same time marked dignity and reserve. A revealing anecdote tells of an American who kept addressing him as "Professor Köhler." One day, the German said, "Why must you be so formal? Why don't you just call me Dr. Köhler?" For an American, a rejection of formality would imply a shift to a first-name basis; for Köhler, it was a step from the prestigious "Professor" to the commonplace "Doctor."

After his work with Wertheimer on the phi phenomenon, Köhler became interested in testing Gestalt concepts in animals. In an early study he used chickens. He placed grains of corn on two cards, one a dark gray, one a medium gray. Grains on the latter could be eaten; those on the dark card were glued down. Soon the hens pecked only at the medium gray card. Now the cards were changed; the darker was taken away and replaced by a light gray card. S-R theory should predict that chickens would continue to peck at the medium card, as it was the one serving as stimulus in the S-R learning task; hence, a connection should have been formed between stimulus and response. In fact, the animals promptly switched to the light gray card. As Köhler pointed out, this was a serious blow to a simple connectionist theory of learning because what had been learned was a *relationship* (peck at the lighter of the visible cards). Spence (1937) developed a Hullian explanation of Köhler's data, using gradients of generalization from the first-trained positive and negative stimuli (p. 212).

Köhler also criticized the application of connectionist theory to Ebbinghaus's work on the learning of nonsense syllable lists. In these experiments, the learner reads a list of syllables several times, and the number correctly recalled is a function of frequency (the number of repetitions). But, noted Köhler (1947), this account is incomplete: "The Subject is not simply exposed to a succession of syllables; rather, he is asked to memorize them. If he follows these instructions, *it is not contiguity alone which establishes the association* . . . without intentional memorization, the learning of a series of nonsense syllables is all but impossible" (pp. 262–263, italics added). The idea is well illustrated by an anecdote (probably apocryphal) to the effect that one of Ebbinghaus's assistants collared a student, placed him in front of the memory drum, and started

Archives of the History of American Psychology

Kurt Koffka and Wolfgang Köhler, important figures in
the expansion of Gestalt theory in psychology

it rolling. After ten repetitions, the assistant asked, "How many can you
repeat?" The student replied, "Was I supposed to *learn* them?" "Mental
set" or attitude determines what one does with a stimulus. Gestalt theory
criticized behaviorist methodology on the ground that many of the so-
called discoveries are functions of the experimental situation and are not
relevant to daily life at all.

The Tenerife Studies   Perhaps because of his willingness to study animals, Köhler was sent to a research station on Tenerife in the Canary
Islands in 1913; his assignment was to study relational learning in anthropoid apes. He had expected to return to Germany late in 1914, but
the outbreak of World War I marooned him on the island. Out of this
experience came a very important research report, *Intelligenzprüfung an
Menschenaffen* ("Intelligence Testing of Anthropoid Apes") in 1917. It
was published in English translation in 1925 as *The Mentality of Apes.*

The chief theoretical concept developed in this study was *insight*. For Köhler, insight meant a restructuring of the perceptual field, resulting in the solution of a problem. The insight experiments included a variety of tasks. For example, a banana might be suspended from the ceiling, beyond the chimpanzee's reach. A box was sitting in a corner of the cage. Several animals solved the problem by moving the box under the banana and climbing on it to reach the fruit. Another problem placed the banana outside the cage, out of reach. A shrub was placed inside the cage. Sultan, Köhler's "genius" chimpanzee, solved the problem by breaking off a branch and using it as a rake to procure the reward.

The operational meaning of insight for Köhler is best illustrated by a description of Sultan's behavior in a more complex task. The fruit had been placed outside the cage, at such a distance that the usual stick would not reach it. Inside the cage were two sticks that could be joined to make one long stick. According to the keeper's account of this test:

> Sultan first of all squats indifferently on the box . . . then he gets up, picks up the two sticks, sits down again on the box and plays carelessly with them. While doing this, it happens that he finds himself holding one rod in either hand in such a way that they lie in a straight line; he pushes the thinner one a little way into the opening of the thicker, jumps up and is already on the run towards the railings . . . and begins to draw a banana towards him with the double stick. (Köhler 1917/1925, p. 127)

What Köhler emphasized in this performance was the sudden "seeing" of a relationship between the two sticks, that they could make one long stick. Other protocols likewise stressed the perceptual nature of the problem-solving activity. Behaviorist critics have commented that there is more trial and error in the experimental reports than would be expected from the theory and some cynics worry about the keeper's sobriety, but it is difficult to conclude that either box stacking or raking, and especially the jointed-stick maneuver, can be explained as random trial and error. The animal had to *see* a relationship to solve these problems.

One disappointment with *The Mentality of Apes* is that it does not carry out the implied promise of "intelligence testing." The term *intelligence* connotes for most of us a matter of individual differences, and Köhler noted that his animals differed; some failed completely on some problems. However, he confined himself to the traditional area of seeking universal laws, in the style of Wundt, rather than identifying parameters of the behavior that could be used quantitatively to measure differences among individuals. Gestalt theorists have generally followed in his footsteps; their research has centered on nomothetic (universal) laws.

A little after Koffka and Wertheimer, Köhler also migrated to the United States. The impression one gets of his departure is that of a dignified aristocrat refusing to allow the upstart Nazis to tell him who could serve on the faculty of the Berlin Institute of Psychology. In 1935, he was ordered to discharge all Jews on the staff; he refused, wrote an indignant letter to a Berlin newspaper, and left Germany. Many of his friends were astonished that he was allowed to leave; it was generally assumed that he would be arrested but, fortunately for American psychology, he was not.

Köhler was the only member of the Gestalt school to be honored by election as president of the American Psychological Association. Perhaps this was a consequence of the publicity he received for his effective debate with Watson, and perhaps of the intriguing studies of chimpanzees. He certainly did his share in bringing the Gestalt theory to a wide American audience. By his constant and sometimes intriguing use of material from modern physics, he also made Gestalt a more respectable system of psychological thought.

Kurt Koffka

Like Köhler, Kurt Koffka, (1887–1941) was recruited into the Gestalt movement by his participation as an observer in the phi-phenomenon studies. He had been born in Berlin, but at least one year of his college training (1904–1905) was received abroad, in Edinburgh. He completed his doctorate under Stumpf in 1908, at Berlin, a year before Köhler. When they met Wertheimer in Frankfurt, both were well trained, young, and talented. However, they had not committed themselves to any specific system or school, and Wertheimer evidently did a thorough job of convincing them that they should join him in his innovative theorizing.

After World War I, it was obvious that the center of world psychology had moved from Germany to the United States. Germany was afflicted with an unstable political and economic situation. Koffka may have anticipated the rise of Hitler, or he may simply have attracted more offers from American schools because of his fluency in English. At any rate, after his visiting professorships at Cornell and Wisconsin he moved to Smith College and remained there until his death in 1941.

Developmental Psychology

Koffka's early work centered on children, and he demonstrated that Gestalt theory provided significant insights into events at that level. In 1921, he published *Die Grundlagen der psychischen Entwicklung* ("Fundamentals of Mental Development"), in which he used the framework of Gestalt theory, which had progressed substantially by that time. Basically he emphasized the inheritance of mental and behavioral tendencies, differentiation of gross movements into finer coordinations, and learning as perceiving and as differentiation of the phenomenal field. This book attracted wide attention when the English translation appeared in 1924 as *The Growth of the Mind*.

Principles of Gestalt Psychology

Whereas Wertheimer was the innovator and Köhler the propagandist and evangelist for Gestalt, Koffka was the methodical systematizer. His major work, *Principles of Gestalt Psychology* (1935), is still an authoritative source for the basic theory (Henle, 1985).

Koffka first asserted a distinction between the geographical environment (the world as seen by physics) and the behavioral environment (the world as perceived by the behaving organism). Darwinian principles would indicate that any species in which these two did not correspond fairly well would die out; hence, human beings obviously have a sensory system that generally, but not invariably, provides a guide to adaptive behavior. None the less, for specific individuals, the perceived environment may differ in important ways from the geographical environment.

It was also necessary, in Koffka's system, to distinguish a psychological field (PF) from the behavioral environment (BE). The psychological or psychophysical field may not include everything in the behavioral environment; one may be unaware of another person's feelings, and yet one's behavior may be modified to take account of them. Similarly, the psychophysical field includes one's awareness of self but does not include unconscious impulses or physiological processes (glandular secretions, for example) that are relevant. These kinds of distinctions make the Gestalt approach compatible with Freud's psychoanalytic theory, to be discussed in Chapter Fourteen.

In the Gestalt view, behavior is molar, not molecular; the task of psychology is to explain and understand the everyday actions of human beings, not an artificial, impoverished laboratory sample. The behavioristic model of atomism is rejected. The metaphor is that of a magnetic field in which each aspect affects all the others, so that it is inaccurate to treat any stimulus in isolation from the field in which it occurs.

In an appeal to the prestige of physics, Koffka—like Köhler—pointed to the value of the field concept for studying gravitation and magnetism. Newton had been criticized for his "mutual attraction of masses" because it implied action at a distance, a possibility repugnant to the physicists of his time. With Albert Einstein, the concept of the gravitational field eliminated the controversy, as each mass was enmeshed in and became a part of the physical field. Note that for the physicist, neither the sun nor the planet "causes" the gravitational field; it is the total situation that can be described by a field. Paralleling this argument, Koffka held that we should think of a "psychological field" (PF), which controls behavior. Figure 12.1, for example, might represent a barking dog (in the physical or geographical environment), perceived as a dangerous beast (in the behav-

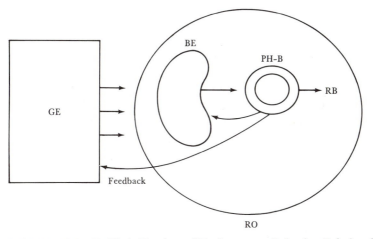

RO

FIGURE 12.1   Koffka's Version of Environment-Behavior Relationships

GE = geographical environment, the physical world; BE = behavioral
environment (how it is perceived by the person RO (real organism). PH-B
= behavior as the behaving person perceives it; this is not necessarily the
same as RB (real behavior as viewed by observers). Feedback has been
added to Koffka's original drawing.   *(Modified from Koffka, 1935, p. 40,*
Figure 2, by permission of Harcourt Brace Jovanovich)

ioral environment). The psychological field (PF) would embrace person,
perceived animal, perceived protective devices, and so on. The perceived
behavior (PH-B) may not be the same as "real behavior" (RB). The person may run screaming for safety but may claim that the action was cool
and controlled.

Obviously, then, Gestalt psychology maximized the difference between
appearance and reality. Most important, Gestalt theory says that we respond to appearances (BE) rather than to "reality" (GE). This position is
in complete contrast with all of the behavioristic theories, which assert
that behavior is in response to a real object in real space.

The psychological field may include other persons, and thus Gestalt
psychology flows easily into social psychology. The field that includes a
young man, a young woman, and little illumination elicits different behavior from that of the same persons on a downtown street corner. It is
a mistake, Koffka held, to deal with any stimulus without regard to the
field in which it is embedded. He would object to Skinner's analysis (Figure 11.3) because the outcome depends on the total field.

To introduce a term not used by Koffka, each psychological field constitutes a *system* in which everything affects everything else. Systems are
not limited to social situations. Each individual may be conceived of as a
system, including a self-image, aspirations and ambitions, and memories

of childhood, all interacting to produce a Gestalt, the personality. Although this seems to accept the analysis of a totality into elements, Koffka held that we can only analyze the larger system into smaller systems (an analogy would be analyzing a corporation into departments, or physiology into a study of digestion or respiration, each a system with intrinsic properties).

Some critics of Gestalt see this as an infinite regress, in which systems enclose systems enclosing systems, as in the verse about "these same fleas have smaller fleas, and so ad infinitum." It is somewhat analogous to the behaviorist's dilemma of defining a response; if the person responding must be observed by another individual, then the recording person should be observed by a second outsider, to verify the occurrence of the recording response, and so on. Gestalt theorists deal with the apparent contradiction as the behaviorists do, that is, by asserting that for practical purposes, the limitation is irrelevant.

Koffka proceeded to define the interrelations of GE, BE, and PF. GE tends to determine the structure of BE (hence, the Gestalt laws regarding grouping, connectedness, contour, and so on, which correspond to features of GE as defined by physics). Köhler had proposed an isomorphic relationship in which a physical Gestalt gave rise to a perceptual Gestalt. However, there are too many exceptions to this rule for it to be accepted as a universal. Isomorphism for Koffka and Köhler seems very similar to Wundt's psychophysical parallelism, but without Wundt's implication of a point-to-point correspondence of physical input and sensory experience. For Gestalt, the relationship is one of matching patterns, not specific points. Koffka offered a diagram (Figure 12.1) purporting to summarize this field theory. The BE is a function of GE, but the response (RB, or real behavior) may also reflect unconscious influences. RO represents the real organism, and PH-B the phenomenal behavior (the response as seen by the responding person). The central circle represents the phenomenal self, or ego.

Koffka (1935) noted that "behavior is *regulated* by the environment" (p. 28). This is a statement of which Skinner could approve. But Koffka meant the behavioral environment, whereas Skinner would point to the physical or geographical environment. What Koffka would concede to Skinner is that the GE can kick back when a response is inappropriate to real conditions; thus over time, the BE will be modified to conform more closely to the demands of the real world. However, the immediate determinant of a response is BE. Look at Figure 12.2. The drawing elicits a familiar response. Now turn the page and look at Figure 12.3. The same physical stimulus (physically identical to the first) is now found to elicit a different percept. Although the example is trivial, the principle is not. As Titchener found it necessary to accept a "context" theory of meaning, and as Hull accepted the rule of afferent interaction, so Gestalt

A|3

FIGURE 12.2   An Illustration of a Common Gestalt Effect

(From a verbal description by J. S. Bruner &
A. L. Minturn, 1955)

discovered that mental set or context may modify the figure or the focal stimulus.

Laws of Perceiving   Koffka (1935) noted the difference between *distant* stimuli and *proximal* stimuli. The distant stimulus is an object or person; the proximal stimulus is a process on the retina, the cochlea, or some other receptor surface. The conscious experience of a situation is a function of the proximal stimuli, which, in turn, depend on the distant stimuli (see Figure 1.3). However, changes in the distant stimuli do not always lead to change in experience (size constancy, color constancy, and shape constancy are examples). Conversely, there may be a constant distant and proximal stimulus situation, yet the experience changes (consider the reversible perspective figures). It seems clear that what is going on *inside* the organism is modifying these stimuli. Perceiving, then, is not a passive reflection of the physical environment but is an achievement of the organism dealing with external imputs.

Figure and Ground   Unless a visual field is homogeneous (as in a thick fog), there are contours in the field, and these set off objects from one another. A young child going to a farm for the first time does not see a "blooming, buzzing confusion" but experiences cow, barn, and food trough as distinct objects. He or she may not be able to name them, but they are separate, segregated from the rest of the field. A given object then becomes the *figure* against a poorly differentiated *ground*.

   Contrast between figure and ground facilitates perceiving. (See Figure 12.4.) If there are two contrasting areas, a contour between them produces two segregated figures. The nature of the configuration determines their properties. Thus Koffka described an experiment in which a card is half-red and half-green. Superposed on both is a gray circle. If a ruler or other divider is laid over the line separating red from green, half of the gray circle will appear green (the one surrounded by red), and the other will appear red (the one surrounded by green). Thus the perceptual quality of the figure is modified by the ground against which it appears.

12 13

FIGURE 12.3   A Change in Context
Changes the Perceived Gestalt

Prägnanz   The figure is defined by its contour. However, there is an intrinsic tendency for this contour to take a regular shape and, if possible, a familiar form. *Prägnanz* is the term used to identify a tendency toward good form—regular, symmetrical, balanced. If a gap appears in the contour, it is likely to be seen as filled; that is, the organism prefers closed figures to incomplete figures.

Proximity and *similarity* influence the formation of Gestalts in the behavioral environment (see Figure 12.4.) If several elements appear in the perceptual field, those close together tend to be organized into one pattern. Similar items also tend to flow together into a pattern, as in Figure 12.4. These principles obviously parallel "laws of association," as stated by the British associationists. However, mere "contiguity" is not adequate to explain the phenomenal experience.

Attitude   One may be expecting a certain friend, and a poorly defined human figure appears in the distance. There is a tendency to shape this figure into the memory image of the friend. An example of how one may be "set" for a certain input and so shape it in the phenomenal field is given in Figures 12.2 and 12.3. The attitude induced by the figure on the left modifies the figure on the right. The use of "attitude" in this context was probably determined by the writings of the Würzburg school.

Attitudes may be a consequence of life experiences rather than of a

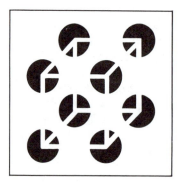

FIGURE 12.4   An Organized Gestalt without Apparent Physical Cues

This may be seen as a grouping of eight circles with white lines across them. Then the figure reverses and the white lines outline a cube. But where are the white lines? *(From D. R. Bradley and H. M. Petty,* American Journal of Psychology, *1977, 90, 253-262; Figure 1, p. 254. By permission of the American Journal of Psychology and the University of Illinois Press)*

laboratory experiment. In Figure 12.5, I represent the situation of persons with radically different social roles and personal histories; the manager will be predisposed to see the "12–13" pattern, but a union leader will be impressed by the "A–B" pattern. Reality depends on what the person brings to the stimulus situation.

Köhler and Koffka pointed out many additional principles relating perceptual Gestalts to physical stimulation. Boring (1950) commented that someone had searched the Gestalt literature and identified 114 "laws" of perceptual organization. Few of us would care to try to learn all of them. Boring (1950, pp. 611–612) offered a condensation that can be useful to anyone studying Gestalt theory.

It is clear from the close link of physical stimuli and perceptual Gestalt that Gestalt theorists are not devoted to a theory of reality as created by consciousness. Rather, they want to establish parallels between configurations in the world of physics and configurations in the world of psychology. In this respect, their work is basic to the development of systems theory, in which a physical system can be broken down, but only into a subsystem or subsystems, each of which has the attributes of a system within itself. Many observers have treated this principle as

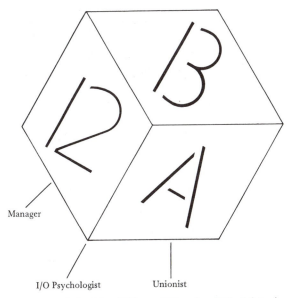

FIGURE 12.5   The Effect of Varying Life Histories on Perceiving

The drawing suggests that the Manager is influenced by the context he brings to industry (12) to see associated events in his fashion (13). The Unionist brings his history (A) and so is inclined to see the associated figure as (B). I/O psychologists try to see both aspects.

evidence of the importance of Köhler's training in physics and his work on physical configurations. Koffka did not give this issue the prominence assigned by Köhler, but nonetheless his treatment of psychological processes flows from the Köhler principle of isomorphism of physical and psychological events.

The Ego   Although Koffka did not label the ego in his drawing of the behavioral field (Figure 12.1), his theory treated it as an important aspect of psychology. Gestalt and psychoanalysis are the only schools explicitly to develop the idea of an ego, or self; Wundt and Titchener had accepted the Humean notion that the self is no more than a bundle of sensations, and Watson modified this view solely by making the personality the sum total of one's response systems. The Gestalt theorists, then, were introducing a novel concept into a laboratory-oriented psychology.

Like BE, the ego is, at bottom, perceptual in nature. The growing child develops segregated perceptual wholes, unitary perceptions of "my body," "my hands," "my toys," and so on. These merge into a percept of the self as a whole. Thus, although the potential for an ego must be innate, its actual formation depends on environmental stimulation and perceptual organization. Only at this point is one able to be "self-conscious," that is, to treat the self like an object or a tool. Contrast facilitates the segregation of the ego; as the child learns that others have toys, demands, and activities, the figure (ego) comes into contrast with the ground (other people).

The ego is a bounded whole, and the average person resents intrusion into this space. Thus we become angry when another individual probes into matters we perceive to be private. Similarly, most of us rebel at being forced to obey the orders of another person; this is especially true if the other person has no socially sanctioned authority to issue commands. Recent research indicates that the average person tries to maintain a physical distance from others, a "personal space."

The Executive   Koffka also found it expedient to postulate the further differentiation within the ego of a system he called "the executive." His logic in this respect is unclear. Some of the attributes of the ego overlap those of the executive. At best, it would seem that the executive was considered an action system, whereas the ego might include other subsystems; for example, the individual's self-image is a component of the ego but may enter into a configuration of executive action, only under special circumstances (those we call *ego involving*).

Motivation   Koffka did not offer any list of human motives. In fact, he treated motivation as if it were externally determined and primarily situational in character. The key concept was *tension*, but this concept could cover a wide range of phenomena, from hunger or pain to a quest for a

Ph.D. degree or a request from a psychologist to fill out a questionnaire. Obviously tensions vary in intensity, as measured by the persistence of efforts to reduce the tension. In this conception, tension for Koffka was much the same as D for Hull: it mobilized energy and sustained activity until the tension was reduced.

A persisting tension induces continuing activity and thus, presumably, further differentiation of the phenomenal field. Tension reduction stops action and so tends to maintain the organization of the field at that point. Seen in this way, tension reduction served the same function for Koffka as reinforcement did for Guthrie; for Hull and Skinner, reinforcement had a strengthening function beyond what Koffka specified.

Tension may be induced by the appearance of objects in the BE. Thus a fruit stand may evoke a feeling of hunger or a tension to approach the fruit and eat it. Koffka (1935) called this attraction value "demand character": "A description of the objects within our behavioural environment would be incomplete and inadequate if we omitted that some of these objects were attractive, others repulsive, and others indifferent" (p. 353). Koffka also included emotion within this category of phenomena; fear, for example, involves repulsion and avoidance, and anger depends on a behavioral environment to which one responds with repulsion plus destructive behavior. It is interesting that in this connection, Koffka had words of praise for William McDougall, the advocate of a comprehensive instinct theory of behavior. In other words, Gestalt accepts the notion that motives and emotions have an innate basis. On the other hand, Koffka conceded that the demand character of some objects was learned, as was true with Hull's secondary reinforcement objects or situations.

Closure Tension reduction is characterized as closure. There is a gap between the organism and the goal object that "demands" closure, and when closure occurs, the tension disappears. Köhler had used this concept in his interpretation of the ape and the jointed stick, as also of the dog that learned to get a bone by going away from it to get around a barrier.

Koffka (1935) pointed out that the same phenomenon can be detected when one is searching for a forgotten memory or for a problem solution. Effort is exerted until the recall is completed, the gap closed: "The stress exists between the Ego and the object, and is relieved by a movement of the organism's body" [not always necessary]. ". . . Such movement as would not be 'adapted' would either leave the stress unaltered or increase it, whereas the 'adapted' movement will decrease and eventually relieve the strain" (p. 373). This explanation does not differ significantly from that of Hull, who used tension reduction as the operative aspect of reinforcement. It is also compatible with Guthrie's view that an "unadapted" response (i.e., an unsuccessful one) leaves tension high, thus resulting in continued activity until the "adapted" response occurs.

Hierarchy of Tensions   Koffka (1935) speculated that control of behavior "from above" implies a hierarchy of tensions. Thus the behavior of a soldier entering combat is described as one in which "the movement actually made is such as to decrease the *total* stress, much as partial stresses may be increased by it" (p. 374). That is, the move toward the combat zone relieves major tensions (e.g., fear of being called a coward or of being court-martialed) as opposed to the tension evoked by the fear of being wounded or killed. Unfortunately, the criterion here of hierarchical potency is behavior, just as it was in Hull's hierarchy of responses. There is no independent criterion by which one can predict the ranking of tensions in potency, although such a ranking can be constructed by close observation, as in clinical diagnosis or therapy.

Memory and Learning   Although most of us would assume that a theory of learning should precede a theory of remembering, Koffka reversed this order. He first developed a theory of the memory *trace*. There must be, he argued, some change in the organism that persists over time, so that it can interact with later stimulus input to elicit behavior learned in the earlier experience. The trace is not a point-to-point connection, a telephone line that has been plugged in, but an organized pattern (one recognizes a melody when it is played in a different key from that in which it was first heard). Koffka did not explicitly accept Köhler's speculation about cortical fields, but his treatment would be compatible with that proposed earlier by Köhler.

The memory trace undergoes changes over time. Most of these follow the rules of perceptual Gestalts. That is, a trace will change from poor form to good form (irregularities are ironed out and familiar elements are exaggerated); missing data will be filled in, and later questioning elicits these as false memories (see, for example, Loftus and Loftus, 1980). New events may also lead to modifications of traces; something analogous to retroactive inhibition may operate as the new pattern dominates over and may block the appearance of the earlier trace. Mere passage of time does not account for forgetting; it is an active process of the replacement of an older by a newer trace. This formulation agrees with those of Hull and Skinner.

Learning was conceived of by Koffka as being a process in which traces of prior experience coalesce with present input to lead to a modification of behavior. In a sense, this is merely a repetition of what he said about forgetting. One deletes the traces that led to maladaptive or unsuccessful outcomes and replaces these with traces calculated to evoke adaptive responses. However, Koffka admitted that one may learn "bad" habits; these, of course, are tension-reducing in some respect. There is, in this system, no place for reinforcement as this concept was used by Hull and Skinner. To the outsider, some of Koffka's examples suggest that a concept like reinforcement is needed to explain why some traces become more potent than others in determining future behavior.

Learning is closely tied to perceiving. The cat in the puzzle box, Koffka asserted, learned to differentiate the lever or button (which opened the door) from its ground, and future responses centered on this part of the behavioral environment. Koffka distinguished this kind of learning task from Köhler's insight experiments by pointing out that in the latter, the box or the stick constituted visual Gestalts; that is, they were already differentiated from the ground. In the puzzle box, there is no perceptible Gestalt that links the lever with the door. Learning, then, may, in some cases, depend on differentiating the field and identifying the crucial element.

Koffka attacked associationist conceptions of learning, as exemplified by Thorndike and by the British associationists; he argued that association implies an external link, whereas Gestalt learning focuses on the *intrinsic relations* of the components of a given system. Unfortunately, the intrinsic relations were not adequately defined. It may seem, for example, that *tree* and *fruit* are intrinsically related, but they do not form any compelling visual organization. Many trees bear no fruit. The role of contiguity in establishing this kind of relationship was ignored by Koffka.

Koffka also conceded that trial and error might be involved in learning, especially in the sense of running around and looking at a task situation from different perspectives. Such variation of behavior could maximize the chance of getting the optimal Gestalt with the key cue as figure. Koffka deprecated the behaviorist emphasis on reflexes, commenting that human and higher animal behavior is far more flexible than it would be if one could only rearrange innate reflexes.

Apparently it is also possible that a new Gestalt emerges from learning, that is, from proximity and repetition. Koffka cited with approval the work on learning to receive transmissions in Morse code, in which learning individual letters occurs first, then recognition of words without spelling them out, and finally the recognition of common phrases without consciously identifying the component words. Although this hypothesis was presumably based on the work of W. L. Bryan and N. Harter (1899), Koffka did not cite them in this regard, probably because they offered an associationist interpretation of the data. Because of the interaction of memory traces, Koffka assumed that mergers could take place inside the organism; some of the recent studies of information processing, to be discussed later, seem to point to a comparable process, that of grouping memories into categories even though the component items of the category have not been experienced together.

The work of Harry Harlow (1949) supported Koffka's speculations about relational learning. Harlow presented rhesus monkeys with three food cups. Two of these had identical covers, (e.g., a circle carved from wood); the third had a different cover, such as a carving of a + sign. Food was always under the "different" lid. The animals soon learned to choose the "odd" item in a triad, even on trials in which both positive and negative symbols were new. This finding is hardly compatible with simple S-R theory; it is evidence for a configurational process of coping with the environment.

Motor Condensation   I have noted the concept of *motor condensation* as proposed by Max Meyer and ratified by Watson. Koffka devised a rather ingenious approach to this phenomenon in terms of Gestalt principles. He suggested that the first repetition of a novel motor act may form a "good Gestalt" (i.e., a form that resists change), but most probably, the act will lead to a trace that is unstable, with unclear contours, irregular and incomplete. Under these circumstances, field forces will tend to push the trace—and hence the later behavior—toward better form. Thus the typist learning to use the machine will indulge in many unnecessary movements; these will drop out as the memory trace attains Prägnanz, or good form (Koffka, 1935, pp. 554–555).

There are two obvious problems in this formulation. One is that the definition of trace stability is circular; if the trace does not change, it is stable. Because this circularity is common in psychological theorizing, we may ignore it. The second problem is that there is no independent criterion of what constitutes an incomplete or irregular form. Koffka would have been reluctant to use a standard set by an external observer, as the BE is inside the responder. At best, we can say that the Koffka hypothesis seems plausible but not open to testing within the limits of his own theory.

Neurologizing   The passion for reducing mental phenomena to events in the nervous system was strongest among the behaviorists; however, Gestalt theorists were not far behind. Wertheimer was fairly cautious in this area, but both Köhler and Koffka indulged in flights of fancy regarding the neurophysiological basis of learning and memory. Köhler (1938) wrote, "Neural events tend to modify slightly the state of the tissue in which they occur. Such changes will resemble those processes by which they have been produced both in their pattern and with respect to other properties" (p. 236). He also propounded a theory of *electrical fields* in the cortex that were isomorphic with the perceptual field. However, his experimental attempts to verify this hypothesis were failures. It is one of the little ironies of history that, some twenty years after Köhler's death, Brenner, *et al.* (1978) found that stimulation of a skin surface induced a *magnetic* field in the somatic projection area of the human cortex.

Koffka also indulged in neurophysiologizing, although less persistently than Köhler. In a discussion (1935/1963) of the effect of successive sound stimuli on perceiving, he wrote:

> The interaction (of sounds) may be due to a leap of electrical potential between the two (cortical) areas, when they are in contact, or between each

of them and the field between them, if they are not adjoining. If stimulation is different in two adjoining areas, then, according to this assumption, the chemical processes in the two corresponding psychophysical areas will lead to different concentrations of the reacting molecules and ions, which, owing to the different velocities of positive and negative ions, must produce a difference of potential. (p. 441)

These remarks are about as remote from reality as Weiss's speculations about proton–electron aggregates determining the learning process. One can explain such fantasies only by assuming that the high prestige of physics, chemistry, and physiology attracts the attention of psychologists, and they seek to add to their own prestige by linking their hypotheses with concepts from these "hard" sciences.

The Americanization of Gestalt

As Titchener brought structuralism from Germany to the United States, so Wertheimer, Köhler and Koffka brought Gestalt theory. However, the Gestalt doctrine had greater success in attracting American adherents, who extended the theory and demonstrated its relevance to new problems. It can be argued that this outcome reflected the greater relevance of Gestalt to general psychology, as compared with structuralism; or it may be that Titchener's strong but somewhat aloof personality limited his ability to attract disciples, as compared with the engaging personalities of Wertheimer and Koffka or the dignified but charming Köhler. At any rate, Gestalt quickly became a recognized part of the American scene.

I have referred earlier to a survey by Coan (1979) in which American psychologists were asked to identify the important figures in the development of psychology in successive decades. Surprisingly, these judgments placed Max Wertheimer among the top five influential leaders for 1910–1919—surprising because he had not begun to publish his original ideas until 1912. A probable explanation is that the judges were aware of the impact of Gestalt in later decades and projected it backward in time; in reality, knowledge of Gestalt thinking in America was minimal during the period 1910–1919. Partly as a result of the severance of German–American communications during World War I, and partly because Gestalt did not reach a "good configuration" as a theoretical system until about 1922, Gestalt had little influence on American psychology until the 1920s. More noteworthy is the fact that these judges placed at least one of the prominent Gestalt theorists in the top five "influential" figures until 1940–1949. Only in the 1950s did the Gestalt group fail to place in the top five.

Muzafer Sherif (1906–   ) published one of the first major American studies based on a Gestalt approach. Sherif was interested in the effect of group pressure on individual decisions. He made use of the auto-kinetic phenomenon (in a dark room, a point of light will seem to move when one stares at it). Sherif got judgments from subjects in isolation about the amount of movement; when the person stabilized at some fig-ure, perhaps ten inches, he or she was placed in a new setting with two other persons. Unknown to the subject was the fact that these were con-federates of the experimenter, primed to give judgments of movements much larger than 10 inches, and averaging, perhaps, twenty inches. The naive subject would soon modify his or her responses to conform with those of the majority. Sherif interpreted this as a case in which the ma-jority judgments induced a mental set so that the subject's responses were perceived as too small, and his or her judgments were modified to pro-duce a better Gestalt. In everyday life, we refer to this as the *bandwagon effect.*

Solomon Asch (1907–   ) continued this line of research, but more rigorously. Instead of the ambiguous autokinetic stimulus, Asch (1956) presented his naive subject with clearly sensed stimuli, such as lines on a visible screen. He found that the subject would conform to a unanimous majority of four and give reports that were obviously unrealistic (Asch noted that some subjects spontaneously informed him later that they did not "see" the longer line but merely changed their verbal response to avoid seeming stubborn. Similar behavior changes are not unusual in political or religious arguments.)

Asch also applied other Gestalt principles in his research. In an inge-nious study of the determination of a part by the whole, he asked his subject to form an impression of an unknown person. He presented a list of adjectives such as the following: "cold, intelligent, vigorous, soft-spoken, dominant, pragmatic." The subjects were asked to write down what kind of personality would be represented by these attributes. An-other group received a similar task, but the adjectives were "warm, in-telligent, vigorous," and so on.

The overall descriptions differed sharply from those of the first group. For example, the "cold" person's intelligence was interpreted as shrewd, cunning, quick to take advantage of others, self-centered, and so on. The "warm" person's "intelligent" attribute, however, meant helpful, a good adviser, and a leader in altruistic causes. Thus the Gestalt induced by the first adjective modified the meaning of the adjectives following it. As Asch (1952) wrote, "The 'same' quality in two persons is often not the same psychologically" (p. 60).

Asch contributed an important textbook in social psychology that sys-tematically developed Gestalt positions. For example, he criticized Floyd Allport's behavioristic social psychology (1924) as "dehumanized," cold, and mechanistic. Allport (1924) had written, "The significance of social behavior is exactly that of non-social, namely, the correction of the individual's biological maladjustment to his environment" (p. 3). The manifest implication is that *all* behavior is egocentric and is directed to removing biological deficits and frustrations. There was no room in Allport's psychology for altruism, loyalty, or self-sacrifice. As in Hobbes's view, cooperation was feasible if and only if it contributed to the welfare of the cooperator.

Asch conceded that Allport was probably correct with respect to language learning, at least with regard to the first year or so of life. This was the circular reflex theory (see p. 189). After the first year, however, the child begins to develop rules of grammar and semantics that cannot be dealt with in behavioristic formulas. (See Chomsky, p. 231). Asch noted that the Gestalt view on these issues was very similar to that of Jean Piaget.

Firing in a different direction, Asch ridiculed the European social psychologists who had espoused the "group mind" concept (see, e.g., LeBon, 1918). Asch (1952) held that these psychologists were "ignoring the fact that group realities must be distributed in individual centers" (pp. 253–254). This moves back toward the Floyd Allport position, leaning away from the Gestalt precept that the group has a reality of its own; Asch defended his view by noting that in such studies as the majority opinion experiments, the evidence for group influence comes from individual judgments, in their conscious or unconscious acceptance of group norms.

Asch demonstrated the utility of such basic Gestalt principles as Prägnanz (good form), closure, and whole–part relations in interpreting a wide variety of social phenomena. One curious omission in his 1952 book is the lack of any reference to the work of Alfred Adler. Asch wrote an entire chapter on "social interest" but failed to credit Adler with introducing the concept. "Of the fact of social interest there can be no doubt," Asch wrote; "we form a craving for the society of people" (p. 333). Adler had written much earlier (1929): "The high degree of cooperation and social culture which man needs for his very existence demands spontaneous social effort. . . . Social interest is not inborn, but it is an *innate potentiality* which has to be consciously developed" (p. 3; italics added). The word *consciously* in this sentence may be misleading, as Adler had elsewhere emphasized the unconscious nature of such processes. The omission of Adler by Asch may have indicated a reluctance to concede any points to psychoanalytic theory; on the other hand, Asch may only have been protecting a "good Gestalt" by deleting any mention of an outside source for his idea. At any rate, Gestalt and psychoanalytic theory are compatible on this issue (although neither side might concur).

Harry Helson (1898–1977) did not consider himself an orthodox Gestalt writer, but he did contribute in an important way to the understanding of Gestalt theory in the United States, and to a body of experimental research supporting the theory. His earliest contribution formed his

doctoral dissertation. Over some opposition from his adviser, E. G. Boring, and the Harvard faculty, he won permission to do a theoretical dissertation summarizing the German literature on Gestalt theory. Ironically, one notes that Boring, a sturdy Titchenerian, had the bad luck to
have Helson escape from his ideas into Gestalt, as later he saw B. F.
Skinner become a leader in the behaviorist movement. Helson (1925,
1926) publicized Gestalt in a series of articles based on his dissertation;
the ideas may have profited from a seminar at Cornell University with
Koffka when Koffka was a visiting professor there in 1924–1925.

Helson's chief claim to fame is his work on adaptation-level (AL) phenomena. The Greeks had observed that if one hand is placed in hot
water and the other in cold water, then both in a tepid bath, one hand
is experienced as warm, the other as cold. The skin had adapted to the
incoming level of stimulation, and the organism (presumably the brain)
formed a norm, or AL, against which later stimuli were judged. This
argument against treating the stimulus as an absolute physical event had
been familiar for centuries. Helson demonstrated its virtual universality;
it can be shown to function in judgments of beauty, in political attitudes,
in preferred noise level, and so on. He showed that if a person is exposed to stimuli varying on more than one dimension (e.g., color and
weight), the kind of AL that develops will depend on which dimension
is made salient by instructions. Thus a person may be induced to form
a norm for yellow weights and may show no evidence of a norm for blue
weights in the same series. This, of course, resembles much contemporary work on memory, which shows that memory loss in one category
may leave other similar classes of memories undamaged.

The AL for a given stimulus, such as noise or pressure, forms a neutral point, or psychological zero. Thus a factory worker may become
adapted to noise and may ignore it, although it may be intensely annoying to a plant visitor. Helson suggested that one can adapt to a crowded
or a solitary environment, and if circumstances push the individual out
of this normal setting, energy will be mobilized to restore the former
equilibrium. Thus, personality traits may be structured ways of protecting some customary AL.

Helson neatly filled a gap between structuralist and Gestalt theory. His
work began, he noted, in the Titchenerian tradition, with studies on visual adaptation and the loss of intensity of a stimulus as it is repeated.
However, he soon parted company with a theory that insisted that the
physical stimulus and the conscious sensation had a fixed, one-to-one
relationship. He found the AL effect to be more immediate and more
effective in changing the experienced sensation than could be accounted
for by the concept of apperception. Further, his principle of AL could
be applied to such problems as judging the attractiveness of faces, the
seriousness of crimes, and so on. The wide scope of AL theory is exemplified by the papers in M. H. Appley (1971), the outcome of a sympos-

ium in Helson's honor. His work has affected a wide range of research, and J. P. Guilford (1979) praised him by asserting that he had "brought relativity to psychology" (p. 629).

Fritz Heider (1896–   ) likewise extended Gestalt theory into what he called "balance theory." Gestalt writers in general have stressed a tendency toward equilibrium and constancy of a whole despite changes in the parts. Heider applied this notion to interpersonal perceiving and behaving. In doing so, he tackled, not always successfully, the ancient dilemma of action based on what one assumes the other person is thinking. He wrote (1958) that "a person reacts to what he thinks the other person is perceiving, feeling, and thinking, in addition to what the other person may be doing" (p. 1). Köhler had touched on this question in his discussion of "physiognomic perception" (e.g., perceiving a hostile attitude behind pleasant words). Heider's work, in turn, was influential in starting research on "attribution theory," as exemplified by Jones, Nisbett, et al. (1971).

Heider and his wife, Grace Heider, translated Kurt Lewin's *Principles of Topological Psychology* (1936) into English, and one might have expected his theory to approximate Lewin's approach. However, his interpersonal research is more in the vein of Köhler and Koffka than of Lewin. A key concept is *Prägnanz,* or good form. Good forms tend to be symmetrical, balanced, and stable; poor forms tend to be modified to become good forms, by the modification of memory traces or by the deletion of elements that do not fit well. If inconsistent perceptions or attitudes exist within a person's phenomenal field, tension is generated and closure is attempted, to remove the inconsistency and reduce the tension: "A balanced configuration exists if the attitudes towards the parts of a casual unit are similar" (Heider, 1946, p. 107). Thus, if I like President Eisenhower and it is alleged that he did something reprehensible, I may protect a stable equilibrium by refusing to believe the report. If it is incontestable, then I may restore balance by reducing my favorable evaluation of Eisenhower.

Interpersonal perceiving is not the only component of Heider's theory. Interpersonal behavior can also be predicted. If Sam is hostile to Tom, and Tom is hostile to Joe, then the theory predicts that Sam will be friendly to Joe: "My enemy's enemy is my friend." From these prosaic examples, Heider went on to develop a fairly elegant mathematical description of balanced social relationships.

Leon Festinger (1919–   ) followed up Heider's work on balance theory by elaborating on the attitudinal aspect in his theory of "cognitive dissonance." Essentially Festinger proposed that individuals experience tension when they are asked to believe two contradictory statements at the same time (George Orwell made this idea the focus in his concept of "doublethink," in which people learned to believe that war is peace, freedom is slavery, and so on). Festinger extended his principle of dissonance to include instances in which the stimulus input is something different from what was expected, or in which the situation is ambiguous. Tension (anxiety) develops when one is uncertain about the appropriate action.

Because tension is essential for learning in the Gestalt tradition, the tension evoked by unexpected or ambiguous stimuli may be expected to lead to learning. As learning means a behavior change, dissonance predicts modifications—of attitudes and actions.

Festinger's theory set off a flurry of experiments on the effects of dissonance on social interactions. One experiment involved inducing college students to make a speech contradicting the speaker's beliefs as these had been expressed in private. If a small reward was offered for such a speech, and if the subject accepted, more attitude change resulted than if the reward was large. Festinger interpreted this outcome as evidence that making the speech induced dissonance ("Why am I saying such things?"). The dissonance could be reduced by deciding, "I really believe at least part of it." On the other hand, giving the disbelieved speech for a large payment required no self-justification. Thus, contrary to reinforcement theory, the learning was greater with small than with large rewards. Later studies have shown that this effect is variable and that the instances in which it works are more restricted than was originally believed.

Applications of Gestalt Psychology

Like structuralism, Gestalt developed in an atmosphere congenial to "pure science" and hostile to applications. Nonetheless, Gestalt influences can be found in a variety of modern settings. Perhaps most of these are concentrated in the field of education. Wertheimer's major book, *Productive Thinking* (1945), urged a reduction in rote learning and more emphasis on problem solving. He demonstrated with American grade schoolchildren that, with proper handling, they could solve complex geometrical problems. One is reminded of Socrates demonstrating that an illiterate slave could solve the Pythagorean theorem (square of the hypotenuse) if led skillfully through the logic involved. Cognitive psychologists (see Chapter Nineteen) have restored Wertheimer's *Productive Thinking* to prominence.

Köhler is not associated with any significant applications of his theories. He was very much the academic scholar, more excited by new developments in theoretical physics than by changes in the world of industry or even of education.

Koffka has been influential, but mainly in education. His analysis of learning as a process of differentiation in the phenomenal field or the behavioral environment has been cited to justify the "whole method" in teaching reading. This educational practice is now under criticism, and it may be that a compromise—part behavioristic, part Gestalt—will prove to be superior to either separately. It is also possible that the behavioristic rote learning, or phonics method, is superior for some children, whereas the Gestalt approach works better for others.

The Gestalt principle of closure has been widely used in a way that probably causes Gestalt theorists some distress. This is in the field of advertising. For example, many television commercials involve messages that end in an incomplete sentence, for which closure is feasible only by inserting the name of the product. Thus the listener is induced to "close" the message and so to intensify the memory trace of the commercial.

Gestalt psychologists have also pointed out errors in some industrial training programs and job requirements. For example, some fifty years ago, there were vigorous efforts to devise the "one best way" of doing a manual job such as assembly. Engineers would time the motions of the worker separately, find the most efficient variant for each of these movements, and then put these movements together to make "the one best way" (see p. 134). All too often, the result was that this artificial merger of isolated movements from different workers proved seriously inefficient when put into practice; for example, the gain in ballistic motion from linking an arm movement to a shoulder movement can be lost if the former is incompatible with the latter. Most of this problem has disappeared as time–motion engineers have learned to observe the task as a Gestalt, a pattern, rather than as isolated elements that can be cemented together like James Mill's bricks and mortar.

CHAPTER 13

Field Theory: Kurt Lewin

The fourth of the major contributors to Gestalt psychology was Kurt Lewin (1890–1947). A bit younger than the "founders" already discussed, he also deviated sufficiently from their approach to justify separate treatment. Another reason for discussing him separately is that he had a more pervasive influence on American psychology, notably social and industrial psychology, than did Köhler and Koffka.

Lewin had an extraverted personality and a great deal of personal charm, which contributed to his wide influence. He attracted a number of brilliant students, and as around Skinner, an almost cultlike atmosphere developed around him and his theory. He certainly inspired extensive research in social psychology, and some of his early work on motivation and memory has—like Titchener's sensory research—simply become part of general psychology. He has been memorialized since 1947 by an annual award offered by SPSSI (Society for the Psychological Study of Social Issues), of which Lewin was an early and influential member.

Biography

Lewin was born into a middle-class Jewish family in Mogilno, then in Prussia, now a part of Poland. He was evidently, from his early days, an energetic, cheerful person who was not motivated by intellectual affairs and preferred socializing to study. Although he was not a victim of physical mistreatment, he knew that he could not aspire to some careers in Prussia because of the deep Prussian anti-Semitism. This probably accounts for the fervor with which he designed and executed research on the causes and elimination of racial prejudices in the United States.

In his seventeenth year, he encountered, in the Gymnasium in Berlin, an instructor in Greek philosophy who stirred him to pursue intellectual affairs. At this time, the German curriculum still classified all of the sciences, from physics to biology, as philosophy. Kurt obtained a solid scientific background, intending to prepare for the medical profession—one of the few professions to which Jews were admitted.

First enrolled at the University of Freiburg, he found himself interested in research rather than medical practice, and he transferred to the doctoral program in biology. In his biography of Lewin, A. J. Marrow (1969) commented that this biological orientation "would endure throughout his life" (p. 6). The comment is worth noting only because it seems inaccurate; certainly Lewin did minimal speculating about the physiological factors influencing behavior, and his major contributions have no biological referent at all.

Dissatisfied at Freiburg, Lewin transferred to the University of Berlin, hoping for a doctorate in philosophy (biology) and an academic career. Politically he was an active socialist. With other graduate students, he organized evening classes for working-class adults, and his devotion to humanitarian causes endured throughout his life.

At Berlin, Lewin came into contact with Carl Stumpf, who had come into conflict with Wundt over the atomistic analysis of consciousness. Stumpf, it will be remembered, had influenced Köhler and Koffka (as Külpe, another dissenter from Wundt, had set Wertheimer on the road to Gestalt). Stumpf was also the founder of the Berlin Association for Child Psychology, where Koffka did some research and where Lewin began his seminal studies on child behavior.

Lewin had completed all requirements for his doctorate in 1914, when World War I broke out and he had to enter the army. After some delays, his degree was officially granted in 1916. It appears that Lewin spent most of his time in the engineering corps; one of his early papers described how different a landscape looks in peacetime and under war conditions. Hills, watercourses, rock outcrops, and forests were seen as obstacles to farming when he visited the area in peacetime, but during the war, he perceived these as possible artillery emplacements, cover for infantry, routes to outflank an enemy, and so on. Perceiving, he commented, is profoundly modified according to the motivational state of the observer.

It is not clear that Lewin did any industrial work, but another of his early papers (1920) dealt with the system of industrial management devised by Frederick W. Taylor. Lewin had no objection to rationalizing industrial work but he was concerned that under Taylor's system, all of the benefits (or most of them) accrued to management and not to the workers. And of course, he did not share Taylor's antipathy to labor unions. Finally, Lewin made the pioneering observation that working conditions should be evaluated for effects on job satisfaction, not solely on production.

Dr. Miriam A. Lewin

Kurt Lewin, ingenious, persuasive innovator in the application of field theory to personal and social psychology

Nazi persecution led Lewin to emigrate from Germany in 1933. Like the other Gestalt workers, he was fortunate in getting prompt employment, first for two years at Cornell University, then at the University of Iowa Child Welfare Research Station. Here he pioneered in designing research on democratic leadership and authoritarian leadership and their effects on group members. His devotion to democratic ideals was passionate; in fact, Robert R. Sears, head of the Research Station (whose wife was a student in the Lewin program) commented, "The autocratic way he insisted on democracy was a little spectacular" (Marrow, 1969, p. 127).

Although emotionally opposed to militarism, Lewin's hostility to Nazism led him to participate actively in the American war effort. One of his best-known contributions, the group-decision technique for influencing attitudes and behavior, was developed in this context. The U.S. government was urging American housewives to increase their use of nonpreferred meats, brown bread, and so on to free other items for military use. Lewin's experiments on ways to influence food-buying behavior were described in a National Research Council bulletin (Lewin, 1943). Although the statistical significance of his findings can be questioned, the technique itself has been widely imitated and has generally produced the effects he ascribed to it. Like the other Gestalters, Lewin never showed much concern about statistical measures of treatment outcomes.

Although Lewin and his family had been close to the Köhlers in Germany, their relationship cooled in America. Marrow (1969) suggested that this change derived from Lewin's growing prestige, which threatened Köhler's preeminence as a spokesperson for Gestalt, and from the extent to which Lewin ignored the similarity of his ideas to those of Köhler and Koffka. (Lewin's novel vocabulary obscured underlying similarities of conceptualization, and Lewin made no attempt to point out the resemblances.) Marrow (1969) described an incident in which Horace Kallen proposed that Lewin be invited to the New School for Social Research to take the place vacated when Wertheimer died in 1943: "Outsiders . . . were enthusiastic; but not Köhler, the other Berlin gestaltist, then at Swarthmore. Lewin, the innovator, was too heretical for Köhler. . . . Lewin was not invited to join the New School faculty" (p. 159).

This was not the only instance of jealousy among the Gestalt émigrés; Karl Bühler was also hampered in his American career by excessively critical letters emanating from his German colleagues. It must be said, however, that hostilities among the Gestalt group never reached the intensity shown by the German and Austrian psychoanalysts who fled Nazism only to feud with each other in America.

After World War II, Lewin organized a group of social psychologists that became known as the Research Center for Group Dynamics. He was successful in getting financial backing for the new center, and it was established at MIT. After Lewin's death, the center moved to the University of Michigan, where it is still an important part of social psychology.

Field Theory

Although Lewin got the idea of calling his version of Gestalt *field theory* from Köhler's magnetic field metaphor, he may also have used it as a way of differentiating his own theories from those of his predecessors. The difference is trivial; most of the earlier Gestalt ideas are nested in Lewin's concepts. He differed especially in his vocabulary, which was studded with terms not used in earlier Gestalt writings. Lewin himself occasionally conceded that his writings amounted to developing a vocabulary, a set of neutral concepts usable in a variety of psychological systems, rather than a novel theory.

Field theory was something more than the magnetic field metaphor; it also used topology, a branch of mathematics in which regions rather than measures played the key role. It is as if one measured travel from New York City to Chicago by counting the states traversed, instead of by the miles covered. This is graphically represented in Figure 13.1, (Lewin, 1936) in which the course of "becoming a physician" is represented by entering and leaving various regions (requirements). This illustration serves to define a "cognitive map," a concept Lewin introduced which was adopted by E. C. Tolman (see Chapter 18). This is a map of the life space (LS) within which behavior takes place. The LS is equivalent to the behavioral environment (BE) defined by Koffka (see Chapter Twelve, p. 251).

Behavior is conceptualized as a locomotion through the LS. The LS (the field within which behavior occurs) is divided into regions, which are usually represented as those present at a given time. The total field in Figure 13.1 can, of course, be said to exist for the individual even though the future steps are not physically in the field. Locomotion is initiated by valences (positive or negative). Lewin borrowed the term *valence* from chemistry but used it to mean an attraction to or a repulsion from a specific activity or situation.

A *region* is segregated by boundaries. These may be easily penetrated, or they may be highly resistant. Anyone can go to a movie (there is no boundary resistance except the ticket price), but getting into Phi Beta

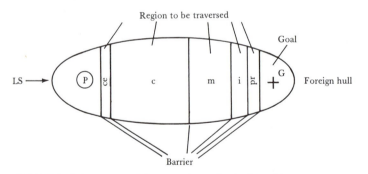

FIGURE 13.1   Career Plan as a Topological Problem

The person (P) aspires to become a physician. To attain this goal he must pass several requirements which in Lewin's system are represented as regions: ce = college entrance examinations; c = college; m = medical school; i = internship; pr = setting up a practice. The field is divided into regions, admission to each requiring penetrating a barrier. LS = the person's life space; Foreign hull = the rest of the environment, not perceived by the person. *(Modified from Lewin, 1936, p. 48, Figure 4; reprinted by permission of McGraw-Hill Book Co.)*

Kappa is more difficult. The boundary, then, may function as a barrier to locomotion. There are relations between the toughness of the boundary and the attractiveness of the group or activity, but we must pass over these points. Some of Lewin's definitions are circular: a positive valence is defined as one eliciting approach behavior, and approach behavior is explained by the positive valence. (Note the similarity to Skinner's "A reinforcer is anything that reinforces.")

The presence of a valence in the field is accompanied by a vector (represented by the arrow in Figures 13.2 to 13.5.) It is not correct to say that the valence *causes* the vector; rather, if there is a valence, there must be a vector; they are simply functions of the field. Lewin used the length of the arrow to suggest the amount of energy channeled into approaching a positive valence or escaping a negative valence. However, he did not propose any metric for reducing the vector to a quantity.

The Field at a Given Time Like the other Gestalters, Lewin treated behavior as a function of the field at a point in time, not as an outcome of historical events (compare "causes," p. 12). This turns out to be unimportant because, as in Figure 13.1, the future can be represented in LS by aspirations and expectancies, and the past by memory traces. Thus, although Lewin insisted that he was proposing an ahistorical explanation of behavior, this was true only in the sense that "my behavior now is a function of how I have been modified by my past."

LS is clearly a function of perception. Like Koffka's geographical environment and behavioral environment, Lewin wrote of a "foreign hull" around LS (see Figure 13.1), the foreign hull consisting of objects or persons of which one is unaware. This assumption is necessary to avoid lapsing into Bishop Berkeley's view that what one perceives is the only reality. An item in the foreign hull can enter the LS if it is perceived.

Lewin shared with the other Gestalt workers the concept of *physiognomic perception*. This idea refers to attributing human qualities to objects, or emotions to humans. A landscape may impress the viewer as inviting or forbidding. One rarely sees just a human face; it is a smiling face, a hostile face, or a sad face. LS, then, is an interaction product; the physical stimuli are to some extent molded by the observer.

Overlapping Regions An interesting derivation from field theory relates overlapping regions, or instances in which the boundary is not clearly defined. Lewin used the case of the adolescent to clarify the point. A child has a definite LS in which some activities are open and others are forbidden. An adult LS is also clear: one must avoid childish things but has many opportunities not open to the child. Adolescents, Lewin noted, do not perceive clear alternatives. They may wish to enter adult regions but are unsure whether this is permissible. Conversely, adolescents may see adults as demanding more than is feasible. This uncertainty corresponds, Lewin noted, to the position of the "marginal man." In theoretical terms, overlapping regions translate into the idea that ambiguity leads to anxiety.

There are, of course, many applications of the overlapping-regions concept. An industrial foreman is no longer "one of the boys" in the factory and may also feel unaccepted by upper management as "one of them." The physically handicapped person is likely to feel that the environment is uncertain and poorly structured.

Tension   Regions may become tense. Lewin never truly clarified this idea; it is part of the valence–vector complex. Any strong valence will induce a corresponding vector; simultaneously, Lewin held, the region becomes "a state of tension." If a hungry person becomes aware of food in preparation, tension is generated, and this tension persists until the food is ingested or the person leaves the field. Academic matters may acquire tension at examination time and may be ignored after the period has passed. Figure 13.2 shows the simplest case, of a child attracted by some positive valence (e.g., a toy); the tension will persist until the child obtains the toy or goes away from the situation.

An important role for the tension concept is in connection with persistence of behavior, memory events, and defensive behavior. Tense systems may endure after the perceived valence disappears. One who strives for the restoration of a desired state of affairs is illustrating how tensions endure over time. Freud theorized that sexual tensions may persist and may motivate many varieties of behavior (see Chapter Fourteen).

Tension and Memory   A logical extension of the foregoing point is that tense systems will be remembered longer than non-tense systems. Two of Lewin's Berlin students did ingenious experiments on this hypothesis: M. Ovsiankina engaged nursery-school children in such activities as cutting out paper patterns and molding animals in clay. Some of these activities were interrupted without explanation, while the child was allowed to complete others. When some free time was made available, 80 percent

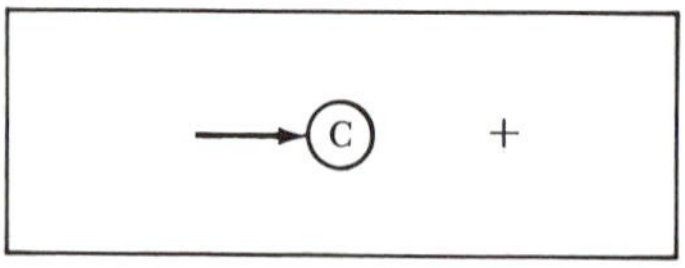

FIGURE 13.2   Motivation according to Lewin

The child (C) is attracted by a positive valence (+); the vector is indicated by the arrow. *(Modified from Lewin, 1935, p. 118, Figure 1, by permission of McGraw-Hill Book Co.)*

of the interrupted tasks were completed, and far fewer of the tasks that had been completed were picked up again.

B. Zeigarnik, whose name has become a part of the professional vocabulary of psychologists for the following study, tested the hypothesis that persisting tensions would lead to better memory. Using older children and the Ovsiankina procedure, Zeigarnik found that on memory tests, the children recalled 2.5 times as many interrupted as completed tasks. For adults, the corresponding figure was only 1.9 (i.e., the advantage of interrupted tasks was smaller); it is possible that some adults interpreted the interruption as a signal of failure to finish in the allotted time. In this case, forgetting might have been a protective device.

Lewin was alert to opportunities to test his theories on happenings outside the laboratory. Marrow (1969), who studied with Lewin and later wrote a biography of him, illustrated the tension-memory relationships with the following anecdote: Lewin and some students were talking over coffee and cake in a Berlin cafe. Donald MacKinnon, one of those present, described the occurrence to Marrow: "Somebody called for the bill and the waiter knew just what everyone had ordered. Although he hadn't kept a written reckoning, he presented an exact tally to everyone. . . . About a half hour later Lewin called the waiter over and asked him to write the check again. The waiter was indignant. 'I don't know any longer what you people ordered,' he said. 'You paid your bill' " (p. 27). Lewin's interpretation was that a tense system is easily recalled, but that when the tension is erased (i.e., the bill is paid), the memory likewise is cleared.

Substitute Satisfactions   Tensions may also be removed by the provision of a substitute goal. If a child modeling a dog, for example, is given a chance to model a camel, the "dog" tension is likely to disappear. This concept is roughly equivalent to the Freudian concept of sublimation, in which a forbidden activity is replaced by one that is socially acceptable.

The effectiveness of substitute goals is related to the problem of "level of aspiration." Remember that the goal that has not been attained is still present in LS as a desirable outcome. If the person perceives this unattained goal as rather easy to achieve, not much tension is generated; and if it is seen as completely out of the question, the tension is likely to be replaced by despair. Maximum effort, then, is generated if the goal is perceived as being within one's "level of aspiration"; that is, it can be attained with an acceptable level of effort.

Satiation   Action was treated by Lewin as if it were locomotion, and actions have some properties appropriate to that metaphor. One of these is *satiation*. This term, traditionally used with regard to the satisfaction of a motive, can also apply to behavior. Lewin (1935) speculated that the repetition of a simple action can lead to satiation in the sense that the act is no longer satisfying any vector and actually develops aversive qualities (a negative valence): "By reason of the repetition, an originally positive valence of the act changes to a negative" (p. 254).

One of the chronic dilemmas of industrial psychology is the fact that the gratification of a motive reduces its effectiveness in energizing behavior. That is, if a desire for recognition is seen as an important source of dissatisfaction, procedures can be introduced to provide some satisfaction of this desire; thereupon, the workers desire some other positive valence. Lewin's work suggests that the satiation of an act contributes to this discontent. Many factory and office workers spend up to eight hours daily making essentially the same movements. Hull (p. 205) would predict the development of reactive inhibition (Ir) in that situation; Lewin called it satiation.

Equilibrium   Lewin's theory of motivation can be called an equilibrium theory in the sense that valence–vector tensions set up a disturbance, and action continues until the equilibrium is restored. This bears a superficial resemblance to Hull's tension reduction, but there are important differences. Perhaps the main one is that Lewin included all kinds of social intentions as vectors, whereas Hull emphasized the physiological drives and the equilibrium as homeostatic. Lewin's tendency toward equilibrium has a close kinship to Koffka's "closure" in the sense that a gap between person and goal induces tension that persists until the gap is closed. Equilibrium is an attribute of LS, and corrective action will persist until the disturbance is removed (Lewin, 1951, pp. 218–222).

Conflict   One of Lewin's most popular ideas was his treatment of conflict. As just noted, equilibrium is disturbed if one valence is present in the LS; tension will persist until the valence is reached. However, equilibrium is more extensively disrupted if two conflicting valences appear. Lewin's valence–vector system provides a convenient way of classifying conflicts and predicting their outcomes.

Type I (+ +) conflicts occur when the person finds himself or herself between two attractive valences and can't grasp both. As Figure 13.3 indicates, the person will be pushed in opposite directions. If the two valences are about equal, the vectors will be equal, and decision will be difficult. If, however, the person moves closer to one, it will be seen as larger, and so he or she will move in that direction (and perhaps return to the second after the first has been captured). Conflicts of this type rarely have any pathological or disruptive significance.

Type II (− −) conflicts occur when the person is between two negative valences. Here the two vectors cause vacillation, and a common outcome is that the person tries to escape (i.e., leave the field). As Figure 13.4 suggests, the barriers that prevent escape may have to be strengthened to keep the person in this unpleasant situation.

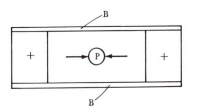

FIGURE 13.3 Lewin's Type I Conflict

The person (P) is attracted in opposed directions by positive valences. The outcome will depend on which valence is perceived as more potent (this would be represented by a stronger vector toward that goal.) B = boundary. *(From Lewin, 1935, p. 123, Figure 7, by permission of McGraw-Hill Book Co.)*

Type III (+ −) conflicts are the most destructive of all three types. As Figure 13.5 indicates, a prototype of this variety is the Freudian desire–anxiety combination. A person may be tempted to engage in a forbidden sexual pleasure (libido) but is deterred by anxiety and prospective feelings of guilt. This type of conflict is obviously quite difficult to resolve because the two opposing valences are perceived as inhering in the same external situation. Further (although Lewin did not explore this point), as the sex drive is inherent in the organism, one cannot run away (as is possible in the Type II conflict).

It will be noted that this treatment of conflict does not differ dramatically from that proposed by John Dollard and Neal Miller (1950). Their analysis, Hullian in origin, stressed the approach–withdrawal gradients

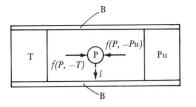

FIGURE 13.4 Lewin's Type II Conflict

This type of conflict involves two negative valences, e.g., an unpleasant task and a threat of punishment if the task is not completed. One likely outcome here is that the child tries to escape from the field (dotted arrow) and must be confined within the field by strong barriers (B). In this diagram, $f(P,-T)$ = force away from task; $f(P,-Pu)$ = force away from punishment; l = tendency to the leave the field. *(Modified from Lewin, 1951, p. 78, Figure 8, by permission of Harper & Bros., publishers.)*

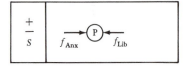

FIGURE 13.5   Lewin's Type III Conflict

Type III conflicts involve a single goal region with both positive and negative valence. The person is attracted to and then afraid of the object,
person or activity involved. Compare Figure 10.2, p. 214, showing the behavioristic treatment of this conflict. In this example, S = sexual activity,
f_{Lib} = libido, f_{Anx} = anxiety.

and the generalization that, on average, avoidance reactions become intensified as the organism approaches the goal (see Figure 10.2, p. 214):
Thus the rat may want food but may fear the shock; at a distance, the
food attraction is stronger, but nearness to the shock causes the fear
response to take over. There is one advantage in the Lewinian analysis:
as it deals with stimuli, the path is indicated by which the conflict may
be resolved (e.g., by removing or distorting one of the valences).

It is perhaps worth noting that the Lewinian analysis can also throw
light on some Freudian principles, which cannot be done with the Dollard–Miller formulation. Freud, in his *Psychopathology of Everyday Life*
(1938), cited cases of slips of the tongue, "meaningful" accidents, forgetting of names, and so on. Lewin would have analyzed these in terms of
resultant vectors. In Figure 13.6, I have shown how a concealed negative
valence may affect the course of action so that it reflects both the conscious and the unconscious intents. Consider the case of a college professor discussing faculty ratings by deans, in which he intended to say,
"The faculty should evaluate the administration," but substitutes the word
evacuate for *evaluate*. The latent hostility has deflected the behavioral intent just enough to give some expression to this negative component.

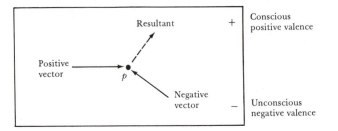

FIGURE 13.6   A Lewinian Interpretation of a Slip of the Tongue

The actual behavior is a resultant of positive (conscious) vector and negative (unconscious) vector.

Locomotion and Learning   Learning is facilitated by tension because it induces locomotion, which makes probable a modification of the LS. Locomotion, of course, need not be physical. One faced with a negative valence (an impending examination, for example) will exert effort to cope with the problem.

The essential phenomenon in learning is a restructuring of the LS. In Figure 13.7, we have a representation of a child inside a U-shaped barrier. As long as the LS does not extend around the ends of the barrier, the child simply stays and struggles to reach the attractive valence. After failing to push through the barrier, the child suddenly turns away from the goal, moves out the open end of the U, and has a clear path to the desired toy. Note that this is merely a visual representation of Köhler's concept of insight. It might involve what Watson called trial-and-error behavior, except that a Gestalt theorist would insist that the restructuring of the field *preceded* the actual movement toward the goal.

Another way of defining learning is to see it as a differentiation of the LS. This treatment follows Koffka. In a strange city, one must identify landmarks, major traffic arteries, locations of stores, and other facilities (Figure 13.8). Lewin treated this as acquiring a *cognitive map*. One need not physically traverse terrain in order to differentiate significant features from a blurred notion of where things are located. Similarly, an employee in a factory must learn to recognize safety hazards, differen-

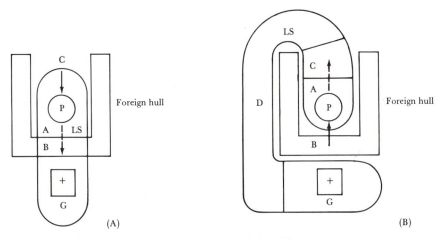

FIGURE 13.7   Learning as Restructuring of the Life Space

(A): The child (P) is blocked from an attractive toy (+) by the U-shaped barrier. (B) The child "sees" the possibility of an end-run around the barrier and reaches the goal (G). Note that this involved drawing some of the "foreign hull" into LS. *(From Lewin, 1951, pp. 72–73, Figures 6 and 7, by permission of Harper & Row, publishers.)*

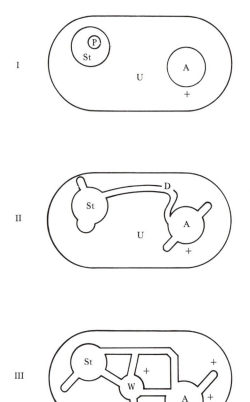

FIGURE 13.8   Learning conceptualized as Differentiation of Life
Space:

I   Person (P) is at station (St) and
    wishes to reach apartment (A).

II Person learns to take bus D to
    reach A.

III Person learns path to work
    (W) and useful locations (+).

This example illustrates how
Lewin used the concept of a "cognitive map" as a model of learning. *(From Lewin, 1951, pp. 70–
71, Figures 3, 4 and 5, by permission
of Harper & Row, publishers)*

tiate among managers, and if possible, see how his or her work fits into
the total activity of the enterprise. Goodman (1968) had managers draw
"maps" of their organization and showed the functional significance of
an inaccurate or incomplete map. A clinical psychologist learning to differentiate areas on the Rorschach blots or a physiologist learning to identify
fuzzily bounded cortical areas illustrates the importance of differentiation as an aspect of learning. Koffka described the process of learning
to mail a letter in a strange country. The first step is to learn to identify
the mailbox; the act of dropping the letter in was acquired early in life,
but the LS must be differentiated (the mailbox must be correctly perceived) for the new behavior to be learned.

Learning also involves *organizing* the LS. A chemistry student would
have a tough time coping with the various elements if it were not for the
periodic table. Economists have to classify observations in terms of some
kind of system before these observations become meaningful. Psychologists organize their subject matter by theories or by methodologies. As
was noted earlier, very little learning of professional material is passive.

One must manipulate it and structure it to establish a durable memory structure.

A weakness of the Lewinian approach to learning is found in the area of motor skills. Although it is possible, in principle, to say that one learns to perceive the correct form of a movement and to organize the movements into complex patterns, most psychologists find the logic unsatisfactory. Motor learning seems more compatible with behavioristic thinking than with a Gestalt approach.

Thinking and Imagination   Problem solving and fantasy were, of course, conceptualized in perceptual terms by Lewin. He proposed that in addition to the real LS, the one corresponding to physical objects, we can also postulate a dimension of reality–irreality, by which he meant that in imagination one can move through barriers and boundaries that are impermeable in real LS. Thus, planning how to operate with high-tension electrical equipment can be pursued more safely on the irreal level than on the real, trial-and-error level. Fantasy may enable a person to discharge some tension by imagining a solution to a problem. Classical economists are often accused of solving all of their problems by *assuming* that the conditions exist for a solution. Psychological theorists also often move from the level of reality to a more workable level by assuming conditions that remove the barriers to a solution.

Both Hull and Skinner took the position that forgetting is a matter of response substitution; they implied that in theory, a memory trace would endure for life if no other learning affected either the stimulus or the response. Some experimental data support that view; various éxperimenters have reported significant savings in relearning after intervals of twenty years or more. Freud, of course, postulated that neuroses are due to memories that have been repressed but are still active.

To some extent, Lewin's theory seems compatible with those of Hull and Skinner. Certainly the substitute satisfaction experiments indicate that a new activity can displace the tense system alleged to persist. On the other hand, Lewin and his Gestalt colleagues held that the memory trace may be modified by intraorganismic activities, as when a memory of an event is changed to fit the accounts of others or the pattern that one would have wished instead of what happened. It seems necessary at present to conclude that both processes occur; forgetting a specific S-R unit may depend on learning a new activity involving the same stimulus or response; forgetting a complex event may result from transforming the "picture" of the occurrence.

Intelligence   Lewin was almost the first theorist in the mainstream of psychology to offer a theory of intelligence. It was based primarily on the familiar concept of differentiation—in this case, differentiation within the personality. In an essay on the feeble-minded (1935, p. 194), he proposed that degrees of intelligence correspond to the degree of inner differentiation; this would mean that greater intelligence is correlated with knowledge of a wider range of experiences and with the placement of these experiences within a framework of interrelations. A second distinction, he suggested, is that the boundaries between regions are more rigid in the feeble-minded than in normals and, by extrapolation, that very intelligent persons have permeable internal boundaries so that knowledge can communicate easily from one region to another (thus, for example, the more intelligent child can see connections between a bicycle and an airplane, or between a marriage and a business merger, whereas the handicapped child is only confused by such comparisons).

Values   Lewin viewed aspirations for the future as a significant part of the LS. The goal of becoming an airline pilot may help a youngster persist in uncomfortable study and training. Valences may also be modified in pursuit of future values. To use a very simple example, Watson experimented on Little Albert by making a loud, unpleasant noise each time the child reached for the white rat. The valence changed, the former plus valence became negative.

In professional training, the same changes can be shown to occur. A premedical student may abhor the sight of blood; but as he or she goes through biology and anatomy, dissections and operations may become positive rather than negative. (One of the attractive features of Lewin's elaborate symbol system is that so many kinds of perceptual phenomena can be categorized under the same symbolic heading.)

Emotion   One manifestation of a disturbance of equilibrium is what we call *emotion*. A technique developed by Dembo (1931) and widely imitated today is interposing a barrier blocking the pathway to a goal. Dembo had her subjects solve anagrams, giving them very easy ones at first, then more difficult ones. Then she handed out one that was insoluble (a barrier to the completion of the task). The subjects became agitated, complained, tensed, and showed other signs of emotional arousal. After they gave up on this anagram, she administered other fairly easy ones, and the performance was much worse than on the warm-up series. Lewin theorized that strong emotions "dedifferentiate" the LS; that is, the sharpness of figure–ground separation is lost, and familiar cues are not evaluated in the customary fashion. This resembles the popular notion of "blind rage"—and, of course, "Love is blind." The importance of the theory in this context is to predict outcomes of other kinds of tension-arousing situations, predictions that cannot be made by the theories discussed earlier.

The Hypothetical Pure Case   In addition to his theoretical contributions, Lewin wrote extensively about the logic of experimentation and of psychology in general. One point on which he and Skinner agreed was that sound research can be done on a single case. The reservation Lewin had was that the case must be chosen very carefully to represent the key elements in the situation. He pointed to the familiar example of gravity; the formula for predicting the rate of acceleration of a body falling toward the center of the earth holds *only* for objects falling in a vacuum. Now, one would never discover this principle by observing the rates of falling of leaves, snowflakes, stones, raindrops, and so on. No matter how large the number of objects used, the finding would never match the theoretical value.

In effect, Lewin suggested that much modern psychological research is like timing the fall of snowflakes. Psychologists have attempted to iron out the effects of individual variations among persons by using numbers of cases and wiping out (as "error variance") the effects of such variations. In an analysis of variance, the experimenter's main purpose, the "main effect," is maximized and the personal variation is discarded because it shows that the controls imposed by the experimenter were not entirely effective. Lewin used the term *phenotype* to identify the usual appearance, and *genotype* to identify the pure case. Unless an experiment is designed to include all of the essential elements of the genotype, the results will not transfer to nonlaboratory situations. The same point was made by M. Brewer (1986), who used the term *analogue* for the experimental design that faithfully mirrors all of the indispensable components of the field situation. Unfortunately, she did not offer a formula either for deciding which elements are indispensable, or for assessing the accuracy of replication of these elements in the laboratory. Thus researchers, including Lewinians, are still thrown back on trial and error in their own problem-solving behavior.

Personality Theory

It is entirely proper that a person concerned with single cases should also theorize about personality. Lewin's approach to individual personalities grew logically out of his concepts of life space, its division into regions, and locomotion through these regions, as these concepts were described above in terms of laws of behavior in general.

The first step in the formation of personality is the internalization of life space. Not only does the person respond to environment in the here-and-now; inner representations of this environment become established. Thus the individual may "look at" the remembered life space and may plan actions. As the LS becomes more differentiated, so the inner milieu also differentiates. The person sees life as involving a region for the family, for the church, for a job, for sports, and so on. Each of these regions comes to form an articulated part of the total life span (Figure

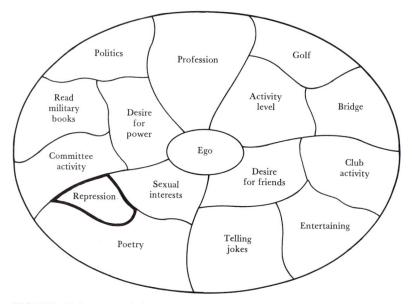

FIGURE 13.9   A Lewinian Representation of a Total Personality

Regions (interests, activities) around the periphery are easily changed and
do not elicit strong emotions if placed under pressure; central regions
designate activities perceived as important; strong emotions are associated
with interference at these levels.   *(From Stagner, 1974, p. 195, Figure 8.3,
by permission of McGraw-Hill Book Co.)*

13.9). In behavioral terms, the person may have habits that come into
play at a church service that are isolated from others in the region conceptualized as business activities. The difference from a Hullian view,
then, would simply be that the related habits are bound together into a
segregated system (Hull might cope with the problem by postulating some
common stimulus that is a part of the complex for business behavior).

The concept of boundary is important here. The self, Lewin suggested, begins to form as the boundary between "me" and "not me" is
recognized. The boundary becomes firmer as the isolation of the self
amid other human beings is consciously accepted. Regions are also delin-
eated by internal boundaries, and some of these regional boundaries
may become quite rigid. In phenomenal terms, this is an area experienced as threatening or unpleasant. Approaching such a dangerous area
sets up strong negative valences and vectors away from the region. Freud,
of course, called this "repression."

The adult personality usually becomes rather complex, with regions
corresponding to habits, perceptions, and valences associated with a sin-

gle group or activity. Thus sports might constitute a region for one person but not for another. Family, church, and profession are some of the commonly observed regions. It should be remembered that these differentiations within the personality correspond to regions in the LS; there are groups that provide rewards and punishments, guidance and frustrations, all of which the person acquires. As William James once wrote, "A man has as many selves as there are groups whose opinion he values."

Peripheral and Central Regions   Lewin, probably influenced by Freud, called attention to the fact that some regions within the personality are superficial and evoke little action if they are threatened. Other regions seem to lie "deeper" within the structure, and a threat to one of these evokes strong anxiety and efforts to defend the personality from this danger. This kind of distinction is actually fairly widespread; for example, some executives who have attended "sensitivity training" return to the workplace, and associates say "He has changed on the surface but not underneath."

Unity of Personality   It would be easy to criticize Lewin for overemphasizing the divisive components in this view of personality. Lewin conceded that the personality is a unified whole, or Gestalt. Nevertheless, "If there were not this sometimes astoundingly complete segregation of different psychical systems from each other, if there were instead a permanently real unity of the mind . . . no ordered action would be possible" (1935, p. 55). One cannot *simultaneously* pursue the goals of food, sex, intellectual achievement, and financial gain. The unity of the individual, then, is preserved by permitting the dominance of one region (interest area or social role) until tension there is reduced; then the dominance shifts to another region. This corresponds to Hull's hierarchy of responses, except that Lewin focused on categories rather than S-R units. It also anticipates Maslow's hierarchy of motives (see Chapter Seventeen).

The Self   A differentiated region within the LS as internalized may be labeled the *self*. The unifying feature of this region is that it is central to the personality and has links with all of the other, relatively segregated regions. The self also acquires attributes of its own, as a function of adult evaluations and also of success or failure. Thus, after a failure, the level of aspiration is lowered, and the effort expended on subsequent endeavors is minimized. School teachers consider such a child to be demoralized; he or she is described as having a poor self-image. According to Lewin, the self-image is a central component of the self, although it is not identical with the self or Ego.

Social Psychology

Lewin was also unique in offering a theory that embraces social psychology as well as the traditional psychology of the individual. His writings point up two aspects of social psychology: the impact of a group on an individual member and the characteristics of groups as groups, without the specification of particular individuals. Both topics require an answer to the question: In what sense is a group *real?*

Around the turn of the century, there was a popular theory postulating the existence of a "group mind." Gustave LeBon (1918) was perhaps the most widely known author advocating this theory. He wrote of France in 1914 as "rising as one man" to fight the Germans. The implication was that a group mind compelled all of the French to act. Now, everyone (certainly including LeBon) knew that this was just not true. Many of the French opposed the war; some even helped the Germans. There is no mind that can control the members of a nation, a church, a labor union, or even a baseball team.

Lewin proposed that instead of a group mind, we postulate a boundary around the group; individuals cooperate with the group in part for fear of being ejected from it, and in part because they experience the group as a positive valence. Each individual has a representation of the group in his or her LS, and typically this region has a positive valence. However, an outside observer can also have a percept of the group as an organized whole, but without valence or even with a negative valence. Thus we can obtain data about the group as seen from inside and from outside. We can also collect information about the properties of the group as an entity (e.g., its tightness of organization, the ease of joining, the power of its leader, and the cooperation among its members).

The study of group effects on members may be said to have started with research by Lewin, R. Lippitt, and R. K. White (1939) on the effects of autocratic and democratic leadership styles. These authors reported a rather clear increase in aggressive behavior under autocratic leadership. Lewin interpreted this finding as indicating that under an autocrat, individual motives are frustrated (impulses to take some action are blocked by the leader), and increased tension is found both within the group and within individual members. Sherif (1936) and Asch (1956), both apparently influenced by Lewin, conducted ingenious experiments that showed that a majority opinion can induce a minority member to change to conform to the majority. Lewin (1935) conceptualized this process in terms of a "field of force" emanating from the group and constraining the behavior of the member. More than one field may be operating in a given situation: discussing a child with severe personality problems, Lewin wrote "The *fields of force* dominating the life space of the child (C) are, above all, those of the father (F), of the grandmother (G), and of the tutor (J)" (p. 147). Lewin tried to picture this (see, e.g., Figure 13.10), but the clarifying effect of his individual diagrams seems to be lost. At any rate, it is clear that, as in a magnetic field, the pressures on the individual will derive from poles of power, the persons able to impose and withdraw valences.

One of the impacts of the group on the individual is to modify the LS. Before becoming a member of a labor union, a worker might have a moderately favorable perception of his employer. However, after listening to his coworkers recount mistreatments, his percept changes. Thus, the majority opinion shapes the views of the individual. As Lewin's students have demonstrated, a group decision to act in a certain fashion has a strong influence on the subsequent behavior of the group's members.

Janis (1972) described this process of establishing a common reality, a shared version of truth, as "shared delusions." That is, the group members reinforce each other for asserting a view of reality, and eventually all come to believe it. The danger, as Janis commented, is that this "reality" may not correspond to elements of the "foreign hull," the reality

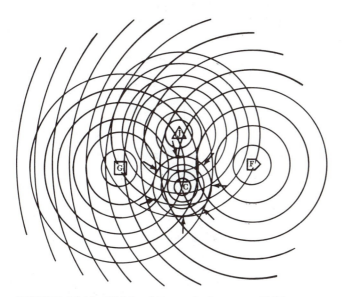

FIGURE 13.10   Fields of Force Acting on a Child

C = child; G = grandmother; J = tutor; F = father. Lewin tried here to represent the pressures acting on the child, pushing for action in different directions. *(From Lewin, 1935, p. 148, Figure 18a, reprinted by permission of McGraw-Hill Book Co.)*

not a part of the LS. The example Janis used was the group around President Kennedy in 1961 when the disastrous Bay of Pigs invasion was being planned. The only opponent of the plan, George W. Ball, was effectively thrown out of the group. He was not told of meetings, did not receive memos, and was given no chance to express his dissident view of the real situation. Sometimes the minority of one is correct.

Lewin also proposed that the concept of tension could be applied to a group. Thus, in a factory situation, workers may be subject to pressures to increase production (e.g., in wages, relations to their supervisor, chances of promotion, and liking the company). But there are also pressures to hold production down (e.g., fatigue, fear of piece-rate cuts, anger at the supervisor, or fear of the disapproval of fellow workers; see Figure 13.11. Lewin hypothesized that production could be increased by two alternative methods: (1) increasing upward pressure and (2) decreasing downward pressure. The first would increase total tension in the group and might lead to "going out of the field," for example, going on strike. The second would decrease the total tension level. To decrease downward pressure, the workers were asked to vote to increase their standard output by some 10 percent. This removed fear of criticism by fellow workers, and the outcome was a fairly substantial increase in production. Control groups who were simply lectured about the company's financial hardships showed no such improvement. A complete account is given by L. Coch and J. R. P. French (1948).

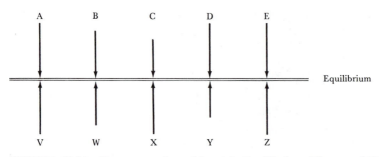

FIGURE 13.11   Representation of Lewin's Equilibrium Theory of Group Behavior

Lewin (1951) conceptualized the output of a group, e.g., in a factory, as stabilizing at a point where pressure for higher output is just balanced by pressures against higher output. If upward pressures (V–Z) are increased, production may go up but so will tension. If one of the negative forces (A–E) can be removed, production increases but total tension actually decreases. *(Suggested by Lewin, 1951, p. 216, Figure 28)*

Practical Applications

Lewin was fond of saying "Nothing is so practical as a good theory." The Coch and French study just mentioned seems to confirm his opinion. We recall, of course, Albert Einstein's dictum that theory tells us what observations to make.

Lewin and his organizational offspring, the Research Center for Group Dynamics, fostered a wide variety of social investigations with practical implications. For example, what is the optimal strategy for opposing a bigot who is spouting antiblack, anti-Catholic, anti-Jewish, or anti-Oriental prejudice? The experimental results indicated that appealing to a stronger valence (e.g., patriotism) was the best technique, and various liberal organizations now advise their members to use this procedure.

The Research Center has also been active in research on discrimination in housing projects and similar problems dear to Lewin's heart. In some cases, it appears that good common sense rather than field theory has dictated the design of a study, but on the whole, the results indicate that Lewin provided some good theoretical guideposts for the design of social research.

Criticisms of Lewin

Probably the deepest criticism of Lewin's field theory relates to the distinction between the life space and the foreign hull. Almost everyone (including Lewin) agrees that there is a physical world out there, which does not depend on someone perceiving it to make it real. It is also generally agreed that behavior based on the LS is doomed to failure if the LS does not coincide substantially with foreign hull. Lewin did not deny this, but he pointed out that this did not invalidate his theory. It is precisely because people act on false notions of reality that we have so many accidents and regrettable failures. As demonstrated by Stratton (1897), it is almost impossible to behave on the basis of what you *know* to be real when your senses are telling you that something else is real.

Another widespread criticism is that Lewin offered not a theory but a vocabulary. Lewin actually accepted this assertion and viewed it as not being a criticism at all. He was trying, he stated, to devise a neutral vocabulary that could be used by varying theorists to maximize communication between them. Thus *valence* could be a neutral way of referring to goals, aspirations, ideals, food, sex, threats, pains, and so on. It was Lewin's hope (1936, p. viii) that precision of meaning would be achieved by the use of his symbols.

Some critics have viewed Lewin as excessively abstract, and others have treated him as being short on abstractions. G. S. Brett (1962) wrote of Lewin's work as "an example of methodology run riot, and of the substitution of methodological blue-prints for fertile hypotheses" (p. 715). On the opposite side, Gordon Allport (1961) cited Lewin as being the source of many seminal ideas for productive research. There is a perceptible tendency for his work to be viewed harshly by the "experimentalist" tough-minded psychologists, and favorably by the "humanist" tender-minded writers.

Lewin's Students

Sahakian (1975) introduced a discussion of Lewin's students with the provocative title, "The Women in Lewin's Life." Because Ovsiankina, Zeigarnik, and Dembo happened to be female, the illusion was created that he had some special appeal for bright young women. Actually, a count of his students suggests that he had about an equal number of male and female students (of course, this balance was unusual, given the usual male preponderance). For example, in the United States, Lewin's best-known students have been Ronald Lippitt, Ralph K. White, Alex Bavelas, J. R. P. French, Jr., Dorwin Cartwright, Pauline Sears, Roger Barker, Leon Festinger, and Alvin Zander, an impressive group of social psychologists.

Lewin also attracted Americans before he left Berlin. Perhaps the best known at the time was J. F. Brown, but Donald MacKinnon and Norman R. F. Maier are also well-known in American psychology. MacKinnon's later work was mostly on personality, and that of Maier on problem solving. Maier's work is reminiscent of Köhler's with the chimpanzees, studying insight in human problem solution. Lewin, after all, thought like a Gestalt psychologist even if he used a somewhat different vocabulary from that of his colleagues.

J. F. Brown (1902–1970) deserves special mention because of his bold extrapolations of Lewin's concepts. Brown went to Germany to study with Lewin before the Nazis came to power; one of his early publications (Brown, 1931) dealt with field effects on perceived speed of movement. He became intrigued by field theory in general and its social relevance in particular. His interest in societal behavior and politics was stimulated, he once remarked, by the fact that, while he was running an experiment in Lewin's Berlin laboratory, noise outside compelled him to stop. He found that the Nazi Brown Shirts were holding a street rally outside; this incident reinforced his conviction that science could not huddle in its laboratory and ignore the outside world.

Brown's book *Psychology and the Social Order* appeared in 1936. In that publication, he offered some significant extrapolations of Lewin's ideas.

He amplified the concept of *boundary*, for example, showing how economic depression might cause a nation to strengthen its boundaries to exclude foreigners and foreign commodities. Membership in the nation becomes more salient for individuals in time of war; and persons seen as working against national policies are ejected from the group. Crises, Brown suggested, tend to make groups more homogeneous, suppressing individual dissidents and exaggerating at least the public support for group goals.

Although Brown used valences and vectors as Lewin had, Brown noted the extent to which group influences may endow a neutral object with valence. Thus, cutting down our national forests was a neutral item for most Americans until speeches and publicity led a majority to react negatively to that practice. Workers may be relatively unconcerned about a proposed merger of their employer with another company until union officials point out that the new management has a history of blocking unionism.

Brown's book did not receive an enthusiastic welcome at the time of publication, mainly because of his open espousal of Marxism. Since the mid-1970s, it has made something of a comeback as a new spirit has invaded social psychology. Brown's attempt to tie Lewin's "universal" concepts to the historical conditions existing at a specific time may be responsible. Social psychology in the 1980s has been influenced both by the existential emphasis on the here and now, and by Lewin's assertion that behavior is determined by "the field at a given time." These approaches are compatible with current developments among behavioristic thinkers. In opposition to this contemporary emphasis, the psychoanalysts, especially the orthodox followers of Sigmund Freud, have focused on the past history of the individual. The following chapter elaborates on this and other distinctive features of Freudian theory.

CHAPTER 14

Psychoanalytic Theory: Sigmund Freud

A plausible case can be made for treating structuralism as an extension of British empiricism, and behaviorism as a rebellion against structuralism. Similarly, Gestalt theory was developed explicitly as a protest against the atomistic assumptions of Wundt and Titchener. The situation is not so clear with respect to psychoanalysis, which grew out of a clinical tradition rather than from the philosophical speculations of Locke and Hume or from the laboratory ventures of Fechner, Wundt, and Titchener. And yet there is an apparent relationship. The structuralists inherited the rational idea that human actions are conscious and logical; Freud demonstrated that much of human behavior is unconsciously determined and irrational. Further, we know that Freud was thoroughly acquainted with British empiricism (he translated one of J. S. Mill's books into German) and that he knew a fair amount about Wundt's version of psychology. He spoke, at times, as if he perceived a rivalry between Wundt's and his conception of psychology; Wittels (1924) illustrated Freud's sense of humor by quoting his remark about Wundt: "We cannot help thinking that the old psychology has been killed by my . . . doctrine; but the old psychology is quite unaware of the fact, and goes on teaching as usual" (1924, p. 130).

Freud knew that Wundt, along with hundreds of other psychologists, had every right to study consciousness. Freud studied consciousness too. It is difficult if not impossible to study unconscious processes except as they distort conscious phenomena—dreams, fantasies, memory reports, and so on. Freud was, however, hostile to the laboratory procedures of the Wundtians. Instead, he used the case study method, studying persons suffering from symptoms that interfered with their daily lives. Thus the material was much richer in detail but was also open to many interpretations because there was no procedure by which observations could be repeated or situations modified so that one could judge the amount of change in behavior. One respect in which Freud did not differ from the "scientific" psychologists was in his search for universals; despite his reliance on the study of a single personality, he sought to develop nomothetic principles.

Historically speaking, it is intriguing that all four of these major psychological theories developed almost simultaneously: Wundt's 1879 laboratory has been taken as the founding of scientific psychology, and the work of Titchener and others consolidated structuralist theory promptly. Behaviorism has been dated to 1913 and Watson's "manifesto," but Max Meyer and others were offering such ideas earlier. Gestalt is customarily dated from 1910 and Wertheimer's phi phenomenon. And Freud's first publication forecasting his revolutionary ideas came in 1893. These coincidences remind one of Figure 1.1, p. 3, in which it was suggested that scientific knowledge had differentiated out from philosophy sufficiently to provide the empirical basis for a new discipline emerging from the domain of philosophy.

Freud's writings dominate psychoanalytic theory. None the less, some dissenters from his system have proposed analytic psychologies worth exploring. This chapter lays out the major ideas of Freud, and Chapters Fifteen and Sixteen discuss a few of the revisions of his theories.

Biography

Sigmund Freud (1856–1939) was born into a relatively poor Jewish family in Freiberg, in what is now Czechoslovakia. Both his father and grandfather had been rabbis, although they were not full-time members of the clergy. They probably influenced the boy toward a keen interest in ideas and a willingness to spend hours daily on his studies. He was academically quite precocious.

Economic losses and threats of mob violence caused Jakob Freud, the father, to leave Freiberg. The family moved briefly to Leipzig, and later to Vienna. After some dismal years, he began to prosper and was able to pay for Sigmund's higher education. The train trip from Leipzig to Vienna serves to illustrate Freud's later theories about distortion of memory. He wrote (in adult life) that he had been shocked to see his mother naked in the compartment when he was only two and a half years old. The records show that he was at least four at the time; in other words, his memory, like those of his later patients, had played tricks on him.

Freud received his M.D. in 1881, after delaying to do research in histology and neurology. He was fortunate to establish a cordial relationship with Josef Breuer, a very successful Viennese physician who not only referred patients to the younger man but lent him money and gave him introductions to important people.

In 1884, Freud began experimenting with cocaine and just barely missed getting the credit for its tremendous value as an ophthalmic anesthetic. Unfortunately, he began taking it orally (with, he claimed, no adverse effects) and recommended it to a friend, Ernst von Fleischl-Marxow, who not only became addicted but died from an overdose. (Freud felt especially guilty because he had told Fleischl that it could safely be injected.) Freud managed to cure his own addiction; however, the incident probably reinforced his bias against chemical curative procedures.

Freud had a tremendous curiosity and experimented with the various "cures" in vogue at the time: hydrotherapy, electrotherapy, massage, rest cures, and hypnosis. He had somewhat better results with hypnotic treatment and for a time came to rely heavily on it. France was then the world center for studies of hypnosis and psychopathology generally; Freud managed to get a travel grant (very difficult for a Jew) and spent several months in Paris studying under Jean-Martin Charcot. Later he was enabled to spend some months with Hippolyte Bernheim in Nancy, the other major center of clinical research on hypnotic phenomena. Freud's keen interest in research showed on this latter visit: he took with him a patient he had unsuccessfully treated with hypnosis. Bernheim hypnotized her but had no more luck than Freud in removing her symptoms.

Other data influenced Freud to abandon hypnosis. Many of his patients were relieved of their symptoms for a few days or weeks, then relapsed. Freud began his search for a more durable treatment. This was the beginning of his slow, methodical progress toward the therapy now known as psychoanalysis.

The major breakthrough came from his close association with Josef Breuer. In 1880, Breuer had been called in to treat a young woman who was anorexic, partially blind, and partially paralyzed. Bertha Pappenheim (later to become famous in medical literature as "Anna O.") had been examined by neurologists and others, who found no organic basis for her symptoms. Breuer accurately diagnosed her problem as "hysteria," a fashionable ailment in the well-to-do circles of Vienna. He tried hypnotic treatments, but—perhaps accidentally—he deviated from the usual procedure. Instead of telling her that her symptoms would disappear, he instructed her, while in the trance, to talk about how she felt and what was bothering her. She began to recall incidents from her past when a symptom had appeared, and to his astonishment, Breuer noted that the symptom often vanished permanently after such hypnotic recall. He also found that the induction of a trance was not essential; when she began to reminisce in a dreamy fashion, she dredged up unpleasant memories, and the same remarkable curative result often followed.

This patient developed what Freud was later to call a strong positive transference to Breuer. She would eat only when he fed her and insisted on holding his hand or having him touch her forehead. She was fluent in English and sometimes talked only in that tongue. She commented on this process of digging up memories and thus ending symptoms, calling it "chimney sweeping" and "the talking cure." Breuer was fascinated by the new insights he was obtaining and probably also became excessively affectionate toward her. His wife objected, and Breuer told Pappenheim that she was now cured, so he would not be seeing her anymore. At this point, she went into an outburst, claiming she was pregnant with Breuer's child, and going into pseudolabor pains. Breuer panicked and left town with his wife.

It was only a few months later that Breuer began to tell his young friend, Freud, about the case. It made a strong impression on Freud, who later noted that on November 18, 1882, he had first become aware of the power of unconscious processes to produce symptoms of psychopathology. Meanwhile, he pursued his practice and the use of hypnosis. It was four years later, in 1886, before he returned to his study of the "talking cure," using Breuer's method with his own patients. Finally, in 1893, the two physicians published the first articles on "the case of Anna O."

Although the Breuer-Freud reports imply that Anna O. made a complete recovery with the "talking cure," this was not correct. She was hospitalized shortly after the break with Breuer and, for years, was in and out of institutions (see Ellenberger, 1972), although by the age of thirty she had recovered sufficiently to initiate propaganda for social reforms leading to the profession now called social work. She also became a friend of Freud's wife, Martha.

Critics have questioned the accuracy of the details recorded in the Breuer–Freud publications, noting that over a span of more than ten years, memory distortions could have mangled the facts in the case. Freud's position (later, at least) was that the theory that had evolved from the case was far more important than factual details. He did not, however, try to apply the theory to himself: Had he projected some of his own attributes into the case and so found evidence to confirm the conclusion he had unconsciously developed?

As Freud began to publish his conclusions regarding the role of sexual motivation in producing hysterical symptoms, he came under vicious personal attack. He was accused of defaming children (previously alleged to be sexually innocent until adolescence), of damaging family life (by conjuring up incest fantasies of child toward parent and vice versa), and of undermining society by recommending an easing of the rigid constraints on discussions of sexuality. Ironically, Freud himself ultimately agreed that some frustration of sexuality is indispensable to civilized living, but he maintained that freer discussion of sex could be beneficial to the social order.

Freud himself explained his focus on sex as the dominant, almost the only, human motive by describing three incidents occurring in his early career (Freud, 1914, p. 13). The first related to Breuer himself, who once commented on a neurotic woman that "these things are matters of the marriage bed." Second, Freud mentioned a clinic with Charcot in which the latter remarked "C'est toujours la chose genitale," that is, sex is always the root factor. Finally, Freud described an occasion when Chrobak, an obstetrician, asked him to take a patient, a young married woman with intense anxiety attacks. Chrobak explained that after eighteen years of marriage, she was still a virgin, and he added that the proper prescription was one "which we cannot prescribe. It is: Penis normalis, dosim, repetatur!" It is typical of the spirit of the times that both Breuer and Chrobak denied Freud's report, and Charcot probably would have also, had he still been alive. Given what Freud demonstrated regarding memory distortions, we do not know whether to believe him or his mentors.

Freud may also have been influenced by the intensity of his own sexual enjoyment; he wrote that "one of the forms in which love manifests itself, sexual love, gives us our most intense experience of an overwhelming pleasurable sensation and so furnishes a prototype for our strivings after happiness" (1933, pp. 37–38).

Other influences favoring Freud's focus on sex were the writings of Havelock Ellis and Richard von Krafft-Ebing. Krafft-Ebing was a practicing psychiatrist who collected bizarre cases of abnormal sexual behavior. He was the presiding officer at the Vienna Medical Society meeting where Freud read his epochal 1896 paper on the sexual determinants of hysteria. At the time, Krafft-Ebing was critical, but he later came to support Freud's theories and endorsed him for a professorship in the university. Ellis was not a medical doctor, but his *Studies in the Psychology of Sex* may have influenced Freud's thinking.

Freud himself insisted that it was the free associations of his patients that led him to a sexual diagnosis. Two questions are worth raising on this point: First, did Freud persist in pursuing a dream or other datum until a link to sex was discovered? And second, did he have a highly restricted sample population? He noted that some patients stopped seeing him because of his questions about sex. Thus it may be that those who stayed in therapy were those for whom this line of questioning was appropriate. American studies (Fiedler, 1950; Heine, 1953) have shown that therapists of different schools almost invariably find that their patients exhibit diagnoses compatible with the therapist's preferred theory.

In 1902, Freud decided he wanted to discuss his ideas with a sympathetic group of physicians. He invited about half-a-dozen men to meet with him on Wednesday evenings to listed to his speculations and respond or offer their own perceptions of the phenomena under discussion. One of the younger members was Alfred Adler; others included Wilhelm Stekel, Max Kahane, and Rudolf Reiter. Only Adler and Stekel are now remembered.

Adler, although fourteen years younger than Freud, did not hesitate to disagree with Freud. At first, the older man tolerated these arguments, but when Adler rejected the concepts of penis envy and the castration complex in favor of inferiority feelings and the will to power, Freud forced him out of the Vienna Psychoanalytic Society in 1911, after having made him president of the society in 1910! Freud seems to have been too rigid and self-centered to tolerate any but devoted disciples around him. After Adler, other members withdrew one by one: Stekel, Carl Jung, and Otto Rank being the most notable.

Freud felt isolated from the orthodox medical community, and perhaps this is why he dominated the embryo psychoanalysts so rigidly. And this may be why he was so delighted to be invited by G. Stanley Hall to lecture at Clark University in 1909. He also received an honorary degree from Clark. He commented that this was the only academic recognition he had received so far. It was at the close of these lectures that William James is said to have thrown his arm around Freud's shoulders and said, "The future belongs to your work."

Freud insisted on staying in Vienna during the rise of Nazism. When told that the Brown Shirts were burning his books in the streets, he placidly remarked, "Three centuries ago they would have burned *me*." Seized by the Nazis in Vienna in 1938, he was ransomed by a wealthy patient, Marie Bonaparte; moved to London; and died there in 1939.

Freud suffered severe pain for years with cancer of the jaw. Schur (1972), Freud's personal physician in England, reported that Freud had extracted from him a promise of a peaceful death if the pain became excessive, and that in March 1939, Freud insisted that Schur keep his promise. Schur stated that he deliberately gave Freud an overdose of morphine, thus ending his life.

Methodology

Freud had full medical training and did biological research before setting up a medical practice. He was not, therefore, a novice in the field of methodology. He wrote of cross-checking his findings and of testing hypotheses about his patients' problems. Obviously this testing could not be rigorously controlled, but he tried to follow careful procedures in collecting information. At that time no experimental models allowed for the operation of unconscious processes; since World War II, extensive progress has been made in testing hypotheses about unconscious phenomena.

As I have already noted, Freud experimented with hypnosis as a method of treatment and also as a way of gathering information from patients. It was the latter aspect that excited him. He observed Charcot and Bernheim inducing posthypnotic acts, for which the person would invent an

excuse. Freud inferred that the suggestion given under hypnosis operated unconsciously to trigger the conscious act. He also found that with
repeated questioning about the reason for the action, the patient would
eventually recall that "You told me to do it." This suggested that even
deeply buried memories could be uncovered by persistent and pointed
questioning.

Freud applied the method first of all to himself. His *Psychopathology of
Everyday Life* (1901) deals with memory lapses, incorrect identifications,
slips of the tongue, and accidents in daily life. Most of the examples
come from Freud's own actions. On forgetting the name of a patient
whom he knew well, he probed for his own associations of ideas and
found that her name happened to be the same as that of another patient
who was long overdue on paying his bill. Freud believed that "accidents"
are often motivated by unconscious considerations. On one occasion he
broke a beautiful marble statuette of Venus; his associations convinced
him that it was a sacrifice of thanksgiving for the recovery of a seriously
ill relative. He misspelled the name of a well-known scientist and found
that this individual had the same name as another Viennese scientist who
had angered Freud by harsh criticism of *The Interpretation of Dreams*. Slips
of the tongue have even got into popular slang as "Freudian slips." Freud
mentions a man who was distressed by his wife's reluctance to bear a
child. Speaking of the tale of Odysseus' wife and her weaving, he commented on "Penelope at her womb." The literary reference to her "loom"
became transposed to fit the man's real concern (see Figure 13.6).

The same method was used in the interpretation of dreams. Freud
made it a practice to write down the details of a dream as quickly as
possible because of the speed with which they are forgotten. Dream
interpretation, he found, is a tedious process. Typically he took specific
details of the dream and produced free associations; thus a dream of an
ocean voyage might be associated with escape from unpleasant chores in
his practice. Freud always insisted that any given dream should be related to other aspects of the person's life; there is no universal dream
symbolism. For example, a young man reports a dream: "She let me put
my car in her garage." This seems to be a dream of intercourse; the car
(penis) is placed in her garage (vagina). However, it may happen that
the associations indicate anxiety and an anticipation of personal problems: "she" turns out to be "mother" and the garage a symbol of protection and security.

From such observations Freud abstracted the attribute "unconscious
determination" and used it as a centerpiece of his theorizing (see Figure
1.3). At the same time, he acknowledged that unconscious phenomena
could be studied mostly through the detection of influences on conscious
events. The emotional state involved in each of the foregoing examples
distorted a conscious memory or action, determining its form or appearance.

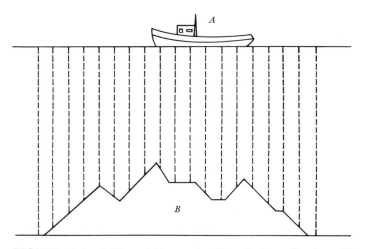

FIGURE 14.1   A Way of Illustrating Freud's Identification of Unconscious Complexes

An observer (A) is in a boat searching for an invisible object under the water. By putting down probes, the shape of the hidden object (B) may be ascertained.

The process of arriving at a diagnosis of any specific unconscious state required careful and persistent probing. A diagram (Figure 14.1) may help one to understand Freud's logic. An observer in a boat (A) cannot see an object under the water (B). However, by putting down successive probes, the inquirer may be able to arrive at a fairly accurate description of the object.

Determinism

It is apparent that Freud carried his philosophy of rigid determinism further than did Hull or Skinner. Hull had introduced an "O" factor to account for some failures of prediction. Skinner conceded that not all operants could be predicted. Freud assumed that even the apparent accident was determined, usually by unconscious emotional urges.

This facet of Freud's thinking has been recognized only recently. Not so long ago H. J. Eysenck (1963) asserted that psychoanalysis "has never been taken very seriously by people with some regard for the principles of scientific method." But in 1978, A. E. Kazdin, a behaviorist, wrote that Freud "assumed a determinism whereby every behavior, thought, and idea, however minor, was caused by underlying mechanisms" (p. 18).

In contrast to the nomothetic psychologists, who tried to extract com-

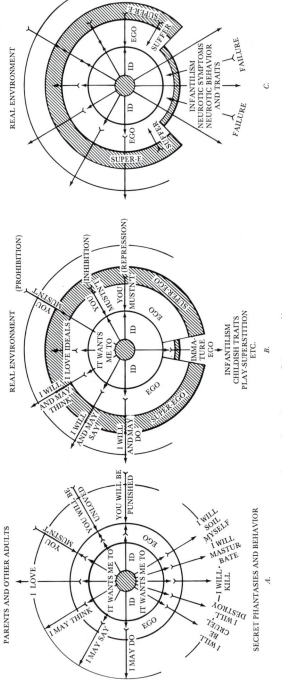

FIGURE 14.2 Hendrick's Version of Freud's Theory of Personality Formation

(A): The id (innate demands) seeks immediate gratification of all needs—the pleasure principle. Parents and other adults begin to impose controls. (B): The normal adult accepts societal controls of most id impulses, and the ego may devise circuitous ways of getting satisfaction while avoiding punishment—the reality principle. (C): The neurotic personality shows incomplete superego formation and an ego not successful in finding substitute satisfactions. (*From Hendrick, Facts and Theories of Psychoanalysis, © 1935, reprinted by permission of Alfred A. Knopf, Inc.*)

mon principles by comparing large numbers of persons, Freud opted for collecting many observations about a single individual and seeking common principles and recurrent themes. A similar procedure has been advocated by Gordon Allport (see Chapter 17).

The Theory

It would be more appropriate to refer to Freud's "theories" than to his "theory," as he constantly modified his conceptualization of mental processes throughout his career. We can, however, identify a few constants and then note changes in certain limited areas.

The Metaphors

Freud used a variety of metaphors in his attempt to convey his abstruse conceptions to his colleagues. One of the earliest was the *membrane metaphor*, a kind of semipermeable membrane that separated conscious from unconscious material. Memories pass easily from conscious to unconscious, but only with difficulty in the reverse direction. In Figure 14.1, the membrane can be treated as the surface of the water; the observer, above it (in the conscious area), cannot see the hidden complex but can get glimpses of it by observing distortions in conscious processes (e.g., memory lapses, slips of the tongue, and dreams). Freud conceived of the unconscious material as pushing against the membrane and thus having an influence on conscious speech, thought, and action.

The *hydraulic metaphor* may have been inspired by Descartes, who had written of the "animal spirits" in his analogy to the automated statues in the French Royal Gardens. Freud treated the libido (motivational energy) as fluid exerting pressure on psychic structures (e.g., habits, speech, and creativity). If the pressure rises too high for the system to tolerate, a break occurs, and a neurotic symptom develops. With increasing maturity, the person develops a kind of reservoir in which excessive pressure can be contained until a socially acceptable outlet can be discovered.

A third metaphor was *geographical*. Freud hypothesized a threefold division of the total personality into the id, the ego, and the superego. The metaphor is that of an iceberg, with most of the personality under the surface (in the unconscious.) The id is described as the raw impulses and emotions, virtually completely unconscious; the superego, composed of societal demands and prohibitions, is unconscious except for a few conscious beliefs in moral or ethical behavior; and the ego, corresponding to most of what we have called psychology up to this point (i.e., perceiving, planning, and acting), makes up most of the "conscious" or visible portion of the iceberg.

Another kind of metaphor was proposed by Ives Hendrick (1935), an orthodox Freudian (Figure 14.2). It has some similarity to Lewin's vector diagrams, with forces emanating from the id, encountering frustrations from the "real" environment, and being sometimes redirected by the ego. Note also that the presence of a "real" environment suggests the presence of a "perceived" environment, as in the Gestalt theories.

Instinct Theory

Freud grew up in an era in which instinct theory was predominant among biologists; he was undoubtedly indoctrinated with this approach in his medical training. It will be recalled that William McDougall postulated a large number of human instincts; Freud pruned the list drastically and emphasized the flexibility of the human species in diverting energy from the same instinctual source into diverse behavioral patterns.

Sex Versus Ego Instincts

In an early formulation, Freud postulated two major instincts (or groups of instincts; he vacillated somewhat on this point). The sexual impulse, or pleasure-seeking tendency, was conceived of as coming into conflict with the ego, or survival instincts (e.g., hunger, fatigue, and pain). The theme of conflict runs through all of Freud's theorizing; this is merely the earliest example.

The sex–ego conflict gives rise to the ego as a structure within the personality (it is not in any way a personification of the ego instincts). Briefly, the sex impulse actuates pleasure-seeking behaviors which sometimes encounter environmental prohibitions. For active pleasure-seeking, the child may be punished by parents, by other persons, or by the physical environment. As a result of the association of the libidinal impulse with pain, anxiety is experienced when the same impulse arises again. Anxiety then becomes the main coercive agent restraining the instinctual impulses from demanding total and immediate gratification.

Eros Versus the Death Instinct

Partly as a consequence of his horror at events of World War I, Freud decided that he had misidentified the polar opposites in human instinctual life. In a revision of his earlier theory, he coalesced sex and survival impulses into a new category, which he called "Eros" (the name of the Greek god of love). Although this category retains the predominance of the sexual aspect in its name, it proposes that the sex and survival impulses can coexist peacefully and that many actions combine sexual pleasure with gratification of survival needs.

In opposition to Eros, Freud placed a difficult concept that he called the "death instinct." (It is often referred to in the literature as Thanatos—the Greek god of death—to parallel Eros; however, there is no evidence that Freud ever accepted this term.) Conflicts of the death instinct with Eros were seen as inevitable; attacking others is not likely to lead to sexual pleasure and, indeed, may threaten survival. If the death instinct were introverted (i.e., turned against the self), it might motivate suicidal behavior. Mainly it was extraverted, turned against the external world and for the most part against barriers to pleasurable gratifications.

Critics argued that the assumption of a "death instinct" was incompatible with Darwinian logic, according to which innate attributes are selected so as to maximize individual or species survival. Freud held that in normal life, this energy was indeed used in the service of survival; it was not normally directed inward. He did, nonetheless, defend the hypothesis on logical grounds. Fechner had argued earlier that all living matter eventually returns to nonliving matter, that metabolism is composed of both catabolism and anabolism (the buildup and breakdown of tissues). Freud also pointed out that wars and riots are too popular, give rise to too much destruction, to be explained on a goal-seeking basis, and that some individuals clearly derive pleasure from destructive and aggressive actions.

The energy of the sexual instinct, or of Eros in the revised theory, was called *libido*. This concept looks alarmingly like Descartes's "animal spirits." Freud originally described it as flowing through tubes and as exerting physical pressure. As the naïveté of this view became apparent, the libido became an abstraction, a way of labeling a kind of energy that could become attached to love objects (and could be withdrawn from them if that action became appropriate). It is the history of the libido, the pleasure-seeking drives of the individual, that constitutes the core of psychoanalytic thinking about personality.

No such energy was postulated for the death instinct. (One of Freud's associates, Paul Federn, proposed the term *mortido*, but it never achieved wide acceptance.) The instinct, however, could be domesticated into an *aggressive* drive, which, in turn, could be drawn into the service of other instincts; for example, in many cultures, an aggressive male is more attractive to females than males who lack this trait.

Freud was emphatic in his assertion that the major determinant of pleasure seeking was sexual. In his *General Introduction to Psychoanalysis* (1916/1949), he asked a very broad question

> We may put the question whether a main purpose is discernible in the operation of the mental apparatus; and our first approach to an answer is that this purpose is directed to the attainment of pleasure. It seems that our entire psychical activity is bent upon *procuring pleasure* and *avoiding pain*, that it is automatically regulated by the *Pleasure Principle*. . . . Pleasure is *in some way* connected with lessening, lowering, or extinguishing the amount of stimulation present in the mental apparatus; and . . . pain in-

volves a heightening of the latter. Consideration of the most intense pleasure of which man is capable, the pleasure in the performance of the sexual act, leaves little doubt upon this point. Since pleasurable processes of
this kind are bound up with the distribution of quantities of mental excitation and energy, we term considerations of this kind *economic* ones.
(p. 311; italics in original)

Thus still another metaphor creeps in; the economic metaphor involves
a cost–benefit analysis of the pleasure–pain balance in a given activity.

As the child matures, pleasure–principle behavior is replaced by the
reality principle, which holds that the individual seeks to maximize pleasure and to avoid pain *in the long run.* This means that the person will
tolerate an immediate discomfort if it is perceived as the path to a greater
pleasure at a later time. This is characteristic of mature adults. But of
course, it is possible—in fact, easy—to find personalities in some contexts
functioning at the reality level but in other situations acting at the pleasure–principle or infantile level.

Anxiety and the Reality Principle

Freud held that the basic principle governing all instinctual manifestations was the pleasure principle. That is, for the very young child, instincts demand immediate and total gratification. And indeed, this is the
one period of life in which such demands may be tolerated. As the child
matures, the adult world begins to demand delay of gratification, to limit
the degree of gratification permitted, and to specify the forms it can take
and the circumstances under which it is permitted. The child who refuses to accept these societal constraints is classified as infantile; neurotic
and psychotic adults show limited areas of behavior in which they manifest infantile tendencies (see Figure 14.2C, page 300).

Adults or the physical world may punish infantile actions. The resulting pain, when recalled, becomes anxiety. The child changes from behavior obeying the pleasure principle to behavior based on the reality
principle as anxiety imposes limits on infantile gratification. The reality
principle states that the individual develops behaviors that maximize
gratification in the long run, that is, that minimize anxiety and punishment while still allowing the achievement of instinctual satisfaction. Some
anxiety, then, is indispensable for socialization.

Actually, Freud's perception that the pleasure principle and the reality
principle were not adequate to explain all behavior led him to formulate
the death instinct hypothesis. Sometimes people engage in actions that
lead directly to painful consequences. Thus a child may reenact going to
the hospital or being in an accident; the memories can hardly be pleasant, and Freud had earlier ascribed them to something he called a "repetition compulsion," although he later decided that an independent instinct of destructiveness must be operative.

In his famous letter to Albert Einstein ("Why War?") Freud wrote that "when human beings are incited to war they may have a whole number of motives for assenting—some noble and some base, some of which they speak openly and others on which they are silent. There is no need to enumerate them all. A lust for aggression and destruction is certainly among them" (1932, pp. 281–282).

How can one energize opposition to such an instinct? Freud proposed that "If willingness to engage in war is an effect of the destructive instinct, the most obvious plan will be to bring Eros, its antagonist, into play against it. Anything that encourages the growth of emotional ties between men must operate against war" (1932, pp. 283–284). Regrettably, as of the 1980s, Freud's prescription has not been very effective. Of course, as G. K. Chesterton remarked about Christianity, it has not yet been tried.

Cathexis

To the extent that Freud wrote about learning, it was in terms of attaching the libido to objects or persons; he called this attachment "cathexis." Some psychoanalysts whose native tongue was German have suggested that Freud's term, *Besetzung*, translates better as "investment"; one *invests* a certain amount of love in one's mother or father. Cathexis, however, has become the standard term for attachment of libido to a person or situation. "Anti-cathexis" has been used for a negative value (dislike) of a person, but Freud never made it clear that these anti-cathexes involved the death instinct. Logically it would seem necessary to postulate some form of attachment of the death instinct to negatively-valued stimuli.

Vicissitudes of Libido

Freud's theory of psychosexual development is a theory of varying gratifications of the libido. Much of the time, he wrote as if these stages were maturational and innate, not dependent on learning. For the most part, non-Freudians perceive them as learned aspects of the child's adaptation to social constraints. As already noted, parental pressures may induce the young person to associate anxiety with certain expressions of the libido; this association, naturally, leads to the inhibition of such activities.

The Oral Stages The earliest weeks of a baby's life are spent mostly sleeping or sucking. The breast, a source of survival, becomes a major object-cathexis, and the mouth, as the body part directly involved, is also invested with libido. Freud hypothesized that during the first few months of life, libido is attached mainly to the lips and to the breast. Gratification is brought to the child without effort on his or her part, and so this stage is passive (no libido is invested in any effortful activity). If the degree of gratification is either excessively high or excessively low, a fixation may occur at the oral passive level, and the corresponding adult personality will be characterized by demanding dependency, expecting others to provide care and gratification without the person's own exertion.

After the emergence of teeth, the baby becomes capable of more aggressive relations with the environment (bitting rather than sucking). This is called the oral-sadistic stage; fixation here is said to eventuate in a sarcastic, "biting" kind of adult personality.

It should be noted that the adult manifestations of fixation at one of these early phases may be treated, in the theory, as an outcome of either overgratification or overdeprivation. Students are sometimes puzzled by this alternative, seemingly contradictory approach. Freud's explanation was not particularly involved. If the infant is overindulged in sucking, he or she may develop a demand that this situation continue; that is, there is an expectancy that others will continue to provide pleasures without effort on the part of the recipient. If, however, the infancy period is characterized by deprivation, then an expectancy of deprivation may underlie a kind of whining demand that more of these gratifications be forthcoming, that other persons provide nurturance without questioning and without limit. The important theoretical point, of course, is that these expectancies are unconscious; thus a person may repeatedly act in such a way as to appeal for rescue and care, when the problem situation could have been avoided with a bit of common sense. Thus an oral-passive person is likely to deny possessing such attributes, although they are highly visible to family and friends. In other words, these infantile gratifications and frustrations may engender libidinal fixations that determine the course of behavior without any conscious recognition.

The Anal Stages   Active conflict with the environment (parents) begins at the stage of toilet training. Like the oral phase, the anal phase has two stages: anal-retentive and anal-expulsive. During the oral period, the act of defecation has been uninhibited; as it is preceded by some discomfort, the expulsion of feces can become reinforcing or pleasurable. Freud claimed that when toilet training begins, the child may show a preponderance of either anal-expulsive or anal-retentive behaviors. If the parent is excessively demanding of conformity, the child may withhold the bowel movement as an assertion of resistance to control. Or he or she may find gratification in expulsive behavior (i.e., having movements at other than the prescribed time).

The anal stages do not separate neatly as the oral stages do. Thus we can consider these behaviors only as alternatives that may appear whenever toilet training begins. In adult life, libidinal fixation on pleasurable stimulation of the anus may be associated with homosexual tendencies; it is also (in the anal–retentive type) associated with miserliness and pedantry (an obsession with trivial details). The anal–expulsive vestiges are associated with vulgar attacks on others, as in some fiction and during some political campaigns (1915).

The Phallic Stage The focus on pleasurable sensations from mouth and lips, and later from the anal area, is replaced at the age of three or four years by an interest in pleasure from stimulating the genitals. Freud called this the "phallic stage" because the genitals are of autoerotic significance rather than being associated with the opposite sex. Libido is invested in the sex organs, and little boys particularly are likely to find pleasure in exhibiting theirs.

The Oedipus Complex At the age of four or five, the autoerotic component of the phallic stage begins to give way to a desire for the love of the opposite-sexed parent. The girl invests heavily in her father and becomes hostile to her mother. Boys are more likely to invest in the mother, to attempt to displace the father. But hostility toward the father is not likely to succeed; he is big and powerful, and he can overcome any childish display of antagonism. The normal solution to this conflict is for the child to *identify* with the same-sexed parent, thus gaining a fantasy mating with the (still beloved) other parent.

Vestiges of poorly resolved Oedipal complexes are found in young women who fall in love with much older men, those chronically critical of their mothers, and so on. Young men who regularly get into fights with authority figures and become infatuated with women resembling the mother illustrate the male variety of the Oedipal pattern.

Freud proposed that the male Oedipal reaction was ended when parents threatened castration. The female castration complex was assumed to have been activated earlier as the girl child became aware of the male organ and her lack of one: "Whereas in boys the Oedipus succumbs to the castration complex, in girls it is made possible and led up to by the castration complex" (Freud, 1925, p. 195). The vestiges of a castration complex were alleged to appear in adult reactions to injury or to loss of power.

Latency If the Oedipal complex is successful assimilated, male children identify with the father, females with the mother. The libidinal impulses that elicited dire threats from the adult world are repressed, and a latent period of life begins. Freud believed that this latency lasted until puberty; modern observers suggest that the latency period may have disappeared from American society.

Genital Sexuality At puberty (or earlier, if stimulated sexually), the young person again experiences active sexual desires. Members of the opposite sex, who have been scorned during the latency period, now are perceived as tremendously attractive. If all goes well, the person will establish a conventional relationship with a person of the opposite sex. Freud, something of a Victorian in his ethical values, assumed that monogamy was the ideal state, although recognizing that many influences operated against it as a permanent pattern of behavior.

As I have suggested elsewhere, Freud was assailed in many quarters for destroying the myth of the innocence of childhood. Merely by talking of such topics, it was said, he was encouraging sexual promiscuity among the young. This criticism has a strangely modern ring in he 1980s, with noisy debates about the effect of sex education on the young.

Thoughtful critics of the stage theory stress the limited amount of empirical support for it, as well as the wide variation within families and social groups with regard to the postulated stages. Freud had an inveterate habit of extrapolating far beyond his data. His insistence on universals associated with sex differences has caused many women's groups to attack him; such an attack obviously is not relevant to the status of the theory as such. Freud's overemphasis on heredity means that he offered few propositions as to conditions that modify the process of personality formation. Freud's hypotheses about homosexuality, sadism and masochism, irrational aggression, passive dependency, and so on often appear to be speculations about extreme behavior without any real clues as to the determining conditions involved.

On the positive side, the theory has provided a vocabulary and a set of categories that facilitate discussions about personality. If an industrial psychologist characterizes a bright young male applicant for a managerial position as "having an unresolved Oedipal problem," she is implicitly or explicitly predicting clashes with authority figures and an inability to inhibit certain aggressive impulses. Similarly, tendencies toward anal-retentive or passive-dependent behavior become more meaningful to those acquainted with the Freudian theory.

Theory of Neurosis

In his interpretation of the case of Anna O., Freud theorized that an emotion blocked from expression may induce a certain symptom as an indirect expression (note that the ego can deflect libido to some extent from one object to another). Freud showed that Anna O.'s symptoms were associated with her (unexpressed) love for her father and the trauma induced by his lingering illness. As Freud began to use the "talking cure" with other patients, he found that many of them showed early memories in which sex and distress or frustration were associated. His early writings present a theory in which traumatic experiences of a sexual character account for repression of the memory but unconscious persistence of the anxiety, and in which this unconscious memory supports the contemporary neurotic symptoms. In Freud's practice, when a supporting memory was dragged up into consciousness, the symptom often disappeared.

Freud knew that incest was not rare in Vienna. Indeed, he admitted that in two of his cases, rape had actually occurred, although he never reported this to the police. But when he inquired of the families of the patients regarding such alleged traumas, the family would defend the accused person. For some reason, Freud decided to accept these denials, concluding that the reported trauma had not "really" happened. After ruminating about this difficulty, he concluded that the reports were out-comes of the daughters' erotic desires for sexual relations with the father (or perhaps with a father substitute). In this theory, a fantasied rape could have the same traumatic outcome as a physical assault. If a com-mon emotional state or libidinal impulse could form an associative link, then, Freud suggested, the female children could have formed sexual desires for their fathers or other adult males, daydreamed of being se-duced by this person, felt guilty about having such thoughts, and so involved the sexual impulse in the neurosis. (See Freud, 1914).

If we consider the Zeitgeist of Vienna in the 1890s, Freud's reasoning is comprehensible but unjustifiable. He knew that the society allowed male sexuality fairly complete freedom, while restricting females se-verely. He also knew of the common practice of "blaming the victim" (i.e., the male charging the female with "seductive behavior"). The fe-male child was thus placed in the painful situation of being traumatized and then blamed for the trauma.

In recent years, empirical data have accumulated to show that Freud's early insight (that many neuroses are due to physical sexual trauma) was correct, and that his fantasy theory was incorrect or, at best, of limited value. One well-controlled study (Storm, 1986), queried fifty adult women who had been victims of sexual abuse as children, compared with fifty matched cases who had come for counseling on matters not involving incest. The abused group had a much higher frequency of nervous breakdowns, suicide attempts, eating disorders, and diagnoses of mental illness.

The Masson Fracas

Orthodox Freudians accepted the fantasy thesis and implemented it with their female patients for some seventy years. It was not until the 1970s that questions began to be raised. Much publicity has recently been given to a young psychoanalyst, J. M. Masson, who had the good fortune to be appointed administrator of the Freud Archives and thus had access to mounds of letters and other unpublished material.

Masson (1984) propounded the theory that Freud's switch from the rape theory to the fantasy theory had a personal motivation. Jakob Freud, Sigmund's father, was married three times, and Sigmund was born eight months after the third wedding; hence Freud could have assumed that his father was guilty of immoral behavior. (See also Balmary, 1982.)

Masson spent a great deal of time identifying significant passages in Freud's letters that had been censored by Anna Freud (Sigmund's daughter and an important psychoanalytical figure in her own right), by Ernest Jones (Freud's official biographer), and by other devotees of the Freudian doctrine. This censorship should surprise no one; all histories include some data and exclude other items, reflecting the bias of the historian. (This is true of the present book, as of all others.) Masson relied heavily on Freud's letters to Wilhelm Fliess, a surgeon with whom Freud became very intimate. As archivist for the Sigmund Freud Archives, Masson had access to the uncensored originals of these letters. (His publication of the censored material cost him his job.)

Masson (1985) published the uncut letters with notes calling attention to passages expunged from the earlier publications. Many of these were trivial and suggest that Masson may have been expressing his annoyance at his treatment. For example, Freud wrote, "I sleep during my afternoon analyses," a condition some clients suspect of contemporary therapists. He also described his failures; on April 25, 1900, he recorded, "The patient whom I treated for 14 days and then dismissed as a case of paranoia has since hanged herself in a hotel room." Other revelations are even more disturbing: of a particular dream analysis, he commented, "I can have dreams like that to order." Whether he "dreamed to order" the instances recounted in *The Interpretation of Dreams* (1938) is a worrisome thought. Did his theory dictate the kinds of dreams Freud recorded?

The focal point of the Masson publications is the charge that Freud had made an indefensible switch in his theory of neurosis, perhaps as a result of his unconscious defense against the suspicion that his father, too, had been guilty of sexually seducing a minor. Masson charged that the evidence favored the original theory (physical traumatic experience) and that Freud altered his views for personal reasons. Masson cynically commented that if analyses were automobiles, every one since 1901 ought to be recalled.

Viennese society of the 1890s was certainly rife with adultery, prostitution, venereal disease, and incest. But the Zeitgeist forbade admission of these phenomena. Only recently has it been possible to get reasonably unbiased studies of sexual crimes, even in America. B. Justice and R. Justice (1979) offered clear evidence that incest, especially father–daughter intercourse, is far more common than we would like to believe. With the increased number of divorces and second marriages, stepdaughters seem to have become especially vulnerable. In Freud's day, fathers had little contact with child rearing and so may have perceived a nubile daughter as an attractive sex object, not as a child to be nurtured and protected.

There is another respect in which the Masson volume (1985) is important. Orthodox analysts have relied on Freud's clear thinking and freedom from bias as outcomes of his self-analysis. The Fliess letters provide a picture of a neurotic, ambivalent, easily misled, and intensely emotional person. They leave the reader with grave doubts about the therapeutic outcome of Freud's self-analysis.

This in no way detracts from Freud's remarkable achievements in documenting the major role played by unconscious processes in human thought and behavior. Western psychology has been irrevocably modified by his theories.

Freud and Feminism

Freud's theorizing about sex differences (not about sexuality in general) has been severely criticized by feminists since the mid-1930s. The fantasy theory of neurosis was seen as an effort to "blame the victim," as many present-day courts blame rape victims for having behaved in a "sexually provocative" manner. New fuel has been added to these flames with the Masson revelations. However, Freud's basically biased view of the female sex as a class was obvious long before the recent publications. His phrase "Anatomy is destiny" meant that the possession of a male or a female sex organ determined psychological attributes. He was firmly convinced that women were weaker and less rational than men and should be subservient to them. After translating J. S. Mill's essay on liberty, in which Mill advocated equality of the sexes before the law, Freud is said to have exclaimed, "But Mill is just crazy!"

In his treatment of two favorite concepts, penis envy and the castration complex, Freud wrote imaginatively but unconvincingly. He assumed that if a small boy saw a girl's vulva, he would not be impressed; after all, not much meets the eye. A young girl seeing a penis, he speculated, "behaves differently. She makes her judgment and her decision in a flash. She has seen it and knows that she is without it and wants to have it" (1925, p. 191).

Freud believed that in therapy, getting down to the castration complex in males (fear of loss of the penis, and therefore being like a female) and to penis envy in females meant excavating the fundamental causes of neurosis. But in describing his therapeutic tactics, Freud destroyed the myth of the detached analyst taking a neutral stance with regard to the patient's problems:

> At no point in one's analytic work does one suffer more from the oppressive feeling that all one's efforts have been in vain and from the suspicion that one is "talking to the winds" than when one is trying to *persuade a female patient* to abandon her wish for a penis on the ground of its being unrealizable, or to *convince a male patient* that a passive attitude towards another man does not always signify castration and that in many relations in life it is indispensable. (1937, p. 356; italics added).

The young girl seeing a penis was assumed, first, to want one and, second, to fantasize that she had one and has lost it (castration). From this hypothetical deprivation Freud deduced some highly unfavorable judgments about women in general:

> Character traits which critics of every epoch have brought up against women—that they show less sense of justice than men, that they are less ready to submit to the greater necessities of life, that they are more often influenced in their judgments by feelings of affection and hostility—all these would be amply accounted for by the modification in the formation of their super-ego [based on the castration complex]. (1925, p. 197)

This critical view seems to have a clear resemblance to the classical Hebrew view of sex differences (see Chapter Two), and to have ignored the contemporary Viennese stereotypes as reasons for female behaviors. As will be noted later, Alfred Adler broke with Freud chiefly over the issues of penis envy and castration complex: Adler said that social constraints were far more important than these speculative anatomical influences on sex differences in behavior.

The Structure of Personality

As the individual matures, the libido undergoes many cathexes and anticathexes. But this process goes on in an environment that imposes many constraints and some compulsions on the person, particularly with respect to the abandonment of infantile gratifications. Freud largely ignored the perceptual and cognitive aspects of this process, but he proposed a theory of the structuring of personal dynamics that is widely quoted, if not accepted.

He began with the innate basis of need and motive—what he had in his early theory conceptualized as the sexual and the ego instincts. These, he proposed, form a single structure, the id. (The German term is *das Es*, "the It," and he used this to mean primitive impulses having no self-reference, as suggested in the Hendrick diagram, Fig. 14.2.) The id was described as the subhuman part of personality, raw demands for food, sex, comfort, relief from pain, and so on. The infant personality is all id, as the process of learning about the environment has not yet begun. In adult life, the id is completely unconscious—although Freud did seem to allow for violent rage and panic fear as uninhibited expressions of id impulses.

As the id impulses seek gratification, the primitive ego begins to form. Sensing and perceiving operate first to guide the person to sources of satisfaction; and as social controls begin to be imposed, the ego serves the function of evading these controls or of devising ways to satisfy the id demands without encountering punishment. The ego has no fund of libido to use in motivating behavior, but by arousing anxiety, it can borrow energy from the id and turn it against impulses that threaten to involve pain and punishment.

Early in life, certainly after the Oedipus conflict is solved, a new personality structure beings to develop. This is a set of impulses corresponding fairly well to the traditional idea of morals, ethics, or conscience. Freud called this evolving system the superego (in German *das Über-Ich*), because it mobilizes energy to control both the id and the ego. As before, Freud postulated that the superego has no libidinal energies of its own but channels the libido from the id storehouse to energize socially approved behavior. As in ego, the mechanism is predominantly that of anxiety, fear of loss of love of the parents, which diverts energy from the id and turns it back on the id impulses to restrain them (see Figure 14.2).

The superego was sometimes described as involving two systems, one of taboos ("you must not") and the other of ideals ("you ought to"). The former derives mainly from anxiety over future consequences, the latter mainly from identification with the parents (especially the identification with the like-sexed parent at the conclusion of the Oedipal phase). This distinction has virtually disappeared from recent psychoanalytic literature.

G. K. Leak and S. B. Christopher (1982) interpreted Freudian structural theory as being compatible with the sociobiological approach that has recently become popular. This is an attempt to identify survival characteristics and to relate them to psychological theory. After examining the id and superego concepts, these authors "suggest that the id reflects selection for adaptation to the *nonsocial* environment and the presence of competitors, whereas the superego is a set of tendencies evolved in response to the selection pressures of *social* living" (p., 317; italics added). This view does not amount to endorsing the position that the superego is innate; their view is that the "selection pressures" of social living operate anew on each individual. Although this idea may be compatible with Darwinian thinking, I doubt it. Indeed, a look at reproductive statistics would suggest that those lacking in superego restraints are reproducing faster than the rest of the population. However, it must also be noted that, in the dark days when the death penalty for crime was ubiquitous and was carried out in many situations, there was no indication that the succeeding generations had superior superego constraints.

Criticisms of the Theory

It is worth noting briefly that this structural theory of personality has been widely criticized on the grounds that the id, the ego, and the superego show no necessary internal link, no functional unity. Although Freud wrote as if some individuals are born with high id energies and other persons with low levels, there is no evidence to confirm this. And among adults, the intensity of drives, such as hunger and sex, varies within the same person as well as among individuals. Thus the term *id* becomes a convenient symbol for innate dynamics but does not seem to have any underlying unity.

The same applies to the superego. Freud wrote of this system as if it were a little person inside the head issuing instructions and prohibitions. Actually, a behavioristic conception of habits of approach and avoidance seems more persuasive. When Freud wrote of a "severe superego," he implied a unified structure, whereas a person might have very rigid taboos, perhaps with regard to sex with children, but not limiting other indulgences. This is a major point of dispute in personality theory; see Chapter Twenty for further details.

This tendency to personify psychic processes accounts for many hostile criticisms of Freud. He spoke of censorship (forcing guilty thoughts down into the unconscious) as *die Zensur,* implying again a person rather than an impersonal process. The punitive aspect of the superego became "the demon," and so on. Freud wrote in literary rather than scientific terms; but it is not very difficult to infer what observables he was referring to, even in his flights of literary imagination.

The conflict between id and superego may impose extreme stress on the ego functions. Thus, in Freud's typical formula for neurosis, the id demands, the superego forbids, and the ego is stuck with the task of working out a compromise that may salvage some impulse gratification without evoking excessive guilt (see Figure 14.2). Obviously most of us manage this, although Freud assumed that everyone (including himself) was a bit neurotic. Some of his critics have said that this self-reference was an understatement.

Defense Mechanisms

The struggle between the id, the ego, and the superego creates intensely unpleasant feelings. The individual devises coping mechanisms, ways of dealing with these conflicts, through perceptual distortions, learned habits, forgetting, and so on. It was in his analysis of these phenomena that Freud came closest to the concerns of the structuralists, the behaviorists, and the Gestalters. Even so, his interest was always in the energy distribution, not in the cognitive or behavioral events.

Primary and Secondary Process   The earliest interaction of the id and the ego occurs (so Freud asserted) shortly after birth. The demand for food causes the primitive ego to hallucinate the breast (infants often go through sucking movements while asleep). He called this hallucination "primary-process" thinking because it indicates a direct impact of impulse on percept. Primary-process thinking is rare in normal adults but explains hallucinations and the delusions of psychotics.

Secondary-process thinking corresponds to the relatively realistic perception of the external world. Logic and adaptive behavior illustrate this category. But perceiving and thinking at this level are not free of libidinal influence.

Infantile omnipotence is a case of primary-process thinking. The infant behaves as if it possessed magical powers: "What I wish is what happens." Soon the ego realizes that it is not omnipotent, that social and physical limits exist. This realization is painful, as many temper tantrums indicate. There is not a good phrase for the opposite of infantile omnipotence, but essentially, the child learns to abandon egocentric thinking, to see reality as adults see it, and to recognize limitations even on the powers of adults, but especially of the self.

Repression The most pervasive mechanism in the Freudian list is repression. It involves imposing a barrier on the entry into consciousness of ideas of forbidden pleasures. One way to avoid punishment for overt sexual behavior is to deny that one has a sex drive (Cf. Origen, Chapter Two). Refusal to "see" phenomena that are readily apparent to others is usually based on repression; to recognize the phenomenon would be to convict oneself of immoral impulses, so the idea is forcibly evicted from awareness.

Repression is intimately involved with Freud's membrane metaphor. He postulated the existence of a *Reizschutz*, a shield against excessive stimulation. The assumption was indispensable, he argued, because the infant would be destroyed by "an external world charged with the most powerful energies. . . . It would be killed by the stimulation emanating from these if it were not provided with a protective shield against stimuli. . . . *Protection against* stimuli is an almost more important function for the living organism than *reception* of stimuli." (1920, p. 27; italics in original). This idea is, of course, compatible with his view—notably with regard to the death instinct—that the ultimate aim of living is nirvana, a quiescence, an absence of tension.

The structuralists had been concerned with adaptation, habituation, and thresholds, not to mention eye blinks and body movements to minimize external stimulation. They had not asked about the *function* of these organismic properties. Freud viewed them as protective and symbolized them with his selective membrane.

Later Freud extended the *Reizschutz* concept to cover internally activated stimuli. Just as the organism may be threatened from the outside, dangerous instincts may threaten to get the child in trouble. To blank out these urgings from within, the *Reizschutz* may selectively tune out or become unaware of forbidden impulses. This may be accomplished by focusing the attention elsewhere, by engaging in routine acts that prevent daydreaming, and so on. Freud referred to this function as *die Zensur* (the censor) and credited it with censoring the content of dreams, thus forcing the ego to transform sexual objects into symbolic representations. (It is not clear why Freud used personifications like *die Zensur* and *das Ich* when an impersonal term would have served as well. His practice has been criticized by literal-minded scholars—and applauded by those with a literary turn of mind.)

The ego, as the aspect of personality in direct contact with the environment, is the seat of perceiving, learning, reflecting, and coping in general. The "mechanisms of defense" are thus ego functions. Experimental psychologists have subjected some of these to experimental confirmation. Thus perceptual vigilance confirms the hypothesis that the objects needed for impulse gratification will be salient in the phenomenal field (see Chapter Nineteen). Perceptual defense, by contrast, occurs as the ego shuts out either external or internal stimuli that threaten punishment or anxiety. *Sublimation* occurs when energy from a tabooed impulse, such as a sexual drive focused on a forbidden person, is channeled into socially desirable activities such as social work, art, or music. *Displacement* is the general term for object substitutions, as when hostility is displaced from the parent to a foreigner. P. Kline (1972) summarized literally hundreds of experiments designed to test Freudian hypotheses; a surprising number meet a rigorous empirical standard.

According to Freud's theory, the ego has no energy of its own and so borrows from the Id, using anxiety as the tool. By evoking an image of punishment, the ego summons up anxiety from the id and uses this energy to block the sexual impulse from being acted out. Anxiety reduction also serves as a reinforcing agent for behavior; thus, if a symbolic ritual at bedtime reduces anxiety enough to permit undisturbed sleep, the habit is reinforced and maintained.

The ego is also involved in perceptual distortions, such as misinterpreting a smile as an erotic invitation, or a frown as a castration threat. Freud did not hesitate to charge critics with distortions and blindness; sarcastically he wrote that "one hears of analysts who boast that, though they have worked for dozens of years, they have never found a sign of the existence of a castration complex. We must bow our heads in recognition of the greatness of this achievement . . . a piece of virtuosity in the art of overlooking and mistaking" (1925, p. 192). What Freud ignored was that "overlooking and mistaking" were charges that could at least as easily be leveled against him for claiming to find the castration complex everywhere.

The handicap imposed on the therapist by Freud's dogmatic attitude can be well illustrated by a reminiscence of Richard Sterba, an orthodox analyst. Sterba, who had gone to Vienna for analysis shortly before Freud proposed his theory of the death instinct, wrote of their difficulty in changing the focus of probing the patient: "Analysts had great difficulty in accepting this new orientation in the theory of drives. . . . Freud's followers had been educated to become libido hunters and detectives" (1982, p. 75). Thus, where they had once focused all attention on manifestations of the libido, they must now search also for evidence of the death instinct. It is clear that the analytic training had induced a kind of conceptual blindness and selective vigilance. Analysts, no less than other psychologists, are also human.

Physical Symptoms   When Anna O. was watching over her dying father, she developed a paralysis of the right arm. This had first occurred when she was sitting in an uncomfortable chair late in the afternoon and had shut off circulation in the arm by her strained position. Breuer and Freud concluded that this and others of her physical symptoms were *conversions* of libidinal energy into behavior. They interpreted the paralysis as a symbolic punishment for not having done enough for her father. Repression is involved in the sense that the person "denies" the existence of the arm; Anna lost sensitivity in the arm as well as movement. (Freud had pointed out early in his career that the hysteric behaves as if the laws of anatomy did not exist; there was no combination of physical defects that could have caused Anna's symptoms; and further, when Breuer hypnotized her and had her recall the first occasion when this paralysis appeared, it went away.)

Projection   Repressive denial of a forbidden wish is not easy to accomplish. The wish (some internal state) triggers sensations, an awareness of desire, and constant turmoil because of the approach–avoidance conflict. One device of the ego is to project the dangerous emotional state onto others; paranoid thinking is an obvious example: "I want to harm them, but that thought is unworthy of me, so I see them as trying to harm me." Strong sexual desire may lead one to "see" sexual advances in the behavior of the other person. Cheaters on examinations and tax returns report that all around them are people engaging in the same unethical behavior.

Rationalization   With increasing verbal facility, the childish ego is able to devise excuses for forbidden actions. Freudians treat this as a device by which the individual evades guilt feelings by changing conscious perceptions of the situation. So a child who has injured this baby brother says, "It was an accident," and an adult male charged with the sexual abuse of an adolescent girl may claim, "I was only helping her to grow up."

Reaction Formation   Probably none of the "Freudian mechanisms" has evoked so much criticism as that known as *reaction formation*. In this phenomenon, a prudish censorial attitude is ascribed to a powerful sex drive; because this drive frightens the possessor, he or she develops a behavior pattern of denouncing sex as evil, and of demanding censorship of publications offering titillating sexual stories or illustrations. (Cynics have commented that this behavior allows the censor to have it both ways: he or she can look at all kinds of "dirty pictures" while maintaining a posture of protecting others from this danger.)

Similarly, reaction formation would explain some cases, for example, of great bravery in combat as an attempt to deny intense fear and the impulse to desert. Certainly some decorated soldiers have insisted that this explained their behavior. Critics, none the less, have ridiculed a theory that says that a strong emotion may produce a behavior *or its exact opposite.*

Conjunctive and Disjunctive Logic   It is appropriate to examine the logic of the Freudian interpretation. Most psychologists have been reared on *conjunctive* logic, that is, seeking formulations in which A leads to B without qualifications. This logic is common in the physical sciences: heat applied to an iron bar always causes it to expand. So the experimental psychologist seeks "uniform monotonic relationships" in which prediction is unequivocal.

Medicine, however, gives us ample examples of disjunctive logic. Consider the allergies. A specific pollen may, even in the same patient— certainly, across patients—induce sneezing *or* eye burning *or* hives *or* shock reaction. The prediction thus must be disjunctive: A may lead to B or to C or to D. It is, of course, possible that some intrapersonal or interpersonal variation determines which of these outcomes will occur. Similarly, the behaviorist may uncover cases in which the same stimulus elicits differing behaviors in different personalities. Positive verbal reinforcement does not always work; F. V. Bishop (1967), R. D. Timmons and C. D. Noblin (1968), and others have demonstrated that persons showing symptoms of the "oral character" condition easily, but that "anal characters" often show reverse conditioning; that is, they react negatively to experimental reinforcement. (Such studies, incidentally, provide empirical support—not confirmation—of Freud's theory of psychosexual development.)

The same disjunctive logic appears in the interpretation of dreams. A dream of being raped, for example, may, for one person, be interpreted as wish fulfillment, and for another, as fear fulfillment. Every unconscious symptom must be interpreted within a context of other symptoms and personality structures.

The Nature of Reality

Freud was not under any delusions about the overwhelming passion that some of his female patients developed for him. He understood that these emotions were cathected to illusory perceptions, to distortions of his appearance and personal qualities. He knew that his patients distorted what they observed in their home environments. He knew that the changes produced by therapy were changes not in the geographical environment, but in the perceived world, the world of personal experience.

To understand the phenomenon of insight in therapy, we must accept a dualistic interpretation of "reality." Freud understood that "geographical reality" was not the same as "experienced reality." Having an excellent background in philosophy, Freud realized that one's fantasies could influence behavior as much as could the physical world. He cited Immanuel Kant to show the importance of the perceiver, in opposition to the British empiricists, who had so belabored the role of experience. "Kant warned us," Freud wrote, "not to overlook the fact that our perceptions are subjectively conditioned and must not be regarded as identical with that which is perceived though unknowable" (*Standard Edition*, vol. 23, p. 196). Kant referred here to the fact that one perceived the superficial attributes of an object, but that the underlying reality, the *Ding-an-sich* (the "thing in itself") remains unknown and beyond the possibility of knowledge. (Cf. the problem of "knowing" that a book is composed of electrons and protons.)

E. S. Casey (1972) pointed out the dualistic nature of Freud's concept of reality. Immediate experience includes the phenomenal percept, the direct experience (not in Titchener's sense, but in the Gestalt conception). Behind this there is an assumed but undefinable reality, an external event that has some kind of existence even though what we know is the phenomenal aspect. In this respect, Freud foreshadowed Koffka's "geographical environment" and "behavioral environment." Unconscious dynamics, of course, modify the phenomenal or behavioral world. That is, in theory one can assume that there is a man, a biological organism, out there, but whether he is friend or foe, aid or destroyer, depends on perception. Similarly, the theory assumes that the unknowable reality remains relatively unchanged, whereas phenomenal reality changes with experience, with love, anger, success, or failure.

Freudianism as a Cult

I have noted that John B. Watson attracted a following of enthusiastic disciples who accepted all of his dicta unquestioningly and criticized any who cast doubt on the behavioristic doctrine. Skinner has had a similar vogue, with devotees publishing a journal devoted to Skinnerian research, and expressing themselves in superlatives such as "positive reinforcement always works." Kurt Lewin was also successful in attracting devotees who issue annual awards to a scholar who has applied Lewinian principles successfully. However, it seems undebatable that the most intense "cult of personality" is the one that has developed around the Viennese genius Sigmund Freud. Not only does this movement engage in vigorous debates about "what Freud really meant"; it also exhibits a sharply defined in-group versus out-group boundary. Alfred Adler and Carl Jung were exiled for daring to disagree with the founder of psychoanalysis. In the United States, the orthodox have split into feuding sects and have engaged in bitter name-calling as well as in battles over the control of training institutes and facilities.

Perhaps the attribute of Freudianism that accounts for the extreme bitterness of these fratricidal feuds is the intense emotional commitment usually made by a person on the way to becoming a psychoanalyst. The requirement that one be analyzed (by a member of the majority faction) involves much discomfort, probably substantial expense, and the love–hate relationship typically developed with the training analyst. These variables undoubtedly intensify the emotional attachment to the doctrine and the hostility to whatever is perceived as threatening to the orthodox ideology.

Neurologizing

Like most of the psychological theorists we have examined, Freud believed that the "ultimate" explanation of human behavior and experience depends on our understanding of the nervous system. This stance is even more plausible in his case than in that of Watson or Köhler: Freud had full medical training and even ran a general medical practice for a time. But like Wundt, he really preferred research and apparently was not satisfied until his practice with neurotics began to bring in enough money so that he did not have to accept other kinds of patients.

Given this background, it is natural that he would hypothesize physiological substrata for many psychological phemomena. For example, he viewed heredity as accounting for individual differences in the total fund of libido available to a person, and he professed to find evidence of endocrine involvements in various neurotic behaviors. (It is now fairly clear that there are such differences, although their source and significance remain in doubt.)

In the early 1890s, Freud wrote a "Scientific Project" purporting to offer neurophysiological explanations for his observations of neurotic patients. An example is given in Figure 14.3. An incoming stimulus tends to evoke a painful association (A–B). An inhibitory process occurs at B which deflects the neural activation into the pattern C, D, E, F—a more pleasant or acceptable series of thoughts.

The question that has arisen about all of these neurological hypotheses applies just as well to Freud. Do we have any conception of how some process at B could deflect the neural activation into a different channel? Indeed, is it not likely that multiple neurons are involved in every stim-

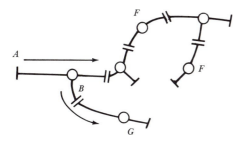

FIGURE 14.3   Freud's Hypothetical Neurological Explanation of Defense Mechanism

An incident (A) initiates a process which might activate G, guilt feeling regarding some past memory. A barrier at B prevents the impulse from flowing to G; instead, it is diverted to F (fantasies of pleasurable events not associated with guilt). *(Redrawn from Freud, Standard Edition, Vol. 1, p. 324)*

ulus input and every facilitative or inhibitory process elicited? In what way have we improved our understanding of the neurotic anxiety or obsessive act by this neurological speculation? Clearly, we know far more about neurotic symptoms than we do about the determiners of synaptic resistance at choice points in the central nervous system.

K. H. Pribram (1962) thought that the "scientific project" demonstrated Freud's brilliant scientific insights and the logical nature of his theorizing. So far, there has been little empirical evidence that Pribram was right. Jonathan Winson (1985) offered some evidence that he perceived as supporting Freud's neurology. Winson purports to have data linking brain activities to the unconscious processing of information during sleep. He made a good deal of the fact that Freud had postulated the determination of some dynamic aspects of personality during critical periods of development (see the earlier discussion of the oral, anal, and phallic stages). To support these speculations, Winson cited the experiments that show that kittens deprived of any experience with vertical lines for their first five months never acquire the ability to respond accurately to problem stimuli in which the crucial cue is a vertical line. Although no one doubts the "critical period" data, their relevance to personality development is profoundly obscure.

Given his medical training, it is not surprising that Freud overemphasized the biological side of psychology. He certainly ignored obvious cultural influences that might have accounted for his findings. Many critics have accused him of an "enormous sampling error" in assuming that phenomena observed in Vienna in the 1890s would hold for America in the 1920s, or in primitive cultures, for example.

Freud and the "Psychologist's Fallacy"

William James warned his readers to beware the psychologist's fallacy, which he defined as the tendency to find in an observation whatever was necessary to support the psychologist's theory. Although this polemic was directed against Titchener and the search for elementary sensations, it could have applied to Freudian theory. Freud trained his disciples as meticulously as Wundt and Titchener did, and he put great pressure on them to find evidence of libidinal cathexes, penis envy, Oedipal conflicts, and other components specified by the theory. Masson's criticisms, cited earlier, and Sterba's report of his difficulty in conforming to Freud's theoretical alterations illustrate the point.

Gordon Allport (1937) summed up this criticism of Freudian theory concisely: "Psychoanalysis is doctrinaire. . . . Its design is traced upon the patient, and then—mirabile dictu—is discovered to exist there" (p. 12). As with Titchener's concept of the stimulus error, the psychoanalyst hears what is expected, not necessarily what the patient is saying.

Practical Implications

Freud's theories have had an extraordinarily wide impact on literature, the arts, and social psychology. Industrial psychology shows some effects, and these seem to be increasing in the 1980s. As was noted in Chapter Seven, American business people found little of interest in structuralism, with its pure science and its rigorously artificial experiments. Behaviorism had a much wider influence; developments in industry called for a focus on responses, not on sensations and images. Gestalt did not affect applied activities to any great extent.

The consequences of psychoanalytic theorizing were important. For professional psychologists, it reinforced the functionalist emphasis on real-life practical events, rather than experimentalism. Freud recognized that there are two kinds of reality: one that is experienced and one that can be measured by physical devices. He also knew that behavior is shaped by the experienced reality, not necessarily by the physics-defined reality. Few psychologists will question that, after being briefly pushed aside by J. B. Watson in the 1920s, psychoanalytic views on child rearing increased in popularity, and most mental health professionals hold that the analytic view, with its recognition of sexuality and aggression in the child, as well as the inevitable conflict of child with parent and society, is clearly preferable to the distant formality in parent–child relations espoused by Watson.

Some of the vestiges of psychoanalysis now found in industrial psychology were discarded by Freud but kept in the prescriptions of other psychologists. Thus *catharsis,* as defined by Charcot and Breuer, in which reliving an intense emotional experience was alleged to release tension and to have curative effects, was dropped by Freud early in his career. He found that some patients could undergo this catharsis under hypnosis several times with no benefit. On the other hand, we find American industrial psychologists endorsing the policy; A. Zaleznik (1986) proposed that industrialists plan their lives to include some vigorous physical activity to permit the catharsis of accumlated tensions. Zaleznik focused on the executive's need to inhibit responses of anger; such inhibition is, of course, necessary to the smooth functioning of a corporation. He did not, however, consider the more intense frustrations and accumulated tensions of workers on regimented jobs, nor the more severe punishment encountered by a worker who gives vent to his or her anger.

R. N. McMurry (1944) used Freudian theory in his examination of union–management conflicts. Oedipal rebelliousness was proposed as an explanation for some worker protest against managerial controls and for the irrational hostility that McMurry perceived in some union officials. He also speculated about the displacement of intrafamily hostilities into the workplace. He was, on the other hand, willing to concede that some industrial executives unconsciously play out the role of *pater familias,* the all-powerful father who dominates his children, the workers, and is good to them when they are submissive.

H. Levinson (1972) made extensive use of psychoanalytic theory in his consulting work in organizational development; he reported a wider range of irrationalities among executives that did McMurry. Walter Neff (1968) also applied analytic theory to the work situation. Some social psychologists are using the pleasure principle and the reality principle to explain the difference between the typical worker and the homeless, lethargic, apathetic drifter. The reality principle says that one should work hard and save money for emergencies, but when life is an unending emergency, the individual falls back on the pleasure principle, seeking immediate gratifications such as alcohol, drugs, and sex.

Freud in America

Shortly after Freud visited Clark University in 1909, he was attacked widely by Americans. J. J. Putnam, a neurologist at Harvard Medical School, attacked his ideas as "immoral." (Putnam later became a supporter of Freud.) Freud was accused of endorsing free love, an end to sexual inhibitions, and complete permissiveness. As Freud was himself something of a prude, this outburst showed more about the attackers than about Freud himself.

Freud's reception by intellectuals, especially writers and artists, was very different. His doctrines certainly had much to do with the increase in the number of penetrating novels and dramas exploring human motivations and emotions (Hale, 1971).

Although until the Nazis arrived Freud was not actively persecuted in Austria by anti-Semites, many of the less prestigious Jewish analysts were jailed or mistreated, and there was a substantial immigration of analysts into the United States in the 1930s. Most of these found a receptive situation; many wealthy Americans sought analysis, and it became a prestige item to boast of "my psychoanalyst." The influence of these emigres was substantial in the development of training programs in clinical psychology, although the most important factor in that expansion was the need for people to work with war-scarred veterans in 1945, and Freudianism is of minimal value in work with traumatic neuroses. The use of diagnostic devices such as the thematic apperception test (Murray, 1938) and the Rorschach Ink Blot Test (Rorschach, 1921) became merged with psychoanalytic doctrines as the interpretation of protocols began to be based on Freudian hypotheses. Until the rise of behavior modification in the 1960s and 1970s, most major clinical training programs had at least some Freudian exponents. Today a fair proportion of training programs rely more heavily on Skinner or on the cognitive behaviorism that will be discussed in Chapter Eighteen.

Many of the brilliant rebels against Freud also came to the United States: Alfred Adler, Erich Fromm, Karen Horney, and Otto Rank were important contributors to the variety of ideas that now compete in American clinical psychology. Their ideas will be sketched in later chapters.

The main consequence for American psychology of Freud's work is obviously in the stimulation of much research and theorizing that offers alternatives to Freud. Mention has been made of Hull's associates who investigated and debated concepts like frustration tolerance, approach–avoidance conflicts, verbal cues for drive arousal, and the learning of symptoms. Clinical psychologists have studied differences in therapeutic procedures and outcomes, stimulated in large part by the controversy between psychoanalysts and behavior modifiers. There can be little question that American psychology would be a vastly different discipline today had Freud never written.

CHAPTER 15

Psychoanalysis: The Neoanalysts (I)

Freudian theory produced more than the usual amount of rebellion. This can be ascribed primarily to the personality of Freud himself, although it is true that, given the ambiguities of unconscious phenomena, differences of interpretation are highly probable. At any rate, we know that Freud was dogmatic, authoritarian, and rigid in many ways. He was proud of his innovative theories and hostile to anyone who seemed to criticize them. Like Wilhelm Wundt, he demanded that his disciples stay within defined limits in modifying his theories. When he believed that some revisionary follower had gone too far, Freud felt no hesitation in excommunicating the offender.

Of the numerous deviants who met this fate, three were of special significance for theorizing in America: Alfred Adler, Carl Gustav Jung, and Otto Rank. Each became, for a time, Freud's favorite, the heir apparent to leadership of the psychoanalytic movement, and each was expelled for the sin of disagreeing with the master.

One of the favorite dicta of the psychoanalysts is that you cannot analyze another person until you have yourself been analyzed. Cynics reply by asking: Who analyzed Freud? The answer is that Freud did it himself. His self-analysis lasted at least ten years, from 1897 to 1906. M. H. Marx and W. A. Hillix (1973) considered the analysis a success, writing that one tangible outcome was that Freud could "stand on his own feet" and so minimize his tendency to depend on others, such as Breuer and Fliess. From another viewpoint, Freud's self-analysis must have been a failure, as it did not reduce, and may even have increased, his need to be a powerful authority figure. Because the events described in this chapter occurred after ten years of self-analysis, the judgment that Freud's analysis failed would seem to have support.

Alfred Adler

The first of the brilliant young disciples to be expelled from the Freudian movement was Alfred Adler (1870–1937). Adler came into Freud's orbit by defending Freud's recently published *Interpretation of Dreams* (1900). A Viennese medical journal published a hostile review of the book, and Adler wrote a rebuttal that was logical and persuasive. As a result, Freud invited him, in 1902, to join in forming a group to discuss the theses of that book plus other ideas of interest. Only three others were invited to the Wednesday evening sessions; Wilhelm Stekel is the only one whose name is remembered today for contributions to psychology.

Biography

Adler was born in Vienna in 1870, into the family of a wealthy grain merchant. As a boy, he was sickly and undersized for his age. One story that probably has significance for his career relates to a severe illness, in the course of which he heard the physician tell his father, "Your boy is lost." Young Alfred decided this was a "bad" doctor and determined that he would become well and learn to be a "good" doctor.

This story suggests that Adler generated at an early age a mental attitude favoring compensation for handicaps. (It may also have been a memory error projected back into time, after Adler had developed his theory of compensation.) His interest in sibling rivalry is also an apparent outcome of boyhood. In his autobiography, Adler wrote, "I did my utmost to excel at running, jumping, and rushing around—activities of which my elder brother was constantly making me aware . . . my elder brother was the only one with whom I did not get along well, and he never took part in our games" (Bottome, 1939, p. 10). The implied contradiction between the two sentences suggests that Adler preferred not to notice his rivalry with his sibling.

Evidence of a compensatory theme in Adler's development is common. He pushed himself through medical school rapidly, obtaining his medical degree in 1895. He set up a practice in ophthalmology but changed to general practice, and later to psychiatry. He retained some general practice (see his discovery of Otto Rank, Chapter Sixteen) and even functioned as Freud's personal physician (for organic problems only!) for a few years.

Adler's intellect and drive impressed Freud, who insisted that the Vienna Psychoanalytic Society elect Adler president in 1910, to the marked annoyance of some other members of the group. Adler was also granted the position of editor of the *Zentralblatt für Psychoanalyse*, a journal founded by Freud to provide a publication outlet for case studies and theoretical articles. It should be noted that these honors to Adler were part of a complicated maneuver by Freud in which he made Carl G. Jung president of the International Psychoanalytic Society; Adler's appointments were intended to reassure the Viennese members that they still had Freud's blessing.

Adler's psychology and social attitudes were probably influenced by his small size and physical inadequacy in boyhood. At any rate, he showed a great deal of concern about "the underdog," becoming active in the Austrian Socialist Party. After a stint as an army physician in World War I, Adler undertook a series of humanitarian projects. He was an early advocate of children's rights, founding the first Child Guidance Clinic in Vienna, and later persuading the school authorities to set up a whole series of such clinics.

As early as 1922, Adler was warning his fellow Austrians that the position of women was unjustifiable and undesirable. The enforced inferiority of women, legally and culturally, was—he asserted—unfair and discriminatory: "The dominance of man over woman deprived him of the highest sexual pleasures and must in a more highly developed civilization lead women to rebellion against their feminine role" (1928/1966, p. 168). This prediction was not validated until the twentieth century, when the feminist movement, at least in Western countries, finally won many concessions in the political, legal, and economic spheres.

In some respects, Adler was unique in that his efforts on behalf of women and children were compatible with his theorizing, whereas most psychologists maintain a rigid barrier between their theoretical views and their public behavior. This point will be developed later.

There is another aspect, however, in which Adler failed to show this consistency. He had protested Freud's dictatorial control over his followers, but he followed the same tactic himself. Alfred Marrow (1969) contrasted the egalitarian attitude of Kurt Lewin with the attitude of "Adler, who held court in the Cafe Siller in Vienna and banished all who did not demonstrate their allegiance" (p. 27). The tactics of Freud and Adler in this regard remind us of Lewin's thesis that a small group maintains its equilibrium by ejecting a disturbing member, a phenomenon described in detail by Irving Janis in *Victims of Groupthink* (1972).

Adler's Theories

When Adler was denounced by Freud in 1911 and resigned his post as president of the Vienna Society, it was over a clear-cut opposition of theoretical positions. Freud was still adamant in his theory that the libido was sexual, and that the ultimate dynamic in human behavior was pleasure seeking, sexual either in fact or in symbolism. Adler was propounding a theory of the libido as general, a kind of life energy that could motivate action for a wide variety of goals. Sex was one of these but was not accorded primacy.

The development of Adler's ideas is important. His earliest contribution centered on compensation for a physical defect, and he used as a model (which could also be called a metaphor), the physiological changes by which the body tries to defend itself against deficiencies. Consider the case in which one kidney is damaged or diseased. The other kidney typically enlarges and often becomes capable of providing all the cleansing action normally afforded by two kidneys. Adler's report on these physiological coping efforts was included in a monograph, *A Study of Organ Inferiority and Its Psychical Compensation* (1907/1917). In this essay, he described behavioral compensations in addition to the purely physiological type, hence the word *psychical*.

Adler noted (eight decades ago) that noisy environments at work lead to deafnesss, and he called for industry to take measures to reduce these assaults on organismic integrity. Only in recent years has this proposal received much attention, and much still needs to be done to meet Adler's criticism.

The "Masculine Protest"   By 1907, Adler was already convinced that a person could channel much energy into compensation for felt inferiority, and that this need not have any sexual implication. However, trying to soothe Freud, he first couched his inferiority thesis in sexual terms. He wrote, and spoke, of a "masculine protest" in which women, and men with handicaps, mobilized energy to overcome their inferior status. This was an attempt to absorb penis envy and the castration complex into his concept of struggle against inferiority. Adler denied that the anatomical difference between the sexes was crucial; the real source of psychological differences between males and females was power. Austrian society was male-dominated; Adler held that female neuroses were often (if not always) ways of protesting against an inferior status and of attaining a kind of power indirectly, the power of the sick over the well. But the masculine protest could be extended further; the small or handicapped male could behave in a loud, aggressive, combative manner to compensate for a felt inferiority. And of course, some women adopted masculine dress and manners instead of neurotic symptoms.

The "Will to Power"   After Freud temporarily tolerated and then attacked Adler on the issue of the masculine protest, demanding that Adler concede the sexual nature of the libido, a head-on collision was inevitable. In February 1911, Adler presented his theses to a series of meetings of the society, and Freud rebutted him incisively and sarcastically. At the end of these debates, the group resolved that Adler's ideas were incompatible with psychoanalysis, and Adler resigned his post as president. (Some hold that Adler was expelled, others that he voluntarily withdrew from the society; the records are unclear.) Eight other members went with Adler, of a total of thirty-five; the society lost almost a quarter of its membership in this battle.

At this time, Freud offered his famous critique of Adler, invoking the Oedipus complex to explain the latter's actions: "The son always tries to destroy the father." Adler tartly replied that this was merely another instance of sibling rivalry (thus placing himself on a par with Freud rather than in an inferior status.) What is particularly entertaining about this exchange is the way in which each used his favorite theory to attack the other.

Adler and his followers immediately set up an independent group, provisionally called the Society for Free Psychoanalysis (meaning free from Freud's domination). But the inevitable jokes about this name led Adler to change it to the Society for Individual Psychology, a name indicative of the shift in theoretical emphasis. The *Journal of Individual Psychology* was founded later to compete with the Freudian journal.

The power struggle over, Adler set about elaborating on his theory of power. As Heinz and Rowena Ansbacher (1956) noted, this theory went through even more changes than Freud's libido theory. From "striving against inferiority," it moved to a "will to power." Later Adler called it "striving for superiority" and "striving for perfection." He also wrote of "moving from a minus to a plus position," a formula reminiscent of Lewin's concept of valence, and also of "overcoming," or mastering the environment. Finally he decided that the basic motive was "social interest."

The theory held that the organism is so constituted, presumably by natural selection, that it seeks mastery of the physical environment. Thus humans build houses and roads and dams, manipulate physical resources, and so on. In this respect, the theory may account for some of the phenomena Freud had conceptualized as "repetition compulsion" (e.g., when a child reenacts a painful scene, behavior superficially antithetical to the pleasure principle). Adler held that the child was trying to establish mastery, to assert control over the event.

The will to power obviously extended also to the social environment. Adler had already attacked Viennese society on the issue of women's rights. And he did not try to conceal the borrowing of some of his ideas from Friedrich Wilhelm Nietzsche; Adler wrote, "Much of our view of the enhancement of the self-esteem as the guiding fiction is included in Nietzsche's 'will to power' and 'will to seem.' Our view touches in many points also on those of Féré and older authors, according to whom the feeling of pleasure is founded in a feeling of power, that of displeasure in a feeling of powerlessness" (Ansbacher and Ansbacher, 1956, p. 111). On the other hand, Adler denied explicitly that he was advocating a personal course of seeking more power; in fact, he wrote, "The views of Individual Psychology demand the *unconditional reduction* of the striving for power and the development of social interest" (Ansbacher, 1972,

p. 13). Thus Adler was not, as some detractors claimed, a forerunner of Nazism but, as his socialistic politics showed, an advocate of distributed power.

Theory of Neurosis   Shortly after the break with Freud, Adler began making more explicit some of the implications of his theory of motivation: "Every neurosis can be understood as an attempt to free oneself from a feeling of inferiority in order to gain a feeling of superiority" (1913/1959, p. 23). This statement was a challenge both to Freud's early theory of neurosis as being due to rape or seduction, and to his later view of neurosis as being due to fantasied sexual experiences.

Human Potentialities   Unlike Freud, Adler also considered the relevance of his theory to positive aspects of human behavior. Instead of "striving for superiority," he shifted to a theory of an innate "striving for perfection." Because this concept later came to fruition in the "human potential" movement in America, it merits a detailed explanation:

> As for the striving for perfection, for superiority, or for power, some had always known about it, but not thoroughly enough to spread this knowledge to a larger mass or to illuminate the fundamental significance of this striving for the structure of the entire personality. Only *Individual Psychology* has pointed out that this striving for perfection is found in every individual and fills every individual. . . . It is not necessary to inoculate man with the desire to develop into superman. . . .
>
> I should like to emphasize first of all that striving for perfection is innate. This is not meant in a concrete way, as if there were a drive which would later in life be capable of bringing everything to completion and which only needed to develop itself. The striving for perfection is innate in the sense that it is a part of life, a striving, an urge, a something without which life would be unthinkable. (Ansbacher and Ansbacher, 1956, p. 104)

The transition from striving for mastery over the environment to striving for perfection was made rather subtly, with little exposition of the logic involved. Adler offered many analogies to justify his development of the idea of perfection, but none is clearly logical. For instance, he spoke of "an urge from below to above." But just why perfection should be equated with being "above" others is not clear. It appears that what Adler was proposing was perfect achievement of the person's ideal, the aspiration that the person sought to actualize. It did not necessarily imply perfection as viewed by observers. Ansbacher and Ansbacher (1956), devoted followers of Adler, relate "striving for perfection" to Kurt Goldstein's concept of "self-actualization," later adopted by Abraham Maslow and other humanists. Goldstein (1939) wrote, "In the innumerable repetitions of children, we are not dealing with the manifestation of a senseless drive for repetition [Freud's repetition compulsion], but with the tendency to completion and perfection" (p. 196). There are also obvious similarities here to a motive of "competence" or "need for achievement" (White, 1959; Atkinson, 1964). Carl Rogers and other humanists have used similar concepts.

Social Interest In his later years, Adler again reformulated his theory of psychic energy and called it "social interest." Once more, the logic is vague. He treated his revision as merely an extrapolation of his power and perfection theories. This phase of his theorizing is of considerable importance for contemporary psychology; he suggested the study of social comparisons, dissonance, attribution theory, and so on. It might also be seen as a forerunner of sociobiology, an effort to tie social-psychological phenomena to innate species-specific behavior tendencies.

According to Adler, the human species is biologically inadequate to the dangers of isolated living. But through cooperation with others, the individual is capable of coping with carnivores, natural disasters, food shortages, and so on: Group life proved to be a necessity. Although Adler did not explicitly formulate the idea, it seems necessary to assume that he thought that some biological mutation had introduced social interest into the innate makeup of the human being, and that this had led to survival advantages, hence to its expanding place in the genetic matrix.

Social interest, Adler argued, bears on three major problems of human existence: communal life, work, and love. His motivational theory, therefore, provides an underpinning for social and industrial psychology as an alternative to Freud's pervasive interest in sex and love.

Theory of Personality Adler went beyond Freud also in developing a theory of personality that incorporated aspirations and ambitions. Adler proposed that social interest can become attached to some future goal (of course, such goals can also be based on a will to power or a desire for superiority). The goal does not exist in the present but is fantasized as an achievement of the future. Adler thus called it "fictional"; it is a goal only in imagination and sometimes is not even conscious. A person may behave in a way that reveals to others a striving for a particular status or social role and yet deny it to herself or himself and to others. Adler also conceived of the goal as being the end of a series of behaviors calculated to achieve it; thus he evolved the term "fictional finalism" to identify such life goals.

The introduction of this future-oriented formulation caused Adler to be criticized as teleological, that is, as visualizing the determination of behavior not by the past but by some future purpose. Adler did not deny that he was using a future goal as a determinant of behavior, but he denied that this approach was teleological because the immediate determinant of behavior was a fantasy, an imagined outcome, which existed in the present, not in the future. Determinism, then, could be a function of a conscious (or unconscious) mental state that pointed to the future; this was not equivalent to saying that the future determined the behavior. In contrast to Freud's emphasis on early childhood as the determinant of the adult personality, Adler provided a place for an orientation toward a future goal without implying a teleological mystery. It was indeed clear to Adler, if not to some of his critics, that the outcome of a person's career might easily be quite different from the individual's conscious aspiration. For example, a determined but irrational drive for political power may lead to failure because of mistakes based on unconscious emotional states.

Style of Life   Adler was striving for a truly "individual" psychology, in the sense of understanding each person as a unique case, in opposition to what he perceived as Freud's emphasis on assumed universals (e.g., the Oedipal conflict and the castration complex). In 1912, Adler took a major step by introducing into his theory the concept of a "life plan" which guided the person's decisions and behavior. Much of the life plan was unconscious and was at times quite different from the conscious aims and aspirations of the individual. It was distinctive and unique to a particular person. Adler later adopted the term "life style," using it in the sense of a characteristic of a specific person, not of a demographic group. Adler (1913) wrote, "We may look upon every single manifestation in life as if in its past, present, and future there were contained traces of a superordinated guiding idea" (p. iii). And in a later essay, he offered the following perceptive generalizations: "we learn from experience only to the extent that the style of life permits" (1937, p. 777). The unified life style made for self-consistency and unity of personality.

Style in this context is idiographic; it is the characteristic of a unique person. The life style has the property of controlling "from above" the acquisition of specific skills, beliefs, customs, and hopes of the individual. "Every individual represents both a unity of personality and the individual fashioning of that unity. The individual is thus both the picture and the artist. He is the artist of his own personality" (Ansbacher and Ansbacher, 1956, p. 177).

Adler recognized this as a concession to Gestalt theory. The whole determines the parts. A person who has the life style of an academic scholar will reject opportunities to flout custom. Contemporary social commentators use this Adlerian concept regularly. The "hippie lifestyle" and the "yuppie lifestyle," for example, have become trite phrases. Adler intended the term for a more specific purpose, as the way in which a particular person planned and organized his or her life and daily activities.

Adler noted that inner personality tendencies are likely to be revealed in times of change. Under normal conditions, the habits and social roles function smoothly, and the life style may not be so obvious. But if the environmental demands change, then the hierarchy of responses operates; new habits are developed that conform to the life style.

Equilibrium Theory   One respect in which Adler adhered to Freud's doctrines was in the importance of equilibrium. Freud had emphasized the role of the nervous system in restoring equilibrium after it had been disturbed by environmental or instinctual pressures. (So, we note, had Hull, Koffka, and Lewin.) Adler put his equilibrium hypothesis as follows:

> As soon as the equilibrium, which must be assumed to govern the economy of the individual organ or the whole organism, appears to be disturbed due to inadequacy of form or function, a certain biological process is initiated in the inferior organs. The unsatisfied demands (for functional outcomes of the relevant organ) increase until the deficit is made up through growth of the inferior organ, of the paired organ, or of some other organ which can serve as a substitute, completely or in part. (Ansbacher and Ansbacher, 1956, p. 25)

Along with the compensation may go overcompensation, or the subsuming of other biological functions under that affected by the postulated inferiority. Adler wrote:

> In favorable cases of compensation the inferior organ has the better developed and psychologically more potent superstructure . . . as far as drive, sensitivity, attention, memory, apperception, empathy, and consciousness are concerned. In the favorable case, an inferior nutritive apparatus may muster the greater psychological potency in all relations to nourishment. But it may also be superior in everything related to the gaining of food, since its superstructure will dominate and draw the other psychological complexes into its orbit. (Ansbacher and Ansbacher, 1956, p. 26)

Adler thus postulated a hierarchy of functions in which the focal function, the "inferior" organ, can determine the processes of perceiving, associating, remembering, and so on. Thus he predicted that a person with a defective digestive apparatus would think more about food than others, notice more cues regarding food, form more associations of neutral topics with food, and perhaps even create new recipes. This high frequency of thoughts about food might have the result, for example, that more neutral stimuli would acquire food associations simply on the basis of the frequency of contiguous occurrence in time. The same logic would dictate, in Freud's system, that a person with a strong sex drive would form a surplus of associations with sex.

Adler also agreed with Freud in assuming that the protection of basic equilibrium was a fundamental attribute of our biological heredity. Without using the term *Reizschutz* to designate a protective membrane, Adler wrote:

The protection of all these organs (sensory and motor) became so necessary that it was approached from two sides: through the sensations of pain and of pleasure (disturbance of equilibrium led to pain, restoration led to pleasure). But this was not enough, and thus a third safeguard developed in the form of the organ of prudence, the organ of thinking, the brain, In the laboratory of nature, all three safeguards can be found. While peripheral defects or accentuated pain and pleasure sensations may arise in the inferior organ, the most variable part, the central nervous system, takes over the final compensation. (Ansbacher and Ansbacher, 1956, p. 57)

As the Ansbachers commented, this idea amounts to adopting Walter Cannon's principle of homeostasis as the physiological mechanism underlying compensation.

The Uniqueness of Personality   Finally, it is important to note that Adler, alone of all the theorists we have so far considered, wrote of the uniqueness of the individual personality: "The uniqueness of the individual cannot be expressed in a short formula, and general rules—even those laid down by Individual Psychology. . . . should be regarded as nothing more than an aid to a preliminary illumination of the field of view in which the single individual can be found. . . . We assign only limited value to general rules and instead lay strong emphasis on flexibility and on empathy into nuances" (Ansbacher and Ansbacher, 1956, pp. 194–195).

Adler thus opened up a new area of psychological speculation. Most of his predecessors, from the Greeks to Wundt and Titchener, had limited their speculations to broad generalizations. Adler was the first to concede that although the human species is generic, the specific individual is unique and cannot be reduced to a set of equations or statistical deviations from a mean.

Comparison with Freud

Adler did not disagree with Freud about the central role of unconscious processes and particularly of repression. Similarly, he took over his mentor's formulations of the defense mechanisms, rationalization, sublimation, projection, and identification.

Where the two differed was, first, on the nature of the libido, and second, on the role of the environment. In regard to the libido, Adler viewed it as a general drive for survival, for equilibrium, or for mastery of the environment; he rejected the Freudian thesis of sexuality as the basic drive. The role of the environment was somewhat more complicated; Freud had recognized the importance of parents and the larger society in shaping the superego; Adler treated the person–culture relationship as an interaction. Adler's psychology is primarily an ego psychology, in which conscious or unconscious processes of perceiving, learning, and remembering lead to ways of behaving that restore equilibrium and that foster power or superiority.

Both Freud and Adler treated psychology as a study of development, but Freud emphasized a series of psychosexual stages that seemed almost inevitable, innate, and deterministic. Adler's view emphasized the unique individual, facing inferiorities and compensating for them in distinctive ways. His writings influenced the development of "humanistic psychology," to be discussed in Chapter Seventeen. Clearly Adler leans more to the "tender-minded" orientation than does Freud.

Practical Applications

Adler's theories have been widely influential in such areas as juvenile delinquency, where both compensation for inferiority and striving for superiority have been found to be common dynamic factors in criminal behavior, especially aggressive, assaultive acts. Abusive husbands and fathers seem often to suffer from Adlerian complexes.

Industrial psychologists find the striving for power and for autonomy (freedom from being controlled by others) to be major considerations in good management. Victor Vroom (1964), Lyman Porter (1973), and Edward Lawler (1973) are representatives of the industrial-organizational psychologists whose positions on industrial motivation have strong similarities to that of Adler.

Carl Gustav Jung

Those who believe that Freud was an exceptionally brilliant observer of human nature must be astounded at his repetitious errors in his selection of "leaders" for the psychoanalytic movement. It is probable that an industrial personnel specialist would have done better. Indeed, a "Freudian" interpretation of Freud's behavior would suggest that he had an unconscious wish to fail in selecting a successor (i.e., to continue to be the unquestioned leader).

Regardless of how one feels about this, it is impressive that Freud successively chose Adler, Jung, and Rank for a prestigious position in the psychoanalytic movement, and that each eventually broke away to found a new, competitive school of psychoanalysis. For various reasons, the defection of C. G. Jung is particularly interesting.

Biography

Carl Gustav Jung (1875–1961) grew up in Basel, Switzerland, where he spent most of his life. He earned an M.D. from the University of Basel in 1902, the year when Freud first organized his psychoanalytic society. Even before this, Jung had been involved in psychiatric work; he had an appointment in 1900 as assistant to the famous Eugen Bleuler, then the leading world figure in the study of schizophrenia. An intriguing fore-shadowing of Jung's later development is found in his doctoral disser-tation, *On the Psychology and Pathology of So-called Occult Phenomena*. This concern with fringe areas of psychology continued throughout his life. From Bleuler, he also learned about the use of hypnosis to treat nervous disorders, and about the phenomena of unconscious motivation and posthypnotic suggestion. He visited Paris and attended many lectures by Pierre Janet, the illustrious successor to Charcot.

Unlike Adler, Jung did not suffer from childhood diseases but was plagued throughout his adult life with various illnesses. At various times, he had to withdraw from professional work entirely, in order to rest and recuperate. On the other hand, he was quite restless and traveled widely, to India, North Africa, and America, in search of anthropological obser-vations that might support his theories that related the progress of hu-man civilization to attributes of the individual personality.

Jung first became acquainted with Freud in 1906. By 1909, he had won Freud's enthusiastic praise, and he accompanied Freud on his trip to America for G. Stanley Hall's symposium (see Chapter Fourteen). After Freud had given his lectures on the theory of psychoanalysis, Jung read a paper describing his own researches on word association, in which he systematized Wundt's method of obtaining free verbal associations (see Jung 1904/1918).

In 1910, Freud decided to set up an international organization dedi-cated to spreading the gospel of psychoanalysis. To emphasize the fact that Vienna would not continue to dominate the scene, he made Jung the first president of the International Psychoanalytic Society, to the great annoyance of Adler and several other members of the Vienna circle. The brouhaha over this move apparently pushed Freud into making Adler president of the Vienna society, a kind of consolation prize.

Freud had sound reasons for the selection of Jung. He wanted to free psychoanalysis from the status of being a Viennese provincialism, and also to end the appearance that the movement was limited to Jewish physicians. Freud was quite frank about the latter point; he once wrote, "I nearly said that it was only by his [Jung's] appearance that psycho-analysis escaped the danger of becoming a Jewish national affair" (quoted by P. Roazen, 1975, p. 227). He apparently gave Jung credit for over-coming any cultural anti-Semitism Jung may have felt (Jung was the son of a Protestant minister in a time when religious hostilities were ram-pant). In a letter to Karl Abraham, Freud wrote that Jung "as a Christian . . . finds his way to me only against great inner resistance. His associa-tion with us is the more valuable for that" (Roazen, 1975, p. 226).

As Freud and Jung became better acquainted, points of divergence began to appear. A source of difficulty may have been in their personal morals. Freud was a rather prudish Victorian (although it was charged by Jung after their split that Freud had had an affair with Freud's sister-in-law, Minna). Jung, on the other hand, described himself as polygamous, and his behavior validated the label. For example, A. Carotenuto (1982) reported on the case of Sabina Spielrein, a teen-aged Russian patient of Jung's. She came under Jung's care in 1904 (before his association with Freud) and soon became his mistress. Despite this impropriety, the treatment must have been somewhat successful because, in 1905, she enrolled in medical school, obtained her medical degree, and eventually joined Freud's Vienna group, becoming a professional psychoanalyst. (Her most famous analysand was Jean Piaget.) When she asked Freud for help in straightening out her feelings about Jung, he wrote to Jung for information. Jung wrote a vicious letter attacking Spielrein, claiming that she had "kicked up a vile scandal solely because I denied myself the pleasure of giving her a child" (Carotenuto, 1982, p. 159). Not making his excuse explicit, Jung was hiding behind the defense later espoused by Freud himself, that "the patient is really to blame for this fuss." On the other side of the coin, we note that Jung gave Spielrein credit for developing the theory of the death instinct, and he charged that Freud expropriated it for his own use without giving her any recognition.

A much longer-lasting affair was one that Jung had with another patient. Paul Roazen (1975) wrote that "to outward appearances Jung remained the upright representative of conventional family behavior. Nevertheless, Antonia Wolff, a psychiatrist and former patient of Jung's, became his long-standing lover" (p. 231).

The break with Freud came in 1913, after Jung had published his *Psychology of the Unconscious.* In this book, he had openly modified the libido theory. It is also true that at this time, Jung complained about the burden of work connected with the International Psychoanalytic Society, but most observers agree that it was the theoretical controversy that made a break inevitable. Jung soon imitated Adler and founded his own school of analysis, which he called "analytical psychology" to differentiate it from psychoanalysis and from individual psychology.

Despite this mutual hostility, Jung continued to urge many of his students and fellow physicians to study with Freud. As late as 1914, well after the rupture of relations, Freud wrote that "most of my followers and co-workers at the present time came to me by way of Zurich" (quoted by Roazen, 1975, p. 226).

The Theory

Like Adler, Jung had questioned the sexual definition of the libido. He wished to make the term identical with life energy, with whatever kind of energy a person can mobilize and use for any purpose: for sexual goals, for mastery, or for self-actualization. However, he denied that he was being mystical. "A concept of life-energy has nothing to do with a so-called life-force," he wrote, "for this latter, as force, would be nothing more than a specific form of a universal energy. . . . I have suggested that we call the hypothetically assumed life-energy, libido" (1926/1942, p. 17). And to clarify the separation from Freud, he added, "unfortunately, Freud was led, by a quite comprehensible overvaluation of sexuality, to reduce to the latter (i.e., to sex) those transformations which represent other specific forces of the mind coordinate with sexuality, and this has brought upon him the justified reproach of pansexualism" (1926/1942, p. 19).

The properties of Jung's libido, however, parallel those set down by Freud: it can be transferred from one love object to another but is not lost (conservation of the libido); it can be directed inward, on the self; and it tends toward entropy, toward equilibrium.

The orientation of the libido identifies one of Jung's major contributions to American psychology. In noting that the libido may be directed outward, on objects or persons, or that it may be directed inward on the self, he arrived at the concepts of extraversion and introversion. These must be considered as alternative outlets for a single dynamic process; thus Jung wrote that "regression can proceed along two lines, either as a retreat from the outer world, introversion, or as a flight into extravagant external experiences, extraversion" (1926/1942, p. 45). Thus schizophrenia was characterized as the ultimate of an introverted pattern of libido distribution.

In his definition, Jung made it clear that these orientations should be applied to specific acts or impulses, not to a total personality. There are, he said, four major psychological functions: sensing, thinking, feeling, and intuiting. Each of these may show an orientation inward, toward the self, or outward, toward the environment. Unlike Adler, Jung did not insist on an internally consistent personality orientation. Each of these four functions could vary independently.

Clearly this concept was not intended as a justification for classifying individuals into pigeonholes, as introverts or extraverts. Unfortunately, many American psychologists seized on the distinction and began making up "personality tests" to identify the respondent as an introvert or an extravert. Jung should bear some of the responsibility for this distortion of his idea, as he, too, wrote carelessly, as if the terms embraced the total personality, for example: "The earliest mark of extraversion in a child is his quick adaptation to the environment, and the extraordinary attention he gives to objects. . . . Apparently he develops more quickly than an introverted child" (1926/1942, p. 303). At any rate, more Americans think of Jung in connection with introversion and extraversion than with any of his other concepts.

The Unconscious   Superficially Jung's concept of the unconscious resembles that of Freud; it comprises processes that may affect and modify conscious thoughts, acts, and choices. However, there is one important difference. Jung wrote, "The unconscious is perhaps best understood if we take it as a natural organ with an energy specific to itself. If, as a result of repression, its products are not admitted into consciousness a sort of damming up results, an unnatural inhibition of a purposive function; as though the bile, the natural product of the function of the liver, were impeded in its discharge into the bowel" (1926/1942, p. 148). Now this sounds deceptively like Freud's hydraulic metaphor, but it is not the same. Jung was concerned with a blockage of ideas and images *generated by the unconscious,* and held there by repression, whereas Freud focused on material once conscious, now repressed into the unconscious and penned there. Jung's unconscious is thus endowed with more functions and a greater significance than Freud's.

The Collective Unconscious   The disagreement regarding the unconscious is further emphasized by Jung's concept of the "collective unconscious," a psychological phenomenon presumably shared by all members of the human race. The hereditary status of the collective unconscious is not always clear. At times, Jung wrote as if it were a matter of natural selection: some unconscious impulses worked against survival and were eliminated, whereas others aided survival and were selected. At other times, he seemed to adopt a Lamarckian perspective and to treat the collective unconscious as a set of racial experiences, implying the inheritance of acquired characteristics.

In Jung's theory, the content of the collective unconscious is made up mainly of *archetypes,* generalized concepts of a somewhat mystical nature. Thus the archetype *Mother* is not the same as one's awareness of a specific mother. It is rather a personification of a nurturing, caring, affectionate presence. The archetypes, however, are not innate ideas in the sense of Descartes. Jung treated them rather as a kind of prewiring, a potential to develop a certain conception when appropriate stimuli are encountered. In this format, it is comparable to the "inherited wiring diagram" postulated by Noam Chomsky (1972), a readiness to acquire a certain kind of linguistic behavior.

Archetypes change with physiological changes. Jung proposed that we possess archetypes for *man* and *woman,* maleness and femaleness; and these may change at puberty. "As a result of puberty," he wrote, "a new archetype becomes constellated: in the man it is that of woman, in woman it is the archetype of man" (1926/1942, p. 127). According to Munroe (1955), the archetypes differ from personal symbols as these were described by Freud; archetypes "belong to the collective unconscious and in this sense transcend the experience of the individual" (p. 553). These archetypes are necessarily limited in number; they correspond to fundamental human situations, such as a need for protection, an effort to overpower an opponent, a strong sexual attraction, and anxiety—in other words, universal problem situations that might plausibly enter in some way into racial heredity.

Munroe (1955) commented also that the archetypes constitute the aspect of Jung's theorizing that has been especially intriguing to creative artists. Novelists seem to be drawn to the use of archetypes in structuring depictions of a person in a tense crisis situation.

The archetype is a kind of mythological element—indeed, Jung assumed that the universality of certain myths verified his speculation about the existence of these archetypes. Thus, the Mother, the Savior King, the Devil, and comparable figures are evoked because there is an inner need for such characters to exist, and if they do not exist, people will create them. Some of the argument suggests that archetypes fill a role somewhat like that of Adler's "social interest," filling an innate need.

The Structure of Personality   Some students find Freud's tripartite personality (id, ego, and superego) complex and puzzling. By comparison, Jung's structure is even more complicated. The following is a highly skeletonized summary of his views (see Figure 15.1).

The first major division of personality is into conscious and unconscious components. The conscious personality is made up of percepts, habits, memories, aspirations, and so on. The unconscious is composed of the personal unconscious (like Freud's) and the collective unconscious (made up of archetypes.)

Early in life, the child develops a *persona*, a mask of socialized behavior. Children learn to smile when their parents expect it, to lie politely

FIGURE 15.1 Jung's Conception of the Personality

Terms are defined in the text. Note the recognition of the Persona or "mask" one presents to others; the distinction between the personal unconscious and the collective unconscious; and the Shadow, an unconscious mirror-image of conscious personality developments. *(From J. Jacobi: The Psychology of C. G. Jung, 1962, p. 126, Figure 6, by permission of the Yale University Press)*

when asked if they love their relatives, and to deny aggression and, a little later, fear. Social roles (e.g., a facade for business purposes or a religious mask) are examples of Jung's use of the *persona* concept.

Animus and *anima* are parts of the unconscious. As has already been suggested, they are likely to emerge at puberty when sex-role differentiation becomes an important psychological problem. Jung used the term *animus* to identify a masculine component in a female person and *anima* for the corresponding feminine element in a male. Each of us, then, is bisexual; however, the cross-sexed component is normally unconscious. In a time of crisis, a man who is normally self-assertive and independent may show a need for care and nurturance; this need would be ascribed to the latent feminine element in his personality. The converse, of course, would apply to a woman. The historical evolution of these aspects of Jung's theory suggests that Jung wanted to cope with Freud's assertion of complexes like fear of castration or Adler's version of the "masculine protest." All three theories provide niches for similar empirical phenomena.

Jung felt that one major goal of psychotherapy was to help the person accept this cross-sexed component as a part of the self. A male should not be ashamed to recognize feminine wishes and emotions in himself, and a woman should accept and exploit her masculine aspects. If Jung was correct, many marital troubles would be alleviated if husband and wife understood their own inner impulses and attributes that are socially ascribed to the opposite sex.

Another aspect of the unconscious is the *shadow*. Although the shadow partakes of the qualities of an archetype, it is more closely related to personal experience than are the archetypes. If a person overextends a conscious aspect of personality, the shadow responds in a dialectical fashion by expanding the opposite trend in the unconscious. As Munroe (1955) put it, Jung "presents all of his theses with an antithesis—a shadow, which is unconscious and which lengthens with one-sided exaggeration of the conscious modes" (p. 562).

Clearly, impulses assigned to the shadow are impulses consciously disavowed by the possessor. Jung ascribed the Freudian mechanism of projection to the shadow: "It is in the nature of political bodies always to see the evil in the opposite group, just as the individual has an ineradicable tendency to get rid of everything he does not know *and does not want to know* about himself by foisting it off on somebody else" (1957– 1958, p. 102).

The Self Like Adler, Jung postulated the presence of an inner structure, a unity, that he called the self. The self for Jung was an integration of the various conscious *and unconscious* components of the personality. One portion of the self he labeled the ego; this, which is closely associated with the persona, or social mask, and which acts as a kind of executive in decision making, corresponds fairly well with the ego of Freudian theory. It is the functional area within the personality that copes with the environment: sensing, perceiving, reasoning, and other cognitive functions. The self may be involved in a pursuit of libidinal goals but does not know of the unconscious biases which distort perceptions of others as well as memory and action.

The ego includes the *persona*, but extends beyond it. It would involve impersonal skills and learning which has no dynamic implication. The self includes the *persona* but integrates all of these components into a loosely unified whole. The self is the total personality, but there are some elements that the individual normally would not acknowledge.

The self develops by a process of *individuation*. In Jung's usage, this is not a splitting off of subsystems, but a process of unifying, of becoming *indivisible*. Thus, as an individual comes to accept her or his persona, animus, anima, and shadow, she or he makes progress toward an undivided self. Here, once more, we get the suggestion that Jung, like Adler, was an ancestor of the humanistic movement. (Jung used the term *self-actualization* in much the same way that Rogers and Maslow used it later.) Jung wrote that "individuation means precisely the better and more complete fulfillment of the collective qualities of the human being" (quoted by Woodrow, 1964, p. 311).

Implications for American Psychology   In terms of American disciples, Jung would come out a poor third after Freud and Adler. There are, however, a fair number of Jungian analysts practicing in this country. Jung's impact on theorizing has likewise been less than that of Freud and Adler. He is credited with introducing the term *complex* into psychology to refer to a system of ideas with a strong emotional coloring; Freud and Adler adopted this term but, of course, focused on concepts central to their theories—Adler on the inferiority complex, Freud on the Oedipus complex. The free association test, which Jung adopted from Wundt and perfected, is still a widely used clinical procedure.

Literary people have made some use of Jung's archetypes in planning novels or dramatic works. But most "scientific" psychologists find the whole structure of Jung's theorizing to be excessively mystical and divorced from empirical confirmation.

Jung's one major contribution to American psychology, then, has been the dimension of introversion–extraversion in behavior and as an aspect of personality. When we see that most American users have distorted this idea of Jung's, this is very faint praise.

Jung may have been a factor in the upsurge of interest in Hindu psychology after World War II. He was a propagandist for the use of Yoga techniques, as in meditation, which became a popular fad during the 1960s and 1970s. And I have noted that in his concept of the self, he contributed to the formation of the school of humanistic psychology. Thus his influences have been diverse and sometimes hard to sort out from other conditions favoring theoretical changes.

Freud Versus Jung

There is a temptation to say that Freud represented the deterministic natural-science approach to psychology, and that Jung sponsored a mystical, quasi-religious approach. G. Murphy and J. K. Kovach (1972) expanded on this polarity in an eloquent passage:

> Jung was a prophetic figure. The term is not used either in terms of adulation or of denigration . . . in the broadest sense, both Freud and Jung were prophets, and they were prophets with very different messages. Freud, the agnostic, found the world impersonal, inscrutable, "oceanic" both in its gift of joy and in its exquisite cruelty . . . As prophet, he saw the sweep of vast forces by which man was caught and against which he could make only a Job-like protest. For Jung, however, there was an increasingly large place for intuitive contact with the majestic and the divine, a willing encouragement of the patient and of the doctor to move freely and without resistance in the direction of mystical aspirations . . . a guide to a sublimely challenging world to which man is genuinely attuned (pp. 293–294).

The meaning of this exuberant praise is not quite clear, although most psychologists would probably agree with the intent of the passage. They would, however, note one error, in that Freud explicitly denied knowing of the so-called oceanic feelings beloved of Jung.

A key contrast between Freud and Jung concerns the issue of orientation in time. Freud, a hard-core determinist, emphasized the past and considered no analysis complete until it had uncovered major portions of the patient's childhood, usually with an eye to inducing an altered perception of these early events. Jung, in his therapy, stressed the present; he did not deny that the present complex must have been formed at some earlier time, but the task of the analyst lies in understanding the present personality and in devising ways to restructure it for better functioning. Beatrice Hinkle (1916), an American follower of Jung, defined the distinction this way: "Jung does not ask from what psychic experience or point of fixation in childhood the patient is suffering, but what is the present duty or task he is avoiding, or what obstacle in his life's path he is unable to overcome? What is the cause of his regression to past psychic experiences?" (quoted in Munroe, 1955, p. 543). This emphasis on the here and now is also found in existentialist theory, as well as among behavior therapists.

Freud, Adler and Jung

The defection of Adler and Jung from the Freudian camp can, in both cases, be described as Oedipal (or as sibling rivalry if one prefers the Adlerian option). Each was a brilliant person who profited from Freud's innovative thinking and moved on beyond Freudianism to a related but distinctive theoretical position. Neither was willing to submit to the authoritarian constraints imposed by Freud as the price of his approval.

It is ironic that Freud had elevated each of them to leadership roles in the psychoanalytic movement. This probably speaks well for his perception of their talents. His conflicts with them do not speak well for the success of Freud's self-analysis. He had not attained enough emotional equilibrium to tolerate outright criticism of his theory.

Adler in particular carved out a domain that might be called the social psychology of psychoanalysis. The theories of the remaining "neoanalysts" show marked similarities to the Adlerian thesis—granting that Adler stated his views in so many alternate forms that it is easy to find a suitable match with one's own ideas. Freud and Jung, then, clung to the biological side of psychology; Adler, Horney, Rank, and Fromm explored the social side.

CHAPTER 16

Psychoanalysis: The Neoanalysts (II)

It is possible to accept the Freudian dictum that the field of psychology includes both conscious and unconscious processes, without accepting Freud's libido theory. This is the criterion for classifying psychologists in this area: Many members of the Vienna school achieved considerable success working within Freud's boundaries. But as Adler so keenly pointed out, the human being is not doomed by his or her biological destiny. Life is a continuing interaction between biological endowment and societal pressures. Several psychologists have achieved high status in this field of social psychoanalysis. Their writings strongly suggest that they were driving an opening for closer cooperation of the analysts with the "scientific" psychologists. This is an important component of the contemporary theoretical scene.

Otto Rank

The third major defector from the Vienna Psychoanalytic Society was Otto Rank (1884–1939). He does not, however, illustrate the role of Oedipal aggression between teacher and pupil. His is rather a pure case of sibling rivalry; he was harassed by other members of the inner circle around Freud, without a clear-cut rift developing between himself and Freud.

Biography

Like a majority of the Vienna Group, Rank was Jewish. Unlike most of them, he was poor. His father was an alcoholic, not abusive, but irresponsible. Young Otto left school at an early age to help his mother financially. His theoretical writings center on the child's relations with the mother, where Freud had emphasized the father. It may well be that Rank's childhood influenced him to make this shift in emphasis.

Although the family was poor, it did have a family physician; and one of the pleasant accidents of life was that the physician was no other than Alfred Adler. Young Otto, who was a voracious reader, had read many of Freud's works and asked Adler if there were some way he could meet Freud. Adler agreed to introduce him, and so in 1906, Otto Rank presented to Freud an essay he had written on "The Artist." Freud was impressed with the young man's perceptivity and intellectual skills; he arranged for Rank to become secretary of the Vienna circle if the youngster would go back to school. Rank complied and by 1912 had earned his Ph.D. from the University of Vienna.

Rank was the first nonmedical member of the society. He has been described as a man of vast learning, particularly in the field of classical mythology. Freud and Jung shared a belief that the myths that enjoy wide acceptance reflected some deep unconscious need for the kind of figure, or situation, central to the myth. Thus, before Jung's departure, he and Freud encouraged Rank in this specialization.

It was not until 1920 that Rank began, with Freud's encouragement, to practice psychotherapy. Meanwhile he had become a co-editor of *Imago*, a new psychoanalytic journal, and supervised the revision and republication of *The Interpretation of Dreams*. Freud, amazingly, inserted two of Rank's essays into one revision of the book; but after Rank broke away from the Vienna group, these were deleted from later editions.

Some students of the psychoanalytic movement have held that Rank was, in purely intellectual terms, the brightest person in the Vienna Psychoanalytic Society. This may have contributed to the sniping and criticism that ultimately led to his withdrawal. Ernest Jones and Karl Abraham were apparently the leaders in the hostile movement. Jones particularly bombarded Freud with letters criticizing Rank and alleging various deviations by Rank from orthodox Freudian doctrine. It is not clear how much of this criticism Freud believed, but he did nothing to ease Rank's position or to suppress the infighting. Eventually Rank quietly withdrew from the Vienna group, and moved to Paris and then to America. He finally resigned from the Vienna society in 1929.

In the United States, Rank achieved considerable success and acceptance. He helped to found the school of social work at the University of Pennsylvania, and many social workers still consider his doctrine very useful in dealing with helpless, apathetic persons (and even, to some extent, with aggressive ones). Rank was intrigued to discover that he could charge much higher fees for analysis than had been customary in Europe, and he found this a solution to his chronic problem of inability to finance an extravagant wife. After he decided to settle permanently here, he divorced her and married his secretary, but he survived this event by only two months.

The Theory

Rank deviated from the orthodox Freudian position by placing heavy emphasis on a child's relations with its mother. Influenced, no doubt, by his own childhood, he began to emphasize the anxiety set off, first, by the pain of birth itself and, second, by the demand that the child become independent and give up the protective nest provided by maternal care.

The theory was first put together systematically in Rank's early book, *The Trauma of Birth* (1929). This is probably his best and most creative work. Unfortunately, it has been misinterpreted, perhaps as widely as Jung's writings. Although it opens with a discussion of the physical stress on the infant at birth, it focuses on the anxiety induced by separation from the mother. The trauma of birth provides a prototype, a basic pattern of anxiety that can be reactivated by a variety of circumstances. Rank argued that all later anxieties are modeled on this first experience, although they differ in intensity, in duration, and in the particular circumstances that trigger them.

In his later writings, Rank downgraded the importance of the physical trauma of birth and placed more stress on fears of loss of security, as well as on fears of being stifled by excessive protection. Thus, loss of the warm, protective environment of the uterus was replaced by the loss of home, nurturance, comfort, and so on. But being overprotected, smothered with affection and control, also induced anxiety. In a way, Rank reproduced Freud's evolution from the physical sexual trauma to the fantasied sexual trauma as his theory evolved from the pain of birth to the pain of separation.

Rank developed the thesis that the personality is in conflict between the fear of life and the fear of death. Life is threatening because it means giving up protection and support. Death is symbolic of the loss of freedom to act independently. Affection can take the form of preventing any independence, any autonomy. One might feel dead if overwhelmed by such excessive care and protection. Guilt feelings about forbidden acts may set off anxiety (punishment by severing the umbilical cord and cutting the child off from maternal pleasures).

E. Menaker (1982), a follower of Rank, described the change from the earlier to the later form of the theory as follows: "Rank himself gave up the literal interpretation of anxiety as deriving from separation of mother and child in the birth experience, to adhere to a metaphorical interpretation of this separation. Not physical separation of the two, but their psychological separation as it takes place through the development of individuation now became the paradigm for anxiety" (p. 77). *Individua-*

tion was the term used by Jung for becoming a unique individual; Rank meant essentially the same process but called attention to separation from the parent figure as an indispensable part of this process.

Polarization   Freud had always couched his theories in polarized impulses: sex versus survival instincts in the early phase, the libido versus the death instinct in the later theory. Rank accepted this structuring of thought; his polarity was between the craving for security and the desire for independence. As in approach–avoidance conflicts in general, the opposition of these two tendencies gives rise to vacillation, uncertainty, and anxiety. And anxiety, of course, is the dynamic force impelling the person to engage in neurotic behaviors, such as demanding nurturance, assuming helpless passivity, and blocking on making decisions, or, alternatively, rejecting parents, demanding complete freedom, and refusing to exercise even limited caution. Both tendencies easily extend into the "neurotic" realm; both are regularly found in the same person, as when adolescents denounce their parents but call for help when in trouble.

Group Relations   Rank's theory is relevant to Lewin's theory about small-group processes. The group may be attractive as a source of affection, companionship, and security, but it may also become a threat by demanding conformity and denying any opportunity to express one's individuality. Rank suggested that the basic conflict is between a fear of being isolated from the group (of loneliness) and a fear of being suppressed (that is, forced to conform to group codes and behaviors).

Empirical Support   Like Freud, Rank insisted that his patients had led him to develop this theory: "one noted that people, theoretically and therapeutically entirely uninfluenced, showed from the very beginning of their treatment the same tendency to identify the analytical situation with the intrauterine state" (1929, p. 6). The logic is interesting. By "theoretically uninfluenced," he presumably meant that Freud's patients knew of Freud's beliefs and would try to respond to them, whereas Rank's patients did not know of his biases and so would not try to confirm them. One wonders whether this suspicion (that patients would try to please the therapist by providing memories appropriate to the theory) was widespread among the Vienna analysts. It is unlikely that Rank realized how easily he could direct the chain of associations by reinforcing words and facial expressions.

It is instructive to recall the research of Fred Fiedler (1950) on Freudian, Adlerian, and Rogerian therapists. Patients reported that all three varieties of therapy involved very much the same procedures; there was nothing distinctive about the therapy itself. And they were about equally pleased with the result. But when Fiedler asked about diagnosis, the three groups of patients separated neatly; each accepted a diagnosis that fitted the theoretical predilection of the therapist. It seems possible that therapy continues until the patient has learned to perceive situations as the therapist does, or at least to use words in ways acceptable to the therapist.

Determinism and Free Will In addition to his emphasis on mothering, Rank was unique in another respect. Where Freud had been rigidly deterministic in his thinking, Rank raised objections. Freud placed the proximate causes of conflict in the external world, in sexual trauma (or later, in fantasied trauma). Rank proposed that we recognize the importance of *determinism from within*. "Only in the individual act of will," he wrote, "do we have the unique phenomenon of spontaneity, the establishing of a new primary cause" (1945, p. 44). This proposal agrees with "common sense," in that the psychologist who decides to conduct an experiment is doing something spontaneous, not elicited by an outside stimulus. In his emphasis on spontaneity, Rank almost seemed to be anticipating the "liberation-of-the-self" groups of the 1960s and 1970s.

Creativity is closely linked to this idea of free will or independent personal choice. A truly creative act is one that has not been performed before, and that thus has not been reinforced and is not coerced by the environment. For Freud, creative performances arose out of conflict between biological impulse and outer constraints. Rank was the first major theorist to speak up for the creative will, for a self-initiated creative action. This, of course, implies responsibility and the risk of failure; the artist must feel secure in order to be truly creative.

Research on creativity has focused mainly on the attributes of persons who have demonstrated creativity. This focus does not reveal much about the process itself. The issue of "will" as a psychological phenomenon is being nibbled at around the edges; for example, Charles Kiesler (1971) demonstrated that when a person makes a public commitment to a specific policy or act, the probability that the act will be carried out is significantly increased.

The Unique Personality Rank joined Adler in supporting the necessity of studying the unique personality. Where Freud had spent his time seeking for universal phenomena such as Oedipal complexes, penis envy, and libidinal cathexes, and Jung had pursued the task of sorting bits of data into evidence for shadow, persona, animus, and so on, Rank spoke up for the study of persons in a context of their uniqueness, their difference from all other human beings. To quote Menaker (1982) again, "It obviously became essential therapeutically to safeguard the patient's potential for the spontaneous expression of his unique personality. This could best be done by an acceptance, on the part of the therapist, of the patient as a 'person' regardless of the particular point in emotional development at which he stood at a given time" (1982, p. 10). Thus Rank seems to have been well in advance of Carl Rogers in proposing the doctrine of "unconditional acceptance."

Rank's Influence

Although Rank has not received much attention from the writers of textbooks, he has influenced theoretical developments in American psychology. Henry Murray (1938) obviously borrowed from Rank for his category of "claustral complexes." In his *Explorations in Personality* (1938), Murray wrote, "Under this heading we shall group all complexes that might conceivably be derived from the prenatal period or from the trauma of birth. The following may be distinguished: 1. a complex constellated about the wish to reinstate the conditions similar to those prevailing before birth; 2. a complex that centres about the anxiety of insupport and helplessness; and 3. a complex that is anxiously directed against suffocation and confinement" (p. 363).

Rank's theory has also influenced therapeutic experiments. L. H. Silverman and J. Weinberger (1985) described a therapeutic ploy that involved showing (at subliminal exposure speeds) a message like "Mommy and I are one." This treatment seems to imply the hypothesis that the separation anxiety is intense and that reassurance (subconsciously) of unity with the mother could be beneficial. The results differed by sex. Male schizophrenics showed improvement in pathological symptoms after repeated showings of "Mommy and I are one," but no improvement occurred in a group given showings of "Daddy and I are one." This outcome would fit Rank's prediction. Unfortunately, the case is not that simple. Female schizophrenics exposed to "Mommy and I are one" showed no improvement, but they did get better when shown repeated versions of "Daddy and I are one." This outcome is compatible with Freudian theory but cannot be said to support Rank's view.

The Zeitgeist

Although Rank got his first acceptance in the United States before World War II, it was after that conflagration that he was recognized as a major prophet. To the young people emerging from the war, the relief of having survived may have been tremendous. Certainly they showed strong desires for independence. Rank never became a cult hero like Herbert Marcuse, but his warnings about being "smothered" by parents found receptive ears. Thus, Rank legitimized the rebellious demand for freedom from control that reached its peak about 1968. It is worth noting (and Rank would not have been surprised) that these same rebellious youngsters joined in groups that demanded maximum conformity in music, clothing, sexual behavior, and so on. A group can serve an anxiety-reducing role only at the cost of smothering other aspects of the unique individuality of the group member.

In a way, it is Rank who should have been credited with the phrase "This is the age of anxiety." However, he has many competitors for that designation, and the evidence is murky. Certainly he found a key principle in the relation of parents and children in the modern situation.

Rank achieved a considerable popularity among artists and writers, perhaps because he emphasized the notion of creativity as a major psychological issue. The novelist Anaïs Nin, who was analyzed by Rank and later helped him in many ways, gave praise and support to Rank and his ideas.

Karen Horney

Another prominent antagonist of the orthodox Freudian group was Karen Horney (1885–1952). Horney had been analyzed by Karl Abraham, a member of the original Vienna circle, but she early adopted many of the deviant ideas of Alfred Adler. Her support of Adler may have been due in large part to Adler's espousal of "feminist" causes in opposition to Freud's male chauvinism. Judiciously, Horney left Germany in 1932, and she worked with the Chicago Psychoanalytic Institute for two years. In 1934, she moved to New York and the orthodox Freudian New York Psychoanalytic Institute. Becoming dissatisfied with orthodox doctrines, she broke away and founded the American Institute of Psychoanalysis.

Horney's rebellion against Freud can be traced primarily to his male chauvinism: his pejorative view of females in general, as well as his thesis about penis envy and the castration complex and the thesis that "Anatomy is destiny." Echoing Adler's critique, she held that many of the behaviors ascribed by Freud to innate female patterns were outcomes of social restrictions and limitations.

Although she did not reject Freud's theory of psychosexual development in all respects, Horney opposed the biological determinism that was implicit in many of Freud's pronouncements. She wrote that "psychoanalysis should outgrow the limitations set by its being an instinctivistic and a genetic psychology" (1939, p. 8). She also questioned the libido theory, offering in its place a dynamic based on anxiety. Most human beings need and seek affection from others, but this does not prove the presence of a libidinal impulse: "Without recognizing anxiety as the dynamic force behind the need for affection, we cannot understand the precise conditions under which the need is enhanced or diminished" (1937, p. 149). The concept of "basic anxiety" as she used it appeared to combine Rank's "fear of life" and "fear of death"; that is, Horney conceptualized anxiety as the fundamental dynamic in human behavior, and this anxiety stemmed from the helpless, powerless status experienced by every infant and child.

Adults, of course, experience anxiety also. In fact, Horney conceived a neurosis as the reactivation of basic anxiety by some realistic situation rather than by reminiscences or fantasies. Every human being can experience "a feeling of being isolated and helpless in a world potentially hostile" (1945, p. 41).

The Neurotic Personality of Our Time (1937) was one of the first books to suggest that ours was "the age of anxiety." Given the worldwide economic depression of 1929–1939, the atrocities of the Nazi regime from which she had fled to the United States, and the looming prospect of a war, she would seem to have been justified in this characterization. The world had become a strange and threatening place full of incomprehensible dangers.

Another feature of the time was what she called "alienation," which she linked to chronic anxiety and to felt powerlessness, closely similar to what later researchers would call "learned helplessness." The individual may perceive the self to be surrounded by impenetrable barriers blocking any avenue of self-enhancement or even of love and affection. The alienated person feels forced to adopt a mask (cf. Jung's persona), which is often at odds with the "real" personality, that is, with the preferred autonomous behavior pattern. These ideas foreshadowed the thinking of the existentialists and the humanistic psychologists about the need for a person to experience an "authentic self" rather than a pretended self.

Cultural Approach   Horney's emphasis on these environmental factors underscores her rejection of Freud's biological theories in favor of the cultural determination of psychological traits: "Freud's disregard of cultural factors not only leads to false generalizations, but to a large extent blocks an understanding of the real forces which motivate our attitudes and actions" (1937, pp. 20–21.) Modern Freudianism, she charged, had "come into a blind alley, manifesting itself in a rank growth of abstract theories and the use of a shadowy terminology" (p. 21). And she attacked the orthodox therapeutic procedure in which "the task of analyzing is fulfilled by discovering either the sexual roots . . . of an impulse or the infantile pattern of which it is supposed to be a repetition" (p. 33).

In Horney's view, the child's anxiety is a function of the social environment. Like Adler, she stressed the powerlessness of the child in the face of adult control of rewards and punishments—as Skinner would say, the available reinforcements. The root of neurosis, Horney claimed, is "an insidiously increasing, all-pervading feeling of being lonely and helpless in a hostile world" (1937, p. 89).

Not all children, however, react by becoming apathetic and alienated. Some who have abandoned hope still burn with rage, which may be displaced onto irrelevant victims in irrational crime. Thus to "basic anxiety" Horney added "basic hostility" as a dynamic factor of great psychological importance. Phobias may develop from such anger: "sometimes the danger is felt to threaten him from his own ungovernable impulses—fear of having to jump down from a high place, or to cut someone with a knife; sometimes the danger is entirely vague and intangible" (1937, p. 60). Thus sex may be an instrument of hostility, reversing Freud's theory that hostility derives from sexual impulses. Horney's view on this point is now widely accepted.

Coping with Anxiety and Hostility   The basic task facing each individual is how to cope with these impulses of anxiety and hostility. As Horney classified behaviors, there are three basic orientations: (1) toward people; (2) away from people; and (3) against people. Thus she (no doubt unintentionally) paralleled the threefold emotional thesis of John B. Watson, who identified love, fear, and anger as the basic emotional states. Simply fitting a behavior pattern into one of these three orientations is not enough to guide therapy; Horney proceeded to identify ten "neurotic needs," which could become the focus of therapeutic efforts:

1. The need for affection and approval—sensitivity to signs of rejection, extreme efforts to please others.
2. The need for a protector—a pattern resembling Rank's "fear of independence."
3. The need to avoid risks—the person lives in a narrow world, has low aspirations, and prefers not to be noticed.
4. The need for power—an extreme version of Adler's "will to power."
5. The need to exploit others—to dominate and use family members or others.
6. The need for prestige.
7. The need for personal admiration.
8. The need for achievement—the hard-driving, incessantly ambitious person, now called "Type A."
9. The need for independence—being excessively sensitive to attempts by others to hem the person in and to impose limits on his or her range of options, an extreme version of Rank's need for autonomy.
10. The need for perfection—obsessively seeking to eliminate all errors and to produce a perfect product; an extreme of Adler's "striving for perfection."

Horney did not allege that there was any innate tendency to develop one or another of these "neurotic needs." In fact, they do not derive from the theory in any logical fashion; they seem merely to be a classification of the neurotic disturbances she had encountered in her therapeutic endeavors.

Cognition   One trait that Horney shared with Freud—and indeed with almost all "analytic" psychologists—was a lack of concern for cognitive processes. Like Freud, she viewed these as feeble tools manipulated by powerful unconscious forces. Occasionally she conceded that a cognitive event might be relevant: "It makes a great deal of difference whether the reaction of hostility and anxiety is restricted to the surroundings which forced the child into it, or whether it develops into an attitude of hostility and anxiety toward people in general" (1937, p. 88). One is reminded of Watson's work with Little Albert, in which the "conditioned fear" generalized to a fur muff, Watson's hair, a Santa Claus mask, and so on. In cognitive terms, then, Horney was saying that emotions are less pathological when narrowly specific than when widely generalized. If all human beings are triggers for anxiety or for hostility, this is more serious than a phobia for red-headed men or people with foreign accents.

Sometimes the neurotic responds to suffering by escaping into Nirvana (i.e., by denying reality and merging with the cosmic soul, as promised in the Upanishads). Horney also suggested that the neurotic could abandon the self in some great cause, religious, esthetic, or political, thus escaping from felt personal inadequacy into a world of powerful abstractions lacking personal reference.

The Basic Conflicts Perhaps the most valuable of Horney's theses is summed up in her examination of culture conflicts. In contrast to Freud, who focused on conflict of instinct against social norms, Horney argued that the basic conflicts are endemic to the culture itself:

1. The conflict between egoistic pursuits (the demand for success) and altruism (concern for others) is a chronic problem in Western civilization. Horney was not referring to selfishness in the sense of id demands, but in the pressure to be first. The child is urged, prodded, and bribed to strive to be on top. Sometimes this becomes "Winning isn't the best thing; it's the *only* thing." Meanwhile the child gets training (less intense) to be helpful to others, not to take advantage of someone's weakness, to be humble, and to do good without hope of reward. Any child who tries to live up to both sets of teachings is going to have problems.

2. The second cultural contradiction, Horney asserted, was between stimulating human needs and blocking their gratification. "Conspicuous consumption" is represented in movies and magazines and on TV and radio; possessors of wealth and power are pictured as beautiful and successful. But for the average citizen, life, if not solitary, is likely to be "nasty and brutish"; in other words, the economic system allows only a small percentage of the population to wallow in luxuries. Thus, one's physical standard of living is in constant dissonance with the ideal existence purveyed by the media.

3. The third major cultural contradiction is between individual freedom and the observed reality of constraints and limitations. The child is told, "You are free, you are responsible, you can do anything if you try hard enough; if you fail, it is your own fault." The culture then stacks the cards so that the vast majority of children move into a society that denies freedom, imposes legal and economic handicaps, frustrates edu-

cational aspirations, and generally gives the lie to the fantasy of personal freedom. As Skinner wrote in *Beyond Freedom and Dignity* (1971), scientific determinism conflicts with the theory that human beings are free, autonomous individuals.

Despite pointing out these contradictions within the culture, Horney came out as being more optimistic than her colleagues. As Ruth Munroe (1955) wrote about Horney, "Self-interest in the true sense involves the satisfaction of *all* the powers of the individual, which automatically include love and consideration for his fellows" (p. 350). This optimism undoubtedly influenced Maslow (who acknowledged Horney as one influence on his thinking) in his development of the idea of self-actualization as a major motive (see Chapter Seventeen). At least Horney found the major conflicts out there in the environment, not inside the biological organism; as the behaviorists have pointed out, it is a lot easier to change the milieu than to change the biological unit.

Significance of Horney

Horney will be remembered for her vigorous attack on Freud's masculine-centered doctrine, as well as for her keen observation of the internal contradictions of our society. Although many of her ideas mirror those of Alfred Adler, she wrote more clearly and more persuasively, and (unlike Adler) she did not change the focus of her theorizing even though she wrote many books.

Horney will also be remembered for another contribution. In her books *New Ways in Psychoanalysis* (1939) and *Self-analysis* (1942), she opened up the possibility that intelligent individuals could analyze their own emotional problems. (After all, Freud claimed to have done so.) When we consider the number of neurotic vestiges that Freud manifested after his analysis was ostensibly complete, we may have doubts that Horney's recommendation of self-analysis is sound. At any rate, she evoked a storm of criticism from the orthodox analysts, who had been indoctrinated with the belief that one must be analyzed by someone who has been analyzed. This counterargument would be more persuasive if there were some evidence that trained analysts are, in fact, better adjusted and more mature in their decisions and actions than people who have not undergone psychoanalysis. Such evidence, regrettably, is hard to come by.

Erich Fromm

The last of the neoanalysts to merit special discussion here is Erich Fromm (1900–1980). Like Rank, he was not a medical doctor; he earned a Ph.D. in sociology and, also like Rank, was at first welcomed into the analytic circle as a bringer of a new perspective, only later to be criticized as heretical.

Fromm's first contribution—and in the eyes of many judges, his most brilliant work—was *Escape from Freedom* (1941), a penetrating examination of the German people's acceptance of Nazism. As the title implies, the main theme is that the Weimar Republic had brought freedom from the authoritarian controls of the empire, but also economic disaster and widespread suffering. The typical German, Fromm concluded, sought to regain a kind of infantile security by complete submission to Hitler's "New Order." In this kind of escape from freedom, what the citizen escapes is the obligation to make decisions and so to be responsible if these decisions lead to failure. Following Rank, Fromm held that in times of trouble, people will abandon freedom to regain a feeling of security. (This idea also has a detectable resemblance to Horney's "neurotic need for a protector," that is, someone who will make the tough decisions and guarantee the followers' security.) In a rigidly hierarchical society, people know their places and their obligations. Everything which is not compulsory is forbidden. This, incidentally, is the kind of security envisioned by those who admire the Middle Ages, with their feudal structure of obligations and responsibilities. There is no ambiguity and (supposedly) no anxiety.

Fromm also shared Horney's cultural determinism: "The most beautiful as well as the most ugly inclinations of man are not part of a fixed and biologically given human nature, but result from the social process which creates man. . . . Man's nature, his passions, and anxieties are a cultural product" (Fromm, 1941, pp. 12–13). He followed Adler and Horney in his concern with the felt helplessness of the individual: "This very helplessness of man is the basis from which human development springs; *man's biological weakness is the condition of human culture*" (1941, p. 33; italics in original). All three, then, were at odds with Freud's thesis that the repression of sexual impulses was the foundation of culture.

The foundation of human freedom, Fromm argued, is actually in freedom from instinctual demands. If individuals are, as Freud held, doomed by their instincts to seek certain goals, to perform certain acts, and to encounter certain conflicts, they are not free. True *human* existence begins as instincts weaken, "when the way to act is no longer fixed by hereditarily given mechanisms. In other words, *human existence and freedom are from the beginning inseparable.* Freedom is here used . . . in its negative sense . . . namely freedom from instinctual determinism of his actions" (Fromm, 1941, p. 32; italics in original). Fromm denied that this position was anti-Darwinian; rather, he held that flexibility and freedom from mechanical actions had been a positive value for the survival of the human species.

Social Theorizing   Given his sociological background, it is no surprise that Fromm's reputation is largely based on his acute perception of social problems. I can describe only briefly some of his books examining institutions and practices, which show the range of his knowledge and the courage of his convictions. *Man for Himself* (1947) is not, as it sounds, an apologia for selfishness, narcissism, and greed; rather, it is an appeal for an openness to others, a loving and cooperative relationship as opposed to exploitation and rivalry. *The Sane Society* (1955) sets forth arguments for Fromm's ideal of a humanistic-communistic society, in which everyone would labor happily for the common welfare. *Revolution of Hope* (1968) deals with humans' relations with their natural environment, a kind of human ecology. *The Anatomy of Human Destructiveness* (1973) focuses on aggression, not in Freud's instinctual terms but on a frustration–aggression basis.

Marx Versus Freud   An interesting angle on Fromm's way of thinking is given by his comparisons of Karl Marx with Sigmund Freud. In his last book, *Greatness and Limitations of Freud's Thought* (1980), Fromm criticized Freud on the grounds that he diverted attention from the "real" problem of modern life: Freud's "concentration on sex actually deflected from the criticism of society and hence had in fact partly a politically reactionary function" (p. 134).

Fromm scolded Freud for failing to follow through on his own discoveries: "Freud's discovery was potentially revolutionary because it could have led people to open their eyes to the reality of the structure of the society they live in and hence to the wish to change it in accordance with the interests and desires of the majority. . . . The concentration on sex actually deflected from the criticism of society" (p. 134). Freud, Fromm said, was not truly radical. The "real" source of psychopathology was our sick society, our sick economic system, our exploitative interrelationships. People needed to be awakened to the fact of industrial slavery. Fromm even went so far to compare Marx and Freud, and to conclude that Marx was the better psychologist, a conclusion that suggests that even a brilliant person like Erich Fromm can make an enormous mistake occasionally.

Psychoanalysis and Neoanalysis

Freud's great contribution came as a corrective to the psychological tradition that had treated conscious experience as the central topic of psychology, without providing a place for unconscious modifiers of consciousness. The neoanalysts deserve a place in history for their modification of Freud's biological, instinct-based theory into a cultural, social-psychological theory. Thus we see a dialectical relationship in which one poses a thesis, others state an antithesis, and later observers devise one or another synthesis of these contradictions. The advance of theory, especially in psychology, seems to follow Hegel's principle of dialectics, that the statement of one view almost automatically encourages someone to present an opposing view.

Regarding the relationship of these psychodynamic theories to structuralism, behaviorism, and Gestalt, theories that focus narrowly on cognitive functions in an impoverished environment, it is clear that all of the analytic theories put pressure on "scientific" psychologists to look outside the laboratory and to find out what is going on in the social environment.

These theories suggest that "scientific" psychology is guilty of ignoring a large segment of human behavior. The association of ideas may be a constantly recurring theme in psychology, but the failure to set this cognitive process in a context of desires, emotions, inhibitions, and maladjustments has been detrimental to the development of a real science of human behavior.

CHAPTER 17

Humanistic Psychology

There is a capsule history of psychology which states that psychology was once the study of the soul, but then it lost its soul and became the study of the mind; later it lost its mind, and became the study of consciousness; and with the behaviorists, it lost consciousness. Although there is more than one grain of truth in this summary, it has met with periodic opposition from those who wish to study personality, imagination, creativity, and esthetics. These critics of the "tough-minded" approach to human behavior banded together to form a "humanistic" school and a mutual support group, the American Association for Humanistic Psychology. In 1961, a new journal was founded (the *Journal of Humanistic Psychology*) as a publication outlet for research and speculation in areas generally perceived by more traditional journal editors as falling outside the boundary of acceptable psychology.

The movement was new only in the sense that it represented a resurrection of questions that had long been ignored by psychologists. The classical philosopher-psychologists would have assumed that all psychology was humanistic. The decisive moment in the split of "scientific" psychology from this humanist tradition came with René Descartes, whose "anthropocentric predicament" led him to treat animals as mere machines. This orientation led to the reflexology of Ivan Pavlov and so to behaviorism. But the human component also suffered from Cartesian logic. Descartes advised all scientists to slice a problem into its smallest parts and to study these separately. This dictum grew and· elaborated into the microscopic analysis of consciousness by the structuralists. It also gave rise to the reflexology of the Russian objectivists, and later to the microanalysis of Meyer, Watson and Weiss. Nobody paid any attention to Mary Whiton Calkins and her arguments for the self as a major component of psychology. Thus on one side were psychologists studying flatworms, pigeons, white rats, and goldfish, and on the other, those studying sensations, images, sensory adaptation, and contrast effects. The whole complex human being—with a capacity for forming economic and political institutions, creating esthetically pleasing objects or symbols, and developing religious or philosophical systems—disappeared.

In America, the "tender-minded" psychologists protested in vain during the first half of the twentieth century. It was mainly after World War II that humanistic psychology achieved some status in the discipline. A Division of Humanistic Psychology within the American Psychological Association was chartered in 1972, and by 1985, it had 788 members. Thus the "humanistic" movement represented a small but not insignificant segment of American psychology.

The "founding father" of humanistic psychology in America was A. H. Maslow (1908–1970). In 1954, he wrote to some friends (Erich Fromm, Karen Horney, Gordon Allport, Carl Rogers, and Kurt Goldstein) suggesting that the time had come to set up a formal organization of like-thinking individuals. The bias of the group toward a neoanalytic psychology is obvious in the list of founders. Kurt Goldstein was the only Gestalt-oriented person involved, although many others have joined since that time. The resultant meetings led to the formation, in 1962, of the American Association for Humanistic Psychology (AAHP).

Interestingly, the manifesto of this group did not resemble Watson's in proclaiming a split within psychology. The official statement of purpose of the AAHP offered the following definition: "Humanistic psychology is primarily an orientation toward the whole of psychology rather than a distinct area or school. It stands for the respect of the worth of persons, respect for differences of approach, open-mindedness as to acceptable methods, and interest in explorations of new aspects of human behavior." (AAHP, 1962, p. 2).

The claim that this was a *new* code for psychologists would be rejected by behaviorists, Gestalt psychologists, and psychoanalysts. All would argue that they "respect the worth of persons" and—except when denouncing each other—show approval for differences of approach. The emphasis in the "humanist manifesto" centered more on the subject matter of psychology. The topics of "love, creativity, self, growth, . . . spontaneity, objectivity, autonomy, . . . transcendental experience, [and] peak experience" identify the significant additions made by humanists to the psychological agenda.

The extent to which these topics are new can also be questioned. William James discussed the experience of religious conversion, and of other mystical experiences. He also invested considerable time in psychic research and was open-minded about such alleged phenomena as telepathy and clairvoyance.

C. G. Jung also broke ground for the AAHP. After his break with Freud, Jung elaborated his theory of a "collective unconscious," of memories based on ancestral experiences, of the male unconscious in female personalities (and vice versa), and of mystical experiences based on the eruption into consciousness of some one of these components.

Alfred Adler's ideas also appear in the humanistic publications. As an early advocate of child guidance and a critic of society for crippling so many individual personalities, he opened a path for a psychology dubious about some social demands. Karen Horney and Erich Fromm, among the founders of AAHP, adhered to many of Adler's theoretical propositions.

Otto Rank is another of the neoanalysts whose theories appear in the humanistic literature. The most apparent is his concept of the "fear of dying," the mental orientation characterized by a fear of being suppressed by societal demands, and of losing one's identity and freedom of decision. The humanists have been ardently (and perhaps excessively) critical of overconformity and loss of the "authentic" self.

Gestalt ideas are also apparent. The quest for wholeness, for the *unified* personality, reflects Gestalt theorizing. Kurt Goldstein is generally credited with persuading his colleagues of this fundamental principle of humanistic psychology.

It is clear, then, that humanism is part of the broad progression from the atomism of Wundt and Titchener—and the behavior fragments of Watson, Hull, and Skinner—to the holism of Gestalt and the dynamism of psychoanalysis. Humanism rejects the analysis of perceptions, emotions, or behavior. Because traditional psychology relied on an analytic methodology, this cut the humanists off from the effective use of the historical materials in the discipline. They opposed the use of impoverished environments to eliminate complex stimuli, and of restrictive response alternatives that limit the person to one or two actions. They prefer to sacrifice experimental rigor in order to achieve relevance.

The "Third Force"

Of military analogies and metaphors there is no end. The neoanalysts and personality researchers who came together to form the "humanistic" movement designated themselves as the "third force" in American psychology. (The two earlier forces were behaviorism and orthodox psychoanalysis.) Just why they ignored Gestalt theory—and especially the Lewinians—is not clear. Many of their ideas have a distinct Gestalt coloration. At any rate, the humanists perceived themselves as crusading for a new and different approach to psychological theory and research.

The reasons for the rejection of behaviorism and orthodox analytic theory have been diverse. Generally speaking, the emphasis has been on the atomism and mechanism of the behaviorists—especially Skinner, but the arguments apply equally to Watson and Hull. On the Freudian issue, the criticism has been that orthodox theory does not allow for the study of the entire person (instead, the Freudians have looked for Oedipal reactions, anal fixations, libidinal cathexes—in short, have been studying segments instead of the total personality).

On the question of unconscious processes there is no unanimity among the humanists. Most concede that unconscious events influence conscious phenomena, but they object to assigning a major role to this principle. Unconscious material can become conscious under appropriate conditions. (Freud held the same, but his "conditions" were those of extreme probing and guidance by an analyst.)

The humanists perceived themselves as rebelling against both the mechanism of the behaviorists and the imperialism of unconscious processes as portrayed by the psychoanalysts. Their central concept was the self, and this self had the attributes of consciousness, planning, and flexibility. It could function as a determinant of behavior in the sense that an incoming stimulus might be evaluated and classified in terms of existing habit and belief systems, which thus determined "from above" the kind of response to be made. This is a very different self from the Freudian ego, which functions mostly as a mediator between the demands of the id and the prohibitions of the superego.

So far, no single spokesperson has been agreed on as an acceptable representative of humanistic psychology. To show the range of consensus, as well as the areas of minor disagreement, I have selected A. H. Maslow, G. W. Allport, C. R. Rogers, Gardner Murphy, and Rollo May as exemplars.

Abraham Harold Maslow

A. H. Maslow (1908–1970) initiated the formation of the American Association for Humanistic Psychology and so might be called the founding father of the movement. He was born in Brooklyn and attended the University of Wisconsin for both undergraduate and graduate training. His doctoral dissertation (1936), with Harry Harlow, dealt with dominance hierarchies in a colony of rhesus monkeys in the Madison zoo. This would not seem to be an auspicious basis for becoming a humanistic psychologist, although it can be noted that Harlow was humanistic in ideology even though almost all of his research dealt with animals. Maslow's friends in graduate school attest that he was already disposed toward a humanistic philosophy at that time.

His real education came after his return to New York City. Unemployed for a year after his doctorate, he was given a research assistantship by E. L. Thorndike at Columbia University. After work hours, Maslow contrived to meet with many of the refugee scholars who had been given shelter at the New School for Social Research. Among the people he credited with influencing his thinking were Max Wertheimer, Bela

Archives of the History of American Psychology

Abraham Maslow, the epitome of the "tender-minded"
psychologist; sensitive, insightful, speculative

Mittelman, Abram Kardiner, and Karen Horney, as well as Americans
like Ruth Benedict. After several years at Brooklyn College, Maslow moved
to Brandeis University, where he remained until illness forced him into
premature retirement and a move to California, where he died in 1970.
He had been elected president of the APA in 1968 but was unable to
read his presidential address because of poor health.

Theory of Motivation   The concept most generally associated with Maslow is the hierarchy of motives. This idea represented either an advance
or a regression, depending on one's perspective, from the behavioristic
limit on motivation to physiological drives, and from the Freudian insistence on sex as the only motive. The hierarchy approach was suggested in an article in 1943 and was expanded in his *Motivation and Personality* in 1954. It has been widely discussed and is often accepted as a
basis for understanding industrial, political, and social behavior.

The theory postulates a hierarchy of needs, which emerge as determinants of human behavior in a certain order; that is, when a "lower" need is satiated, the next higher one tends to dominate behavior:

1. At the base or foundation, Maslow placed the physiological needs: hunger, thirst, and the maintenance of other homeostatic equilibria. He did not specifically list freedom from pain, although it must be included in this group.
2. When these basic drives are satisfied, they weaken, and the "safety" needs take over. These are connected with anticipation of danger and are measures to protect one against threatened deprivation. In some writings, Maslow referred to these as "security" needs, and this would seem to be a preferable label.
3. When safety needs have been met, belongingness and love needs emerge. Like Freud, Maslow extended sex to include friendship, affiliation, and similar relations.
4. When the love needs are met, the need for esteem, for respect by others, comes to the fore. In this area, Maslow mainly relied on the ideas of Adler. Most humans show a certain spontaneous quest for prestige and attention. Maslow did not offer any details about this need, presumably accepting Adler's views on compensation for inferiority, on will to power, and on social interest. (He acknowledged Adler as a source of ideas in a general way.) Maslow did distinguish between applause and achievement, although both seem to fall in this category. Surprising to those who knew Maslow was his citation of the novelist Ayn Rand in this connection. His social philosophy was quite remote from her version of "rugged individualism."
5. The need for self-actualization influences the behavior of some individuals who have achieved satisfaction of all the preceding motives. Self-actualizing may include creativity or remolding the environment to resemble one's dreams or ideals. Maslow was ambiguous about this category; he referred to doing what one is skilled to do (a musician must make music), but it may also imply embarking on a new career ("What a man *can* be, he *must* be"—1954, p. 91).

These are the five "basic needs" in Maslow's theory. One is puzzled, then, to find them followed by a discussion of a "cognitive" need (a need to know) and an "esthetic" need, (a motive toward the enjoyment of beauty in one or many forms). Maslow's treatment does not identify these as basic needs, but it is clear that they may operate concurrently with the lower needs and hence do not fit into the hierarchy. It is also unclear whether these can be satiated to the point of becoming unimportant, as the "lower" needs can.

The theory emphasizes a progression, as one satisfies first the physiological demands, then the security needs, and so on. An individual operating on a higher need (e.g., for prestige) may be forced back to a lower level by the occurrence of a threat to the lower need (e.g., a physiological threat). But Maslow also conceded that some individuals break the hierarchical order; an artist may undergo severe deprivation at the physiological or safety level in order to "actualize" her or his talent. Maslow treated these instances as exceptions and offered no logic for fitting them into the theory.

The instinct theorists (notably William McDougall) had postulated somewhat similar lists of motives, but without Maslow's hierarchical arrangement. Maslow hesitated about calling his basic needs "instincts," but he accepted the notion of some degree of hereditary determination; he adopted the adjective *instinctoid* to show this connection. One distinction of *instinctoid* from *instinctive* is that instinctoid needs may fade and disappear, whereas true instincts could not. Thus the theory calls for a hereditary predisposition, but not for a rigid determinism, with respect to these basic needs.

Maslow did not offer any logical explanation of the sequence stated in his hierarchy. One may particularly question his placing the love needs in third place. As reproduction is indispensable for species survival, it would seem plausible that the sex drive would be coequal in potency with the physiological drives.

The unique value of the Maslow theory of needs lies in the concept of the hierarchy. It has long been known that a satiated need weakens and that some other motive then activates behavior. Maslow provided some predictions about which unsatisfied motive would emerge as the new determiner of behavior.

Cognition   Another area of concern to Maslow was cognition. This was not an interest in adaptive cognition, as in the perception of objects or persons; rather, he wrote extensively about what, in a broad sense, might be called "esthetic" cognition. He used the term "B-cognition" (cognition-in-being) to contrast with "D-cognition" (cognition relevant to the deprivation of some needed substance). Thus, D-cognitions are those studied by structuralist and Gestalt psychologists, dealing with the attributes of objects that relate to survival. By contrast, the B-cognitions include "the parental experience, the mystic, or oceanic, or nature experience, the aesthetic experience, the creative moment, the therapeutic or intellectual insight, the orgasmic experience" (Maslow, 1962, p. 69). Further, B-cognitions are *"detached from relations, from possible usefulness, from expedience, and from purpose"* (p. 70; italics in original). The B-cognitions, then, relate to enjoyment, but not necessarily to adaptation. Maslow's poetic approach contrasts with the cool analytical style of experimental writers on perceiving; he sided with Cattell when Cattell accused scientific psychology of "viewing the body of nature with eye of an anatomist rather than a lover."

Peak Experiences   A special category of B-cognitions received the label of "peak experiences." These are mystical states, "oceanic experiences." Maslow (1962) wrote, "The emotional reaction in the peak experience has a special flavor of wonder, or awe, of reverence, of humility and surrender before the experience as before something great" (p. 82). And again, "The person at the peak is godlike not only in senses that I have touched upon already but in certain other ways as well" (p. 87). Being godlike is a very tempting idea; St. Augustine and St. Thomas Aquinas endorsed the goal of spiritual ecstasy long ago. Jung would argue that the desire to be godlike is part of the wish to have powers beyond those of ordinary mortals, a part of the collective unconscious, a recurrent reaction against the limitations of human capacity. It is thus hardly surprising that humanistic psychologies have a strong appeal to young people; this is heady stuff when compared with the austere logic of Hull or of Koffka.

Maslow regrettably did not offer any discussion of the antecedent conditions giving rise to peak experiences; in fact, he did not explicitly recommend any particular study of them. He did offer some tentative hypotheses about the aftereffects of some peak experiences, notably, possible therapeutic consequences; however, as we do not know the antecedents, we cannot induce these as part of a therapeutic process.

Avoidance of Knowledge as Defense   One further aspect of Maslow's theory of cognition deserves mention: the proposition that curiosity, or the need to know, may be frustrated by the individual's fear of knowledge. This is approximately equal to Freud's concept of repression, and to his emphasis on resistance in therapy as developing out of a fear of learning about one's sex drives and other forbidden material. As Maslow (1962) wrote, "Often it is better not to know, because if you *did* know, then you would *have* to act" (p. 63). Censors of school textbooks hold that it is better for children not to know certain facts (e.g., about sex or about theories such as evolution). The Germans living near Dachau during World War II protected themselves from guilt feelings by carefully avoiding knowledge of what was going on in the death camp.

Personality   Maslow's contribution in the area of personality is an extension of the need for self-actualization. He began by noting that mental health should not be identified with an absence of neurosis. He wrote of "intrapsychic health," which involves such attributes as self-awareness, felt personal security, independence of the social environment, and a willingness to conform to social customs or to abandon them for some "higher" purpose. He criticized orthodox psychoanalysis for giving the impression that the unconscious was no more than a source of neurotic symptoms. A psychology based on the study of abnormal personalities must be, he said, a "cripple psychology."

On this point, Maslow revealed an acceptance of Asian ideas, of Hinduism and Zen Buddhism: If reality is pathological, simply withdraw from it. If societal demands are irrational and oppressive, ignore them. The self-actualizing person can stand against the environment if it becomes necessary, either by fighting back or by ignoring it.

So far, the argument seems acceptable. But he then proceeded to pose such a sweeping indictment that virtually everyone would be pathological: "What we call 'normal' in psychology is really a psychopathology of the average, so undramatic and so widely spread that we don't even notice it ordinarily. The existentialist's study of the authentic person and of authentic living helps to throw this general phoniness, this living by illusions and by fear into a harsh, clear light which reveals it clearly as sickness" (1962, p. 15).

As a rule, Maslow did not deign to offer any empirical data in support of his speculations. In the case of the "self-actualizing" personality (those who have achieved the gratification of basic needs and have ascended to the level of self-actualization), he did offer a crude research design. Negatively, his target person must be free of neurotic traits; positively, such individuals must be using their talents and capacities to the fullest extent possible. College students proved to be too immature to meet his criteria. Finally, he opted for a study of the biographies of historical personages (e.g., Abraham Lincoln, Thomas Jefferson, and William James), plus a few living public figures such as Eleanor Roosevelt and Albert Einstein. None of these was actually interviewed; only public data were examined. It would seem obvious that this procedure allowed unlimited opportunities for selective perception; the results probably show more about Maslow's theory of self-actualization than about the persons studied: "Data here consist not so much in the usual gathering of specific and discrete facts as in the slow development of a global or holistic impression" (1954, p. 203).

Maslow enumerated several attributes that he reported as cutting across most, if not all, of his self-actualizers: (1) efficient perception of reality; (2) acceptance of self, of others, and of nature; (3) spontaneity—this may include a rejection of conventional social codes when they are perceived as absurd; (4) problem centering—not on personal problems, which have already been solved, but on social or environmental problems; (5) detachment—a need for privacy; (6) autonomy, or independence of the culture and of the environment; (7) mystic experiences and oceanic feelings; (8) *Gemeinschaftsgefühl*—identification with and sympathy for humans in general; (9) a preference for a few deep friendships rather than wide superficial socializing; (10) a democratic character structure—freedom from prejudice, especially as regards race or religion; (11) creativeness; and (12) a resistance to enculturation (a certain detachment from their own culture.)

Almost any reader is likely to examine this set of attributes and agree that such a person, if found, would be good to know. However, we have no evidence that self-actualization produces such personalities, or whether these personalities are capable of achieving the state Maslow called self-actualizing. It is also probable that some tyrants might qualify, as well as a number of capitalists. If we omit race prejudice, Adolf Hitler might qualify, and Josef Stalin might come close. These frightening figures were attempting to mold their environment to *fit their ideals,* were autonomous, detached, sure of themselves, and so on. Maslow would, of course, have had nothing but personal revulsion for either man. The issue, however, is: just how detached and autonomous a person may become without also losing the quality that Maslow called sympathy or empathy with others. Indifference to societal constraints may be fine for a Gandhi or a Martin Luther King, but it is not a kind of behavior one would advocate for growing children.

There is, in fact, a certain idealization of the child in Maslow's writings. "The healthily spontaneous child," he wrote, "reaches out to the environment in wonder and interest. . . . In this process, that which gives him the delight-experience is fortuitously encountered. . . . He must be safe and self-accepting enough to be able to choose and prefer these delights" (1954, p. 58). This sounds enough like Freud's pleasure-principle, the characteristic of the infantile personality, to be disturbing. And we do not know what "delights" should be forbidden: alcohol, drugs, and sex? Maslow, it should be noted, early in his career endorsed the idea of the "unconditional gratification" of children; in later years, he abandoned this theory in favor of placing carefully chosen limits on the child.

Tension Reduction and Tension Increase   S. R. Maddi and P. T. Costa (1972) suggested that some of the inconsistencies in Maslow's theorizing might be ironed out by an examination of the motives leading to tension reduction, as opposed to those leading to tension increase. Traditional psychology has emphasized tension reduction. Maslow's self-actualizing person seems capable of accepting challenges, of entering into situations in which tension is increased, and of finding this experience exhilarating. Deficiency motives fall into the traditional pattern; being-motives, such as curiosity and creativity, show enjoyment of tension increases.

Maslow also urged tolerance of ambiguity. This was perhaps fortunate in that his own writing often seems ambiguous. He wrote of the person (presumably a self-actualizer) as follows: "The person in the peak experience feels more integrated (unified, whole, all-of-a-piece) than at other times. He also looks (to the observer) more integrated in various ways . . . e.g., less split or dissociated, less fighting against himself, less split between an experiencing self and an observing self, more one-pointed, more harmoniously organized, more efficiently organized" (1962, p. 98). It seems clear that Maslow considered peak experiences to be good for one, but beyond that, the reader may feel as William James felt about describing all the boulders on a New England farm.

Carl Ransom Rogers

Carl R. Rogers (1902–1987) was expounding a humanistic philosophy of psychology before Maslow; Maslow has been given priority here because of his role in organizing the humanistic psychologists. Rogers provides us with an illustration that may be valuable for an understanding of the genesis of novel theories.

Biography

Rogers described his parents as hard-working upper-middle-class Americans. His father had a college degree in engineering, and his mother had attended college but never graduated. Rogers considered it odd, therefore, that they were either indifferent to or critical of intellectual pursuits.

Rogers reported a good deal of sibling rivalry in his early years. He felt that his parents preferred an older son, Ross, and apparently the two boys had frequent conflicts. On the other hand, Carl and his younger brother, Walter, had good relations. There is, one must add, little evidence that Carl Rogers's theories were affected in any way by this family constellation.

Rogers described himself as a chronic daydreamer and a social isolate. It is possible that the tension level in the family was higher than would be inferred from his description, as he developed a duodenal ulcer and had to be hospitalized. Before then, he had been active in YMCA and church activities. (Note that several prominent individuals in the history of psychology underwent serious illnesses in childhood, among them Descartes, James, and Hull, as well as Rogers. It may be that illness and confinement lead to thinking about human behavior and so to a career in psychology. Adler, of course, would emphasize the role of compensation for a handicap as motivation for exceptional achievement.)

In 1924, Rogers enrolled at Union Theological Seminary, where he met Goodwin Watson and Theodore Newcomb, both important figures in twentieth-century psychology. Deciding to become a professional psychologist rather than a minister, he transferred to Columbia University, where he came in contact with Alfred Adler, and, of more importance personally, with Leta Hollingworth, a professor of clinical psychology.

Rogers was quite explicit about the intellectual conflicts to which he was subjected at Columbia. In the doctoral program, he was required to learn and accept the rigorous requirements of the experimental laboratory in the person of E. L. Thorndike (Chapter Eight.) In his placement in a child guidance clinic, he was surrounded by Freudians and was expected to acquire both the vocabulary and the interpretations appropriate to that variety of psychology. Rogers perceived these conflicting influences as the starting point for his invention of nondirective therapy and his theory of a self-psychology. It does not appear that he was influenced by Mary Calkins's theory of the self.

The Metaphor

Rogers's psychology is neatly encapsulated by his preferred metaphor, which was biological—more precisely, botanical. A seed, he noted, if given water and nutrients, grows up into a plant. If the environment is normal, it grows to be a normal, fully developed representative of its species. Humans, he reasoned, would likewise grow up to be normal, well-adjusted specimens of *Homo sapiens* if they were simply allowed to grow, unhampered and undamaged by environmental conditions.

The Theory   Rogers hypothesized that every person is born with the potential to develop into a normal personality. The individual has an innate impulse or drive to grow and develop; Rogers called this drive the "principle of self-enhancement." By this, he did not imply egotism, just as Maslow's self-actualizing people are not explicitly egotistical. Actually, Rogers applied self-enhancement so widely that it resembled Freud's libido or Adler's striving for perfection. Conceptually it has more in common with Adler than with Freud; Rogers was acutely aware of the ease with which libido theory could become a rationalization for pleasure seeking without social responsibility. He evaded this charge against his own theory by defining self-enhancement so widely as to include everything from eating (nourishing the self) to religion (expanding the self through a relationship to God). Thus all of Maslow's hierarchy can be absorbed into this single impulse. This kind of all-embracing theory has been called "monistic dynamism" by Calvin Hall and Gardner Lindzey (1970, p. 530). This monistic theorizing is clear in Freud and Adler, each of whom influenced Rogers's thinking.

In accord with the metaphor, the self tends to grow, to express itself, and to develop its full potential. As with a tree, inadequate nutrition or adverse external conditions may produce sickly, ineffectual, or distorted growth. This sounds as if it were going to fit Maslow's criticism of the "cripple psychology," but in fact, theories of normal healthy personality tend to be mirror images of theories exploring the pathological personality.

Organismic Experience and Phenomenal Experience   The theory begins with a clearly Gestalt orientation. The emphasis is on perceiving and assimilating, not on responses. Various things happen to the developing organism (the child). Everything that has an effect is defined as "orga-nismic experience." But not all experience is reflected in conscious awareness. The limited portion of which the child is conscious Rogers called "phenomenal experience." This is not Freud's conscious–uncon-scious dichotomy; it has more in common with Lewin's life space and foreign hull. Rogers recognized the importance of events and memories which were not adequately represented in awareness.

Two outcomes may arise from this split between organismic and phe-nomenal experience. They may be *congruent* (i.e., there is no conflict between the two with respect to the self or to others), or they may be *incongruent* (i.e., the phenomenal field distorts or censors the organismic experience). Incongruent material, then, corresponds roughly to what is repressed, in Freudian terminology. And as in the Freudian system, un-conscious material may influence conscious processes, leading to misper-ceptions and erroneous behavior (Rogers, 1959).

An important source of incongruity and hence of personality disturb-ance occurs in the socialization of the child. Children, in their egocentric self-aggrandizement, often express antisocial feelings. The child may say, "I don't like my baby brother." Parents will insist, "Of course you love your baby brother." The outcome of this conflict may be resentment of the parents, repression of a hostile attitude toward the baby, or a hostile perception of the self for harboring "bad" thoughts.

It is this line of reasoning that led Rogers to his famous doctrine of "unconditional gratification." He did not mean it quite as it has often been interpreted. Parents must protect "baby brother" and other poten-tial objects of the child's aggression. Rogers urged only that parents es-chew any comments that the older child is "bad," or efforts to force incompatible statements such as "I really love him." Unconditional grat-ification, then, had a restricted meaning for Rogers, which has been mis-interpreted widely. Rearing a child with true "unconditional gratifica-tion" (i.e., allowing the active expression of all impulses) will produce egocentric self-aggrandizers.

A more fortunate way of expressing the theory is "unconditional ac-ceptance." Rogers's view of therapy include viewing the client as a hu-man being worthy of respect and acceptance. Again, Rogers did not im-ply approval of the client's behavior. One may give "unconditional acceptance" to a rapist and still send the rapist to jail.

Tension Reduction Rogers's theory of motivation focused on positive goals rather than on tension-reduction. However, he often conceded that the phenomenon of closure (closing the gap between the self and the desired object) is accompanied by tension. One might say that Rogers's phenomenal field was not quite congruent with his organismic experi-ence, which included the occurrence of tension; he simply refused to recognize it as such.

Repression, for Rogers, was less coercive than for Freud. Rogers conceded that some material is not accessible to conscious inspection, but that, without deep analysis, it can be recovered and inspected in a therapeutic situation if the client feels unconditional acceptance from the therapist. If this material is then integrated into a phenomenal field, the pathological symptoms should disappear.

The Self   Rogers's theory is often called a *self theory*. It does not stress the concept of self much more than the neoanalysts or Koffka and Lewin. It may be that the central place of "self-enhancement" justifies the label.

For Rogers, there were three selves: the phenomenal self (the self as perceived by the person), the "real" self (including disapproved attributes that are not accessible to consciousness), and the ideal self (based on family and other cultural values, perhaps including some features of the phenomenal self). However, a major aspect of personality diagnosis for Rogerians is the discrepancy between the phenomenal self and the ideal self. This discrepancy induces tension (often organismic, not conscious), and tension induces a restructuring of the phenomenal field, perhaps including the phenomenal self.

Rogers's definition of the self was complex: "the organized, consistent, conceptual Gestalt composed of perceptions of the characteristics of the 'I' or 'me' and the perceptions of the relationships of the 'I' or 'me' to others and to various aspects of life, together with the values attached to these perceptions. It is a gestalt which is available to awareness though not necessarily in awareness" (1959, p. 200).

The Role of the Group   Rogers recognized that although the individual's self-image or self-concept is shaped mainly by experiences within the family, outside groups can also be important. A major source of pathology is the pressure to conceal certain impulses or actions in order to avoid social disapproval.

From this generalization came the idea that groups might be formed in which individuals would be encouraged to abandon their constraints on self-description and to admit to the possession of "bad" impulses or irritating characteristics. From this theorizing came the "encounter groups," in which everyone was urged to bare his or her own inner self but to be accepting of the bad features of others. The effect would be, Rogers thought, that each person would come to be less self-critical and also more accepting of others. Not everyone responded that way; some groups became very sadistic, attacking a particular person and reinforcing feelings of inferiority or unacceptable traits.

Some enthusiasts decided that if the encounter group met for the purpose of baring oneself, the process could be accelerated by baring the body. Hence, "nude encounter" groups became popular for a time, mostly in Southern California but sporadically in other cities where being "sophisticated" was highly valued. One is reminded of the fad for psychoanalysis in the 1920s, when society figures competed for the "best" analysts and bared their unconscious impulses (as the analyst had identified them) at cocktail parties.

It is reasonable to assume that Rogers had nothing to do with either the sadism seen in some encounter groups or the nudism seen in others. Once an idea is published, it is out of the theorist's control and may be picked up by charlatans. Misinterpretation is rife; Freud was blamed for the weakening of conscious sexual taboos, with the inaccurate charge that he was encouraging sex before, during, and outside of marriage. Rogers has been similarly victimized.

Relation to Scientific Psychology

Where other humanists, like Maslow, concentrated on denouncing the theories and methods of experimental or "scientific" psychology, Rogers extended an olive branch. Humanistic psychology, he held, was not intended to replace the science built up by Titchener, Hull, and Skinner, but to extend and supplement this structure: "The Newtonian, mechanistic, linear cause-effect behaviorist view of science is not thrown out, but it is seen as simply one aspect of science, a perfectly good way of investigating some questions, but definitely inappropriate for others" (Rogers, 1985, p. 16).

Whether other Rogerians, or even Rogers himself, acted on this advice can be debated. A distinguished psychologist remarked on the widely publicized debate between Rogers and B. F. Skinner that he "did not see Skinner giving Rogers any positive reinforcement, nor did Rogers give Skinner unconditional acceptance." It is perhaps easier to be tolerant and calm in the privacy of one's study than in a combative public debate.

Rogers demonstrated his desire for a friendly relationship with "scientific" psychology by initiating one of the earliest research programs dealing with the process of psychotherapy. C. R. Rogers and Rosalind Dymond (1954) devised several innovative approaches to what had seemed an area not compatible with objective data collection. These approaches included audio recordings of therapy sessions (in later years, audiovisual tapes were made) and the use of Stephenson's Q-sort technique. Recording constituted a breakthrough because traditional therapists were confident that such an intrusion would cause patients to inhibit the free report of their problems. The Rogers study proved this objection to be unfounded.

The Q-sort technique merits brief description as one idiographic method that has been under-utilized. This procedure, devised by William Stephenson (1953), permits a person to record a self-description in readily quantifiable form. Using a packet of (usually) 100 cards, each bearing a single descriptive statement, the individual is asked to sort them to provide a self-picture. The cards must be distributed according to the normal curve; thus one cannot select all of the desirable attributes and place them in the affirmative category. It is necessary to pick a most applicable statement, some a bit less applicable, a large number in the middle group, and a few in the "not-applicable" categories. Thus each person must identify favorable and unfavorable attributes.

Rogers's method asked a client to sort the cards once for self-description, once for "ideal self," once for "how my mother sees me," and so on. Pre-therapy sortings often produced a negative correlation of the real self with the ideal self. After therapy, most such correlations were positive and fairly high; in other words, the client now perceived the real self to be approaching the pattern of the ideal self-image.

There can be little doubt that Rogers, by boldly initiating rigorous research methodology into the study of psychotherapy, fostered important steps forward in the study of personality and the acquisition of desirable attributes.

Gordon Willard Allport

Gordon W. Allport (1897–1967) had, like Rogers, been advocating a "humanistic" psychology for many years before Maslow set about organizing the AAHP. His was a philosophical and esthetic approach to psychology; he was not dedicated to empirical research or to what we have been calling "scientific" psychology.

Born in Indiana, the son of a physician, Allport went to Harvard University prepared to compete with his older brother, Floyd (see Chapter Nine) who was then in the doctoral program in psychology. Gordon won his B.A. in 1919, when Floyd obtained his doctorate. The two seem not to have been very friendly; in his autobiography, Floyd told of an occasion when his wife rattled off a list of Floyd's good points to Gordon, who promptly replied, "And is he still stubborn, lazy, and procrastinating?" This remark was particularly surprising because Gordon, in his interpersonal relations, was generally quite gentle and uncritical.

In contrast to Floyd's behaviorism, Gordon became a champion defending humanistic approaches against the encroachment of "scientific" doctrines. In 1927, Morton Prince donated to Harvard University some $80,000 (a small sum today, but seen as large at that time) on condition that a psychological clinic be established. H. A. Murray was brought in as clinic director. According to Nevitt Sanford, there was strong opposition from the scientific wing of the department (led by E. G. Boring and K. S. Lashley) to the reappointment of Murray in 1934. At that time, Gordon Allport led the defenders of Murray and the clinical aspect of psychology. Although Sanford did not allude to the later split of the department, in which the "pure science" proponents kept the title, De-

Archives of the History of American Psychology

Gordon W. Allport, a tender-minded systematizer of self
theory and idiographic research

partment of Psychology, and the humanist clinicians joined with sociology and cultural anthropology to form a new Department of Social Relations, the intensity of the struggle made this outcome virtually inevitable.

Gordon Allport won his doctoral degree in 1922, three years after his
brother. His mentor was E. B. Holt, whose orientation was behavioristic;
it is clear that he did not win Gordon to his views. On the other hand,
Gordon's aggressive opposition to behaviorism is more often attributed
to his conflict with his brother—an example of Adler's "sibling rivalry."

Gordon Allport never distinguished himself as a researcher. And his
students were allowed to do unusual tasks to earn their degrees. For
example, Allport allowed Henry S. Odbert to do a dictionary study (it
was called a "psycholexical" investigation) on the diversity of terms in
English for attributes of personality. Allport's forte was philosophical,
and it is likely that he attracted students with a similar orientation. Among
these, to mention some outstanding contributors to American psychology, were Jerome S. Bruner, Roger Brown, Gardner Lindzey, Herbert
Kelman, Stanley Milgram, and Kenneth Gergen. Gordon Allport was
elected president of the APA in 1939.

Allport's theoretical stance can best be described by the same phrase
used for Carl Rogers: a "self psychology." In his first major book, *Personality: A Psychological Interpretation* (1937), Allport introduced ideas that
he was still supporting at the time of his death in 1967.

Psychology of the Individual

Allport, like Rogers, placed the concept of *self* at the center of psychology. He believed that although sensing, perceiving, learning, and reasoning are important processes, each of them is important in relation to a person, a self. From his viewpoint, it is not so significant that seeing goes on, but that *I* see. His view, then, was at a polar opposite to that of David Hume, for whom the self was no more than a collection of perceptions or ideas.

To avoid the metaphysical implications of the concepts of self and ego, Allport relied on the term *proprium* as a neutral concept free of historical excess baggage (1961, p. 127). In doing so, he acknowledged the influence of William James with regard to the distinction between the "knower" and the "known."

Propriate Functions In his 1961 volume on personality, Allport identified seven aspects of the proprium. They were presented with the following labels:

1. *Sense of bodily self* refers to kinesthetic and other interoceptive sensory experiences, and also to the combinations of these with the visual awareness of bodily movements, touch, temperature, and the like. In infancy, these may resemble James's notion of consciousness as a "blooming, buzzing confusion" or Titchener's discussion of sensations completely devoid of meaning. However, over a (fairly short) period of time, they become integrated into a sense of "my own body."
2. *Continuity of self-identity.* Memories of past sensations build an awareness of the self as a continuing entity. Being called by one's name by adults and remarks about past events reinforce this continuity.
3. *Self-esteem and pride.* Social comparisons are made with peers, regarding bodily size, agility, possessions; there is an awareness of family and its status.
4. *Extension of self.* Ethnocentric thinking begins as the child identifies self with groups (e.g., family, neighborhood, city, nation, and religion).
5. *The self-image.* The formation of the self-image actually starts at birth but probably does not become conscious until the age of five or six. It ties together the bodily, family, and social group elements already mentioned.
6. *Self as coping mechanism.* Later still, the child becomes aware of intellectual abilities, skill in solving problems, acting independently of parents, and so on. It is now possible for the child to think about her or his own thinking.
7. *Propriate striving.* Desire for self-esteem may become focused on an ambition, an aspiration. There is a tremendous difference between

an ambition autonomously adopted by the individual and one imposed on him or her by parents or others. Self-determined choice has
the motivational power of the self, or proprium; an imposed goal
mobilizes far less energy and may even be unconsciously sabotaged
by the individual.

It will be noted that Allport unobtrusively introduced a developmental
theory into his discussion of the proprium. Although all seven of these
aspects of self ultimately become merged into one complex Gestalt, Allport suggested that the observer can watch these aspects differentiate
from the confused aggregate that is the behavior of the infant and can
also see them reintegrated into the complex adult personality.

It is also easy to see that Allport did not bother with elaborating a
theory of sensing or perceiving. He was concerned not with how information gets inside the organism, but with the way in which each individual personality grasps this information and uses it in the service of the
self. To emphasize this distinction, he adopted the term *proception* to
stress the notion that what he was discussing was perception plus self-
relevance. Thus a professional psychologist usually pays attention to any
random mention of "psychology" but is not selectively sensitive to mentions of medicine, chemistry, or sociology.

Functional Autonomy   Allport left one other concept as his unique contribution to psychological theorizing: the idea of *functional autonomy*, which
refers to such phenomena as secondary drive; secondary reinforcement,
in the behaviorist language. Compare the phrase "mechanisms become
drives," a slogan of the functionalists.

Allport (1961, p. 220) laid down certain broad considerations essential
to a theory of human motivation (as distinguished from animal drives):
(1) the *contemporaneity of motives,* a rejection of the Freudian theory that
adult motives are never separated from their infantile roots; (2) *plural-
ism,* in opposition to monolithic theories such as libido or social interest,
and approval of Maslow's distinction between deficiency and growth motives; and (3) *fusion of dynamic force with cognitive processes,* an approval of
the Gestalt hypothesis that cognition of a certain situation carries within
itself the motivational energy to impel action. Allport proposed the term
intention to identify this fusion of motive with cognition. Thus, a young
woman may form an intention to win a Ph.D. degree in psychology. This
intention then becomes an organizing force; some environmental opportunities become less attractive whereas others are more appealing; acquisition of certain skills is pursued with energy, and others are neglected; and so on.

Allport conceded that this emphasis on intention minimized the role
of unconscious processes. For example, he contrasted the answers of a
psychoanalyst and a consulting psychologist, each being asked, "What is

the most important question you can ask a person in order to understand his or her personality?" The analyst asks for fantasies, for clues to
the unconscious conflicts and complexes; the consultant asks for intentions ("What do you want to be doing five years from now?") The consultant may realize that the unconscious forces may bias the intention;
however, he or she is still concerned with the intention itself. As Allport
might put it, action is most often based on conscious, not unconscious,
impulses.

Functional autonomy, then, is the principle that activities take on motivational energy over time. The sailor who retires likes to live by the sea
and get out on it when possible. The bus driver goes on a holiday tour
by bus. Habitual actions resist efforts to block them, as many who try to
quit smoking discover. An orchestra member plays his or her instrument
when there is no audience and no occasion to learn a new composition.
Allport held that these acquired drives are far more potent than the
secondary drives mentioned by Hull; the distinctive feature is that functional autonomy applies to habits that have self-relevance, to some intention or ambition.

Allport noted that we can distinguish between primary reinforcement
and functional autonomy very easily. If a child comes to my door and
receives a cooky, he comes back. If the cookies stop and the visits continue, then the behavior is due not to primary reinforcement but to an
interest in me or my milieu. This distinction by Allport is relevant to the
use of "token economies" in mental institutions and special classes. The
token maintains some desired habit as long as it is available, but when
tokens are removed, the preferred behavior may weaken and disappear.
Only when the token is used to establish an action that becomes valued
in itself does the procedure really succeed.

Idiographic Research   Given his continuing interest in the self as a unique
person, it is not surprising that Allport did not feel attracted to nomothetic research. He did help prepare a test to measure ascendance and
submission, with his brother Floyd, and one to measure personal values,
with P. E. Vernon. He also participated in research on expressive movements with Vernon. However, his position led him to support the idea
of idiographic research, research that seeks common and replicable findings within a single person. The basic methodological principle is that
instead of examining a universe of individuals, we examine a universe
of actions of a single person. If orderly relations exist within this universe, principles can be adduced which hold for that person only.

Allport cited with approval the research of Alfred Baldwin (1942) in
which he analyzed over a hundred letters written by a woman over a
period of eleven years (from age fifty-nine to age seventy). Baldwin tab-
ulated recurring topics in the letters and then sought for regularities in
the associations of these topics. For example, she showed a paranoid

attitude in her relations with other women and was very jealous of her son. Baldwin wanted to know how these ideas were associated in "Jenny's" mind. He found that when she wrote something favorable about her son, the next topic generally was nature or art (positive values for Jenny); when she wrote something unfavorable, she mentioned her own self-sacrifices and made hostile comments about other women. Baldwin concluded that enduring clusters of cognitive-affective material formed unique features of this specific personality. Clearly, idiographic research is possible, but so far, it has not become popular, perhaps because the collection of the requisite "universe of acts" is difficult. It is easier to get a few measures on a large number of persons and thus to establish nomothetic relationships, that is, principles that apply to the total population studied, but not to any specific individual within that population.

Semantic Space Edwin Lawson (1978) devised an idiographic method that fits some of Allport's requirements. Rather than collecting the behaviors of a person, Lawson collected a person's judgments on a variety of topics, including the self, using Osgood's "semantic differential" (see Chapter Ten). Lawson devised a method for reducing this mass of judgments (ratings) to a three-dimensional model that revealed meaningful clusters and significant distances. One woman, for example, placed her self-image in the center of a cluster including God, father, virtue, and power; another cluster, at some distance from the first, included husband, sin, death, and weakness. One does not need a Ph.D. in clinical psychology to interpret this model of her semantic space. (For a more extensive example, see Figure 17.1. The subject, a female college student, put herself in a cluster with boy friend, love, and a career but placed family, college, and hometown in a remote space close to "weak" and "passive.") This technique for plotting a person's semantic space may also develop into a valuable idiographic tool.

Despite his persuasive writing and his personal charm, Allport never founded a "school," perhaps because his stress on uniqueness ran counter to the American tradition of mass research on large populations. He did, however, instill strong personal loyalties in the students who worked with him, and his influence is discernible in much of the research on personality since 1937.

Rollo May

Among the humanistic psychologists, another important contributor has been Rollo May (1909–   ). May is best known for his introduction of existentialism to American audiences, a reflection of his dissatisfaction with orthodox psychoanalysis. He was trained in New York City, and his comments on that training are significant: "It was argued by competent

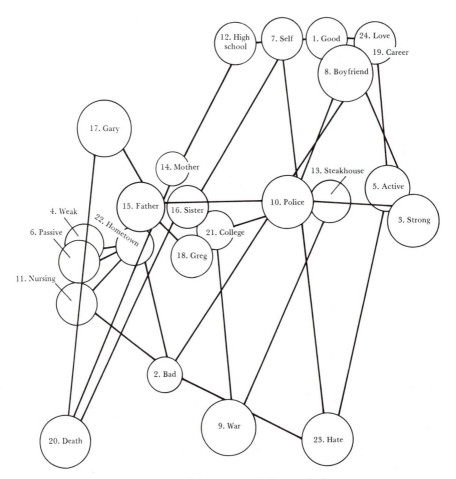

FIGURE 17.1   Lawson's Map of One Person's Semantic Space

Each respondent checks nine 7-step scales, three from Osgood's (1957) Evaluation factor, three from the Potency factor, and three from the Activity factor. Lawson (1978) has a computer program which generates a 3-dimensional model (the third dimension in this illustration is indicated by the size of circles). Items close together are closely associated, according to the correlations of judgments.   *(Courtesy of Dr. E. D. Lawson)*

and experienced analysts," he wrote of these trainers, "that whether or not the patient was a gangster or a responsible member of society was no business of theirs—their task was only to help him become free to do better *whatever he wished*" (1969, p. 169; italics in original). May assailed this detached attitude as a violation of social ethics. We can sympathize with his indignation; it hardly seems proper for a therapist to help someone be a better-adjusted confidence man, embezzler, or safecracker. But there is another side to the coin: Is it wise to assign to psychotherapists the role of deciding what social values should be inculcated during therapy? Visions of *1984* or *Walden Two* cast shadows on the image of the high-minded therapist who decides what is good for the patient or for society.

May argued eloquently for his thesis that therapists should consciously take a stand on value orientations. He asserted that the policy of neutrality on values "actually separates and alienates the person from his world, removes whatever structure he had to act within or against, and leaves him with no guideposts in a lonely, worldless existence" (1969, p. 169).

The same comment may be made with respect to much work in industrial psychology, which rarely involves any discussion of whether a proposed management policy is beneficial to the society in general but is focused on how to achieve the goals set by management. The position of humanistic psychology, quite simply, is that psychologists cannot shrug off the values of society, although they may consciously reject those values and seek to modify them. We have seen this tradition in European psychology, where Adler, Fromm, and many other neoanalysts adopted a socialist position in opposition to their social milieu.

May argued plausibly that societal freedom must include the freedom to oppose existing social practices. This argument resembles Maslow's argument that the self-actualizing person may, on occasion, rise above conforming to established social conventions in order to further some higher value. The rub, of course, lies in deciding which value is higher. For May and Maslow, the answer was obvious, but for many other social reformers, the "higher value" may be something harmful to human beings. (For example, many social psychologists deplore the intrusion of religious considerations into political elections, on the ground that, given a diversity of religions, victory for one means oppression for others.)

Powerlessness   May (1972) continued to explore the implications of this conflict of the individual with the society. Adler had demonstrated the ubiquitous character of the will to power and its potential damage to society; Karen Horney expanded on this conclusion by pointing out the destructive consequences of powerlessness. May (1972) agreed with her:

> A great deal of human life can be seen as the conflict between power on one side (i.e., effective ways of influencing others, achieving the sense in interpersonal relations of the significance of one's self) and powerlessness on the other. In this conflict our efforts are made much more difficult by the fact that we block out both sides, the former because of the evil connotation of "power drives," and the latter because our powerlessness is too painful to confront. Indeed, the chief reason people refuse to confront the whole issue of power is that if they did, they would have to face their own powerlessness (pp. 20–21).

It is puzzling to the historian that the key role that Adler played in the explication of power motives has been so widely ignored. Maslow did not mention Adler, nor did Gardner Murphy in his *Human Potentialities*. Allport noted Adler's concept of *life style* but did not mention his theory of the will to master the environment or the striving for perfection. Of this group, only Rollo May has given Adler credit for his contributions to the psychology of power.

The "Human Dilemma" Descartes had posed for psychologists the "anthropocentric dilemma," or the issue of the similarity of humans to lower animals. If humans are the center of the universe, perhaps an anthropocentric psychology is justified; but are humans really that central? In turn, Rollo May (1967) faced the psychological profession with what he called the "human dilemma," which he defined as "man's capacity to experience himself as both subject and object at the same time" (p. 8). This problem had been pointed out by William James, but he had questioned the "same time" posited by May. James noted that these two experiences typically alternate; one first experiences the self in action, as subject, and then retrospectively examines what went on (i.e., treating the self as object). The mainstream of American psychology, of course, adopts the "self-as-object" posture and avoids consideration of the "self as subject, as knower."

May's resolution of the "human dilemma" is not very clearly stated. He did suggest that choosing one's own set of values is crucial: "One can take over rote values (more accurately called 'mores,' 'standards') from the church, or the therapist, school, American Legion, or any other group in the culture. But the act of valuing, in contrast, involves a commitment on the part of the individual which goes beyond the 'rote' or automatic situation. This, in turn, implies some conscious choice and responsibility" (1967, p. 220).

Existentialism May also deserves credit for playing a major role in the introduction of existentialism to American psychologists. Although this philosophical orientation has not become widely known or adopted in the United States, it is more-or-less closely related to the humanistic doctrines described in this chapter.

May (1958) defined existentialism as "the endeavor to understand man by cutting below the cleavage between subject and object which has bedeviled Western thought and science since shortly after the Renaissance" (p. 11). Further, he commented that "the existential psychologists and psychiatrists do not at all rule out the study of dynamisms, drives, and patterns of behavior. But they hold that these cannot be understood in any given person except in the context of the overarching fact that here is a person who happens *to exist, to be,* and if we do not keep this in mind, all else we know about this person will lose its meaning" (p. 12). The existentialist, then, focuses on concrete reality, on the person in the situation. An amusing illustration was used by May: Three apples plus three apples equals six apples. But the mathematical statement could, he commented, apply just as well to three unicorns. His point was that there is a great difference between reality and abstraction, between a statement about a present reality (an apple) and an idea that has no physical referent (a unicorn). Since Plato, we have been looking for abstractions that hold without regard to concrete reality; it is time, assert the existentialists, for science, especially psychological science, to get back to the real world of living, breathing human beings.

It could be said that existentialism marks the culmination of a trend that began with Wundt and the analysis of consciousness. There has been a steady increase in the concern with complex stimuli and complex responses; there is a questioning of the validity of the single-stimulus–single-response unit, the impoverished environment and the constrained response alternatives. The more complex is the more difficult, but the humanist–existentialist doctrine would hold that difficulty is a price we should willingly pay to study real psychology.

Gardner Murphy

Another important researcher in the field of personality is Gardner Murphy (1895–1979). Murphy did not endorse the extreme variety of humanistic psychology posed by Maslow; he is perhaps best described as an experimental humanist, or a humanistic experimentalist. His major contribution, *Personality: A Biosocial Approach to Origins and Structure* (1947), identified connecting links between the nomothetic principles of "scientific" psychology and the "tender-minded" theories later to be proposed by Maslow and his colleagues.

Murphy was trained in the functionalist tradition, earning his Ph.D. at Columbia University in 1923. R. S. Woodworth and E. L. Thorndike were major influences on his training. However, he quickly developed expertise in the relatively new field of social psychology and in 1931 he and his wife, Lois B. Murphy, gave the field a shape and name by publishing *Experimental Social Psychology,* a summary of studies using "scientific" methods as contrasted with the tradition in social psychology of using anecdotes, anthropology, and sociology as raw material.

Like William James and Clark Hull, he was handicapped through much of his career by illness. His limited physical energies may have contributed to his low research productivity in the decade after his doctorate and the fact that he was not given tenure at Columbia University. In 1940 he accepted a full professorship at the City College of New York, a recognition of his scholarly stature but depriving him of the pleasure of working with doctoral candidates. In 1952 he accepted an appoint-

Dr. Lois B. Murphy

Gardner Murphy, a synthesizer who explored the common areas of nomothetic psychology and personality
theory

ment as Director of Research at the Menninger Foundation in Topeka,
Kansas, where he stayed until retirement in 1972.

Murphy resembled Rogers in his theoretical position, emphasizing
connections between the psychoanalytic conception of personality, Allport's self-psychology, experimental studies of perceiving and learning,
and Gestalt theory. He rejected extremes of environmentalism and of
nativism. He wrote critically of the "situation error" (attributing too much
potency to the environment) and the "organismic error" (too much emphasis on the biology of the organism). He offered a compromise between Allport's insistence on uniqueness and the dimensional analysis of
psychologists measuring personality traits, suggesting that we recognize

personality types and consider how the same "trait" might function quite differently in persons belonging to different types.

Murphy's most significant contributions were in this domain of re-interpreting the two traditions to bring them closer together. For example, he proposed the concept of "canalization" as a substitute for Freud's "cathexis"; he incorporated the data Hull had treated as "secondary drives" and tied the concept to Allport's "propriate striving." He made the important point that Hull's phenomena are subject to extinction, whereas the other varieties of canalization are not, and deduced from this some variables important to the understanding of personality. He linked motivation with perceiving: "the structure of motive patterns tends to become the structure of cognitive patterns" (1947, p. 351). As might be guessed from that sentence, Murphy and his students made important contributions to the "New Look" movement in research on perception.

Motivated perceiving, or "autistic" perception, as Murphy labeled it, reflects the influence of rewards and punishments, but it may also function as a way of imposing a meaningful structure on a scene of disorganization. R. Schafer and Murphy (1943) used an ambiguous figure, a reversible Gestalt in which two "faces" can be seen in succession but not simultaneously. One finding was that, by rewarding one "face" and not the other, they could train a subject so that the second "face" was never seen. Another observation was that, if no rewards were given, the subject would still eventually settle on one "face" and ignore the other (pp. 371, 380); they interpreted this phenomenon as a need to get rid of the ambiguity involved in seeing the two faces in the same drawing. This would appear to give some support to Maslow's "cognitive need", or to Adler's desire for mastery of the environment.

Murphy conceded that the physiological drives stressed by Watson and Hull were important; however, he proposed that these dynamic tendencies can fuse into a kind of generalized motive which he called "self-enhancement," thus resembling the humanistic doctrines cited in preceding pages. He borrowed from Kurt Lewin the concept of tension, and pointed out—as Lewin had—that tensions spread: "however much we emphasize the functional distinctness of the various individual drives and of the various classes of drives, we must keep constantly in mind that the tension system is a system, that tensions spread through the body, that no one region is ever active without arousing others, and that no drive can ever exist in an otherwise undriven body" (1947, p. 120). Thus he rejected the isolable, segmented drives of behaviorism in favor of a motive as generalized as Freud's libido—even more generalized, in fact.

Given his concern for self-enhancement, the concept of self obviously must be clarified. Murphy considered that the self began as self-image (much as Allport, 1937, had done), but that it became abstracted and expanded beyond the limits of perception: *"In short, the self becomes less and less a pure perceptual object, and more and more a conceptual trait system"* (1947, p. 506; italics in original). The concept of trait will be explored in Chapter Twenty.

Murphy and his students opened up various new fields of investigation. Since Ebbinghaus, the experimental ideal had been to find learning tasks which had never been encountered before, i.e., prior learning was zero. Murphy suggested that it was important to see how social attitudes and personality patterns modified the learning process. An early study (Levine and Murphy, 1943), demonstrated that persons favorable to communist ideas learned pro-communist verbal passage more rapidly than did anti-communists; and the anti-communists learned a passage hostile to communism faster than the pro-communist subjects. Thus, the meaning or content of the learning task varied the speed of learning according to its compatibility with pre-existing mental sets.

While I do not believe Murphy ever called himself a "humanist", his acquaintances agree that this was an appropriate category for him. His book on *Human Potentialities* (1958) and his presidential address to the American Psychological Association, "The Freeing of Intelligence" (1945), contributed to the intellectual foundations of the humanistic movement.

Role Versus Person

Murphy's position at the intersection of the fields of social psychology and personality psychology is not unique. Over 3000 psychologists belonged to the Division of Personality and Social Psychology of the American Psychological Association in 1986. The two areas are perceived as closely related. Floyd Allport (Chapter Nine) had emphasized the learning of socially required behavior, corresponding to a social role, and much of this learning took the form of reinforced trials leading to conformity with adult requirements. However, as Freud demonstrated (Chapter Fourteen), the interaction of child and parent in this process often produces either personality eccentricities or outright pathology.

The existentialists took a strong stand against forced conformity, urging that children be free to develop their unique personalities. Most of the "humanistic" group—notably Maslow and Rogers—criticized the acquisition of social roles at the cost of personal development. More conservative psychologists have pointed out that true individualism leads to social chaos; the "rugged individualist" upsets the smooth functioning of social interaction by refusing to behave in accordance with role prescriptions.

The humanist criticism of social conformity is that it leads to the formation of a "mask" (compare Jung's *persona*) which is not an authentic representation of the "real" personality. Certainly some social practices merit this criticism. Decades ago, "the man in the gray flannel suit" epitomized the conformist, the person who lost individuality in gaining group acceptance. William James (Chapter Six) had pointed out how business molds the behavior of employees. Recently women aspiring to executive jobs have been advised to "dress for power". Social behavior involves much mechanized behavior which may be perceived as stifling individual expression.

Erving Goffman (1959) pointed out that many individuals engage in "impression management," that is, voluntarily pretended to attributes not spontaneously present. An example might be that of Skinner (Chapter Eleven) whose autobiography presented a view of his rigorous time scheduling, and which he later conceded to be a pose. Others develop styles in speaking, "ingratiating," and suppression of emotions as ways of making a desired impression on persons in the interaction. This kind of behavior is obviously compatible with the humanists' insistence on self-actualization or self-enhancement; a skill may be acquired in order to present a suitable "mask" to one's friends and associates.

It is this emphasis on appearances as opposed to realities that the humanists have criticized. Thus we observed the rise of nondirective therapy, in which the individual is encouraged to recognize his or her "real" self; similar are the "encounter groups," T-groups, sensitivity training, and so on, in which masks are discarded—sometimes ripped off by harsh critics. That these manipulations produce changes in observed behavior is pretty well established; the duration of the changes is not. Follow-up studies are rare, but the trend is toward forgetting the learning that occurred in the group session and regressing to former behavior patterns.

Unfortunately, the advice to cast off the mask of a social role and conformity behavior became an excuse, in many instances, to free the id from restraints and to foster infantile, pleasure-principle behavior. It is difficult to assess the net outcome of these social changes; perhaps, on the whole, they have been beneficial. Sheldon Korchin (1976), a clinical psychologist, commented:

> The encounter movement started . . . as a protest against the growing sense of a loss of a sense of psychological community in contemporary America. At its best it is a groping toward new social institutions and new life styles to replace those which no longer serve our profound needs for intimacy and community. At its worst it perverts and cheapens those needs . . . In a time of deteriorating social values, it may also represent a frenzied quest for individual pleasure and indulgence which serves as an escape from confronting the true problems. (p. 422)

Industrial Effects   The humanistic movement has also had an impact on industrial-organizational psychology. Douglas McGregor (1960) adapted some of Maslow's ideas to the working environment with his "Theory X" and "Theory Y." Theory X represented the traditional managerial ideology, which depicted workers as lazy and irresponsible; Theory Y proposed that workers will channel energy into work that they enjoy, and where they have a chance to participate in decisions that influence working conditions and supervision.

McGregor pointed out that industrial executives rarely characterize themselves as lazy and irresponsible; they reserve such adjectives for descriptions of workers. Further, he said that workers resent such labels, and that the antagonism makes industrial relations more, not less, difficult.

There is some evidence that a switch to Theory Y thinking in specific companies has been followed by better cooperation, less wastage, fewer strikes, and more profitability. Other executives prefer the ego satisfactions of dominance and arbitrary decision-making power to the risky situation of participatory management.

Can Humanism Be Scientific?

The five authors reviewed in this chapter—Maslow, Rogers, Allport, Murphy and May—would insist that humanistic psychology can be scientific, but on its own terms. These terms include a preservation of the complexity of the stimulus environment and a provision for complexity in responses. This stipulation may make research more difficult, but we have plenty of examples from other sciences that with progress goes difficulty (momentary thought about cyclotrons and orbiting laboratories will confirm this). Further progress may depend on adapting methods like William Stephenson's Q-sort or Gordon Allport's idiographic universe to comparing the structure of one uniquely defined personality with that of another. Computers make possible the construction of models mapping the cognitive-affective space of an individual in three dimensions (Lawson, 1978). The work of Milton Rokeach (1973) on beliefs and value structures may also lead to methodological innovations useful in this area.

Scientific harmony will not be furthered by exuberant claims by humanists such a that of Shaffer (1978) that "the world is seen freshly, perhaps akin to the experience of the very young child before he has acquired the rudiments of language" (p. 153). The innocence of childhood may be admirable, but its intellectual comprehension leaves something to be desired. Scientific psychology will not be benefited by a regression to childish cognitions.

CHAPTER 18

The Neobehaviorists

The mechanistic and analytical schools of psychology provoked opposition and alternative theories. Titchener's structuralism led to functionalism (a small deviation) and Gestalt (a major change from the emphasis on sensations). Watsonian behaviorism not only led to more sophisticated versions, as in the work of Hull and of Skinner, but also pushed some psychologists into approval of the "consciousness" systems: structuralism and Gestalt. Hull and Skinner, in turn, set off a movement that I have called *humanistic psychology* to emphasize personality and complex cognitive processes. Orthodox Freudianism spawned neoanalytic theories that shifted psychodynamics from a purely biological base to an environmental approach.

It would be nice for the historian if these developments had taken place neatly, one after the other, in a visible sequence. Unfortunately, human beings operate in less predictable ways. The foundations of what I call *neobehaviorism* antedate Clark Hull's most sophisticated publications. These foundations were laid by E. C. Tolman and his students.

Neobehaviorism, as it is conceptualized here, is a fusion of concepts from Watsonian behaviorism with conscious processes, primarily derived from Gestalt theory. Such ideas as intentions, stimulus learning, expectancy, and planning had been rejected by J. B. Watson, Max Meyer, and A. P. Weiss. In their wish to banish consciousness completely, they shut off any utilization of conscious processes in human behavior.

When Tolman published his major theoretical contribution, *Purposive Behavior in Animals and Men* (1932), he challenged two taboos of the period. One was the concept of purpose, which had been officially banned by mistaken Darwinians who saw purpose as a mystical concept associated with instinct and thus as misleading. The second was the rejection of consciousness, which Watson had advocated so persuasively. Tolman sought to reinstate purpose as a feature of behavior, and to insert conscious processes into equations for predicting behavior. The functionalists had tried to mix conscious with behavioral concepts, without much success. Neobehaviorism, in the last half of the twentieth century, has been more successful.

Edward Chace Tolman

The reunification of conscious and behavioral psychology received its first major push from Edward Chace Tolman (1886–1959). Tolman wrote that in his early years, he was intrigued by Watson's evangelistic behaviorism, and he expressed reservations mainly about Watson's speculative neurology, pointing out that hiding the determinants of action in cortical synapses differs from Titchener's study of consciousness only in replacing one set of unknowns with another. On the other hand, Tolman laid himself open to somewhat the same criticism with his concepts of implicit processes such as expectancies and intentions.

Tolman called these concepts "intervening variables" and asserted that logic supported their use if they could be anchored to observable data. Hull, we note, accepted the intervening-variable idea from Tolman and likewise claimed to validate such operations by measurable effects of observable behavior (See Figure 10.1).

Curiously enough, Watson had foreshadowed the Tolman position. In 1913, he wrote, "If you will grant the behaviorist the right to use consciousness in the same way that other natural sciences employ it—that is, without making consciousness a special object of observation, you have granted all that my thesis requires." But he did not follow up on his own idea and, in fact, became more rigidly opposed to any insertion of conscious data into his predictions. Because Hull and Skinner accepted this aspect of Watsonian doctrine, American psychology was dominated by mechanistic thinking for several decades.

Biography

Tolman once commented that his family background included a Puritan tradition of hard work and a Quaker tradition of plain living and high thinking. His career choice was affected at least to some extent by sibling rivalry. His older brother, Richard (later a renowned physicist), preceded Edward through high school and the undergraduate program at MIT, leaving behind him an academic record that Edward felt he could not match. Thus, after earning a degree in electrical engineering, Edward transferred to Harvard University for graduate study in psychology. He received a doctorate in psychology from Harvard in 1915 and, after three years at Northwestern University, moved to the University of California at Berkeley, where he spent the rest of his life.

Before finishing his graduate studies, Tolman spent some time in Ger-

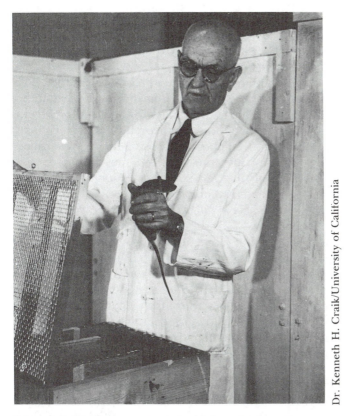

Dr. Kenneth H. Craik/University of California

Edward C. Tolman, a systematic thinker who incorporated conscious events as responses into his theoretical
system

many, where he met with Kurt Koffka and other noted psychologists.
He was also influenced somewhat by Hugo Münsterberg at Harvard, so
he was well informed regarding the German traditions in psychology.
Besides Münsterberg, Tolman worked with William McDougall, who
stressed the importance of purpose and of instincts in human behavior,
and his thesis adviser, E. B. Holt, who had adopted a vigorously behavioristic position. (As American universities began to break with the Germanic tradition of one professor per department, and with the authoritarian control of the younger faculty by the professor, students began to
be exposed to a variety of viewpoints and to perceive themselves as free
to pick and choose among faculty theorists.)

It is not clear just when Tolman met Kurt Lewin, but he documented
various points of agreement with Lewin's field theory. One important
terminological borrowing was the concept of *valence,* in the sense of

Koffka's *demand character;* Tolman used this term for the attractive or repelling quality of external objects and persons. Tolman also adopted the term *cognitive map* from Lewin to identify the quasi-perceptual outcome of many forms of learning.

By 1922, Tolman's disappointment with Watson had reached the point where Tolman called for a "nonphysiological behaviorism," a position he never abandoned. In this respect, he anticipated Skinner, although in most respects the two differed markedly on theoretical issues. Tolman sharpened Watson's "implicit movements" by devising the class he called "intervening variables," factors operating between the reception of a stimulus and the occurrence of an overt response. Skinner, of course, never accepted this as a legitimate psychological concept.

When Tolman's *Purposive Behavior in Animals and Men* appeared in 1932, many critics hailed it as a new and refreshing approach, but others wrote harshly of the neologisms coined by Tolman, such as *sign-gestalt-readiness, discriminanda,* and *manipulanda.* The book established Tolman's status as a major theorist, and he was elected president of the American Psychological Association in 1937, only five years after the book's publication.

Tolman was a large and genial man who inspired unusual devotion among his students. However, he discouraged them from becoming "disciples" of his system. He played a major part in the development of the Berkeley program as one of the best in America for scientific psychology.

Tolman's Quaker tradition may have received its most conspicuous expression immediately after World War II, when anti-Communist hysteria spread across legislatures, newspapers, and universities. The Board of Regents of the University of California ordered every faculty member to sign an oath denying any Communist affiliations, beliefs, or acquaintances. The Berkeley faculty (like those on the other University of California campuses) complained bitterly about this attempt to coerce belief systems, but most signed the oath on the last permissible day. Tolman and a few others led a successful legal and publicity battle against the requirement of an oath, which they finally won after several years. It was remarkable that Tolman did not allow personal bitterness to influence his way of conducting the campaign, and as Crutchfield (1961) wrote in his obituary of Tolman, "It is a fitting tribute to the dignity and integrity with which Tolman waged this struggle that in 1959 the Regents . . . conferred upon him the honorary LL.D. degree." (p. 140).

The Theory

Like most theories, Tolman's ideas evolved over time. I can sketch only some of the key concepts in the 1932 volume and a few modifications that appeared later; specifically, I will select those changes that show Tolman's evolution from being a behaviorist to being a neobehaviorist.

The first debate arose over Tolman's use of the concept of *purpose.*

Biologists in general objected to the idea of purpose as it related to sub-human behavior on the grounds that these animals could not foresee future situations and merely behaved in a deterministic fashion (i.e., their behavior was determined by the past, not the future). Weiss (1929) had suggested (see Chapter Nine) that the movement of a drop of water from the clouds to the earth's surface, to streams and lakes, and so ulti-mately to the ocean, defined purpose for him. Tolman argued that "im-mediate purposivism" included such behaviors as a rat searching for food, and that this concept had no implication of anthropomorphizing (of at-tributing human capacities to lower animals). Similarly, if human beings persist over years in a course of action (such as graduate study in psy-chology), a concept of purpose seems indispensable to understanding the behavior. There are simply not enough supportive stimuli and inter-mediate rewards to explain long-term projects that are carried through to completion. Thus, Tolman concluded, the Watson–Weiss theory was inadequate to either human or animal behavior.

Tolman was also more concerned with *motivation* than Watson or Weiss. "Physiological quiescences or disturbances" initiate restless activity in an-imals and humans. More precisely, disturbance starts action, and quies-cence ends it. The ultimate reinforcement is thus physiological quies-cence, a view shared by Hull and Freud. Tolman, however, shifted focus from the interior of the organism to the outside environment. *Incentives* (valences) guide behavior and terminate a sequence of efforts. One tries to reach a positive valence and to escape from a negative valence. There is, however, a hierarchy of incentives, in that some will elicit more effort and persistence than others.

Cognition, Tolman held, is an important part of the motivational pro-cess. The organism cognizes (perceives) potential goal objects and also the paths and barriers to be traversed. In a specified environment, such as a maze, the animal forms *goal expectancies* that can be tested by objec-tive methods. There is also evidence that rats can develop a *cognitive map* of a maze or other obstacle course. Objects that must be dealt with in the course of achieving a goal are known as *discriminanda* (items which must be discriminated); as Koffka and Lewin pointed out, learning in-volves, at least in part, identifying the parts of the environment that must be acted on. (Skinner used to rub food on the pedal in his lever-pressing experiments, so that the rat would become active in the vicinity of the pedal; this would increase the probability that the operant, press-ing the pedal, would occur.) Some discriminanda only serve as guide-posts, such as the lights in a discrimination box. Others must be manip-ulated, like the string in Thorndike's puzzle box or the lever that opened the door in Guthrie's version of the puzzle box.

Sensory Learning   The first major theoretical innovation in Tolman's theorizing involved sensory learning. Watson and his colleagues had as-serted the indispensability of a response: all learning conformed to the

S-R formula. Tolman argued that another type of learning, abbreviated as *S-S learning*, was important. In this regard, he was reviving the British associationists' thesis that all learning is an association of ideas, as opposed to an association of responses. S-S learning had actually been demonstrated already in Pavlov's laboratory, specifically in relating a neutral stimulus to a conditioned stimulus, so that the previously neutral item evoked the conditioned response.

Tolman's discussion of the acquisition of S-S associations differs from that of Koffka mainly in that Tolman minimized the importance of the innate "organization" of the stimulus field. Tolman held that repeated contiguity could establish a "sign-gestalt," that is, a kind of expectancy that, given A, the complex ABC would appear.

The term *discriminandum* exemplifies another aspect of sensory learning. To cope with an environmental problem, the organism must first identify the significant stimuli to be dealt with. Some drinking fountains operate with a hand control (wheel or lever), but some require pressure on a foot pedal. Until the "discriminandum" (the thing that must be discriminated) has been identified, the thirsty person gets no water.

In the foregoing example, the pedal could also be treated as a "manipulandum" (the thing that must be manipulated). Some discriminanda are not manipulanda; a signal light in a Skinner box may merely indicate that rewards will be available if the lever is pressed. Tolman found it convenient to distinguish the two, but in most instances, they coincide.

Place Learning A special version of sensory learning is place learning. Rats were allowed to obtain food by following a circuitous route to the goal. Then the familiar path was blocked, and the animals were allowed to choose from a number of runways. A large percentage chose the path that pointed to where the goal had been, disregarding the paths that started in the direction of the training maze. Tolman interpreted this result as evidence that the animal had learned not responses of running and turning, but a spatial relationship.

Latent Learning Tolman proposed a distinction between learning and performance (Hull apparently adopted this idea from Tolman). He, unlike Hull, postulated learning without reinforcement. This variety of learning he called "latent" because it was not revealed until a reinforcement was added to the situation. Tolman and Honzik (1930) allowed rats to explore a maze from start to finish for ten days. One group was fed in the goal box, immediately. The others were fed in their home cages, two hours later. As might be expected, Group II showed virtually no learning. However, on day 11, food was placed in the goal box for all animals. On Day 12, the Group II animals made fewer errors than those reinforced for all eleven days. The authors interpreted this result as evidence that learning took place on Days 1–10, but that there was no incentive to rush through the maze; when food was available, the animals made use of their latent learning to go through with virtually no errors.

The Cognitive Map   Although the concept of the cognitive map does not appear in the 1932 book, it was later (Tolman, 1948) added to expand the coverage of sensory learning. In this article, Tolman made an explicit contrast between Watson's metaphor of a "complicated telephone switchboard" and his own metaphor of the central nervous system as being "more like a map control room. The stimuli . . . are not connected by just simple one-to-one switches to the outgoing responses . . . but are worked over and elaborated." Tolman borrowed not only Lewin's concept of the cognitive map but also Köhler's isomorphism; Tolman assumed that the map details inside the organism paralleled the field relationships in the external environment.

Response Learning   Tolman did not ignore the importance of response learning. Indeed, he defined his sensory learning constructs in such a way that they could be related to overt responses; this, he felt, justified calling his theory behavioristic.

The most important development in this area was vicarious trial-and-error. Tolman called attention to the behavior of his rats "running back and forth" in a maze as if seeking for clues to the correct turn. Krechevsky (1932), later known as David Krech, christened this tentative incomplete behavior as "hypotheses"; that is, he suggested that the rat was checking on an expectancy that "turning left will get me to the food." Still later, Karl Muenzinger (1938) translated Krech's "hypothesis" into "vicarious trial-and-error" (VTE). This almost reunified Tolman with Watson, as the latter had postulated incomplete or tentative movements as a replacement for the conscious planning of an action. Tolman did not see it this way; he actually became more "cognitive" and less response-oriented in his later years.

Molecular Versus Molar Responses   Tolman objected to Watson's "muscle twitchism." This criticism was not entirely fair; in his research, Watson used maze learning, puzzle solving (rats digging through sawdust for food), conditioned emotional responses, and so on. On the other hand, in his theorizing, Watson did try to reduce behavior to a single stimulus connected to a single response. The difference from Tolman is much like the difference drawn by Weiss between biophysical and biosocial responses. Tolman was impatient with the notion that one could identify a specific receptor–connector–effector link. He emphasized that he was studying molar behavior, behavior organized with reference to achieving some environmental consequence (much as in Skinner's notion that an operant is an act that changes the relation of the organism to the environment.)

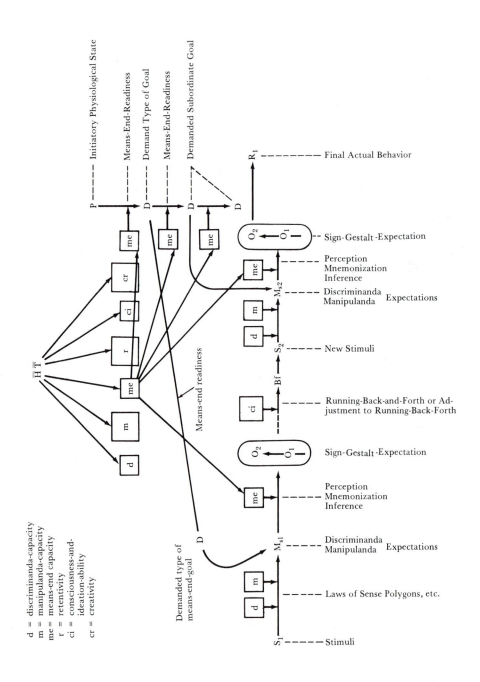

d = discriminanda-capacity
m = manipulanda-capacity
me = means-end capacity
r = retentivity
ci = consciousness-and-ideation-ability
cr = creativity

In general usage, the molar–molecular debate is one facet of the controversy over the analysis of behavior (or consciousness) into minute components. Tolman insisted that psychologists do not need physiology as an explanatory realm, and he never engaged in neurological speculation.

Summary on Tolman

Tolman provided us with a schematic drawing (Figure 18.1) analogous to that drawn later by Osgood for Hull's behavior model (Figure 10.1). In Figure 18.1, Tolman attempted to portray the interaction of the environment and the organism to produce behavior.

The diagram is unique in that it incorporates capacity along with other variables. Discriminanda capacity is, of course, sensory, and manipulanda capacity is motor. Retentivity is an essential, and it is probable that individual differences in these variables affect learning, as well as the use of learned activities in more complex processes such as planning.

Any specific act involves moving from left to right through the diagram, with the exception that a motive (an initiatory physiological state) is shown on the right. This state activates a means–end readiness (i.e., a readiness to engage in some act that may reduce the physiological tension). This acts on the perception of the environment (discriminanda and expectations); although Tolman was not explicit on this, it can be assumed that this process sensitizes the organism to some stimuli and blocks out others. A "sign-gestalt-expectation" is formed; the organism anticipates that some specified set of stimuli will provide an opportunity to satisfy the motive. Various cognitive processes may occur in discovering this behavioral opportunity (hypotheses, perceiving, and inference), all of which finally eventuate in a molar act.

The skeleton view presented in this diagram is considerably more complex than that in the Osgood–Hull diagram. This is realistic; Tol-

---

FIGURE 18.1   Summary of Tolman's "Purposive Behavior" Theory

In the upper left corner Tolman listed various capacities which are different from one organism to another, and which are indispensable for learning. In the upper right is the sequence of events in a specific learning task: drive (e.g., hunger), readiness to respond, expectancy as to goal demanded, and subsidiary goals if relevant. Across the base line, from left, are the stimulus situation, rules governing sensory information, perception and inferences, expectancy as to the behavior most likely to lead to the goal, and so on to the actual behavior. *(From Tolman, E. C., 1932,* Purposive Behavior in Animals and Men, *p. 407, Figure 72, by permission of Irvington Publishers)*

man's theory is significantly more complex than is Hull's. It has actually been simplified here; feedback from VTEs and changes of location play a part, and other complicating influences are ignored. The importance of incentives is underestimated in the diagram; the "demanded type of goal" may influence the choice of environments and actions. On the whole, the diagram represents Tolman's theory with fair accuracy.

It is interesting that Tolman even made a place for sensory psychology as taught by Titchener (e.g., laws of sense polygons and psychophysics) and Gestalt formulations in this formula. The diagram is thus a virtual summary of psychology according to Tolman.

Tolman's Social Psychology

Stimulated by World War II, Tolman (1942) applied his "purposive behaviorism" to the psychology of international conflict. The treatment was derivative of Dollard and associates' book, *Frustration and Aggression* (1939). Tolman's view is both more systematic and more far-reaching than the Dollard volume (see Chapter Ten).

Tolman elaborated on the role of prior learning in determining the course of current learning. This is another feature often ignored by his predecessors, and also by Hull and Skinner. Tolman suggested (Figure 18.2) that the individual comes to a social situation with prior learned tactics for self-assertion, and with membership in various groups with associated collective techniques for dealing with blockages of behavioral intentions.

There is more than a trace of Freud in this analysis. Tolman did not hesitate to incorporate repression in his schema, as well as defense mechanisms (note, for example, that aggression may be inverted into oversolicitude for others, or into self-punishment, which are varieties of reaction formation). More often aggression is directed outward, as in crime, scapegoating, domineering over inferiors, and so on.

Tolman proposed that some of the dynamic for war comes from individuals, in the displacement of aggression from domestic frustrations, and that some comes from groups; the individual members must learn techniques of attacking the enemy. There is no place here for an instinct of pugnacity. An optimistic note is found in the diagram: Tolman suggested that we might reduce the frequency of wars by a federation of nations into some international organization.

Determinism from Above   Tolman also specified that determinism may operate "from above" rather than from elementary processes. Thus a person with a strong habit of attending church on Sunday is more likely to reject an invitation to a Sunday morning round of golf than is a person without a church-going habit. This principle can also extend to verbal and mental processes: A confirmed pacifist will vote against increased

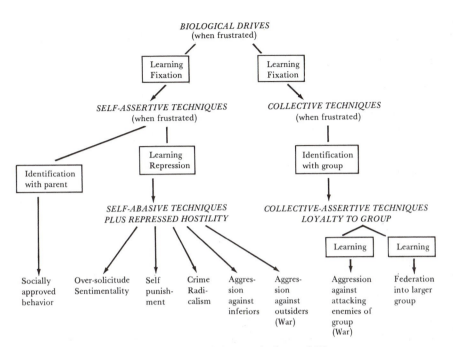

FIGURE 18.2   Tolman's Analysis of the Psychology of War

The ultimate motive is placed in biology but not in an instinct of pugnacity; rather, it is a biological need which is frustrated. The person learns
techniques of coping with frustration, under the influence of parents,
peer groups, and national institutions. Aggression may be directed
against individuals (crime, cruelty) or against groups (ethnic hostilities,
national wars).   *(From Tolman, E. C., 1942, Drives Toward War, Figure 2,
p. 74, by permission of Prentice-Hall, Inc., Englewood Cliffs, New Jersey)*

military expenditures, even if these are advocated by a friend. For a
skilled baseball player, the demands of the situation determine whether
to throw to first, second, third, or home base, although each of these
moves is of roughly equal strength in terms of Hull's hierarchy concept.
The specific response (throwing) is determined by the context.

Moderator Variables and Individual Differences   Tolman broke with the
Watsonian tradition in another way. He hypothesized the operation of
intraorganismic factors that moderate the "main effects" of the stimulus
situation. In Figure 18.3, these factors are designated as *H, A, T,* and *E*
(heredity, age, training, and endocrine-physiological states). In effect,
Tolman asserted that the level of these four variables could modify the
usual course of stimulus–central-processing–response. For heredity, he
could cite the excellent animal studies of the inheritance of some capac-

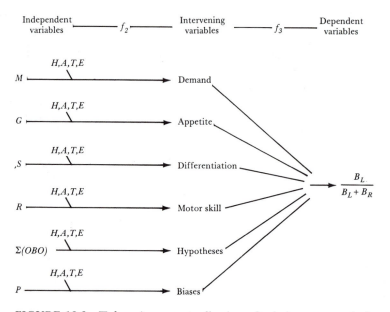

FIGURE 18.3   Tolman's conceptualization of relations among independent variables, intervening variables, and dependent variables.

M = maintenance schedule of animal
G = goal object
S = external stimulation
R = response repertoire of animal

H = heredity
A = age
T = prior training
E = endocrine or physiological variables

$\Sigma(OBO)$ = Hypotheses regarding correct turn
P = response biases
B_L = behavior of turning left
B_R = behavior of turning right
*(From Tolman, 1938, p. 16. Reprinted by permission of the American Psychologi-
cal Association.)*

ity that affects the speed of maze learning. The importance of age and
of prior training needs no comment. The addition of the endocrine-
physiological variable reflects developments of the time in the study of
such factors as thyroxin and testosterone, which might and often did
influence the speed of learning.

What is particularly important to the student of psychological theory
is that this is a major break in the millennial tradition that all laws apply
to all human beings regardless of status. Tolman forged a link between

nomothetic psychology (the laws of universal applicability) and the psychology of individual differences. This is not intended to depreciate the work of J. M. Cattell and the researchers on intelligence and personality variables; consideration will be given to their work in Chapter Twenty. However, up to this time, the major theorists had placidly ignored the relevance of the individual-difference theories and research to general psychology. Tolman set a standard that, although not uniformly imitated, has prompted more attention to the interaction of moderator variables with general laws of behavior.

Tolman represented a convergence of various historical trends. We remember William James's thoughtful remark that a blind instinct is no longer blind after one encounter with a stimulating environment. Tolman took this remark and converted it into the idea of expectancy: One anticipates that Act A will lead to Consequence B. Tolman (1932) reacted to Descartes's "anthropocentric predicament" by asserting that he would assume a substantial similarity of human to animal psychology: "I shall continue to go ahead imagining how, *if I were a rat,* I would behave as a result of such and such a demand combined with such and such an appetite." Margaret Washburn had advocated this approach to animal behavior, and even Titchener (1911) conceded that if one wanted to study animal behavior, one should "try as far as possible to put himself in the place of the animal . . . and then, from the character of his human consciousness, he attempts—always bearing in mind the limit of the animal's nervous system—to reconstruct the animal's consciousness" (p. 31).

Tolman's Students

Like Titchener and Hull and Skinner, Tolman attracted a group of outstanding students, among them D. T. Campbell, Henry Gleitman, Julian Hochberg, and David Krech. Yet there was no Tolman school, no sign-Gestalt system. Campbell (1979) asked somewhat ruefully how it happened that Tolman's theories had been explored only by those remaining at Berkeley; doctorates who wandered off to other institutions also chose other theoretical models to explore. As I have suggested earlier, this probably resulted from Tolman's unassuming modesty and his preference for encouraging students to follow their own hunches rather than clarifying minor details of his theories. Tolman was modest about his own achievements, and he would never have attempted to coerce students to follow in his footsteps.

Although Tolman was elected president of the APA in 1937, it cannot be truthfully said that his theories were highly respected until after World War II. The changes in the Zeitgeist, including much more concern about social and clinical psychology, created a situation more favorable to the complex, integrated perspective he offered.

Julian B. Rotter

The first evidence of this receptivity to "purposive behaviorism" after World War II is found in the success of *Social Learning and Clinical Psychology* (1954) by Julian B. Rotter (1916–   ). The title provides clues to two important developments of the time. First, Rotter wrote about social learning, not laboratory learning. Although he did not ignore the vast accumulation of experimental data on learning by animals and humans, his emphasis shifted from white rats and pigeons to human beings. Second, Rotter shifted the focus from laboratory to clinic; he was responding to the cries for help from the returning veterans of the war, whose consciousness and behavior had been tragically disrupted by the international conflict.

Rotter was born in 1916 and earned a doctorate at Indiana University in 1941. It is safe to assume that this was a heavily behavioristic climate. Clinical psychology had not, in 1941, become a major focus of graduate training as it has been from about 1950 to the present. Social psychology was barely recognized in 1941. Rotter, then, represented an about-face that, in the absence of further evidence, was generated by the demands of the society and the hospitals after the war. At any rate, he picked up concepts from Tolman and from Lewin and welded them into a new theoretical approach.

Social Learning Theory

The first point of distinction in Rotter's work is that he propounded a *social* learning theory. Note that the work of Watson, Hull, and Skinner (and even Tolman) had emphasized one-individual learning. That is, learning occurred within one rat or one dog or one child, but not in interaction with another of the same or a different species. Rotter held that most of the important learnings in life are learnings from parents, from teachers, and from peers. He thus decided to focus on an interacting pair rather than on an isolated person. It was particularly true with respect to clinical psychology, then dominated by Freud and some neoanalysts, that the crucial events were child–parent, male–female, and similar interactions. Very few people learn nonsense syllables or acquire conditioned eye-blink reflexes. A *relevant* theory of learning had to be one applicable to human interactions.

Rotter's theory, like Tolman's, was primarily a theory of learning. He began with the concept of a "meaningful environment," which can be taken as a close approximation of Koffka's behavioral environment, Lewin's life space or Rogers' phenomenal field. It is the environment as experienced by the responding organism; it may correspond closely to the physical environment, although both errors of perception and incomplete information may result in a meaningful environment that is separated to some extent from the physical world (Rotter, 1954).

Rotter adopted from Hull the practice of announcing his postulates and then trying either to relate these to existing empirical research or to suggest suitable research to test the postulate. His first postulate was the one just cited, namely, that behavior is a function of the meaningful environment. He could, of course, point to Gestalt studies and to the work of Tolman and his colleagues in demonstrating discrepancies between the physical world and the apparent determinants of behavior.

A second postulate seems to have derived from Tolman and Skinner. Rotter announced that biological processes need not be considered in his analysis of behavior. Although granting that something happens in the brain during a response, he held that nothing of psychological significance could be derived from speculation about neurological bases or physiological processes.

Rotter's third, and central, postulate was that the learning with which psychological theory is concerned is *social* learning, that is, learning in a social context (home, school, or work) in response to social stimuli (e.g., parental praise and reproof on teacher instructions). Although not arguing that animal experiments are useless, Rotter espoused the discontinuity theory by insisting that human behavior does not necessarily obey the same general laws that had been induced from animal studies. Note that this goes beyond Tolman's theoretical structure; Tolman might have agreed in principle, but in practice, he held that animal behavior and human behavior are subject to the same laws.

Actually, Rotter's position reminds us of the concept of *biosocial* response as proposed by Weiss (see Chapter Nine). Weiss had been concerned with a class of behavior that determined a person's status in society. Reading, playing the piano, manufacturing commodities—any of these and comparable activities have an impact on how one is perceived by one's peers. Although Weiss did not make the extrapolation to the idea that most learning is also social, it seems logical enough. One does not acquire any such responses except by imitation of another person or by instruction. Only a microscopic fragment of social behavior is truly developed within the person, without external stimulation.

Rotter pushed this third postulate further. One does not react solely to what another person does. Sally is concerned not only about her feelings for John, but also by her perception of his feelings for her. The employee is influenced by what he thinks the employer is planning. Two rivals watch each other's moves for evidence to support a prediction about what is likely to happen next. Rotter was thus getting out of the laboratory into the everyday world. (Of course, this same phenomenon of guessing what the other intends goes on in the laboratory also; students are notorious for trying to outguess the psychological experimenter.)

Because our knowledge of the consciousness of the other is limited and often unverifiable, the possibility is left open that much of behavior will be determined by intraorganismic states, not by the objective stimuli beloved of Watson and Skinner. "Attribution theorists," who ascribe much of human behavior to the assumptions that one person makes about the attributes or intentions of another, have followed in Rotter's footsteps; the chief difference is that attribution theory is a theory about perceiving, but as perceived reality determines behavior, there is no conflict of theories here.

Role of Reinforcement   Rotter accepted the view of Hull and Skinner regarding the essential status of reinforcement. Generally speaking, Rotter followed Skinner on this point. The child who behaves cooperatively in nursery school and is rewarded for doing so will show an increased probability of such responses on later occasions. From this, one can deduce the importance of planned reinforcements of young children for doing chores, playing peacefully, helping other children, and so on, much as Skinner promulgated in his utopia, *Walden Two* (1948).

Surprisingly, Rotter did not explicitly recognize the tendency of humans to impose their own idiosyncratic perceptions on external events. Parents sometimes reward a child for being cooperative and the child interprets their action to mean a reward for not making noise. The work of behavior modifiers (clinicians using operant conditioning techniques) reveals many instances in which the parent's perception of an interaction and the child's view of the same event are dramatically different. Success in this field depends heavily on the perceptive diagnosis of exactly what behavior is being rewarded in what way.

Expectancy   The role of feedback has been increasingly stressed in recent theorizing. Watson and Hull had recognized only internal feedback (the reduction of homeostatic tensions); Skinner emphasized external feedback (the changing relation of person to environment). Rotter adopted this latter view and extended it much further in time than Skinner would. He noted that much of everyday behavior (e.g., studying by a college student) is energized by an expectation of reinforcement at some remote time. Feedback at periodic intervals (like semester grades) provides what Hull would have called secondary reinforcement; more important for Rotter, it reinforces the expectation that the ultimate goal will be achieved.

Rotter deviated from Skinner in another respect. Skinner's dictum was that one reinforces a response; one does not reinforce a *person*. Rotter held that reinforcement for a response has a dual function: increasing the probability that the response will recur and increasing the person's evaluation of the self as competent. Essentially, Rotter paralleled the neoanalyst concept of ego strength: if a person develops a generalized expectancy of success, the self-evaluation will improve, and failure (if it occurs) will not be demoralizing. This notion will be expanded somewhat in the discussion of differences in personality in Chapter Twenty.

Expectancy, of course, is a two-way street. The pupil may expect to succeed, but the teacher may expect him or her to fail. If this teacher expectation is communicated, whether consciously or not, the behavior of the pupil will be less effective (Rosenthal, 1976.) Expectancies may also flow from subordinates to superiors. Factory workers who have been told that a given supervisor is a hard driver will generally observe evidence that supports their expectation.

The dynamics of behavior were treated almost entirely in terms of achieving an expected goal, rather than in terms of any physiological state. Rotter (1954) stated that "all goal-directed behavior may be considered to lead toward psychological homeostasis, satisfaction, or security" (p. 196). He did not, however, define "psychological homeostasis." By analogy, we can infer that a state of psychological equilibrium may be disturbed by some internal or external process, and that behavior will continue until the gap is closed between the expected and the perceived state of affairs. In that case, the term *homeostasis* could be defended.

Rotter's 1954 book and the substantial flow of research it triggered suggest that he played an important role in the move from "mature behaviorism" to neobehaviorism. Other psychologists have picked up his ideas and extended them even further.

Albert Bandura

A major contributor to the neobehaviorist tendency in psychological theorizing is Albert Bandura (1925–   ). He earned his Ph.D. degree at the University of Iowa; although he was majoring in clinical psychology, he found the general atmosphere to be favorable to Hull's brand of behaviorism, largely because of the presence of Kenneth W. Spense.

Although he is widely known for his work in behavior modification, Bandura developed a theoretical stance that is distinctly different from that of B. F. Skinner and his devotees who apply Skinnerian models to the elimination of undesirable behavior patterns. Bandura worked extensively with aggressive adolescents (mostly juvenile delinquents), phobias, and similar specific psychological maladjustments. He was elected president of the APA in 1974.

Theoretical Proposals

Bandura began his separation from traditional behaviorism by questioning the basis for conditioning. Mere contiguity was not enough, he concluded; a cognitive mediating process was involved. He was thus disposed to introduce a cognitive element into his theories about various aspects of human behavior. This trend may have arisen out of his specialization in clinical work; it was probably also influenced by his contacts with Robert R. Sears, director of the Iowa Child Welfare Research Station during part of Bandura's study at Iowa. There may also have been residuals from Kurt Lewin's stay at the Research Station, although Bandura and Lewin did not overlap their tenures there.

A prolific writer, Bandura published (with R. H. Walters) a book on *Adolescent Aggression* in 1959, and again with Walters, *Social Learning and Personality Development* (1963). At this point, he had already developed his individualistic approach to theory. His first deviation from orthodox behaviorism was in his emphasis on *modeling*. (In the nineteenth century, this was called *imitation*, but the term *imitation* fell on evil times, and when Bandura resuscitated the concept, he found it appropriate to use a new label.) Now, popular psychology has always held a brief for imitation in the origin of delinquency; "He fell into bad company," the saying goes, and "like father, like son" merged imitation and heredity as causes of behavior.

Actually, modeling was not an invention of Bandura. Mary Cover Jones (1924a), a student of John B. Watson, used modeling in her behavior change experiments. To eliminate a conditioned fear of a white rabbit, she placed the child (Peter) in a high chair with food, then brought the animal into the room. After some repetitions, Peter would eat with the rabbit nearby, and eventually with the rabbit on his chair. This was widely interpreted as proof that the food–rabbit combination would eliminate fear as the rabbit–noise combination had established it. What has generally been ignored is the fact that Jones also brought into the room children who were not afraid of the animal, petted it, carried it around, and so on. In principle, food alone might have worked; Bandura's work suggested that the fearless models alone might also have worked.

Bandura distinguished between live modeling and symbolic modeling. In the former, the model is a person present in the laboratory. In the latter, the model is usually a character in a movie, or occasionally, word–still-picture combinations. As might be guessed, "symbolic modeling is less powerful than live demonstrations of essentially the same behavior" (Bandura, 1969, p. 180). However, Bandura found that symbolic modeling could be made more effective by the inclusion of several different persons as models in the film, and perhaps by a variety of "threat" animals in the film. No doubt, the number of repetitions of the modeled stimulus would also be relevant.

Reinforcement   Bandura conceded that reinforcement facilitates the effect of a model on behavior. He differed explicitly with Skinner on the action of a reinforcer. As Figure 18.4 indicates, Skinner had—at least early in his career—treated reinforcement as "working backward" to increase the probability of repeating the response. Later Skinner modified

Reinforcement Theories

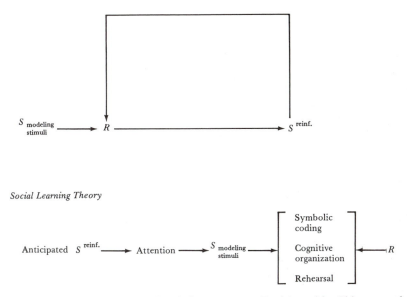

FIGURE 18.4   The Role of Reinforcement as Envisioned by Skinner and by Bandura

Skinner's reinforcement theory proposed that reinforcement works backward in time to "strengthen" a response. Bandura's social learning theory stresses a conscious variable, expectation of reinforcement, as focusing the organism's attention on the modeling stimuli, which are then classified and perhaps rehearsed mentally before the overt response. *(From Bandura, 1977, p. 38, reprinted by permission of Prentice-Hall, Inc., Englewood Cliffs, New Jersey)*

this position to say that the reinforcement affects "a class of responses" but never clarified how such a principle would operate. Bandura picked up from Tolman the idea of expectancy; in the figure, the "anticipated" reinforcer attracts the person's attention to the modeling stimulus. This may be followed by coding or rehearsal, leading to the desired act.

Conscious Awareness   Although Bandura called himself a behaviorist, he did not hesitate to incorporate conscious awareness into his behavior analysis. Figure 18.5 shows his comparison of different theories in their treatment of awareness as a variable in changing behavior. In this usage, the nonmediational theory (Skinner, 1953; Thorndike, 1931) admits awareness after the fact and without any function. The independent-systems theory (Verplanck, 1962) is like psychophysical parallelism (i.e.,

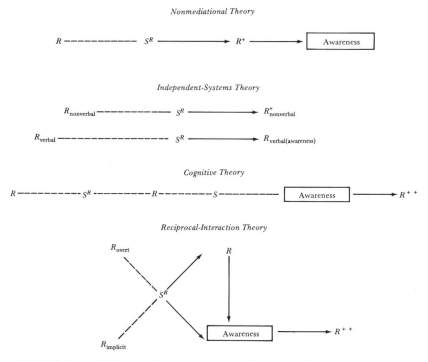

FIGURE 18.5   Different Ways of Conceptualizing the Relation between Awareness and Overt Responses

For identification of the theories represented, see text.   *(From Bandura, 1969, p. 565, Figure 9-1, reprinted by permission of Holt, Rinehart and Winston)*

the verbal and nonverbal chains run off without affecting each other). Cognitive theory Bandura ascribed to Donald Dulany (1962) and Charles Spielberger and L. D. DeNike, (1966); this theory assigns a role to awareness in selecting among responses alternatives. Why Bandura did not cite Tolman in this category is a mystery. The fourth theory, reciprocal interaction theory (Farber, 1963) assumed that overt and implicit responses interact, again a feature of Tolman's theory. Without explicitly saying so, Bandura seems to have put himself in the reciprocal interaction group. In this formulation, "hypotheses" are formed. Correct hypotheses lead to successful behavior; incorrect hypotheses are extinguished. Bandura also pointed out that verbal instructions may speed up learning, by directing attention and emphasizing certain hypotheses. This is a bit encouraging; some college professors had begun to doubt that their verbal efforts had led to improved learning.

Bandura also assigned a prominent place in his theory to attention.

Wundt and Titchener had discussed attention at length, and Köhler had suggested that most formal learning would never occur without the instruction to "pay attention." Everyday learning, of course, occurs without a verbal command to pay attention but is nonetheless dependent on attention. Witnesses to crimes rarely agree about what happened because they attended to different aspects of the event.

This explains why Bandura placed expectation of reinforcement ahead of attending in his time sequence. It also means that we must ascertain what kinds of reinforcement will be attractive to the person we wish to influence. At this point, the individual difference features recognized by Tolman ought to be incorporated into the Bandura formula.

Coding   As shown in Figure 18.4, Bandura suggested that the individual may engage in coding, organizing cognitions, and rehearsal. Coding may be important. An instructor modeling a particular behavior, such as psychotherapy, may need to be sure that the trainee codes the symbolic material appropriately. One does not use the same tactics with a belligerent adolescent as with an autistic child. The rule holds even more widely; certain behavior may be coded as "how to deal with an angry customer," while another may be "how to help a customer reach a decision." Unless the learner codes the situation correctly, unfortunate results may follow.

Most modeling therefore includes cognitive training as well as behavioral modification. Irwin Sarason and V. J. Ganzer (1969) noted that in their work with disadvantaged adolescents (modeling interviews for jobs and similar roles), the modeling was far more likely to be effective if it was immediately followed by a group discussion of just why the role should be played a certain way and how the imitator had failed to reproduce it. In other words, *conscious* examination of the behavior pattern made it more easily imitated.

Peripheral Versus Central Processes   Titchener, Watson, Hull, and Skinner had emphasized peripheral processes (physical stimuli, reception, muscular action, and feedback from the environment). The Gestalt and psychoanalytic theories emphasized central phenomena. As might be inferred from the preceding pages, Bandura occupied an intermediate position, being concerned with both sets of events. His basic interest was in changes in overt behavior, so he had to recognize peripheral determinants, but he also found evidence to support the importance of consciousness, coding, symbolic cues, and so on. On the whole, the central components got top billing. He wrote, "Theoretical formulations emphasizing peripheral mechanisms began to give way to cognitively oriented theories that explained behavior in terms of central processing of direct, vicarious and symbolic sources of information" (1977, p. 192). Conscious anticipation based on prior experience or on the nature of the immediate stimulus situation is the basic learning phenomenon.

Much of Bandura's writing seems to assume the operation of Festinger's cognitive dissonance. Bandura postulated the development of implicit standards of "good performance" and "poor performance," much as Rotter had. Failure to perform in accordance with the preferred norm initiates tension: "Perceived negative discrepancies between performance and standards create dissatisfactions that motivate corrective changes in behavior" (Bandura, 1977, p. 193). Koffka would call this "closure," the closing of a perceived gap between performance and the internalized norm of behavior.

Self-monitoring   As the term *imitation* from classical psychology has been replaced by *modeling,* so *introspection* has been replaced by *self-evaluation, self-observation,* or *self-monitoring.* The behaviorists who use the social learning approach (Rotter, Bandura, and Staats, especially) have abandoned the insistence on outside observers. The individual is perceived as competent to report on his or her own actions.

Bandura made a good point with regard to the Rogerian approach to improving the self-image by way of emphasizing achievement and success: What if the individual can't think of any cases in which he or she has achieved anything? "In many cases . . . unfavorable self-attitudes stem from behavioral deficits and are repeatedly reinforced through failure experiences occasioned by the person's inability to meet realistic culture expectations. . . . Here the primary concern must be with self-development rather than self-exploration" (Bandura, 1969, pp. 614–615). Thus, we first help the person develop some *successful* response patterns, then encourage self-evaluation.

Self-efficacy   Bandura introduced the term *self-efficacy* to label the individual's self-evaluation. He did not, however, offer an explicit definition of the self. From the context, one can infer that the self-image is crucial: if the person's perceptions of himself or herself in 'action are linked to unpleasant or punitive outcomes, conscious self-efficacy will be low.

It seems curious that neither Bandura nor Staats (who also advocated self-evaluation and self-reinforcement) mentioned Alfred Adler in their major writings. Bandura (1969) wrote that "expectations of *personal mastery* affect both initiation and persistence of coping behavior" (p. 193). He might well have added that such expectations are so widespread that they may be innate. Indeed, the assertion of dissonance effects suggests that most of us are constantly evaluating our own performance in comparison with the performance of others. This is one of the lines of evidence cited by Adler for his theory.

Other Features of Bandura's Theory   Although it was not a matter of major concern to Bandura, he took time out to criticize the Pavlovian conception of conditioning: "Originally, conditioning was assumed to result automatically from events occurring together in time. Closer examination revealed that it is in fact cognitively mediated". (1977, p. 67). This is perhaps too sweeping a statement. It is difficult to link cognitive mediation with a conditioned eye blink. On the other hand, Bandura has much empirical support for his view of conditioning anticipation: "A conditioned stimulus . . . often activates anticipatory responses that bear little resemblance to the unconditioned response. [See Figure 9.3] It would, therefore, seem more plausible to view conditioning outcomes as reflecting the operation of mediating mechanisms rather than the direct coupling of stimuli with responses evoked by other events" (1969, p. 444). An instance of this anticipatory responding was given earlier in this book (the discussion of the CR in Chapter Nine).

Desensitization and *counterconditioning* are aspects of the behavior therapy program advocated by Bandura. Desensitizing involved presenting the aversive stimulus (e.g., a live snake in a case of snake phobia) under carefully regulated conditions. Counterconditioning differs only in that the aversive stimulus is made the signal for a positive state of affairs (e.g. food, praise, or peer approval). As might be expected, Bandura proposed that these reinforcements be accompanied by a verbalization of the preferred course of action, thus establishing a symbolic behavior control for future occasions.

There can be no question that Bandura has had a significant impact on American psychology. By his ingenious merger of concepts involving consciousness with concepts of the more traditional behavioristic pattern, he has gone a considerable distance toward minimizing the gap between psychologists who define psychology as the study of experience and those who restrict it to the study of behavior. His work in sponsoring applications of these concepts has also served to increase communication between the clinical and personality-oriented psychologists on the "humanist" side with their laboratory-bound "scientific" colleagues.

Applications

Much of Bandura's theorizing has been tied intimately to quasi-clinical work on the modification of juvenile delinquency, the elimination of phobias, and so on. In these projects he has demonstrated the utility of modeling, especially symbolic modeling. Unemployed young men, for example, need to acquire some socialized skills in order to hope for success in applying for jobs. Bandura suggested that in many cases, aggression is the preferred mode of response to a frustration simply because the individual has no alternative responses to use. By instilling socially approved alternative behaviors, Bandura has had considerable success in reducing recidivism in such cases.

Efforts to apply the Bandura technique in institutions have been criticized on the grounds that the behavior modifiers have found it necessary to impose some degree of deprivation before the reinforcers available will be effective. Thus an adequate but boring diet may lay the groundwork for using food incentives for prosocial behavior. Similarly, deprivation of TV and similar privilages may cause the individual to value them more highly and so to modify her or his actions in order to win these reinforcements.

The Bandura studies on phobias have also been criticized on the grounds that many individuals appear to be cured in the laboratory but relapse in an everyday environment. The theoretical issue here is generalization. If the "tolerant" behavior to a snake stimulus is practiced only in the laboratory, it may not generalize to a wilderness setting. Bandura has recognized this problem, but it is not always clear just how one maximizes the generalization of a new response.

Bandura has also expressed concern with industrial psychology, although apparently not to the extent of practicing it. He noted that Skinner recommended immediate reinforcement to industrial workers because it motivates increased production. Bandura (1977) saw a potential societal maladjustment in this policy of piecework payments: "When industrialists commanded exclusive power, they paid workers at a piecerate basis and hired and fired them at will. As workers gained coercive economic strength through collective action, they were able to negotiate guaranteed wages on a daily, weekly, monthly, and eventually on an annual basis" (p. 210). In effect, Bandura was arguing that persons in positions of power should not use knowledge of psychological principles to exploit others.

In a later article, Bandura (1982) noted that "studies of social and political activism indicate that detrimental conditions prompt forceful action, not in those who have lost hope, but in the more able members whose efforts at social and economic betterment have met with at least some success" (p. 143). Clearly his concept of behaviorism covers substantially more territory than those of any of his predecessors except Skinner.

Arthur W. Staats

Another variant on neobehaviorism has been promulgated by Arthur W. Staats (1924–   ). Staats, who received his Ph.D. in psychology at the University of California at Los Angeles in 1956, has published extensively both on behavioral theory and on child psychology. His theory differs from that of Bandura and Rotter sufficiently to justify its being summarized in some detail.

Staats sought to incorporate Gestalt principles into a social behavioristic theory. He suggested that "smaller unitary responses can be grouped into large configurations of responses, and then the learning principles will apply to the whole rather than to the unitary responses" (1975, p. 52). Where most behaviorists would emphasize the acquisition of the smaller (reflex) responses, Staats stressed the Gestalt character of learned configurations and their inseparability once the pattern has been acquired.

As regards the role of consciousness, he went along with Rotter and Bandura. Behavior is controlled by the *perceived* environment, and intentions, images, and so on play a part in determining the response that will be emitted in a given stimulus situation.

Conditioning of Images   Staats placed more faith in Pavlovian conditioning than did his predecessors. He even went so far as to treat images as conditioned responses in which the conscious sensation is the unconditioned response. This theoretical stance, although certainly acceptable to most psychologists, seems hardly necessary. It may merely indicate that Staats was very thorough in covering all aspects of the problem.

Conditioning is also the base for the change from simple innate needs to the complex motives affecting adult behavior. Behavior is activated by anticipated pleasures and pains. These become conditioned to environmental and conscious signs and symbols, so that one may be motivated by a religious ideal as well as by more earthy symbols, such as money. Staats has not, however, emphasized the role of consciousness in conditioning as much as Bandura did.

The A-R-D Theory   The conditioning of affective states is one of the basic principles of Staats's theory. He calls it an A-R-D theory, the letters referring to attitude, reinforcement, and directive processes. The term *attitude* here almost replicates the formulation of Wilhelm Wundt, who had written that "every motive is *a particular idea with an affective tone* attaching to it" (1896, p. 231; italics in original).

Staats was not the first to identify attitude as a determinant of learning. Levine and Murphy (1943) demonstrated that people learn material more quickly when it is congruent with their attitudes, more slowly when it conflicts with their attitudes. This, of course, might be merely a function of familiarity. Staats had something more in mind: a dynamic influence. Just as food can be a reinforcer for a hungry pigeon, so a vivid patriotic phrase may be a reinforcer for a patriotic citizen. Staats also extended "attitude" to include phenomena not ordinarily in that category; for example, attitude toward another person, attitude toward a specified career, or attitude toward moral-ethical standards.

In the A-R-D formulation, attitudes are conceived of as conditioned positive or negative perceptions of situations, corresponding to the Lewin–Tolman use of *valence*. A positive attitude defines a tendency to approach the object perceived. Although conceding the role of innate factors, Staats has made the point that very little adult behavior is set off by raw physiological needs. Instead, he has emphasized that hunger may elicit food-seeking behavior, in the course of which some substances are found to "taste good" and hence trigger a positive attitude; objects that are unpleasant become nuclei of negative attitudes. Ultimately, behavior is activated by the presence of, or images of, such attitude objects.

Reinforcement, of course, needs no definition. What is interesting about the Staats formulation is that attitudes can also serve as reinforcers. A desire to watch a ballet performance may set off a search for a theater, and the arrival at the theater reinforces the learning that evolved during the search.

Attitudes, obviously, can also be directive. Knowledge of the location of the attractive object directs action to reaching that location. It thus appears that the Staats theory is simpler than might be thought at first. The essence of the theory is that objects, persons, or situations can become signs of pleasure or of unpleasantness and then may direct behavior and reinforce it.

Learning Staats has embraced both contiguity and reinforcement as learning principles. He is thus more catholic than Bandura, who stressed reinforcement more heavily. Staats cited a number of predecessors, mostly Hullians, who had proposed two-factor theories in earlier years (Staats has been more methodical than many of his colleagues in acknowledging the contributions of his predecessors. Bandura and Rotter gave few references which would confirm the sources of their ideas.) Basically, Staats's view parallels that of Mowrer (1956), which cited Pavlov's variety of conditioning for the formation of dynamic states (attitude, for Staats), and reinforcement for instrumental responses. Thus contiguity accounts for the acquisition of reinforcers, and these in turn account for coping behavior. It is not always clear whether Staats is relying on the conditioning of autonomic nervous system responses for the formation of attitudes; he often suggests that conscious feelings of pleasure and unpleasantness affect perceiving directly. The visceral response principle seems to be favored; Staats did not propose a perceived environment (life space or behavioral environment) as a part of his system.

Patterns of Association Staats resurrected some ideas from Ebbinghaus with regard to the formation of associative connections. It will be recalled (see Chapter Five) that Ebbinghaus had identified remote associations as well as direct associative linkages between items in a series. Staats proposed (Figure 18.6) that we think of any sentence as offering opportunities for the linking not merely of the words in that sentence, but also, by way of stimulus generalization, of other words having the same position and/or functional significance in the language. Long before children reach maturity, they have acquired such a large network of associations

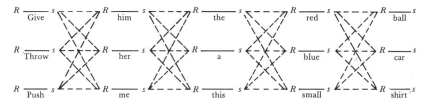

FIGURE 18.6   A Sophisticated Version of the Language Chaining Phenomenon

Remote associations and place associations make possible the formation of
a network so that almost any word can be linked to any other word.
(From Staats, 1975, p. 46, Figure 2.11, by permission of Dr. Arthur W. Staats.)

that almost any word has a connection with a tremendous variety of
other words.

What, then, directs verbal behavior? Staats has placed great stress on
the concept of the hierarchy of responses, on determination from above.
It would seem, as in Hull's hierarchy of responses, that the sHr unit
which had been most often reinforced would stand at the top of the
hierarchy. Staats accepted this idea but noted that this process can go on
in parallel with other learning. In the case of ordinary use of speech
(Figure 18.6), certain connections (noun to verb, for example) occur very
often and so are strengthened; connections from an adverb to a noun
occur rarely and so are not elicited as often. Thus Staats holds that he
has devised a reasonable and naturalistic explanation for the overlearn-
ing of normal grammatical speech connections.

Concept Formation   Another contribution to the formation of language
hierarchies comes through an examination of concept formation. Consider the analysis offered by Staats (Figure 18.7). A child encounters a
dog, and this encounter elicits a "mediating response" (meaning), which
provides a "mediating stimulus" (sm), which triggers vocalization of the
word *dog*. But much of the time, an adult will indicate that another relevant word is *animal*. A similar process goes on for an observation of a
cow, of a pig, and so on. As these incidents accumulate, the number of
repetitions of *animal* can easily outnumber all of the repetitions of single
percept-vocalizing pairs. The stimulus *animal,* then, can become a selective device directing attention to a group of specific examples of the
concept, and excluding many other associated terms, such as *house, tree,
automobile,* and so on.

The principle is not of great importance in connection with simple
visible data such as cats, dogs, and canaries. Determination from above
becomes much more important when the abstractions involve such concepts as *stealing, cheating,* and *lying.* Moral values can control behavior

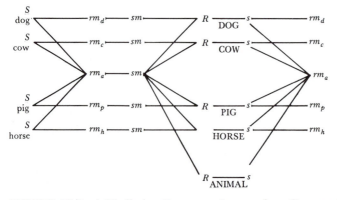

FIGURE 18.7   A Mediating Response Approach to Concept Formation

Staats proposed that the child acquires names which serve as mediating responses for the animals represented by these names, but also that the abstract idea "animal" can become conditioned to all of these stimuli and generalize to new names.   *(From Staats, A. W. 1961, p. 194, Figure 3, by permission of Dr. Staats and the American Psychological Association)*

only when they have become firmly associated with language responses that rank high in the individual's response system.

   Other frequently reinforced concepts or generalized labels include religious values, political policies, racial prejudices, and aesthetic choices. When the biased individual learns that some person or movement is "———" (any hostile stereotype will do), a whole array of antagonistic, denigrating verbal responses move into a favored position to be expressed. Attacking behavior of a nonverbal kind may also be alerted for action. This notion that the abstract label may be strengthened by an association with a wide variety of other words offers a rather useful formulation of how the process of "determination from above" can fit into a behavioristic system.

   Staats holds that this version of language theory has been firmly grounded in laboratory work and can be applied to the process of child development outside the laboratory:

> The construction of classic hierarchical theory requires the present field of study be elaborated to include functional human behavior in all of its complexity, not just the events of the basic learning laboratory. Then it can be realized that the principles of learning are themselves the higher-order principles . . . the empirical, elementary principles of learning must take a position at the apex of the theoretical structure . . . The task of basic learning theory is the selection, elaboration, derivation and systematization of a set of basic learning principles . . . [to] serve as a foundation for the more general theory of human behavior. (1975, p. 15–16)

What, concretely, did Staats mean by these generalizations? Among basic skills, he identified such phenomena as learning to follow directions (to use verbal symbols to guide overt behavior), learning sets, habits of attending, the discrimination of speech sounds, and the acquisition of goals. If these basic skills are acquired in early childhood, they will facilitate further skill acquisition, notably academic and professional skills. But it is clear that these foundation skills are also relevant to learning nonacademic performances as well. Thus Staats agrees with Bandura that values can control both the learning of new responses and the behavior of the person after the actions have been learned. They are in agreement also that psychologists must come out of the laboratory and cope with issues of human behavior outside experimental constraints.

Linking by Emotion   An essential part of Freudian theory is that certain overt and implicit processes are linked in a complex by associations with a single emotional state. Thus a feeling of guilt over some action or omission may become linked with other occasions on which guilt was experienced. In a therapeutic interview, opening up one memory of a humiliating or embarrassing event may release a flood of memories in which the same emotion was central. Figure 18.8 offers an example in which the linking emotion is positive. The stimuli are of the type Lewin would call positive valences. On the right are various kinds of approach responses. It is obvious that a child who learns one tactic for getting desired objects (e.g., "crying for") will probably try the same in connection with desired but unattainable objects in later life. However, the response would not be elicited by an unpleasant stimulus because there is no learned link with this array of responses.

Staats noted that there are two hierarchies here, one of stimuli and one of responses. Although Staats has emphasized responses, as a behavioristic theorist must, he has not ignored the fact that each person also constructs a hierarchy of desirability for goal objects (cf. Maslow, Chapter Seventeen) and also a hierarchy of aversions. These hierarchies are presumably based on the intensity of experienced pleasure or pain in early encounters with these objects.

It will be instructive to compare this diagram with Figure 1.4, and to consider how intraorganismic processes may block out certain stimuli or may inhibit certain responses. Differences in personality can often be analyzed in such terms.

Proactive Transfer and Inhibition   Another useful contribution by Staats is his resurrection of the phenomena of transfer, positive and negative. The functionalists had discovered that learning of one association, A–B, may facilitate or hinder the subsequent learning of A–C. The learning of A–C may also facilitate or inhibit the recall of A–B. It is curious that neither Hull nor Skinner made much of this phenomenon.

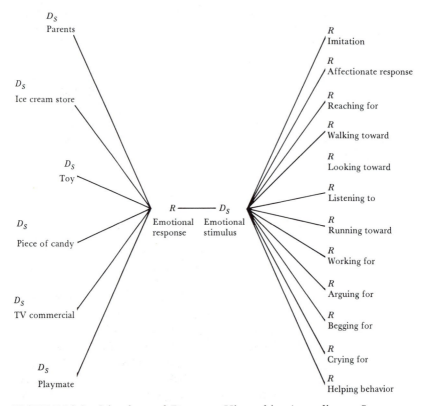

FIGURE 18.8   Stimulus and Response Hierarchies According to Staats

The child may (usually unconsciously) develop a hierarchy of stimulus objects from those most desirable to those minimally desirable, and a hierarchy of goal-attaining responses, ranked in terms of probability of success.   *(From Staats, 1975, p. 110, Figure 4.3, by permission of Dr. Staats and Dorsey Press)*

Staats contrived a way of formulating this issue that permits past learning to be treated as either an independent or a dependent variable (Figure 18.9). In this formula, BBR (the basic behavioral repertoire) is a *dependent* variable in relation to past stimuli, but it is an *independent* variable in relation to the here-and-now. The response to the present stimulus situation, then, is a joint function of input and prior learning: for example, a person who fears crowds will be predisposed to take evasive action in a crowd situation.

The Reinvention of the Self   This logical device permitted Staats to insert a "self-concept" into his psychology. He conceived of the self as a collection of responses linked to images of the self, including body im-

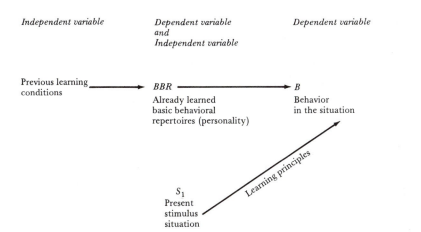

Independent variable

*Dependent variable
and
Independent variable*

Dependent variable

Previous learning
conditions

BBR
Already learned
basic behavioral
repertoires (personality)

B
Behavior
in the situation

S_1
Present
stimulus
situation

Learning principles

FIGURE 18.9   Proactive Facilitation and Inhibition

Behavior in the immediate present is a joint function of the current stimulus situation and of past learning, which may be facilitative or inhibitory, as summarized in the "basic behavioral repertoire." *(From Staats, 1975, p. 69, Figure 3.1, by permission of Dr. Staats and Dorsey Press)*

age, descriptions by others, self-achievements, and other observables. This "omnibus" definition of the self is reminiscent of Hume, for whom the self was only a bundle of ideas, or for Watson, a bundle of responses. In apparent contradiction to his phrasing but not to his intention, Staats treated the self as one of the determinants of a response: "the individual constitutes a stimulus to himself" (1975, p. 68). The self-concept "included an outline of the manner in which the individual learns to describe himself" (p. 61).

The perceived self can become a stimulus for behaviors that cannot be accounted for solely on the basis of environmental stimuli. Reactions to the self may mediate overt behavior. Staats used the familiar observation that two individuals may observe a third and may reach opposed conclusions regarding the correct way to respond: "To illustrate, one individual who sees someone tending to avoid him will label the other's behavior as shyness, and this verbal response will elicit overt behaviors to make the person feel more at ease. Another individual, in response to the same social behavior, may say that the other person does not like him, and this will elicit overt behaviors of an avoidant or aversive kind" (1975, pp. 67–68). Thus the implicit response (What does he think of me?) may determine the overt action. It will be recalled that Bandura also emphasized this type of mediating response in his "reciprocal determinism" thesis. It is also confirmed by the "attribution theory" research; see, for example, Jones et al., 1971.

Parallel Response Systems   The self-concept rests in part on perceptions of one's own responses. This suggested to Staats that improved learning might result from a planned linking of response systems. He applied this notion to the child's learning of numbers. Traditionally, the child memorizes number sequences: "One, two, three, four . . ." Staats hypothesized that an inability to use these responses in a practical situation results from the isolation of the response. He started training children to say the numbers while manipulating objects (Figure 18.10). In this case, the child says, "One" and takes one penny from the table; "Two" and takes a second; "Three" and takes a third. Staats argued that practicing these parallel responses gave the child an operational (kinesthetic) cue to go along with the vocal response of saying the number. He claimed that children taught this way acquired numerical skills well beyond their age level (Staats, Brewer, and Gross, 1970).

"Conditioning" Personality   Another ingenious if not convincing experiment devised by Staats involved "conditioning" personality descriptions. Subjects were asked to make responses describing their interactions with others; when the response indicated getting along well, the experimenter responded, "Good," "Fine," and so on. When these individuals later took a personality inventory, they described themselves as more sociable than before the experiment. Unfortunately, Staats did not take his own advice and get overt behavior as a validation measure. It is quite possible that, like T-group experiences and some forms of behavior therapy, the results are quickly forgotten (Staats et al., 1962).

Staats et al. (1973) showed that verbal stimuli (items from the Strong

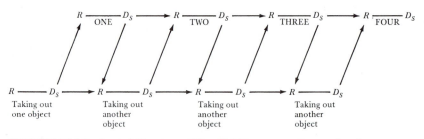

FIGURE 18.10   Staats' Version of Parallel Responses Strengthening Learning

If a child engages in two linked responses, e.g., saying the number and taking the object, learning is speeded. Staats speculated on an intensifying effect of the second response on memory for the first. Compare Münsterberg's study of intensification of a sensation by an accompanying response, Chapter 8.   *(From Staats, 1975, p. 447, Figure 12.1, by permission of Dr. Staats and Dorsey Press)*

Vocational Interest Blank) could be used as (1) classical conditioning stimuli; (2) reinforcers; and (3) discrimination stimuli. Items that the individual had marked "like" could be used as "unconditioned stimuli" in a verbal conditioning experiment, and the positive affect was transferred to the nonsense syllable associated with such items. These authors also used these items as reinforcers, and as guidance (discriminative) stimuli (Staats et al., 1973, p. 251). One defect of this study is that subjects who suspected the purpose of the experiment were excluded from the data; the procedure can be defended, of course, and the results are less ambiguous than if these subjects had been retained.

The purpose of the experiment was to show that "all stimuli that elicit an emotional or attitudinal response in the individual also have two other behavioral functions. An attitudinal stimulus will serve as a reinforcing stimulus when it is presented following any instrumental behavior. . . . In addition, a stimulus that elicits an emotional response [may function] as a discriminative [goal] stimulus" (Staats et al., 1973, p. 252).

Not surprisingly, Staats had a further goal in designing these experiments. He was planning a critique of psychoanalytic psychotherapy. Much of the analytic process consists of verbal reports by the patient of self-referent memories. To some of these (sex-related or aggression-related), the analyst is likely to say, "Good," or by nonverbal means to indicate that progress is being made. Thus, Staats speculated, verbal conditioning may be operating. This cast doubt, Staats commented, on the use of patient reports in shaping theories about personality dynamics; "it might be the influence of the psychotherapist that was reflected in the patient's statements" (1975, p. 292).

The Staats technique of using attitudinal material as reinforcing stimuli for behavior change was developed, apparently independently, by J. A. Varela (1971). Where Staats used reported interests as reinforcers, Varela prepared a graded series of attitudinal statements which served as reinforcers for decisions by the subject. For example, he described a case of a man who disliked the idea of having a medical check-up and had postponed it for years. Varela began with a strong positive valence: "I love my family very much." When the subject agreed, Varela continued with "My health is much worse now than when I was a young man." So, in a Socratic fashion, Varela led the man to phone and make an appointment for a complete medical examination. Varela was using attitude statements as Skinner had used grains of corn in shaping pigeons' behavior. Varela's success supports the Staats theory that verbalizations can be used as reinforcers in changing behavior.

Social Psychology   Most of the research directed by Staats has been focused on the behavior of individuals. However, he has not hesitated to speculate about the relevance of his theory to larger populations. For example, he treated the economic law of supply and demand as an exercise in deprivation–satiation operations. If consumers of a product are relatively satiated (low demand), the price will fall; if the consumers are deprived of a product, demand will be high, and the price will rise. Staats also noted (without apparently seeing its significance) that if successive units of a commodity are supplied, the value of each additional unit diminishes. This is actually a manifestation of the familiar Weber fraction, in which perceived differences diminish as the level of stimulation increases.

Staats also resembles Bandura, Skinner, and Tolman in relating his theory to political and economic power. A-R-D resources are those that human beings require for survival. Students of politics have discovered that "there are certain classes of people who, through their possession of power (A-R-D) resources, have an inordinate influence upon the society" (Staats, 1975, p. 505). Staats even offered the "Watergate" scandal of the 1970s as another example of the application of A-R-D control to manipulate public policy (p. 507).

Other Neobehaviorists

Many other psychologists have espoused theoretical positions meeting my criterion of the treatment of conscious events as responses. J. W. Brehm (1966) offered a minitheory on "reactance," or the tendency of individuals to react against influence attempts. Skinner had mentioned the possibility that control measures might evoke an aversive response, but he never amplified on the possibility. It seems clear that many human beings resist being conditioned or being persuaded to change an established habit or attitude.

Victor Vroom (1964) developed a theory of motivation known as V-I-E (valence, instrumentality, and expectancy), which closely resembles Staats's A-R-D. Vroom frankly adopted Lewin's concept of valence, which carries with it the positive–negative, approach–avoidance connotations; Vroom made somewhat less effort to deal with the origins of valence than Staats applied to his "attitude" concept. However, Vroom worked out, within an industrial context and in substantial detail, the perceived instrumentality of a given action and the perceived expectancy that the outcome would be desirable.

Perhaps the most optimistic development in psychological theorizing of the last century has been the effort to put consciousness and behavior back together. Both Titchener and Watson preached a divisive approach to psychology. The innovations described in this chapter may lead us back to a conception of psychology that takes in the whole of human behavior and experience.

CHAPTER 19

Neostructuralism

The demise of Titchenerian structuralism has been taken for granted for the last thirty years or more. E. G. Boring (1950) wrote, "Somehow Titchenerism in America had been sustained by his magnificent personality. With his death it suddenly collapsed" (p. 420). A similar dogmatic verdict was issued by A. R. Gilgen (1982) with the pronouncement— "Structuralism became virtually extinct by the 1920s" (p. 15). (Titchener died in 1928). That structuralism in America was for a time buried under a flood of behavioristic criticism is certain. Whether this development was fatal is quite another matter. There is considerable evidence that structuralism, if not traveling under that name, is a persistent and respectable influence on American psychology in the 1980s.

We have described the neoanalysts as psychologists holding some point of agreement with Sigmund Freud, but disagreeing on matters such as the role of the social environment in the shaping of personality and psychopathology. Similarly, "neobehaviorism" was treated as a theoretical development with roots in the work of Watson, Hull, and Skinner, but deviating primarily in the recognition of conscious processes as responses.

"Neostructuralism," then, can be recognized by the fact that it (1) places the primary focus of psychology on consciousness; (2) endorses an atomistic, elementaristic mode of analysis; and (3) spreads out from original structuralism into studies of responses and learning, concedes that some perceptual units are better described as configurations than as conglomerations of elements, and attempts to incorporate motivational phenomena into research on perceiving. For example, hypotheses derived from psychoanalytic theory have been applied to studies of perceptual constancy and variation.

Generally speaking, the theoretical tendencies grouped here as "neostructuralist" have their origin in Titchenerian problems (sensory and perceptual consciousness) but without the rigidity imposed by Titchener's structuralist theory. Like neoanalysis and neobehaviorism, this cluster of approaches to the study of psychology can be perceived as steps toward mergers of conflicting points of view, incorporating more sources of variation and adding more flexibility with respect to the modes of interaction of the variables.

The "New Look" in Perception

Immediately after World War II, a new trend in perceptual research and theorizing introduced studies of motivational effects on perceiving. E. C. Tolman (Chapter Eighteen) probably had some influence on this trend; George Klein (1970) credited David Krech, a Tolman doctorate, with christening this movement the "new look." Gardner Murphy (Chapter Seventeen) helped shape it. Its outstanding feature has been research on motives, emotions, and values as they affect perceptual constancies and errors in perceiving. The latter concern grows naturally out of Freud's analysis of perceptual errors in everyday life (Chapter Fourteen).

The earliest perceptual research had been based on the assumption that the senses give us information about the "real" physical environment. Wundt and Titchener focused on the manipulation of physical stimuli and used as dependent variables introspective reports. Külpe and Wertheimer likewise concentrated on purely cognitive factors, somewhat more complex than those used by their predecessors, but excluding any kind of dynamic factor. Although Köhler wrote about "physiognomic" perceiving, in which humanlike attributes were incorporated into precepts of physical objects, he did not devise any theoretical formula for incorporating dynamics into his experimental manipulations.

As so often happens, the dating of the "new look" movement is ambiguous. As early as 1936, Nevitt Sanford was studying the effect of a physiological drive (hunger) on perceiving and responding. In one study, he showed ambiguous drawings and found that hungry subjects "saw" more food-related objects than those tested just after eating. He also presented incomplete words and had subjects complete them. For the hungry group, ME–– was likely to be completed as *meal* or *meat* rather than *mean* or *meet*. At about the same time, Heinz Ansbacher (1937) demonstrated that value (cost) influenced perceiving. He pasted postage stamps of different values on cards, let the subject handle them, and then exposed them briefly in random order. Even though the observer frequently could not tell which stamp was being exposed, those of higher cost were "seen" as being more numerous than the cheaper stamps. And Siipola (1935) demonstrated that mental set modified the perception of words. She presented misspelled words tachistoscopically at very short exposures; one group was told that the list would contain names of animals or birds; the other, words about travel. She found that *sael* was read as *seal* by the first group and as *sail* by the second. Other results supported this finding; the errors were determined by expectations.

The "new look" researches proper began in 1947 with work by Jerome S. Bruner (1915–   ) and his colleagues at Harvard University. One of the earliest in this series of studies was by Bruner and Leo Postman (1947a) on *perceptual vigilance*. Freud had hypothesized that unconscious processes sensitize the person to certain classes of stimuli (e.g., sexual or threatening) so that they would be recognized more rapidly than others. Bruner and Postman presented neutral stimuli and anxiety-arousing stimuli to their subjects in a tachistoscope at very short exposure times. Statistically, anxiety-arousing words were identified within shorter times than words in the neutral set.

One of the most widely cited studies in the "new look" area was by Bruner and C. C. Goodman (1947). In this experiment, life history was the independent variable. Children from well-to-do homes were compared with children from a poor neighborhood. The task was to set a circle of light equal to a dime or a quarter. The poor children grossly overestimated the size of a quarter; the dime was exaggerated somewhat; and a penny was estimated at only slightly more than its "real" size. The authors interpreted the data to mean that a quarter had a greater relative value for the poor group, and that this greater value had led to the overestimation. An alternative interpretation might be that the poor children rarely handled coins and so had no internal standard as a guide to a realistic setting.

Perceptual Defense

Freud's *Reizschutz* (Chapter Fourteen) was described as a system by which the infant protects itself against dangerous external stimuli, and that later is used to block conscious awareness of anxiety-arousing ideas and images. A number of "new look" studies have confirmed that many individuals defend themselves against threatening stimuli by simply "failing to see" them.

Bruner and Postman (1947b) applied an idea based on Jung's studies of word association. Jung found that if a patient blocked on a stimulus word, took a long time, blushed, or stammered, the word probably evoked some unconscious complex. Jung's interest was, of course, in identifying the complex; Bruner and Postman simply wanted an index of anxiety or guilt feelings. They administered a word-association test to a large group of students, then took for each person a set of words with delayed reaction times and a set with normal times. These words were then presented in the tachistoscope. The recognition times resembled the reaction times; words with slow response times were recognized only at long exposure times. The interpretation was that the person defended against threatening words by refusing to recognize them.

Various other studies have used vulgar sexual and excretory words in such experiments. These were criticized on the grounds that the subject might be embarrassed to say these words to a strange experimenter. Variations of method that eliminated speaking the word still resulted in evidence favoring "defense," but the slowing of response time from neutral words was decreased.

Theoretical Implications

One of the theoretical tangles introduced by the "new look" experiments is that of mutual contradictions. In various experiments, some nonsense syllables were paired with electric shock, and others were not. On the perceptual threshold test, the anxiety-arousing signals were seen clearly more slowly than the neutral syllables. The tangle arises from the fact that the person must have recognized the syllable at very short exposure times in order to activate a blocking mechanism; in other words, it may be that perceptual defense is merely an extension of perceptual vigilance. The concept of *subception* was proposed by McCleary and Lazarus (1949) to identify this phenomenon.

The studies involving meaningful words raised the criticism, too, that taboo words were rarely seen in printed form. To test with nonverbal material, Westerlundh (1985) used pictures. One drawing, for example, showed two persons facing each other. At a speed too fast for conscious awareness, a castration drawing was exposed over the visible picture. When the observer gave a verbal description of the scene, the reports included hostile or aggressive words not found in the reports from persons exposed to a subliminal scene of affection.

The Westerlundh study, like that of Perky (1910), showed that conscious reports could be modified by stimuli too weak to reach the level of conscious recognition. In other words, there must be some activation of perceptual processes below the threshold of conscious recognition. Leibniz (Chapter Four) and Helmholtz (Chapter Five) had both postulated some such process a century earlier; the "new look" studies provided limited confirmation.

The interest in manipulating stimulus conditions or organismic conditions to test for modifications of perception has waned. However, there are some obvious implications for theories of psychology. First, perceiving is not an isolated function. It is influenced by drive states and by expectancies. Floyd Allport (1955) proposed that we use the term *directive state* to identify such influences. In this case, a directive state might be conceived of as facilitating the emergence of certain responses by changing the input of stimuli, or by changing the rank order of the responses in a hierarchy. Staats (Figure 18.9) proposed that such states be considered independent variables helping to determine the specific response to be emitted in a certain situation. Gestalt theory suggests that when the physical forms are ambiguous, the kind of Gestalt to emerge can be influenced by intraorganismic conditions.

Information Processing

Another major development since World War II has been in an area generally known as *information processing*. The "new look" experiments showed that a response cannot be tied to a specified physical stimulus; the response is a joint product of stimulus and directive state, and the latter can be manipulated independently of the former. Thus the "information" on which the person acts is modified by these directive states.

What about the *unlearned* processing of information? Titchener showed that absolute thresholds and differential thresholds have effects on consciousness, as do contrast, adaptation, and other variables. Information-processing research in the last half of the twentieth century has greatly expanded the scope and modified the theoretical context of such investigations.

John Locke pointed out two hundred years ago that all of our information comes from the environment. Even if we accept the rationalist modification, that the organism restructures and abstracts from the incoming data, it is still true that behavior must be guided by and directed toward the environment. It follows that intensive study of how human beings receive information, process it, store it, and utilize it is urgently needed.

Wundt, Titchener, Cattell, and James thought that they were engaged in exactly that pursuit. They were concerned about receptor processes and about conscious perception, apperception, and memory. Although Wundt and Titchener advocated the analysis of these experiences into elements, they—along with their colleagues—agreed that this was an important phase of adaptation to the demands of survival.

The same holds for research on information processing today. Cognitive psychology is composed, for the most part, of the study and interpretation of the stimulus side of psychology, including how a person transforms and reconstructs the inputs from the environment. The behaviorists had considered this a pseudoproblem. In their view, an organism responds to the "real" world. Survival is possible because the individual is behaving in ways compatible with the requirements of the real world. We must keep this in mind if it appears that problems of illusion, misinterpretation, and error seem to get an undue amount of attention from researchers working on the stimulus side. They feel compelled to bludgeon the behaviorists into recognizing that the percept is neither objective nor veridical. Information is, as Freud might have said, what gets through the filters and protective devices. And this is by no means a fair sample of what is out there in the external world.

Introspection as Method   Introspection as the basic procedure for gathering psychological data suffered during the middle of this century. It has made a substantial comeback since about 1970. To quote Michael Posner (1978): "All people have a window on the operation of their own minds available to them alone" (p. 1). As Posner proceeded to point out, not all windows are equal. The introspective window is valuable for certain kinds of data, but much in human life is not revealed to introspection. Within a restricted sphere, on the other hand, introspection is not merely a useful tool; it is the only tool.

At the same time, one notes that the term *introspection* is being used in ways rather different from its use in structuralism. Posner (1978), for example, wrote that "the largest use of introspection in current psychological investigation is in the study of memory. Recall and recognition both rely on subjects being able to introspect into their past experiences to decide whether a given event is or is not familiar" (p. 3). Most behaviorists would reject the notion that this is introspection, and the same goes for Titchener. Posner, of course, could argue that a person who says, "Yes, I saw that one" is *not* repeating the response given on first contact with the stimulus. It seems necessary to assume that the individual searches among stored items (memory traces) for a match to the one being presented (see Figure 19.1). Search, then, could be treated as an introspective operation, but it would not be a report on the *search process;* rather, it would be a report on what the search had produced. And this outcome is not available to an outside observer; hence it can be considered a process of introspection.

The Computer as Metaphor   As a recent arrival in the psychology laboratory, the computer has only recently been available as a metaphor. It is used by most, if not all, information-processing psychologists. This, of course, tends to emphasize the similarity of contemporary work to that of the classical structuralists. A computer program must center on the atomistic components of a stimulus (loops, diagonals) in order to identify a nonsense syllable. The Gestalt approach is impossible to use with present-day computers, although some observers believe that ultimately, holistic recognition by computers will be possible.

The computer also exemplifies the processes of search and retrieval, which are the core of most research in this area. Given a pattern or template, the computer can search a large number of records and identify matches quickly.

In the early days of computer work, *serial* processing of data was the only available mode. This meant that one operation had to be completed before the next one was initiated. This has now been replaced by parallel processing, in which various questions may be asked of the data simultaneously. Thus one program might be searching for "letter width" while another is searching for "closed loop." When these parallel-processing techniques are perfected, the speed of optical scanning will undoubtedly be increased greatly.

Filters   Titchener had emphasized the importance of lower thresholds, the point at which the human observer can no longer detect a stimulus. Modern work may focus on upper thresholds. There is already a widespread concern with noise in the workplace, and with evidence of chronic hearing loss among workers in noisy environments.

Most theorists assume the existence of filters that prevent or minimize the occurrence of such overload. These filters may be simple, as in the case of a receptor threshold, or complicated, as in the case of choices among sensory channels. It is particularly difficult to grasp the concept of a filter that limits the number of bits of information per second that gets into the processing mechanism (the central nervous system, presumably). Donald Broadbent (1963) proposed a filtering system based on sensory channels and channel capacities. According to this view, a flood of information impinges on the sensory receptors—a higher amount, of course, at some times than at others. Filters may reduce this flow; for example, with practice one may be able to exclude sounds from consciousness. Visual filters are also manipulable to some extent.

Broadbent did not take into account perceptual defense, the "new look" studies, or selective emotional filters. Freud incorporated these in his concept of the *Reizschutz* (see Chapter Fourteen). Social psychologists have also commented on the "dialogue of the deaf," in which two persons appear to hold a conversation: each talks, but neither listens. Similarly, certain content (e.g., sexual) may be excluded by this mechanism. Conversely, we can imagine that some individuals selectively *amplify* some messages (e.g., about sexual availability). Thus there may be a misinterpretation of the other person's intentions, resulting from this magnification of the emotional content of a communication.

Attending   One feature of the selective filter hypothesized by Broadbent is that it can be "tuned" to a certain sensory channel or to a certain topic. Titchener would have called this "voluntary attention," just as the effects of distracting stimuli were ascribed to "involuntary attention." What one experiences in a complex situation depends on the direction of one's attention. R. S. Wyer and T. K. Srull (1980) wrote, "Mary's representation of herself slapping John at dinner may include the expression on John's face, the feelings of anger that led her to commit the act, and the stinging sensation of her hand hitting John's cheek" (p. 231). They could have added her awareness of others viewing the incident and even her memory of being slapped in a comparable situation. In other words, the analysis of information input means attending to some details and not to others.

Coding   Information which gets past the filter is coded as the first step in processing. By *coding* is meant the categorization of the message, a step preliminary to putting it into memory storage. The simplest coding is simply by sensory modality, that is, by receptor channel. Language coding may involve multiple coding, inasmuch as a written message may also be recorded in the auditory system. Some information may be coded for both smell and taste, although, of course, most observers cannot distinguish these. Multiple coding is held to account for the storage of the same information in different parts of the cerebral cortex. Brain injury cases reveal that some information (e.g., written material) may be lost, but that the same item in auditory form is still available.

More complex codes are used for meaningful materials (see Figure 19.1). These may be cognitive, as new information about brain function, for example, may be sorted and stored with other physiological items. Coding may also be emotional; evidence that one is inferior in some task performance may be stored with other data relating to inferiority, and that regarding superior achievement may be coded "irrelevant" and eliminated from storage. (This example is based on Carl Rogers; see Chapter Seventeen.)

Coding is an efficiency measure. Posner and Rogers (1978) defined *abstraction* as "the recoding of information in a reduced or condensed form." This, of course, is an indispensable feature of the theorizing process itself; when one uses a term like *discriminative operant response,* an amazing amount of information is conveyed to the reader familiar with psychological research. (There is an associated danger; if the coding is incorrect, much information is lost.)

Posner and Rogers also hypothesized that coding could proceed without consciousness. This hypothesis is compatible with Freudian theory, and it is also appropriate to the studies of perceptual defense, in which empirical research confirmed a selective rejection of incoming material before it has reached conscious awareness. According to this view, the "code" (dangerous) may be identified in a very brief exposure time, triggering the defensive measure of blocking the sensory channel. Offhand this finding would seem to contradict Wundt's finding that a report on feeling was usually slower than one on sensation, but the early work on feelings led to ambiguous results, so there is not necessarily a contradiction here.

Coding of Responses   It should be noted that coding may apply to responses as well as to stimuli. When Skinner commented that "we reinforce a *class* of responses "he opened the door for one to label one's own behavior and so perhaps to categorize it differently from others. To a critical remark, a person may respond with a defensive posture that he or she classifies as cool and rational but that is heard by the critic as hasty and irrational. It seems likely that some of the data on the "conditioning" of personality traits, described in Chapter Eighteen, may depend on the subject's coding of responses as sociable, or submissive, or insensitive. Failures of communication, of course, are mostly associated with biased coding by the listener.

Storage   The number of storage levels is a matter of dispute among the information processors. Lachman, Lachman, and Butterfield (1979) proposed that we distinguish among the "sensory register" (often called the *icon* or very-short-term memory); the "short-term store"; and the "long-term store." Any input material works its way through these successive storage stages. Some material may be lost (forgotten) at each stage. Information is held in the sensory register for only one or two seconds; if the channel to the short-term storage is overloaded, much of the incoming information will be lost. Small amounts of material seem to move directly to the long-term store, but most goes through the short-term stage first. Rehearsal is said to reduce the amount of loss. However, as noted earlier, the environmental conditions that result in efficient storage are hardly mentioned. Learning, it would seem, obeys different principles and is thus excluded from the information-processing analysis.

The time intervals in these studies are very short. Material can be lost from the VSTS (very-short-term storage) in 0.4 seconds if the person is distracted momentarily. The procedure is generally the same as that used by J. M. Cattell (1898), except, of course, that more precise control of time is characteristic of modern studies. D. J. K. Mewhort (1969) noted that "the differentiation between familiar and unfamiliar material takes place in the time interval between input to memory and retrieval from it" (p. 360). Thus it is necessary to postulate still further processing that can be detected only by variations in output. There is no evidence of conscious involvement; like the experiments of the Würzburg school, these researchers require us to assume the operation of unconscious processes.

Long-term storage appears to use multiple locations. Brain injury cases provide persuasive evidence that memory storage by categories occurs at least some of the time. Some aphasias have involved the loss of one's native tongue but the retention of a foreign language learned in maturity. One interesting stroke victim lost large segments of memory but gradually regained most of them. His conspicuous loss was that of the names of vegetables. He could describe them but could not name them.

Priming   The structuralists had written of mental set or directed attention. Posner (1978) used the term *priming* to identify the same phenomenon. In his research, it involved presenting a pre-task stimulus that might facilitate or inhibit performance on the task. Thus, in one experiment, it was shown that priming on a response (saying "Same" or "Different") speeded the reaction on a task calling for the same response. Stimulus priming involved some method (such as saying a sentence) which called attention to a subject-matter area, and then presenting words within or outside that area. The response times were faster for items within the category. Coding, then affects not only memory storage, but also re-trieval.

R. M. Shiffrin (1970) offered a hypothetical system of organized stor-age that may serve to clarify the priming concept and also to amplify the relationship of information processing to the work of Titchener. In Fig-ure 19.1 is shown Shiffrin's hypothetical storage system. This, of course, is long-term storage. Bits of information are accumulated about some observed object, animal, or person. These coalesce into a rounded form, but the separate items are still used for identification. A search set is

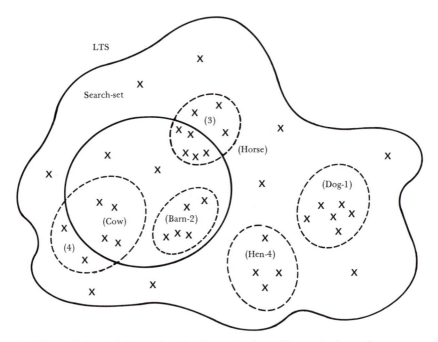

FIGURE 19.1   A Scheme for the Organization of Items in Long-Store Memory

The outer boundary represents total Long-Term Storage (LTS). Within it, the heavy black circle encloses a "search-set" within which one seeks identification of a perceived object. The dotted figures indicate stored memories or concepts. Each x indicates a specific attribute or bit of infor-mation.   *(From Shiffrin, 1970, p. 377, by permission of the author and Aca-demic Press)*

induced by the experimenter (e.g., an important asset for a farmer?). The observer scans various cognitive structures and decides that the barn fits the criteria best. The supposed formation and identification processes are atomistic, not holistic.

S. E. Palmer and R. Kimchi (1986) have been even clearer in their endorsement of an atomistic approach to the reception or retrieval of information. They wrote, "Any complex (i.e., nonprimitive) informational event at one level of description can be specified more fully at a lower level by *decomposing* it into (1) a number of components, each of which is itself an informational event, and (2) the temporal ordering relations among them that specify how the information 'flows' through the system of components" (p. 39). Thus, in opposition to Gestalt theory, Palmer and Kimchi asserted that the analysis into components will *more fully* describe and explain the event.

Physiological data have also been cited to support atomistic analysis. The work of D. H. Hubel and T. N. Wiesel (1954) showed that certain attributes of a visual stimulus set off preselected cortical cells. These cells are highly selective; some receive only diagonal lines, some verticals, and so on. Posner (1978) seems to have been tempted by the idea of a single-receptor—single—cortical—cell link in reception and storage. Ulrich Neisser (1967), however, expressed doubt that this was possible: "Most of the data about human pattern recognition cannot be accounted for by analyzers of this sort" (p. 83).

Many years ago, Lashley (1954) pointed out a basic fallacy with this kind of cell-to-cell linkage. The human eye, he noted, is in virtually continuous motion. Saccadic movements occur on an average of four to five times per second. Thus, any fixation lasting as long as one-half second would involve two or three fixations at different loci on the retina. Yet the phenomenal experience, the visual pattern, is stable. There must be, Lashley concluded, a corrective mechanism somewhere in the system that rules out the effects of the saccadic movement.

Volition   Wilhelm Wundt (1896) had characterized the "will" as a human function in anthropomorphic terms: "But when the will has once discovered that its voluntary muscles enable it to do almost anything it wishes, it, and not the reflex, is master" (p. 226).

Endel Tulving (1972) waxed equally anthropomorphic in his discussion of memory:

> Let us think of episodic and semantic memory as two information processing systems that (a) selectively receive information from perceptual systems or other cognitive systems, (b) retain various aspects of this information, and (c) *upon instructions* transmit specific retained information to other systems, including those *responsible* for translating it into behavior and conscious awareness (p. 385; italics added).

Tulving has clearly attributed to these "systems" some human properties such as responsibility, transmitting instructions, and acting on instructions.

Lest it be thought that Tulving's anthropomorphizing was a rare exception, here is a quotation from Wyer and Srull (1980): "The system consists of four primary storage units. . . . In addition, there are five processing units . . . a Preencoder, an Executive Unit, an Encoder-Organizer, an Integrator, and a Response Selector" (pp. 229–230). Choices are made: "The Encoder interprets new or previously acquired items of information by designating them as exemplars of concepts or schemata that already exist in Permanent Storage" (p. 244). Freud's personalizing of mental functions looks like Ockham's razor compared to this flight of fancy.

There are, naturally, some psychologists working in the field who reject this anthropormorphic thinking about information processing. Ruminating about such theorizing, Posner (1978) commented, "A ghost haunts experimental psychology and many of our demonstrations and results. The ghost is homunculus, the little man inside. What use is a psychological theory that postulates a man in the head whose behavior must itself be explained by the psychological theory?" (p. 151)

The other side of this coin is that, not the homunculus, but the person being tested may foul up the experiment. In a passage reminiscent of Titchener's plaint (see Chapter Seven) about the ingenuity of college students who invented novel forms of noncompliance with his instructions, Tulving (1985) paid tribute to the creativity of his subjects and their skill at frustrating his experimental manipulations.

> We assume that both memory systems and memory tasks . . . are composed of, or can be broken down into, more elementary constituents (I have referred to them in this article as operating components), but we do not yet know how to relate one to the other in the world of empirical observations. . . . The difficulty is compounded by the clever and inventive strategies that learners and rememberers frequently use when confronted with laboratory tasks, *strategies that drive wedges between what the experimenter thinks he or she is observing and what the observed organism is in fact doing* (pp. 395–396; italics added).

Tulving's faith in the structuralist hypothesis (of analyzing data into the smallest components) is also revealed here. (Compare Sternberg's view; see Chapter Twenty.) The Cartesian tradition dies hard.

The Vocabulary Problem   As with the original structuralist observers, there is a vocabulary problem to be faced. Information processors have not agreed on terminology. M. White (1985) described an effort to find out how much mutual agreement had developed within this field. The conclusion was: not much. After an extensive literature survey, White issued the following gloomy report: "Many concepts were referred to by many different names, even in the same book. *Icon* affords a good example. This was variously called iconic memory, iconic storage, preattentive memory, preperceptual visual store, sensory buffer, visual information store, visual memory, visual sensual memory, visual sensory register, visual sensory store, and visual storage system" (p. 118).

There are at least two ways of looking at such lists. One is to agree with Watson that introspection as a technique is useless because of differences in the reporting of observations; and the second is that the field of information-processing research could benefit from some conceptual clarification. It might be instructive if someone looked at the history of chemistry and counted the number of different terms used for oxygen in the days before verbal uniformity developed.

The Memory Trace Information-processing theory intersects with traditional learning theory at the point of the memory trace. The trace in the VSTS is evanescent; it must be transferred quickly or it will be lost. Transfer to a more durable storage may involve reinforcement; some data indicate that about one-half second is the optimal interval between the conditioned stimulus and the unconditioned stimulus in a Pavlovian design. However, in the case of instrumental learning (Mowrer), much longer time intervals still support permanent memory traces; the same holds for Skinner's operant conditioning.

It must be noted, first, that a child does not *learn* to make a transfer from STS to LTS (or any other transfer postulated by a theory). Although empirically it appears that reinforcement must be a factor, we also have the experiments of Guthrie and his students that question reinforcement. It may be that, as Guthrie hypothesized, the first pairing of a neutral and a reinforcing stimulus leads to the formation of a trace, but this trace may be transferred into LTS only by repetition. Clearly, repetition prevents the loss of STS material and fosters its transfer to LTS.

Loss of information may occur at any transfer point. If STS material is not transferred within about one second, it vanishes. But inhibitory processes can also operate. If one tries to transfer several items into long-term memory, some will usually be lost. This problem is rarely mentioned in the information-processing (IP) literature, but Hull's theory offers some suggestions; so does Freud's view.

Lachman, Lachman and Butterfield (1979) pointed out that the IP literature conflicts with neobehaviorist ideology: "They [neobehaviorists] generally minimized innate ideas, capacities and instincts as suitable accounts of behavior, preferring the *tabula rasa* notion" (p. 41). The IP psychologists are described as being more nativist: "We are more willing to consider that innate abilities underlie many important human capacities" (p. 42). The IP studies have made a strong case for the notion of innate *capacities* and *processes;* most modern psychologists resist the postulation of "innate *ideas.*"

Like theorists of other schools, the IP proponents have been aggressive in pushing the outer limits of their ideas. W. K. Estes (1979) illustrated this tendency well when he wrote, "Just as the physical sciences can be conceived as the study of energy in its many aspects, the behavioral and social sciences can be characterized in terms of their concerns with the processing and transformation of information" (p. 1). Thus, IP psychologists have taken the world for their oyster.

Cognitive Psychology

At some point IP psychology began to be treated as cognitive psychology. The change was probably motivated by the desires of many psychologists to study complex processes such as problem solving, which do not fit into the IP model experiments. Neisser (1969) is generally credited with triggering the change to "cognitive psychology." T. J. Knapp (1986) observed that *information* is a concept widely used in computer science and communications theory; hence, it is not distinctively psychological. (Thus we seek to differentiate *our* area from that of others!) Neisser's invention of the new term provided a more acceptable label for psychologists.

Neisser, of course, was not inventing a new concept. The psychology of cognition goes back to the philosophical psychologists like Herbart, and was developed in terms of innate capacities by the Scottish school. T. V. Moore published a book on *Cognitive Psychology* in 1939; although it had a distinctly philosophical flavor, it made use of the research of Wundt and the Würzburg school. Moore's definition of his subject matter showed its ties to the Scots and also to IP psychology: he proposed to "throw light on the problem of how knowledge gets into the mind." Cognitive psychology, then, was "that branch of general psychology which studies the way in which the human mind receives impressions from the external world and interprets the impressions thus received" (p. v). Clearly this embraces the information-processing research.

After the publication of Neisser's book, cognitive psychology flourished. New journals were founded: *Cognitive Psychology,* founded in 1969, *Cognition* in 1972, and *Memory and Cognition* in 1973. Psychology faculties began to introduce courses in the area, which opened a market for textbooks using—and sometimes limited to—cognitive concepts.

Why were the theories of learning proposed by Hull, Skinner, Lewin, and others perceived as failing to deal with "how knowledge gets into the mind"? As has been noted earlier, the behaviorists had preferred to study learning in animals, necessarily simpler and more mechanical than human learning; further, most behaviorists rejected conscious material, and much of what children study in school is conscious and symbolic, not overt responding. With an echo of John B. Watson's manifesto of 1913, L. E. Bourne (1973) aggressively asserted that cognitive psychology's domain included all human activity: "No behavior is noncognitive. No behavior is without competence. Behavior itself . . . is characterizable in terms of a set of parameters or attributes which fall into the categories cognition, competence, intention, and performance—all psychological, all behavioral—*nothing less*" (p. 315; italics in original). Bourne was not claiming that all behavior is conscious, but he was counterattacking the behaviorist eviction of consciousness from scientific psychology.

Frederic Bartlett

Neisser considered Sir Frederic Bartlett (1886–1969) the true founder of cognitive psychology; Neisser also praised Tolman for his sturdy defense of expectancies and cognitive maps in the face of entrenched opposition. Bartlett, a Cambridge University psychologist, studied the Ebbinghaus method of measuring memory for nonsense syllables and concluded that this would never provide insights into the everyday role of remembering as the basis for adaptive behavior. He advocated a "naturalistic" way of studying human behavior, in contrast to the rigidly controlled laboratory conditions made standard by Wundt.

Bartlett earned his status as the founding father of cognitive psychology with his pioneering work *Remembering* (1932). In this book, he reported numerous studies on memory for drawings and stories, both more realistic than the nonsense syllables. One methodological innovation was to have the same person make repeated recalls of the same material; another was to have one person's recall become the stimulus for the next individual to learn.

Bartlett's interest was not in the *outcome*, the remembered material, but in the *processing* that went on between learning and recall. He pointed out that "In a . . . constantly changing environment, literal recall is extraordinarily unimportant. . . . Condensation, elaboration, and invention are common features of ordinary remembering, and these all very often involve the mingling of materials belonging originally to different 'schemata'" (1932, p. 204). Note that a *schema* is a general outline or skeleton of a story, on which details can be strung like ornaments on a tree. In other words, remembering is a constructive process in which one retrieves a sketch of the original material and then adds to, subtracts from, or modifies this structure. As Freud had alleged, Bartlett found that emotional similarities in stories caused them to become associated and led to the details of one slipping into the recall of another.

This view of memory as a transformational process (in which the item as recalled may have only a modest resemblance to the original stimulus material) justifies making it fundamental to cognitive psychology. Locke, it will be recalled, postulated *sensation* and *reflection* as the basic psychological processes. Reflection in Bartlett's pattern involves much more than a mirror image; reflection, as he used the term, means mulling over, rearranging, and putting into a more plausible form. Bartlett's emphasis on a tendency toward closure and toward a good Gestalt have caused some proponents of Gestalt to claim Bartlett for their school, but he was not committed to their set of postulates. None the less, his views (like those of Neisser) have much in common with those of Koffka and of Lewin in particular. The behavioral environment is not identical with the geographical environment. And remember Freud's distinction between physical trauma and fantasied trauma. All of these trends converge on the development of a cognitive psychology. We see again the emergence of the "appearance-versus-reality" motif so important in the historical development of scientific psychology.

Schema   Bartlett's research convinced him that the memory trace has something of the quality of a skeleton or a stripped-down version of what happened. This he called a *schema,* a diagram or summary of what was observed. At the time of recall, one activates a schema of the event and adds details as they seem appropriate; that is, memory is a reconstructive process. Studies of "real-life" memory, as opposed to lists of nonsense syllables, indicate that much of purported recall is reconstruction. An interesting example comes from the London blitz of 1940. Observers at the scene tape-recorded victims' accounts of what happened. About forty years later, many of these people were interviewed and asked to describe events in the blitz. Only a very small percentage of the details given in the "blitz" interviews appeared in the follow-up study—and conversely, many of the details given in the 1980s could not be located in the original transcripts.

The concept of the schema is related to a somewhat more widely used term: *frame of reference*. This frame consists of generalized beliefs and information about the topic or context of an event. Lashley (1950) wrote an informative analysis of his own memory processes: "When I read a scientific paper, the new facts presented become associated with the field of knowledge of which it is a part. Later availability of the specific items of the paper depends on a partial activation of the whole body of associations. . . . I believe that recall involves the subthreshold activation of a whole system of associations which exert some sort of mutual facilitation" (pp. 497–498). While Lashley did not use the word *schema*, he pointed to a linkage with a whole set of memories, not a single S-R association such as his mentor, Watson, had envisioned. (See also Northway, 1940.)

Problem Solving

One reason for the switch from information-processing psychology to cognitive psychology was to affirm the relevance of studies of reasoning and problem solving. The Würzburg school had devised an experimental design in which a simple task was timed; then another task was added, and the two-step procedure was timed; then a third and even a fourth task might be employed. The researchers took the time for the one-step task and subtracted it from the time used for the two-step operation; the difference was assumed to measure the duration of the "higher" mental activity.

R. J. Sternberg (1979) devised an information-processing study using a common intelligence-test item. For example, he might present the following analogy: "LAWYER is to CLIENT as DOCTOR is to PATIENT (true or false?)" He would obtain the time required to recognize *Lawyer;* then the time to identify the *Lawyer–Client* relationship; then three of the elements; and finally all four. By subtracting the time at each step from that of the next higher step, he assumed that he was measuring the time needed for the additional task. This logic is called the assumption of *serial processing.* Sternberg figured that his typical subject spent 54 percent of the total time encoding the content of the problem; inference required an added 12 percent of the time; mapping the paired analogy took 10 percent of the total time; another 10 percent was used for application; and 17 percent was used for the response.

The subtractive method proves that some additional process has been introduced, but the exact time involved is speculative. *Parallel* processing is probably involved. J. M. Cattell (1886) had demonstrated in Wundt's laboratory that adding a new unit of the same task does not give a uniform increase in processing time. He had subjects respond by naming one letter; then he widened the exposure window so they could see two letters at the same time, and the time per letter dropped; when the window allowed three letters to be seen, the time dropped further. Clearly, while the letter was being identified and the name located and pronounced, the next letter was being identified, and so on.

Palmer and Kimchi (1986) seemed to support the serial processing theory. "In stage theories," they wrote, "each operation has a specific duration. . . . Before the end of this time interval the operation has no output, and at the end its output is assumed to be fully available as input to the next operation" (p. 54). And they concluded, "In one form or another, stage models have dominated IP theories of flow dynamics ever since [the Sternberg work]" (p. 45).

George Mandler (1985) did not agree with the Palmer and Kimchi judgment. He asserted that most scholars now prefer a parallel processing approach. But this approach, he conceded, leads to another theoretical snag. He asked, "How does a parallel system produce linear output?" He suggested that a solution might be found in the unity of consciousness; when processing is complete, awareness of the answer is triggered, and action follows.

Constructivism

The role of the active organism is the main theme of the cognitive psychologists. Bartlett's conception of remembering was that a stimulus may reactivate a stored part or a memory trace; this then draws in associated material to fill out details that are not recorded as part of the schema. It follows that much of what passes for recall is really reconstruction, a phenomenon familiar to many professionals who deal with "facts" about the commission of crimes. Interpolated events (after the crime) often get incorporated into the memory of the event itself, the stereotypes about the behavior of certain kinds of persons or details of past experiences with such persons become intertwined with the actual events.

Although constructivism does not play an active part in IP psychology, the conception of the organism as innately endowed with certain capacities and routines for processing (e.g., transferring material from STS to LTS) is compatible with the active organism in Bartlett's approach. And this kind of organism seems more adaptable to the needs of the neobehaviorists—with the interpolation of expectations and intentions into a behavior cycle—than the extreme environmentalism postulated by Hull and Skinner.

Bartlett (1932) offered still another criticism of the specific S-R theory of a behavioral unit. When one is playing tennis, each stroke may be considered a single response to a specific stimulus, the ball. This, he argued, is grossly oversimplified. If I swing my racket at a ball, the specific act is modified by my estimate of the speed of the ball, my bodily posture, the nearness of the net, the location of my opponent, and my conception of tennis strategy. These differences have generally been ignored by behaviorists, who have written as if one pedal press were interchangeable with another. (Indeed, they are; but this simple identity does not hold for everyday skilled behavior.)

Attribution Theory

A specialized offshoot of cognitive psychology developed in the 1970s. It involves a constructivist process in which the observer attributes a "cause" to some unit of behavior. E. E. Jones and R. E. Nisbett (1972) summarized a number of studies in which observers attempted to infer the factors behind the action. This phenomenon is reminiscent of the Gestalt use of the concept of *physiognomic perception,* in which human emotions were perceived as inhering in inanimate objects, or in which a person's appearance was endowed with properties which could not be physically visible.

One of the interesting problems uncovered by attribution theory research is the difference between an Actor and an Observer. When an Actor does something and is asked, "Why did you do that?" the answer is typically put in terms of the environment: "He was trying to bully me," or "She was being flirtatious." But an Observer watching the action tends to ascribe the "cause" to an inner trait of personality of the Actor; "He is typically aggressive," or "He is only interested in women."

Jones and Nisbett (1972) pointed out that this difference in interpretation may be a function of information processing; in fact, Actor and Observer may not even pick up on the same information from the event. As Jones and Nisbett wrote, *"different aspects of the available information are salient for actors and observers"* (p. 85; italics in original).

From the viewpoint of theory, one might expect behaviorists to emphasize the judgment of the Observer (trait explanation) because of the traditional behaviorist preference for data not based on introspection. However, the emphasis on the situation is also compatible with a behaviorist view. Jones and Nisbett suggested that the implicit trait interpretation given by the Observer is only a projection, and that this consistent pattern "is in the eye of the beholder." Others have argued that the situational determination of action is also "in the eye of the beholder." Not much theoretical advance can be expected from this kind of argument.

From Gestalt to Neo-Gestalt?

As I have already noted, many of the IP and cognitive psychology speculations overlap with Gestalt propositions (see Chapter Twelve). A major difference is that Gestalt tended to emphasize figure–ground relations as determined by physical stimuli; that is, the Gestalt was physical before it became phenomenal. The theoretical bias of the psychologists reviewed in this chapter is toward a constructivist or active organism interpretation; according to this view, the person may construct a configuration in the absence of appropriate physical inputs. The term *neostructuralism* is thus not entirely suitable, although the IP research has been primarily atomistic.

On the basis of configurational studies, L. C. Robertson (1986) suggested that "cognitive psychology" is really a neo-Gestalt phenomenon. He noted interpretations showing that the whole message may determine the way in which the parts are perceived, the memory work on transformation of chaotic messages into "good form," the closure of in-complete patterns as in the addition of details to memory schemata, and so on.

An alternative view would be that the gap between structuralist and Gestalt psychology has been closing. Just as neobehaviorist thinking has incorporated both conscious and overt responses, so the IP approach incorporates both structuralist and Gestalt ideas. It would seem that we can be cautiously optimistic that theoretical controversies and contradic-tions are being ironed out. This does not, of course, imply that the tender-versus-tough dichotomy will vanish, nor the emphasis on "pure science" versus "humanistic" psychology. But the development of a vocabulary acceptable to both schools may improve communication in the future.

CHAPTER 20

Theories of Individual Differences

A tradition has grown up in American psychology which segregates the domain of general psychology (the psychology of universal laws) from differential psychology (the psychology of individuals). Few psychologists would be so brash as to say that "individual-differences" thought and research cannot be considered "psychology"; yet most histories completely ignore the development of concepts relative to research on and application of measures of individuals. Theoretical writings especially have tended to ignore completely the field of differential psychology. There is a large body of work on aptitudes, achievements, attitudes, and personality traits, but there has been virtually no critical notice of this material by the theoreticians.

The reason is not exactly simple. Some of it may be the Wundt–Titchener tradition that psychology must be kept "pure" and untainted by practical applications. More of it, I suspect, is simply academic tradition. The British empiricists, the French mechanists, and the German physiologists sought abstract truths. The Scottish faculty psychology and the Francis Galton tradition were perceived as separate and distinct from that orientation. In the meantime, applied work based on measures of individual differences has multiplied to a point where it demands thoughtful consideration.

The case for a psychology of individual differences goes back, of course, to J. M. Cattell and Francis Galton, but the major theorists of general psychology declined to incorporate the Cattell-Galton subject matter into their theories. Titchener, as an obvious example, paid no attention to variations among his observers in sensory acuity, sensory threshold, speed of adaptation to stimuli, and so on. Similarly, Watson denied the relevance of individual differences ("Give me a dozen healthy infants . . ."), as had Meyer. Clark Hull developed an elaborate scheme for determining the probability of a response being learned by a hypothetical, perfectly average member of the species under investigation, but ignored differences in motivation, speed of acquisition, retentivity, rate of loss of a habit unit over time, and so on.

The first of the "mainstream" theorists to take explicit account of individual differences was E. C. Tolman (1932). Tolman wrote the H, A, T, E, variables into his equation for predicting learning; heredity and age were variables almost completely ignored by his colleagues; training and physiological variables were occasionally mentioned but not in the context of individual differences. Tolman recognized the relevance of such researches to general psychology, but his lead has not been widely followed.

The result has been the development of a separate body of theory devoted explicitly to the sources of differences in ability and personality among members of a given species. Generally this has been known as "differential psychology."

Intelligence

A cynic once defined *intelligence* as "what the intelligence tests measure." This probably was not a deliberate echo of Skinner's "a reinforcer is anything that reinforces"; it was a reflection of a pragmatic attitude that the tests had predictive value so they must be measuring some attribute of human beings.

If we approach the topic of intelligence operationally, we find that the tests present stimuli calculated to elicit specific responses. Each test item, then, constitutes the s in a given sHr (habit strength) unit. The test constructor, however, is primarily interested in a sample of these units and the relative standing of each test taker in his or her group. Figure 20.1 shows one way of conceptualizing the relation of specific observable responses and hypothetical "abilities." Each x in the diagram represents a single habit. A solid circle indicates a clustering or habits that are linked by associative bonds so that if one is emitted, there is a high probability that the others will also be available. The process by which this cross-item linkage is established was examined earlier, in Chapter Ten. A relevant analysis is that of Staats (1975), whose theory of hierarchy formation was shown in Figure 18.6. Hull's habit hierarchy concept had a different orientation (determining which of various possible responses would be elicited by the stimulus); Staats was concerned with linkages among the responses themselves. Briefly, if Johnny can correctly solve 8×9, there is a high probability that he can also solve $15 + 31$. The stimuli are not the same, but they belong to the same class.

It is impossible for a test to cover every example of numerical behavior; the psychologist therefore prepares a *sample* of habit-strength units

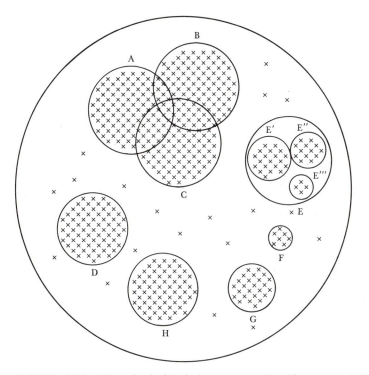

FIGURE 20.1   Hypothetical Relations among Specific Acts and General
Abilities or Personality Traits

x = a specific observable act

Circles = clusters of acts which occur together more often than chance
        would permit

Overlapping circles = abilities or traits which have some common vari-
        ance but also some unique variance

E', E", E''' = integrated clusters within a given domain, relatively inde-
        pendent of each other

(From Stagner, 1937, p. 137, reprinted by permission of McGraw-Hill Book Co.)

and determines empirically that they do, in fact, form a positive correlation matrix or, in Staats's term, a hierarchy.

At first glance, this statement of the intelligence-testing situation seems
to load the cards in favor of an environmentalist theory of the origin of
intelligence. Not so. The psychologists advocating a hereditarian view
can accept the same data and fit them into a genetic theory.

Information Processing

An alternative to the formulation just suggested has been offered by the
information-processing psychologists (see Chapter Nineteen). Posner

(1978) pointed out that a very useful test item is immediate memory span; another is repeating numbers or letters backward. Both skills increase steadily up to about age sixteen; and this can be interpreted as a maturation (heredity) effect. However, Posner suggested that speed of processing and ease of retrieval depend on familiarity, and that letters, numbers, words, and so on, become far more familiar with increasing age, so that the same child will generally show an increase in the number of tasks successfully executed. Training *(T)* was another of Tolman's variables; it is obvious that a child never exposed to numerical information will not develop habits of dealing effectively with numerical problems. To the extent that these factors affect "intelligence," we are dealing with the influence of "nature" versus "nurture," an issue long disputed in the psychological literature.

Intelligence: Early Developments

Like the nomothetic speculation of the British empiricists and rationalists, early discussions of intelligence had very little in the way of empirical backing. The history of psychology as discussed in earlier chapters suggests that theoretical concepts improve as research and data collection provide some anchoring points for theorizing.

Galtonism

It is convenient to begin a discussion of intellectual capacity with Sir Francis Galton. Galton, a believer in monarchy and aristocracy, held that noble birth carried with it a high probability of intellectual brilliance. His early book, *Hereditary Genius* (1869/1972), listed the eminent positions and accomplishments of aristocratic families. As his criterion of accomplishments included government posts which were open only to the aristocracy, his hypothesis was self-confirming.

Galton objected violently to the democratic notion that differences in accomplishment could be due to home environment and schooling. "I have no patience," he wrote, "with the hypothesis occasionally expressed . . . that babies are born pretty much alike. The experiences of the nursery, the school, the University, and of professional careers, are a chain of proofs to the contrary" (1869/1972, p. 56). Not surprisingly, views of intelligence as being determined by heredity have been denounced ever since by opponents of an aristocratic social order.

Galton was a true scion of the British empiricists: "Nothing is in the intellect unless it was first in the senses." He therefore theorized that superior sensory acuity, the ability to make sensory discriminations and to judge sensory inputs, should be excellent items to include in a test of intellectual capacity. However, he went beyond the Lockean empiricists by collecting masses of data and subjecting them to statistical analysis. This tradition has continued; most research in the field of individual differences is heavily sprinkled with number crunching.

Galton's experiments with sensory testing encouraged J. M. Cattell (who worked with Galton for a year or more after leaving Wundt and Leipzig) to institute a similar testing program for students applying for college admission. He was gravely disappointed when his student Clark Wissler (1901) published the correlations of sensory tests with college grades, which were uniformly near zero.

Studies of Immigrants   Galton was not the only researcher to allow prejudice to overrule a critical examination of the data. Several distinguished American psychologists uncritically accepted test scores purporting to show the intellectual inferiority of immigrant men who were tested in the U.S. Army during World War I. R. E. Fancher (1985) summarized the affair:

> Compared to native-born American whites, immigrants from northern Europe scored slightly lower, and those from southern and eastern Europe decidedly so. . . . Yerkes' colleague Carl Brigham made much of these findings in his book, and explained them on a genetic-racial basis. . . . Brigham asserted that the higher intelligence of native Americans and northern Europeans was due to their superior "Nordic" blood, as opposed to that of the inferior "Alpine" and "Mediterranean" racial types (p. 128).

Floyd Allport (1924b) looked at the data on racial differences and (unfortunately) agreed that the results could be interpreted as evidence of racial inferiority. We should not, he wrote, be alarmed at a charge of racism: "Scientific caution is to be commended, but it may be overdone" (p. 312).

Galton rose to the occasion with a "selective migration" hypothesis which must have bothered some American scientists. He had written long before these data on immigrants were collected that America attracted some undesirable characters:

> Whenever during the last ten or twelve generations, a political or religious party has suffered defeat, its prominent members, whether they were the best, or only the noisiest, have been apt to emigrate to America. . . . Every scheming knave, and every brutal ruffian, who feared the arm of the law, also turned his eyes in the same direction. . . . If we estimate the moral nature of Americans from their present social state, we shall find it to be just what we might have expected from such a parentage (1865, p. 320).

It might have been embarrassing to Galton, Brigham, Yerkes, and others if they had read a familiar passage from Cicero before citing race as an explanation for low mental performance. Cicero wrote to a friend, "Do not obtain your slaves from Britain because they are so stupid, and so utterly incapable of being taught." Or they might have heeded the Moorish scholar Said of Toledo, who observed, "Races north of the Pyrenees are of cold temperament and never reach maturity; they are of great stature and of a white color. But they lack all sharpness of wit and penetration." (The two quotations are from Thomas and Sillen, 1972, p. 23.)

It is astonishing to observe how far bigots will go in seeking evidence to support their prejudices. N. Weyl and S. T. Possony (1963) attempted to use paleoanthropology for this purpose; they wrote that "modern man emerged in Europe in substantially his present form 250,000 years ago, in China 150,000 years ago, but in Africa and north Borneo only 40,000 years ago. The Negro race, according to this evidence, differs by one to two hundred thousand years in evolutionary development" (p. 37). One can only imagine their chagrin when the Leakeys found fossils of primitive humans in northern Africa over a million years old; by Weyl and Possony's bizarre criterion, the black race ought to be the most mature and advanced of all subspecies of human beings.

Intelligence Tests and Intelligent Concepts

Shortly after the pioneering, if unsuccessful, work of Galton and Cattell, the quest for practical measures of intellectual capacity got under way in France. The leader of this development was an established psychologist, Alfred Binet (1857–1911). Binet had published a book, *Animal Magnetism* (1886), criticizing Anton Mesmer and his disciples; *Psychic Life of Microorganisms* (1887), an example of the kind of speculation about animal consciousness that irked John B. Watson; and other works dealing with applied psychology. Although Binet acknowledged being unable to read German, it is reasonably certain that he was familiar with the work of Wundt, Stumpf, and others.

Binet was not picked arbitrarily by the French government to head a project aimed at the early identification of mentally handicapped children. In fact, he had been propagandizing and lobbying for action to help the schools; only a few years had gone by since the nation had opened the schools to all children free of charge, and many disadvantaged children were doing poorly and dropping out. Binet helped found *La Société Libre pour l'Étude Psychologique de l'Enfant* and was its president when the government asked him to work on the project. It is quite possible that this was the first major government research grant to a psychologist.

Functional Age

Binet's major contribution to child psychology was the notion that mental capacity could be assigned an age level based on the tasks correctly performed by children at that age. Binet coined the phrase "mental age" (MA) to specify the age level at which a child was functioning; that is, one who could just solve problems typically solved by seven-year-olds, but not by six-year-olds, was assigned an MA of 7. Binet did not use the term *functional age,* which was introduced in 1953 by Ross McFarland to apply to adults as well as children.

Binet and his collaborator, Théophile Simon, decided that the path outlined by Galton and Cattell was not promising. They opted for simple everyday tasks such as counting, naming familiar objects, parts of the body, and the uses of objects, and interpreting proverbs. (Memory span was the only item common to their preliminary test and the Cattell battery.)

Binet took a strictly functionalist view of the problem. He was searching for a measure for "a fundamental faculty . . . this faculty is judgment, otherwise called good sense . . . the faculty of adapting oneself to circumstances" (quoted in Dennis, 1948, p. 417). But he suffered from a conflict, an ambivalence, about the origin of intelligence. At one point we find him saying, "It is understood that we here separate natural intelligence and instruction" (quoted on Dennis, p. 416), and at another, that it was necessary to inquire about acquired information as part of the measurement process. And in still another passage, Binet claimed, "We believe that we have succeeded in completely disregarding the acquired information of the subject" (quoted in Dennis, p. 416).

Binet was, however, opposed to the "fixed-level" theory of intelligence. He criticized the view that "The intelligence of an individual is a fixed quantity, a quantity that one cannot augment. . . . We must protest and react against this brutal pessimism" (quoted by Kamin, 1979, p. 91). Binet advocated the development of "mental orthopedics," a profession devoted to correcting children's handicaps and returning them to the normal educational process. It is interesting that he recognized the "stigma" problem that has proved a stumbling block for much remedial education in the United States. He also had some critical words for his fellow professionals: "When the child is taken to the clinic, the physician listens a great deal to the parents and questions the child very little, in fact scarcely looks at him, allowing himself to be influenced by a very strong presumption that the child is intellectually inferior" (quoted in Dennis, 1948, p. 414).

The concept of mental age seems to have been made explicit only in 1905: "Understanding the normal progress of intellectual development among normals, we shall be able to determine how many years such an individual is advanced or retarded" (quoted in Dennis, p. 415). Thus a child who could not pass the tasks which most of those in the same age group did pass was considered retarded. Binet's recommendation was that these children receive special tutoring and return to their regular class; today's educators will recognize this as a familiar problem.

William Stern

Binet had set up age norms and had assigned to a given child a mental age based on passing tests up to a set of norms (i.e., the point beyond which the child could not solve the problems presented). However, the MA alone seemed inadequate; one child of six might get an MA of 8, and another twelve years old might get an MA of 8. William Stern (1871–1938) proposed a solution that has become a familiar concept: the intelligence quotient, (IQ). He defined this "mental quotient" as "the ratio of mental to chronological age" (p. 42), and he wrote, *"This quotient shows what fractional part of the intelligence normal to his age* a feeble-minded child attains" (1914, p. 80; italics in original).

Stern recognized that some of the mensurational problems had not been eliminated by his innovation. He noted, first, that the difference in IQ predicts a higher rate of growth and a higher ceiling for the child of higher IQ, and second, that the tests passed by children of a given IQ are not always the same.

Stern realized that differences in home environment might enable one child to do better on one class of test items than another child. He thus approached the concept of "fluid intelligence" and "crystallized intelligence" proposed by R. B. Cattell (1963); as conceived by Cattell, fluid intelligence was determined mainly by inherent or maturational factors, whereas crystallized intelligence reflected environmental advantages. Fluid items included the information-processing variety of tasks: memory span, backward digit span, and perceptual discriminations. Crystallized items involved vocabulary, everyday information, and so on.

The work of Binet and Stern assumed—implicitly if not explicitly—that intelligence was some kind of capacity of the organism which facilitated learning about objects, customs, and language usage in the child's immediate environment. If a given child could be assigned an M.A. or an I.Q., this implied an all-around attribute which could show in a variety of tasks. Yet it was perfectly obvious that two children might have the same mental age, yet pass different tests to earn this score. This led to the development of theories of general plus special abilities.

Charles E. Spearman

The first theorist to make explicit the theory of general abilities supplemented by special abilities was Charles E. Spearman (1836–1945), a follower of Galton. Spearman's reputation is based in part on his statistical innovations, but his theory of intelligence is still widely cited (Spearman, 1927).

Spearman's theory of "individual psychology" involved several interesting assumptions. The first and most widely accepted was that performance on a specific test item was a function of general aptitude *(g)*, and of one or more specific *(s)* variables. Performance in arithmetic was found to depend on *g* plus a specific numerical variable. There may be a large number of *s* variables, since they depend partly on the environmental stimulus to which a response must be made. Less attention has been paid to some other general factors specified in Spearman's theory (some psychologists call them "group" factors in order to leave *g* as the undisputed general variable manifested in all "intelligent" performances). At any rate, these were: *c*, labeled retentivity or mental inertia; *o*, a variable somewhat like Hull's oscillation factor—in other words, a tendency toward fluctuations in performance, which Spearman found to vary considerably among his subjects; and *w*, a variable of "will power" or self-control, the ability to keep focused on a task. (Many American psychologists merged *c* with *g* and rejected *o* and *w*, the latter two because they appeared to be personality dimensions rather than intellectual capacities.) According to Spearman's formulation, performance on a given cognitive task would be a function of *g*, *c*, *o*, and *w*, along with s_1, s_2, and other specifics that depend on the nature of the stimulus material, which might be numerical or visual, for example. It would appear that Spearman viewed the general factors as being determined chiefly by heredity, and the specific factors by environment. However, he conceded that *g* and *w* might be modified by a decidedly favorable or unfavorable environment.

One way of representing Spearman's theory visually is shown in Figure 20.2. This figure, devised by Anne Anastasi (1976), suggests that there are overlaps in either stimulus variables or response variables, and that extensive overlap could be produced by a general factor. The figure does not, of course, offer any hypothesis as to how this overlap comes about.

Spearman generally favored the use of symbolic or abstract test items,

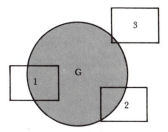

FIGURE 20.2   Spearman's Theory as Diagrammed by Anastasi

G = general intellectual ability (*g* in Spearman's style) 1, 2, and 3 = specific abilities. Performance on tasks in area 1 will be markedly influenced by *g*, whereas performance in area 3 will be virtually independent of *g*. *(From Anastasi, 1988, p. 382, reprinted by permission of Macmillan Publishing Co.)*

in part because they predicted school and other performances fairly well. As industrial psychologists have learned, such abstract skills may be of little value in the selection of employees, although they have better predictive value in the choosing of graduate students.

Spearman did not commit himself as to the nature of g. It is heavily involved in symbolic processing, and some psychologists have treated it as ability to learn, while others emphasize only the learning of abstractions. Spearman (1923) agreed with the Lockeans that all knowledge came through the senses, but he emphasized that the organism did not simply soak up information; the observations were differentiated, dissected, and compared. He specified two kinds of mental products ensuing from reflection on sensory data: *eduction of relations,* (what is the relation of HOUSE to ROOF?) and the *eduction of correlates* (what is the opposite of COLD?) These obviously come under the heading of information processing as this area was defined in Chapter Nineteen. They are, however, influenced by learning; an exception must be noted in that persons very low on g may seem completely incapable of grasping such abstractions.

It should be noted that Spearman was advocating a form of "determination from above," i.e., the shaping of a response by a prior mental set. This might be an instruction to give examples of a class, e.g., vertebrates, or to take some specifics and develop a generalized concept (horse, cow, pig, sheep would educe a concept of "domesticated animals"). The role of g in this process may involve selective attention and selective inhibition of responses not compatible with the instructions.

Cyril Burt

A successor to Spearman, and like Spearman an important influence on American thinking about intelligence, was Sir Cyril Burt (1883–1972). Burt had only minimal training in psychology, but was energized by a lifelong admiration for Francis Galton. When Burt's psychology mentor, William McDougall, learned of this enthusiasm for Galton, he assigned young Burt to try out some of Galton's testing devices. In this connection, Burt worked briefly with Charles Spearman. He also won a scholarship that enabled him to study in Germany.

Burt's early research used teachers' ratings of "intelligence" as the validating criterion for his tests. In general, the pattern of correlations that he obtained resembled those of Spearman, and Burt interpreted them as confirming Spearman. But he went further. He found that pupils at private schools (confusingly labeled "public schools") did better on tests than those from a local grammar school (in American terms, a public school). Burt leaped to the conclusion, derived from Galton, that as the private-school boys came from upper-class families, they were *inherently* brighter than the sons of local merchants and artisans (Burt, 1966).

Regrettably, Burt is best known for his discredited studies of mono-zygotic (identical) and dizygotic (fraternal) twins. He apparently did ad-minister intelligence tests to some pairs of twins and found that the iden-ticals correlated with each other more highly than did the fraternals. Unfortunately, it appears that he wanted to keep publishing without doing more testing; his later articles added to the number of cases reported, yet the correlation coefficients remained identical. Leon Kamin, an American critic of the heredity thesis, found so many unchanged coef-ficients with changed numbers of cases that he concluded this was statis-tically impossible.

Later Leslie Hearnshaw, a psychologist and a friend of Burt's, was asked to do Burt's biography. He was distressed to find that, during the period of the later papers, Burt had tested no new subjects and that the research assistant alleged to have helped him did not exist. He had even gone so far as to invent a fictitious student thesis, to which he referred as the source of some of his data. Hearnshaw (1979) found that Burt, an ambitious man, wanted the prestige of a successful scientific career without doing the usual amount of work. Psychologists, we must con-clude, are only human; but it is distressing that we must gaze suspi-ciously at any especially dramatic finding.

There have been several scientific scandals in which an assistant, knowing what the superior wanted to find, faked the evidence accordingly. Paul Kammerer, a Viennese biologist, was a victim of such an assistant. Errors may also occur accidentally. L. E. Travis, of the University of Iowa, re-ported some data around 1930 that seemed to show a very high corre-lation (+0.80) of knee-jerk latency with IQ. Regrettably, when he had a new assistant measure the knee-jerk records without knowing the IQ's, the correlation dropped to about +.05. (Travis notified his colleagues of the error.)

Louis Leon Thurstone

Not every psychologist studying the measurement of "intelligence" has accepted the assumption of a "general" ability. A pioneer in the factorial study of intelligent behavior was L. L. Thurstone (1887–1955), probably the first modern figure to reject the g hypothesis (the faculty psycholo-gists had postulated a variety of mental abilities but without supporting data). Like Tolman, Thurstone had an undergraduate degree in engi-neering and a talent for mathematics—he developed the first widely-used computational routine for sorting out factors from a correlation matrix.

Thurstone considered that the variations among persons on cognitive performances were too great to justify the g concept. He held that his data pointed to the existence of seven independent clusters of ability; these were respectively Verbal Comprehension, Word Fluency, Number

Facility, Spatial Visualization, Associative Memory, Perceptual Speed, and Reasoning. He called these the "Primary Mental Abilities" (1938). It must be noted that, while factor analysis gives an illusion of precision and objectivity, critics looked at Thurstone's data and disagreed with his interpretations. Assigning a numerical value to a phenomenon does not guarantee an objective underlying reality.

To the extent that mental testing is a valuable adjunct to counseling and guidance, Thurstone's seven primary mental abilities constituted an important improvement over the M.A. and I.Q. A profile of seven variables can suggest career opportunities where the person will be at an advantage and warn against careers in which deficits of ability may constitute a serious handicap.

Such observations indicate that Thurstone was not quite the embodiment of the "tough-minded" scientist he might seem to have been. He shared with the humanistic psychologists a concern for the unique individual personality. In 1923 he wrote—obviously dissenting from Titchener and from the behaviorists with their emphasis on environmental variables—"I suggest that we dethrone the stimulus. He is only nominally the ruler of psychology. The real ruler of the domain which psychology studies is the individual and his motives, desires, wants, ambitions, cravings, aspirations. The stimulus is merely the more or less accidental fact. . . ." (1923, p. 364.) This emphasis on the individual was also exemplified in his presidential address to the American Psychological Association in 1933 which was titled "The Vectors of the Mind."

Raymond Bernard Cattell

Studies of the clustering of performances in the area of ability (as also of personality) necessarily become statistically complicated. As I noted above, a factored matrix does not interpret itself, and different "rotations" of the vectors can prompt different hypotheses about the way these are related in the symbolic functioning of the person. A follower of Spearman and Burt who migrated to America and influenced the development of this aspect of psychology was R. B. Cattell (1905–   ).

Cattell was trained by Burt at the University of London. However, most of his professional life was spent in the United States. He and Thurstone were probably the most prominent of the psychologists making major use of factor analysis as a research tool. He agreed with Thurstone on the key issue of group factors as against Spearman's g, but he claimed that his factor rotations led to a different theory about the structure of intelligence.

One of the problems with exhaustive manipulation of test correlations is that the statistical result is no more trustworthy than the reliabilities of the individual performances on which the computations are based. Cattell had a fondness for brief tests of what he considered to be primary intellectual abilities, and these short work-samples were inevitably unreliable, or at least of dubious reliability. (The reliability of an individual test in one of his batteries was often below $+.50$; this leaves one with grave doubt as to the legitimacy of calling this a measure of any unified skill or capacity.) Statisticians also question using such tests in second-order and third-order factor analysis.

In the field of ability testing, probably Cattell's major contribution has been a conceptual one. He proposed that we recognize *fluid* intelligence (G_f) and *crystallized* intelligence (G_c). The first would correspond to the sort of intelligence Galton was seeking (i.e., some kind of organismic quality—probably innate—involving the speed of perceiving and learning), whereas crystallized intelligence involves the acquisition of the information and skills demanded by the culture. J. L. Horn, trained by Cattell, originally found evidence supporting the G_f and G_c dichotomy but later decided that a minimum of four "intelligences" was requisite (Horn, 1985). In the meantime, a fair number of studies supporting (and at least a few casting doubt on) Cattell's two varieties of intelligence have been published. The outcome of this debate is still in doubt.

Joy Paul Guilford

The most elaborate and sophisticated theory of intelligence so far is that proposed by J. P. Guilford (1897–   ). Guilford, one of the last students to work with E. B. Titchener, did his doctoral thesis with Karl M. Dallenbach, a devoted structuralist. In the earlier portion of his career, Guilford moved from psychophysics to *Psychometric Methods* (1936), to *Personality* (1959), and then *The Nature of Human Intelligence* (1967).

Guilford's approach is primarily empirical; he has been skeptical of the value of a theoretical system: "I have never had ambitions to attempt to build a system of psychology, perhaps because I noted from my Cornell experience how restricting it can be" (1967, p. 186). Many, if not most, psychologists would agree, at least with the idea that structuralist theory was restrictive. On the other hand, it seems likely that Guilford's work on intelligence was based on an unstated theory because of the systematic thinking revealed in the research.

One example of this theoretical orientation is his criticism of his colleagues for overdoing their devotion to the principle of parsimony (see the discussion of Ockham's razor in Chapter One). In developing his "structure-of-intellect" model, Guilford not only hypothesized several new factors but devised tests for them. These tests led to the identification of about twenty new "factors of intellect" and a prediction that even more would be identified.

The SOI (structure of intellect) model is based on information-processing assumptions. Guilford began his work by trying out large numbers of tests on rather large populations. (He was aided by sizable grants from

the U.S. Navy, which was concerned about selection tests that could predict success in a naval career.) By the time he had accumulated some
forty factors, Guilford began to search for a rational structure that would
reveal something more than an empirical association.

At some point, Guilford generated an insight that led him to a three-
dimensional model. He noted that his group could be sorted out on
three independent dimensions, or continua. One was the kind of *processing* involved: comprehension, remembering, and fluency of ideas. A second depended on the kind of *input* involved: visual, symbolic, and semantic. Finally, he settled on a characterization of the third dimension
in terms of *products:* classes, relations, and systems.

When he attempted to plot these, Guilford produced a cube, a model
of intellect (Figure 20.3). This is the final form of the model, and it has
four kinds of contents, five kinds of operations, and six kinds of products. This generates 120 possible "varieties of intelligence," although

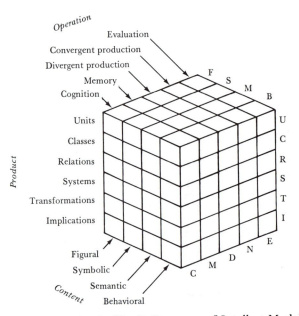

FIGURE 20.3   Guilford's Structure-of-Intellect Model

The three dimensions of the cube are: bottom, left to right, content of
the intelligent act (figural, symbolic, semantic, or behavioral); vertical, top
to bottom: products of the intelligent act (units, classes, relations, systems,
transformations, and implications); and top, front to back: operations
(cognition, memory, divergent production, convergent production, and
evaluation).   *(From Guilford, 1967, p. 63, Figure 62, reprinted by permission
of McGraw-Hill Book Co.)*

Guilford's model does not require that each be completely independent of all the others. In fact, not all of them have yet been confirmed by research; Guilford (1985) estimated that he and his colleagues had identified about 98 to his satisfaction. This is truly a remarkable achievement.

The assignment of specific tests to a box in Figure 20.3 was done by logic as much as by magnitude of factor loading. Guilford (1967) wrote, "if one collects a half-dozen verbal factors in one set, and an appropriate . . . half-dozen nonverbal factors in another," one would be led to assign them to parallel locations. Thus Guilford eventually arrived at his SOI model. This model has three independent dimensions: content, operation, and product. For the content dimension he found four categories: figural, symbolic, semantic, and behavioral. For operations five different kinds were located: evaluation, convergent production, divergent production, memory, and cognition. The logic becomes apparent when we note that cognition is basic, memory is basic to the remaining tests, evaluation depends on competence at divergent and convergent production. The third dimension involved the product resulting from the mental operation; he identified six varieties, the simplest being units, then classes, relations, systems, transformations, and implications. The neat way in which these categories mesh is apparent from Figure 20.3.

Guilford's theory of intelligence takes off from an information-processing approach. He wrote, "intelligence should be defined as *a systematic collection of abilities or functions for processing information of different kinds in various forms*" (1985, p. 231; italics in original).

The SOI model is not only sophisticated and complex; it is also comprehensive. It has been criticized for excessive complexity and coverage. Guilford replied that in dealing with complex phenomena, we are likely to need complex theories. He noted that where early investigators had found little validity in sensory tests, his data related visual and auditory inputs in a meaningful way to other cognitive performances. His tests were not, of course, a simple matter of visual acuity or differential threshold; it involved operations such as remembering and evaluation. Learning performances were also differentiated and were shown to have meaningful relations with other tests. Tests of creativity were also fitted into the SOI model.

The intriguing parallel between a three-dimensional SOI model, Wundt's tridimensional theory of feeling, and Osgood's (1957) three-dimensional semantic space was explored by Guilford and R. Hoepfner (1971, p. 349). Whether these parallels indicate that psychological reality is Euclidean or Einsteinian is a topic beyond the scope of this book. Guilford and Hoepfner did develop the relationship between their SOI model and faculty psychology: "It was not the faculty psychologists' type of thinking that should have been condemned. Where they were wrong was in their choice of faculty concepts and for regarding them as unitary powers or functions when they are decidedly not. The main trouble with

the faculty psychologists was that they lacked empirical methods for discovering unitary or unique functions and for checking up on their hypotheses regarding them" (1971, pp. 348–349). This is a familiar problem in the history of any science. Speculation often outruns technology;
to take a specific example, the phi phenomenon (Wertheimer) could not
have been tested until stroboscopic lighting was available.

R. J. Sternberg

Another psychologist who treated intelligence as an example or perhaps
an evaluation of information processing was R. J. Sternberg (1949–   ).
Sternberg (1985) offered a threefold breakdown of intelligence: *metacomponents* were described as "higher-order control processes used for
executive planning, monitoring, and evaluation of.one's performance in
a task" (p. 62). This seems to be related to Staats's "hierarchy" concept
but does not parallel the Guilford SOI model. The metacomponents include identifying a problem, diagnosing it, choosing established action
patterns that may cope successfully (these are called *components*), monitoring feedback, and so on. A second level is *performance components,* such
as encoding information, inferring relevant relations within the information, and examining past solutions for relevance in the new situation.
These components correspond to some of Guilford's "varieties of intelligence." Finally, intelligence involves learning new information that may
help one to cope with the problem. To no one's surprise, this led to the
conclusion that ability to learn, especially verbal material, is an important
component of intelligence.

According to Sternberg, intelligence may involve rejecting some high-
probability responses in favor of others lower in the hierarchy. Consider,
for example, an analogies item: "TREE:ANIMATE :: PENCIL : (a) IN-
ANIMATE, (b) PAPER." Here, the linkage of *pencil* to *paper* is obviously
closer than any link to *inanimate.* But the intelligent response is *inanimate;* thus, the high-probability response must be inhibited if one is to
achieve a correct response.

Other varieties of ability, such as mechanical aptitude, are of concern
to vocational counselors and employment managers. These abilities have
not, so far, inspired any theoretical speculations of significance, and so
are not included here. On the other hand, several varieties of individual
differences in psychological attributes are relevant to the consideration
of cognitive theory; they are sketched briefly in the following pages.

Cognitive Style

In the period just after World War II, there was a sudden outpouring
of perceptual studies, called the "new look" (see Chapter Nineteen). These
involved the use of procedures developed by the structuralists, but in

the service of hypotheses generated by Gestalt and psychoanalytic theory.

Another development that was intimately implicated with these studies
of perceptual dynamics was the concept of *cognitive style*. Like intelligence, cognitive style cuts across all the domains of reception and processing of informational inputs. I shall mention only a few of the styles
that have been discovered as characteristic features of a specific individual's cognitive functioning.

Field Dependence   Gestalt psychologists pointed out that although most
of the meaning of a visual (or other perceptual) experience is carried by
the figure, we must not ignore the ground. Indeed, many Gestalt experiments demonstrated that a change in the ground modifies the figure.
Witkin, et al. (1962) speculated that there were consistent individual differences in field dependence or independence. One of their successful
procedures was the "rod-and-frame" test. This consisted of placing the
person in a dark room in front of a lighted square (the frame). Inside
the square was an illuminated rod. Square and rod could be moved independently; the experimenter tipped the square to one side or the other
and asked the subject to set the rod at the true vertical. Some individuals
were strongly influenced by the frame (ground), tipping the rod as much
as ten or fifteen degrees in the direction of the tilted frame. These qualified as field-dependent; the position of the rod (figure) was modified by
the frame (ground). Others set the rod at or close to the true vertical,
ignoring the tilt of the frame; they were considered field-independent.
Witkin et al. found that this dimension was consistent in other tasks; e.g.,
if a simple figure is embedded in a complex drawing, the field-independent persons found it more quickly than the field-dependent persons.

Correlates of this cognitive style indicated that it had extensive effects
in many aspects of behavior. Dependent cases, for example, were more
susceptible to propaganda, more suggestible, and more influenced by
majority opinion in the Sherif-Asch type of experiment.

The extent of this generalization can be illustrated by the work of
S. A. Rudin (1955). He hypothesized that this cognitive style would affect the self-percept, as well as conformist behavior. Specifically, field-
dependent persons would be more affected in their perceptions of people by the social situation than would field-independent individuals.

Rudin's design was quite simple. Using the rod-and-frame test, he selected a group of "dependent" and a group of "independent" persons.
All of them took a self-description test using Osgood's semantic scales
(see Chapter Ten). The instructions were to "think of yourself giving a
speech in front of a class. Now describe yourself in that situation." Later
the subjects were asked to "think of yourself lost in a dark and dangerous forest. Now describe yourself in that situation." Using several such
imaginary contexts, Rudin demonstrated that the field-independent sub

jects changed their descriptions of themselves only slightly; the field-dependent individuals showed large changes in self-image as the context changed. This finding seems to indicate the generality of the cognitive style across physical and social domains. (For further details see Rudin and Stagner, 1958.)

Rigidity   Another cognitive style, which may overlap somewhat with field dependence, has been called *rigidity*. The following test was devised by G. S. Klein and P. Holzman (1950). They took a task used by Harry Helson in his AI (adaptation level) research and used it to prospect for individual differences. The observer saw squares projected on a screen, and was asked to judge their sizes. The series began with five squares, varying from two to six inches on a side, shown at random. After three runs through these five, the experimenter surreptitiously removed the smallest (two-inch) square, replacing it with a seven-inch square. This was repeated until the set ranged from ten inches to fourteen inches.

Each subject formed an AL of about four inches on the first round. But as the physical stimuli changed, some observers changed, keeping accurate track of the physical stimuli. Others held onto their original AL; the authors reported that one subject was, just before the end, judging a thirteen-inch square to be only four inches on a side. Klein and Holzman labeled the dimension "rigidity–flexibility," based on the fact that some subjects held to a prior standard in the face of environmental change. These authors also used the terms *levelers* and *sharpeners,* based on the tendency of the rigid group to level out changes in the stimuli, whereas the others exaggerated or at least kept pace with the changing stimuli. In other tests, the sharpeners reproduced drawings and exaggerated irregularities, whereas the levelers smoothed out the contours of the drawings. Personality differences were also found to distinguish between levelers and sharpeners.

Tolerance of Ambiguity   Another perceptual style that seems intriguing has been studied by Else Frenkel-Brunswik (1949). In connection with her work on the "authoritarian personality" project, she concluded that some of the persons she interviewed were very uncomfortable in the face of uncertainty about political issues. They became anxious if it appeared that their established views might be incorrect.

The test she developed has an obvious similarity to the changing squares of Klein and Holzman. She devised drawings that changed step by step (e.g., a cat clearly outlined changed subtly, becoming fuzzy, eventually changing into a dog). Some observers clung to the "cat" percept almost to the end of the series; others called the figure unclear or detected the emerging "dog" before it was well defined.

The personality variables associated with this style were similar to those noted by Klein and Holzman. Rigid individuals indulged in black–white thinking (all judgments were extreme; no middle ground was recognized). Flexible persons (tolerating the ambiguity) were also more flexible with regard to political issues. This polarized thinking, of rigid personalities, Frenkel-Brunswik reasoned, was a defense against the anxiety evoked by uncertainty. As the psychoanalysts have pointed out, individuals with a strong need for security often become very anxious in ambiguous situations. This connection suggests that the environment, especially early parent–child relations of consistent or variable treatment of the child, may affect the formation of a cognitive style.

Personality Traits

Although both cognitive and personality variables are aspects of ID (individual difference) psychology, they have traditionally been kept in different logical compartments. This is unfortunate, as they interact in much of human behavior.

T. Wolf, a biographer of Binet, stated that Binet never approved of a dividing line between the intellectual and dynamic aspects of the individual child. Wolf (1973) quoted Binet as saying that "the separation between abilities and personality traits is artificial and the two domains need to be rejoined in interpreting an individual's test scores" (pp. 217–218). The argument is that performance may be as much a function of energy mobilization, control of attention, and persistence, as it is of intellectual capacity.

Over the last fifty years, evidence to support Binet has accumulated impressively. One of the earliest studies (Stagner, 1933) demonstrated that predictability of performance was a function, in part, of personality. College students were separated on the basis of personality test scores into fairly homogeneous groups. Those with favorable scores (dominant, emotionally stable, and self-sufficient) had high correlations of ability with grades. Those on the other end of the three dimensions (submissive, neurotic, and dependent) showed low predictability. The data were interpreted as meaning that a surplus of negative emotions (worry, hostility, depression, anxiety, and guilt) led to highly variable behavior; one such person might concentrate on study to compensate for a problem, whereas another would ignore academic demands in favor of rumination over the unpleasant aspects of life.

Trait Measures In principle, any attribute of personality that can be named can also be measured. Inventories use the following method: If an adjective such as *dominant* is hypothesized to indicate a consistent trait of personality, a number of acts involving dominance or submission may be presented to the respondents. If the items intercorrelate highly (if dominant answers go together, and submissive responses occur together), the trait hypothesis can be accepted.

Perhaps the first such inventory used in American psychology was the Woodworth Personal Data Sheet. First used during World War I, it was devised by R. S. Woodworth and was administered to thousands of soldiers, although it is not clear that much use was made of the data. The inventory consisted of lists of symptoms reported by neurotics, and the theory was that an increasing number of symptoms predicted a greater likelihood of psychiatric breakdown in combat. An account can be found in H. L. Hollingworth (1920). It is important mainly for the quantitative view of traits (i.e., using an inventory score as an index of probability that the trait label properly applies to a specific person).

In recent years, the number of inventories has increased, along with their complexity. One of the most widely used is the Minnesota Multiphasic Personality Inventory (MMPI), published by S. R. Hathaway and J. C. McKinley (1940). This test resembles the Woodworth inventory in that most of the items were lifted from psychiatric case histories. The earliest scoring was based on the similarity of response patterns to those of a group of psychiatric patients (schizophrenics, depressives, and so on). Another, apparently more sophisticated, test is the California Psychological Inventory (Gough, 1987). The scores for this inventory are based on a factor analysis of the intercorrelations of the answers. The method of interpreting the scores is also interesting: A person is first classified as falling into one of four types (called alpha, beta, gamma, and delta); then the individual scores are compared with norms for that group. This procedure, Gough claimed, resulted in more accurate insights into the person's temperament and probable behavior than use of the trait score alone.

Other widely used inventories are those by Cattell (1956), Guilford (1956), and A. L. Comrey (1966). The use of such inventories is quite common in student counseling, employee selection, marital conflict resolution, and so on.

Personality differences have also been studied by the use of the Rorschach inkblots (1921), the Thematic Apperception Test (Murray, 1938), and various other projective methods. These procedures assume that a person "sees" in these ambiguous materials phenomena that reflect the respondent's personality; in other words, they rely on the difference between physical environment and perceived environment emphasized by Gestalt and humanistic psychologists.

The two questions asked regarding all tests of cognitive capacity, cognitive style, and personality relate to *reliability* and *validity*. The reliabilities of personality inventories vary but are reasonably high (+.75 is probably an average figure). The validity of personality measures is more complicated: What theory is the researcher trying to validate? Several predictive studies have shown that personality scores predict managerial success as well as or better than intelligence (see Bentz, 1967; Harrell and Harrell, 1973; Stagner, 1984).

Various theoretical interpretations of these validity studies have been offered. R. Stagner (1984) noted that a trait can be considered a generalized way of perceiving a class of situations, and that such perceptions would guide behavior; for example, a dominant person will see a committee meeting as something to take over, whereas a submissive individual may see it as an opportunity to let others make decisions. Traits also function as "directive states," inhibiting some responses and facilitating others (see discussion of Staats, Chapter Eighteen). Traits may influence the focusing of energy on a task. Personality, then, may affect one's use of one's abilities in a variety of ways.

Origins of Individual Differences

A perennial ground for debate among ID psychologists relates to the issue of origins. The faculty psychologists had generally opted for a nativist interpretation of differences in cognitive capacities or in emotional tendencies. Behaviorists have favored environment, with an emphasis on learning verbal skills and on acquiring conditioned emotional reactions. Not all are as exuberant as John B. Watson (Chapter Nine) whose claim, "Give me a dozen healthy infants . . .", went well beyond what most of his successors would endorse. At any rate, the controversy has centered for years on "nature versus nurture" or "heredity versus environment."

Hereditary determination of intelligence has been espoused by large numbers of psychologists. I have noted that Alfred Binet rejected this hypothesis but conceded that heredity might play a part. He had also proposed "mental orthopedics," a helping skill that would bring the retarded child up to normal. Curiously enough, many American psychologists, who might be expected to endorse an egalitarian philosophy regarding intelligence, dropped the ideal of equality in favor of innate, unchangeable differences.

The opinions of professional psychologists about the intelligence levels of immigrants to the United States were cited earlier. These can almost certainly be attributed to ethnocentric prejudice, the psychologists being of "Nordic" stock and disposed to find evidence of their superiority. But even Binet had, from time to time, used the term *natural intelligence* as distinguished from acquired knowledge, so the conceptual problem was widespread. Galton, of course, had asserted the hereditary superiority of the aristocrats of Britain.

The study of identical twins has been one of the most useful conceptual tools of the hereditarian school. Fraternal twins are born when two ova are fertilized at the same time; identical twins result when one fertilized ovum splits into two, producing two babies. Thus identical twins have an identical DNA genetic constitution, whereas fraternal twins have no more resemblance in DNA than do other siblings. The crucial experiment is the separation of identical twins at birth, so that their heredity is identical but their environment is different; these are contrasted with fraternal twins, in whom heredity varies somewhat, but environment is almost identical. (No two environments are ever identical; babies bring out different responses from parents, and parental preferences may affect fraternal twins even though no one sees the differences.) These studies have not led behaviorists to abandon their emphasis on environment; Watson and, more recently, Skinner left no doubt that in their view, heredity was relatively insignificant.

This debate, of course, goes back to Locke and Leibniz. Locke had fostered the "blank slate" proposition; each baby was there, ready to be shaped by experience. Leibniz had insisted on a quality of the person, "intellect," which determined what information a child could assimilate and what complex processes could utilize this material. Gestalt and information-processing theories stem from the Leibniz tradition; behaviorism has developed out of the Lockean philosophy.

The Case for Heredity

The assumption of hereditary determination of mental capacity goes back to the Scottish school, and was accepted by Binet, who used the phrase *natural intelligence* and repeatedly referred to his efforts to exclude school materials from his test items. He seems to have assumed an innate capacity resembling Spearman's *g*. However, he rejected the hypothesis that mental ability is fixed and unchangeable.

Early research on heredity favored an emphasis on innate determination of intelligence. Burks (1942) and Burt (1966) studied identical twins and found them to be much more alike than fraternal twins. A refinement of these studies focused on identical twins reared apart as compared with those reared together and found that environment did not have a major influence.

Arthur Jensen (1969, 1973) advocated a theory of hereditary intelligence. Unfortunately, he cast it in a context of racial discrimination. He began with the observation that black children have, in a large number of studies, gotten average IQ scores about 15% below white children of the same age and school level. Jensen proposed an index of heritability:

$$h^2 = \frac{V_g}{V_p}$$

Archives of the History of American Psychology

Anne Anastasi, a gifted expert on measurement who developed the connections of statistical theory to individual-difference theory

which simply defines heritability as the ratio of genetic variance to population variance. Jensen reported that this index was about 0.80 (others have obtained smaller values). He therefore concluded that IQs of black children were innately inferior to IQs of white children. Not surprisingly, he was widely attacked as a "racist." Such epithets may be emotionally satisfying but they do nothing to solve a theoretical issue.

Anne Anastasi criticized Jensen for a hidden assumption: the hypothesis that intelligence is unitary, resembling Spearman's *g* rather than the more complex conceptions of Thurstone, Cattell, and Guilford. Like Binet, she objected to the "fixed-level" view of intelligence; an IQ is an index of "ability level at a given point in time" (1988, p. 362). She faulted the Jensen hypothesis on three grounds: "First, the concept of heritability is applicable to populations, not to individuals . . . in trying to establish the etiology of a particular child's mental retardation, the heritability index would be of no help" (p. 365). Environment may account for 100% of the variation in a single child's ability.

"Second, heritability indexes refer to the population in which they were found at the time . . . increasing environmental homogeneity would reduce the variance attributable to environment, and hence raise the heritability index . . . Third, heritability does not indicate the degree of modifiability of a trait" (p. 367). She asserted that behavior is always an interaction product of heredity and environment. Thus, if in a population all received identical diets, *no variance* could be attributed to food; but an improvement in diet might elevate the performance of everyone in the group.

The point has been made earlier (p. 461) that motivation and personality influence successful use of one's intelligence. Jensen, abandoning his focus on heredity, conceded that performance might be due mainly to environment: "There is potentially more we can do to improve school performance through environmental means than we can do to change intelligence *per se*" (1969, p. 59). He proposed the concept of *teachability* as the proper focus of environmental studiesx teachability included habits of attending, attitude to teachers, inhibition of irrelevant responses, and so on. It seems certain that if Jensen had recommended research on teachability, he would have been less disliked, and less famous.

The Case for Environment

Given our taboos on sex and parenthood, it is not surprising that no one has proposed experimentation with human reproduction to see if the intellectual capacities of children could be improved by selective breeding. On the other hand, there is considerable social support for efforts to improve the environments of young children after they are born. For obvious reasons, these are called *intervention studies*.

Marie Skodak did one of the first intervention studies at the University of Iowa (it does not appear that Lewin was involved, although he was on the staff there at the time of her investigation). Skodak (1939) followed up 154 babies placed for adoption shortly after birth. She estimated the IQs of the biological mothers to be about 80. After two years in the foster home, the average IQ of the babies was about 100, higher, she thought, than that of their mothers by a significant quantity. Most of the assumed twenty-point gain still persisted at age four.

The Milwaukee project is the popular name for a long-term intervention that enrolled infants and had staff personnel working with them eight hours a day for a full year. The mothers had IQs of 75 or less. The researchers (see Garber and Heber, 1982) had as their aim the prevention of mental retardation; the chances of retardation, for a child of low socioeconomic status with the mother's IQ 75 or less, would be far higher than for the average infant. For the children, the program included teaching simple skills but stressing language development; the staff were mostly paraprofessionals. For the mothers, the program offered job training, home management, and remedial education. The data showed a highly significant advantage for the experimental over the control children (the mean IQ was 120 for the experimentals, 94 for the controls). One puzzling item was that the controls, with an expected IQ of 75, scored 94. Another unexpected finding was that the siblings of the experimental children also seemed to benefit.

The North Carolina project involved family counseling and medical assistance for both experimental and control groups of infants. However, unlike the Milwaukee project, no systematic effort to teach parenting skills was included in the Carolina study. The program for the children involved day care for approximately nine hours a day. The training emphasis was on language development. C. T. Ramey, D. MacPhee, and K. O. Yeates (1982) reported that at age three and a half, the experimental children were significantly superior to the control group on seven of eight tests. Figure 20.4 shows the superiority of the experimentals on the Bayley MDI (Mental Development Index) at 18 months, and on the Stanford–Binet at 24 and 36 months.

One side issue is worth noting. The children were divided on the Ponderal Index (PI), a measure of fetal nutrition and development at birth; the superiority of the experimentals, with both high and low PI scores, is obvious in the chart. A second comparison (not shown) demonstrated that "difficult" (temperamental) children scored low at all ages; however, the experimental "difficult" cases had surpassed the control "easy" cases by age thirty-six months.

Ramey et al. (1982) added a theoretical note of their own: "One of the principles of General Systems Theory is that the organism is active rather than reactive. . . . An active organism constantly adapts to the environment *while modifying it*" (pp. 108–109; italics added). This is, of course, an implicit argument for heredity; it opposes the heavy emphasis on nurture by the behaviorists. It might seem to support the Jensen claim that nature accounts for 80 percent and nurture for 20 percent of intellectual status. On the other hand, it may be necessary to modify these figures, too. S. G. Vandenberg and G. P. Vogler (1985) offered an estimate of the heritability of intelligence on the order of .35 to .40, quite a drop from .80. Is this a result of cultural change across the United States, or merely an undetected change in our methods of measurement? Future historians of psychology may be in a better position than we are today to answer such questions.

Another methodological issue was pointed out by E. R. Hilgard (1987). He observed that the environmentalists generally favor the statistical

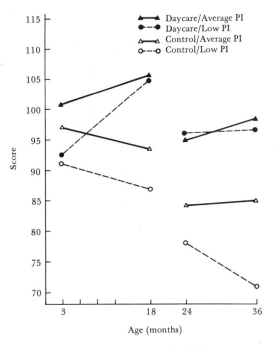

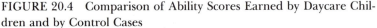

FIGURE 20.4   Comparison of Ability Scores Earned by Daycare Children and by Control Cases

The children were tested at three and eighteen months with the Bayley Scale and at twenty-four and thirty-six months with the Stanford-Binet. Average PI = normal physical condition at birth; Low PI = underweight, poor physical status at birth. Note that regardless of grouping, Daycare scores increased or remained steady, while the control children regressed.   *(From Ramey, McPhee and Yeates, 1982, reprinted by permission of Ablex Publishing Co.)*

analysis of differences in mean scores for experimental and control children. Nativists show a decided preference for correlational statistics. The first group seeks to establish *treatment effects*, whereas those supporting a genetic explanation use statistics reflecting the *attributes of the organism*. It may be that future investigators will find ways to combine the two approaches and to reduce or end this controversy.

Theoretical Speculations

The neobehaviorist approach to intelligence has best been developed by Staats (1975; Staats and Staats, 1963). This analysis offers a theoretical approach to the development of abstract and symbolic thought which is illustrated in Figure 20.5. Staats suggested that the child acquires verbal responses to attributes of physical objects, so that an abstraction, such as

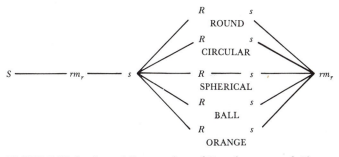

FIGURE 20.5   Staats' Conception of Development of Abstract Coding

This diagram shows a hierarchy of responses which the child may acquire in interaction with parents, peers, and teachers. The suggestion is that acquisition of abstractions and verbal labels for these facilitates the kind of learning called "intelligence." *(From Staats, 1961, p. 204, Figure 4, reproduced by permission of the Author and the American Psychological Association)*

spherical is built up, and that this, in turn, can provide the essential "prior learning" for mathematical and physical laws relating to spheres.

Essential to the Staats theory is the notion that specific behavioral units such as those in Figure 20.5 can become part of the "prior learning" and can be built into a hierarchy of functionally related responses. One way of visualizing this was shown in Figure 20.1, which suggests that specific cognitive or affective learning can become integrated into more inclusive units. This diagram, although originally designed to show how specific acts could become organized into personality traits, can also apply to Guilford's or similar models of intelligence.

An essential step in Staat's logic was the assumption that past learnings (the basic behavior repertoire shown in Figure 18.9) can determine what is learned in a novel situation. Thus, the child who has not learned such abstractions as "spherical" will be at a disadvantage in geometry or physics. If one has not learned the meaning of correlation, factor analysis will be impossible of acquisition. The broad generalization is that these prior learnings make possible activities such as planning, inhibiting or activating lower-order processing, search, retrieval, and so on, as well as evaluation of one's own performance. It will be noted that there is nothing here contradictory to Guilford's or Staats's formulation; they are complementary, not contradictory.

Sociobiology

Another theoretical controversy has blossomed since the mid-1960s. This involves a new theory by the intriguing name of *sociobiology*. It had its official beginning with the publication by E. O. Wilson (an entomologist) of a book entitled *Sociobiology: The New Synthesis* (1975). In this book, Wilson elaborated on a theory that has its roots in McDougall, the faculty psychologists, and Darwin, built around the question of the survival value of psychological traits. It is interesting that Wilson is the second entomologist to make a stir in psychological circles—the first being A. C. Kinsey of "sexual behavior" fame.

Although sociobiology has been attacked as "racist," Wilson's focus was specieswide, not pointed at group differences within the human race. He tried to emphasize the possible contribution of the genotype to behaviors such as cognition, socialization, and altruism. There can be little doubt that the information-processing skills have contributed greatly to human survival on the planet.

Altruism can be cited as a specific example of how sociobiological theory differs from current orthodox thinking. Altruistic behavior in an extreme form involves the death of a specific individual to permit the survival of relatives. Thus it seems superficially anti-Darwinian. "Natural selection" assumes the survival of the individual to make possible the production of children who will increase the probability of the survival of the species. Wilson's argument is that, in a fair number of situations, altruistic behavior (self-sacrifice) contributes to species survival, as when a mother dies defending her children. The logic is that of Thomas Hobbes, who argued that a *consistent* quest for individual survival would endanger the species; as an alternative, Hobbes offered the "social contract" by which individuals within a limited area agree not to attack each other but to cooperate against outsiders.

Any human behavior that can be observed must be at least compatible with genetic constraints. Humans can't fly without artificial supports; birds can. Humans can't remain indefinitely under water; fish can. There are broad species-specific characteristics which are beyond debate; they are genetically determined. Speaking Chinese is a matter of environment, but the ability to acquire spoken and written language is innate. Adler argued that social interest, or the drive to mingle in groups and to have social relations with other humans, is an inborn tendency of the species. If so, genetically determined altruism is not inconceivable.

The sociobiologists have not, however, given adequate attention to human history. Young princes have been notorious for killing each other off to win the throne or some other prize. Wilson, as an entomologist, must have known of the bad habit shown by a newly emerged queen bee; she goes around and kills all of her unhatched sisters before doing anything else. That genotype is certainly not altruistic.

It can also be argued that husbands and wives probably do more mutual sacrificing than any other social group, yet the genetic similarity here is limited, especially in exogamous societies. Perhaps the determinant of altruism is unusually susceptible to manipulation by environmental pressures.

Wilson (1975) also expressed himself with regard to the debate about the heritability of intelligence. Surprisingly, he wrote, "I see maybe 10% of human behavior as genetic and 90% environmental. Lewontin (a critic of sociobiology) would see it as zero percent genetic and all environmental" (cited by D. Goleman, 1986).

Dobzhansky (1973), an outstanding geneticist, offered the following comment on genotypes: "Inhabitants of the whole world share in the common gene pool of the species. . . . [But] the population of our species is complexly subdivided into a variety of subordinate Mendelian breeding populations. In each of these, the probability of marriage within is greater than between populations. [These] breeding populations are more often than not overlapping" (p. 24). He asserted that even in a caste-ridden society like India, there is some overlap of gene pools and, in the United States, an overlap of the black and white gene pools.

Dobzhansky also commented that "people vary in their capacities to take advantage of opportunities that they meet" (p. 39), and he noted that intelligence measurements have predictive value over a long time period of predicting success (e.g., income).

Gene Pools The crucial point in Dobzhansky's commentary on psychology is that there are different gene pools involved in human reproduction, and that much of the "racial differences" controversy has arisen because of confusion over these categories. As Dobzhansky noted, there is a specieswide gene pool that carries the determinants of human form and function. These are universal in the species but may be and often are species-specific (i.e., not shared with the lower animals).

Then there are partially independent gene pools for breeding populations (e.g., Eskimos, Mongolians, Africans, and Caucasians). These subordinate pools carry determinants for skin color, facial attributes, and so on. It is noteworthy that even a simple trait like skin color requires at least nine genes for complete determination. Finally, there is a gene pool for a given family tree; obviously this pool overlaps with the subpopulation pool and also with the specieswide pool. However, the heredity of a specific child includes all three of these gene pools. The conclusion is that twin differences are primarily functions of the family pool, which has only a limited overlap with the subspecies (ethnic group) pool; hence, heritability of height (or intellect) may not involve the ethnic group genes at all.

An Interaction Hypothesis It is simple logic to insist that the child's IQ is a function of both heredity and environment, because, without heredity, there is no organism, and without environment, the organism quickly ceases to exist. Thus the treatment of IQ as H × E has been common. Sandra Scarr-Salapatek (1971) elaborated on this: She arranged data on IQ tests for black and white children by socioeconomic status and found a significant interaction. The two "races" did not react in the same way to differences in environment. So far, this has not led to a significant breakthrough, perhaps because our notion of "effective environment" is too restricted; it may be that some different enrichment will be more influential than those kinds tried in research so far.

Fallacies

I have noted some misconceptions in the discussion of ability, cognitive styles, and personality traits. It is worthwhile to conclude this bit of psychological history by echoing the warning of B. Mackenzie (1984). Mackenzie suspected that proponents of either nature or nurture tended to have unconscious assumptions that caused the individual psychologist to ignore some evidence and to exaggerate other data. Mackenzie nominated two major fallacies that were preventing rational solutions to this conflict.

One of these he called the "sociologist's fallacy" which he characterized as follows: If two groups differ on a measure of cognitive ability, and if they also differ on a measure of environmental opportunity, the latter must be deemed the cause of the former. Some of us might call this a Marxist fallacy, or even a behaviorist fallacy. Mackenzie held that other alternatives must be explored; the syllogism is fallacious.

Conversely, he hypothesized a "hereditarian fallacy," which takes this form: If two groups differ on a measure of cognitive ability, and if no environmental determinant can be identified, the origin must be genetic. This assumption is equally unjustified, Mackenzie argued; there are still alternatives (such as Scarr-Salapatek's interaction hypothesis) that may clarify the origins of individual differences in psychological functions.

Hans Eysenck (1981), who took his Ph.D. with Cyril Burt, has aggressively supported the hereditarian theory: "We conclude, therefore, that a simple model giving a heritability of something like 80% for IQ is both realistic and defensible" (p. 52). The details of evidence that he presented are too extensive to reproduce here.

Leon Kamin, who earned his Ph.D. at Harvard University, has debated with Eysenck, notably in the jointly published volume, *The Intelligence Controversy* (1981). Kamin challenged many of the factual assertions made by Eysenck and presented evidence that heritability of IQ may be as low as 40 percent, rather than the 80 percent urged by Eysenck. Regrettably, both authors have cited statistical studies without reproducing the relevant data (which would have made a large and unwieldy volume); this leaves even an informed reader confused about what can be believed.

We can probably conclude that the information-processing components of intelligence are predominantly determined by heredity, and that the content (knowledge of everyday life, abstract concepts, and verbal problem-solving) depends much more on environment. The exact ratio of these factors must be left to further study and interpretation.

CHAPTER 21

Psychotherapy and Behavior Modification Theories

The history of theorizing recounted so far has centered on the "normal adult mind." We have this legacy from Wundt and Titchener, and for the most part, we go along with it. One can argue, in fact, that there are far more "normal" people than "pathological" individuals around us; hence the greater concentration on the normal is only a matter of common sense. Cynics, however, speculate that the "normal adult mind" is a fiction, that each of us has some (perhaps minor) symptom of psychological disturbance. And certainly, the pathological cases demand attention. Thus, psychological theorizing has expanded to cover abnormal phenomena.

The history of psychotherapy can conveniently begin with Sigmund Freud. I noted in Chapter Fourteen that he studied hypnosis with Charcot and Bernheim and attempted to use it as they had, to remove neurotic symptoms. He dropped the method because of the frequency of relapses (the suggestion failed after a time) and of symptom substitution (a paralysis might be replaced by a loss of memory or an anesthesia). Such relapses still plague psychotherapists and behavior therapists alike.

Freud had also proposed a theory of therapy as catharsis, or abreaction. If a patient "relived" a traumatic event, the emotion would be discharged and the symptom relieved. Regrettably, he found that catharsis might only amount to rehearsal, and that the symptom might appear to be even more intractable than before.

Psychoanalytic Psychotherapy

Freud's final theory of therapy built on the concept of *insight.* This involved the excavation of repressed memories, almost invariably from very early childhood, and, to some extent, "reliving" the forgotten experience. According to James Strachey (1957), both insight and abreaction were essential components of a successful treatment: "If the original experience, along with its affect, can be brought into consciousness, the affect is by that very fact discharged or 'abreacted,' the force that has maintained the symptom ceases to operate, and the symptom itself disappears" (p. xix).

The term *insight* as used here has apparent similarities to the usage of Köhler and Lewin. Köhler wanted to emphasize the restructuring of the perceived environment when his animals perceived a relationship theretofore hidden. Lewin pointed out that such restructuring could often reduce tension and so modify behavior. It appears, however, that Freud took precedence, developing his idea before the Gestalt theory was formulated. My point is only to call attention to the convergence of these theories, not to establish priority.

It will be recalled that Freud had abandoned his sexual trauma theory of neurosis in favor of a fantasized sexual experience. It must be assumed, therefore, that insight included an acceptance of the diagnosis (the seduction was really a fantasy) before therapy could be completed.

Freud also instructed his students to allow the patient to associate freely about any topic—to pick up and explore further those topics that seemed relevant to the hidden problem. This implied that the therapist did not decide what the basic problem was and persuade the patient to accept this view. There is, unfortunately, some doubt about how faithfully Freud followed his own advice. In an essay, "Analysis Terminable and Interminable" (1937) he wrote that it was very frustrating to him to try to "persuade a female patient to abandon her wish for a penis" (p. 311) or to convince a male patient that castration was not an inevitable consequence of submission to another male. Obviously this description implies a highly directive therapeutic style, as opposed to the neutral stance which he recommended that his trainees adopt. Of course we have no data indicating how frequently Freud violated his own rules; the "persuading" may have been a rarity. On the other hand, it may have been his standard procedure.

Another problem relates to directing the flow of free associations. Numerous analysands have commented that the therapist seems alert and interested when sexual matters are mentioned but seems bored and indifferent when the train of ideas centers on work or family. Behaviorists have argued that typical analytic therapy consists of verbal conditioning: the analyst "rewards" one line of verbalization and extinguishes others.

Transference and Countertransference   In the case of Anna O., Breuer found that Anna had developed an intense love for him (this is called *transference*) and that he had to some extent reciprocated her affection (*countertransference*). The terms derive from an assumed transfer of the intense love felt by a child for one parent or both. There is some reason to believe that any continued relationship that involves one person confiding intimate biographical details to another will foster this kind of irrational affection. Young people in training to become analysts are warned of these hazards, but the reports of surveys of sexual liaisons between therapists and patients indicate that the warning often does not work.

Insight   The analysis of the transference is intended to help the patient understand the unconscious impulses behind both the transference and the neurosis. Thus, if Anna had been encouraged to see her love for Breuer as an offshoot of her love for her father, she might then have been able to see the origins of her neurotic symptoms and be able to abandon them.

Insight as used here means that the individual becomes able to "see" relationships that had not before been recognized. An oversimplified diagram will perhaps clarify this idea. Figure 21.1 builds on an earlier illustration of putting an item in a new context. If a daughter, for example, has for years seen her mother as dictatorial, suppressive, and unfeeling, insight may make it possible for her to see her mother as protective, well-intentioned, and loving. (If one has seen only the A–B sequence, a shift to seeing the 12–13 sequence can be illuminating.)

A behaviorist could, of course, offer an alternative interpretation, namely, that one response (rejection and rebellion) has been replaced by another (acceptance and cooperation). In the absence of any specific training by the therapist, this alternative seems improbable.

For most of the period before World War II, the psychoanalytic model dominated American training programs for clinical psychologists. Modifications were offered that involved shortening the period of treatment, introducing the interpretation of symbols earlier in the process, and making positive suggestions for changing daily behavior. However, the consensus was that digging out unconscious material and making it conscious was an essential part of therapy.

All of this changed after World War II. There were two major contributing causes: one was the tremendous influx of wounded veterans (including psychological as well as physical trauma cases), and the other was the surge of attempts to apply conditioning principles to the elimi-

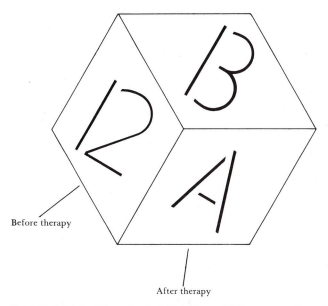

Before therapy

After therapy

FIGURE 21.1 Hypothetical Relation of Therapy to Perceiving

"Insight" therapy is alleged to help the client see past events and present situations from a different perspective, often leading to a significant change in behavior.

nation of pathological symptoms. Before examining these, it will be helpful to pay a brief visit to the ideas developed out of Clark Hull's behaviorism by John Dollard and Neal Miller.

Therapy Based on Learning Theory

Hull's theory of learning provided a base from which John Dollard and Neal Miller (1950) formulated a theory concerning psychotherapy. They admitted that this theory was closely modeled on Freud's approach, but they introduced formal concepts such as reward and reinforcement, trial and error, inhibition, and generalization. The approach–withdrawal analysis of conflict situations was an important part of their diagnostic and therapeutic formulations (see Figure 10.2, p. 214).

In this theory, transference is also accepted and is treated as a process of generalizing from stimulus figures in childhood to stimulus figures in the present situation, specifically the therapist. Dollard and Miller warned against scolding the patient but did recommend emphasizing that the therapist is *not* the father or mother against whom hostility is being directed.

Labeling Dollard and Miller treated the unconscious as merely a convenient collective term for ongoing processes that cannot be verbalized. The person is anxious or depressed but has no words to identify the memories that have triggered such emotions and may not even be able to verbalize the emotions themselves. Thus a substantial part of therapy is learning verbal labels for describing internal states, plus using these labels as control devices for coping with emotional states.

Labeling may take many forms. For example, the patient may be able to use the word *angry* accurately to describe others, but in talking about his wife, he is incapable of using the word *angry,* although it is obvious that this emotion is active. Sometimes the mere process of talking over such previous inhibitions enables the patient to attach the familiar word to the novel experience and so to achieve the possibility of applying verbal controls to the formerly vague inner experience. The therapist may also detect that the person "knows" a certain word–emotion relationship, may reward this word when it is used, and so may increase the probability that the word will be correctly used more and more often. Some therapists ask the patient to rehearse verbalizations about previously "forgotten" events in order to increase response probabilities even more. In the case of unlabeled fear or depression or hostility, the individual may be encouraged to try out different words, to see if the applicable one will "stand out" in memory and become an effective part of the vocabulary.

Discrimination is facilitated by labeling. Dollard and Miller made a point of the fact that young children often get sexual functions and eliminative functions mixed up in their thinking. Teaching precise labeling and detached feelings about these aspects of existence helps the patient separate intermingled ideas, so that behavior relevant to one does not interfere with the other.

Directive remarks seem to be somewhat more characteristic of the "learning theory" version of therapy than of the Freudian version. (We must, of course, keep in mind that Freud was not always as nondirective as he claimed, and it is probable that his followers often became quite direct.) Dollard and Miller (1950) illustrate their tactic by asking a patient, "Aren't you acting toward your mother-in-law as you did as a child toward your own mother?" (p. 320). The patient's attention was directed toward an unconscious fixation that had developed, of identifying the mother-in-law with the mother; with repetition, this identification was recognized and could then be taken apart to permit a new approach to the mother-in-law.

Rogers's Nondirective Therapy

I noted earlier (Chapter Seventeen) that Carl Rogers experienced a profound conflict in his graduate training, getting a functionalist-experimental view in his basic course work and a dose of Freudian theory in his internship. He resolved this conflict by adopting not a Dollard–Miller learning-theory version of therapy, but a virtually novel type, which he called "nondirective therapy." Rogers proposed to eliminate the interpretation of dreams and symbolism in favor of helping the patient to solve realistic problems. In Rogers's metaphor, the therapist is a tool—for example, a mirror. The patient can use this tool to accomplish tasks that otherwise would be too difficult.

C. H. Patterson (1966) stated that Rogers's development of nondirective (or client-centered) therapy was influenced by the views of Otto Rank. This is quite possible, as Rank had advocated helping the patient to become autonomous and self-developing.

A Cognitive Approach The most radical aspect of Rogers's approach to therapy was that it emphasized cognitive processes. Freud and the neoanalysts had stressed unconscious emotions and drives, and even the Hullians built their approach around the idea of nonverbalized (hence, unconscious) processes. Rogers held that the need to find order in one's experiences (Maslow's "cognitive need") was a major asset which the therapist could exploit to facilitate the removal of pathological or undesirable behavior and thinking.

It will be recalled that Rogers distinguished between *organismic* experience and *phenomenal* experience (Chapter Seventeen). Organismic experience covered everything that had happened to the person; phenomenal experience included only the experiences of which the person had been aware. Thus the conscious–unconscious dichotomy recurs, but this time without the invocation of a repressive force.

Rogers was far more optimistic about human nature than Freud had been. Rogers believed that it was not necessary to provide training to inhibit a destructive instinct; given love and security, each of us will behave in cooperative, constructive, trustworthy ways. (This was Skinner's view as expressed in *Walden Two*.) An essential basis for Rogerian therapy, then, is an *unconditional acceptance* by the therapist of the patient. Rogers believed that any therapeutic relationship based on this principle would result in positive changes in the patient.

Basic Concepts Rogers's theory of motivation emphasized self-enhancement: "the inherent tendency of the organism to develop all its capacities in ways which serve to maintain or enhance the organism" (1959). This resembles Goldstein's principle of self-actualization and Maslow's principle of the same name.

The *phenomenal field* is virtually identical to Lewin's life space and Koffka's behavioral environment. Although Rogers adopted no term like *foreign hull* for events outside the phenomenal field, he made it clear that such an area existed. Between the phenomenal field and the foreign hull, there is an area of experiences *available* to consciousness. Their relation to the phenomenal field is something like Wundt's distinction between *Blickfeld* and *Blickpunkt;* there is a clear focal area in the phenomenal field, but there are vaguely perceived background features that can be brought into focus by special techniques. Even without clear perception, a person's behavior may be modified by this hazy material. To describe this process Rogers adopted the term *subception* to designate perceiving somewhat short of optimal clarity. This is the logic by which Rogers took account of what the psychoanalysts had called the *unconscious.*

Diagnosis Undesirable behavior and self-destructive ruminations result from occasions when the phenomenal experience and the organismic experience differ substantially. A child may say, "I don't like my baby brother!" Parents insist, "Of course you love him." The child may yield consciously and say, "I love him," but the experience of hostility is remembered, although blocked from verbalization. Therapy often consists primarily of resurrecting such gaps in experience and closing them so that the patient can say, "Of course I resented him at the time, but now we get along well."

For Rogerians, diagnostic emphasis falls on the self-image. A prime candidate for Rogerian treatment is one who achieves well but denigrates the self as inadequate, unlovable, and antisocial. The improvement of the self-image is one major goal of the therapy. In the example just cited, the unstated thought "I was bad because I did not love my baby brother" can give rise to self-criticism, guilt, depression, and inability to function constructively.

The Therapeutic Process As originally practiced, nondirective therapy avoided both praise and criticism of the individual. The effort of the therapist was to help the patient to see himself or herself as did others. Much of the process involves labeling. There is a need for the patient to see the self as normal, functional, and acceptable. Such perceptions are emphasized to conflict with and to inhibit self-critical ruminations. Explorations of the "evidence" supporting these inferiority sentiments often lead to awareness that the incompetence was a misperception. However, it is likely that the erroneous self-image will persist for some time.

Growth   Rogers was consistent about his botanical metaphor. He often wrote of therapy as a way of encouraging the patient to develop. "The individual and not the problem is the focus," he wrote. "The aim is not to solve one particular problem, but to assist the individual to *grow*, so that he can cope with the present problem and later problems in a better-integrated fashion" (1942, p. 28). This is at odds with both orthodox psychoanalysis, where the focus is on hidden conflicts, and behavior therapy, which is explicitly concerned only with symptoms. For Rogers, the progress of therapy was not gauged by problem solving; it was more a matter of experiencing feelings: "You say you felt depressed when your brother made Phi Beta Kappa? Can you tell me more about that?" By asking for repetition and rewording of reports, the therapist tries to help the patient perceive the self in a new way (see Figure 21.1) and to accept antisocial feelings as facts of life. Unconditional acceptance, one notes, is not the same as approving of antisocial behavior. Rogers believed (this is not easy) that he could "accept" a murderer while disapproving of the crime.

C. H. Patterson (1966) suggested that the process of self-recognition and restructuring in Rogerian therapy might include "getting behind the mask." The mask is, of course, that facade of socialized acts that runs counter to deeply held feelings. I may think my boss is a rogue elephant, but I have to mask this feeling. In many important social relationships, the mask and the self differ so widely that we could label the personality as being *dissociated*.

The purpose of therapy might be encapsulated in the remark by one patient: "I have all these masks for different groups and different occasions, but I keep wondering if one of them is the real me." If Rogerian therapy is successful, the patient will have found "the real me" without necessarily discarding the masks. They are now perceived as simple tools or skills for getting a job done. Often the masks undergo some modification so that they will integrate more with the nuclear self.

Conditioning as Therapy

Back in 1919, John B. Watson had discussed with his student, John J. B. Morgan, a program for the use of conditioning procedures to cure undesirable or maladaptive behavior. One of Watson's students, Mary Cover Jones, demonstrated the reconditioning of a child (Peter) who feared a white rabbit. The child was fed and then the rabbit was introduced; it was taken away when Peter stopped eating. The next day, Peter tolerated a longer stay of the rabbit in the room and a closer approach. After about two weeks, Peter tolerated the rabbit on his high chair (Jones, 1924a). This, of course, was a reversal of the "Little Albert" treatment.

Aversive Conditioning   Behaviorists have followed up on Watson's idea. The conditioned-response paradigm, or some variant of it, has been used in much "behavior therapy." This group of behavior modifiers denies the thesis of an underlying (unconscious) component of pathological behavior. The symptom is a unit of behavior. Eliminate it, and you eliminate the problem. Although this logic agrees with the general theories enunciated by Watson, Hull, and Skinner, it has not always been successful.

One of the earliest instances in the literature was described by English Bagby in his *Psychology of Personality* (1928): "The patient, a university sophomore, sought assistance in connection with a strong impulse to gnaw the back of his right hand. The tendency had existed for a period of two months and already a large callous area had developed. The patient appeared to be quite ashamed of his inability to secure control of this habit" (p. 7).

As an aversive stimulus, Bagby applied a bitter-tasting ointment to the hand so the youth would get an unpleasant taste if he repeated the chewing:

> On the third day the young man reported that the inclination to bite his hand was no longer troubling him. However, he called attention to a new symptom. He found himself almost constantly beset by moral worries [over ridiculously trivial matters.] . . . Finally, however, the patient came to report that his distressing condition had completely disappeared and that he was again serene. But, in the course of the conversation, it was observed that he repeatedly bit his *left* hand. . . . When the fact was called to his attention, he gave unmistakable evidence of surprise and chagrin. (p. 7)

The case parallels Freud's early experiences with hypnosis. A symptom might disappear only to have a substitute pop up; or in other cases, the disappearance was only temporary. It was this phenomenon of persistence that led Freud to his thesis of unconscious determination.

Hans Eysenck has been one of the more aggressive anti-Freudians who have expanded the behavior therapy movement at a rapid rate. He has frequently made assertions like "There is no underlying complex or other 'dynamic' cause which is responsible for the maladaptive behavior; all we have to deal with in neurosis is conditioned maladaptive behavior" (1963.)

Eysenck bolstered this claim by describing a case that had come to his attention, of a man who loved his wife but none the less was irresistibly attracted to a neighbor and was having an affair with her. Eysenck applied a straight aversive conditioning procedure; he showed a photo of the neighbor and then administered an electric shock to the man's thigh. Then he showed the wife's photo; no shock. Presentation of each photo with the shock or nonshock consequence, over a period of several days, led the man to assert that the neighbor no longer looked attractive, and he did not feel tempted to continue the affair.

In such cases, the skeptic cries out for a follow-up study. For how many weeks or months did the aversive conditioning last? What was the effect on the marriage? Did the man develop any alternative pathological or maladaptive symptoms?

The major premise of this approach can be stated as follows: All behavior is composed of discrete units; any unit can be inhibited by activation of an incompatible response; therefore we can cure this maladaptive behavior by conditioning a conflicting response to the eliciting stimulus. What is ignored is the kind of phenomenon studied by Bandura and Staats (Chapter Eighteen), in which higher-order response systems develop and determine the occurrence or nonoccurrence of specific units within this higher system.

Extinction as Therapy   There are dozens of examples of the direct aversive treatment advocated by Eysenck. There are even more that derive from Skinner's operant conditioning; specifically, there have been many studies that attempted to eliminate maladaptive behavior by the process of extinction (i.e., nonreinforcement).

One of the early cases in this category is that of T. Ayllon and J. Michael (1959). The patient, a paranoid schizophrenic, represented an extreme challenge to any kind of therapy. The authors described

> Helen, whose delusional talk had become so annoying that the other patients had resorted to beating her in an effort to keep her quiet. Her delusional conversations centered around her false belief that she had an illegitimate child and the man she claimed was responsible was pursuing her. . . . Prior to the application of extinction, 30-minute intervals were observed to determine the relative frequencies of the delusional and rational (sensible) content of her conversations. It was felt that the nurses' attention to her had been maintaining this psychotic kind of speech. The nurses were instructed not to pay any attention to her psychotic talk but to reinforce sensible conversation. If another patient started to fight with [Helen], the nurses were instructed to stop the fight but not to make an issue of it. By the ninth week, the frequency of Helen's delusional talk was drastically reduced (Lundin, 1969, p. 75).

In fact, Helen's episodes decreased from about eight per day to two per day. Unfortunately, the "cure" was temporary:

> Then, the rate drastically increased because, it is supposed, a social worker entered the situation. The patient told the nurses, "Well, you're not listening to me. I'll have to go see [the social worker] again, 'cause she told me that if she could listen to my past she could help me" (Lundin, 1969, pp. 75–76).

It is obvious that the treatment did not result in the extinction of the undesirable behavior, as it was reactivated at a high level after a single reinforcement. What may have happened is that the treatment resulted in conditioned inhibition: in the presence of anyone wearing a hospital uniform, she inhibited her delusional speech. None the less, the delusions were still there.

Wolpe's Reciprocal Inhibition   In 1958, Joseph Wolpe published *Psychotherapy by Reciprocal Inhibition,* in which he described a novel approach to what he called psychotherapy but is generally classified as behavioral therapy. He focused on fear and anxiety cases and applied systematic desensitization as a major technique, with progressive relaxation as an accompaniment. Desensitization would, in behaviorist terms, be called *extinction.* The procedure required the patient to draw up a list, a hierarchy of fear-arousing situations; the aim of the therapy was to extinguish fear in these situations. Wolpe relied on imagination (in contrast to Bandura, who used live snakes—see Chapter Eighteen). The patient would imagine the least frightening situation, and Wolpe would make suggestions for relaxation. When the first level no longer stirred fear, they moved on to the next higher anxiety level, and so on.

Obviously two principles were being applied: extinction, as the stimuli were repeated (in fantasy) without being reinforced by fearful happenings; and reconditioning, as the stimuli now became associated with muscular relaxation.

Ellis and Rational Emotive Therapy   Albert Ellis (1977) offered a cognitive-behavioral therapy that he labeled "rational emotive therapy" (RET). The procedure was based on a theory that neurotic symptoms were outcomes of irrational belief systems (e.g., a phobia for high places was based on an unreasonable fear of falling). The approach is thus neobehaviorist, not one derived from Watson or Hull. Ellis required "homework" of his patients, including reading about irrational emotions and repeating optimistic sentences. He also instructed the patient in behavioral matters (how to act in a more self-assertive fashion, for example) and insisted that these be practiced. Much of the RET material related to how the patient perceived the environment. As H. I. Kalish (1981) put it, Ellis held that "people get into behavioral difficulties, not because of the things that occur to them but because of the way they view these occurrences (their attributions)" (p. 362). This is reminiscent of Freud's decision that neuroses were not due to sexual trauma, but to sexual fantasy.

It will be noted that Ellis's concept of "rules guiding behavior" can fit comfortably into Bartlett's "schema" or into Staats's "basic behavioral repertoire." The attempt to change these basic belief systems is the basis for calling the system *rational;* Ellis tried to combine cognitive education with emotional reconditioning.

The foregoing sketch does not even list several well-known patterns of behavior therapy, primarily because this book is about theories and not about therapies. The examples cited provide a basis on which we can construct a discussion of how the theory affects the procedure.

Cognitive Behavior Therapies

The foregoing pages described therapies based on Pavlov, Hull, or Skinner; that is, they rely mainly on contiguity conditioning. Other experts in this field have turned to "cognitive behavior therapy," which builds on language and symbolic processes. M. J. Mahoney (1974) divided the cognitive therapies as follows: Mediational Model I (covert conditioning); Mediational Model II (information processing); and Mediational Model III (cognitive learning).

Mediational Model I does not differ greatly from the behavioral models already described; in fact, Mahoney classified Wolpe as an instance of this category. Admittedly, Wolpe made use of some cognitive processes, especially in the desensitization phase. Other techniques in this group are "thought stopping" as a treatment for ruminations about deprivations, frustrations, and inferiorities; "coverant control," in which the patient is encouraged to generate subvocal slogans of a positive nature; and covert conditioning, a method using vivid imagery, often of a disgusting type, in association with the disapproved behavior.

Mediational Model II was apparently inserted into Mahoney's scheme for purposes of symmetry. He described some ways in which information processing (see Chapter Nineteen) might be relevant to therapy, but he gave no instances.

Mediational Model III centers on the work of Abert Bandura. There are, however, others whose work should be classified in this group. Aaron Beck, Milton Erickson, and J. R. Cautela, as well as some of Mahoney's own therapeutic ventures, deserve mention.

Aaron T. Beck has contributed substantially to the literature on cognitive behavior therapy. His logic resembles that of Ellis. For example, he attempts to make his patients conscious of such errors in thinking as *arbitrary inference* (e.g., treating a failure to say "hello" as evidence of hostility); *overgeneralization* (as when a single incident occurs and the patient applies it to the entire human race); and *magnification* (the tendency to exaggerate how much one has been injured by some incident).

Michael J. Mahoney has also been prolific in spreading the gospel of behavior therapy. Mahoney, who has a fondness for puns and also an affinity for acronyms, gives his patients a five-step program called *adapt* for obvious reasons: (A) *acknowledge* the emotion (anxiety or anger); (D) *discriminate* the key elements in an event that has just occurred; (A) *assess* the logical bases and adaptive functions of your images and self-descriptive statements; (P) *present* alternatives (consider modes of behaving other than what you are about to do); and (T) *think* praise (reward yourself when you really act on this model (1974, p. 175).

Milton H. Erickson pioneered in the use of hypnosis to help individuals suffering from intractable pain, notably in terminal cancer cases. The procedure is properly categorized as a behavior therapy because the hypnotic trance is studded with suggestions about things the person is going to do, activities that will—by posthypnotic suggestion—be pain-free, or relatively so. We know that Freud experimented with hypnosis but mainly used direct suggestion to make the symptom disappear without providing a substitute. Erickson's results imply that a positive suggestion can dominate the unitary consciousness where a purely inhibitory suggestion cannot (1982). Erickson, and other authors in the same volume, offer techniques for turning the hypnotic function over to the patient, thus enhancing a feeling of self-control.

The use of psychological methods to control organic pain puts some patients in a double bind. If the hypnotic suggestion works, then it seems that the pain was psychological rather than physiological; if the method doesn't work, the pain is physiological but intolerable. L. B. Sachs (1982) recommended explicit instruction to the patient that the pain is organic, that the hypnotic procedure can modify organic pain just as the patient can modify breathing or heart rate, and that the fear of having "an imaginary pain" is based on a delusion. It is possible that the failure to provide this patient instruction is a major cause of unsuccessful applications of suggestion in this and other behavioral enterprises.

Imagery Imagery is involved in Wolpe's desensitization or covert conditioning technique. It has been used more directly by other therapists, notably J. R. Cautela. Cautela (1967, 1973) has dealt with obesity cases due to chronic overeating by encouraging the patient to visualize a fine meal, then to feel nausea, and finally to vomit all over the table. Suggestions regarding the odor, the taste, and the social embarrassment are vivid and persuasive. Then the patient is encouraged to imagine washing up and feeling wonderful (Cautela, 1967). In a later article, Cautela (1973) argued that this constituted a covert punishment process; it could just as well involve changing the valence of the food from positive to negative by the association with unpleasant consequences.

Some of the behavior modification experiments have verged on the bizarre. I. Kirsch and D. Henry (1977) asked persons afflicted with a public speaking phobia to imagine being before an audience and disturbed by anxiety. When the individual reported feeling anxious, he was given an electric shock "to punish the anxiety." These authors claimed many successes with this treatment, but it seems theoretically impossible.

Follow-up Studies of Psychotherapies

There has been an extended debate about the effectiveness of psycho-analysis as a therapy for neurotics, beginning with an article by Eysenck (1952) that made the startling suggestion that as many neurotics without treatment showed improvement as those who underwent psychoanalysis. Since that time, a dozen or more studies have sought to increase the number of patients and the number of analysts, to control for the length of the treatments, the proportion of dropouts, and so on, in an attempt to get at a firm estimate of the beneficial consequences of psychotherapy. In recent years, the follow-up of behavior therapy cases has also begun. I shall first consider the studies on psychotherapy (i.e., the "talking cure").

Howard, Kopta, Krause, and Orlinsky (1986) consolidated the data from fifteen reports of improvement in therapy. These reports covered over 300 therapists and 2,500 patients. Thus it cannot be said that only a few cases were involved; regrettably, the other side of this coin is great variability in the type of therapy, the competence of the therapist, the presenting symptoms and seriousness of the problem, and worst of all, the criteria for judging improvement. The findings are summarized in Figure 21.2, which shows the increase in the proportion of patients reported as improved in relation to the number of interviews completed. It will be noted that this looks like a typical laboratory learning curve. It is encouraging that the curves for therapists' judgments and patients' self-judgments are reasonably parallel. The data are complicated by the fact that many of the nonimproved dropped out of therapy; thus, after eight sessions, about half the patients felt that they had improved, but many of the remaining half stopped therapy at this point. We do not know if these patients would have shown improvement later, nor do we know if they went to other therapists.

An attempt to use a questionnaire, providing similar criteria to all therapists, for judging improvement was reported by P. S. Gallo and E. Lynn (1981). Their conclusion was rather discouraging: "Psychotherapy has a real, measurable, and *quite weak* effect upon the adjustment scores that constitute the dependent measure" (p. 1197; italics added). They also broke down the sample according to different types of therapy and reported that "different types of psychotherapy have a real, measurable and *quite weak* effect upon the adjustment scores" (p. 1197; italics added).

I noted in Chapter Fourteen the comment by Masson that, if psycho-analysis were an automobile, all cases since 1901 should be recalled. These surveys suggest that the verdict would be the same even if Freud had not abandoned his realistic theory for a fantasy theory.

S. J. Rachman and G. T. Wilson (1980) came to an equally discourag-

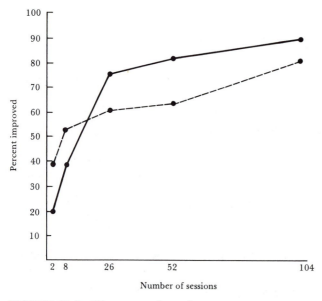

FIGURE 21.2   Therapy as Learning

The relationship of number of repetitions (therapy sessions) to improvement as rated by therapist (solid line) and by patient (dotted line).   *(From
Howard, K. I., Kopta, S. M., Krause, M. S., and Orlinsky, D. E., 1986,* The
Dose-Effect Relationship in Psychotherapy. *American Psychologist, 41, 159–
164, reprinted by permission of American Psychological Association)*

ing conclusion: "there is modest evidence to support the claim that psychotherapy can produce beneficial changes. The negative results still
outnumber the positives, and both are exceeded by the number of un-
interpretable results. The strength and breadth of the persisting, un-
qualified faith in the value of psychotherapy rests on an insubstantial
foundation" (p. 93).

Follow-up of Behavior Therapy

Although behavior therapy became popular long after psychotherapy,
there are about as many follow-up studies of such treatments as there
have been of psychoanalytic therapies. One reason is that behavior therapies have developed out of laboratory experiments, so their advocates
are acutely aware of the need for validation studies. Another reason is
that these psychologists, being mostly critics of traditional psychotherapy, have felt obligated to report on successes and failures.

Sad to say, this willingness did not convert itself into solid, persuasive data. For the most part, follow-up has consisted of a telephone call or a brief questionnaire that focused on the undesirable response that was being treated. The number of studies using actual physical interviews is very small. Thus, information on substitute symptoms is rare—and untrustworthy in most cases. Further, we have little information on the number of cases in which the person felt the need to seek further help elsewhere. D. Chambless (1985), in a follow-up of agoraphobics, noted that those most prone to relapse had more than that one problem, often had marital difficulties, and had in some cases encountered environmental stresses. Clients who were poorly educated and of low socioeconomic status relapsed more often. (Rachman and Wilson did not mention this aspect in their survey of psychotherapy, perhaps because poor people rarely even enter traditional psychotherapy.)

Behavior therapy has often been recommended for behavior problems of a less serious nature. Overeating, nail biting, smoking, and similar problems have often been treated by aversive or positive conditioning. The treatment of narcotic addictions and alcoholism has been less common. Success figures of 65 percent to 75 percent have been reported for the minor problems treated. Unfortunately, the relapse rate is quite high. In a well-controlled study, S. Shiffman (1985) found that, in follow-ups of persons who had been considered completely successful at the termination of treatment, about 75 percent had relapsed within one year. The plot of time against the continuance of nonsmoking looked very much like Ebbinghaus's curve of forgetting; casually, at least, one could say that the individual acquires a new habit (nonsmoking) but forgets it just as verbal material is forgotten—perhaps because of an intensification of the factors that led to original smoking, perhaps to new learning that has interfered with the nonsmoking habits. It is thus doubtful that Rachman and Wilson (1980) were justified in their optimistic conclusion that behavior therapy "must be viewed as the single most significant development in the effective treatment of clinical disorders in recent times" (p. 194).

Importance of Context   A point that recurs in discussions of the behavior therapies is that a "cure" may be accomplished in the laboratory or clinic but may dissolve in the outside environment. A snake phobia may disappear while an experimenter in a white coat with an impressive laboratory manner handles the snake and encourages the patient to do the same. But when the patient goes to Yosemite National Park, the phobia reappears. The context has changed. Hull had found that the stimulus surround of an experiment often had an important effect on learning; rats that had learned a maze in one position sometimes seemed confused when it was moved to a new position with a change in lighting and similar (usually ignored) sources of stimulation. Hull added "afferent stimulus interaction" to his behavior formula in an attempt at least to recognize these effects, even though he could not always control them.

The problem, again, is the impoverishment of stimuli. In the interest of rigor, all stimuli that can be excluded are blocked out. But in the everyday world, where the behavior therapy has to operate, these stimuli are constantly present. The problem of the transfer from laboratory or clinic to "real life" thus becomes crucial. (It must be added that the same holds for psychotherapy, with the exception that such treatments seek to establish *internal* states that will guide behavior, as opposed to the external controls relied on by the behavior therapist.) The problem of *transfer,* then, is still a fundamental issue in treatment procedures. As in the case of Helen (see p. 483), the addition of a single person to the staff may be enough to wipe out the elaborate training process and its effect.

Negative Outcomes of Psychotherapy

Therapies may fail because of the move from the clinic to the streets, but therapies also fail in a more direct and impressive manner. I shall first look at the arguments regarding failure in psychotherapy, then in behavior therapies.

Freud had his failures; he wrote to Fliess of one patient who committed suicide after he had dismissed her as untreatable. Less prestigious analysts have also admitted to failures. Rather than look at cases, we can take a look at the explanations offered for these mishaps. Generally, three factors seem to be involved: (1) the characteristics of the patient; (2) the mode of treatment; and (3) the behavior of the therapist.

One valuable study dealing with failures was the Psychotherapy Research Project at the Menninger Foundation (Kernberg et al., 1972). The authors divided 42 cases into three categories: success (10 cases); failures (11 cases); and partial success (21 cases). Regarding the failures, they concluded that 7 had been misdiagnosed (an important finding, as the contemporary tendency is to minimize the importance of accurate diagnosis). The misdiagnosis took the form of underestimating how sick these individuals were. Second, the failures showed "low ego-strength," an inability to inhibit self-defeating behaviors such as the use of alcohol and drugs, an unwillingness to cooperate with the therapist, angry attacks on the therapist, and so on. The successes were, by and large, with the people who least needed therapy; they could probably have managed without it.

Another major source of failure was the family. Just as the "real-life" context is important in behavior therapy, so it is in psychotherapy. Families who criticized the patient, indulged his or her binges, carped about the therapist, and so on were found in 10 of the 11 failure cases.

With regard to treatment, the failures were individuals who failed to develop a good positive transference but who developed a high-level negative transference (e.g., hostility, angry accusations, and criticism of the therapist's competence.) Among the 11 failures, there were 10 therapists, 9 psychiatrists, and 1 psychologist; among the successes, 7 psychiatrists and 2 psychologists—no real difference. The success group actually had fewer years of professional experience than the therapists in the failure cases.

D. T. Mays and C. M. Franks (1985), commenting on the Kernberg et al. study, observed that the one factor open to improvement was the family. If individual therapy had been combined with family counseling, some of the failures could probably have been prevented.

Negative Outcomes: Behavior Therapy

There are reports also of suicides among patients in behavior therapy programs. Because behavior therapy usually focuses on a single action pattern rather than on the total personality, as in psychotherapy, this is perhaps a bit more excusable; still, it must be counted as a failure. Failure rates are mostly calculated on the basis of inability to eliminate the undesirable behavior; thus, Chambless (1985) mentioned that among agoraphobics, 65 to 70 percent improved after treatment (by subtraction, the failure rate was 30 to 35 percent).

Perhaps the first critical look at follow-up of behavior therapy cases was done by A. E. Bergin (1963). He used the term *deterioration* to apply to some patients; however, that term has become controversial. We need to distinguish between persons who show no improvement and persons whose symptoms become more severe during treatment.

C. R. Barbrack (1985) looked at the follow-up reports on behavior therapies and concluded that the situation is confused. Reports of actual worsening of patients are rare (perhaps because the therapists prefer not to publish them); another reason, he insinuated, was that editors of behavior therapy journals reject manuscripts reporting failures—this is a device for protecting an established belief system. Barbrack put the point amusingly: "In short, the failure of behavioral treatments has been aversive to many in the behavioral community" (p. 79). One is reminded of the Mahoney study (see Chapter Eleven) in which editorial consultants rejected research reports that seemed to challenge their theoretical commitments.

Catharsis Versus Intensification A defect that may be inherent in some systems was identified by Eysenck (1982). In many procedures (e.g., Wolpe's), anxiety imagery is elicited, and anxiety is raised to a fairly high level. Although the theory is that this procedure will habituate and weaken the anxiety, Eysenck pointed out that it may intensify the anxiety instead. Studies of aggression suggest that aggressive acts generate more, not less, aggression. The same may hold for anxiety.

The rather high percentage of patients who drop out of behavior therapy may be due to such excessive anxiety. In her follow-up study, Chambless (1985) found that some "improved" agoraphobics were now taking anxiety-reducing medication, and that others had entered treatment with other therapists.

The personality of the patient may also be a factor, not necessarily as in psychotherapy, where it is the "weak ego" that is often considered a failure. Persons who experience "internal fate control" (see Chapter Eighteen) may resist being manipulated by a behavior therapist, even if they have sought treatment in the first place. In a summary of studies by Stolz, Wienckowski, and Brown (1975), the following conclusion seems significant: "For many persons, it is highly reinforcing to be resistant to attempts to alter their behavior and highly aversive to succumb to external control" (p. 1037). Although these authors garbled their theoretical vocabularies (if behavior doesn't change, then the stimulus applied was not a reinforcer), the message is clear. Some individuals, even if they seek help, cling to established behavior patterns and resist influence attempts. The resistance may even be unconscious, although most behaviorists would rule out such an explanation.

The humanistic critique of behavior therapies revolves around this same issue. Whereas humanists have traditionally favored psychotherapy (the split described in Chapter One was between experimentalists and therapists), they have not taken kindly to behavior therapies. What might have been seen as a rapprochement (tough-minded scientists trying to collaborate on solving personal problems) has instead been seen as a process of dehumanizing the curative process. The behavior therapies not only derived from laboratory research; they also relied heavily on mechanical repetitions of instructions and rote memory for self-instruction. They eliminated the aspects of personality most dear to the humanists—values, emotions, intuitions, and mystical experiences—not to mention the vagaries of the human soul.

The focal point of criticism has typically been the issue of free will or free choice. A. Wheelis (1973) put it this way: "All such [behaviorist] treatment takes the person as object and seeks to achieve the desired change by manipulation. . . . If one's destiny is shaped by manipulation one has become more of an object, less of a subject, has lost freedom" (p. 104). The choice seems to be one of continuing to be a crippled but free subject, or of becoming a more comfortable and effective object.

Bandura (1969) posed the argument on the behaviorist side: "To the extent that the client serves as the primary decision-maker in the value domain, the ethical questions that are frequently raised concerning behavioral control become pseudo issues" (p. 101). To which Mahoney (1974) drily commented that in a deterministic universe, the individual's "free choice" is not free at all. Most of us, however, like to believe we have some freedom of choice and can opt to enter therapy or decline. And it is unlikely that a person voluntarily entering a therapy program will consider this a loss of freedom; it is rather an attempt to maximize freedom.

Values of Behavior Therapists   Of interest in this dispute is the question: What values characterize the psychologists specializing in behavior therapy? L. Krasner and A. C. Houts (1984) extended the work of R. W. Coan (1979) and G. A. Kimble (1984) using the set of values shown in Figure 1.5. Their focal group was composed of 82 psychologists who identified themselves as engaged in behavior modification, who had published at least one article in the area, and who had been cited in other behavior-modification publications. The control was composed of 37 psychologists who had published at least one article, and who were not engaged in behavior modification work.

The results closely resemble the findings of Coan (1979) and Kimble (1984). Compared with the controls, the behavior therapists emphasized facts as opposed to theories, supported "impersonal causality" versus personal will, focused on behavior instead of consciousness, favored atomistic (analytical) approaches to problems, and endorsed physical environmentalism and objectivism. Thus they closely resembled the experimentalists whose views were summarized in Chapter One.

The behavior modifiers leaned to conservatism in social philosophy, and to "social Darwinism." They broke with traditional conservatives on one point: they opposed social-ethical constraints on their research and practice. (This opposition may have been a reflection of unfavorable publicity over some behavior therapy with juvenile delinquents that had appeared not long before the survey was made.) In short, although the behavior modifiers purported to be concerned with curing undesirable behaviors, their approach was essentially the detached, impersonal posture adopted by experimental psychologists in general.

Humanists have also criticized the behavior therapists for ignoring diagnosis and for simply treating the symptom. One psychologist told of curing a patient who was grinding his teeth (to the point of damaging them) by having gold and silver fillings installed so that tooth grinding gave him a weak but unpleasant electric shock. When asked about the condition causing the tooth grinding the therapist indicated that this did not concern him. It is this complete lack of interest in the patient as a person that is most often criticized by psychotherapists.

Ethics and Therapies

Many observers would question the ethics of treating a symptom with no attempt to evaluate the person's history or personal problems. Of course, the question of ethical standards has been around for a long time. Freud's work was denounced because it was held that he encouraged sexual liberty to the point of license. Although Freud denied this charge, some analysands, seeing their moral controls as vestiges of an unhappy childhood, have abandoned their behavior controls for a time. It is also clear that in a fair number of cases, the patient, involved in a transference "love" for the analyst, has seduced the analyst. And in other cases, the therapist, wrapped up in a countertransference passion, has seduced the patient. Recent surveys confirm that the incidence of sexual relations in the therapy situation is high enough to justify some concern.

Behavior Therapy   The sexual issue has hardly arisen with regard to behavior therapies, except in the area of specific sexual malfunction. On the whole, contacts between therapist and patient in behavior therapies are relatively brief, do not involve a discussion of intimate emotions, and produce only small transient transference effects. These factors may explain why clinical-psychology training programs have shifted from a major focus on training in dynamic psychotherapy to an emphasis on behavior therapies. The professorial staff has less to worry about with regard to the behavior of their trainees.

Societal Norms   A much wider issue than sex is that of the extent to which a therapist, of whatever persuasion, is entitled, or even obligated, to change the patient's behavior in the direction of socially approved actions. I noted earlier the discomfort that Rollo May experienced on learning that his psychoanalytic mentors excluded any consideration of ethical values as goals of therapy; they held that their duty was to make the person more efficient, even if that meant a "more efficient gangster" (see Chapter Seventeen). Generally speaking, this has been the stance adopted by behavior therapists, too. They do not propose to dictate the standards of behavior to which the patient should conform. Like May's instructors in psychoanalysis, the behaviorists avoid advising the client regarding ethical standards. They are especially sensitive to the charge that they are making the client over into a robot.

The criticism of psychoanalysis—that it is a device for strengthening the status quo in society—was often heard in the 1960s, when adolescent rebellion against childhood socialization reached a peak. But the objection has a long history. Even some analysts (notably Erich Fromm) disapprove of therapy that deflects energy (libido) from social reform to personal happiness.

The charge that psychoanalysis is merely a device for adjusting patients so that they will love the status quo goes back to the beginning of the twentieth century. Max Eastman, a well-known left-wing writer, told of being analyzed by Smith Ely Jelliffe (who had been analyzed in Europe and adhered to orthodox Freudianism). When Jelliffe offered the interpretation that Eastman's political ideas represented "hostility to the father working itself out in prejudiced radicalism" (Hale, 1971, p. 385),

Eastman became indignant. It is likely that Adler, Fromm, and Horney would have supported Eastman, as they held capitalism to be a causal factor in behavior disorders and would see Eastman's radicalism as good societal therapy.

This position also has its dangers. There has been extensive criticism in the United States of the Soviet practice of putting dissenters in mental hospitals and treating them for irrational behavior. It can be argued (perhaps with tongue in cheek) that anyone who openly criticizes communist doctrines inside the Soviet Union must be a bit unbalanced mentally. But unless we wish to use the same tactics with our own dissenters, we must beware of advising psychotherapists and behavior change experts to adjust the patient to the realities of life in the United States.

Integration

In this area of behavior change, signs of theoretical and procedural integration have developed. H. Arkowitz and S. B. Messer (1984) invited prominent figures from the traditional practice of psychotherapy and others from the behavioral therapies to write essays on the points of convergence or divergence of the two approaches. The result was a rather encouraging set of agreements and disagreements. Arkowitz (1984) provided a historical essay in which he asserted that many psychodynamic therapists have adopted a variety of behavior management techniques from the psychologists. He quoted P. London (1964) on the value of behaviorist methods of removing symptoms; London commented that insight might also be useful, and that behaviorists had "tended, apparently somewhat unwittingly, to disregard the efficacy of thinking as a means of controlling human behavior" (1964, p. 128). In other words, it might help the patient to improve if the therapist explained possible causal factors while also prescribing corrective exercises.

One point which became clear in the essays was that behavior therapists often do much more than they report in the literature. Suggestions were common and interpretations were occasionally offered. The emotional climate—the relationship of therapist to patient—also had a major impact on success or failure.

Behaviorists are also picking up ideas from psychodynamic approaches. J. M. Rhoads and B. W. Feather (1972) advocated a combination of systematic desensitization and interpretive therapy. They considered this mixture particularly helpful in some cases of traumatic phobias (e.g., a fear of driving a car after being in a wreck). The use of directed fantasy sessions (instead of free associations) was proposed as a way to uncover links to childhood fears that may have been reactivated by the adult trauma. These authors proposed a therapeutic goal of anxiety reduction as opposed to complete insight into the bases of the symptoms.

Psychoanalytic concepts have been viewed more sympathetically than in the past. P. Wachtel (1982) commented on *resistance* in behavior therapy. Some patients chronically promise to follow a set of rules, then quickly break the behavioral routine prescribed. Wachtel found that in some instances, the patient is being reinforced by family members for maintaining the symptom, and that this reinforcement may intensify resistance to the therapist's instructions.

The papers in the Arkowitz–Messer book suggested that the resistance to the integration of psychoanalytic and behavioral theories evoked resistance about as strong as the traditional resistance of analysands to exposing hidden emotions. Several papers were mainly defensive of an established position. These resistances were recognized by others in the group; Arkowitz quoted E. Wolf (1966) to the effect that integration was necessary and desirable "however passionately some or many of us choose to resist it." Resistance occurs in therapists, too.

The successes of behavior therapies have been reinforcing to practitioners in this area, and these reinforcements have affected self-images. P. C. Kendall (1982) commented, "Behavior therapy has gained a sense of self-acceptance and can now be self-critical and self-evaluative . . . The time is ripe for integration". (p. 560). One may feel surprise at a behaviorist's use of terms like *self-critical* and *self-evaluative,* and may still approve of moves which will bring the tough-minded scientists and the tender-minded humanists into closer cooperation.

CHAPTER 22

The Two Cultures of Psychology

The history of psychological theories bears witness to the variety of ways of thinking about human behavior and experience in modern times. Incidental comments comparing concepts across theories have suggested that communication across theoretical schools is quite difficult. The situation is not unlike that described by the British scientist-novelist C. P. Snow in his provocative account of the "two cultures":

> There have been plenty of days when I have spent the working hours with scientist and then gone off at night with some literary colleagues. . . . I felt that I was moving among two groups—comparable in intelligence, identical in race, not grossly different in social origin, . . . who had almost ceased to communicate at all, who in intellectual, moral and psychological climate had so little in common that instead of going from Burlington House or South Kensington to Chelsea, one might have crossed an ocean (1964, p 2).

This was the origin of Snow's thesis of "two cultures": science and the humanities.

The history of psychology parallels Snow's description very closely. From William James's "tough-minded" and "tender-minded" psychologists to R. W. Coan's elaborate factor structure of objectivistic and subjectivistic psychologists (1979), the pure scientists and the humanistic school have criticized each other but have not indulged in constructive communication. Sigmund Koch (1981) recognized this dichotomy but seemed to despair of improving the situation.

Not all observers agree on just where the boundary between the factions should be drawn. Lee Cronbach (1957) identified the schism as lying between the experimentalists and the correlational psychologists. W. A. Owens (1968) proposed that the division lay between those who

controlled antecedent conditions (a small slice of personal history, manipulated in the laboratory) and those who tried to measure the larger
personal history (i.e., the individual's biography). Both agreed that the
experimental approach involved discarding the variance due to individual differences—as Cronbach put it, casting into the outer darkness of
"error variance" what should have been considered evidence for differences in response to the treatment of personalities or groups within the
sample studied.

Is there a need for combining personal with nomothetic studies? Evidence indicates that such a program might help clear up some of the
misunderstanding between clusters of psychologists. G. A. Forsyth and
D. R. Brown (1968) noted that the experimentalist tends to report how
the "typical" subject responded to the treatment; yet there may be no
"typical" subject in the group. They cited a study by Strongin, Bull and
Korchin (1941), who found a significant decrease in reading efficiency
under threat of electric shock. But a case-by-case examination showed
that all of the loss was due to a small group, 14 percent of the group
tested. The modal subject did not change in efficiency at all. DeNike and
Spielberger (1963) showed (see Figure 11.2) that a small cluster of five
subjects could produce a "significant" difference in a study of verbal
conditioning. Bishop (1967) and Timmons and Noblin (1963) demonstrated that "anal" personalities differed from "orals" in standard laboratory procedures. Probably many other studies could be found that indicate that "personality," however fuzzy the concept may be, cannot be
ignored by experimentalists.

Even when psychology had not established an identity separate from
philosophy, these lines of fragmentation had begun to show. Von Helmholtz wrote of a division between science and philosophy; Buxton (1985)
quoted him as saying, "The philosophers accused the scientific men of
narrowness; the scientific men retorted that the philosophers were crazy"
(p. 427). Stanley Hall praised Wundt for showing aspects of psychology
that were of importance to both science and humanities students. Even
Titchener talked about unifying the structuralists and the functionalists.
However, he humorously cited G. T. Ladd's remark that religious leaders were always talking about unifying the Christian sects, but each wanted
unification by having the others join his or her denomination.

The Need for Conceptual Anchors

When I add another reference to E. B. Titchener, my colleagues ask me
why I have this obsession with him and his ideas. The answer is quite
simple: Every intellectual frame of reference has to have an anchor point,
a definition of the dimensions that are under discussion. If a person
exclaims, "That is big!" the listener will want to know if the referent is
an elephant or a mouse. The same rule holds for the examination of

theories. It is difficult to do a conceptual analysis of a theoretical system without contrasting it to another system.

In Muzafer Sherif's (1936) study of social norms, a major discovery was that the judgments of peers provided an anchor to which the responses of the experimental subject were related. In Harry Helson's (1964) work on adaptation level, the individual worked out his or her own zero point and used it as a reference. It seems helpful to apply these ideas in comparing theories. Titchener himself made this clear when he proposed that the zero point for sensation be the absolute threshold, below which a stimulus elicited no conscious sensation, and that the unit of distance be the "just noticeable difference."

For the evaluation of theories, Titchener serves a slightly different purpose. As a fairly well-known and rigid theorist, he can serve as a reference point to which other theorists can be compared. Rigidity is useful (even if undesirable) because it makes the reference point steady. It would be difficult to use either Wundt or James in this role, because each engaged in mutually contradictory speculations at different times and places.

I have deliberately used Titchener, therefore, as a kind of marker for comparisons. Watson resembled Titchener on many points, the major exception being Watson's rejection of consciousness. Wertheimer and his colleagues retained consciousness but rejected atomism. Freud differed in focusing on dynamics as opposed to cognition, and also in emphasizing unconscious processes as opposed to a restrictive consciousness theory.

This need not be interpreted as requiring that each novel theory be a conscious rebellion against structuralism. The contrasts noted are heuristic, convenient descriptive devices. The differences are logical rather than emotional.

The Psychology of the Psychologist

Perhaps the split between the "two cultures" is itself a function of psychological determinants. With regard to theorists clinging to a mechanistic or a finalistic (purposive) view of psychology, Karl Lashley (1923) suggested that this is "wholly a matter of temperament; the choice is made upon an emotional and not a rational basis" (p. 344).

Mahoney (1974), writing from the viewpoint of cognitive behavior therapy, said that "the human being is a frequently deluded organism whose beliefs and behavior are stubbornly molded by perceptual bigotry" (p. 289). As psychologists are also human beings, it behooves us to consider whether we have deluded ourselves with excessive rigidity of beliefs about psychology. But other critics, seeking to use psychological models for psychologists, have used the method mainly to criticize their opponents. Jerome Kagan (1967) described structuralism and classical behaviorism as "absolutistic, outer directed, and intolerant of ambiguity" (p. 131). This was an indirect suggestion that these schools were authoritarian; the three terms used were said by T. W. Adorno, (1950) to be typical of the authoritarian personality. What Kagan may not have anticipated is that many "tough-minded" psychologists would applaud his characterization; they are indeed "outer-directed," focusing on the environmental determinants of behavior, and intolerant of the ambiguity that creeps into complex researches on personality where probabilities, not rigorous predictions, are the rule. The point was made by Rom Harré (1984) that "those who work in the 'experimental' tradition . . . make the implicit assumption that men, women and children are high-grade automata, the patterns of behavior are thought to obey something like natural laws" (p. 4). Again, the experimentalist may have no objection to being described as a high-grade automaton (many would protest if called "low-grade" automata). It is exactly this attribute of detached, impersonal precision that is attractive to many "pure science" psychologists.

Egocentric Thinking

Jean Piaget (1928) described the earliest stages of childhood thought as egocentric. By this, he meant the ability to see as real only what was perceived, to disregard the possibility that matters looked different to others. Thus he found that young children could not "take the place of another" (i.e., imagine themselves in a different location seeing the environment from a different angle). They continued to report the physical environment as it appeared from where they were observing.

Piaget noted that egocentrism declines as parents and peers coerce the child into conceding that reality might be seen differently by others; indeed, the child typically comes to accept adult definitions for many aspects of reality (1928, p. 279). The youngster also moves from egocentrism to ethnocentrism: "What is real is defined by what *my group* sees as real." It is relatively rare for even adults to reach the stage where they can look at reality from several different points of view—a stage I have called *altrocentrism* (Stagner, 1978).

Egocentric thinking gives rise to a phenomenon known as the *dialogue of the deaf*. This is a common occurrence in political and social disputes, where everybody talks and nobody listens. It can be documented easily in psychological debates, for example, by looking at the bibliographies appended to polemics. The advocates of the scientific approach rarely cite anyone from the humanistic side, and vice versa.

The dialogue of the deaf often begins in graduate school, where professors often actively discourage familiarity with or support of theories other than their own. It continues in the journals, where editors accept only articles that conform to their norms, often including theoretical biases.

It is also found in the job market; department chairpersons and committees select new teaching faculty with views that "fit" the departmental climate, instead of seeking to guarantee a diversity of theoretical convictions. And of course, in industrial and clinical institutions, the same trend is even more egregiously displayed.

In Chapter One, data were presented from a study by Gregory Kimble (1984) comparing the values of psychologists holding affiliations with different divisions of the American Psychological Association (APA). The profiles for two of these divisions (experimental and psychotherapy) were shown in Figure 1.6. The figures shown make it clear that the "two cultures" are divided on several major issues of significance. These include scientific versus humanistic values; determinism; objectivism; laboratory versus field research; nomothetic versus idiographic laws; and elementism versus holism. Each of these dimensions is of importance to any efforts at unification of the profession.

The two cultures of psychology have developed symptoms comparable to those described by Snow, that is, an inability to communicate, a lack of interest in communicating, and a mutual indifference shading over into active distaste for one another. These symptoms are believed by many observers to be hazardous to the health of psychology.

A Historical Note

The authors cited in this chapter have generally written as if this intradisciplinary feuding were a new development. Actually, American psychology went through a period of fission in the 1930s. In 1935, some practitioners were developing applied psychology, specifically in the clinical and industrial areas. Persons active in this movement found themselves unable to obtain any support from the APA, which was dominated by experimentalists devoted to the "pure science" belief system. After agitating unsuccessfully for "equal time" and equal effort from APA officials, these psychologists chose to set up a new organization, and in 1936, the American Association for Applied Psychology (AAAP) was organized.

At the same time, unemployment, the rise of fascism, and fears of war motivated a group of social psychologists to petition the APA officers for lobbying efforts to create state and federal jobs for psychologists, for official stands on political and international issues, and for job placement services at conventions. The "pure science" devotees in control of APA declined to assume these tasks, and a result was that in 1936, the Society for the Psychological Study of Social Issues (SPSSI) was formed.

Interestingly enough, neither those joining AAAP nor those with SPSSI showed any marked tendency to withdraw from APA. By organizing a mutual support group, the applied psychologists were able to work for licensing, quality control of practitioners, and other professional goals. The social psychologists, through organization, became able to lobby, to issue political statements on matters involving psychological considerations, and to protest encroachments on free speech for psychologists.

Within ten years, in 1946, the pure science group conceded the necessity of recognizing the process of differentiation, in knowledge and in economic concerns, places of employment, and so on. The APA was converted to a federation of divisions, or special-interest groups. The AAAP dissolved and became Division 12 (clinical psychology) and Division 14 (industrial psychology) of the new APA. The members of SPSSI voted to retain their specialized organization but also to continue as an APA affiliate, known now as Division 9. However, in the 1980s, friction between the scientists and the practitioners has again intensified.

Sources of Schism

What psychological principles are relevant to this fragmentation process? One fairly obvious factor is *information overload*. No one could possibly read all of the technical journals now being published, dealing with psychological issues and research. Human individuals defend themselves against the exasperation of overload by sharply restricting their intake of technical material. Thus the clinician drops any plans to read on physiological psychology, on perceptual processes, on laboratory studies of learning, and so on. The industrial psychologist likewise concentrates on research and speculation related to the industrial-organizational sphere. Neuropsychologists abandon most of the applied literature in favor of keeping up with some of the interesting work in neurophysiology. Thus each subgroup loses touch with the others. Further, with new concepts and new phenomena being discussed, vocabularies grow further apart and communication is more painful.

Specialization is also fostered by the reward system. To produce a significant contribution, one must concentrate on a narrow field. Anyone who tries to appeal to two or more of these differentiated groups will probably be viewed as an outsider by each group. The risk of seeming uninformed is much greater. Academic prestige is attained by demonstrating a high level of mastery in one area, not competence in several areas. Publications are the major source of status, and accomplishment here is favored by specialization.

A Role for Organizational Psychology?

I have already suggested that individual psychology can contribute to our understanding of the schism that has resulted in the "two cultures" phenomenon. Another tempting hypothesis is that the work of organizational psychologists may be relevant. Industrial psychologists have expanded their domain since the mid-1950s from the psychological problems of the individual worker or executive to problems which inhere in the organization perceived as a functional system. These include problems of communication, recruitment, and group interactions. The difficulties facing organized psychology may thus benefit from research and theorizing on industrial organizations.

An organizational psychologist called in as a consultant on corporate problems encounters many instances in which difficulties have arisen not because of incompetent executives or rebellious workers, but as a consequence of the way the organization functions. Poor communication between different groups within a corporation, for example, can lead to costly mistakes in management. The reward system may be functioning in such a fashion as to pit executives against one another instead of fostering mutual cooperation. Economic and power rewards are most important here, but subgroup loyalty may also be a factor.

Do these phenomena have analogues in scientific psychology? Certainly the problem of communication across specialty lines is an important consequence of the increased differentiation of areas within psychology. Clinical, physiological, social, industrial, and cognitive psychologists report that it is hard to understand people in other specialties. Each area develops its own vocabulary to designate the ideas and data of importance inside the area. As this process goes on, communication with psychologists outside the specialty becomes more difficult.

The reward system encourages specialization and discourages spending time and energy on the "total field" of psychology. As a rule, rewards for psychologists are not controlled by a single power figure, as in a corporation. For academic psychologists, rewards are related mainly to research and publication; these are easier to accomplish within a recognized specialty than by integrative speculation or investigation. Professional recognition is based chiefly on the detailed exploration of a single problem. If an individual aspires to lead a "school" or system of psychology, success will be made more probable if the person specializes.

Walter Firey (1948) offered a persuasive analysis of the conditions under which a corporation tends to split into a number of contending factions. Corporate functioning is optimized when all participants perceive that their economic rewards, security, power, and so on can best be achieved by the cooperation of all divisions. Fission is furthered if one group tries to advance its own power or security at the cost of others. Such conflicts develop between departments (e.g., production against sales). Each group seeks to maximize its budgetary allocations, its power to make decisions, and the bonuses or other benefits to its members. Some entertaining examples have been collected by Melville Dalton (1959).

The relation between differentiation and communication is emphasized when we consider the role of psychological journals. We recall that

Wundt founded *Philosophische Studien* as an outlet for studies done at Leipzig or within Wundt's theoretical framework. This goal automatically implied keeping articles out that reflected poorly on Wundt. Wertheimer and his colleagues founded *Psychologische Forschung,* Titchener set up the *American Journal of Psychology;* and Hall's rival publication, *Psychological Review,* provided space for nonstructuralist research. As Mahoney (1977a) demonstrated, systematic factors operate to favor the acceptance or rejection of research studies. Arthur Staats (1983) described an episode in which an editor kept adding reviewers for a paper until he got enough unfavorable comments to support his decision against publication.

Corrective Action

The foregoing analysis has stressed the centrifugal factors tending to break up the discipline of scientific psychology into segregated specialty groups. Yet there are other influences—weaker, admittedly—fostering integration. We see this on a large scale in conferences on the unity of science and the need for cross-disciplinary cooperation. It is also visible within psychology; for example, R. R. Grinker (1956) reported on a five-year interdisciplinary effort to develop a "unified theory of human behavior." The APA has also sponsored conferences on graduate training that have endorsed in principle the idea of reunifying psychology. The Grinker conferences did not seem to have any impact on psychological thinking; and although APA can influence training programs on details, the general philosophy and content emphasis of graduate programs remains under the control of individual departments and institutions.

Grinker gave a rather gloomy assessment of the five-year program he chaired. The participants—psychiatrists, psychologists, sociologists, anthropologists, and philosophers—rarely changed their positions as a result of intense discussion. He noted that "individuals grouped themselves less according to emphasis on particular aspects of observation, or on theory versus empiricism, but more in terms of their personal, habitual ways of viewing the world" (p. 366). In other words, exposure to divergent ways of conceptualizing human behavior did not succeed in modifying established belief systems.

The Grinker report does not prove conferences to be futile, but it raises a warning signal that putting convinced exponents of certain theories into a room and getting them to talk is not guaranteed to modify any theoretical convictions. The failure to modify beliefs also casts some doubt on the utility of cognitive dissonance as an instrument of change. The conference may be perceived as an opportunity to defend a specialized theoretical system rather than as an excuse to change.

Let me return to my metaphor of the industrial-organizational psychologist asked to help with a corporate problem. Setting up conferences where leaders of contending factions can interact may be beneficial, but unless there are some rewards for changing, we should not expect much in the way of results. In inducing organizational change, the I-O psychologist would prefer to set up task forces that include members of noncooperating groups but make it clear that rewards will be forthcoming if a sound solution is developed. Sherif, Harvey, White, Hood, and Sherif (1961) got adolescent gangs to cooperate by creating a crisis that could be solved only by joint action. Ordinarily we cannot create a crisis to order—and would not for ethical reasons—but it is possible to offer rewards for joint productivity. Thus the APA might encourage joint efforts in such combinations as humanistic psychology with verbal learning, using the methodology proposed by W. A. Owens (1968), or any other procedure that would be useful. Publicity and prestige rewards would motivate many psychologists to join in such problem-solving efforts.

Expanding the Frame of Reference

At times, conflict resolution is facilitated if the disputants can see the issues within a larger framework. Thus, labor–management controversies may be set aside when an entire industry seems to be on the verge of bankruptcy. This situation is irrelevant for a science such as psychology, but it may still be feasible to devise a more comprehensive view of the relevant issues. J. R. Royce and A. Powell (1983) proposed a new matrix of motives and values within which specific problems could be nested (Figure 22.1). This is a cross-cultural framework, bearing some resemblance to the sketch of Greek, Hebrew, and Hindu philosophies of person–environment relations offered in Chapter Two. It has elements of Gestalt theory in that the emphasis is on the relation of a part (the person) to a whole (society). In a perhaps whimsical passage, Royce and Powell suggested that these cultural perspectives represent a search for social meaning, a "self-image" of society, or a generalized image of the human species. Within each of these combinations of the transmission of values, some kinds of perceiving and learning are blocked by value systems. Motivation is also involved in the matrix. Although a Lewinian conception of valences and vectors would seem to be immediately applicable, many other views could be fitted into the scheme.

Extensive social rewards could derive from such an intellectual effort. The problem of alienation, for example, is a rapidly growing and alarming phenomenon. But we do not have much in the way of either theory or research to help government officials and/or social philosophers to plan public policy. There has been a great deal of verbalization but little investigation of the psychological implications of aid to families with dependent children, medical programs for drug users, required job train-

The Most Valuable Aspect of Individual Human Beings

IDEAL WAYS INDIVIDUAL HUMAN BEINGS WORK TOWARD THEIR GOALS	RELATIONS WITH OTHERS IN THE WORLD	ACCOMPLISHMENTS	INNER DEVELOPMENT AND ASCENDANCY OVER THE WORLD
Interacting and being a part of the world	Individual humans are an integral part of society (Communal society)	Individual humans are achievers within the social context (Kibbutz society)	Individual humans are alienated from society and the focus is on "here-and-now" actualization (Epicurean society)
Thinking about and manipulating the world	Individual humans are replaceable parts of society (Socialistic society)	Individual humans are achievers and are set apart from each other by their achievements (Technological society)	Individual humans are contemplators of their individual nature (The Academy of Ancient Greece)
Transcending the abstract and physical world	Individual humans must always conform to the social myth of the state (Fascistic society)	Individual humans are ethical and spiritual achievers and are judged by those achievements (Protestant subculture)	Individual humans are integrated with society, but they reach beyond society for transcendental meaning (Humanistic society)

(From Royce & Powell, 1983, p. 225, Table 10–2, reprinted by permission of Prentice-Hall, Inc., Englewood Cliffs, N.J.)

ing, required unskilled work on public projects, and so on. Perceiving, learning, motivating, and similar basic processes are intimately involved in all of these policy proposals. Efforts to solve them may well have the incidental benefit of optimizing the relations between the specialties within psychology.

Culture and the Unconscious

The problem in applying an analysis such as the one offered by Royce and Powell (1983) is that each of us has unconsciously adopted so many values and belief systems from our culture that it is not any longer feasible to make a voluntary change to a different value system. A distressed individual in treatment with Carl Rogers may concede that oneself as perceived does not conform to one's ideal self. Any person may, in theory, desire to be not merely integrated with society but cathected also with some mystical transcendent reality. But behavior in accordance with that ideal is difficult because of thoroughly indoctrinated individualistic competitive patterns of motivation and action. Most of this conflict is unconscious and, in any event, is going to resist change.

The analogy can be carried over to the culture of the graduate school and the indoctrination of young psychologists. Professors have ways of reinforcing agreement with their preferred theories, and the aspiring graduate student is likely to accept these without question. There are exceptions—consider the case of Skinner and the Harvard faculty—but on the whole, students accept the views of a majority of the faculty or of the dissertation adviser.

Appeals to the mature psychologist, then, to examine value systems and theoretical rigidities are likely to fail. Seymour Sarason (1981), asking for such changes, admitted the difficulties: "One's own culture is both ally and adversary: an ally in providing continuity and an adversary in making it so difficult, and often impossible, to examine certain ideas, to challenge certain values, and to transcend one's own context" (p. 173).

The Boundaries of Psychology

The Royce–Powell schema defines psychology so broadly as to include most of the social sciences. Perhaps this is necessary if we are to attain the all-embracing perspective needed. Other psychologists, as is well-known, prefer to set the boundary for their discipline at the human skin.

Tough-minded psychologists have a predilection for this narrower definition. It has the advantage, as they see it, of leaving open the possibility of reducing psychological generalizations to biological laws. This fits in with a major belief system for the group, namely, that in the short run, all psychological events will be explained by studies of brain function and, in the long run, by deductive extrapolation from atomic physics. Be it noted that such belief is still a matter of faith; psychology can still provide more help to neurophysiology than the latter can offer to psychology.

One low-cost solution to a problem is to draw boundary lines so that the problem is excluded. Thus, if we ban dreams and fantasies from the realm of scientific psychology, we put an end to the theoretical controversy over consciousness, but we also lose valuable clues to psychopathology and creative thought. At present, it would appear that we have much more to gain from an exploration of the wide-ranging theories than from narrowly focused approaches.

This book has sought to clarify the process of theory formation and the interaction of theorists of different schools. A status report would have to conclude that we have a multiplicity of theories, each of which seems to have some value. To optimize our situation, we must try to merge these diverse views into a more widely generalized interpretation of basic psychological processes. This is the task facing the younger generation of psychologists.

The foregoing discussion is based on the implicit assumption that unification in the area of theory is desirable. Most psychologists will agree with this assumption in principle, while ignoring or opposing it in practice. A second assumption is that a common subject matter, the behavior and conscious experiences of human beings, offers an opportunity to achieve unification; that is, in principle, laws can be developed that will apply across the spectrum from sensation to creativity.

I do not intend this extrapolation to extend over into physics. Clark Hull, like A. P. Weiss and other early behaviorists, hoped that physics and psychology would some day intersect; he predicted that "the theoretical physicists will ultimately deduce as theorems from electrons, protons, etc., the six postulates which we have employed as the basis for the deduction of adaptive behavior. If this deduction were accomplished we should have an unbroken logical chain extending from the primitive electron all the way up to complex purposive behavior. Further developments may conceivably extend the system to include the highest rational and moral behavior" (1937, p. 29).

In opposition to this view, we could pose the doctrine of emergent properties: The level of functioning may change the relevant attributes in ways not linked to the properties of the next lower level. It is obvious, for example, that human behavior is somehow related to the properties of neurons; but the human nervous system, with its billions of neurons arranged in intricate linkages, acquires properties that seem to be independent of the properties of the single cell. Such theories avoid what seems to be oversimplification (reducing behavior to neuron firing and muscle twitching) in favor of molar principles governing molar phenomena.

The outcome of these debates may well depend on the emotional values of the various groups involved. History, after all, is written by the winners. A theory may come to widespread acceptance because of the energetic devotion of its sponsors. As W. B. Yeats wrote:

> The best lack all conviction, while the worst
> Are full of passionate intensity.

It would be wrong to imply that advocates of the fragmentation of psychology are "the worst" in any sense. But in other respects, Yeats was right: advocates of tolerance and compromise often seem to be passive and lacking in energy, whereas specialists manifest energy and effort. This psychological distinction may determine the outcome of the competition among theories.

Bibliography and
Author Index

This Bibliography includes most of the works consulted in preparing the fore-going text. For the most part, each item is referenced to one or more pages in the text. Not all of these, however, will actually be cited on the page shown. Space would not permit that, and in many cases the page merely indicates the topic in connection with which the paper was examined. There are also a few very general books which are relevant to so many passages as to become top-heavy; for example, Edna Heidbreder's *Seven Psychologies* deals with many of the same theories and could be cited in scores of contexts. Similarly, a book like Zusne's *Biographical Dictionary of Psychology* is an appropriate accompaniment to this book, but it would be impractical to cross-reference all of its entries.

There are, on the other hand, many individuals named in the text without any citation of a publication. In these cases the name will be found in the General Index which follows the Bibliography.

Sigmund Freud presents a special problem because of the numerous editions and reissues of books and essays. I have adopted the policy of dating each paper as of the original publication, but appending the volume in which it appears in the *Standard Edition of the Complete Works of Sigmund Freud,* edited by James Strachey, so that it can be identified with precision.

ABELSON, R. P., ARONSON, E., McGUIRE, W. J., NEWCOMB, T. M., ROSENBERG, M. J., & TANNENBAUM, P. H. (Eds.) 1968. *Theories of Cognitive Consistency: A Sourcebook.* Chicago: Rand McNally. [264–265]

ADLER, A. 1907/1917. *Study of Organ Inferiority and Its Physical Compensation.* New York: Nervous & Mental Diseases Publishing Co. [328]

―――― 1913/1959. *The Neurotic Constitution.* New York: Dodd Mead & Co. [330, 332]

―――― 1924/1927. *Practice and Theory of Individual Psychology.* New York: Harcourt, Brace & Co. [331]

―――― 1927. *Understanding Human Nature.* New York: Greenberg, Publisher, Inc. [328]

—— 1928/1966. The psychology of power. *Journal of Individual Psychology,* *22,* 166–172. [328]

—— 1933/1964. *Social Interest: A Challenge to Mankind.* London: Faber & Faber. [331]

—— 1937. Psychiatric aspects regarding individual and social disorganization. *American Journal of Sociology, 42,* 773–780. [332]

—— 1970. *Superiority and Social Interest.* Evanston, Illinois: Northwestern University Press. [331]

ADORNO, T. W., FRENKEL-BRUNSWIK, E., LEVINSON, D. J., & SANFORD, R. N. 1950. *The Authoritarian Personality.* New York: Harper. [500]

AFL-CIO. 1979. The intimidation of job tests. *American Federationist,* (Jan.), 1–8. [147, 452]

ALBEE, G. W. 1983. Political ideology and science: A reply to Eysenck. *American Psychologist, 38,* 965–966. [472]

ALLPORT, F. H. 1924a. *Social Psychology.* Boston: Houghton Mifflin. [92, 187–190, 262]

—— 1924b. Social aspects of the measurement of intelligence. (Review of Brigham, 1923.) *Journal of Abnormal and Social Psychology, 19,* 311–313. [447]

—— 1955. *Theories of Perception and the Concept of Structure.* New York: Wiley. [426]

—— 1974. Autobiography. (In Boring, E. G., & Lindzey, G., Eds., *History of Psychology in Autobiography,* Vol. 6.) Englewood Cliffs, N.J.: Prentice-Hall. [374]

ALLPORT, G. W. 1937. *Personality: A Psychological Interpretation.* New York: Holt, Rinehart, & Winston. [375]

—— 1940. The psychologist's frame of reference. *Psychological Bulletin, 37,* 1–28. [375]

—— 1943. The productive paradoxes of William James. *Psychological Review, 50,* 95–120. [112]

—— 1946. Personalistic psychology as science: A reply. *Psychological Review, 53,* 132–135. [378]

—— 1955. *Becoming: Basic Considerations for a Psychology of Personality.* New Haven, Conn.: Yale University Press. [376]

—— 1961. *Pattern and Growth in Personality.* New York: Holt, Rinehart, & Winston. [376–379]

AMERICAN ASSOCIATION FOR HUMANISTIC PSYCHOLOGY (AAHP). 1962. *Constitution.* Washington, D.C.: The Association. [360]

AMES, A., JR. 1951. Visual perception and the rotating trapezoidal window. *Psychological Monographs, 65,* No. 7. [23]

AMOORE, J. E. 1964. Current status of the steric theory of odor. *Annals of the New York Academy of Science, 116,* 457–476. [24]

AMSEL, A. 1982. Behaviorism then and now. (A review of Watson, J. B. 1919. *Psychology from the Standpoint of a Behaviorist.*) *Contemporary Psychology, 27,* 343–346. [176]

ANASTASI, A. 1970. On the formation of psychological traits. *American Psychologist, 25,* 899–910. [451]

—— 1988. *Psychological Testing* (6th ed.) New York: Macmillan. [351, 451, 464, 466]

ANGELL, J. R. 1907. The province of functional psychology. *Psychological Review, 14,* 61–91. [152–154]

—— 1904/1909. *Psychology: An Introductory Study of the Structure and Function of Human Consciousness.* New York: Henry Holt & Co. [153]

ANSBACHER, H. L. 1937. Perception of number as affected by monetary value of objects. *Archives of Psychology,* No. 215. [424]

—— 1972. Adler's "striving for power" in relation to Nietzsche. *Journal of Individual Psychology, 28,* 12–24. [329]

—— & ANSBACHER, R. R. (Eds.) 1956. *The Individual Psychology of Alfred Adler. A Systematic Presentation in Selections From His Writings.* New York: Basic Books. [327, 329, 330, 333, 334]

APPLEY, M. H. (Ed.) 1971. *Adaptation-Level Theory: A Symposium.* New York: Academic Press. [263–264]

ARDREY, R. 1966. *The Territorial Imperative.* New York: Dell Publishing Co. [110]

ARGYRIS, C. 1968. Some unintended consequences of rigorous research. *Psychological Bulletin, 70,* 185–197. [283]

ARKOWITZ, H. 1984. Historical perspective on the integration of psychoanalytic therapy and behavior therapy. (In Arkowitz, H., & Messer, S. B., Eds. *Psychoanalytic Therapy and Behavior Therapy: Is Integration Possible?)* New York: Plenum Press. [495]

ARNHEIM, R. 1986. The two faces of Gestalt psychology. *American Psychologist, 41,* 820–824. [253]

ARVEY, R. D. 1986. General ability in employment: A discussion. *Journal of Vocational Behavior, 29,* 415–420. [450]

ASCH, S. E. 1946. Max Wertheimer's contribution to social psychology. *Social Research, 13,* 81–102. [262]

—— 1952. *Social Psychology.* Englewood Cliffs, N.J.: Prentice-Hall. [262]

—— 1956. Studies of independence and conformity: A minority of one against a unanimous majority. *Psychological Monographs, 70,* 9 (Whole No. 416). [286]

—— 1968. Wolfgang Köhler. *American Journal of Psychology, 81,* 110–119. [246]

ATKINSON, J. W. 1964. *An Introduction to Motivation.* New York: Van Nostrand Reinhold. [331]

AVERILL, J. R. 1982. *Anger and Aggression.* New York: Springer-Verlag. [180]

AX, A. F. 1953. The physiological differentiation between fear and anger in humans. *Psychosomatic Medicine, 15,* 433–442. [180]

AX, A. F., & BAMFORD, J. L. 1968. Validation of a psychophysiological test of aptitude for learning social motives. *Psychophysiology, 5,* 316–332. [194]

AX, A. F., LLOYD, R., GORHAM, J. C., LOOTENS, A. M., & ROBINSON, R. 1978. Autonomic learning: A measure of motivation. *Motivation and Emotion, 2,* 213–242. [194]

AYLLON, T., & MICHAEL, J. 1959. The psychiatric nurse as behavioral engineer. *Journal for Experimental Analysis of Behavior, 2,* 323–334. [483]

BAGBY, E. 1928. *Psychology of Personality.* New York: Henry Holt & Co. [482]

BAKAN, D. 1965. The mystery-mastery complex in contemporary psychology. *American Psychologist, 20,* 186–191. [14]

—— 1966. Behaviorism and American urbanization. *Journal of the History of the Behavioral Sciences, 2,* 5–28. [184]

BALDWIN, A. L. 1942. Personal structure analysis: A statistical method for investigating the single personality. *Journal of Abnormal and Social Psychology, 37*, 163–183. [378]

—— 1946. The study of individual personality by means of the intra-individual correlation. *Journal of Personality, 14*, 151–168. [378]

BALDWIN, J. M. 1895. *Mental Development in the Child and the Race: Methods and Processes.* New York: Macmillan. [91]

—— 1897. *Social and Ethical Interpretations in Mental Development.* New York: Macmillan. [91]

—— 1913. *History of Psychology.* New York: Putnam. [160]

BALMARY, M. 1982. *Freud and the Hidden Fault of the Father.* (Trans. by Ned Lukacher.) Baltimore, Md.: Johns Hopkins University Press. [309]

BALZ, A. G. A. 1952. *Descartes and the Modern Mind.* New Haven, Conn.: Yale University Press. [47, 50]

BANDURA, A. 1962. Social learning through imitation. (In Jones, M. R., Ed., *Nebraska Symposium on Motivation.*) Lincoln, Nebraska: University of Nebraska Press. [406]

—— 1969. *Principles of Behavior Modification.* New York: Holt, Rinehart, & Winston. [406, 411, 492]

—— 1973. *Aggression: A Social Learning Analysis.* Englewood Cliffs, N.J.: Prentice-Hall. [409, 489]

—— 1977a. *Social Learning Theory.* Englewood Cliffs, N.J.: Prentice-Hall. [409, 410, 412]

—— 1977b. Self-efficacy: Toward a unifying theory of behavioral change. *Psychological Review, 84*, 191–215. [410]

—— 1978. The self system in reciprocal determinism. *American Psychologist, 33*, 344–358. [410]

—— 1982. Self-efficacy mechanism in human agency. *American Psychologist, 37*, 122–147. [410]

—— & MISCHEL, W. 1965. Modification of self-imposed delay of reward through exposure to live and symbolic models. *Journal of Personality and Social Psychology, 2*, 698–705. [411]

—— & WALTERS, R. W. 1959. *Adolescent Aggression.* New York: Ronald Press. [406, 411]

—— & —— 1963. *Social Learning and Personality Development.* New York: Holt, Rinehart, & Winston. [406]

BARBRACK, C. R. 1985. Negative outcome in behavior therapy. (In May, D. T., & Franks, C. M., Eds., *Negative Outcomes in Psychotherapy.*) New York: Springer Publishing Co. [491]

BARCLAY, L. 1982. Social learning theory: A framework for discrimination research. *Academy of Management Review, 7*, 587–594. [412]

BARITZ, L. 1965. *Servants of Power.* New York: Wiley. [412]

BARKER, R. G. 1968. *Ecological Psychology: Concepts and Methods for Studying the Environment of Human Behavior.* Stanford, Cal.: Stanford University Press. [489]

BARTLE, P. M. 1984. Lillian M. Gilbreth: In Memoriam. *Newsletter, Division 26,* American Psychological Association, (October), 1–3. [134]

BARTLETT, F. C. 1932. *Remembering: A Study in Experimental and Social Psychology.* Cambridge, England: Cambridge University Press. [437, 440]

—— 1958. *Thinking: An Experimental and Social Study.* New York: Basic Books. [440]

BASS, A. R., & FIRESTONE, I. J. 1980. Implications of representativeness for generalizability of field and laboratory research findings. *American Psychologist, 35,* 463–464. [489]

BECK, A. T. 1976. *Cognitive Therapy and the Emotional Disorders.* New York: International Universities Press. [485]

BECKER, C. B. 1986. Reasons for the lack of argumentation and debate in the Far East. *International Journal of Intercultural Relations, 10,* 75–92. [39]

BECKER, E. 1973. *The Denial of Death.* New York: Free Press. [347]

BEEBE-CENTER, J. G. 1932. *The Psychology of Pleasantness and Unpleasantness.* New York: D. Van Nostrand Co. [136]

BEIER, E. G. 1985. Setting new trends. *American Psychologist, 40,* 248. [237]

BEKHTEREV, V. M. 1913a. *Objective Psychologie.* Leipzig: Tuebner. [164]

—— 1913b. *La Psychologie Objective.* Paris: Alcan. [164]

—— 1933. *General Principles of Human Reflexology.* (Trans. by E. Murphy & W. Murphy.) New York: International Publishers. [164]

BEN-DAVID, J., & COLLINS, R. 1966. Social factors in the origins of a new science: The case of psychology. *American Sociological Review, 31,* 451–465. [97]

BENJAMIN. L. T., JR., & PERLOFF, R. 1982. A case of delayed recognition: Frederick Winslow Taylor and the immediacy of reinforcement. *American Psychologist, 37,* 340–342. [184]

BENTLEY, M. 1900. The synthetic experiment. *American Journal of Psychology, 11,* 405–425. [489]

BENTZ, V. J. 1967. The Sears experience in the investigation, description, and prediction of executive behavior. (In Wickert, F. R., & McFarland, D. E., Eds. *Measuring Executive Effectiveness.*) New York: Appleton-Century-Crofts. [463]

BERGIN, A. E. 1963. The effects of psychotherapy: Negative results revisited. *Journal of Counseling Psychology, 10,* 244–250. [491]

BERKELEY, G. 1710/1963. *A Treatise Concerning the Principles of Human Knowledge.* LaSalle, Ill: Open Court Publishing Co. [99]

BERKOWITZ, L., & DONNERSTEIN, E. 1982. External validity is more than skin deep. *American Psychologist, 37,* 245–257. [489]

BERNFELD, S. 1944. Freud's earliest theories and the school of Helmholtz. *Psychoanalytic Quarterly, 13,* 341–362. [298]

BERNREUTER, R. G. 1933. Theory and construction of the Personality Inventory. *Journal of Social Psychology, 4,* 387–405. [462]

BINET, A. 1883. Le raisonnement dans les perceptions. *Revue Philosophique, 15,* 406–432. [448]

—— 1890/1977. *On Double Consciousness.* (Trans. by H. G. Baldwin.) Washington, D.C.: University Publications of America. [448]

—— 1892. *Mental Imagery.* (In Robinson, D. N. 1977. *Significant Contributions to the History of Psychology.*) Washington, D.C.: University Publications of America. [448]

—— 1948. The development of the Binet-Simon scale. (In Dennis, W., Ed., *Readings in the History of Psychology.*) New York: Appleton-Century-Crofts. [449]

—— & HENRI, V. 1896. La psychologie individuelle. *L'Année Psychologique, 2,* 411–465. [449]

—— & SIMON, T. 1911/1977. The development of intelligence in children. (In Robinson, D. N., Ed., *Significant Contributions to the History of Psychology, 1750–1920.*) Washington, D.C.: University Publications of America. [449]

BIONDO, J., & MACDONALD, A. P., JR. 1971. Internal-external locus of control and response to influence attempts. *Journal of Personality, 39,* 408–419. [404]

BISHOP, F. V. 1967. The anal character: A rebel in the dissonance family. *Journal of Personality and Social Psychology, 6,* 23–36. [498]

BLAKE, R. R., & MOUTON, J. S. 1961. Group competition under win-lose conditions. *Management Science, 7,* 420–435. [286]

BLOCK, J. 1961. *The Q-Sort Method in Personality Assessment and Psychiatric Research.* Springfield, Ill.: Charles C Thomas. [373]

—— 1971. *Lives Through Time.* Berkeley, Cal.: Bancroft. [463]

BLUMENTHAL, A. L. 1975. A reappraisal of Wilhelm Wundt. *American Psychologist, 30,* 1081–1088. [94]

—— 1980. Wilhelm Wundt and early American psychology: A clash of cultures. (In Rieber, R., & Salzinger, K., Eds. *Psychology: Theoretical-Historical Perspectives.*) New York: Academic Press. [94]

—— 1985. Wilhelm Wundt: Psychology as the propaedeutic science. (In Buxton, C. E., Ed. *Points of View in the Modern History of Psychology.*) New York: Academic Press. [94]

BORING, E. G. 1921. The stimulus error. *American Journal of Psychology, 32,* 449–471. [122, 322]

—— 1929. The psychology of controversy. *Psychological Review, 36,* 97–121. [125]

—— 1929/1950. *A History of Experimental Psychology.* New York: Appleton-Century-Crofts., [82, 133, 423]

—— 1933/1963. *The Physical Dimensions of Consciousness.* New York: Dover Publications. [133]

—— 1946. Mind and mechanism. *American Journal of Psychology, 59,* 173–192. [125, 133]

—— 1969. Perspective: Artifact and control. (In Rosenthal, R., & Rosnow, R. L., Eds. *Artifact in Behavioral Research.*) New York: Academic Press. [405]

——, LANGFELD, H. S., WERNER, H., & YERKES, R. M. (Eds.) 1952. *A History of Psychology in Autobiography.* Worcester, Mass.: Clark University Press. [199–201]

BOTTOME, P. 1939. *Alfred Adler: A Biography.* New York: G. P. Putnam's Sons. [326]

BOUCHARD, T. J. JR., & MCGEE, M. 1981. Familial studies of intelligence: A review. *Science, 212,* 1055–1058. [464]

BOUCHARD, T. J. JR., & SEGAL, N. L. 1985. Environment and IQ. (In Wolman, B. B., Ed. *Handbook of Intelligence: Theories, Measurements, and Applications.*) New York: Wiley. [465]

BOWER, G. H. (Ed.) 1977. *Human Memory: Basic Processes.* New York: Academic Press. [437]

BRADLEY, D. R., & PETRY, H. M. 1977. Organizational determinants of subjective contour. *American Journal of Psychology, 90,* 253–262. [254]

BRAMEL, D., & FRIEND, R. 1981. Hawthorne, the myth of the docile worker, and class bias in psychology. *American Psychologist, 36,* 867–878. (See also *American Psychologist,* 1982, *37,* 855–861.) [357]

BRANDT, L. W. 1979. Behaviorism—the psychological buttress of late capitalism. (In Buss, A. R., Ed. *Psychology in Social Context.*) New York: Irvington Publishers. [184]

BREHM, J. W. 1966. *A Theory of Psychological Reactance.* New York: Academic Press. [422]

BRENNAN, J. F. 1982. *History and Systems of Psychology.* Englewood Cliffs, N.J.: Prentice-Hall. [2]

BRENNER, D., LIPTON, J., KAUFMAN, L., & WILLIAMSON, S. J. 1978. Somatically evoked magnetic fields of the human brain. *Science, 199,* 81–83. [260]

BRENT, S. B. 1978. Motivation, steady-state, and structural development: A general model for psychological homeostasis. *Motivation and Emotion, 2,* 299–332. [195]

BRETT, G. S. 1912. *History of Psychology* (3 Vols.) London: G. Allen & Unwin.

—— 1922/1965. *History of Psychology* (Edited and abridged by R. S. Peters.) Cambridge, Mass.: M. I. T. Press. [38, 50, 52–54, 73, 290]

BREUER, J., & FREUD, S. 1895. *Studies on Hysteria.* London: Hogarth Press. SE 2. [295]

BREWER, M. 1986. Experimental research and social policy: Must it be rigor versus relevance? *Journal of Social Issues, 41,* 159–176. [283, 489]

BREWER, W. F. 1974. There is no convincing evidence for operant or classical conditioning in humans. (In Weimer, W. B., & Palermo, D. S., Eds. *Cognition and the Symbolic Processes.*) New York: Halstead. [437]

BRIGHAM, C. C. 1923. *A Study of American Intelligence.* Princeton, N.J.: Princeton University Press. [447]

BRINGMANN, W. G. 1986. Edwin Garrigues Boring: In Memoriam. *History of Psychology Newsletter, 18* (4), 93–127. [122]

——, BALANCE, W. D. G., & EVANS, R. B. 1975. Wilhelm Wundt 1832–1920: A brief biographical sketch. *Journal of the History of the Behavioral Sciences, 11,* 287–297. [86]

—— & TWENEY, R. D. (Eds.) 1980. *Wundt Studies.* Toronto: C. J. Hogrefe. [86]

BROADBENT, D. E. 1969. Word-frequency effect and response bias. (In Haber, R. N., Ed. *Information-Processing Approaches to Visual Perception.*) New York: Holt, Rinehart, & Winston. [429]

BRODY, N. 1985. The validity of tests of intelligence. (In Wolman, B. B., Ed. *Handbook of Intelligence: Theories, Measurements, and Applications.*) New York: Wiley. [444]

BROME, V. 1978. *Jung.* New York: Atheneum. [335–337]

BROUGHTON, J. M. 1981. The genetic psychology of James Mark Baldwin. *American Psychologist, 36,* 396–407. [154–155]

BROWN, H. C. 1916. Language and the associative reflex. *Journal of Philosophy, Psychology, and Scientific Method, 13,* 645–649. [187]

BROWN, J. F. 1934. Freud and the scientific method. *Philosophy of Science, 1,* 323–337. [298–299]

—— 1936. *Psychology and the Social Order.* New York: McGraw-Hill. [290–291]

—— 1940. *Psychodynamics of Abnormal Behavior.* New York: McGraw-Hill. [319]

BROWN, T. 1820/1970. *Lectures on the Philosophy of the Human Mind.* New York: Random House. [70]

BROWNELL, K. D., MARLATT, G. A., LICHTENSTEIN, E., & WISCON, D. T. 1986. Understanding and preventing relapse. *American Psychologist, 41,* 765–782. [488–489]

BROZEK, J., & EVANS, R. B. (Eds.) 1977. *R. I. Watson's Selected Papers on the History of Psychology.* Hanover, N. H.: University Press of New England. [17]

BRUNER, J. S. 1965. The growth of mind. *American Psychologist, 20,* 1007–1017. [424]

—— & ALLPORT, G. W. 1940. Fifty years of change in American psychology. *Psychological Bulletin, 37,* 757–776. [424]

—— & GOODMAN, C. C. 1947. Value and need as organizing factors in perception. *Journal of Abnormal and Social Psychology, 42,* 33–44. [425]

——, GOODNOW, J. J., & AUSTIN, G. A. 1956. *A Study of Thinking.* New York: Wiley. [436]

—— & KLEIN, G. S. 1960. The functions of perceiving: New Look retrospect. (In Kaplan, B., & Wapner, S., Eds. *Perspectives in Psychological Theory.*) New York: International Universities Press. [424]

—— & MINTURN, A. L. 1955. Perceptual identification and perceptual organization. *Journal of Genetic Psychology, 53,* 21–28. [424]

—— & POSTMAN, L. 1947. Emotional selectivity in perception and reaction. *Journal of Personality, 16,* 69–77. [425]

BRUNSWIK, E. 1939. The conceptual focus of some psychological systems. *Journal of Unified Science, 8,* 36–49. [4]

—— 1943. Organismic achievement and environmental probability. *Psychological Review, 50,* 255–272. [12]

—— 1952. *The Conceptual Framework of Psychology.* Chicago: University of Chicago Press. [12, 20]

BRYAN, W. L., & HARTER, N. 1899. Studies on the telegraphic languages. *Psychological Review, 6,* 345–375. [259]

BURGHARDT, G. M. 1985. Animal awareness: Current perceptions and historical perspective. *American Psychologist, 40,* 905–919. [163]

BURKS, B. S. 1942. A study of identical twins reared apart under differing types of family relationships. (In McNemar, Q., & Merrill, M. A., Eds. *Studies in Personality.*) New York: McGraw-Hill. [463, 466]

BURNHAM, W. H. 1917. Mental hygiene and the conditioned reflex. *Pedagogical Seminary (Journal of Genetic Psychology), 24,* 449–488. [145]

BURT, C. 1966. The genetic determination of differences in intelligence. *British Journal of Psychology, 57,* 137–153. [452]

—— 1972. The inheritance of general intelligence. *American Psychologist, 27,* 175–190. [452]

BURTT, H. E. 1929. *Psychology and Industrial Efficiency.* New York: D. Appleton & Co. [184]

BUSS, A. R. 1975. The emerging field of the sociology of psychological knowledge. *American Psychologist, 30,* 988–1001. [184]

—— 1978. The structure of psychological revolutions. *Journal of the History of the Behavioral Sciences, 14,* 57–64. [2]

—— (Ed.) 1979. *Psychology in Social Context.* New York: Irvington Publishers. [184]

———— & POLEY, W. (Eds.) 1976. *Individual Differences: Traits and Factors.* New York: Halstead (Wiley). [452]

BUXTON, C. E. (Ed.) 1985. *Points of View in the Modern History of Psychology.* New York: Academic Press. [498]

CACIOPPO, J. T., & PETTY, R. E. 1981. Electromyograms as measures of extent and affectivity of information processing. *American Psychologist, 36,* 441–456. [429]

CALKINS, M. W. 1894. Association I. *Psychological Review, 1,* 476–483. [157]

———— 1896. Association: An essay analytic and experimental. *Psychological Review Monograph Supplements, 1,* No. 2. [157]

———— 1899. Attributes of sensation. *Psychological Review, 6,* 506–514. [156]

———— 1906. A reconciliation between structural and functional psychology. *Psychological Review, 13,* 62–80. [155]

———— 1908. Psychology as a science of the self. *Journal of Philosophy, Psychology, and Scientific Method, 5,* 12–19, 64–68, 113–121. [156]

———— 1909/1921. *A First Book in Psychology.* New York: Macmillan. [155–157]

———— 1921. The truly psychological behaviorism. *Psychological Review, 28,* 1–18. [156]

———— 1927. The self in recent psychology. *Psychological Bulletin, 24,* 205–215. [156]

CAMPBELL, A. A. 1938. Interrelation of two measures of conditioning in man. *Journal of Experimental Psychology, 22,* 225–243. [210]

———— & HILGARD, E. R. 1936. Individual differences in ease of conditioning. *Journal of Experimental Psychology, 19,* 561–571. [210]

CAMPBELL, B. A., & PICKLEMAN, J. R. 1961. The imprinting object as a reinforcing stimulus. *Journal of Comparative and Physiological Psychology, 54,* 592–596. [204–205]

CAMPBELL, D. T. 1965. Ethnocentric and other altruistic motives. (In Levine, D., Ed. *Nebraska Symposium on Motivation.*) Lincoln, Nebraska: University of Nebraska Press. [470]

———— 1974. "Downward causation" in hierarchically organized biological systems. (In Ayala, F. J., & Dobzhansky, T., Eds. *Studies in the Philosophy of Biology: Reduction and Related Problems.*) Berkeley, Cal.: University of California Press. [416]

———— 1975. On the conflicts between biological and social evolution and between psychology and moral tradition. *American Psychologist, 30,* 1103–1126. [470]

CAMPUS, N. 1974. Transituational consistency as a dimension of personality. *Journal of Personality and Social Psychology, 29,* 593–600. [461]

CANNON, W. B. 1929. *Bodily Changes in Pain, Hunger, Fear, and Rage.* New York: D. Appleton. [180]

CAROTENUTO, A. 1982. *Diario di una segreta simmetria. (A Secret Symmetry).* Trans. by A. Pomerano, John Shepley, & Krishna Winston. New York: Pantheon Books. [337]

CASEY, E. S. 1972. Freud's theory of reality: A critical account. *Review of Metaphysics, 25,* 659–690. [319]

CASON, H. 1922. The conditioned pupillary reaction. *Journal of Experimental Psychology, 5,* 108–146. [177]

———— 1930. Common Annoyances. *Psychological Monographs, 40* (Whole No. 182). [461]

CATANIA, A. C. 1973. The psychologies of structure, function, and development. *American Psychologist, 28,* 434–443. [138–139]

—— 1975. The myth of self-reinforcement. *Behaviorism, 3,* 192–199. [410]

CATTELL, J. M. 1886a. Über die Zeit der Erkennung und Benennung von Schriftzeichen, Bildern, und Farben. *Philosophische Studien, 2,* 635–650. (The time it takes to see and name objects. *Mind, 11,* 63–65.) [148, 150, 439]

—— 1886b. Psychometrische Untersuchungen. *Philosophische Studien, 3,* 305–335. (Ph.D. thesis.) [150]

—— 1898. The biological problems of today: Psychology. *Science, 7,* 152–154. [431]

CATTELL, R. B. 1945. Principal trait clusters for describing personality. *Psychological Bulletin, 42,* 129–161. [454–455]

—— 1956. Validation and intensification of the Sixteen Personality Factor Questionnaire. *Journal of Clinical Psychology, 12,* 205–214. [462]

—— 1963. Fluid and crystallized intelligence. *Journal of Educational Psychology, 54,* 1–22. [455]

—— & DREVDAHL, J. E. 1955. A comparison of the personality profile (16PF) of eminent researchers with that of eminent teachers and administrators, and of the general population. *British Journal of Psychology, 46,* 248–261. [462]

CAUTELA, J. R. 1967. Covert sensitization. *Psychological Reports, 20,* 459–468. [486]

—— 1973. Covert processes and behavioral modification. *Journal of Nervous and Mental Disease, 157,* 27–36. [486]

CHAMBLESS, D. 1985. Follow-up Research on Agoraphobics. Unpublished paper, American Association for Behavior Therapy, Houston, November. (ERIC, Document Reproduction Service, No. ED 268454.) [489, 491, 492]

CHANDLER, M. J. 1973. Egocentrism and antisocial behavior: The assessment and training of social perspective-taking skills. *Developmental Psychology, 9,* 326–332. [406]

CHEIN, I. 1947. The genetic factor in ahistorical psychology. *Journal of General Psychology, 36,* 151–172. [273]

CHOMSKY, N. 1959. Review of Skinner's *Verbal Behavior. Language, 35,* 26–58. [231, 263, 339]

—— 1972. *Language and Mind.* New York: Harcourt Brace Jovanovich. [231]

CHRISTOPHER, S. B., & LEAK, G. K. 1984. Freud and sociobiology. *American Psychologist, 39,* 184–185. [313]

COAN, R. W. 1968. Dimensions of psychological theory. *American Psychologist, 23,* 715–722. [19, 20, 135, 239, 261]

—— 1973. Toward a psychological interpretation of psychology. *Journal of the History of the Behavioral Sciences, 9,* 313–327. [19, 20, 21]

—— 1979. *Psychologists: Personal and Theoretical Pathways.* New York: Irvington Publishers. [19, 20, 135, 239, 261, 439, 497]

COCH, L., & FRENCH, J. R. P., JR. 1948. Overcoming resistance to change. *Human Relations, 1,* 512–532. [288]

COFER, C. N., & APPLEY, M. H. 1964. *Motivation: Theory and Research.* New York: Wiley. [180]

COHEN, D. 1979. *J. B. Watson: The Founder of Behaviorism.* London: Routledge & Kegan Paul. [171, 175]

COMBS, A. W. 1952. Intelligence from a perceptual point of view. *Journal of Abnormal and Social Psychology, 47,* 662–673. [248]

COMREY, A. L., & JAMISON, K. 1966. Verification of six personality factors. *Educational and Psychological Measurement, 26,* 945–953. [462]

CRAIK, K. H. 1986. Personality research methods: An historical perspective. *Journal of Personality, 54,* 18–51. [462]

CRONBACH, L. J. 1957. The two disciplines of scientific psychology. *American Psychologist, 12,* 671–684. [497]

CRUTCHFIELD, R. S. 1961. Edward Chace Tolman: 1886–1959. *American Journal of Psychology, 74,* 135–141. [392]

CUNY, H. 1965. *Ivan Pavlov: The Man and His Theories:* New York: Paul S. Eriksson. [165, 168]

DALTON, M. 1959. *Men Who Manage.* New York: Wiley. [503]

DANZIGER, K. 1979. The social origins of modern psychology. (In Buss, A. R., Ed. *Psychology in Social Context.*) New York: Irvington Publishers. [184]

―――― 1980. The history of introspection reconsidered. *Journal of the History of the Behavioral Sciences, 16,* 241–262. [137]

DARWIN, C. 1859. *The Origin of Species.* New York: Hurst. [139, 229]

DAVIS, H., & HURWITZ, H. M. B. (Eds.) 1977. *Operant-Pavlovian Interactions.* Hillsdale, N.J.: Lawrence Erlbaum Associates. [168]

DECI, E. L. 1972. Effects of contingent and noncontingent rewards and controls on intrinsic motivation. *Organizational Behavior and Human Performance, 8,* 217–229. [237]

―――― 1975. *Intrinsic Motivation.* New York: Plenum Press. [237]

DEKKER, E., & GROEN, J. 1956. Reproducible attacks of asthma: A laboratory study. *Journal of Psychosomatic Research, 1,* 58–67. [481]

DEMBO, T. 1931. Der Ärger als dynamisches Problem. *Psychologische Forschung, 15,* 1–144. [282]

DeNIKE, L. D., & SPIELBERGER, C. D. 1963. Induced mediating states in verbal conditioning. *Journal of Verbal Learning and Verbal Behavior, 1,* 339–345. [232, 233, 498]

DENNIS, W. 1948. *Readings in the History of Psychology.* New York: Appleton-Century-Crofts. [140, 449]

DESCARTES, R. 1649/1955. *The Passions of the Soul.* (Trans. by E. S. Haldane & G. R. T. Ross.) New York: Dover Press. [50]

―――― 1901. *Discourse on Method.* (Trans by J. Veitch.) New York: Tudor. [48, 51, 99]

―――― 1927. *Treatise on Man.* (R. M. Eaton, Ed.) New York: Scribner. [47]

DETTERMAN, D. K., & STERNBERG, R. J. (Eds.) 1982. *How and How Much Can Intelligence Be Increased?* Norwood, N.J.: Ablex Publishing Co. [466, 468]

DEWEY, J. 1896. The reflex arc concept in psychology. *Psychological Review, 3,* 357–370. [100, 151, 152]

―――― 1922. *Human Nature and Conduct.* New York: Holt. [152]

DIAMOND, S. 1984. Leibniz's aphorism in different contexts. (In *Psychology in its Historical Contexts: Festschrift in Honor of Josef Brozek.*) Valencia, Spain: Monografias de la Revista de Historia de la Psicologia. [73–75]

DIPBOYE, R. L., & FLANAGAN, M. F. 1979. Research settings in industrial and organizational psychology: Are findings in the field more generalizable than in the laboratory? *American Psychologist, 34,* 141–150. [489]

DOBZHANSKY, T. 1973. *Genetic Diversity and Human Equality.* New York: Basic Books. [471]

DOLEZAL, H. 1975. In honor of Robert Brodie MacLeod: Psychological phenomenology face to face with the persistent problems of psychology. *Journal of the History of the Behavioral Sciences, 11,* 223–234. [195]

DOLLARD, J., DOOB, L. W., MILLER, N. E., MOWRER, O. H., & SEARS, R. R. 1939. *Frustration and Aggression.* New Haven: Yale University Press. [214, 398]

—— & Miller, N. E. 1950. *Personality and Psychotherapy.* New York: McGraw-Hill. [213, 417, 478]

DORSEY, J. M. 1976. *An American Psychiatrist in Vienna, 1935–1937, and His Sigmund Freud.* Detroit, Mich.: Center for Health Education. [297]

DULANY, D. E. 1967. Awareness, rules, and propositional control: A confrontation with S-R behavior theory. (In Horton, D., & Dixon, T., Eds.: *Verbal Behavior and S-R Behavior Theory.*) Englewood Cliffs, N.J.: Prentice-Hall. [408]

EBBINGHAUS, H. 1885/1964. *Über das Gedachtnis.* (On Memory). New York: Dover Publications. [94–97, 246]

—— 1908. *Grundzüge der Psychologie. (Foundations of Psychology.)* Leipzig: Veit. [96, 118]

EBER, M. 1983. Freud, sociobiology, and contemporary psychoanalysis. *American Psychologist, 38,* 496–497. [313]

EDEN, D., & SHANI, A. B. 1982. Pygmalion goes to boot camp: Expectancy, leadership, and trainee performance. *Journal of Applied Psychology, 67,* 194–199. [405]

EDWARDS, A. L. 1954. *Manual for the EPPS (Edwards Personal Preference Schedule).* New York: The Psychological Corporation. [462]

EHRENFELS, C. VON. 1890. Über Gestaltqualitäten. *Vierteljahrschrift wissenschaftliche Philosophie, 14,* 249–292. [241]

EINSTEIN, A. 1961. *Relativity: The Special and the General Theory.* New York: Bonanza Books. [7]

ELLENBERGER, H. F. 1972. The story of "Anna O.": A critical review with new data. *Journal of the History of the Behavioral Sciences, 8,* 267–279. [294, 295]

ELLIOTT, R. M. 1931. Albert Paul Weiss, 1879–1931. *American Journal of Psychology, 44,* 707–709. [185, 187]

ELLIS, A. 1970. *The Essence of Rational Psychotherapy: A Comprehensive Approach to Treatment.* New York: Institute for Rational Living. [484–485]

—— 1977. The basic clinical theory of rational-emotive therapy. (In Ellis, A., & Grieger, R., Eds. *Handbook of Rational-Emotive Therapy.*) New York: Springer Publishing Co. [484, 485]

ELLIS, H. 1859/1942. *Studies in the Psychology of Sex.* New York: Random House. [296]

EMMELKAMP, P. M. G., & KUIPERS, A. C. M. 1979. Agoraphobia: A follow-up study four years after treatment. *British Journal of Psychiatry, 134,* 352–355. [489]

ENDLER, N. S., & MAGNUSSON, D. 1976. *Interactional Psychology and Personality.* Washington, D.C.: Hemisphere Publishing Corporation. [462]

EPSTEIN, S. 1979. The stability of behavior. I. On predicting most of the people much of the time. *Journal of Personality and Social Psychology, 37,* 1097–1126. [462]

———— 1980. The stability of behavior. II. Implications for psychological research. *American Psychologist, 35,* 790–806. [462]

ERICKSON, M. H. 1985. The case of Barbie: An Ericksonian approach to the treatment of anorexia nervosa. *Transactional Analysis Journal, 15,* 85–92. [486]

ERON, L. D. 1987. The development of aggressive behavior from the perspective of a developing behaviorism. *American Psychologist, 42,* 435–442. [411]

ESPER, E. A. 1964. *A History of Psychology.* Philadelphia: W. B. Saunders. [216]

ESTES, W. K. 1954. Kurt Lewin. (In Estes, W. K., Koch, S., MacCorquodale, K., Meehl, P. E., Mueller, G. G., Jr., Schoenfeld, W. N., & Verplanck, W. S., Eds. *Modern Learning Theory..*) New York: Appleton. [279]

———— 1979. Experimental psychology: An overview. (In Hearst, E. *The First Century of Experimental Psychology.*) Hillsdale, N.J.: Lawrence Erlbaum Associates. [436]

EVANS, R. B. 1972. E. B. Titchener and his lost system. *Journal of the History of the Behavioral Sciences, 8,* 168–180. [115]

EVANS, S. H. 1967. A brief statement of schema theory. *Psychonomic Science, 8,* 87–88. [440]

EYSENCK, H. J. 1952. The effects of psychotherapy: An evaluation. *Journal of Consulting Psychology, 16,* 319–324. [482]

———— 1963. Behavior therapy, spontaneous remission and transference in neurotics. *American Journal of Psychiatry, 119,* 868–879. [299, 482]

———— 1970. *The Structure of Human Personality.* (Rev. Ed.) London: Methuen. [461]

———— 1971. *The IQ Argument: Race, Intelligence, and Education.* New York: Library Press. [472]

———— 1982. Political ideology and science. *American Psychologist, 37,* 1288–1289. [491]

———— & KAMIN. L. 1981. *The Intelligence Controversy.* New York: Wiley. [472]

FANCHER, R. E. 1985. *The Intelligence Men: Makers of the IQ Controversy.* New York: Norton. [140, 448–452]

FARKAS, G. M. 1980. An ontological analysis of behavior therapy. *American Psychologist, 35,* 364–374. [481–485]

FECHNER, G. T. 1860/1966. *Elements of Psychophysics.* (Trans. by H. Adler.) New York: Holt, Rinehart, & Winston. [83–85, 101, 105]

———— 1851/1906. *Zend-Avesta, oder über die Dinge des Himmels und des Jenseits.* Leipzig: Voss. [38, 84, 85]

FEENEY, E. L. 1973. At Emery Air Freight: Positive reinforcement boosts performance. *Organizational Dynamics, 1,* 41–50. [235–236]

FESTINGER, L. 1957. *A Theory of Cognitive Dissonance.* Stanford, Cal.: Stanford University Press. [266]

FIEDLER, F. E. 1950. A comparison of therapeutic relationships in psychoanalytic, nondirective, and Adlerian therapy. *Journal of Consulting Psychology, 14,* 436–445. [296]

FIREY, W. 1948. Informal organization and the theory of schism. *American Sociological Review, 13,* 15–24. [503]

FISHER, S., & FISHER, R. 1955. Relationship between personal insecurity and attitude toward psychologcial methodology. *American Psychologist, 10,* 538–540. [21]

FLAVELL, J. H. 1963. *The Developmental Psychology of Jean Piaget.* Princeton, N.J.: D. Van Nostrand Co. [8, 9]

——— 1986. The development of children's knowledge about the appearance-reality distinction. *American Psychologist, 41,* 418–425. [23]

FLORES D'ARCAIS, G. B. 1975. *Studies in Perception: Festschrift for Fabio Metelli.* Milano, Italy: Aldo Martello-Giunti Editore. [135]

FOA, E. B., & EMMELKAMP, P. M. G. (Eds.) 1983. *Failures in Behavior Therapy.* New York: John Wiley & Sons. [493]

FÖRSTERLING, F. 1986. Attributional conceptions in clinical psychology. *American Psychologist, 41,* 275–285. [480]

FORSYTH, D. R., & STRONG, S. R. 1986. The scientific study of counseling and psychotherapy. *American Psychologist, 41,* 113–119. [495]

FORSYTH, G. A., & BROWN, D. R. 1968. Stimulus recognizability judgments as a function of the utility of physical dimensions in recognition-discrimination studies. *Perception & Psychophysics, 3,* 85–88. [498]

FOX, D. R. 1985. Psychology, ideology, Utopia, and the Commons. *American Psychologist, 40,* 48–58. [493–495]

FREDERIKSEN, N. 1986. Toward a broader conception of human intelligence. *American Psychologist, 41,* 445–452. [458]

FREEMAN, E. 1936. *Social Psychology.* New York: Henry Holt & Co. [357]

FREEMAN, G. L. 1948. *Energetics of Human Behavior.* Ithaca, N.Y.: Cornell University Press. [192–195]

FRENKEL-BRUNSWIK, E. 1942. Motivation and behavior. *Genetic Psychology Monographs, 26,* 121–265. [325, 357]

——— 1949. Intolerance of ambiguity as an emotional and personality variable. *Journal of Personality, 18,* 108–143. [460]

FREUD, S. [The dates used for Freud's writings are those shown in the Standard Edition (London: Hogarth Press) edited by James Strachey, as the date of first publication, or completion of the MS. For each publication I have indicated the volume of the Standard Edition (SE) in which it can be found. Pages, however, are based on the separate publications.]

FREUD, S. 1953. *The Standard Edition of the Complete Works of Sigmund Freud.* (James Strachey, Ed.) London: Hogarth Press.

——— 1896. The aetiology of hysteria. *Wiener klinische Wochenschrift* (21 April), *9,* 20. SE 3 [294]

——— 1900. *The Interpretation of Dreams.* SE 4, 5 [298, 310]

——— 1901. *The Psychopathology of Everyday Life.* SE 6 [278–298]

——— 1905. *Three Essays on the Theory of Sexuality.* SE 7 [303, 306]

——— 1910. *Five Lectures on Psychoanalysis.* (Clark University Series.) SE 11 [302, 323]

——— 1911. *Formulation on Two Principles of Mental Functioning.* SE 12 [303, 314]

——— 1914. *On the History of the Psychoanalytic Movement.* SE 14 [296, 308]

——— 1915. *Instincts and Their Vicissitudes.* SE 14 [306]

——— 1916. *General Introduction to Psychoanalysis.* SE 15–16 [305, 306, 308, 312, 314]

—— 1920. *Beyond the Pleasure Principle.* SE 18 [313, 315]

—— 1921. *Group Psychology and the Analysis of the Ego.* SE 18 [316]

—— 1923. *The Ego and the Id.* SE 19 [313, 316]

—— 1925. *Some Psychological Consequences of the Anatomical Distinction Between the Sexes.* SE 19 [307, 311, 312]

—— 1926. *Inhibitions, Symptoms, and Anxiety.* SE 20 [304, 316]

—— 1932. *Why War? Letter to Einstein.* SE 22 [305]

—— 1933. *New Introductory Lectures on Psychoanalysis.* SE 22 [296, 305, 306, 307, 314, 317]

—— 1937. *Analysis Terminable and Interminable.* SE 23 [311]

—— 1940. *An Outline of Psychoanalysis.* SE 23 [304, 312, 314, 319]

FRIEDMAN, P. 1970. Limitations in the conceptualization of behavior therapists: Toward a cognitive behavioral model of behavior therapy. *Psychological Reports, 27,* 175–178. [485]

FROMM, E. 1941. *Escape from Freedom.* New York: Farrar & Rinehart. [55, 356]

—— 1947. *Man for Himself.* New York: Holt. [357]

—— 1955. *The Sane Society.* New York: Rinehart. [357]

—— 1959. Psychoanalysis and Zen Buddhism. *Psychologia, 2,* 79–99. [37]

—— 1973. *The Anatomy of Human Destructiveness.* New York: Holt. [357]

—— 1980. *Greatness and Limitations of Freud's Thought.* New York: Harper & Row. [357]

FUCHS, A. H., & KAWASH, G. F. 1974. Prescriptive dimensions for five schools of psychology. *Journal of the History of the Behavioral Sciences, 10,* 352–366. [17]

FURUMOTO, L. 1979. Mary Whiton Calkins (1863–1930): Fourteenth President of the American Psychological Association. *Journal of the History of the Behavioral Sciences, 15,* 346–356. [155–157]

—— & SCARBOROUGH, E. 1984. Placing Women in the History of Psychology Course. Eastern Psychological Association, September, 1984. [157]

GALL, F. J. 1825/1965. On phrenology, the localization of the functions of the brain. (In Herrnstein, R. J., & Boring, E. G., Eds. *Source Book in the History of Psychology.*) Cambridge, Mass.: Harvard University Press. [76]

GALLO, P. S., JR., & LYNN, E. 1981. The variance accounted for in meta-analysis of psychotherapy outcomes—A reply to Willson. *American Psychologist, 36,* 1196–1198. [487]

GALTON, F. 1865. Hereditary talent and character. *Macmillan's Magazine, 12,* 318–327. [447]

—— 1869/1972. *Hereditary Genius.* Gloucester, Mass.: Peter Smith. [140–141]

—— 1883/1908. *Inquiries into Human Faculty and Its Development.* London: Macmillan. [141–142]

GANTT, W. H. 1973. Reminiscences of Pavlov. *Journal of the Experimental Analysis of Behavior, 20,* 131–136. [165]

GARBER, H., & HEBER, F. R. 1977. The Milwaukee Project: Indications of the effectiveness of early intervention in preventing mental retardation. (In Mittler, P., Ed. *Research to Practice in Mental Retardation,* Vol. 1.) Baltimore: University Park Press. [466–467]

GARDNER, R. W. 1953. Cognitive styles in categorizing behavior. *Journal of Personality, 22,* 214–233. [430, 459]

—— 1969. Organismic equilibration and the energy-structure duality in psychoanalytic theory: An attempt at theoretical refinement. *Journal of the American Psychoanalytic Association, 17*, 3–67. [303]

GARNER, W. R. 1970. Good patterns have few alternatives. *American Scientist, 58*, 34–42. [254]

GENTNER, D. R., & NORMAN, D. A. 1984. "The typist's touch." *Psychology Today, 18*, 66 ff. [170]

GERGEN, K. J. 1985. The social constructionist movement in modern psychology. *American Psychologist, 40*, 266–275. [440, 507]

—— & GERGEN, M. M. (Eds.) 1984. *Historical Social Psychology.* Hillsdale, N.J.: Lawrence Erlbaum Associates. [434]

GHISELLI, E. E. 1960. The prediction of predictability. *Educational and Psychological Measurement, 20*, 3–8. [462]

GIBSON, J. J. 1967. On the proper meaning of the term "stimulus." *Psychological Review, 74*, 533–534. [195]

—— 1975. Three kinds of distance that can be seen, or how Bishop Berkeley went wrong in the first place. (In Flores d'Arcais, G. B., Ed. *Studies in Perception.*) Milano, Italy: Aldo Martello-Giunti Editore. [99]

GILBRETH, F. B. 1911. *Motion Study.* New York: D. Van Nostrand Co. [134]

—— 1914. *Primer of Scientific Management.* New York: D. Van Nostrand Co. [134]

—— & GILBRETH, L. M. 1916. Effect of motion study upon the workers. *Annals of American Academy of Political and Social Science, 65*, 272–276. [134]

GILBRETH, L. M. 1914. *The Psychology of Management.* New York: Macmillan. [134]

GILGEN, A. R. 1982. *American Psychology Since World War II: A Profile of the Discipline.* Westport, Conn.: Greenwood Press. [402, 423]

GODDARD, H. H. 1917. Mental tests and the immigrant. *Journal of Delinquency, 2*, 243–277. [447]

GOFFMAN, E. 1959. *The Presentation of Self in Everyday Life.* Garden City, N.Y.: Doubleday & Co. [187, 220, 387]

GOLDSTEIN, K. 1939. *The Organism.* New York: American Book Co. [360]

GOLDSTONE, S., & GOLDFARB, J. L. 1964. Adaptation level, personality theory, and psychopathology. *Psychological Bulletin, 61*, 176–187. [264]

GOLEMAN, D. 1986. Anatomy of a fierce academic feud. *New York Times, Education Life* (9 November), pp. 58 ff. [471]

—— & SCHWARTZ, G. E. 1976. Meditation as an intervention in stress reactivity. *Journal of Consulting and Clinical Psychology, 44*, 456–466. [38]

GOODMAN, M. 1982. Biomolecular evidence on human origins from the standpoint of Darwinian theory. *Human Biology, 54*, 247–264. [139]

GOODMAN, P. S. 1968. The measurement of an individual's organizational map. *Administrative Science Quarterly, 13*, 246–265. [280]

GOUGH, H. G. 1987. *CPI: California Psychological Inventory Administrator's Guide.* Palo Alto, Cal.: Consulting Psychologists Press. [462]

GRAY, J. 1980. *Ivan Pavlov.* New York: Viking. [165]

GREENO, J. G. 1978. Nature of problem-solving abilities. (In Estes, W. K., Ed. *Handbook of Learning and Cognitive Processes,* Vol. 5, *Human Information Processing.*) Hillsdale, N.J.: Lawrence Erlbaum Associates. [458]

GREENWALD, A. G. 1980. The totalitarian ego: Fabrication and revision of personal history. *American Psychologist, 35*, 603–618. [298, 435]

GREGG, L. (Ed.) 1969. *Cognition in Learning and Memory.* New York: Wiley. [436]

GREGORY, R. L. 1981. *Mind in Science: A History of Explanations in Psychology.* Cambridge, England: Cambridge University Press. [4]

GRIFFIN, M. C., & BEIER, E. G. 1961. Subliminal prior solution cues in problem solving. *Journal of General Psychology, 65,* 219–227. [425]

GRINKER, R. R. (Ed.) 1956. *Toward a Unified Theory of Human Behavior.* New York: Basic Books. [504]

GRUBER, C. 1972. Academic freedom at Columbia University 1917–1918. The case of James McKeen Cattell. *American Association of University Professors Bulletin, 58,* 297–305. [149]

GUILFORD, J. P. 1936. *Psychometric Methods.* New York: McGraw-Hill. [455]

—— 1957. *Personality.* New York: McGraw-Hill. [462]

—— 1959. Three faces of intellect. *American Psychologist, 14,* 469–479. [455]

—— 1961. Factorial angles to psychology. *Psychological Review, 68,* 1–20. [455]

—— 1967a. *The Nature of Human Intelligence.* New York: McGraw-Hill. [455]

—— 1967b. Autobiography. (In Boring, E. G., & Lindzey, G., Eds. *A History of Psychology in Autobiography.*) New York: Appleton-Century-Crofts. [455]

—— 1985. The structure of intellect model. (In Wolman, B. B., Ed. *Handbook of Intelligence: Theories, Measurements, and Applications.*) New York: Wiley. [457]

—— & HOEPFNER, R. 1971. *The Analysis of Intelligence.* New York: McGraw-Hill. [457]

—— & ZIMMERMAN, W. S. 1956. Fourteen dimensions of temperament. *Psychological Monographs, 70,* Whole No. 417. [462]

GUMP, P. V., & KOUNIN, J. S. 1959–60. Issues raised by ecological and "classical" research efforts. *Merrill-Palmer Quarterly of Behavior and Development, 6,* 145–152. [489]

GUTHRIE, E. R. 1935. *The Psychology of Learning.* New York: Harper & Row [191, 192]

—— 1938. *The Psychology of Human Conflict.* New York: Harper & Row. [191]

—— 1942. Conditioning: A theory of learning in terms of stimulus, response, and association. (In National Society for the Study of Education, *Forty-First Yearbook.*) Chicago: University of Chicago Press. [191]

—— 1944. Personality in terms of associative learning. (In Hunt, J. McV., Ed. *Personality and the Behavior Disorders.*) New York: Ronald. [462]

—— 1946. Psychological facts and psychological theory. *Psychological Bulletin, 43,* 1–20. [191]

—— & HORTON, G. P. 1946. *Cats in a Puzzle Box.* New York: Rinehart. [191]

GUTHRIE, R. 1976. *Even the Rat Was White.* New York: Harper & Row. [447]

GUTTMAN, N. 1977. On Skinner and Hull: A reminiscence and projection. *American Psychologist, 32,* 321–328. [201, 238]

HABER, R. N. 1966. Nature of the effect of set on perception. *Psychological Review, 73,* 335–351. [424]

—— (Ed.) 1969. *Information-Processing Approaches to Visual Perception.* New York: Holt, Rinehart, & Winston. [430]

HALE, N. G., JR. 1971. *Freud and the Americans: The Beginnings of Psychoanalysis in the United States, 1876–1917.* New York: Oxford University Press. [323, 494]

HALL, C. S., & NORDBY, V. J. 1973. *A Primer of Jungian Psychology.* New York: New American Library. [335–342]

HALL, D. T., & NOUGAIM, K. E. 1968. An examination of Maslow's need hierarchy in an organizational setting. *Organizational Behavior & Human Performance, 3,* 12–35. [363.]

HALL, G. S. 1904. *Adolescence: Its Psychology and Its Relations to Physiology, Anthropology, Sociology, Sex, Crime, Religion, and Education* (2 Vols.) New York: Appleton. [144]

—— 1907. *Youth: Its Education, Regimen, and Hygiene.* New York: Appleton. [144]

—— 1911. *Educational Problems.* Vol. 1. New York: D. Appleton. [143]

—— 1912. *Founders of Modern Psychology.* New York: D. Appleton. [144]

—— 1922. *Senescence: The Last Half of Life.* New York: Appleton. [144]

—— 1923. *Life and Confessions of a Psychologist.* New York: Appleton. [144]

HALSTEAD, W. C., & RENNICK, P. 1962. Toward a behavioral scale for biological age. (In Tibbits, C., & Donohue, W., Eds. *Social and Psychological Aspects of Aging.*) New York: Columbia University Press. [449]

HARLOW, H. F. 1949. The formation of learning sets. *Psychological Review, 56,* 61–65. [259]

—— 1953. Mice, monkeys, men, and motives. *Psychological Review, 60,* 23–32. [259]

—— 1969. William James and instinct theory. (In MacLeod, R. B., Ed. *William James: Unfinished Business.*) Washington, D.C.: American Psychological Association. [116]

—— & HARLOW, M. K. 1949. Learning to think. *Scientific American, 181,* 36–39. [259]

——, —— & MEYER, D. R. 1950. Learning motivated by a manipulation drive. *Journal of Experimental Psychology, 40,* 228–234. [259]

—— & STAGNER, R. 1933. Effect of complete striate muscle paralysis on learning. *Journal of Experimental Psychology, 16,* 283–294. [131]

HARRÉ, R. 1984. *Personal Being.* Cambridge, Mass.: Harvard University Press. [500]

HARRELL, T. W. 1972. High earning MBAs. *Personnel Psychology, 25,* 525–530. [463]

—— 1977. An organizational change triggered by a survey: The Army Air Forces in World War II. *Academy of Management Review* (October). [286]

—— & HARRELL, M. S. 1973. The personality of MBAs who reach general management early. *Personnel Psychology, 26,* 127–134. [463]

—— & HARRISON, R. 1938. The rise and fall of behaviorism. *Journal of General Psychology, 18,* 367–421. [182]

HARROWER, M. 1983. *Kurt Koffka: An Unwitting Self-Portrait.* Gainesville, Fla.: University Presses of Florida. [249]

HART, J. J. 1982. Psychology of the scientist, XLII. Correlation between theoretical orientation in psychology and personality type. *Psychological Reports, 50,* 795–801. [21]

HARTLEY, D. 1749/1966. *Observations on Man, His Frame, His Duty, and His Expectations.* Gainesville, Fla.: Scholars' Facsimiles and Reprints. [65]

HARTMANN, E. VON. 1869. *Psychologie des Unbewussten. (Psychology of the Unconscious.* Trans. by W. C. Coupland.) New York: Harcourt, Brace, & Co. [9]

HASHER, L., & ZACKS, R. T. 1984. Automatic processing of fundamental information: The case of frequency of occurrence. *American Psychologist, 39,* 1372–1388. [435]

HASTIE, R., OSTROM, T. M., EBBESEN, E. B., WYER, R. S. JR., HAMILTON, D. C., & CARLSTON, D. E. 1980. *Person Memory: The Cognitive Basis of Social Perception.* Hillsdale, N.J.: Lawrence Erlbaum Associates. [218, 434, 435]

HATHAWAY, S. R., & McKINLEY, D. J. 1940. A multiphasic personality scale. I. Construction of the schedule. *Journal of Psychology, 10,* 249–254. [462]

HEARNSHAW, L. S. 1979. *Cyril Burt, Psychologist.* Ithaca, N.Y.: Cornell University Press. [452–453]

HEARST, E. (Ed.) 1979. *The First Century of Experimental Psychology.* Hillsdale, N.J.: Lawrence Erlbaum Associates.

HEATH, R. G. (Ed.) 1964. *The Role of Pleasure in Behavior.* New York: Harper & Row. [68]

HEBB, D. O. 1978. Open Letter: To a friend who thinks the IQ is a social evil. *American Psychologist, 33,* 1143–1144. [472]

HEBER, R. 1968. *Rehabilitation of Families at Risk for Mental Retardation.* Madison, Wis.: University of Wisconsin Regional Rehabilitation Center. [467]

HEDGES, L. V. 1987. How hard is hard science, how soft is soft science? *American Psychologist, 42,* 443–455. [17]

HEFFERLINE, R. F., KEENAN, B., & HARFORD, R. A. 1959. Escape and avoidance conditioning in human subjects without their observation of the response. *Science, 130,* 1338–1339. [225]

HEIDBREDER, E. 1933. *Seven Psychologies.* New York: Appleton-Century.

HEIDER, F. 1946. Attitudes and cognitive organization. *Journal of Psychology, 21,* 107–112. [265]

—— 1958. *Psychology of Interpersonal Relations.* New York: Wiley. [265]

HEINE, R. W. 1953. A comparison of patients' reports on psychotherapeutic experience with psychoanalytic, nondirective, and Adlerian therapists. *American Journal of Psychotherapy, 7,* 16–23. [296]

HELMHOLTZ, H. L. F. 1856/1924. *Treatise on Physiological Optics.* Rochester, N.Y.: Optical Society of America. [81, 82, 86]

HELSON, H. 1925. The psychology of Gestalt. *American Journal of Psychology, 36,* 342–370, 494–526. [263–265]

—— 1926. The psychology of Gestalt. *American Journal of Psychology, 37,* 25–62, 189–223. [263–265]

—— 1933. The fundamental propositions of Gestalt psychology. *Psychological Review, 40,* 13–32. [263–265]

—— 1947. Adaptation level as a frame of reference for prediction of psychophysical data. *American Journal of Psychology, 60,* 1–29. [264]

—— 1964. *Adaptation-Level Theory.* New York: Harper & Row. [264, 499]

HENDRICK, I. 1935. *Facts and Theories of Psychoanalysis.* New York: Alfred A. Knopf. [300]

—— 1943. Work and the pleasure principle. *Psychoanalytic Quarterly, 12,* 311–329. [303]

HENLE, M. 1978a. Gestalt psychology and Gestalt therapy. *Journal of the History of the Behavioral Sciences, 14,* 23–32. [259]

—— 1978b. One man against the Nazis—Wolfgang Köhler. *American Psychologist, 33,* 939–951. [248]

—— 1985. Koffka's *Principles* after fifty years. Unpublished paper, American Psychological Association, 1985. [250]

HERON, W., DOANE, B. K., & SCOTT, T. H. 1956. Visual disturbance after prolonged perceptual isolation. *Canadian Journal of Psychology, 10,* 13–16. [194]

HERRNSTEIN, R. J. 1977. The evolution of behaviorism. *American Psychologist, 32,* 593–603. [197]

—— & BORING, E. G. (Eds.) 1965. *A Source Book in the History of Psychology.* Cambridge, Mass.: Harvard University Press. [1]

HEYDUK, R. T., & FENIGSTEIN, A. 1984. Influential works and authors in psychology: A survey of eminent psychologists. *American Psychologist, 39,* 556–559. [19]

HIGH, R. P., & WOODWARD, W. R. 1980. William James and Gordon Allport: Parallels in their maturing conceptions of self and personality. (In Rieber, R. W., & Salzinger, K., Eds. *Psychology: Theoretical-Historical Perspectives.*) New York: Academic Press. [376]

HILGARD, E. R. 1936. The nature of the conditioned response. I. The case for and against stimulus substitution. *Psychological Review, 43,* 547–564. [196]

—— 1973. A neo-dissociation interpretation of pain reduction during hypnosis. *Psychological Review, 80,* 396–411. [486]

—— (Ed.) 1978. *American Psychology in Historical Perspective: Addresses of the Presidents of the APA, 1892–1977.* Washington, D.C.: American Psychological Association.

—— 1986. *Divided Consciousness* (Expanded Edition). New York: Wiley. [294]

—— 1987. *Psychology in America: A Historical Survey.* San Diego, Cal.: Harcourt Brace Jovanovich. [467]

HINKLE, B. 1916. *Psychology of the Unconscious.* (Transl. of Jung's *Wandlungen und Symbole der Libido.*) New York: Moffat, Yard, & Co. [337, 343]

HO, D. Y. F. 1985. Cultural values and professional issues in clinical psychology: Implications from the Hong Kong experience. *American Psychologist, 40,* 1212–1218. [321]

HOBBES, T. 1651/1974. *Leviathan.* Baltimore: Penguin. [53, 54, 99]

HOFFMAN, H. S., & SOLOMON, R. L. 1974. An opponent-process theory of motivation. III. Some affective dynamics in imprinting. *Learning and Motivation, 5,* 149–164. [302]

HOGAN, R. 1975. Theoretical egocentrism and the problem of compliance. *American Psychologist, 30,* 533–540. [14, 386]

—— 1976. *Personality Theory: The Personological Tradition.* Englewood Cliffs, N.J.: Prentice-Hall. [462]

—— & EMLER, N. P. 1978. The biases in American social psychology. *Social Research, 45,* 478–534. [290]

—— & SLOAN, T. 1985. Egoism, altruism, and psychological ideology. *Journal of Social and Clinical Psychology, 3,* 15–19. [507]

HOKANSON, J. E. 1970. Psychophysiological evaluation of the catharsis hypothesis. (In Megargee, E. I., & Hokanson, J. E., Eds. *The Dynamics of Aggression.*) New York: Harper & Row. [475]

HOLLINGWORTH, H. L. 1920. *Psychology of Functional Neuroses.* New York: D. Appleton-Century Co. [462]

HOLMES, D. S. 1984. Meditation and somatic arousal reduction: A review of the experimental evidence. *American Psychologist, 39,* 1–10. [38] (See also *American Psychologist,* 1985, *40,* 717–731, for discussion.)

HOMME, L. E. 1965. Perspectives in psychology. XXIV. Control of coverants, the operants of the mind. *Psychological Record, 15,* 501–511. [231]

HORN, J. L. 1985. Remodeling old models of intelligence. (In Wolman, B. B., Ed. *Handbook of Intelligence: Theories, Measurements, and Applications.*) New York: Wiley. [455]

—— & CATTELL, R. B. 1967. Age differences in fluid and crystallized intelligence. *Acta Psychologica, 26,* 107–129. [455]

HORNEY, K. 1937. *The Neurotic Personality of Our Time.* New York: W. W. Norton. [351–354]

—— 1939. *New Ways in Psychoanalysis.* New York: W. W. Norton. [351, 355]

—— 1942. *Self-Analysis.* New York: W. W. Norton. [355]

—— 1945. *Our Inner Conflicts.* New York: W. W. Norton. [352]

HORTON, D., & DIXON, T., (Eds.) 1967. *Verbal Behavior and S-R Behavior Theory.* Englewood Cliffs, N.J.: Prentice-Hall. [231]

HOTHERSALL, D. 1984. *History of Psychology.* New York: Random House. [167]

HOVLAND, C. I., HARVEY, O., & SHERIF, M. 1957. Assimilation and contrast effects in reactions to communications and attitude change. *Journal of Abnormal and Social Psychology, 55,* 244–252. [127]

HOWARD, K. I., KOPTA, S. M., KRAUSE, M. S., & ORLINSKY, D. E. 1986. The dose-effect relationship in psychotherapy. *American Psychologist, 41,* 159–164. [488]

HUBEL, D. H., & WIESEL, T. N. 1959. Receptive fields of single neurones in the cat's striate cortex. *Journal of Physiology* (London), *148,* 574–591. [433]

HULL, C. L. 1920. Quantitative aspects of the evolution of concepts. *Psychological Monographs, 28* (Whole No. 123). [200]

—— 1928. *Aptitude Testing.* Yonkers-on-Hudson, N.Y.: World Book Co. [200]

—— 1931. Goal attracting and directing ideas conceived as habit phenomena. *Psychological Review, 38,* 487–506. [205]

—— 1933. *Hypnosis and Suggestibility: An Experimental Approach.* New York: D. Appleton-Century Co. [200, 207]

—— 1937. Mind, mechanism, and adaptive behavior. *Psychological Review, 44,* 1–32. [208, 508]

—— 1943. *Principles of Behavior.* New York: Appleton-Century-Crofts. [202–206, 276]

—— 1951. *Essentials of Behavior.* New Haven, Conn.: Yale University Press. [15, 202–205]

—— 1952. *A Behavior System.* New Haven, Conn.: Yale University Press. [206–211]

HUME, D. 1748/1955. *An Enquiry Concerning Human Understanding.* New York: Liberal Arts Press. [63, 64, 99]

—— 1739/1960. *A Treatise of Human Nature: Being an Attempt to Introduce the Experimental Method of Reasoning Into Moral Subjects.* Oxford: Clarendon Press. [62, 63]

HUMPHREYS, L. G. 1986. Commentary. *Journal of Vocational Behavior, 29,* 421–437. [431]

HUNT, J. McV. 1984. Orval Hobart Mowrer (1907–1982). *American Psychologist, 39,* 912–914. [216, 217]

ICHHEISER, G. 1970. *Appearances and Realities: Misunderstandings in Human Relations.* San Francisco, Cal.: Jossey-Bass. [500]

JACOBI, J. 1943. *Psychology of C. G. Jung.* (Trans. by K. W. Bash.) New Haven, Conn.: Yale University Press. [340]

JACOBSON, E. 1930. Electrical measurements of neuromuscular states during mental activities. III. Visual imagination and recollection. *American Journal of Physiology, 95,* 694–702. [184]

—— 1938. *Progressive Relaxation.* (2nd ed.) Chicago: University of Chicago Press. [184]

JAMES, W. 1890/1950. *Principles of Psychology* (2 Vols.) New York: H. Holt & Co. [100–111]

—— 1892. *Psychology: Briefer Course.* New York: H. Holt. [100–111]

—— 1895. Experimental psychology in America. *Science, 2,* 626. [101]

—— 1907. *Pragmatism.* London: Longmans, Green. [21, 109, 184]

—— 1910/1962. The moral equivalent of war. (In *Essays on Faith and Morals.*) New York: Meridian, 1962. [110]

—— 1920/1969. *Letters of William James* (2 Vols.) Boston: Atlantic Monthly Press. New York: Kraus Reprint. [102]

—— 1960. *William James on Psychical Research* (Ed. by G. Murphy and R. O. Ballou.) New York: Viking. [39, 360]

JANET, P. 1920. *The Major Symptoms of Hysteria.* (2nd ed.) New York: Macmillan. [101]

JANIS, I. L. 1972. *Victims of Groupthink.* Boston: Houghton-Mifflin. [287, 288, 327]

JAYNES, J. 1970. The problem of animate motion in the 17th century. *Journal of the History of Ideas, 13,* 219–234. [48]

—— 1976. *The Origin of Consciousness in the Breakdown of the Bicameral Mind.* Boston: Houghton-Mifflin. [181]

JENKINS, N. 1957. Affective processes in perception. *Psychological Bulletin, 54,* 100–127. [425]

JENSEN, A. R. 1969. How much can we boost IQ and scholastic achievement? *Harvard Educational Review, 39,* 1–123. [464]

—— 1973. *Educability and Group Differences.* New York: Harper & Row. [464–466]

JONES, E. E., KANOUSE, D. E., KELLEY, H. H., NISBETT, R. E., VALINS, S., & WEINER, B. 1971. *Attribution: Perceiving the Causes of Behavior.* Morristown, N.J.: General Learning Press. [265, 419]

—— & NISBETT, E. E. 1971. The Actor and the Observer: Divergent perceptions of the causes of behavior. (In Jones et al. *Attribution: Perceiving the Causes of Behavior.*) Morristown, N.J.: General Learning Press. [265, 419]

JONES, M. C. 1924a. A laboratory study of fear: The case of Peter. *Pedagogical Seminary (Journal of Genetic Psychology), 31,* 308–315. [481]

—— 1924b. The elimination of children's fears. *Journal of Experimental Psychology, 7,* 382–390. [406, 481]

JOURARD, S. M. 1971. *Self-Disclosure: An Experimental Analysis of the Transparent Self.* New York: Wiley Inter-Science. [372]

JUNG, C. G. 1906/1918. *Diagnostische Assoziations-Studien.* (*Studies in Word Association.* Trans. by M. D. Eder.) New York: Moffat, Yard. [336]

—— 1910. The association method. *American Journal of Psychology, 21,* 219–240. [336]

—— 1916. *Psychology of the Unconscious.* (Trans. by B. Hinkle.) London: Moffat, Yard. [337, 339, 341]

—— 1921/1971. *Psychological Types.* (Trans. by H. G. Baynes.) Princeton, N.J.: Princeton University Press. [338]

—— 1926/1942. *Contributions to Analytic Psychology.* (Trans. by H. G. Baynes & C. F. Baynes.) London: Kegan Paul, Trench, Trubner, & Co. [337, 338, 339]

—— 1957–1958. *The Undiscovered Self.* Boston: Little, Brown. [341]

JUSTICE, B., & JUSTICE, R. 1979. *The Broken Taboo: Sex in the Family.* New York: Human Sciences Press. [310]

KAGAN, J. S. 1955. Differential reward value of incomplete and complete sexual behavior. *Journal of Comparative and Physiological Psychology, 48,* 59–64. [216]

—— 1967. On the need for relativism. *American Psychologist, 22,* 131–142. [500]

KAHN, R. L., WOLFE, D. M., QUINN, R. P., & SNOEK, J. D. 1964. *Organizational Stress: Studies in Role Conflict and Ambiguity.* New York: Wiley. [503]

KAMIN, L. J. 1974. *The Science and Politics of IQ.* Potomac, Md.: Erlbaum. [449, 472]

KANT, I. 1781/1929. *Critique of Pure Reason.* (Trans. by J. Watson.) New York: St. Martin's Press. [75, 319]

KANTOR, J. R. 1968. Behaviorism in the history of psychology. *Psychological Record, 18,* 151–166. [162]

KAPLAN, K. J., SCHWARTZ, M. W., & MARKUS-KAPLAN, M. 1984. The family: Biblical and psychological foundations. *Journal of Psychology and Judaism, 8,* 77–199. [33]

KARPF, F. B. 1953. *The Psychology and Psychotherapy of Otto Rank.* New York: Philosophical Library. [347–349]

KARSTEN, A. 1928. Psychische Sättigung. (Satiation.) *Psychologische Forschung, 10,* 142–154. [275]

KATZ, D. 1930. *The World of Colour.* London: Kegan Paul. [253]

KAWASH, G., & FUCHS, A. F. 1974. A factor analysis of ratings of five schools of psychology on prescriptive dimensions. *Journal of the History of the Behavioral Sciences, 10,* 426–437. [19]

KAZDIN, A. E. 1978. *History of Behavior Modification.* Baltimore, Md.: University Park Press. [299]

KELLEY, H. H., & MICHELA, J. 1980. Attribution theory and research. *Annual Review of Psychology, 31,* 457–501. [265, 419]

KELLY, G. A. 1955. *Psychology of Personal Constructs* (2 Vols.). New York: Norton. [388]

KENDALL, P. C. 1982. Integration: Behavior therapy and other schools of thought. *Behavior Therapy, 13,* 571. [496]

—— & HOLLON, S. (Eds.) 1984. *Cognitive-Behavioral Interventions.* New York: Academic Press. [485]

——, PLOUS, S., & KRATOCHWILL, T. T. 1981. Science and behaviour therapy. *Behaviour Research and Therapy, 19,* 517–524. [485]

KENDLER, H. H. 1981. *Psychology: A Science in Conflict.* New York: Oxford University Press. [497]

—— & SPENCE, J. T. 1971. Tenets of neobehaviorism. (In Kendler, H. H., &

Spence, J. T., Eds. *Neobehaviorism: A Memorial Volume to Kenneth W. Spence.*) Englewood Cliffs, N.J.: Prentice-Hall. [389]

KERNBERG, O., BURSTEIN, E., COYNE, L., APPLEBAUM, A., HORWITZ, L., & VOTH, H. 1972. Psychotherapy and psychoanalysis: Final report of the Menninger Foundation's Psychotherapy Research Project. *Bulletin of the Menninger Clinic, 36,* Nos. 1–2. [490]

KESSEL, F. S., & BEVAN, W. K. 1985. Notes toward a history of cognitive psychology. (In Buxton, C. E., Ed. *Points of View in the Modern History of Psychology.*) New York: Academic Press. [436]

KIESLER, C. A. 1971. *The Psychology of Commitment: Experiments Linking Behavior to Belief.* New York: Academic Press. [422]

KIMBLE, G. A. 1984. Psychology's two cultures. *American Psychologist, 39,* 833–839. [20, 493, 501]

———— & SCHLESINGER, K. (Eds.) 1984. *Topics in the History of Psychology.* Hillsdale, N.J.: Lawrence Erlbaum Associates. [2]

KING, W. P. (Ed.) 1930. *Behaviorism: A Battle Line.* Nashville, Tenn.: Cokesbury Press. [185]

KINTZ, B. L., DELPRATO, D. J., METTEE, D. R., PERSONS, C. E., & SCHAPPE, R. H. 1965. The experimenter effect. *Psychological Bulletin, 63,* 223–232. [105]

KIRSCH, I. 1985. Response expectancy as a determinant of experience and behavior. *American Psychologist, 40,* 1189–1202. [393]

———— & HENRY, D. 1977. Extinction vs. credibility in the desensitization of speech anxiety. *Journal of Consulting and Clinical Psychology, 45,* 1052–1059. [486]

KITCHER, P. 1985. *Vaulting Ambition: Sociobiology and the Quest for Human Nature.* Cambridge, Mass.: M. I. T. Press. [470]

KLEIN, G. S. 1970. *Perception, Motives, and Personality.* New York: Alfred A. Knopf. [424–426]

———— & HOLZMAN, P. 1950. The "schematizing" process: Perceptual attitudes and personality qualities in sensitivity to change. *American Psychologist, 5,* 312. [437, 440, 460]

KLEIN, K., & SALTZ, E. 1976. Specifying the mechanisms in a levels-of-processing approach to memory. *Journal of Experimental Psychology: Human Learning and Memory, 2,* 671–680. [430, 431]

KLINE, P. 1972. *Fact and Fantasy in Freudian Theory.* London: Methuen & Co. [316]

KNAPP, T. J., & ROBERTSON, L. C. 1986. *Approaches to Cognition: Contrasts and Controversies.* Hillsdale, N.J.: Lawrence Erlbaum Associates. [436]

KOCH, S. 1981. The nature and limits of psychological knowledge: Lessons of a century qua "science." *American Psychologist, 36,* 257–269. [497]

KOFFKA, K. 1921/1924. *Die Grundlagen der Psychisches Entwicklung (The Growth of the Mind.* Trans. by R. M. Ogden.) London: Routledge & Kegan Paul. [249]

———— 1922. Perception, an introduction to the Gestalt-theorie. *Psychological Bulletin, 19,* 531–585. [253]

———— 1935/1963. *Principles of Gestalt Psychology.* New York: Harcourt, Brace, & World. [250–255]

KÖHLER, W. 1917/1925. *Intelligenzprüfung an Menschenaffen. (Mentality of Apes.* Trans. by E. Winter.) New York: Harcourt Brace. [248]

———— 1929/1970. *Gestalt Psychology.* New York: Liveright. [246]

—————— 1938. *The Place of Value in a World of Facts.* New York: Liveright. [260]

—————— 1940/1960. *Dynamics in Psychology.* New York: Grove Press. [260]

—————— 1959. Gestalt psychology today. *American Psychologist, 14,* 727–734. [261]

KOHUT, H. 1971. *The Analysis of the Self.* New York: International Universities Press. [372]

KOLERS, P. A. 1964. Apparent movement of a Necker cube. *American Journal of Psychology, 77,* 220–230. [254]

KORCHIN, S. 1976. *Modern Clinical Psychology: Principles of Intervention in the Clinic and the Community.* New York: Harper & Row. [387]

KOUNIN, J. S. 1941. Experimental studies of rigidity. *Character and Personality, 9,* 251–272, 273–282. [272, 460]

KRASNER, L., & HOUTS, A. C. 1984. A study of the "value" systems of behavioral scientists. *American Psychologist, 39,* 840–850. [493]

KRASNOGORSKII, N. I. 1908. (About conditioned reflexes in children.) *Russkii Vrach,* No. 28, 930–932. (See Burnham, 1917.) [145]

—————— 1909. Über die Bedingungsreflexe in Kindesalter. *Jahrbuch der Kinderheilkunde, 69,* 1–24. [145]

KRAWIEC, T. F. (Ed.) 1978. *The Psychologists: Autobiographies of Distinguished Living Psychologists* (Vol. 3). Brandon, Vermont: Clinical Psychology Publishing Co.

KRECHEVSKY, I. 1932. "Hypotheses" in rats. *Psychological Review, 39,* 516–532. [395]

KROUT, M. H., & TABIN, J. K. 1954. Measuring personality in developmental terms: The Personal Preference Scale. *Genetic Psychology Monographs, 50,* 289–335. [305–308]

KUENNE, M. R. 1946. Experimental investigation of the relation of language to transposition in young children. *Journal of Experimental Psychology, 36,* 471–490. [212]

KURTZ, P. W. 1956. Human nature, homeostasis, and value. *Philosophy and Phenomenological Research, 17,* 36–55. [505]

LACHMAN, R., LACHMAN, J. L., & BUTTERFIELD, E. C. 1979. *Cognitive Psychology and Information Processing: An Introduction.* Hillsdale, N.J.: Lawrence Erlbaum Associates. [435]

LACHMAN, S. J. 1972. *Psychosomatic Disorders: A Behavioristic Approach.* New York: Wiley. [481]

LADD, G. T. 1891. *Elements of Physiological Psychology.* New York: Scribner. [160]

—————— 1892. Contributions to the psychology of visual dreams. *Mind, 1,* 299–304. [123]

LAIRD, D. A. 1925. A mental hygiene and vocational test. *Journal of Educational Psychology, 16,* 419–422. [338]

LA METTRIE, J. O. DE. 1748/1912. *L'Homme Machine.* (*Man the Machine.* Trans. by G. C. Bussey & M. W. Calkins.) La Salle, Ill.: Open Court Publishers. [52]

LAMIELL, J. T. 1981. Toward an idiothetic psychology of personality. *American Psychologist, 36,* 276–289. [378]

LANDIS, D. 1963. *Conditioned Salivation to a Negative After-Image.* Unpublished Ph.D. dissertation, Wayne State University. [413]

—————— & SOLLEY, C. M., JR. 1965. Classical conditioning to a negative after-image. *Psychological Record, 15,* 553–560. [413]

LASHLEY, K. S. 1923. Behavioristic interpretation of consciousness. *Psychological Review, 30,* 237–272, 329–353. [182, 489]

——— 1929. *Brain Mechanisms and Intelligence.* Chicago: University of Chicago Press. [183]

——— 1950. In search of the engram. *Proceedings, Society for Experimental Biology, 4,* 454–482. [183, 438]

LATHAM, G. P., & SAARI, L. M. 1979. Application of social learning theory to training supervisors through behavioral modeling. *Journal of Applied Psychology, 64,* 239–246. [412]

——— & YUKL, G. A. 1975. Assigned versus participative goal setting with educated and uneducated woods workers. *Journal of Applied Psychology, 60,* 299–302. [236]

LAWLER, E. E., III. 1973. *Motivation in Work Organizations.* Monterey, Cal.: Brooks/Cole. [335]

LAWSON, E. D. 1978. An easy semantic differential technique: Construction of a three-dimensional model. ERIC, ED 163 033. [379, 380, 388]

LAZARUS, A. A. 1983. Distorting the point: A reply to Wolpe. *American Psychologist, 38,* 1028. [489]

LAZARUS, R. S. 1984. On the primacy of cognition. *American Psychologist, 39,* 124–129. [109]

——— & FOLKMAN, S. 1984. *Stress, Appraisal, and Coping.* New York: Springer. [192]

LEAHEY, T. H. 1980. *History of Psychology.* Englewood Cliffs, N.J.: Prentice-Hall.

——— 1981. The mistaken mirror: On Wundt's and Titchener's psychologies. *Journal of the History of the Behavioral Sciences, 17,* 273–282. [137]

LEAK, G. K., & CHRISTOPHER, S. B. 1982. Freudian psychoanalysis and sociobiology: A synthesis. *American Psychologist, 37,* 313–322. [313]

LEARY, D. E. 1979. Wundt and after: Psychology's shifting relations with the natural sciences, social sciences, and philosophy. *Journal of the History of the Behavioral Sciences, 15,* 231–241. [91]

LEBON, G. 1918. *The Psychology of the Great War.* (Trans. by E. Andrews.) New York: Macmillan. [286]

LEEPER, R. W. 1943. *Lewin's Topological and Vector Psychology.* Eugene, Ore.: University of Oregon Press. [272]

——— 1944. Dr. Hull's *Principles of Behavior. Journal of Genetic Psychology, 65,* 3–52. [201]

——— 1963. Learning and the fields of perception, motivation, and personality. (In Koch, S., Ed. *Psychology: A Study of a Science,* Vol. 5.) New York: McGraw-Hill. [201]

LEFCOURT, H. M. 1983. *Research with the Locus of Control Construct.* Vol. 3. *Extensions and Limitations.* New York: Academic Press. [404]

LERNER, M. 1985. *Occupational Stress Groups and the Psychodynamics of the World of Work.* Oakland, Cal.: Institute for Labor and Mental Health. [288]

LEUBA, C. 1940. Images as conditioned sensations. *Journal of Experimental Psychology, 26,* 345–351. [413]

——— 1955. Toward some integration of learning theories: The concept of optimal stimulation. *Psychological Reports, 1,* 27–33. [194]

LEVINE, F. M., & FASNACHT, G. 1974. Token rewards may lead to token learning. *American Psychologist, 29,* 814–820. [237]

LEVINE, J. M., & MURPHY, G. 1943. Learning and forgetting of controversial material. *Journal of Abnormal and Social Psychology, 38,* 507–517. [413]

LEVINSON, H. 1972. *Executive Stress.* New York: Harper & Row. [288, 323]

LEWIN, K. 1917. Kriegslandschaft. (War landscape.) *Zeitschrift für Angewandte Psychologie, 12,* 440–447. [269]

——— 1920. *Die Sozialisierung des Taylorsystems. (Socialization of the Taylor System.)* Berlin: Verlag Gesellschaft und Erziehung. [269]

——— 1935. *Dynamic Theory of Personality.* (Trans. by D. K. Adams & K. E. Zener.) New York: McGraw-Hill. [272–278]

——— 1936. *Principles of Topological Psychology.* (Trans. by F. Heider & G. M. Heider.) New York: McGraw-Hill. [265, 279–281]

——— 1943. Forces behind food habits and methods of change. *Bulletin, National Research Council, 108,* 35–65. [270–288]

——— 1951. *Field Theory in Social Science.* (D. Cartwright, Ed.) New York: Harper & Bros. [288–289]

———, LIPPITT, R., & WHITE, R. K. 1939. Patterns of aggressive behavior in experimentally created "social climates." *Journal of Social Psychology, 10,* 271–299. [286]

LEYS, R. 1984. Meyer, Watson, and the dangers of behaviorism. *Journal of the History of the Behavioral Sciences, 20,* 128–149. [168–175]

LIDDELL, H. S., JAMES, W. T., & ANDERSON, O. D. 1934. The comparative psychology of the conditioned motor reflex, based on experiments with the pig, dog, sheep, goat, and rabbit. *Comparative Psychology Monographs, 11,* 1–89. [167]

LIEBERMAN, D. A. 1979. Behaviorism and the mind: A (limited) call for a return to introspection. *American Psychologist, 34,* 319–333. [428]

LIEBERMAN, E. J. 1984. *Acts of Will: The Life and Work of Otto Rank.* New York: Free Press. [347–349]

LIFTON, R. J. 1971. Protean man. *Archives of General Psychiatry, 24,* 298–304. [387]

LILLY, J. C. 1956. Mental effects of reduction of ordinary levels of physical stimuli on intact healthy persons. *Psychiatric Research Reports, 5,* 1–9. [194]

LOCKE, E. A. (Ed.) 1986. *Generalizing from Laboratory to Field Settings: Research Findings from Industrial-Organizational Psychology, Organizational Behavior, and Human Resource Management.* Lexington, Mass.: Lexington Books. [412]

LOCKE, J. 1690/1956. *An Essay Concerning Human Understanding.* Chicago: Henry Regnery Co. [58–61]

LOEB, J. 1918. *Forced Movements, Tropisms, and Animal Conduct.* Philadelphia: Lippincott. [172]

LOEHLIN, J. C., & NICHOLS, R. C. 1976. *Heredity, Environment, and Personality.* Austin, Texas: University of Texas Press. [463–466]

LOFTUS, E. G., & LOFTUS, G. R. 1980. On the permanence of stored information in the human brain. *American Psychologist, 35,* 409–420. [438]

LONDON, P. 1972. The end of ideology in behavior modification. *American Psychologist, 27,* 913–920. [495]

LORENZ, K. 1950. The comparative method in studying innate behavior patterns. *Symposium, Society for Experimental Biology, 4,* 221–268. [173]

LOVAAS, O. I., FREITAG, G., KINDER, M. I., RUBENSTEIN, B. D., SCHAEFFER, B., &

SIMMONS, J. Q. 1966. Establishment of social reinforcers in two schizo-phrenic children on the basis of food. *Journal of Experimental Child Psychology, 4*, 109–125. [236]

LOWEN, W. 1982. *Dichotomies of the Mind: A Systems Science Model of the Mind and Personality*. New York: Wiley. [428]

LOWRY, R. J. 1971. *The Evolution of Psychological Theory: 1650 to the Present*. Chicago: Aldine-Atherton. [52]

LUCHINS, A. S. 1968. Max Wertheimer. *International Encyclopedia of the Social Sciences*, Vol. 16, pp. 522–527. [243–245]

LUNDIN, R. W. 1969. *Personality: A Behavioral Analysis*. New York: Macmillan. [483]

———— 1979. *Theories and Systems of Psychology*. Lexington, Mass.: D. C. Heath & Co. [115, 238]

MACCORQUODALE, K., & MEEHL, P. E. 1954. EDWARD C. TOLMAN. (In Estes, W. K., Koch, S., MacCorquodale, K., Meehl, P. E., Müller, C. G., Jr., Schoenfeld, W. N., & Verplanck, W. S., Eds. *Modern Learning Theory*.) New York: Appleton-Century-Crofts. [393–395]

MACLEOD, R. B. 1964. Phenomenology: A Challenge to Experimental Psychology. (In Wann, T. W., Ed. *Behaviorism and Phenomenology*.) Chicago: University of Chicago Press. [241–242]

MACKENZIE, B. 1984. Explaining race differences in IQ: The logic, the methodology, and the evidence. *American Psychologist, 37*, 1214–1233. [447, 465–466, 472]

MACKINTOSH, N. J. 1973. Stimulus selection: Learning to ignore stimuli that predict no change in reinforcement. (In Hinde, R. A., & Stevenson-Hinde, J., Eds. *Constraints on Learning*.) London: Academic Press. [429]

MADDI, S. R. 1972. *Personality Theories: A Comparative Analysis*. Homewood, Ill.: Dorsey Press. [13]

———— & COSTA, P. T. 1972. *Humanism in Personology*. Chicago: Aldine-Atherton. [359–361, 368]

MADSEN, K. B. 1968. *Theories of Motivation*. (4th ed.) Copenhagen: Munksgaard; and Kent, Ohio: Kent State University Press. [204, 205]

MAGOUN, H. W. 1981. John B. Watson and the study of human sexual behavior. *Journal of Sex Research, 17*, 368–378. [171, 174]

MAHONEY, M. J. 1974. *Cognition and Behavior Modification*. Cambridge, Mass.: Ballinger Publishing Co. [485, 492, 499]

———— 1976. *Scientist as Subject: The Psychological Imperative*. Cambridge, Mass.: Ballinger Publishing Co. [507]

———— 1977a. Publication prejudices: An experimental study of confirmatory bias in the peer review system. *Cognitive Therapy and Research, 1*, 161–175. [237, 504]

———— 1977b. Reflections on the cognitive-learning trend in psychotherapy. *American Psychologist, 32*, 5–13. [485, 486]

————, THORESEN, C. E., & DANAHER, B. G. 1972. Covert behavior modification: An experimental analogue. *Journal of Behavior Therapy and Experimental Psychiatry, 3*, 117–119. [195]

MAIER, N. R. F. 1949. *Frustration: The Study of Behavior Without a Goal*. New York: McGraw-Hill. [214–215]

MALCOLM, N. 1964. Behaviorism as a philosophy of psychology. (In Wann, T. W., Ed. *Behaviorism and Phenomenology.*) Chicago: University of Chicago Press. [198]

MANDLER, G. 1985. *Cognitive Psychology.* Hillsdale, N.J.: Lawrence Erlbaum Associates. [436, 439]

MANICAS, P., & SECORD, P. F. 1983. Implications for psychology of the new philosophy of science. *American Psychologist, 38,* 399–413. [497, 498]

MARKUS-KAPLAN, M., & KAPLAN, K. J. 1979. The typology, diagnosis, pathologies, and treatment-intervention of Hellenic versus Hebraic personality styles. *Journal of Psychology and Judaism, 3,* 153–167. [33]

MARROW, A. J. 1969. *The Practical Theorist: The Life and Work of Kurt Lewin.* New York: Basic Books. [268–270, 327]

MARUYAMA, M. 1963. The second cybernetics: Deviation-amplifying mutual causal processes. *American Scientist, 51,* 164–179. [195]

MASLING, J., WEISS, L., & ROTHSCHILD, B. 1968. Relationships of oral imagery to yielding behavior and birth order. *Journal of Consulting and Clinical Psychology, 32,* 89–91. [305]

MASLOW, A. H. 1936. The role of dominance in the social and sexual behavior of infrahuman primates. *Journal of Genetic Psychology, 48,* 261–277. [362]

—— 1937. Personality and patterns of culture. (In Stagner, R., *Psychology of Personality.*) New York: McGraw-Hill. [361]

—— 1943. A dynamic theory of human motivation. *Psychological Review, 50,* 370–396. [363–365]

—— 1954. *Motivation and Personality.* New York: Harper. [363–368]

—— 1955. Deficiency and growth motivation. (In Jones, M. R., Ed. *Nebraska Symposium on Motivation.*) Lincoln, Nebraska: University of Nebraska Press. [368, 369]

—— 1956. Defense and growth. *Merrill-Palmer Quarterly, 3,* 36–47. [366]

—— 1959. Critique of self-actualization. I. Some dangers of Being-cognition. *Journal of Individual Psychology, 15,* 24–32. [367]

—— 1961. Health as transcendence of environment. *Journal of Humanistic Psychology, 1,* 1–7. [367]

—— 1962. *Toward a Psychology of Being.* New York: D. Van Nostrand. [366, 368]

—— 1964. *Religions, Values, and Peak-Experiences.* Columbus, Ohio: Ohio State University Press. [366]

MASSON, J. M. 1984. *The Assault on Truth.* New York: Farrar, Straus, & Giroux. [309–311]

—— (Ed.) 1985. *The Complete Letters of Sigmund Freud to Wilhelm Fliess, 1887–1904.* Cambridge, Mass.: Harvard University Press. [309–311]

MASTERS, J. C. 1984. Psychology, research, and social policy. *American Psychologist, 39,* 851–862. [505]

MASTERS, W. H., & JOHNSON, V. E. 1966. *Human Sexual Response.* Boston: Little, Brown. [174]

MATEER, F. 1918a. *Child Behavior: A Critical and Experimental Study of Young Children by the Method of Conditioned Reflexes.* Boston: Badger. [145]

—— 1918b. Diagnostic fallibility of intelligence ratios. *Pedagogical Seminary (Journal of Genetic Psychology), 25,* 369–392. [449]

MATTHEWS, C. G., & REITAN, R. M. 1963. Relationship of differential abstraction ability levels to psychological test performances in mentally retarded adults. *American Journal of Mental Deficiency, 68,* 235–244. [456–457]

MAX, L. W. 1935. An experimental study of the motor theory of consciousness. III. Direct-current responses in deaf-mutes during sleep, sensory stimulation, and dreams. *Journal of Comparative Psychology, 19,* 469–486. [182]

MAY, R. 1967. *Psychology and the Human Dilemma.* Princeton, N.J.: D. Van Nostrand Co. [7, 382]

——— 1969. William James' humanism and the problem of will. (In MacLeod, R. B., Ed. *William James: Unfinished Business.*) Washington, D.C.: American Psychological Association. [380]

——— 1972. *Power and Innocence.* New York: W. W. Norton & Co. [381]

———, ANGEL, E., & ELLENBERGER, H. F. (Eds.) 1958. *Existence: A New Dimension in Psychiatry and Psychology.* New York: Basic Books. [382]

MAYS, D. T., & FRANKS, C. M. 1985. *Negative Outcomes in Psychotherapy.* New York: Springer Publishing Co. [491]

MCCABE, V., & BALZANO, G. (Eds.) 1986. *Event Cognition: An Ecological Perspective.* Hillsdale, N.J.: Lawrence Erlbaum Associates. [436]

MCCLEARY, R. A., & LAZARUS, R. S. 1949. Autonomic discrimination without awareness. *Journal of Personality, 18,* 171–179. [426]

MCCLELLAND, D. C., ATKINSON, J. W., CLARK, R. A., & LOWELL, E. L. 1953. *The Achievement Motive.* New York: Appleton-Century-Crofts. [331]

MCCONNELL, J. V. 1982. *Understanding Psychology.* New York: Holt, Rinehart, & Winston. [174]

MCCURDY, H. J. 1981. The duality of experience and the perplexities of method. (In Royce, J. R., & Mos, L. P., Eds. *Humanistic Psychology.*) New York: Plenum Press. [378]

MCDOUGALL, W. 1908/1950. *An Introduction to Social Psychology.* (33rd edition.) London: Methuen. [110]

MCGEOCH, J. A., & IRION, A. L. 1952. *Psychology and Human Learning.* (Rev. Ed.) New York: Longmans Green. [154]

MCGREGOR, D. 1960. *The Human Side of Enterprise.* New York: McGraw-Hill. [387]

MCGUIGAN, F. J. 1986. Edmund Jacobson (1888–1983). *American Psychologist, 41,* 315–316. [184]

MCGUIRE, W. J. 1973. The yin and yang of social psychology: Seven koan. *Journal of Personality and Social Psychology, 26,* 446–456. [489]

MCMURRY, R. N. 1944. *Handling Personality Adjustments in Industry.* New York: Harper & Bros. [323]

MCNEMAR, Q. 1964. Lost: Our intelligence? Why? *American Psychologist, 19,* 871–882. [172]

MCPHERSON, F. M., BROUGHAM, L., & MCLAREN, S. 1980. Maintenance of improvement in agoraphobic patients treated by behavioural methods—A four-year follow-up. *Behaviour Research and Therapy, 18,* 150–152. [491]

MCREYNOLDS, P. F. 1985. Metaphors in the History of Motivational Psychology. Unpublished paper, American Psychological Association. [13]

——— 1987. Lightner Witmer: Little-known founder of clinical psychology. *American Psychologist, 42,* 849–858. [474]

MEEHL, P. E. 1950. On the circularity of the law of effect. *Psychological Bulletin, 47,* 52–75. [159]

MEHRABIAN, A. 1979. *Basic Dimensions for a General Psychological Theory.* Cambridge, Mass.: Oelgeschlager, Gunn, & Hain. [20]

MEICHENBAUM, D. H., BOWERS, K. S., & ROSS, R. R. 1969. A behavioral analysis of teacher expectancy effect. *Journal of Personality and Social Psychology, 13,* 306–316. [410]

MENAKER, E. 1982. *Otto Rank: A Rediscovered Legacy.* New York: Columbia University Press. [347, 349]

MENNINGER, K. 1942. Work as sublimation. *Bulletin of the Menninger Clinic, 6,* 170–182. [303]

MEWHORT, D. J. K. 1967. Familiarity of letter sequences, response uncertainty, and the tachistoscopic recognition experiment. *Canadian Journal of Psychology, 21,* 309–321. [431]

MEYER, M. F. 1911. *The Fundamental Laws of Human Behavior.* Boston: Badger. [168]

—— 1921/1922. *The Psychology of the Other-One.* Columbia, Mo.: Missouri Book Co. [168]

MICHOTTE, A. 1963. *The Perception of Causality.* New York: Basic Books. [5]

MILGRAM, S. 1963. Behavioral study of obedience. *Journal of Abnormal and Social Psychology, 67,* 371–378. [286]

MILL, J. 1829/1869. *Analysis of the Phenomena of the Human Mind.* London: Longmans & Dyer. [67]

MILL, J. S. 1843/1900. *System of Logic, Ratiocinative and Inductive.* London: Longmans, Green. [67]

MILLER, N. E. 1944. Experimental studies of conflict. (In Hunt, J. McV., Ed. *Personality and Behavior Disorders.*) New York: Ronald Press. [478]

—— 1959. Liberalization of basic S-R concepts: Extensions to conflict behavior, motivation, and social learning. (In Koch, S., Ed., *Psychology: A Study of a Science.* New York: McGraw-Hill. [403, 478]

—— & DOLLARD, J. 1941. *Social Learning and Imitation.* New Haven, Conn.: Yale University Press. [406]

MILTON, F., & HAFNER, J. 1981. The outcome of behaviour therapy for agoraphobia in relation to marital adjustment. *Archives of General Psychiatry, 36,* 807–812. [491]

MINER, J. B. 1984a. The unpaved road over the mountains: From theory to applications. *The Industrial Psychologist, 21,* 9–20. [503]

—— 1984b. The validity and usefulness of theories in an emerging organizational science. *Academy of Management Review, 9,* 296–306. [503]

MINTON, H. L. 1984. J. F. Brown's social psychology of the 1930s: A historical antecedent to the contemporary crisis in social psychology. *Personality and Social Psychology Bulletin, 10,* 31–42. [290–291]

MISCHEL, W. 1968. *Personality and Assessment.* New York: Wiley. [304, 463]

—— 1973. Toward a cognitive social learning reconceptualization of personality. *Psychological Review, 80,* 252–283. [463]

—— 1976. *Introduction to Personality* (2nd ed.) New York: Holt, Rinehart, & Winston. [463]

MISHLER, E. G. 1976. Skinnerism: Materialism minus the dialectic. *Journal for the Theory of Social Behavior, 6,* 21–47. [230]

MOORE, T. V. 1939. *Cognitive Psychology.* Philadelphia: Lippincott. [436]

MORAWSKI, J. G. 1982. Assessing psychology's moral heritage through our neglected Utopias. *American Psychologist, 37,* 1082–1095. [230, 494]

MORGAN, J. J. B. 1924. *Psychology of the Unadjusted School Child.* New York: Macmillan. [184]

MOSKOWITZ, M. J. 1977. Hugo Münsterberg: A study in the history of applied psychology. *American Psychologist, 32,* 824–842. [146–147]

MOWRER, O. H. 1939. A stimulus-response analysis of anxiety and its role as a reinforcing agent. *Psychological Review, 46,* 553–565. [216–217]

—— 1947. On the dual nature of learning: A reinterpretation of "conditioning" and "problem-solving." *Harvard Educational Review, 17,* 102–148. [216–217]

—— 1948. Learning theory and the neurotic paradox. *American Journal of Orthopsychiatry, 18,* 571–610. [216–217]

—— 1950. *Learning Theory and Personality Dynamics: Selected Papers.* New York: Ronald Press. [216–217]

—— 1956. Two-factor learning theory reconsidered, with special reference to secondary reinforcement and the concept of habit. *Psychological Review, 63,* 114–128. [216–217]

MUENZINGER, K. F. 1927. Physical and psychological reality. *Psychological Review, 34,* 220–233. [251]

—— 1938. Vicarious trial and error at a point of choice: I. A general survey of its relation to learning efficiency. *Journal of Genetic Psychology, 53,* 75–86. [395]

MÜLLER, J. 1838. *Handbuch der Physiologie des Menschen.* (Excerpted in R. J. Herrnstein & E. G. Boring, *A Source Book in the History of Psychology.*) Cambridge, Mass.: Harvard University Press. [80]

MUNROE, R. L. 1955. *Schools of Psychoanalytic Thought.* New York: Dryden Press. [339–341, 343, 351]

MÜNSTERBERG, H. 1913. *Psychology and Industrial Efficiency.* Boston: Houghton Mifflin. [147]

—— 1914. *Psychology: General and Applied.* New York: Appleton. [147]

MURCHISON, C. (Ed.) 1936/1961. *A History of Psychology in Autobiography.* Vol. III. New York: Russell & Russell. (Worcester, Mass.: Clark University Press.) [172]

MURPHY, G. 1929/1949. *Historical Introduction to Modern Psychology.* New York: Harcourt, Brace & Co. [176]

—— 1943. *Human Nature and Enduring Peace.* (3rd Yearbook of the Society for the Psychological Study of Social Issues.) Boston: Houghton-Mifflin for Reynal & Hitchcock. [110]

—— 1945. The freeing of intelligence. *Psychological Bulletin, 42,* 1–19. [386]

—— 1947. *Personality: A biosocial approach to origins and structure.* New York: Harper & Bros. [383–386]

—— 1958. *Human Potentialities.* New York: Basic Books. [386]

—— 1968. *Psychological Thought from Pythagoras to Freud.* New York: Harcourt, Brace, & World. [25, 101]

—— 1969. Psychology in the year 2000. *American Psychologist, 24,* 523–530. [423]

—— & JENSEN, F. 1932. *Approaches to Personality.* New York: Coward-McCann. [305]

—— & KOVACH, J. K. 1972. *Historical Introduction to Modern Psychology* (3rd ed.) New York: Harcourt, Brace, Jovanovich. [343]

—— & Murphy, L. B. 1931. *Experimental Social Psychology*. New York: Harper. [262–263]

—— & —— 1968. *Asian Psychology*. New York: Basic Books. [39]

——, ——, & Newcomb, T. M. 1937. *Experimental Social Psychology* (Rev. Ed.) New York: Harper. [262–263]

Murray, H. A. 1938. *Explorations in Personality: A Clinical and Experimental Study of Fifty Men of College Age*. New York: Oxford University Press. [350, 462]

Myers, I. B., & McCaulley, M. H. 1985. *A Guide to the Development and Use of the Myers-Briggs Type Indicator*. Palo Alto, Cal.: Consulting Psychologist' Press. [338]

Myers, J. G., & Tweney, R. D. 1983. Was Münsterberg a Utopian? *American Psychologist, 38*, 1258–1259. [147, 382]

Nafe, J. P. 1924. An experimental study of the affective qualities. *American Journal of Psychology, 35*, 507–544. [119]

Natsoulas, T. 1978. Consciousness. *American Psychologist, 33*, 906–914. [115]

Neff, W. S. 1968. *Work and Human Behavior*. New York: Atherton Press Inc. [303]

Neisser, U. 1967. *Cognitive Psychology*. New York: Appleton-Century-Crofts. [433, 436]

Nevill, D. D. (Ed.) 1977. *Humanistic Psychology*. New York: Gardner Press. [360]

Newcomb, T. M. 1947. Autistic hostility and social reality. *Human Relations, 1*, 69–86. [251]

Newell, A., & Simon, H. A. 1961. Computer simulation of human thinking. *Science, 134*, 2011–2017. [428]

Nicolás, A. T. de. 1976. *Meditations through the Rig Veda*. Boulder, Colo.: Shambhala Publications, Inc. [37]

Norman, D. A. (Ed.) 1970. *Models of Human Memory*. New York: Academic Press. [432–434]

—— & Rumelhart, D. E. 1970. A system for perception and memory. (In Norman, D. A., Ed. *Models of Human Memory*.) New York: Academic Press. [432–434]

Northway, M. L. 1940. The concept of the 'schema.' *British Journal of Psychology, 30*, 316–325; *31*, 22–36. [438]

Nuttin, J. 1949. "Spread" in recalling failure and success. *Journal of Experimental Psychology, 39*, 690–699. [246]

O'Brien, R. M., Dickinson, A. M., & Rosow, M. 1982. *Industrial Behavior Modification*. Elmsford, N.Y.: Pergamon Press. [236]

O'Donnell, J. M. 1979. The crisis of experimentalism in the 1920s: E. G. Boring and his uses of history. *American Psychologist, 34*, 289–295. [20]

Ogilvie, D. M. 1984. Personality and paradox: Gordon Allport's final contribution. *Personality Forum, 2*, 12–14. [375]

O'Keefe, J., & Nadel, L. 1978. *The Hippocampus as a Cognitive Map*. New York: Oxford University Press. [280]

Olds, J. 1958. Self-stimulation of the brain. *Science, 127*, 315–324. [204]

—— & Milner, P. 1954. Positive reinforcement produced by electrical stimulation of septal area and other regions of rat brain. *Journal of Comparative and Physiological Psychology, 47*, 419–427. [204]

ORNE, M. T. 1959. The nature of hypnosis: Artifact and essence. *Journal of Abnormal and Social Psychology, 58,* 277–299. [294]

——— 1962. On the social psychology of the psychological experiment with particular reference to demand characteristics and their implications. *American Psychologist, 17,* 776–783. [283, 489]

——— 1969. Demand characteristics and the concept of quasi-controls. (In Rosenthal, R., & Rosnow, R. L., Eds. *Artifact in Behavioral Research.*) New York: Academic Press. [283]

ORNSTEIN, R. E. 1977. *The Psychology of Consciousness.* (2nd ed.) New York: Harcourt Brace Jovanovich. [362]

OSGOOD, C. E. 1953. *Method and Theory in Experimental Psychology.* New York: Oxford University Press. [210–211]

——— & SEBEOK, T. A. (Eds.) 1965. *Psycholinguistics.* Bloomington, Ind.: Indiana University Press. [215]

———, SUCI, G. J., & TANNENBAUM, P. W. 1957. *The Measurement of Meaning.* Urbana, Ill.: University of Illinois Press. [215]

OSIER, D. V., & WOZNIAK, R. H. 1984. *A Century of Serial Publications in Psychology.* White Plains, N.Y.: Kraus International Publications.

OSTROM, T. M. 1984. The role of external invalidity in editorial decisions. *American Psychologist, 39,* 324. [237, 504]

OWENS, W. A. 1968. Toward one discipline of scientific psychology. *American Psychologist, 23,* 782–785. [497, 505]

PACKER, M. J. 1985. Hermeneutic inquiry in the study of human conduct. *American Psychologist, 40,* 1081–1093. [4]

PALMATIER, J. R., & BORNSTEIN, P. H. 1980. The effects of subliminal stimulation of symbiotic merging fantasies on behavior treatment of smokers. *Journal of Nervous and Mental Disease, 168,* 715–720. [347, 486]

PALMER, S. E., & KIMCHE, R. 1986. The information-processing approach to cognition. (In Knapp, T. J., & Robertson, L. C., Eds. *Approaches to Cognition: Contrasts and Controversies.*) Hillsdale, N.J.: Lawrence Erlbaum Associates. [433, 439]

PARANJPE, A. C. 1984. *Theoretical Psychology: The Meeting of East and West.* New York: Plenum Press. [37–40]

PARISI, T. 1987. Why Freud failed: Some implications for neurophysiology and sociobiology. *American Psychologist, 42,* 235–245. [313]

PATRY, J.-L. 1983. Evolution and "evolutionary behaviorism." *American Psychologist, 38,* 1026–1028. [471]

PATTERSON, C. H. 1966. *Theories of Counseling and Psychotherapy.* New York: Harper & Row. [479, 481]

PAVLOV, I. P. 1927/1960. *Conditioned Reflexes.* (Trans. by G. V. Anrep.) New York: Dover Publications. [165–168]

PEEKE, H. V. S., & PETRINOVICH, L. (Eds.) 1984. *Habituation, Sensitization, and Behavior.* New York: Academic Press. [127]

PEIRCE, C. S. 1878. How to make ideas clear. *Popular Science Monthly, 12,* 286–302. [109]

PELLEGRINO, J. W. 1985. Anatomy of analogy. *Psychology Today* (Oct.), 49–54. [150, 439]

PERKY, C. W. 1910. An experimental study of imagination. *American Journal of Psychology, 21,* 422–452. [120, 426]

PERRY, R. B. 1935. *The Thought and Character of William James.* (2 vols.) Boston: Little, Brown. [111, 128]

PETERSON, J. 1931. Learning when frequency and recency factors are negative and right responses are painful. *Psychological Bulletin, 28,* 207–208. [204, 224]

PIAGET, J. 1926. *The Language and Thought of the Child.* New York: Harcourt, Brace. [8]

—— 1930. *The Child's Conception of Physical Causality.* London: Kegan Paul. [4]

—— 1928. *Judgment and Reasoning in the Child.* New York: Harcourt, Brace. [9, 500]

—— 1954. *The Construction of Reality in the Child.* New York: Basic Books. [6]

—— 1974. *Understanding Causality.* New York: W. W. Norton. [6]

—— & INHELDER, B. 1969. *The Psychology of the Child.* New York: Basic Books. [2–10]

PILLSBURY, W. B. 1911. The place of movement in consciousness. *Psychological Review, 18,* 83–99. [130, 132]

—— 1919. *Psychology of Nationality and Internationalism.* New York: Macmillan. [133]

—— 1929. *History of Psychology.* New York: Norton. [133]

PLANCK, M. 1949. *Scientific Autobiography.* New York: Philosophical Library. [292]

PLATO. 1909. *Dialogues of Socrates: Phaedo.* (Trans. by Benjamin Jowett.) New York: Collier. [26–30]

POLLAK, E. I. 1983. Will sociobiology really revive Freud? *American Psychologist, 38,* 497–498. [313]

POPPLESTONE, J. A., & McPHERSON, M. W. 1980. The vitality of the Leipzig model of 1880–1910 in the United States in 1950–1980. (In Bringmann, W. G., & Tweney, R. D., Eds. *Wundt Studies.*) Toronto, Ont.: Hogrefe. [93]

PORTER, L. W., & STEERS, R. M. 1973. Organizational, work, and personal factors in employee turnover and absenteeism. *Psychological Bulletin, 80,* 151–176. [335, 503]

PORTEUS, S. D. 1937. *Primitive Intelligence and Environment.* New York: Macmillan. [472]

POSNER, M. I. 1969. Abstraction and the process of recognition. (In Bower, G., & Spence, J. T., Eds. *Psychology of Learning and Motivation,* Vol. 3.) New York: Academic Press. [8, 430]

—— 1978. *Chronometric Explorations of Mind.* Hillsdale, N.J.: Lawrence Erlbaum Associates. [428, 431, 433, 434, 445]

—— & ROGERS, M. G. K. 1978. Chronometric analysis of abstraction and recognition. (In Estes, W. K., Ed. *Handbook of Learning and Cognitive Processing.* Vol. 5. *Human Information Processing.* Hillsdale, N.J.: Lawrence Erlbaum Associates. [8, 430]

POSTMAN, L., & BRUNER, J. S. 1952. Hypothesis and the principle of closure: The effect of frequency and recency. *Journal of Psychology, 33,* 113–125. [65, 204, 257, 395]

POWERS, W. T. 1973a. Feedback: Beyond behaviorism. *Science, 179,* 351–356. [228–229]

—— 1973b. *Behavior: The Control of Perception.* Chicago: Aldine. [25]

PREMACK, D. 1959. Toward empirical behavior laws: I. Positive reinforcement. *Psychological Review, 66,* 219–233. [204, 224]

—— & WOODRUFF, G. 1978. Chimpanzee problem-solving: A test for comprehension. *Science, 202,* 532–535. [248]

PRIBRAM, K. H. 1962. The neuropsychology of Sigmund Freud. (In Bachrach, A. J., Ed. *Experimental Foundations of Clinical Psychology.*) New York: Basic Books. [321]

PRINCE, M. 1885. *Nature of Mind and Human Automatism.* Philadelphia: Lippincott. [374]

PROCHASKA, J. O. 1979. *Systems of Psychotherapy: A Transtheoretical Analysis.* Homewood, Ill.: Dorsey Press. [474–481]

—— 1983. Self-changers versus therapy changers versus Schacter. *American Psychologist, 38,* 853–854. [490]

RACHMAN, S. J., & WILSON, G. T. 1980. *Effects of Psychological Therapy.* (2nd ed.) New York: Pergamon Press. [487–489]

RAMEY, C. T., MacPHEE, D., & YEATES, K. O. 1982. Preventing developmental retardation: A general systems model. (In Detterman, D. K., & Sternberg, R. J., Eds. *How and How Much Can Intelligence be Increased?*) Norwood, N.J.: Ablex Publishing Co. [467]

RANK, O. 1924/1929. *Das Trauma der Geburt. (The Trauma of Birth.)* New York: Harcourt, Brace & Co. [347–350]

—— 1936/1945. *Will Therapy and Truth and Reality.* New York: Knopf. [349]

RATTNER, J. 1983. *Alfred Adler.* (Trans. by H. Zohn.) New York: Frederick Unger Publishing Co. [326]

RAZRAN, G. 1955. A direct laboratory comparison of Pavlovian conditioning and traditional association learning. *Journal of Abnormal and Social Psychology, 51,* 649–652. [166]

REED, H. B. C., & REITAN, R. M. 1963. Changes in psychological test performance associated with the normal aging process. *Journal of Gerontology, 18,* 271–274. [449, 455]

REEVES, C. 1982. Breuer, Freud, and the case of Anna O.: A re-examination. *Journal of Child Psychotherapy, 8,* 203–214. [295]

REICHELT, P. A. 1974. *Moderators in Expectancy Theory: Influence on the Relationships of Motivation with Effort and Job Performance.* Unpublished Ph.D. dissertation, Wayne State University. [404]

REID, T. 1749/1970. *An Inquiry into the Human Mind on the Principles of Common Sense.* New York: Random House Modern Library. [69, 72, 99]

REITMAN, W. 1970. What does it take to remember? (In Norman, D. A., Ed. *Models of Human Memory.*) New York: Academic Press. [431]

RESCORLA, R. A. 1977. Pavlovian second-order conditioning: Some implications for instrumental behavior. (In Davis, H., & Hurwitz, H. M. B., Eds. *Operant-Pavlovian Interactions.*) Hillsdale, N.J.: Lawrence Erlbaum Associates. [166]

—— & SOLOMON, R. L. 1967. Two-process learning theory: Relationships between Pavlovian conditioning and instrumental learning. *Psychological Review, 74,* 151–182. [216]

REYNOLDS, D. K. 1980. *The Quiet Therapies: Japanese Pathways to Personal Growth.* Honolulu: University Press of Hawaii. [40]

RHOADS, J. M., & FEATHER, B. W. 1972. Transference and resistance observed in behavior therapy. *British Journal of Medical Psychology, 45,* 99–103. [495]

RIEBER, R. W. (Ed.) 1980. *Wilhelm Wundt and the Making of a Scientific Psychology.* New York: Plenum Press. [85–94]

———— & SALZINGER, K. (Eds.) 1980. *Psychology: Theoretical-Historical Perspectives.* New York: Academic Press.

RIEFF, P. 1959. *Freud: The Mind of a Moralist.* New York: Viking. [304]

RIEGEL, K. F. 1975. From traits and equilibrium toward developmental dialectics. (In Arnold, W. J., & Cole, J. K., Eds.: *Nebraska Symposium on Motivation.*) Lincoln, Nebraska: University of Nebraska Press. [462]

———— 1976. *Psychology of Development and History.* New York: Plenum Press. [357]

———— 1979. *Foundations of Dialectical Psychology.* New York: Academic Press. [291]

RITCHIE, B. F. 1964. *Edward Chace Tolman.* Washington, D.C.: Biographical Memoirs, National Academy of Sciences. [390]

ROAZEN, P. 1974. *Freud and His Followers.* New York: Alfred A. Knopf. [336–337]

ROBACK, A. A. 1917. The moral issues involved in applied psychology. *Journal of Applied Psychology, 1,* 232–243. [412]

ROBERTSON, L. C. 1986. From Gestalt to Neo-Gestalt. (In Knapp, T. J., & Robertson, L. C., Eds. *Approaches to Cognition.*) Hillsdale, N.J.: Lawrence Erlbaum Associates. [441]

ROBINSON, D. N. (Ed.) 1977. *Significant Contributions to the History of Psychology, 1750–1920.* Washington, D.C.: University Publications of America. [448]

———— 1981. *An Intellectual History of Psychology.* New York: Macmillan. [28, 35, 37, 78]

———— 1986. The Scottish enlightenment and its mixed bequest. *Journal of the History of the Behavioral Sciences, 22,* 171–177. [72]

ROE, A. 1953. A psychological study of eminent psychologists and anthropologists, and a comparison with biological and physical scientists. *Psychological Monographs, 67,* No. 352. [21]

ROGERS, C. R. 1942. *Counseling and Psychotherapy.* Boston: Houghton-Mifflin. [479, 481]

———— 1959. A theory of therapy, personality, and interpersonal relationships, as developed in the client-centered framework. (In Koch, S., Ed. *Psychology: A Study of a Science.* Vol. 3.) New York: McGraw-Hill. [370–372, 480]

———— 1964. Toward a science of the person. (In Wann, T. W., Ed. *Behaviorism and Phenomenology.*) Chicago: University of Chicago Press. [370]

———— 1967. Autobiography. (In Boring, E. G., & Lindzey, G., Eds. *A History of Psychology in Autobiography.* Vol. V.) New York: Appleton-Century-Crofts. [369]

———— 1985. Interview with Carl Rogers. *APA Monitor, 16,* # 5 (May), p. 16. [373]

———— & DYMOND, R. F. (Eds.) 1954. *Psychotherapy and Personality Change: Coordinated Studies in the Client-Centered Approach.* Chicago: University of Chicago Press. [373]

———— & SKINNER, B. F. 1956. Some issues concerning the control of human behavior. *Science, 124,* 1057–1066. [373]

ROKEACH, M. 1960. *The Open and Closed Mind.* New York: Basic Books. [419]

—— 1968. *Beliefs, Attitudes, and Values.* San Francisco: Jossey-Bass. [413]

—— 1973. *The Nature of Human Values.* New York: The Free Press. [388, 493]

RORSCHACH, H. 1921/1942. *Psychodiagnostik. (Psychodiagnostics.)* New York: Grune & Stratton. [96, 462]

ROSENBAUM, M., & MUROFF, M. (Eds.) 1982. *Anna O.: Fourteen Contemporary Reinterpretations.* New York: Free Press. [295]

ROSENBERG, S., & GARA, M. A. 1983. Contemporary perspectives and future directions of personality and social psychology. *Journal of Personality and Social Psychology, 45,* 57–73. [20]

ROSENHAN, D. L. 1973. On being sane in insane places. *Science, 179,* 250–258. [493]

ROSENTHAL, R. 1966. *Experimenter Effects in Behavioral Research.* New York: Appleton-Century-Crofts. [405]

—— & ROSNOW, R. L. 1969. *Artifact in Behavioral Research.* New York: Academic Press. [405]

ROSENZWEIG, M. R. 1984a. Experience, memory, and the brain. *American Psychologist, 39,* 365–376. [321]

—— 1984b. U. S. psychology and world psychology. *American Psychologist, 39,* 877–886. [44]

Ross, D. 1972. *G. Stanley Hall: The Psychologist as Prophet.* Chicago: University of Chicago Press. [144]

ROTTER, J. B. 1954. *Social Learning and Clinical Psychology.* New York: Prentice-Hall. [402–403]

—— 1966. Generalized expectancies for internal versus external control of reinforcement. *Psychological Monographs, 80,* Whole No. 609. [111]

—— 1982. *The Development and Applications of Social Learning Theory.* Westport, Conn.: Greenwood Press. [403]

—— & HOCHREICH, D. J. 1975. *Personality.* Glenview, Ill.: Scott, Foresman & Co. [462]

ROWE, D. C. 1987. Resolving the person-situation debate: Invitation to an interdisciplinary dialogue. *American Psychologist, 42,* 218–227. [467]

ROWE, F. B. 1983. Whatever became of poor Kinnebrook? *American Psychologist, 38,* 851–852. [88]

ROYCE, J. R., & MOS, L. P. (Eds.) 1981. *Human Psychology: Concepts and Criticisms.* New York: Plenum Press. [359–361]

—— & —— (Eds.) 1984. *Annals of Theoretical Psychology.* New York: Plenum Press. [388]

—— & POWELL, A. 1983. *Theory of Personality and Individual Differences: Factors, Systems, and Processes.* Englewood Cliffs, N.J.: Prentice-Hall. [505–507]

RUCKMICK, C. A. 1937. Carl Stumpf. *Psychological Bulletin, 34,* 187–190. [241]

RUDIN, S. A., & STAGNER, R. 1958. Figure-ground phenomena in the perception of physical and social stimuli. *Journal of Psychology, 45,* 213–225. [460]

RUMELHART, D. E., McCLELLAND, J. L., & THE PDP RESEARCH GROUP. 1986. *Parallel Distributed Processing: Explorations in the Microstructure of Cognition.* (2 vols.) Cambridge, Mass.: M. I. T. Press. [439]

RUSSELL, B. 1945. *A History of Western Philosophy.* New York: Simon & Schuster. [60, 75]

RUSSELL, R. W. 1984. Psychology in its world context. *American Psychologist, 39,* 1017–1025. [44]

RYCHLAK, J. F. 1977. *The Psychology of Rigorous Humanism.* New York: Wiley. [386, 479]

SACHS, L. B. 1982. Teaching hypnosis for the self-control of pain. (In Barber, J., & Adrian, C., Eds. *Psychological Approaches to the Management of Pain.*) New York: Brunner/Mazel. [486]

SAHAKIAN, W. S. 1975. *History and Systems of Psychology.* New York: John Wiley & Sons. [72, 99]

SALOMON, G. 1981. Self-fulfilling and self-sustaining prophecies and the behaviors that realize them. *American Psychologist, 36,* 1452–1453. [404]

SALTZ, E. 1970. Manifest anxiety: Have we misread the data? *Psychological Review, 77,* 568–573. [462]

—— 1971. *The Cognitive Bases of Human Learning.* Homewood, Ill.: Dorsey Press. [435]

—— & DiLORETO, A. 1965. "Defense" against traumatic concepts. *Journal of Abnormal Psychology, 70,* 281–284. [426]

SALZINGER, K. 1973. Inside the black box, with apologies to Pandora. A review of Ulric Neisser's *Cognitive Psychology. Journal of the Experimental Analysis of Behavior, 19,* 369–378. [436]

SAMELSON, F. 1979. Putting psychology on the map: Ideology and intelligence testing. (In Buss, A. R., Ed. *Psychology in Social Context.*) New York: Irvington Publishers. [449, 472]

—— 1980a. J. B. Watson's Little Albert, Cyril Burt's Twins, and the need for a critical science. *American Psychologist, 35,* 619–625. [181, 453]

—— 1980b. E. G. Boring and his "History of Experimental Psychology." *American Psychologist, 35,* 467–470. [93]

SANFORD, R. N. 1937. Effects of abstinence from food upon imaginal processes: A further study. *Journal of Psychology, 3,* 145–159. [424]

—— 1983. Gordon Allport and I. *Personality Forum, 1,* 14–20. [376]

SARAL, T. B. 1983. Hindu philosophy of communication. *Communication, 8,* 47–58. [39]

SARASON, I. G. 1969. *Contemporary Research in Personality* (2nd ed.) Princeton, N.J.: D. Van Nostrand. [462]

—— & GANZER, V. J. 1969. Social influence techniques in clinical and community psychology. (In Spielberger, C. D., Ed.: *Current Topics in Clinical and Community Psychology.* Vol. 1.) New York: Academic Press. [409]

SARASON, S. B. 1977. *Work, Aging, and Social Change.* New York: Free Press. [386]

—— 1981. *Psychology Misdirected.* New York: Free Press. [386, 507]

SAVAGE, C. W. 1970. *The Measurement of Sensation.* Berkeley, Cal.: University of California Press. [135]

SCARR, S. 1981. Testing *for* children. *American Psychologist, 36,* 1159–1166. [471]

—— & CARTER-SALTZMAN, M. 1982. Genetics and intelligence. (In Sternberg, R. J., Ed. *Handbook of Human Intelligence.*) Cambridge, England: Cambridge University Press. [471]

SCARR-SALAPATEK, S. 1971. Race, social class, and IQ. *Science, 174,* 1285–1295. [471]

SCHAFER, R., & MURPHY, G. 1943. The role of autism in figure-ground relationships. *Journal of Experimental Psychology, 32,* 335–343. [385, 425]

SCHATZMAN, M. 1973. *Soul Murder: Persecution in the Family.* New York: Random House. [309]

SCHNAITTER, R. 1986. A coordination of differences: Behaviorism, mentalism, and the foundations of psychology. (In Knapp, T. J., & Robertson, L. D., Eds. *Approaches to Cognition: Contrasts and Controversies.*) Hillsdale, N.J.: Lawrence Erlbaum Associates. [497]

SCHUR, M. 1972. *Freud: Living and Dying.* New York: International Universities Press. [297]

SEAGOE, M. V. 1975. *Terman and the Gifted.* Los Altos, Cal.: W. Kaufmann. [470]

SEAMAN, J. D. 1984. On phi-phenomena. *Journal of the History of the Behavioral Sciences, 20,* 3–8. [245]

SEARS, R. R., MACCOBY, E. E., & LEVIN, H. 1957. *Patterns of Child Rearing.* Evanston, Ill.: Row, Peterson. [305–307]

SECHENOV, I. M. 1863/1965. On reflexology and psychology. (Excerpted in Herrnstein, R. J., & Boring, E. G., Eds. *A Source Book in the History of Psychology.*) Cambridge, Mass.: Harvard University Press. [164]

SECORD, P. F. 1982. *Explaining Human Behavior: Consciousness, Human Action, and Social Structure.* Beverly Hills, Cal.: Sage Publications. [389]

SEGAL, E. M., & LACHMAN, R. 1972. Complex behavior or higher mental process. *American Psychologist, 27,* 46–55. [433]

——— & STACY, E. W., JR. 1975. Rule-governed behavior as a psychological process. *American Psychologist, 30,* 541–552. [231]

SELYE, H. 1956. *The Stress of Life.* New York: McGraw-Hill. [192]

SEWARD, J. P. 1942. An experimental study of Guthrie's theory of reinforcement. *Journal of Experimental Psychology, 30,* 247–256. [191]

——— 1954. Hull's system of behavior: An evaluation. *Psychological Review, 61,* 145–159. [272]

SHAFFER, J. B. P. 1978. *Humanistic Psychology.* Englewood Cliffs, N.J.: Prentice-Hall. [360, 388]

SHAKOW, D., & RAPAPORT, D. 1964. The influence of Freud on American psychology. *Psychological Issues, 4, #* 13. [323]

SHEFFIELD, F. D., & ROBY, T. B. 1950. Reward value of a non-nutritive sweet taste. *Journal of Comparative and Physiological Psychology, 47,* 349–354. [215]

———, WULFF, J. J., & BACKER, R. 1951. Reward value of copulation without sex drive reduction. *Journal of Comparative and Physiological Psychology, 44,* 3–8. [216]

SHEPHER, J. 1984. *Incest: A biosocial view.* New York: Academic Press. [309]

SHERIF, M. 1936. *The Psychology of Social Norms.* New York: Harper & Row. [262, 499]

———, HARVEY, O. J., WHITE, B. J., HOOD, W. R., & SHERIF, C. 1961. *Intergroup Conflict and Cooperation.* Norman, Okla.: Institute of Group Relations, University of Oklahoma. [505]

———, TAUB, D., & HOVLAND, C. I. 1958. Assimilation and contrast effects of anchoring stimuli on judgments. *Journal of Experimental Psychology, 55,* 150–155. [264]

SHERMAN, M. 1927. Differentiation of emotional responses in infants. *Journal of Comparative Psychology, 7,* 265–284. [180]

SHEVRIN, H., & DICKMAN, S. 1980. The psychological unconscious: A necessary assumption for all psychological theory? *American Psychologist, 35,* 421–434. [9]

SHIFFMAN, S. 1985. *Characterizing Smoking Relapse Episodes.* Unpublished paper, American Association of Behavior Therapy (Houston). [489]

SHIFFRIN, R. M. 1970. Memory search. (In Norman, D. A., Ed. *Models of Human Memory.*) New York: Academic Press. [432]

SIIPOLA, E. M. 1935. A study of some effects of preparatory set. *Psychological Monographs, 46,* Whole No. 210. [424]

SILVERMAN, L. H., & WEINBERGER, J. 1985. Mommy and I Are One: Implications for psychotherapy. *American Psychologist, 40,* 1296–1308. [350]

SIMPSON, E. L. 1977. Humanistic Psychology: An Attempt to Define Human Nature. (In Nevill, D. D., Ed. *Humanistic Psychology.*) New York: Wiley Inter-Science. [366]

SKAGGS, E. B. 1945. Personalistic psychology as science. *Psychological Review, 52,* 234–238. [376]

SKINNER, B. F. 1931. The concept of the reflex in the description of behavior. *Journal of General Psychology, 5,* 427–458. [222]

—— 1938. *The Behavior of Organisms.* New York: Appleton-Century. [9]

—— 1944. *Principles of Behavior* by Clark L. Hull. *American Journal of Psychology, 57,* 276–281. [238]

—— 1948. *Walden Two.* New York: Macmillan. [404]

—— 1950. Are theories of learning necessary? *Psychological Review, 57,* 193–216. [3, 222]

—— 1953. *Science and Human Behavior.* New York: Macmillan. [407]

—— 1957. *Verbal Behavior.* New York: Appleton-Century-Crofts. [234]

—— 1959. John B. Watson, behaviorist. *Science, 129,* 197–198. [175]

—— 1964. Behaviorism at fifty. (In Wann, T. W., Ed. *Behaviorism and Phenomenology.*) Chicago: University of Chicago Press. [175]

—— 1967. Autobiography. (In Boring, E. G., & Lindzey, G., Eds. *A History of Psychology in Autobiography.*) New York: Appleton-Century-Crofts. [220]

—— 1968. *Psychology in the year 2000.* Address at Wayne State University Centennial, 10 May 1968. [236]

—— 1969. *Contingencies of Reinforcement: A Theoretical Analysis.* New York: Appleton-Century-Crofts. [225]

—— 1971. *Beyond Freedom and Dignity.* New York: Alfred A. Knopf. [235, 255]

—— 1974. *About Behaviorism.* New York: Alfred A. Knopf. [232]

—— 1976. *Particulars of My Life.* New York: Alfred A. Knopf. [220]

—— 1979. *The Shaping of a Behaviorist.* New York: Alfred A. Knopf. [220]

—— 1983a. Intellectual self-management in old age. *American Psychologist, 38,* 239–244. [234–235]

—— 1983b. Interview. *Psychology Today, 17* (Sept.), 25 ff. [220]

SKODAK, M. 1939. Children in foster homes. *University of Iowa Studies in Child Welfare, 16, # 1.* [466]

SMITH, M. B. 1950. The phenomenological approach to personality theory:

Some critical remarks. *Journal of Abnormal and Social Psychology, 45,* 516–522. [370]

——— 1971. Allport, Murray, and Lewin on personality theory: Notes on a confrontation. *Journal of the History of the Behavioral Sciences, 7,* 353–362. [370]

SMITH, M. L., & GLASS, G. V. 1977. Meta-analysis of psychotherapy outcome studies. *American Psychologist, 32,* 752–760. [488]

SNOW, C. P. 1964. *The Two Cultures and a Second Look.* London: Cambridge University Press. [20, 497]

SNYDERMAN, M., & HERRNSTEIN, R. J. 1983. Intelligence tests and the Immigration Act of 1924. *American Psychologist, 38,* 986–995. [447]

SOKAL, M. M. (Ed.) 1987. *Psychological Testing and American Society, 1890–1930.* New Brunswick, N.J.: Rutgers University Press. [447]

SOLLEY, C. M., JR. 1954. *Drive, barrier conditions, and personality variables affecting problem-solving behavior.* Unpublished doctoral dissertation, University of Illinois. [282]

——— & MURPHY, G. 1960. *Development of the Perceptual World.* New York: Basic Books. [6, 8, 246, 424]

——— & STAGNER, R. 1956. Effects of magnitude of temporal barriers, type of goal, and perception of self. *Journal of Experimental Psychology, 51,* 62–70. [282]

SOLLOD, R. N. 1975. Carl Rogers and the origins of client-centered therapy. *Professional Psychology, 9,* 93–104. [479]

——— 1981. Goodwin Watson's 1940 conference. *American Psychologist, 36,* 1546–1547. [479]

SOLOMON, R. L., & CORBIT, J. D. 1974. An opponent-process theory of motivation. I. Temporal dynamics of affect. *Psychological Review, 81,* 119–145. [276]

——— & TURNER, L. H. 1962. Discriminative classical conditioning in dogs paralyzed by curare can later control discriminative avoidance responses in the normal state. *Psychological Review, 69,* 202–219. [131]

SPEARMAN, C. E. 1923. *The Nature of "Intelligence" and the Principles of Cognition.* London: Macmillan. [452]

——— 1927. *The Abilities of Man—Their Nature and Measurement.* New York: Macmillan. [450]

SPENCE, K. W. 1937. The differential response in animals to stimuli varying within a single dimension. *Psychological Review, 44,* 430–444. [246]

——— 1940. Continuous vs. non-continuous interpretation of discrimination learning. *Psychological Review, 47,* 271–288. [212]

——— 1956. *Behavior Theory and Conditioning.* New Haven, Conn.: Yale University Press. [212]

——— 1960. *Behavior Theory and Learning.* Englewood Cliffs, N.J.: Prentice-Hall. [212]

SPERRY, R. W. 1969. A modified concept of consciousness. *Psychological Review, 76,* 532–536. [321]

SPIELBERGER, C. D. (Ed.) 1969. *Current Topics in Clinical and Community Psychology,* Vol. I. New York: Academic Press. [409]

——— & DeNIKE, L. D. 1966. Descriptive behaviorism versus cognitive theory in verbal operant conditioning. *Psychological Review, 73,* 306–326. [408]

SPURZHEIM, G. 1834. *Phrenology, or the Doctrine of Mental Phenomena.* Boston: Marsh, Capen, & Lyon. [76]

STAATS, A. W. 1961. Verbal habit-families, concepts, and the operant conditioning of word classes. *Psychological Review, 68,* 190–204. [416]

—— 1968. *Learning, Language, and Cognition.* New York: Holt, Rinehart, & Winston. [413]

—— 1971. *Child Learning, Intelligence, and Personality.* New York: Harper & Row. [415, 420]

—— 1975. *Social Behaviorism.* Homewood, Ill.: Dorsey Press. [413–416, 419–421, 444, 468, 504]

—— 1981. Paradigmatic behaviorism, unified theory, unified theory construction methods, and the Zeitgeist of separatism. *American Psychologist, 36,* 239–256. [504]

—— 1983. *Psychology's Crisis of Disunity.* New York: Praeger. [504]

——, BREWER, B. A., & GROSS, M. C. 1970. Learning and cognitive development: Representative samples, cumulative-hierarchical learning, and experimental-longitudinal methods. *Monographs of the Society for Research on Child Development, 35,* Whole No. 141. [420]

——, GROSS, M. C., GUAY, P. F., & CARLSON, C. C. 1973. Personality and social systems and attitude-reinforcer-discrimination theory: Interest (attitude) formation, function, and measurement. *Journal of Personality and Social Psychology, 26,* 251–261. [420–421]

—— & STAATS, C. K. 1957. Meaning established by classical conditioning. *Journal of Experimental Psychology, 54,* 74–80. [416]

—— & —— 1963. *Complex Human Behavior.* New York: Holt, Rinehart & Winston. [468]

——, ——, HEARD, W. G., & FINLEY, J. R. 1962. Operant conditioning of factor analytic personality traits. *Journal of General Psychology, 66,* 101–114. [420]

STAGNER, R. 1933. Relation of personality to academic aptitude and achievement. *Journal of Educational Research, 26,* 648–660. [461]

—— 1937. *Psychology of Personality.* New York: McGraw-Hill. [445]

—— 1975. Personality, perceiving, and adaptation level. (In Flores d'Arcais, G. B., Ed. *Studies in Perception: Festschrift for Fabio Metelli.*) Milano, Italy: Aldo Martello-Giunti Editore. [264]

—— 1977. Homeostasis, discrepancy, dissonance: A theory of motives and motivation. *Motivation and Emotion, 1,* 103–118. [195]

—— 1978. Egocentrism, ethnocentrism, altrocentrism: Relations to individual and group violence. *International Journal of Intercultural Relations, 1,* 9–30. [500]

—— 1981. Training and experiences of some distinguished industrial psychologists. *American Psychologist, 36,* 497–505. [136]

—— 1984. Trait theory. (In Endler, N. S., & Hunt, J. McV., Eds. *Personality and the Behavioral Disorders.*) New York: Wiley. [463]

STEELE, R. S. 1985. Paradigm found: A deconstruction of the history of the psychoanalytic movement. (In Buxton, C. E., Ed. *Points of View in the Modern History of Psychology.*) New York: Academic Press. [297]

STEPHENSON, W. 1953. *The Study of Behavior.* Chicago: University of Chicago Press. [373]

STERBA, R. F. 1982. *Reminiscences of a Viennese Psychoanalyst.* Detroit: Wayne State University Press. [316–317]

STERN, W. 1914. The psychological methods of testing intelligence. (In Robinson, D. N., Ed. 1977. *Significant Contributions to the History of Psychology, 1750–1920.*) Washington, D. C.: University Publications of America. [450]

STERNBERG, R. J. 1977. *Intelligence, Information Processing, and Analogical Reasoning.* Hillsdale, N.J.: Lawrence Erlbaum Associates. [439]

—— 1979. Stalking the IQ quark. *Psychology Today* (Sept.), 42–51. [439]

—— (Ed.) 1982. *Handbook of Human Intelligence.* Cambridge, England: Cambridge University Press. [449]

—— 1985a. Cognitive approaches to intelligence. (In Wolman, B. B., Ed. *Handbook of Intelligence: Theories, Measurement, and Applications.*) New York: Wiley. [458]

—— 1985b. *Beyond IQ: A Triarchic Theory of Human Intelligence.* New York: Cambridge University Press. [458]

—— (Ed.) 1986. *Advances in the Psychology of Human Intelligence.* Hillsdale, N.J.: Lawrence Erlbaum Associates. [449]

—— & BERG, C. 1986. Quantitative integration. (In Sternberg, R. J., & Detterman, D. K., Eds. *What Is Intelligence?*) Norwood, N.J.: Ablex Publishing Corp. [458]

—— & DETTERMAN, D. K. (Eds.) 1986. *What Is Intelligence?* Norwood, N.J.: Ablex Publishing Corp. [449]

—— & POWELL, J. S. 1982. Theories of intelligence. (In Sternberg, R. J., Ed. *Handbook of Human Intelligence.*) Cambridge, England: Cambridge University Press. [449]

STERNBERG, S. 1969a. The discovery of processing stages: Extensions of Donders' method. *Acta Psychologica, 30,* 276–315. [431]

—— 1969b. Memory-scanning: Mental processes revealed by reaction-time experiments. *American Scientist, 57,* 421–457. [435]

STIVERS, E. H., & WHELAN, S. A. (Eds.) 1986. *The Lewin Legacy: Field Theory in Current Practice.* New York: Springer. [289]

STOLZ, S. B., WIENCKOWSKI, L. A., & BROWN, B. S. 1975. Behavior modification: A perspective on critical issues. *American Psychologist, 30,* 1027–1048. [235, 492]

STORM, K. A. 1986. *Women Surviving Incest: The Trauma Endured.* Unpublished M.A. thesis, University of Wisconsin (superior). [309]

STRACHEY, J. 1957. Editor's introduction to Breuer and Freud's *Studies on Hysteria.* New York: Basic Books. [476]

STRATTON, G. M. 1897. Vision without inversion of the retinal image. *Psychological Review, 4,* 341–360, 463–481. [125]

STRONGIN, E. L., BULL, N., & KORCHIN, B. 1941. Visual efficiency during experimentally induced emotional states. *Journal of Psychology, 12,* 3–6. [498]

TABIN, J. K. 1985. *On the Way to Self.* New York: Columbia University Press. [306, 307]

TAFT, J. 1936. Preface. (In Rank, O. *Will Therapy: An Analysis of the Therapeutic Process.*) New York: Alfred A. Knopf. [349]

TAYLOR, S. E. 1983. Adjustment to threatening events: A theory of cognitive adaptation. *American Psychologist, 38,* 1161–1173. [366]

TENOPYR, M. 1981. The realities of employment testing. *American Psychologist, 36,* 1120–1127. [431, 452]

TERMAN, L. M., & ODEN, M. H. 1947. *The Gifted Child Grows Up.* Stanford, Cal.: Stanford University Press. [470]

TERRACE, H. S. 1979. *Nim: A Chimpanzee Who Learned Sign Language.* New York: Alfred A. Knopf. [231]

———— 1985. In the beginning was the 'name.' *American Psychologist, 40,* 1011–1028. [231]

THOMAS A., & SILLEN, S. 1972. *Racism and Psychiatry.* New York: Brunner/Mazel. [497]

THOMPSON, R. F. 1976. The search for the engram. *American Psychologist 31,* 209–227. [321]

THORNDIKE, E. L. 1911/1970. *Animal Intelligence: Experimental Studies.* (Rev. ed.) New York: Macmillan; Hafner. [159]

———— 1931. *Human Learning.* New York: Century. [159, 407]

———— 1940. *Connectionism.* New York: Macmillan. [159].

———— & WOODWORTH, R. S. 1901. The influence of improvement in one mental function upon the efficiency of other functions. Psychological Review, 8, 247–261, 384–395, 533–564. [72, 158]

THORNDIKE, R. L. 1954. The psychological value systems of psychologists. *American Psychologist, 9,* 787–790. [20]

THURSTONE, L. L. 1923. The stimulus-response fallacy in psychology. *Psychological Review, 30,* 354–369. [454]

———— 1938. Primary mental abilities. *Psychometric Monographs,* No. 1 [453]

———— 1947. *Multiple Factor Analysis: A Development and Expansion of "The Vectors of the Mind."* Chicago: University of Chicago Press. [453]

TIMMONS, E. O., & NOBLIN, C. D. 1963. The differential performance of orals and anals in a verbal conditioning paradigm. *Journal of Consulting Psychology, 27,* 383–386. [498]

TITCHENER, E. B. 1896. *An Outline of Psychology.* New York: Macmillan. [119]

———— 1898. The postulates of a structural psychology. *Philosophical Review, 7,* 449–465. [118, 119]

———— 1899. Structural and functional psychology. *Philosophical Review, 8,* 290–299. [118]

———— 1905. *Experimental Psychology: Student's Manual.* New York: Macmillan. [124]

———— 1908/1973. *Lectures on the Elementary Psychology of Feeling and Attention.* New York: Macmillan; Arno Press. [120]

———— 1909a. *Experimental Psychology of the Thought Processes.* New York: Macmillan. [115, 221]

———— 1909b. *Experimental Psychology: A Manual of Laboratory Practice.* Vol. I. *Qualitative Experiments.* Part 1. *Student's Manual.* New York: Macmillan. [123]

———— 1911. *A Textbook of Psychology.* New York: Macmillan. [117, 120, 121, 122, 124, 126, 401]

———— 1912a. Description vs. statement of meaning. *American Journal of Psychology, 23,* 165–182. [115]

———— 1912b. The scheme of introspection. *American Journal of Psychology, 23,* 489. [117]

—— 1914a. On "Psychology as the behaviorist views it." *Proceedings, American Philosophical Society, 53,* 1–17. [176]

—— 1914b. Psychology: Science or technology? *Popular Science Monthly, 84,* 39–51. [129, 136]

—— 1918. *A Primer of Psychology.* (Rev. ed.) New York: Macmillan. [119, 126]

—— 1924. The term "attensity." *American Journal of Psychology, 35,* 156. [120]

—— 1925. Experimental psychology: A retrospect. *American Journal of Psychology, 36,* 313–323. [127]

—— 1929. *Systematic Psychology: Prolegomena.* New York: Macmillan. [123]

TOCH, H. 1969. *Violent Men.* Chicago: Aldine. [187]

TOLMAN, E. C. 1932. *Purposive Behavior in Animals and Men.* New York: Century. [390–398]

—— 1938. The determiners of behavior at a choice point. *Psychological Review, 45,* 1–41. [400]

—— 1942. *Drives Toward War.* New York: D. Appleton-Century. [399]

—— 1948. Cognitive maps in rats and men. *Psychological Review, 55,* 189–208. [395]

—— 1949. There is more than one kind of learning. *Psychological Review, 30,* 144–155. [395]

—— & KRECHEVSKY, I. 1933. Means-end-readiness and hypothesis: A contribution to comparative psychology. *Psychological Review, 40,* 60–70. [395]

TOLMAN, E. C., & HONZIK, C. H. 1930. Introduction and removal of reward, and maze performance in rats. *University of California Publications in Psychology, 4,* 257–275. [390]

TRAVIS, L. E., & HUNTER, T. A. 1928. The relation between "intelligence" and reflex conduction rate. *Journal of Experimental Psychology, 11,* 342–354. [453]

—— 1986. Personal communication. 8 Aug. 1986. [453]

TREISMAN, A. M. 1960. Contextual cues in selective listening. *Quarterly Journal of Experimental Psychology, 12,* 242–248. [429]

TRIPLET, R. G. 1982. The relationship of Clark L. Hull's hypnosis research to his later learning theory: The continuity of his life's work. *Journal of the History of the Behavioral Sciences, 18,* 22–31. [207]

TULVING, E. 1972. Episodic and semantic memory. (In E. Tulving & W. Donaldson, Eds. *Organization of Memory.*) New York: Academic Press. [433]

—— 1985. Memory and consciousness. *Canadian Psychology/Psychologie Canadienne, 26,* 1–12. [434]

ULLMAN, L. P., & KRASNER, L. 1975. *Psychological Approach to Abnormal Behavior.* New York: Holt, Rinehart & Winston. [484–485]

UNDERWOOD, B. J. 1957. *Psychological Research.* New York: Appleton-Century-Crofts. [498]

—— 1971. Recognition Memory. (In Kendler, H. H., & Spence, J. T., Eds. *Essays in Neobehaviorism: A Memorial Volume to K. W. Spence.*) New York: Appleton-Century-Crofts. [212]

—— 1975. Individual differences as a crucible in theory construction. *American Psychologist, 30,* 128–134. [498]

—— 1983. *Attributes of Memory.* Glenview, Ill.: Scott, Foresman, & Co. [435]

VALE, J. R., & VALE, G. R. 1969. Individual difference and general laws in psychology: A reconciliation. *American Psychologist, 24,* 1093–1108. [498]

VALENSTEIN, E. S. 1985. *Great and Desperate Cures.* New York: Basic Books. [76]

VANDE KEMP, H. 1980. Origin and evolution of the term Psychology: Addenda. *American Psychologist, 35,* 774. [22]

VANDENBERG, S. G., & VOGLER, G. P. 1985. Genetic determinants of intelligence. (In Wolman, B. B., Ed. *Handbook of Intelligence: Theories, Measurements, and Applications.*) New York: Wiley. [467]

VAN HOORN, W., & VERHAVE, T. 1977. Socioeconomic factors and the roots of American psychology. *Annals, New York Academy of Science, 291,* 203–221. [184]

VARELA, J. A. 1971. *Psychological Solutions to Social Problems.* New York: Academic Press. [421]

VERNON, P. A. 1987. *Speed of Information-Processing and Intelligence.* Norwood, N.J.: Ablex Publishing Corp. [446]

VERNON, P. E. 1933. Biosocial nature of the personality trait. *Psychological Review, 40,* 533–548. [463]

———— 1979. *Intelligence: Heredity and Environment.* San Francisco: W. H. Freeman & Co. [463–466]

VERPLANCK, W. S. 1962. Unaware of where's awareness: Some verbal operants—notates, monents, and notants. (In Eriksen, C. W., Ed. *Behavior and Awareness.* Durham, N.C.: Duke University Press. [407]

VINEY, W., WERTHEIMER, M., & WERTHEIMER, M. L. 1979. *History of Psychology: A Guide to Information Sources.* Detroit: Gale Research Co.

VON BERTALANFFY, L. 1964. The mind-body problem: A new view. *Psychosomatic Medicine, 26,* 29–45. [49]

VROOM, V. H. 1964. *Work and Motivation.* New York: Wiley. [335, 355, 422]

VYGOTSKI, L. S. 1979. Consciousness as a problem in the psychology of behavior. *Soviet Psychology, 17,* 3–35. [49]

WACHTEL, P. L. 1973. Psychodynamics, behavior therapy, and the implacable experimenter: An inquiry into the consistency of personality. *Journal of Abnormal Psychology, 82,* 324–334. [489–490, 496]

WALKER, N. 1956. Freud and homeostasis. *British Journal of the Philosophy of Science, 7,* 61–72. [168, 303–304]

WALLACH, M. A., & WALLACH, L. 1983. *Psychology's Sanction for Selfishness.* San Francisco: W. H. Freeman & Co. [500]

WALSH, R. N., & SHAPIRO, D. H., JR. (Eds.) 1982. *Beyond Health and Normality: Explorations of Exceptional Psychological Well-Being.* New York: Van Nostrand-Reinhold. [366]

WANN, T. W. (Ed.) 1964. *Behaviorism and Phenomenology.* Chicago: University of Chicago Press. [198]

WARREN, H. C. 1921. Psychology and the central nervous system. *Psychological Review, 28,* 249–269. [153]

WASHBURN, M. F. 1908/1936. *The Animal Mind* (4th ed.) New York: Macmillan. [48]

———— 1916. *Movement and Mental Imagery.* Boston: Houghton Mifflin. [130–132]

———— 1922. Introspection as an objective method. *Psychological Review, 29,* 89–112. [130]

———— 1923. A questionary study of certain national differences in emotional traits. *Journal of Comparative Psychology, 3,* 423–430. [132]

—— 1924. Gestalt psychology and motor psychology. *American Journal of Psychology, 37*, 516–520. [132]

—— & ABBOTT, E. 1932. Experiments on the brightness value of red for the light-adapted eye of the rabbit. *Journal of Animal Behavior, 2*, 145–180. [130]

WASSERMAN, E. A. 1973. Pavlovian conditioning with heat reinforcement produces stimulus-directed pecking in chicks. *Science, 181*, 875–877. [165]

WATSON, G. 1940. Areas of agreement in psychotherapy. *American Journal of Orthopsychiatry, 4*, 698–710. [296]

WATSON, J. B. 1903. *Animal Education: The Psychical Development of the White Rat.* (Ph.D. dissertation.) Chicago: University of Chicago Press. [172]

—— 1909. *The Behavior of Noddy and Sooty Terns.* Washington: Carnegie Publication #103. [173]

—— 1913. Psychology as the behaviorist views it. *Psychological Review, 20*, 158–177. [175, 390]

—— 1914. *Behavior: An Introduction to Comparative Psychology.* New York: Holt. [173]

—— 1916. The place of the conditioned reflex in psychology. *Psychological Review, 23*, 89–116. [176]

—— 1917. The effect of delayed feeding upon learning. *Psychobiology, 1*, 51–60. [178]

—— 1919/1924. *Psychology from the Standpoint of a Behaviorist.* Philadelphia: J. B. Lippincott Co. (Rev. Ed. 1924.) [176–183]

—— 1925/1930. *Behaviorism.* New York: W. W. Norton & Co. [177, 183, 353]

—— 1930. Autobiography. (In Murchison, C., Ed. *A History of Psychology in Autobiography.* Vol. 3.) Worcester, Mass: Clark University Press. [171–175]

—— 1936. Letter to T. W. Harrell, 16 June 1936. [172]

—— & McDOUGALL, W. 1929. *The Battle of Behaviorism.* New York: W. W. Norton. [175]

—— & MORGAN, J. J. B. 1917. Emotional reactions and psychological experimentation. *American Journal of Psychology, 28*, 163–174. [184]

—— & RAYNER, R. 1920. Conditioned emotional reactions. *Journal of Experimental Psychology, 3*, 1–14. [180–181]

—— & WATSON, R. R. 1921. Studies infant psychology. *Scientific Monthly, 13*, 493–515. [180, 181]

—— & —— 1928. *Psychological Care of Infant and Child.* New York: Norton. [175]

WATSON, R. I., SR. 1965. The historical background for national trends in psychology: United States. *Journal of the History of the Behavioral Sciences, 1*, 130–138. [183–185]

—— 1967. Psychology: A prescriptive science. *American Psychologist, 32*, 435–443. [183]

—— 1971. Prescriptions as operative in the history of psychology. *Journal of the History of the Behavioral Sciences, 7*, 311–322. [17, 183–185]

—— 1977. *Selected Papers on the History of Psychology.* (Ed. by J. Brozek & R. B. Evans.) Hanover, N.H.: University of New Hampshire. [183–185]

WATSON, R. R. 1920. I was the mother of a behaviorist's sons. *McCall's Magazine* (December). [175]

WEBER, E. H. 1846/1905. *Der Tastsinn und das Gemeingefühl. (The Sense of Touch and Common Sensibility.)* Leipzig: Engelmann. [82]

WEIMER, W. B., & PALERMO, D. S. (Eds.) 1974. *Cognition and the Symbolic Processes.* New York: Halsted Press. [433]

WEINER, B. 1985a. "Spontaneous" causal search. *Psychological Bulletin, 97,* 74–84. [4]

―――― 1958b. *Human Motivation.* New York: Springer-Verlag. [192, 302, 328]

WEISMAN, R. V. 1977. On the role of the reinforcer in associative learning. (In Davis, H., & Hurwitz, H. M. B., Eds. *Operant-Pavlovian Interactions.*) Hillsdale, N.J.: Lawrence Erlbaum Associates. [204, 223]

WEISS, A. P. 1917. Relation between structural and behavior psychology. *Psychological Review, 24,* 301–317. [185]

―――― 1922a. The stimulus error. *Journal of Experimental Psychology, 5,* 223–226. [187]

―――― 1922b. Behavior and the central nervous system. *Psychological Review, 29,* 329–343. [185]

―――― 1924/1929. *A Theoretical Basis of Human Behavior.* (Rev. Ed.) Columbus, Ohio: R. G. Adams Co. [185–187]

―――― 1925. One set of postulates for a behavioristic psychology. *Psychological Review, 32,* 83–87. [185–187]

WELD, H. P. 1931. Review of *A History of Experimental Psychology* by E. G. Boring. *Psychological Bulletin, 28,* 130–145. [93]

WERTHEIMER, M. 1912/1916. Experimentelle Studien über das Sehen von Bewegung. (Experimental studies on the seeing of motion. In Shipley, T., Ed. *Classics in Psychology.*) New York: Philosophical Library. [244–245]

―――― 1945. *Productive Thinking.* New York: Harper. [245]

WESTERLUNDH, B. 1985. Subliminal influence on imagery: Two exploratory experiments. *Psychological Research Bulletin, Lund University* (Sweden), *25,* 6–7. [426]

―――― & SMITH, G. J. W. 1983. Perceptgenesis and the psychodynamics of perception. *Psychoanalysis and Contemporary Thought, 6,* 597–640. [426]

WEYL, N., & POSSONY, S. T. 1963. *The Geography of Intellect.* Chicago: H. Regnery Co. [448]

WHEELIS, A. 1973. *How People Change.* New York: Harper & Row. [492]

WHITE, M. J. 1985. On the status of cognitive psychology. *American Psychologist, 40,* 117–119. [434]

WHITE, P. 1984. A model of the layperson as pragmatist. *Personality and Social Psychology Bulletin, 10,* 333–348. [109, 265]

WHITE, R. K. 1943. The case for the Tolman-Lewin interpretation of learning. *Psychological Review, 50,* 157–186. [280, 393–395]

WHITE, R. W. 1959. Motivation reconsidered: The concept of competence. *Psychological Review, 66,* 297–333. [328, 331]

WICKELGREN, W. A. 1970. Multitrace strength theory. (In Norman, D. A., Ed. *Models of Human Memory.*) New York: Academic Press. [209–216]

WILSON, E. O. 1975. *Sociobiology: A New Synthesis.* Cambridge, Mass.: Harvard University Press. [469–470]

―――― 1978. *On Human Nature.* Cambridge, Mass.: Harvard University Press. [469–470]

WILSON, G. T., & FRANKS, C. M. (Eds.) 1982. *Contemporary Behaviour Therapy.* New York: Guilford Press. [481–485]

WINDHOLZ, G., & LAMAL, P. A. 1986. Priority in the classical conditioning of children. *Teaching of Psychology, 13,* 192–195. [145]

WINSON, J. 1985. *Brain and Psyche*. New York: Anchor Press. [321]

WISPE, L. 1963. Traits of eminent American psychologists. *Science, 141,* 1256–1261. [21]

WISSLER, C. 1901. The correlation of mental and physical tests. *Psychological Review, Monograph Supplements, 3,* Whole No. 16. [150, 447]

WITKIN, H. A., DYK, R. B., FATERSON, H. F., GOODENOUGH, E. R., & KARP, C. 1962. *Psychological Differentiation*. New York: Wiley. [459]

WITTELS, F. 1924. *Sigmund Freud*. New York: Dodd, Mead. [292]

WOLF, E. 1966. Learning theory and psychoanalysis. *British Journal of Medical Psychology, 39,* 1–10. [496]

WOLF, T. H. 1973. *Alfred Binet*. Chicago: University of Chicago Press. [461]

WOLMAN, B. B. (Ed.) 1985. *Handbook of Intelligence: Theories, Measurements, and Applications*. New York: Wiley. [444]

WOLPE, J. 1958. *Psychotherapy by Reciprocal Inhibition*. Stanford, Cal.: Stanford University Press. [484]

———— 1962. Missing the point: A reply to Wogan and Norcross. *American Psychologist, 37,* 1286–1287. [484]

———— 1969. *The Practice of Behavior Therapy*. Oxford: Pergamon Press. [484]

WOODROFFE, J. 1959. *Sakti and Sakta: Essays and Addresses on the Sakta Tantrasastra*. Madras, India: Ganesh & Co. [37]

WOODWARD, W. R. 1982. The "discovery" of social behaviorism and social learning theory, 1870–1980. *American Psychologist, 37,* 396–410. [389]

———— & ASH, M. G. (Eds.) 1982. *The Problematic Science: Psychology in Nineteenth Century Thought*. New York: Praeger. [81]

WOODWORTH, R. S. 1918. *Dynamic Psychology*. New York: Columbia University Press. [158]

———— 1931. *Contemporary Schools of Psychology*. New York: Ronald Press.

WOOLFOLK, A. E., WOOLFOLK, R. L., & WILSON, G. T. 1977. A rose by any other name. . . . : Labeling bias and attitudes toward behavior modification. *Journal of Consulting and Clinical Psychology, 45,* 184–191. [484]

WREGE, C. D., & PERRONI, A. G. 1974. Taylor's pig-tale: A historical analysis of F. W. Taylor's pig-iron experiments. *Academy of Management Journal, 17,* 6–27. [184]

WUNDT, W. 1874/1904. *Principles of Physiological Psychology*. (Trans. by E. B. Titchener.) New York: Macmillan. [87–94]

———— 1880. *Logik* (2 vols.) [94, 103–104]

———— 1892. *Lectures on Human and Animal Psychology*. (Trans. by E. B. Titchener, & J. E. Creighton.) New York: Macmillan. [87, 88, 91, 93, 292, 413, 433]

———— 1900/1920. *Völkerpsychologie. (Social Psychology.)* (10 vols.) Leipzig: Engelmann.

WYER, R. S., JR., & SRULL, T. K. 1980. The processing of social stimulus information: A conceptual integration. (In Hastie, R., et al., Eds. *Person Memory*.) Hillsdale, N.J.: Lawrence Erlbaum Associates. [429, 434]

YERKES, R. M., & MORGULIS, S. 1909. The method of Pavlov in animal psychology. *Psychological Bulletin, 6,* 257–273. [165–166]

YOUNG, P. T. 1927. Studies in affective psychology. III. The "trained" observer in affective psychology. *American Journal of Psychology, 38,* 157–193. [123–124]

YUKL, G. A., & LATHAM, G. P. 1975. Consequences of reinforcement schedules and incentive magnitudes for employee performance: Problems encountered in an industrial setting. *Journal of Applied Psychology, 60,* 294–298. [236]

ZAJONC, R. B. 1984. On the primacy of affect. *American Psychologist, 39,* 117–123. [109]

ZALEZNIK, A. 1986. How managers should handle their anger. *New York Times Magazine* (8 June), Part 2, pp. 83 ff. [323]

ZANGWILL, O. L. 1972. *Remembering* revisited. *Quarterly Journal of Experimental Psychology, 24,* 123–128. [437]

ZEIGARNIK, B. V. 1927. Über das Behalten von erledigten und unerledigten Handlunger. *Psychologische Forschung, 9,* 1–85. [275]

—— 1984. Kurt Lewin and Soviet psychology. *Journal of Social Issues, 40,* 181–192. [268]

ZIELINSKI, J. J. 1978. Maintenance of therapeutic gains: Issues, problems, and implementations. *Professional Psychology, 9,* 353–360. [489–492]

ZIGLER, E. 1986. Intelligence: A developmental approach. (In Sternberg, R. J., & Detterman, D. K., Eds. *What Is Intelligence?*) Norwood, N.J: Ablex Publishing Corp. [448–450]

ZUCKER, R. A., ARONOFF, J., & RABIN, A. I. 1984. *Personality and the Prediction of Behavior.* New York: Academic Press. [461–463]

ZUSNE, L. 1984. *Biographical Dictionary of Psychology.* Westport, Conn.: Greenwood Press.

INDEX